THE LINE IN THE SAND:
THE SHIFTING BOUNDARY BETWEEN
MARKETS AND REGULATION IN
NETWORK INDUSTRIES

THE LINE IN THE SAND
THE SHIFTING BOUNDARY BETWEEN
MARKETS AND REGULATION
IN NETWORK INDUSTRIES

Sarah Potts Voll and Michael J. King, Editors

NERA ECONOMIC CONSULTING

National Economic Research Associates, Inc.
50 Main Street, 14th floor
White Plains, NY, 10606
www.nera.com

Printed in the United States of America.

Sarah Potts Voll and Michael J. King
The Line in the Sand: The Shifting Boundary Between
Markets and Regulation in Network Industries;
edited by Sarah Potts Voll and Michael J. King,
with a foreword by Alfred E. Kahn.
Includes index.
ISBN 978-0-9748788-4-3
1. Economics 2. Regulation 3. Energy
I. Title.

2007932675

CONTENTS

III. Market Power

IV. Security of Supply

FOREWORD

When I became chairman of the New York Public Service Commission in the summer of 1974, I had not the slightest notion that I was assuming the leadership of an enterprise that either was or should have been in the process of going out of business. On the contrary, my preponderant interest was in applying to electric, gas, telephone and water system charges the elementary economic principles I had previously enunciated in the course of my academic career—an intensely regulatory endeavor. One striking but representative—and still highly relevant—achievement of that mission, which I subsequently cited proudly, was that in consequence of our order to all major electric companies of the state to come in with time-of-day electric rate schedules for customers large enough to be equipped economically with the requisite meters, and optionally for residential customers, instead of users of electricity on Long Island paying the previous flat charge of some five cents per kilowatt hour every hour of every day, the metered ones would soon pay rates ranging between 2-1/2 cents at night and 30 cents on summer days when the temperature got above some stipulated level.

Before we could make that kind of change, my colleagues had to act on—and turn down—a petition that I disqualify myself from participating in a case ultimately leading to such a result on the grounds that I had "prejudged the issue", because I had previously proclaimed—among other places in my "Economics of Regulation"—that the real purpose of the prices we set was not, directly, to effect a "fair" apportionment of the aggregate costs we approved, but to induce efficient behavior by customers. In addition, my fellow member of the State Cabinet, John Dyson, prudently and helpfully arranged a meeting with business leaders in the state, in which I was able to assure them that it was not my demagogic purpose, in pressing for marginal cost pricing, to transfer costs from households to businesses—an assurance I felt necessary to confirm, in a subsequent rate case, by accepting the "equitable" distribution of costs among major customer groups produced by the traditional fully-restricted cost allocation methods—no small concession—and applying marginal cost principles to pricing only within each category.

I also testified at that time, by invitation, at the (Senator) Kennedy hearings on the airline industry, which played a substantial role in its deregulation just a few years after; but I had not the slightest inkling of how radically that experience would shortly change the course of my own career. I did however faintly recognize the possible effect on economic history itself: that's why a couple of years later I accepted the job as head of the (now defunct) CAB, declaring prophetically somewhere along the way that I would take as a measure of my success the extent to which there would indeed no longer be a need for such a regulatory agency when I was through.

A quarter century later, I had occasion to review the subsequent experience in commercial aviation, telecommunications and, in electricity, the California deregulatory fiasco, in an article whose title, "The Deregulatory Tar Baby: The Precarious Balance Between Regulation and Deregulation, 1970—2000 and Henceforward",[1] was intended to convey to anyone who remembered the classic 1881 Joel Chandler Harris Uncle Remus tale that—apart from the airlines and, shortly thereafter, trucking—"deregulation" was rarely a single decisive act—a proposition richly documented in the impressive collection of essays that comprise this volume.[2]

Persuaded by the editor—perhaps too easily—that that quarter-century review was still highly relevant to this volume, I have agreed to borrow from it here, with excisions and insertions to increase that relevance. Not surprisingly, as several of these essays clearly suggest, many of the problems and issues I raised then persist.

In the airline industry—thoroughly deregulated in 1978—the common complaint continues to be the severe deterioration in the quality of service—longer lines, cramped seating (outside of first class, disappearance of "free" meals) and crowded planes—is certainly legitimate. But that cramping and crowding has been the product not of "monopoly airlines" but of the intense price competition unleashed by deregulation and thanks largely to the fully 30 percentage point increase in average load factors—from the low 50s to the low 80s—and narrower seating—and the vast, often discriminatory differentials in fares. As to the first of these: under tight price regulation, travelers were confronted with only one choice—generally (indeed inefficiently) good service at cartel prices. The purpose of deregulation was, by unleashing price competition, to offer economy-minded travelers an alternative, low price and necessarily correspondingly lower quality option; and in that it has dazzlingly succeeded. The one clear failure has been that of Congress and federal and state agencies to respond to the predictably increased demand for infrastructure services—air traffic control and airports—and—counter to our continued (and to this day continuing) advice—to price them correctly. As the paper in this volume on transport congestion pricing demonstrates, there are clear economic solutions available. Their enactment, however, evidently requires the political solution of managerial and financial privatization.

The extreme differentiations in airfares following deregulation have, in very important measure, not been discriminatory at all, but reflect the efficient and beneficent competitive elimination of cross-subsidizations—of thinly traveled by heavily traveled, short-haul by long-haul routes—doomed once the price, entry and exit regulations were lifted. On the other hand, it is also commonplace to recognize, in any such industry characterized by extreme economies of scale and scope and pervasive common costs, particularly under the hub and spoke operations adopted by the largest carriers, price discrimination—differential markups above short-run incremental costs—is inescapable if total costs are to be recovered with minimal sacrifice of efficiency.

Deregulation of the US transportation industries—as well as crude oil, natural gas, stock exchange brokerage fees, cable television and wireless telephony—has been comparatively simple, while, unsurprisingly, enforcement of the one residual regulatory provision—of captive shipments by rail—remained highly contentious. In contrast, the tar baby continues—or threatens to renew—its grip on telecommunications and the electricity industries, because of the persistence of elements of natural monopoly—or, in the former, duopoly (of wire telephony and broadband access to the Internet)—that provided the justification for their treatment as public utilities in the first place. For this reason, I still cannot bring myself to deny the regulatory agencies a role in the transition of those public utilities to competition, although the FCC's persistent attachment of intensely regulatory "public interest" conditions to its approvals of mergers and, until finally stopped by the courts, efforts to produce viable *competitors,* even if mere resellers,[3] have convinced me that the primary role of presiding over and establishing the necessary conditions for deregulating an industry should not be entrusted to the agency that regulated them.

Unsurprisingly, I incline to the same view with respect to the electric power industry, at least in the US, given its tumultuous history of the last seven years. As Chapter 13 describes, the effort to deregulate electricity has led to a wide variety of inconsistent monitoring and mitigation schemes. California's particular mistake, to cite one of the most egregious, was deregulating only partially: clearly its mandated reduction and freeze of retail prices, accompanied by deregulation of wholesale prices, proved catastrophic—initially to the distribution companies but then, inevitably, to consumers and taxpayers called upon to bail them out.

Even more fundamentally, the California electric deregulatory fiasco raised the question of whether electricity should have been deregulated at all. Any answer would have to take into account the extraordinary and in some respects literally unique characteristics of the industry—the high degree of interdependence between investments and operations at the transmission and generation levels, the nonstorability of power and consequent need for instantaneous matching of generation and consumption, in consequence of which failure at any point can threaten the stability of the entire grid. As Chapter 17 observes, this susceptibility is compounded by the high inelasticity of demand of most consumers in the short-term, because of the historically high metering costs of confronting them on a real time basis with the wide fluctuations in marginal supply and opportunity costs consequent on the short-run inelasticity of supply at the peak. In these circumstances, Parmesano and Voll's contention, in Chapter 7, that those costs are falling to the point that widespread metering has become economic, implies a profoundly improved climate for effectively functioning deregulated markets.

As Chapter 17 also describes, "deregulation" was hedged about, from the onset, with phased mandated stipulated reductions or, after disappointments, "stabilization" plans or stipulated gradual increases, or deferrals—sometimes by "securitization" of increases: when the optimistic expectations turned out to have been founded on the opposite forecasting errors, the tar baby quickly regained its grip.

I, along with many others, have observed that the deregulation movement in electric power has been an essentially opportunistic response to the enormous forecasting errors of the 1970's, which appeared to have left large regions of the country with a heavy burden of high-cost excess capacity and a consequent wide spread between book costs—the basis for regulated rates—and the costs of new combined cycle plants powered by (once again optimistically anticipated) cheap natural gas. Significantly, there never was and still is no substantial interest in deregulation in states supplied preponderantly by coal-fired generation plants, heavily depreciated on the books, in which, in consequence, regulated rates appeared to have remained consistently below long-run incremental costs. The irony is that despite the general expectation of huge immediate benefits for consumers from deregulation—such as flowed immediately from the release of competition among the airlines—and the consequent expropriation of book equities, regulators and legislators were typically unwilling to put their entire trust in the liberated markets. When those opportunistic expectations turned out to have been founded on the opposite forecasting errors, the tar baby quickly regained its grip.

Other factors besides regulatory opportunism may also have been at fault. The apparent success of the mandatory divestiture of AT&T's putatively naturally monopolistic local service from its potentially competitive long distance service evidently encouraged legislators and regulators to prescribe similar divestitures or structural separations in electric power as well. I have wondered, however, whether the mandate to sever the ties between electric generating companies and their transmission and local distribution networks may have contributed to California's problems by denying it one of the main benefits of vertical integration itself—the incentives it creates for undertaking investments at one horizontal level necessary for the success of operations at another. Continued ownership of generation capable of satisfying a larger proportion of their needs would obviously have protected the major distribution companies that were forced to freeze their retail rate while having to purchase their power in an exploding wholesale market. In those circumstances PURPA would presumably have continued to ensure the possibility of entry by independent power producers as a continuing competitive check on the exercise of vertically integrated monopoly power. Of course, that would have left unresolved the perceived threatened anticompetitive consequences of vertical integration of generation and transmission, a problem with which FERC has continued to struggle: I am constrained to regard the compatibility of vertical integration with open competition as an open issue.

It is no accident that the required regulatory reform in the electric power industry is characterized as "restructuring" rather than mere deregulation. Fully as much as the efforts of the Federal Communication Commission to implement a Congressional decision to open the local telephone business to competition, however, the experience in the US electric power sector illustrates the evils of deregulatory and regulatory opportunism, of excessively detailed design and prescription and misguided populism—promising consumers the benefits of competition while sheltering them from its risks. The central task is to design the inescapable residual regulation in such a way as, through pricing, to ensure the same kind of efficient synchronization of investments and operation as were previously achieved within the vertically integrated and regulated utility companies.

This volume's sections on procurement and security of supply make it clear that the flaws in the design of electricity restructuring have by no means been confined to California. Deregulation is of course an essentially economic and engineering undertaking that must take place in an intensely political context—exposing it to the competition of politically organized groups for protection from competition, as well as of misguided populism. The result can be a California meltdown. At the very least, the deregulators there cannot escape blame for succumbing to a characteristically compulsive tidiness, a high propensity to micro-manage the process: for example, the artificial concentration of purchases and sales forced by California's requirement that the distribution companies purchase all their power in the spot market was directly responsible for the suddenly emerging shortages at times of peak demand and the explosion of prices they produced.

It is not surprising also that observers of that experience were the first to identify apparent exercises of market power because of the newly-discovered susceptibility of spot markets (on which, recall, distribution companies were forced to depend exclusively) to multi-plant producers unilaterally withholding some comparatively small proportion of their capacity, and the consequent apparent insufficiency of competitive discipline at times of peak demand.

But more generally, I suggest, no one should have been surprised by the failure of any market in which the ability of customers to respond to changes in price was so limited. It is the comparative rarity of real-time pricing and metering, precluding an efficient demand-side response to shortages and sky-rocketing energy prices that makes these markets dysfunctional, subjecting policy-makers to the Hobson's choice between caps on prices, to protect defenseless customers, and permitting prices on peak periodically to rise to the politically unacceptable levels necessary if capital costs are to be recovered over time and efficient entry encouraged. The interim resolution has been regulatorily-imposed reserve capacity requirements and separate markets for satisfying them. But, as I have remarked previously[4] and several papers in this volume spell out, if markets were free to fluctuate with the changing balance of supply and demand *and* a sufficient portion of large customers were so metered as to be able to respond by changing their electricity using practices—the very policy, I trust I will be forgiven for mentioning, that was the focus of my efforts at the New York Public Service Commission thirty years ago—such capacity requirements would be unnecessary, and, I presume, genuine deregulation of generation and marketing would be feasible. Notwithstanding the problems that are discussed in this volume, deregulation has been shown to work in the sense that risks are better allocated (generators take the risk of investment decisions), there have been efficiency gains (units run better) and a not insignificant portion of the regulatory burden has been shifted to markets. Customers in restructured states are no longer responsible for the forecasting errors and financial failures of the independent merchants—their shareholders have been. We have been spared endless wrangling over the terms under which transmission should be available to wheel power through utility service territories, or worse still, supply a captive customer. Arcane debates over whether a utility should be allowed to preempt construction of a competing independent power producer by building its own facility have come to a halt. The need for new facilities is now dominated by technical considerations rather than battles between customer classes that were growing quickly and ones that were growing more slowly. Those who argued that running hourly auctions for incremental supplies was too complex an endeavor to be feasible have been proven wrong. Operating efficiencies for power plants, especially nuclear, have never been higher. The search for efficient technologies for CO_2 control is clearly heightened by the promise of extraordinary returns to the winners. In short, the dynamic efficiencies that are the true benefits of competition have begun to emerge. The promise hinted at by these developments makes it even clearer that the impediments to the emergence of competitive electric markets—impediments stemming from the regulatory process itself—should not be allowed to obstruct the emergence of true competition.

The proper residual role for regulation is to preserve and expand the opportunities for independent competitive entry at all levels on the supply side and efficient choice on the demand side.

****

I have been associated with NERA for more than 40 years and during that time have been enjoyed working with many of the authors whose papers appear in this volume. I commend these products of their latest thinking and experience with drawing the shifting line between regulated and unregulated markets—the very problem that has been my central professional concern these last four decades.

ALFRED E. KAHN
Robert Julius Thorne Professor of Political Economy, Emeritus,
Cornell University
Special Consultant, NERA

Notes

1. *Journal of Regulatory Economics,* 21:1 (2002), 35-56.

2. I documented it also in three little volumes, whose titles and subtitles amply reflected my impatience with the "high marginal propensity of regulators and presumed deregulators to meddle" with the process: *Letting Go: Deregulating the Process of Deregulation, or: Temptation of the Kleptocrats and the Political Economy of Regulatory Disingenuousness,* The Institute of Public Utilities and Network Industries (1998), *Whom the Gods Would Destroy, or How Not to Deregulate,* AEI-Brookings Joint Center for Regulatory Studies, (2001), and *Lessons from Deregulation: Telecommunications and Airlines after the Crunch,* AEI-Brookings Joint Center for Regulatory Studies (2003).

3. Alfred E. Kahn, Timothy J. Tardiff and Dennis L. Weisman, "The Telecommunications Act at three years: an economic evaluation of its implementation by the Federal Communications Commission," Information Economics and Policy, 11(4), (1999), 319-365. See also my above cited Whom the Gods Would Destroy, or How Not to Deregulate, Chapter 6; Lessons from Deregulation, Chapter 3.

4. "The Adequacy of Prospective Returns on Generation Investments under Price Control Mechanisms," *Electricity Journal* (March 2002), 37-46.

PREFACE

Beginning with the 1978 deregulation of the US airline industry under the leadership of Alfred E. Kahn, during the last quarter century the network industries worldwide have been exposed to the transforming winds of market forces. In the US, the Public Utilities Regulatory Policies Act of 1978 introduced non-utility generation into the vertically integrated electric utility system. AT&T divested itself of the Regional Bell Operating Companies in 1984, opening the way for competition in long distance service, while the Natural Gas Act of 1985 deregulated the field prices of natural gas producers. The Energy Policy Act of 1992 permitted wholesale customers their choice of supplier and required utilities to transmit power across their territories.

The first mover in Europe was the UK, which following Margaret Thatcher's re-election in 1983 embarked on a comprehensive privatization program. The pre-1984 candidates for privatization had been reasonably competitive firms like British Aerospace, Britoil, Cable and Wireless and Enterprise Oil, but by 1987 the UK had privatized, though not necessarily de-regulated, British Airports Authority and British Air, British Gas and British Telecom, and in March 1990 had restructured and privatized its electric system, and then water through the Water Industry Act of 1993. The trend spread to Europe and was ultimately adopted by the European Union itself. On January 1999, for example, EU Utilities Directive took effect opening electric and gas utilities to competition in its member countries.

Chile, which deregulated its electric system in 1982 and privatized it between 1986 and 1989, was the exemplar for emerging markets. Led by Chile's example and pushed by the Washington Consensus, the economic policy prescriptions promoted by Washington-based institutions that constituted the "standard" free market oriented reform package, the emerging markets of Latin America and elsewhere pursued privatization and/or deregulation programs of their network industries as the preferred engine of modernization and economic growth.

The crux of the transformations in all of these developments was the shifting boundary between regulation and putatively competitive markets. Beginning with vertically integrated, state owned or pervasively regulated utilities, the reforms disaggregated the industries and incrementally moved the boundary between the pieces regulated by public agencies and those disciplined by the market (and sometimes back again). The question of where that boundary should lie is essentially an economic one, depending on company and market structure and informed by the principles of regulatory economics. It is a question about which the economists in the Energy, Environmental, Water, Transport and Auction practice of NERA Economic Consulting have advised and testified, for companies, governments and regulators on six continents over the past three decades.

This book is a result of conversations and debates among colleagues across continents and is designed to identify and consider the issues, methodologies and techniques that will be of concern in the playing field of the network industries in the first decade of the twenty first century. It contains five sections on the energy sector, each with an explanatory introduction, with 21 essays, plus two separate chapters that discuss the water and transport industries.

The first Section contains essays that explore seven aspects of regulation that have evolved in the electricity sector. Chapter 1 provides a framework for the remaining papers in this section by laying out the theoretical rationale for regulation of monopoly utility companies. Chapter 2 describes the foundation of the prudent cost standard in competitive market theory, and critiques the tendency of regulators to second-guess and apply hindsight review to management decisions. Chapter 3 explains why phased development of nuclear power makes sense, given uncertainties about such factors as coal plant costs and the cost of greenhouse gases, and offers new analytical tools for a phased development that can be abandoned at various steps. The following two chapters describe aspects of incentive or price cap regulation. Chapter 4 discusses the components of a price cap formula and provides advice on practical considerations in designing the details of the mechanism to ensure that it achieves the regulatory objectives. Chapter 5 focuses on one element of the price cap formula, the "X-factor", compares two common approaches to determining its level, and finds that one of them, while convenient, is ultimately unreliable and inconsistent with the principles of incentive regulation. Chapter 6 categorizes the types of mergers taking place and concludes that regulators need to focus on the likely long-term effects of the newer types—modifying their use of traditional tools and adjusting their expectations about the size and certainty of direct benefits. Chapter 7 discusses the new role of distribution charges in a world with some level of service unbundling, and argues that rate structures that worked in a world of bundled electricity service and limited options for self-generation may no longer achieve their objectives.

Section 2 addresses several issues of public policy, and in particular, the design of public policies to prevent or remedy market failures. Chapter 8 reviews the financial incentives anticipated under the US Energy Policy Act of 2005 for new nuclear plant construction and operation and questions whether they will be sufficient to produce a real nuclear renaissance. The next two chapters examine the use of new mechanisms to implement public policies. Chapter 9 discusses the market-based instruments and portfolio standards that may be used to comply with regulatory policies that dictate increased reliance on clean, renewable resources. Chapter 10 considers the extensive experience with the use of trading mechanisms to deal with air emissions in the US and, most recently, greenhouse gas emissions in Europe.

Section 3 examines the global issue of market power, beginning with an introduction that lays out the ambiguities associated with that concept, and sets out NERA's perspective on market power in the electricity industry. The three chapters in the section then explain how the issue is approached in Australia, Europe and the US.

Section 4 looks at Security of Supply, a debate driven by supply interruptions in the US and Europe in recent years. In the context of the "time consistency" problem, it asks how different market structures ensure that system capacity will be adequate to satisfy demand. Chapter 14 reviews the conditions necessary to ensure efficient investment in capacity, taking account of the risks faced by investors. Chapter 15 discusses one approach, the Capacity Payment Mechanism (CPM), and the criteria that should govern the choice of a particular form. Chapter 16 focuses on recent innovations in the design of CPMs, including locational incentives to promote efficient coordination of generation and transmission investment. Chapter 17 analyzes the approach of designing systems to ensure that demand response is capable of rationing capacity before prices spike to intolerable levels. It points out that if the market is complete, most of the issue of security of supply and the problem of "time consistency" disappear.

The fifth Section explores strategies for procuring competitive generation services by regulated distribution companies. Chapter 18 examines the drivers of the trend in the US toward full requirements procurements and away from utility portfolio management in those instances in which wholesale markets are growing in competitiveness and sophistication. Chapter 19 explains the Federal Energy Regulatory Commission's (FERC's) standards for approval of a contract between a distribution utility and an affiliated wholesale generator. Chapter 20 contrasts the bidding processes for a full-requirements product in two states in the US, the so-called New Jersey and Maryland models. Chapter 21 then discusses the adoption of open auctions as a new model for power procurement, and compares the power procurement auctions in Brazil and New Jersey, highlighting how the design of the auction can be critical to the outcome.

Finally, two separate essays discuss issues in other network industries, water and transport. Chapter 22 looks at the use of estimates of customers' willingness to pay for service quality increments, which can, and the authors argue should, play an important role in the decisions of regulators and regulated companies. Chapter 23 considers how economic techniques can contribute to determining the best use of existing capacity in the highway, airport and rail sectors.

We hope you will find the explanations and insights in this volume conceptually interesting and a useful analytical resource when confronting the challenges of our evolving network industries.

Sarah Potts Voll and Michael J. King

ACKNOWLEDGMENTS

A work of this scope is a cooperative effort, involving organizers, authors, reviewers, editors, and producers. Credit goes, of course, to the able contributing economists of the Energy, Environment, Water, Transportation and Auction Practice at NERA Economic Consulting for pulling together and presenting their latest thinking in each of their fields. However, the individual chapters were greatly enhanced, and the task of the editor substantially eased, by the thoughtful efforts of the first line of reviewers of each section: David Harrison, Mike King, Jeff Makholm, Gene Meehan, Hethie Parmesano, Michael Rosenzweig and Graham Shuttleworth. Their observations helped clarify the authors' initial thinking and often served to internationalize the resulting essay. Others contributed advice on individual chapters and encouragement to individual authors: John Allison, Oscar Arnedillo, Elizabeth Bailey, Jeffrey Bloczynski, Jennifer Fish, Greg Houston, Francesco Lo Passo, Wayne Olson, Carlos Pabon-Agudelo and Patricia Robl.

The design, production and marketing of the book are the results of the efforts by Adam Findeisen, Arthur Schening and Ben Seggerson at NERA, with the invaluable help of Anita Blumenthal's careful manuscript review and Priscilla Arthur's excellent typesetting skills. We are grateful for their expertise, efficiency, and initiative.

Finally, special thanks to Michael Rosenzweig and Michael King, without whose leadership, support and perseverance this volume would not have been possible.

I

REGULATION

CURRENT ISSUES IN UTILITY REGULATION

Hethie Parmesano

Although the basic goal of utility regulation—substituting for missing competitive forces—has not changed, it is an ongoing effort to determine how to achieve that goal, given changes in such factors as technology, industry structure, market arrangements, investment strategies and consumer preferences change. It is not an easy job, and the sometimes tortured path to new regulatory practices reflects the difficulty of simultaneously achieving conflicting aims. Whatever their chosen method of regulation, regulators have to balance the aims of (1) preventing monopoly profits; (2) ensuring that the regulated companies have a reasonable opportunity to cover the costs of operating, maintaining, and expanding the system, including a reasonable profit; and (3) providing incentives for efficient decisions by consumers and the utility.

This section of the book addresses several aspects of regulation that have evolved with the electricity sector. Although the focus of some of these chapters is on electricity, many of the issues apply equally to natural gas. Some of the papers discuss issues and practices in several parts of the world, while some focus on the US. In many cases, the papers provide lessons from regulation in the US, Europe, South America, and Oceania that illustrate what has and has not worked.

The first chapter, Economic Principles of Regulation, provides a framework for the remaining papers in this section by laying out the theoretical rationale for regulation of monopoly utility companies. It reminds us that regulation attempts to:

- remove monopoly profits so that prices stay close to costs (and consumers can make efficient energy decisions),
- encourage or require the monopolist to expand output toward the efficient level, while
- promoting minimization of costs (both costs of providing service and costs of the regulatory regime), and
- ensuring adequate quality of service.

This chapter describes the mechanisms by which cost-of-service regulation and price-cap regulation pursue these objectives, noting that the differences are largely a matter of the relative emphasis given to cost-saving and efficient pricing.

Both cost-of-service and price-cap regulation typically involve a periodic regulatory review of utility decisions and cost levels. Costs deemed "imprudent" are not included in the prices charged to the utility's captive customers. The difficulty is defining what constitutes a prudent level of cost. Regulators often attempt to determine what the costs of an efficient firm in a competitive market would have been and disallow any costs that are higher. Chapter 2, Rethinking the Implementation of the Prudent Cost Standard, describes the foundation of the prudent cost standard in competitive market theory and explains the numerous ways in which regulated utilities differ from textbook competitive firms.

In administrative rate cases, regulators review a wide variety of management choices and decisions. This process often includes second-guessing and hindsight review. Benchmarking exercises compare the results of management choices to costs of supposedly similar utilities. However, selecting objective and transparent benchmarks is a thorny problem. The best solution may be to use a two-step process. In the first step, the regulator reviews the utility's *decisional prudence* to invest (along with all relevant information available at the time, including expected costs) and pre-approves the investment decision. In the second step, the regulator reviews the utility's *managerial prudence* in carrying out the investment, possibly using benchmarking, but it does not revisit the decision to invest.

An example of historical prudence review is the massive disallowances of nuclear costs in the 1980s and 1990s. For years afterwards, utilities steered clear of even mentioning new nuclear investments, but global warming and the profitability of existing nuclear units is changing that. Chapter 3, Why Planning a Nuclear Plant Is a Good Idea even if Building One Turns out To Be a Bad Idea, explains why phased development of nuclear power makes sense, given uncertainties about factors such as coal plant costs and the cost of greenhouse gases. The chapter offers a simple numerical example and makes the case that *real options analysis* and other new analytical tools support a phased development that can be abandoned at various steps. An education program may be required to convince regulators that such preliminary investments are prudent, even if not "used and useful" in the traditional sense.

Price-cap regulation, also called incentive regulation, RPI-X or CPI-X regulation, or performance-based regulation (PBR), requires the regulator to (1) set an initial price cap (or caps) and (2) establish a formula for adjusting price caps periodically until the next full price review. Regulators in the UK and other European countries now have significant experience with price-cap regulation and there are important lessons to be learned from their successes and mis-steps.

The fourth chapter, Practicalities of Price Cap Regulation, discusses the components of a price cap formula and provides advice on practical considerations in designing the details of the mechanism to ensure that it achieves the regulatory objectives. Key tasks include forecasting a reasonable level of costs, setting a formula that tracks costs, determining how allowed revenues should adjust to changing patterns of demand, and addressing special risks and uncertainties. The chapter emphasizes that a successful price cap program must include minimum quality standards as well as transparent, stable and predictable regulatory methods, including strict criteria for changing the rules.

The typical multiyear price cap formula includes an "X-factor" intended to capture "normal" annual levels of productivity improvement in the industry. The formula rewards utilities that achieve higher levels of productivity improvement by allowing them to keep the excess profits until the next full price review (and vice versa). Chapter 5, Elusive Efficiency and the *X-Factor* in Incentive Regulation: The Törnqvist v. DEA/Malmquist Dispute, compares the characteristics of two common approaches to determining the level of the X-factor. It finds that the DEA/Malmquist procedure is convenient but ultimately unreliable and inconsistent with the principles of incentive regulation.

Another area where regulation affects the utility industry is corporate restructuring—particularly the review of mergers and acquisitions. Introduction of wholesale and retail competition in electricity (and other) sectors around the world was intended to create a more efficient industry by allowing firms to respond to economic incentives rather than just to regulatory orders. Corporate restructuring is one way that firms have sought to respond to the new incentives, with the aims of controlling costs and positioning to enter new markets.

Mergers in the newly competitive sectors have rationales and expected benefits that are different from those of from earlier corporate restructuring, and US regulators have struggled to update their criteria for reviewing the corporate restructuring proposals. Chapter 6, Mergers and

Acquisitions in the US Electric Industry: State Regulatory Policies for Reviewing Today's Deals, describes types of mergers taking place and their benefits and costs. It discusses how state regulators view their merger oversight responsibilities and the tools they have available to protect the public interest. This chapter concludes that regulators need to focus on long-term effects of proposed mergers, to modify their use of tools, and to adjust their expectations about the size and certainty of direct benefits from the newer types of mergers.

Even in jurisdictions with retail competition for generation supply, regulators retain the responsibility to regulate prices for delivery service, which is still a monopoly service. The final chapter in this section, Rethinking Rate Design for Electricity Distribution Service in the US, discusses the new role of distribution rates in a world with some level of service unbundling. The chapter points out that rate structures that worked in a world of bundled electricity service and limited options for self-generation do not achieve ratemaking objectives when applied to distribution rates, and the authors recommend a more appropriate, cost-based rate structure.

1

ECONOMIC PRINCIPLES OF REGULATION

Graham Shuttleworth
Sarah Potts Voll

Principles of Price Cap Regulation

Many regulatory regimes for monopoly utilities operate within a legal and procedural framework that is relatively new and that allows regulators the room to adopt a wide range of methods. This regulatory discretion has permitted innovation in the design of the regulatory framework for monopoly networks, particularly in the design and calculation of price caps, the favoured form of regulation in many regimes. However, for any regulatory method, fundamental economic principles limit the range of sustainable and efficient designs. Some regulatory systems encounter problems with price cap regulation because the chosen methods have not complied with these economic principles. This chapter is intended to explain the nature of monopoly regulation and the fundamental economic principles that underlie it in order to help regulators and regulated utilities avoid errors in the design of regulatory instruments, and to provide a framework for rational debate of regulatory proposals.

Section I of the chapter sets out a statement of the economic principles of price regulation. These principles derive from academic and regulatory sources around the world, and they are not specific to any single regulatory regime or legal system. Instead, they form a set of universally applicable *economic* principles, which, while often abstract or arcane, are expressed in terms that should be accessible and familiar to anyone working within or around monopoly network industries.

This section examines why economic regulation is necessary and identifies the problems it is supposed to cure. On the basis of this analysis, it then sets out the economic objectives of regulation.

Section II then considers how well the traditional form of regulation, known as Rate of Return regulation or Cost of Service regulation, meets these economic objectives.

Since many critiques of these traditional forms advocate Price Cap regulation instead, Section III examines the key differences between these two models of regulation, the incentives under each, and their relative merits with regard to the economic objectives discussed in Section I.

Why Is Regulation Necessary?

The primary method of organising private sector activity is through the operation of a market. Provided that certain basic rules are defined (principally, who owns what resources), markets allow producers to compete against one another, unfettered by any constraint other than supply and demand. If markets meet certain criteria, competition will produce the most efficient possible outcome, including a market price equal to the minimum long-run average cost. However, if these criteria are not met, competition no longer produces efficient outcomes.[1]

One of those criteria is the presence of multiple economic agents, each too small to exert a perceptible influence on price. Therefore by definition, competition is not feasible in cases of monopoly, and a profit-maximising monopoly will raise its prices above its costs. High prices allow a firm to earn monopoly profits that are higher than they need to be and discourage demand that could be met at a cost that consumers are willing to pay. This effect results in a loss of potential efficiency to society. Distaste for monopoly profits and the associated efficiency losses are two reasons why governments intervene in markets.

Monopolies are maintained by barriers that prevent other companies from entering the market. The first course of action is therefore to remove unnecessary entry barriers—for instance, by abolishing legal constraints that limit the number of providers in a market. However, the intrinsic conditions of supply and demand in some markets make it more efficient to concentrate production within one firm than to have competing providers. The resulting monopolies are called "natural monopolies". They usually arise in industries that make long-term investments and face economies of scale. Their behaviour merits permanent regulation to reverse or reduce the undesirable effects of monopoly provision:

- By removing monopoly profits, so that prices are closer to costs; and
- By encouraging or obliging the monopoly to increase its output towards the efficient level without letting the quality of service fall.

Monopoly regulation is therefore intended to set prices lower, and outputs higher, than would happen otherwise. However, monopoly regulation that succeeds in these goals will increase economic efficiency only if regulation itself does not cause an excessive increase in costs. Hence, the design of regulation must also pay attention to the need (1) to encourage the monopolist to keep down the costs of production and (2) to keep down costs of administering the regulatory regime. Here lies the essential tradeoff within all forms of regulation. Setting prices close to costs gives consumers an accurate signal about the cost of their consumption, but setting prices exactly equal to costs—both allowing full cost recovery and reflecting any efficiency gains immediately in prices—will do nothing to promote minimisation of costs. The challenge that faces all regulators of monopoly utilities is to find a way to reconcile these two conflicting outcomes, or to choose a beneficial trade-off between them.

Natural Monopolies and the Need for Regulation

The primary characteristic of a natural monopoly is that the industry experiences such large economies of scale relative to the size of the market that one firm meeting total demand is always cheaper than the total cost of two or more firms, each meeting a share of total demand. Most network utilities experience large economies of scale, either in their business as a whole or in an individual service or in providing a service in each location. In such conditions, continuing competition in the market is either inefficient or impossible. Overall, in cases of natural monopoly, competition does not provide a useful role model for the appropriate form of interventions by government.

Economies of scale do not rule out competition entirely. Consumers can still hold competitions to select the cheapest provider of a service, from among several potential providers. This form of competition is sometimes known as "contestability" or "competition *for* the market" (as opposed to "competition *in* the market"). However, most network utilities experience additional conditions that prevent such competition for the market from taking place. These are the additional conditions (which are sometimes classed as additional conditions of a natural monopoly):

- The industry invests in assets that have very long lives.
- These investments are irreversible (i.e., the assets cannot be withdrawn from the industry without substantial cost or loss of value).
- The level of demand needed to capture economies of scale covers sales to a large number of customers.
- Customers would incur a substantial "transactions cost" if they wished jointly to negotiate a contract with a single supplier.

In an industry with long-lived assets, consumers would need to sign a long-term contract with the provider in order to capture the benefits of "competition for the market". To capture the necessary economies of scale, a group of consumers would need to join together in a "coalition" and to negotiate as a body. Therefore, competition *for* the market typically takes place only when a state-owned entity is being privatised and government, acting on behalf of the consumers, auctions the right to provide service to a particular geographic area, and signs a multi-decade concession agreement with the winning bidder. Even at that unique turning point, as long as the market is a natural monopoly, competition remains inefficient and undesirable. Rather, governments find it is more useful to design interventions as a proxy for the long-term contract that consumers would want to negotiate if they had the power and ability to do so.[2] The role of a sector-specific regulator is to negotiate the terms of service on behalf of consumers and to update those terms if conditions change in unforeseen ways. How the regulator conducts these negotiations defines a regulatory regime.

Economic Objectives of Regulation

Given the conditions of natural monopoly, the next step is to identify key economic objectives that are common to all regulatory regimes.

Definitions of Efficiency Objectives

The starting point for natural monopoly regulation is simply the desire to increase output and to bring prices back down towards the level of costs, including the costs of capital.[3] Such interventions increase *allocative efficiency,* i.e., the efficiency with which consumers choose which products and services to consume (and hence the efficiency with which resources are allocated to different industries). Setting prices in line with costs helps consumers to allocate their expenditure efficiently—and also prevents monopoly profits.

To increase efficiency overall, monopoly regulation must also avoid causing an unnecessary increase in production costs. If prices are set equal to costs at all times, then the monopolist has no incentive to minimise costs, since an effort to cut costs does not produce any increase in profits. It is possible that costs would be allowed to rise and *productive efficiency* would drop, i.e., the company would produce its output less efficiently. Indeed, some criticisms of simple approaches to regulation conclude that setting prices equal to costs would actively encourage inefficient forms of production and higher costs. Therefore, all regulatory regimes offer some incentive for regulated companies to reduce their costs, essentially by reducing profits if the company is inefficient, and/or increasing profits if the company is efficient.

Concomitant Objectives
By applying these general terms—allocative efficiency and productive efficiency—to natural monopolies, more specific objectives emerge as corollaries.

First, natural monopolies in general (and utilities in particular) rely on long-term investments. In order to provide the output that consumers want, regulated industries must be able to attract capital investment; moreover, they must be able to access low-cost sources of finance to keep down costs. This aim has important implications for the process of regulation and, in particular, it means that the regulatory regime should not act as a source of unnecessary risk that might drive up the cost of capital or discourage investment.

Second, the regulatory regime must ensure that the monopolist cannot respond to incentives to cut costs merely by reducing the quality of its output. Under price cap regulation, this form of cost cutting would increase the profits of the regulated firm but would not serve the interests of consumers. Consequently, monopoly regulation must offer the monopolist incentives to provide adequate service quality.

In summary, any system of regulation must try to achieve the following objectives:

- Allocative efficiency (limitation of monopoly profits)
- Productive efficiency, which means:
  - Low-cost provision of service
  - Ability to attract capital for long-term investment
  - Maintenance of adequate service quality

The balance between these objectives may change over time, and hence the appropriate regulatory rules may also change. For example, immediately after privatisation, monopoly regulation in the UK focused on the need to eliminate inefficient production methods; as a result, the industry adopted simple price caps that allowed companies to increase profits by cutting costs. After 10 or 15 years of cost cutting, however, consumers and other authorities began to express concerns about the level of investment and the quality of service. The most recent price controls have therefore included elaborate incentive schemes designed to encourage investment and penalise poor quality service. Other regulatory regimes can expect to pass through the same or similar cycles.

Implications for Monopoly Regulation
The main terms of any regime of monopoly regulation are:

- Legal protection of a monopoly in return for an obligation to meet all reasonable demands for the service;
- A promise that the company will recover its costs, balanced by a restriction on revenues or prices that prevents the company from earning monopoly profits; and
- A set of minimum quality standards that prevents the company from profiting by reducing the quality of service (as a substitute for raising prices).

Profit-maximising monopolies restrict the supply of a product or service in order to drive up the price and raise their profits. The effect of these instruments is to offset the monopolist's natural tendency and, in economic terms, reduce prices from monopoly levels to encourage a move towards allocative efficiency, i.e., towards more efficient choices by consumers, which can be achieved by prices that signal the true cost of products and services. However, an unrestricted privately owned monopoly usually has an incentive to minimise costs in order to maximise profits because prices and costs are not inextricably linked.[4] Any regulatory device that links prices to costs in order to achieve allocative efficiency reduces the incentive for the monopolist to minimise costs. Since unnecessary escalation of costs is undesirable, monopoly regulation is also driven by a concern for cost minimisation, or productive efficiency.

In addition, consistent with the model of regulation as a proxy for negotiations by consumers, regulators of monopoly utilities are also usually given the power to restrict prices. The aim of regulators is to curb monopoly profits and maximise benefits to *consumers,* rather than to seek efficiency or benefits to *society as a whole,* including shareholders.[5] Thus, in some monopoly industries, a reduction in prices will only bring about a small increase in demand, and hence a small increase in allocative efficiency. This extra output may come at the expense of some increase in costs, i.e., a loss of productive efficiency. Prices would still be set equal to costs (as required for allocative efficiency), but the reason for doing so would be the desire to eliminate unnecessary monopoly profits (i.e., profits in excess of the cost of capital). In theory, this creates an apparent tension between efficiency and consumer benefit.

In practice, maximising benefits to consumers also requires pursuing economic efficiency; hence, the apparent conflict between the goals of economic efficiency and consumer benefits is limited. In the long run, consumers benefit most if the regulator can encourage a monopoly to minimise its costs while not limiting its ability "to raise money necessary for the proper discharge of its public duties."[6] In summary, regulation intended to maximise benefits to consumers must still ensure (1) that production is efficient and (2) that prices reflect total costs, including the cost of capital.

Incentives Under Rate of Return Regulation
The type of monopoly regulation known as Rate of Return (ROR) regulation or Cost of Service (COS) regulation has traditionally been practised in the United States. Its associated incentive problems persuaded policymakers to consider alternatives (first in other countries and later back in the US). Technically, a useful distinction can be made between the two terms, although they are usually used synonymously in the US. Here, we will use the term ROR regulation to refer to a regulatory regime in which allocative efficiency is paramount and the regulated firm's prices are reset *frequently* to keep prices at all times equal to the firm's costs, including a fixed rate of return on investment. Effectively, therefore, this type of regulatory regime sets prices by controlling the profit made by the firm and letting the firm pass through its costs to consumers (for which reason this type of regulation is sometimes known as "cost pass-through"). In fairness, ROR regulation does not exist in this pure form, since no regulator would allow a monopoly to earn a guaranteed rate of return, regardless of its efficiency.

The more common form of regulation requires prices to be reset in line with costs relatively *infrequently,* so that the rate of return can vary, at least within certain bounds. In this paper, we refer to this type of regime as COS regulation. Nevertheless, it is useful to consider ROR regulation in its pure form, in order to understand the aims of price cap regulation.

Controlling a firm's profits through ROR regulation is a politically attractive approach; however, criticisms of the approach contend that it:

- Encourages the firm to "over-capitalise" its expenditure,
- Encourages an excessively high quality of supply, and
- Generally lacks incentives to increase efficiency.

We discuss each of these in turn.

Encouraging Capital Spend

A famous criticism of ROR regulation is known as the Averch-Johnson (A-J) effect.[7] The Averch-Johnson model examines how a regulated firm chooses its inputs when the firm is allowed to earn a rate of return greater than its cost of capital. Averch and Johnson argued, "[I]f the rate of return allowed by the regulatory agency is greater than the cost of capital...then the firm will substitute capital for the other factor of production and operate at an output where cost is not minimized".

The analysis concludes that under ROR regulation, the firm has an incentive to over-invest, because by expanding the rate base it can earn a return on all additional investment. Firms may respond to this incentive either through (1) unnecessary capital expenditure that has no impact on relevant measures of the quality of supply ("gold-plating") or (2) substituting capital expenditure for operating expenditure (i.e., using capital intensive rather than least-cost technologies). Thus, the general level of utility rates (or prices) will be higher than under a theoretical optimum.

In the US, however, the A-J effect has always been more intriguing to academics than persuasive to regulators. In the original article, Averch and Johnson term the situation where allowed rates of return are above the opportunity cost of capital as the "interesting case" and not necessarily the probable one. US regulators note that the whole point of cost-of-capital analysis, and in particular their preference for the discounted cash flow methodology, is to ensure that allowed rates of return do in fact equal investors' opportunity cost of capital. As Averch and Johnson themselves observed,

[S]ince the interesting implications of the model rest on the assumption that the allowable rate of return exceeds the actual cost of capital, the question arises as to whether revenues of the industry do exceed factor costs. While it is impossible to treat this question exhaustively here, there is some reason to believe that revenues are generally in excess of costs. We have been told by representatives in both the [telecommunications] industry and in regulatory agencies that justification exists for allowing a return in excess of cost to give firms an incentive to develop and adopt cost saving techniques.[8]

Recent scholars have noted that a "lot of ink was spent on the many papers that developed variations on the A-J model and to test its implications empirically during the 1970s and 1980s" but that "[e]mpirical tests have not been particularly successful".[9] Researchers testing the Averch-Johnson effect using a frontier approach have concluded that previous studies found evidence to support the A-J hypothesis only by assuming technical or productive efficiency so that "any observed overuse of capital may just as easily be caused by lack of cost minimizing behavior by the regulated monopoly as from a distorting capital subsidy".[10] While the researchers found "significant evidence of overcapitalization,...once technical inefficiency is netted out, and a direct link to the return on the utility's rate base relative to its cost of capital is tested for," regardless of how the over-use of capital was measured, there was no statistically significant evidence to support the A-J hypothesis.[11]

In fact, all real regulatory schemes offer more complex incentives than Averch and Johnson imply. The extent to which the Averch-Johnson effect applies must in any case depend upon (1) how generous the allowed rate of return is, or is expected to be in the future and (2) the powers of the regulator to disallow "imprudent" or "inefficient" expenditure. So, on the one hand, the A-J model suggests the following drawbacks:

- In cases where the regulator deliberately provides an incentive rate of return to develop cost-saving techniques or to encourage investment for long-term reliability, the regulator may inadvertently be introducing a capital-using bias in the firm's investment decisions.
- In cases where the allowed rate of return is—and is expected to remain—relatively low (or allows little headroom for the commercial

and political risks involved), ROR regulation would discourage capital expenditure.

On the other hand, the threat of the A-J model is mitigated where ROR regulation is supported by "prudence" reviews under which the firm may be prohibited from recovering the costs of investments that the regulator shows to be inefficient or "imprudent".

Prudence reviews are well established in the US and other jurisdictions have developed similar concepts. In the mid-1990s, the authorities in Hong Kong were keen to minimise regulatory risk in the face of the impending regime change. They agreed to a regulatory regime for the Hongkong Electric Company (HEC), known as the Scheme of Control, which defined a guaranteed rate of return on investment for a period of 10 years. However, the Scheme of Control included a test to see whether or not there was excess generation capacity; if HEC were to fail the test (i.e., if there were apparently excess generation capacity), HEC's shareholders would be prevented from earning a return on new generating units.[12] ROR regulation (or cost pass-through) can provide a strong incentive for investment, but the influence of the Averch-Johnson hypothesis has led regulators in the UK, Australia, and elsewhere to focus more attention on incentives for cost minimisation and less on incentives to promote efficient investment. While there are signs that the emphasis is changing again in the US and Europe, owing to recent concerns over security of supply, it is useful to recognize the implications of Averch-Johnson as the source of price cap regulation.

Encouraging Very High Quality of Supply

One of the implications of the Averch-Johnson model is that the regulated firm with a generous allowed rate of return will resist policies that reduce the need for capacity and favour high quality and reliability of service. These standards require capital expenditure, which earns a higher total profit. One of the common consequences of ROR regulation is a high quality of supply.

A high quality of supply may be socially desirable, but not if it comes at a price that consumers are not willing to pay. Regulators therefore need to evaluate quality standards carefully. However, it would be unwise to assume that regulators must at all times curb the regulated companies' desire to invest. The precise level of investment required to achieve a reasonable quality of service is rarely known with precision. The electricity industries in California and New Zealand (Auckland), and in the rail network in the UK (Railtrack) provide instances where a failure to provide incentives for efficient investment had disastrous results for service provision. The price of over-investment or excess quality of supply may be worth paying, if the cost of under-investment is a catastrophic failure, as in these cases.

However, it is hard to ensure that excess investment will result in additional quality of supply. In many cases, the result is simply gold-plating. For this reason, regulators are normally suspicious of claims that ROR regulation automatically promotes a desirable investment in quality. Regulators prefer to offer separate, explicit incentives for maintaining the quality of supply.

Lack of Incentives to Increase Efficiency

The main drawback associated with ROR (or cost pass-through) regulation is a poor record for promoting productive efficiency and long-term price reductions. A short review period, with an immediate return to the normal rate of return, has a number of effects on the incentives for the regulated firm. While the pass-through of costs to final consumers is allocatively efficient (i.e., prices reflect costs) it provides no incentive for firms to be productively efficient by keeping costs to a minimum. No regulated firm would wish to raise costs in ways that put profits at risk (e.g., by discouraging consumer demand), but ROR regulation offers no extra profit for keeping costs down. In contrast to the concerns raised by Averch-Johnson model, this so-called "x-inefficiency", demonstrated in much of the empirical literature on the effects of US regulation, arises "from imperfections in managerial efforts to minimize the costs of production... [These imperfections lead] to production inside the production frontier and not just at the wrong location on the production frontier."[13] This x-inefficiency leads to some expenditure being wasted, not just to a bias in favour of capital- intensive methods.

Practical Consequences

For these reasons, regulators are generally reluctant to allow monopolies to include all their costs *automatically* in their prices, and in practice, few regulators have ever adopted ROR regulation in the form of automatic pass-through of costs. First, costs are subject to a series of tests, e.g., to ensure that costs were "prudently incurred" or that investments remain "used and useful". Second, under COS regulation, regulators fix tariffs at reviews and then leave them unmodified for some time, until either the regulator or the regulated company prompts the next review. In between reviews, the fixed tariffs allow the company to increase profits by reducing costs—a phenomenon known as "regulatory lag".[14] Bonbright, a widely respected author on regulatory matters, defines regulatory lag as "the *quite usual* delay between the time when reported rates of profit are above or below standard and the time when an offsetting rate decrease or increase may be put into effect by commission order or otherwise" (emphasis added).[15] The incentive this phenomenon provides is limited, or at least unpredictable, since the regulator can trigger a tariff review at any time if the regulated company's cost cutting opens a large gap between revenues and costs.

In practice then, COS regulation (as opposed to the idealised form of ROR regulation described above) provides some incentive for productive efficiency in the form of cost minimisation. Regulated firms protect themselves against a cut in their profits by avoiding imprudent investments, and regulatory lag provides a short-term (if uncertain) incentive to raise their profits by cutting costs.

What Defines the Different Forms of Regulation?

In writings on economic regulation, it is common to find a distinction between two different models. On the one hand, some commentators refer to "traditional" methods of regulation, which they call ROR or COS regulation. As discussed above, regulators do not only regulate rates of return, so ROR regulation does not exist in its pure form. However, many regulatory systems are recognisably similar to COS regulation, in which tariffs are reset every so often in line with the costs of service (rather than the market value of the service).

On the other hand, some policymakers criticise COS regulation and advocate instead the use of Price Cap (PC) regulation. PC regulation is also known as incentive regulation, RPI-X regulation, CPI-X regulation, Performance Based Regulation (PBR), or even as "benchmarking" or yardstick regulation. Advocates present these alternative forms of regulation as a way to introduce incentives for productive efficiency, supposedly in contrast to the situation under COS regulation.

Some academic and regulatory discussions suggest there are huge differences between the intellectual and procedural methods underlying each form of regulation. COS regulation gives regulated firms an incentive to minimise costs to the extent there is a "regulatory lag" between cutting costs and resetting tariffs, whereas PC regulation works most effectively when revenues reflect actual costs. However, all forms of regulation are in fact constrained by the economic objectives set out above. In practice, therefore, the differences between PC regulation and the alternative COS regulation are rather subtle.

Key Differences Between COS and PC Regulation

The traditional form of COS regulation revolves around tariff reviews. Such a review can be opened either by the regulated company or by the regulator (often acting on a complaint from another interested party). A review normally takes place if a change in circumstances causes the company's rate of return to reach a level that is unacceptably high (to the regulator) or unacceptably low (to the company). Although this kind of regulation is sometimes called ROR regulation by reference to this trigger, regulators do not usually fix the company's rate of return, but rather approve a set of tariffs intended to allow the company to achieve a certain rate of return in certain conditions.

During a tariff review, the regulator examines the costs of the regulated company in order to establish whether or not the company should be allowed to recover them, using some standard, such as whether they were prudently incurred. The regulator then calculates a revenue requirement for the regulated company that is sufficient to cover the allowed level of operating costs and depreciation (amortisation of capital costs) and to grant the company a reasonable rate of return. Finally, the regulator approves a new set of tariffs sufficient to recover the revenue requirement defined by these costs—hence the term Cost of Service regulation. The tariffs emerging from any review are valid until the next review.

Price Cap regulation differs from COS regulation in the following respects:

- The period between tariff reviews is pre-specified, so that a tariff review is not triggered by a change in the company's rate of return.
- The outcome of a review may be a form of control defined in terms of total revenues, or average prices, rather than a detailed set of tariffs for particular services, so that, within limits, the regulated firm has scope to adjust the balance of tariffs.
- Controls on total revenues or average prices would allow a regulated company to increase its profits by cutting the quality of service to save costs, so PC regulation usually incorporates a number of minimum quality standards or quality incentives.[16]

· Because the revenue or price control must last for a defined period, the PC formula will contain a number of indices or factors that update maximum revenues in the light of unpredictable or expected changes. For example, including a retail price index (RPI) or consumer price index (CPI) accounts for general inflation, whilst the "x-factor" builds in an annual rate of change designed to match the expected rate of growth in efficiency.

Because of this last point, PC regulation is sometimes also known as "RPI-X" or "CPI-X" regulation. The effect of adopting this approach is to give the regulated company a profit incentive to reduce the costs of providing a given quality of service. Figure1 shows how PC regulation benefits both customers and shareholders in the regulated utility, assuming that the efficiency term X is greater than the inflation index.

Figure1 shows how costs and prices might be expected to change over time under COS regulation and PC regulation. For simplicity, it assumes that costs—and therefore prices—remain constant under COS regulation. However, the dashed line shows a price cap that falls over time. PC regulation allows the company to increase its profits by cutting its costs, so costs are lower than under COS regulation. In the figure, the company is able to reduce its costs faster than the price cap falls. The total cost reduction or efficiency gain is divided between the company's customers and shareholders, in the form of a price reduction (a benefit to customers) that still leaves the company earning higher profits than under COS regu-

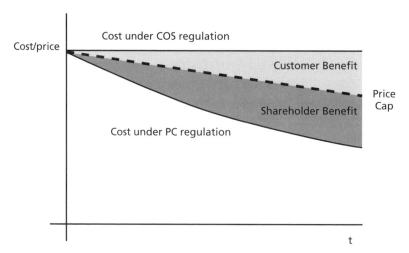

Figure 1.   *Simple Cost of Service Regulation v. Simple Price Cap Regulation*

lation (a benefit to shareholders). Hence, in principle at least, the superior incentive properties of PC regulation create an overall gain, which allows everyone to benefit from a "win-win situation".

Incentives for Cost Reduction from COS and PC Regulation

The standard model for analysing incentive regulation involves a firm with a cost structure of the form $c = c^E + u$. Here, c is the *ex-post* realised cost, whilst c^E is some expected value of costs or benchmark, and u is a term dependent on both chance *and* the firm's effort to reduce costs.[17] It is assumed that the regulator can observe c and has some way of estimating c^E—or at least some way of setting c^E as a reasonable target for costs. Hence, it is possible to calculate u. However, it is not possible for the regulator to break down u into the separate effects of chance and effort. Attempts to provide a reward for effort must take this lack of information into account.

Consider a price control that takes on the form:

$$p = c^E + (1-\gamma)(c - c^E).$$

The parameter γ reflects the level of cost pass-through or profit sharing. If $\gamma=0$ then the firm always obtains its realised cost—the benchmark c^E plus the difference between the difference between the *ex post* costs and the benchmark—and it has no profit incentives to reduce cost. This is a simplistic form of ROR regulation.

On the other hand, if $\gamma=1$ and the benchmark

$$c^E[t] = c^E[t-1] \times \left(\frac{RPI_t}{RPI_{t-1}} - X \right)$$

where RPI_t is the Retail Price Index in year t and X is the rate of expected efficiency growth (defined as a fraction, so that 0.02 means 2 percent annual growth), the term $(1-\gamma)(c-c^E)$ drops to zero and we have a simplistic form of RPI-X Price Cap regulation in which prices change by an index and there are no periodic reviews. The firm may keep any unexpected cost reduction as profit, and this provides optimal incentives for cost reduction. However through time, forecasting errors will widen the gap between p and c, and large abnormal profits (or losses) will result.

Any reasonable incentive scheme must involve intermediate levels of profit sharing, either in an automatic revenue formula or through the medium of periodic reviews. In other words, any reasonable scheme will have $0 < \gamma < 1$. When the degree of cost sharing is low, then the incentives for cost reduction are high, but price may depart from observed cost causing allocative inefficiency and either large monopoly profits or large losses. Note that the scheme still retains a degree of cost sharing if these profits and losses are eliminated at periodic reviews rather than automatically through a revenue or tariff formula between periodic reviews. Abstracting from other factors and assuming similar degrees of risk aversion for the regulator and the monopoly, the optimal form of regulation for businesses with a large level of cost uncertainty will involve a high degree of profit sharing.[18]

Is PC Regulation Better than COS Regulation?

To assess the relative merits of PC regulation and COS regulation, we need to appraise them by reference to the economic objectives for regulation described in section I.C.

Balancing Allocative and Productive Efficiency
As we have described them above, PC regulation will be better at delivering productive efficiency (i.e., lowering costs), whilst COS regulation will be better at maintaining allocative efficiency (i.e., keeping prices in line with actual costs and avoiding monopoly profits). However, no form of regulation can focus entirely on one to the exclusion of the other:

- In practice, COS regulation provides some incentives for cost minimisation—mainly because prices are in fact fixed during the lag between the time when the firm cuts its costs and the time when the regulator sets new tariffs.
- In practice, PC regulation must periodically or gradually realign prices with costs, or else the regulated firm would incur politically unsustainable abnormal profits or financially unsustainable abnormal losses.

Thus *in practice* the difference between COS and PC regulation in *terms of cost saving incentives and allocative efficiency* is a question of degree. As Laffont and Tirole wrote about incentives for cost reduction:[19] "...it would be simpleminded to make a strong distinction between COS and PC regulations. After all in both regimes prices are set by the regulator for some length of time."

In traditional COS regulation, incentives to cut costs are a by-product of the regulatory framework rather than the result of conscious design.

Bonbright expressed this particular view of cost of service regulation in the following terms:

> "What has saved [cost of service] regulation from being a critical influence in the direction of mediocrity and tardy technological progress has been its very 'deficiencies' in the form of regulatory lags and in the form of acquiescence by commissions in fairly prolonged periods of theoretically 'excessive' earnings on the part of companies whose...comparative rates of charge for service have not made them vulnerable to popular attack."[20]

PC regulation moves this aspect of regulation to the foreground and focuses attention on the need to design appropriate incentives for cost reduction. The definition of a fixed regulatory period between reviews *formalises* the kind of "regulatory lags" that provide incentives under COS regulation and so strengthens those incentives. However, it is not sufficient merely to fix the regulatory period. In order to set up a price cap that improves incentives for efficiency and is not "vulnerable to popular attack", regulators must consider two other factors.

Capital Attraction and Quality of Service
Figure1 showed how price caps allow regulated monopolies to increase their profits by *cutting* costs. However, customers also want regulated monopolies to *incur* the cost of long-term investment in order to increase output and to maintain the quality of supply. Regulators therefore have to be careful not to destroy incentives to spend money by over-emphasising incentives to cut spending. The incentive for long-term investment derives from the incentives offered by the review process, not from the price cap formula itself, for reasons that are best explained by reference to Figure 2.

Whenever regulated monopolies invest, they incur the capital expenditure of the investment and the recurrent expenditure of operating it. Recovery of the capital expenditure is spread over many years—in some cases more than 40 years. In all subsequent years, therefore, allowed revenues need to cover not only annual operating expenditures, but also an allowance for costs of depreciation and return on capital.

Given that tariffs or price caps are reviewed every three to five years at most, the allowance for depreciation and return on capital with a 40-year life must survive scrutiny by a regulator on eight or more occasions. In order to provide an incentive for investment, the regulatory scheme must

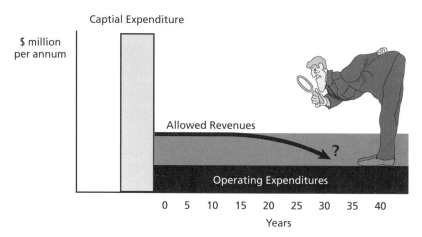

Figure 2. *Long-Term Regulatory Risk*

offer investors a reasonable prospect that these reviews will continue to allow them to recover the investment cost. No individual regulator can offer such long-term assurance on a personal basis; instead, the assurance must derive from guidelines (legal, administrative, procedural) on the way in which each future review will be carried out.

Similarly, successful use of PC regulation requires a supporting set of incentives that discourage regulated monopolies from cutting the quality of service. Hence, PC regulation to encourage cost cutting requires both (1) a clear set of review procedures to provide long-term incentives for investment and (2) additional incentives to maintain quality of service in the short-term. These quality incentives may take the form of minimum standards (with large penalties for falling below them) or graduated incentives (which adjust revenues by a small amount when a measure of quality rises or falls). Because different aspects of service quality need attention at different times, as the regulator updates the regulatory incentives for investment, the process of defining quality standards takes a long time. Again, a key consideration is the extent to which investors believe that they have a reasonable prospect of cost recovery when they invest in expanding the quantity or quality of service.

In the United States, these assurances of cost recovery derive from the Fifth Amendment of the US Constitution, which prohibits all federal and state institutions from depriving individuals (in this case, shareholders) of their property without due process: "No person shall...be deprived of life, liberty or property without due process of law, nor shall private property be taken for public use, without just compensation."

The Fourteenth Amendment applies this provision to state institutions: "No state shall make or enforce any law which shall abridge the privileges or immunities of citizens of the United States; nor shall any state deprive any person of life, liberty, or property, without due process of law...."

Neither amendment rules out the taking of private property. However, due process and just compensation play a vital role in regulation and judicial review. Their application to shareholders' funds in regulated utilities and the right of regulated utilities to a reasonable prospect of cost recovery derives from the US Supreme Court's interpretation of the Constitution in two decisions: *Bluefield* and *Hope*.

The *Bluefield* decision of 1923[21] established that regulators must offer investors "a reasonable rate of return", i.e., a rate of return that is comparable to that available to investors in similar businesses with corresponding risks and uncertainties. The *Bluefield* decision established that the ultimate test of the rate of return was the ability of regulated companies "under efficient and economical management" to attract capital for investment. The *Hope Gas* decision of 1944[22] shed further light on the definition of a reasonable rate of return. The appropriate return on capital must be achievable after recovery of all other costs, particularly the return of capital (i.e., depreciation) and operating costs. In other words, it is not sufficient for a regulator to allow a comparable rate of return; the regulator must also allow revenues that cover a reasonable estimate of other costs as well.

In summary, US regulation can be characterised by the obligation to give regulated firms a reasonable prospect of cost recovery. A reasonable prospect is not, of course, the same as an absolute certainty, as the regulator can prevent firms from recovering costs if they are proven (after following due process) to be "imprudent".

Outside the US, few legal frameworks offer such clear-cut legal protection to shareholders' funds. Therefore, if PC regulation (or indeed any form of utility regulation that delays recovery of capital expenditure) is to provide effective incentives for investment outside the US, it must operate within a detailed framework of accounting rules and review procedures that, at the very least, make it clear (1) what costs the regulated firm should expect to recover and (2) whether the regulator is offering the firm any prospect of recovering them. This framework does not rule out price caps that allow the regulated monopoly's achieved rate of return to vary if the company is in fact more or less efficient than expected.

This legal and procedural framework need not *guarantee* cost recovery; even under COS regulation, cost recovery is normally subject to a "prudence" test. However, any regulatory review procedure must offer investors a reasonable prospect of cost recovery, meaning that investors can expect to recover all their costs (including the cost of capital) if they maintain a reasonable degree of efficiency. To ensure that the benefits of PC regulation will not be offset by the cost of regulatory risk, it is important to adopt accounting methods and price cap review procedures that give investors confidence that they can recover their costs. Then PC regulation can fulfill its promise as a useful weapon in the armoury of monopoly regulators.

Notes

1. The outcome of a market may be efficient without being politically acceptable, or desirable, if the resulting distribution of costs and benefits unduly affects particular individuals. However, here, we will be focusing on economic efficiency as a prerequisite for successful competition or regulation.

2. See G. Shuttleworth, "Opening European Electricity and Gas Markets". Beesley lecture for the Institute of Economic Affairs, London, November 2000, reprinted in *Utility Regulation and Competition Policy,* ed. Colin Robinson, (Cheltenham: Edward Elgar Publishing Ltd., 2002). That lecture lists the conditions that make sector-specific regulation necessary. These include conditions of natural monopoly, i.e., economies of scale/scope, long-lived assets and sunk costs, and customers' inability to capture the economies of scale and scope (transactions costs). Other criteria (switching costs, frequency of repeated cases, and distributional concerns) might also make sector-specific regulation necessary even for markets that do not exhibit natural monopoly conditions, but they are not immediately relevant here.

3. Regulatory economists divide the accounting profits of a regulated company into two parts: the cost of capital, or the rate of return required to reimburse investors, sometimes known as the "normal profit"; and any rent or "super-normal profit" earned above the cost of capital. Unless stated otherwise, when we use the term "costs", we are referring to the economic definition of costs, which includes the cost of capital or a "normal profit".

4. This condition does not hold universally. A monopoly fearful of potential competitors may overinvest, thereby raising total costs but making it easier to survive a price war, in order to deter others from entering the market. However, such behaviour is a reaction to particular market conditions. Private sector monopolies do not have an inherent tendency to overspend in the absence of regulatory interventions or threats.

5. In economic terms, consumer benefits are known as the "consumer surplus", whereas benefits to society are known as "welfare". For a study of the effect of choosing one or other objective, see Richard Schmalensee, "Good Regulatory Regimes," *RAND Journal of Economics,* XX, 3 (Autumn 1989), 417-436.

6. *Bluefield Waterworks & Improvement Co. v. Public Service Commission,* 262 US 679 (1929).

7. See H. Averch and L. Johnson, "Behavior of the Firm under Regulatory Constraint," *American Economic Review,* LII, 5 (December 1962), 1052-1063.

8. Ibid., p. 1061.

9. Paul Joskow, "Regulation of Natural Monopolies," in *Handbook of Law and Economics,* ed. by A. M. Polinsky (Amsterdam: North-Holland, August 2007); available in PDF at Joskow's website, p. 119.

10. Donald F. Vitaliano and Gregory Stella, "A Frontier Approach to Testing the Averch-Johnson Hypothesis," *Rensselaer Working Papers in Economics* (New York: Department of Economics, RPI, June 2006), p. 3.

11. Op. cit., p. 19.

12. In the UK, where there are many supporters of "light-handed price cap regulation", the energy regulator (Ofgem) began (effectively from 2004 onwards) to question whether regulated gas and electricity distribution networks should recover the full cost of investments made during the previous regulatory period. At least initially, Ofgem's criteria for disallowing the cost of inefficient or wasteful investment were too vague and changeable to provide clear incentives to investors. However, Ofgem's attempt to disallow investments shows that even PC regulation needs the support of transparent prudence review procedures—using predefined and objective criteria.

13. Joskow, op. cit., p. 120.

14. See Jean-Jacques Laffont and Jean Tirole, *A Theory of Incentives in Procurement and Regulation* (Cambridge: MIT Press, 1993), p. 15.

15. James Bonbright, *Principles of Public Utility Rates* (New York: Columbia University Press, 1961), p. 53. Bonbright also refers to "regulatory lag" on pages 242 and 262.

16. In COS regulation, monitoring of quality of service is usually performed as a separate function unrelated to the rate case.

17. The discussion is based on R. Rees and J. Vickers, "RPI-X Price Cap Regulation" in M. Bishop et al. (eds.) *The Regulatory Challenge* (Oxford: Oxford University Press, 1995). A technical discussion may be found in J-J. Laffont and J. Tirole, op. cit. as well as in M. Armstrong, S. Cowan, and J. Vickers, *Regulatory Reform—Economic Analysis and British Experience* (Cambridge MA: MIT Press, 1994), 61-64.

18. Schmalensee, op. cit.

19. Op. cit., p. 18.

20. Bonbright, op. cit., p. 262.

21. *Bluefield,* op. cit.

22. *Federal Power Commission v. Hope Natural Gas Co.,* 320 U.S. 591 (1944).

2

RETHINKING THE IMPLEMENTATION OF THE PRUDENT COST STANDARD

Karl McDermott
Ross Hemphill
Carl Peterson

Introduction

During the height of the 2001 regional power crisis in the western United States, Nevada Power Company (NPC) and Sierra Pacific Power Company (SPPC) purchased over a billion dollars of short-term power. The purchases coincided with a period of great regulatory uncertainty in the region, as policymakers began to reevaluate ongoing efforts to deregulate the power industry. Given the uncertainty of their future service obligations under restructuring, the incumbent utilities argued that managers could not reasonably plan for the long term and instead had to depend on short-term purchases in an ever-deteriorating short-term market. The Nevada Public Utilities Commission disagreed and subsequently denied recovery of $437 million of NPC's $922 million in purchased power costs and $55.8 million of SPPC's $205 million in deferred power costs.[1] The question facing the Nevada regulators was the primary regulatory problem facing administrative agencies charged with the control of prices for regulated firms: How does a regulatory body assess the reasonableness of management actions for the purpose of setting rates?

Regulators around the world operate under the presumption that customers should only pay the prudent costs of operating the utility. Throughout much of the history of public utility regulation in the United States, regulators have struggled to establish a standard of prudent costs to verify that the proper balance was achieved between the interests of customers and stockholders of the regulated utility. The essence of the problem is the premise that, by definition, prudent costs are those incurred under competition because in a competitive market only the prudently managed firm would survive. Regulation should therefore serve as a substitute for the market and mimic the competitive market outcome. However, since public utilities in the US are regulated as natural monopolies, unlike firms operating in competitive markets, there are few market prices that can be reliably employed to assess the cost effectiveness of the regulated firm. The result has been a search for a reasoned approach (1) to developing a mechanism to establish a reliable proxy for the competitive costs of providing service[2] and (2) to make the concept operational in a transparent, understandable, and desirable way.

However, the whole concept of mimicking competition begs the question of what "competitive benchmark" is appropriate as a standard for prudence. The purpose of this chapter is to examine the approaches regulators use to assess the reasonableness of costs, with a particular emphasis on identifying the prudent costs included in rates. We will explore the foundation of the prudent cost standard in competitive market theory and explain how that theory is used (and misused) in practice. This analysis will be used to suggest a new approach to addressing the prudent cost standard that could help achieve the balance between customers and utilities that would be more effective for utilities, while maintaining the necessary oversight by the regulator.

The Context for the Prudent Cost Standard

Although regulation has been viewed as necessary when the structure of the industry does not allow for sufficient competition,[3] the standard for efficiency that Western societies typically employ is the outcome of a competitive process. This concept underlies many of the policies toward business in the US and the European Union, including antitrust policies.[4] Given its pre-eminent role, competition has become the cornerstone in the philosophical preconceptions regarding proper economic design. For example, an early observer noted:

> [O]ur ethical conceptions...reflect the ideals of competition: we see unfairness in practices which do violence to the presumed results of free competition and regard as fair and just prices which, being established through competition, correspond to the costs of production.[5]

It was a natural extension of this philosophical outlook to apply the concept to the regulatory process and to envisage a process that would achieve approximately the same results as would occur if competition truly existed in the industry. The literature on regulation in the United States is replete with references to the idea that regulation should imitate, replicate, or simulate the competitive market, or alternatively, serve as its surrogate, replacement, or substitute. For example, in his 1961 classic, James Bonbright wrote:

> Regulation, it is said, is a substitute for competition. Hence its objective should be to compel a regulated enterprise, despite its possession of complete or partial monopoly, to charge rates approximating those which it would charge if free from regulation but subject to the market forces of competition. In short, regulation should be not only a substitute for competition, but a closely imitative substitute.[6]

Following Smith and Bonbright, it would appear that the fundamental notion of just price is tied to the costs of production, and more specifically to the costs of production under a competitive market process. In Bonbright's words, regulation should then compel the industry to operate as if it were a competitive firm.[7] This reliance on the concept of regulation as a substitute for competition has been repeated so many times by so many theorists and practitioners that it has become one of the core myths of regulation.

The problem with applying this concept is that the very reason for the regulation of public utilities is that the fundamental production technology is not consistent with a competitive outcome.[8] Utility investments tend to be very capital intensive and long-lived and, in most cases, irreversible. This has two important implications. First, these characteristics suggest production technology that leads to economies of scale and in most cases to natural monopoly, which in turn implies a noncompetitive outcome. Second, large sunk capital costs also imply *quasi-rents,* which provide opportunity for regulatory opportunism, i.e., once the investment is in place, the regulator has the incentive to set price at just a smidgeon above variable cost, thereby bankrupting the utility. Effective regulation must use a mechanism, such as a legal requirement to ban the expropriation of investments once they have occurred.[9]

In addition, the competitive market operates as a resource allocation process through an intricate set of prices and transaction costs that involve risk and reward trade-offs that are not necessarily available to public utilities. In particular, while a competitive firm can enter or exit any product market based on the expected profits, this entry and exit flexibility is denied to regulated firms. Generally, the utility is also legally obligated to hook up and serve customers at regulated rates, a truncation of the property rights that does not exist in the non-regulated sectors.[10]

Furthermore, the competitive firm is always subject to the unforgiving eye of the competitive benchmark, and that eye uses 20/20 hindsight to punish or reward firms for its decisions, whether or not these decisions were made as part of a reasonable process. But if the competitive benchmark is taken to mean that a firm can earn uncapped profits when decisions turn out well and experience uncapped loses when the firm's decisions turn out badly, it cannot be the standard applied to the utility industry. The utility is generally regulated under a profit cap that would result in a situation of 'heads you win, tails I lose' if 20/20 hindsight were used to review its decisions.

Finally, the operation of competitive markets has implications for how firms operate. In perfectly competitive markets, firms produce where costs are minimized subject to the constraint of the production technology.[11] Conceptually, while maintaining a constant output, an efficient firm produces where the rate of physical transformation of inputs is equal to the rate of economic substitution (the relative prices) of those inputs. This is the familiar case of minimizing costs subject to an output constraint, and one could imagine a fully efficient (or "x-efficient") firm operating at the solution to this minimization problem. Expanding this cost minimization construct to the entire industry, one could draw a unit isoquant, which describes the input possibilities for the production of a unit of the good.[12] An x-efficient firm is a firm that is producing on the unit isoquant. In theory, one could deduce a firm's inefficiency by measuring how far it lies from that isoquant and in practice many regulators use this theory to set the prudent level of costs allowed to be recovered by utilities by estimating that "efficient frontier".

There are several problems with such an approach. First is the practical issue of estimating the efficient frontier. An estimate is just that and all estimation techniques are sensitive to many different assumptions and data constraints. For example, Data Envelopment Analysis (DEA), a linear programming technique, provides no statistical basis to estimate the error of the estimate and is sensitive to the choice of inputs and outputs, which can vary significantly among its practitioners. Such dependence on the practitioner's judgment renders the standard arbitrary, and for the utility subject to the technique, that could mean the difference between sinking and swimming.[13]

Second, even if we could agree on the estimation technique, the idea that the efficient firm is the proper standard is suspect. In simple text-book economics, all firms are x-efficient and operate on the efficient frontier. In reality, the efficient firm is the *highest* standard in the industry and not the standard by which all firms are judged: x-ineffi-ciency exists. In the textbook model, if a firm is more efficient than another firm, it expands production and chases the inefficient firm from the market. However, in reality that is not the way markets work. Differential efficiencies exist as a matter of historical accident, luck, tech-nological change, market imperfections, and a variety of other reasons unrelated to managerial competence. These differential efficiencies cannot be squeezed out of the market and will exist in the long run. This implies that firms with differential efficiency will earn above or below normal profits in the long run, even in a competitive market. Therefore, comparing all firms to the most efficient firm misses the reality of how markets actually operate.

Approaches to Determining Prudent Costs

Around the globe, regulators have been experimenting with ways to capture the notion of prudent costs and replicate the market outcome. Attempts to balance the desire to control with the desire to provide incentives have resulted in experiments with a wide range of administra-tive mechanisms. The two predominant ways to establish prudent costs are the administrative rate case and benchmarking. In the administrative rate case, effective evaluation involves thoroughly evaluating management choices and reviewing a wide range of decisions, both past and present, a review that could lead to second-guessing and hindsight review. This process has often set regulators and managers of utilities at odds, since management often perceives effective regulation as interference with its prerogatives. Alternative mechanisms like benchmarking that do not use a utility's own costs may reduce the review of management choices, but the potential arbitrariness of the benchmark can punish management for perfectly reasonable choices.[14] These mechanisms presume that (1) the level of a company's imprudent costs can be measured by its distance from the least cost, most efficient firm and (2) that distance is solely attributable to inefficient and incompetent management. While these two approaches can be subdivided into multiple methods, we focus on them generically in order to illustrate the differences and obtain lessons from their application.

Administrative Rate Cases

Basic Approach

One of the keys to US regulation is what is known as the "end-result doctrine." Established in the Hope Natural Gas Case,[15] the court held that commissions have considerable flexibility to select among different theories of ratemaking: "Under the statutory standard of just and reasonable it is the result reached, not the method employed which is controlling. It is not theory but the impact of the rate order which counts." Within that flexibility, a very elaborate and comprehensive system has evolved to calculate the legitimate costs of supplying utility service. Under this system, a *total revenue requirement* is determined that is set equal to the total cost of supplying services, including capital costs.[16] It can be summarized in the familiar regulatory equation:

$$TR = TC = [RB - D]\ ROR + OE + d + T$$

Where:
TR = Total revenue (or revenue requirement)
TC = Total cost
RB = Ratebase or value of capital
D = Accumulated depreciation
ROR = Rate of return
OE = Operating expenses
d = Annual depreciation cost
T = Taxes

Conceptually, if the monopoly supplies service efficiently, the total costs of supplying these services would be the *prudently incurred costs.*[17] In implementing the equation, regulators are guided by certain principles. These include:

- **Prohibition on single-issue ratemaking:** Regulation focuses on the total cost of service and avoids problems of piecemeal or single-issue ratemaking. That is, no single cost item, such as inventory, should be the factor that drives the ratemaking decision; what matters to regulators in setting the revenue requirement is (consistent with the end result doctrine) the net result of all cost increases and decreases as well as productivity changes.[18]

· **Prohibition on retroactive ratemaking:** The revenue requirement and, in turn, rates are set prospectively. All attempts at setting just and reasonable rates are for the purposes of looking forward. There is no attempt to rectify past outcomes by making up for lost or excess profits.[19]

· **Prudent investment standard:** Prudence is generally defined in terms of the reasonable person standard. That is, given the information that was known or that should have been known at the time a decision was made, if that decision could have been made by a reasonable person, then that decision is prudent (i.e., prudence is *not* a 20/20 hindsight review). Imprudent management can lead to the exclusion of the costs associated with those actions from the revenue requirement.[20]

· **Used and useful standard:** Utility assets must be sized at any given time such that they are, or can be, used to provide service to customers.[21]

· **Test year:** The test year is used to ensure a matching of revenues and costs. The simplest method is to employ a historic test year where all costs and revenues are known.[22] However, forecast or future test years have been employed, as well as mixtures of historic and future test years.[23]

In an administrative rate case the utility presents a *test year* set of revenues (at current prices) and costs so the regulator can determine the excess or shortfall in revenues relative to the current costs of providing service. The costs and revenues must *match,* that is, the revenues allowed to be recovered are compared to the costs incurred in the same period.[24] Allowable expenses must have a connection with the delivery of service to customers in the period going forward.[25] Often a normalization process is used to remove the effect of extraordinary events, a practice that avoids strategic choice of test periods. Investment cost included in the ratebase must be used and useful in supplying service to customers.[26] Although the used and useful test has a long history in the US, it came to prominence during the age of nuclear expansion. Sometimes used as a substitute for the standard prudence test, it is always applied after the fact and therefore its 20/20 hindsight can be a problem. One particularly troublesome version is the "economic" used and useful test. Under this test, all plant that fails to be equal to or less than a current market value is disallowed[27] so that it is a logical extension of the idea that regulation should mimic competition. This test sounds like the long-since-abandoned fair value standard for evaluating utility assets,[28] rejected by most US regulators because of (1) its circularity for ratemaking purposes, (2) the practical problems of estimating the correct market value, and (3) issues of strategically choosing when to revalue assets.[29]

Evolution of the Prudence Standard
Policymakers have grappled with the concept that the reasonableness of allowed costs can be measured by the hypothetical competitive market outcome since the early days of regulation. However, it was not until the late 1970s that regulators faced the more practical applications of assessing the prudence of the cost overruns and cancellation of a large number of power plant construction projects.[30] Because some of these project additions could add as much as 30 percent to the existing rates, regulators were compelled to examine these projects on a case-by-case basis.[31] Through their decisions and the court reviews, the idea of prudence evolved in the legal battles, not only over utility plant construction and cancellation decisions, but also regarding fuel costs, plant operations, capacity purchases, plant availability and outages, and ultimately the overall prerogative of management.

At the federal level, the traditional definitions of prudence remained largely unchanged. The Federal Energy Regulatory Commission opined,

> Managements of unregulated business subject to the free interplay of competitive forces have no alternative to efficiency. If they are to remain competitive, they must constantly be on the lookout for cost economies and cost savings. Public utility management, on the other hand, does not have quite the same incentive. Regulation must make sure that the costs incurred in the rendition of service requested are necessary and prudent.[32]

What constituted prudent behavior? The FERC defined it by employing a reasonable person standard:

In performing our duty to determine the prudence of specific costs, the appropriate test to be used is whether they are costs which a reasonable utility management ... would have made, in good faith, under the same circumstances, and at the relevant point in time.[33]

But at the state commissions, this period saw the beginning of "prudence reviews" as the primary method for challenging the companies' past decisions and their implication for customer rates. The possibility that state commissions would apply hindsight, that is apply what they know today in order to judge the prudence of company decisions made yesterday, raised a number of legal and policy questions. The desire of the states to adopt concepts of efficiency and prudence that allowed "Monday morning quarterbacking" was constrained by the courts as they reviewed commission decisions. The courts recognized that decision makers did not have crystal balls and could not foresee changing market and economic conditions. In particular, the special circumstances that distinguish a utility from competitive firms, such as the obligation to serve, required that construction and supply decisions be made in advance to avoid system failure and prolonged outages. As courts evaluated commission determinations of prudent costs, prudence, then, as a standard of review, evolved to take into account the utility's special characteristics. The courts found that it is impermissible to allow 20/20 hindsight to bias the review of management behavior:

A prudence review must determine whether the company's action, based on all that it knew or should have known at the time were reasonable and prudent in light of the circumstances which then existed. It is clear that such a determination may not properly be made on the basis of hindsight judgments, nor is it appropriate for the (commission) merely to substitute its best judgment for the judgments made by the company's managers.[34]

And:

The company's conduct should be judged by asking whether the conduct was reasonable at the time, under all the circumstances, considering that the company had to solve its problems prospectively rather than in reliance on hindsight. In effect, our responsibility is to determine how reasonable people would have performed the task that confronted the company.[35]

However, despite the standards applied by the courts and encouraged by the example of the FERC, the prudence disallowances still amounted to as much as 30 percent of the capital costs and as much as $1.4 billion dollars for new plant.[36] Thus, just as a market can inflict losses on firms as a result of market disequilibrium, the regulatory process, through the case-by-case prudence reviews, was able to simulate this competitive adjustment process with a vengeance. Further, prudence reviews were not limited to investment in new electric plant. Debates arose over the approval of the cost of replacement power resulting from plant outages, and jurisdictional battles arose between states and federal agencies over the prudence of utility power purchases.[37] In natural gas, deregulation of markets in the 1980s forced gas utilities to change their purchasing practices from long-term contracts with pipelines to supply portfolio management of purchases directly from gas suppliers.[38] The move to direct market access and purchases from marketers of gas implied that the term structure, price, and the quantity purchased from any one supplier, as well as firmness and other reliability characteristics, were now decision variables whose prudence state regulators could examine when reviewing supply decisions. Believing that the "cost-plus" regulatory process did not systemically provide management an incentive to control cost, commissions also began experimenting with new regulatory tools, like management audits to evaluate utility decision management,[39] and greater attention to the management of end-use efficiency.

As the prudence battle unfolded, it became clear to many in the industry that there was a need restructure the regulatory process to limit the effect of after-the-fact reviews and the concomitant increased risk and cost of capital and reduced incentives to invest. Alternative mechanisms included some form of pre-approval process for new plants, performance-based regulation, competitive bidding for new supplies, and least-cost planning processes intended to increase the parties and information that could be brought to bear on the capacity decisions.

Evaluation of Prudence Reviews
Utility investments are highly capital intensive and tend to be rather lumpy. Traditionally, prudence reviews took place after investment had occurred and only when that investment was "used and useful" for supply

customers. This suggests a tremendous level of risk for investors concerning the price level, and in turn profits, in the post-investment period. The fundamental problem of 20/20 hindsight review of prudence and used and useful examinations is that the uncertainly of cost recovery can leave a utility in a financially vulnerable position. The end-results doctrine, along with the wide latitude given regulators in the US to make decisions based on the record as they see it, presents unnecessary risks that may harm both investors and, in the long run, customers through inefficient investment. The prudence review, at least, allows the utility its "day in court" but clearly does not diminish the unnecessary risks associated with the process.

Benchmarking

In one sense, all rate regulation uses some form of benchmarking. In the own cost/revenue-requirements comparison performed for administrative rate case, the regulator estimates the cost of equity, which implicitly sets a benchmark for returns. Other benchmarking processes use more formulaic or mechanistic approaches. Two of these processes are statistical benchmarking, or simply benchmarking, and yardstick regulation. Benchmarking involves the use of statistical (and mathematical) models to assess the efficiency of the utility for the purposes of assessing relative efficiency and, in turn, allowed costs. Methods such as DEA, stochastic frontier analysis, total factor productivity, and corrected least squares models[40] can either be applied to the actual allowed costs of the firm or be used to assess the productivity (or future productivity growth) that should be expected from the firm for the purpose of setting formulas for changing rates.

Yardstick regulation is one form of benchmarking. A generic yardstick price is set as follows:

$$P_{i,t} = \alpha_i C_{i,t} + (1 - \alpha_i) \sum_{j=1}^{n} f_j\, C_{i,t}$$

Where
$P_{i,t}$ = overall price cap for the utility (i.e., firm i)
α_i = share of the utility's own costs in the price cap
f_j = weight for each firm in the peer group that is the benchmark, and
$C_{i,t}$ = unit cost of each peer group firm.

Note that $\alpha_i = 1$ is the US style rate of return regulation and $\alpha_i = 0$ is a pure yardstick. Prices could also be used in place of costs. Yardsticks come in various forms and can be calculated in many different manners. Issues that regulators need to address include how the initial prices are set, whether the benchmark is of total cost or a single element of cost, whether it is based on utility's own cost or on a peer group's, whether prices will be updated annually based on formula (e.g., RPI-X) and how changes in actual utility costs will be incorporated if they are different from the benchmark.

As Table 1 shows, most statistical methods adapted in practice are found outside the US, while there are some limited examples from the US.[41] (North Dakota uses a form of price yardstick to set annual rates under its price cap plan for Northern States Power and Otter Tail Power[42] and Illinois has used a form of yardstick for setting prices at the beginning of the restructuring period.[43]) Energy regulators in the EU are more prone to use these methods for benchmarking the level of costs than are their US counterparts, in part because the standards of proof are not as demanding in the European context, and European regulators face less pressure to explain their decisions in detail.

In fact, while not much used today, yardstick regulation has an old if somewhat a checkered past in US regulation. During the 1920s and early 1930s it was introduced by advocates of public power[44] who proposed that the costs of publicly owned and operated power systems could provide a standard of reasonable rates for private companies:

> The latest phase of public ownership and operation has a different character and purpose, namely, its use as a "yardstick" for the rates of private companies. This is the outgrowth of a feeling that the system of private operation with public control should be required constantly to meet the test of furnishing service on as good terms as the public could furnish directly. It is felt that without this there is no adequate check on the reasonableness of costs, and that the system of valuing property and allowing a "fair return" on the valuation is full of loopholes, operating in practice too favorably for the companies. The intent of the yardstick policy is to supplement these weak points of regulation by furnishing standards of reasonable cost and by putting the private companies under pressure to meet the cheapness of public service, under possible penalty of being displaced if they fail to meet a fair comparative test.[45]

Table 1.   *Examples of Benchmarking Procedures for Energy Utilities*

Country	Benchmarking Practice
Finland	Data Envelopment Analysis (DEA)
Norway	DEA
Sweden	Reference Network (has used DEA for comparison)
Denmark	Network Volume Model
Spain	Reference Network
Netherlands	DEA, to be updated by yardstick regulation (from 2007)
UK	Regression (with various adjustments)
Northern Ireland	DEA
Australia–New South Wales	DEA, Stochastic Frontier Analysis and Total Factor Productivity (TFP)
Australia–Queensland	Previously used DEA; moved to econometric methods
Australia–Tasmania	Consultant report
Australia–Victoria	Statistical benchmarking
Canada–Ontario	Historical TFP
Japan	Yardstick on rates of comparable groups
US (traditional regulation)	Rate of return (accounting cost)
Brazil	DEA
Chile	Yardstick with reference network
Columbia	DEA
Maine (US–Central Maine Power)	TFP for setting x-factor in price cap
North Dakota (US–NSP/Otter Tail Power)	Yardstick based on prices and negotiated productivity number for x-factor

Adapted from Carl R. Peterson, "Efficiency in the US Electric Industry: Transaction Costs, Deregulation, and Governance Structures," Unpublished dissertation, Department of Economics, University of Illinois at Chicago, 2007; S. Viljainen, K. Tahvanainen, J. Lassila, S. Honkapuro, and J. Partanen, "Regulation of Electricity Distribution Business," Nordic Distribution and Asset Management Conference: Helsinki University of Technology (23 August 2004), Helsinki, Finland. (Table 1) and Jamasb and Pollitt (2001, Table 4).

Thus the director of the Tennessee Valley Authority, a public power entity, described the approach:

> The power policy written into the operations in this limited area [is]...intended to serve as a "yardstick" by which to measure the fairness of rates of private utilities, and to prevent destructive financial practices by the latter. Tennessee Valley Authority Act represents an attempt to regulate public utilities not by quasi-judicial commissions but by competition.... The Authority is required to acquire a market and to set up an area in which to conduct its operations. The result of these operations in this limited area [is]...intended to serve as a "yardstick" by which to measure the fairness of rates of private utilities, and to prevent destructive financial practices by the latter.[46]

These yardstick approaches were criticized as being dishonest due to (1) the differences in financing and taxation of public and private entities and (2) the allocation issues associated with water projects with multiple uses.[47]

Evaluation of Benchmarking

In many ways, benchmarking appears to be a solution to several of the key critiques of American-style regulation. First, on its face, the benchmarks are supposed to be objective and transparent. Second, the traditional incentive to unnecessarily increase capital spending that has long been a criticism of cost-based regulation would seem to disappear. Third, benchmarking the costs to the correct cost level would appear to provide the correct incentive for efficient operation. Fourth, lumpy investment can be addressed through formula rates. Last, it would seem that these methods are less costly to implement than an American-style regulatory system.

However, all is not as it seems.

The concept of benchmarking relies heavily on the competitive market paradigm where many small similar firms compete to produce a homogeneous product in the same market, so benchmarking inherently ignores the reality that utilities are not competitive firms, do not compete in the same market (service territory) and can be very heterogeneous. The difficulty is to distinguish what portion of the inefficient (at least higher cost) operation is due to managerial incompetence and therefore should not be included in regulated rates and what portion is due to the natural operation of markets where different firms are producing under different conditions. Under a mechanistic benchmarking approach, all inefficiency is assumed to be a result of managerial incompetence (or imprudent behavior), yet we know that this is not the case. The approach can be fundamentally unfair to investors in instances where a benchmark fails to adequately address specific issues that drive costs in different utility service territories. While many authors and regulators have recognized these problems, the solutions are generally either (1) more detailed reviews of each case so the regulator obtains adequate information to determine what portion of inefficiency is "reasonable" and what portion is due solely to poor management, or (2) more complicated mechanisms, such as adjustments to the benchmarking models and added incentive mechanisms.[48]

Further, there is no consensus on the appropriate method for benchmarking utility costs.[49] Benchmarking of cost levels would seem to be even more problematic than benchmarking productively and price changes over time. This is due to tremendous discretion provided to those running the benchmarking models that are largely a black box to the public and often to the regulators as well. In contrast, TFP analysis at least has a solid foundation in the economic literature and the econometric methods are well known.[50] As a result, regulators (and the parties to cases) especially in the US see these methods as removing the regulator from its key analytical oversight function. If their decisions are to withstand judicial review, US regulators must provide detailed and transparent reasoning for each decision based on the specific facts related to a particular utility's situation.[51] This does not spell the end of the experiment with incentive regulation in the US, but it clearly signals a time to re-think and re-work the methods that have been used to date, especially those methods that utilize full-cost benchmarking.

Conclusions and Potential Solutions

The saying that the grass is always greener on the other side of the fence may apply to utilities' perceptions of US and European approaches to prudence. Utilities in the US face after-the-fact prudence reviews that tend to create unnecessary risks, and some long for an easier method that at least provides a benchmark to work under. Many in Europe see (full cost) benchmarking as arbitrary, effectively creating an artificial hurdle based on management techniques, and not good regulatory policy. They long for the ability to prove that their costs are reasonable and should be recovered in rates.

Actually, neither approach adequately addresses the dilemma of determining the prudence of all costs incurred by the regulated utility. What is needed is a combination of the approaches resulting in a separate treatment of the major long-term cost categories for which the prudence evaluation has always been most crucial.

The key issue in addressing prudence is the risk associated with the prudence decision itself. In the American-style model with ex post managerial prudence reviews, this risk manifests itself through possible after-the-fact disallowances. In the (full cost) benchmarking model, this risk is related to the inability of the benchmark to accurately estimate the actual costs of running the utility. In both cases, the risk of under-recovery weakens the incentive for investment, and in the end, customers suffer from the resulting underinvestment.[52] To address this fundamental issue, a pre-approval process can be used to set the cost level and capital investment choices prior to investment by the utility. This pre-approval approach has several benefits:

- Investment decisions are made *a priori* when all parties have the same information. This prevents 20/20 hindsight from entering the prudence decision.
- An open process of pre-approval provides the regulator and parties with a transparent method of oversight.
- Changes to the investment plan can be incorporated over time.
- The process is flexible enough to address multiple utility functions.

Three examples of this approach can be found in US regulation.

- **Pre-approval of regulatory parameters (i.e., rate-of-return, type of investment):** As early as 1988, the state of Massachusetts adopted a pre-approval contract approach for the cost recovery of incremental investments.[53] Currently, in Wisconsin contracts with affiliated companies are approved prior to construction of power plants and in Iowa a "rate case" is completed prior to construction in order to determine all financial parameters and choice of technology.
- **Pre-approval of procurement processes:** In New Jersey and Illinois, utilities purchase power for customers through a statewide auction that has pre-approved structure and rules. Costs are then passed through to consumers as prudent.

· **Formula rates or performance-based regulation:** RPI-X and other performance-based regulation programs can operate as a pre-approval.

Regulators and the regulated utilities must decide how to establish a process under which a fair assessment of the utilities' prudent costs can be conducted. If regulators are to avoid the problems concomitant with lengthy after-the-fact reviews without giving up some form of oversight, they must commit to a two-step pre-approval process. In effect this process divides the prudence question into two parts—decisional prudence and managerial prudence—thereby focusing and limiting the reviews in a meaningful way.[54] In step one, the issues surrounding the decision to invest can be examined together with all relevant information at the time and not be subjected to after the fact review. Through its involvement and review of decisions and their expected costs, the regulatory agency, accepts the decision of how and why to move forward. Commissions maintain oversight but that oversight occurs upfront, at the time of the decision. In a second phase of the case, the commission can always ask if the company carried out the decisions well. Thus the regulator preserves an oversight role in examining how the effectively the pre-approved decisions were executed but does not question the decision itself.

The problem in the United States in the 1980s was that major inquiries had never been required before. Utility management had previously not needed to clear its investment decisions and few regulators questioned that their investments were reasonable. Suddenly confronted with major cost overruns for unneeded capacity, regulators questioned the prudence of the investments but had no reasoned process for going back in time to reconstruct the decision process and the relevant information that influenced or should have influenced the decisions. Modern regulation needs to avoid repeating the mistakes of that period and needs to separate the conditions surrounding the making of a decision from the execution of the decisions. The judicious employment of pre-approval processes, in conjunction with cost indexing, performance regulation, or auction processes, can focus the debates over prudence and improve the rationality of the next round of utility investments and rate cases.

Notes

1. See Re Nevada Power Co. 216 PUR4th 557 (Nev.P.U.C. 2002); Re Sierra Pacific Power Co., 218 PUR 4th 1, (Nev. P.U.C. 2002). In disallowing the power costs, the NPUC found that certain NPC actions were imprudent, including: failure to enter into an energy contract with Merrill Lynch, conducting a power procurement strategy in February 2001 that lead to "above average" costs, entering into a forward contract in April 2001, contracting for peak power in September 2001 that turned out to be excessive, and, contracting for off-peak energy in the second and third quarters of 2001.

2. It may be questionable whether regulation can ultimately be a substitute for competition in a market where the technology implies a natural monopoly. However, this chapter will operate under the premise that regulation should substitute for competition, in the sense that firm behavior under regulation should, to the extent possible, imply efficient production (i.e., with a minimum of waste).

3. Traditionally in the US, utilities have been privately owned firms operating under regulatory supervision of the state. However, in parts of the US, as well as many European countries, the preferred option was public ownership of the utility operating under social management. This chapter will not address the issues related to public ownership.

4. There are exceptions to this general rule, such as patent policy and other policies that are related to improving societal outcomes through noncompetitive processes, as well as policies that are aimed at maintaining certain social norms, such as labor market restrictions.

5. Nelson Lee Smith, *The Fair Rate of Return in Public Utility Regulation* (Boston: Houghton Mifflin, 1932), p. 8.

6. James C. Bonbright *Principles of Public Utility Rates* (New York: Columbia University Press, 1961), p. 93) See also, Nelson Smith, *ibid.,* p. 6, Clair Wilcox, *Public Policies Toward Business* (Homewood, IL: Richard D. Irwin, 1966), pp. 476-477; and William J. Baumol and J. Gregory Sidak, *Toward Competition in Local Telephony* (Cambridge, MA: MIT Press, 1994), p. 5.

7. Bonbright dedicated an entire chapter to examining what he referred to as an "intriguing proposition" and remained somewhat skeptical of the efficacy of such a policy, in part due to the complexity of replicating the competitive results under the actual conditions required of a utility's operations.

8. Jerry Hausman, "Power Struggles: Explaining Deregulatory Reforms in Electricity Markets," Comments, *Brookings Papers on Economic Activity: Microeconomics* (1996), pp. 264-266.

9. Richard J. Gilbert and David M. Newbery, "The Dynamic Efficiency of Regulatory Constitutions," *Rand Journal of Economics,* XXV, 4 (1994), 538-554 model investment under various forms of regulation including a legal requirement to allow recovery of "used and useful" investment A discussion of opportunism and its implications for governance structures can be found in Oliver E. Williamson, "Transaction Cost Economics," in R. Schmalensee and R. Willig,

eds., *Handbook of Industrial Organization* Vol. 1. (New York: North-Holland, 1989), pp. 135-182.

10. In fact, in the US, if the government attempted to truncate a nonregulated firm's property rights, without due process and proper compensation, such an action would run afoul of the national constitution.

11. See, e.g., Andreu Mas-Colell, Michael D. Whinston and Jerry R. Green, *Microeconomic Theory* (New York: Oxford University Press, 1995); or Hal R. Varian, *Microeconomic Analysis* (New York: W.W. Norton, 1991).

12. See, e.g., T.J. Coelli, D.S. Prasada Rao, C. J. O'Donnell, and G.E. Battese, *An Introduction to Efficiency and Productivity Analysis* (New York: Springer, 2005).

13. Other techniques, such as regression analysis, may do a better job but still suffer from sensitivities to data requirements and the practitioner's judgment.

14. See, e.g., G. Shuttleworth, "Benchmarking of Electricity Networks: Practical Problems with its Use for Regulation," *Utilities Policy*, XIII (2005), 310-317.

15. Hope Natural Gas Case. *Federal Power Comm'n v. Hope Natural Gas Co.*, 320 U.S. 591 (1944).

16. The discussion of revenue requirement builds on K.A. McDermott, C.R. Peterson and R.C. Hemphill, "Critical Issues in the Regulation of Electric Utilities in Wisconsin," *Wisconsin Policy Research Institute Report,* XIX (2006) 1-68.

17. In theory, "efficiently" would mean production without waste. In practice, the reasonable person standard is applied.

18. Single-issue ratemaking is discussed in: *Citizens Utility Board v. Illinois Commerce Commission,* 166 Ill.2d 111, 651 N.E.2d 1089 (1995); *Business and Professional People for the Public Interest v. Illinois Commerce Commission,* 146 Ill.2d 175, 585 N.E.2d 1032 (1991); *State ex rel. Utility Consumers Council of Missouri, Inc. v. Public Service Commission of Missouri,* 585 S.W.2d 41 (Mo. 1979); and *Pennsylvania Indus. Energy Coalition v. Pennsylvania Pub. Util. Comm'n,* 653 A.2d 1336, 1350 (Pa. Comm. Ct. 1995), aff'd, 670 A.2d 1152 (Pa. 1996). There are limited exceptions to the single-issue ratemaking prohibition related to items that are highly volatile (e.g., fuel or purchase power costs).

19. See, e.g., Stefan Kreieger, "The Ghost of Regulation Past: Current Applications of the Rule Against Retroactive Ratemaking in Public Utility Proceedings," *University of Illinois Law Review* (1991), 983.

20. See, e.g., Gary Allison, "Imprudent Power Construction Projects: The Malaise of Traditional Public Utility Policies," *Hofstra Law Review,* XIII (1985), 507.

21. See, e.g., Jonathan A. Lesser, "Used and useful test: implications for a restructured electric industry" XXIII *Energy Law Journal* (2002), 349-381.

22. Historical test years can be adjusted through *known and measurable* changes to costs that will occur with a very high probability in the short term.

23. See, e.g., Clark E. Downs, "The Use of The Future Test Year in Utility Ratemaking," *Boston University Law Review,* LII (1972), 791, 796.

24. "The matching principle is a fundamental concept of both accounting and ratemaking. A mismatch of reported costs and revenues on an income statement will understate or overstate a firm's earnings. A mismatch of costs and revenues in the calculation of a utility's test year earnings and its revenue requirement will result in deficient or excessive rates—in either case such rates would not be just and reasonable." *Iowa Public Service Co.* 46 PUR 4th 339, (1982).

25. Tests for allowable expenses do not include "hypothetical, uncertain, remote, and conjectural." *Los Angles Gas and Electric Corp. v. RR Com of California* 289 US 57, S. Ct. 637 (1936).

26. See *Union Stock Yard v. United States,* 304 US 470, 475, 58 S. Ct. (1938). See also *Jersey Central Power and Light Co. v. FERC,* 810 F.2d 1168 (D.C. Cir. 1987) and *Duquesne Light Co. v. Barasch,* 488 U.S. 299 (1989).

27. Of course, plant that is below market value is not "written up" to market value.

28. The US Supreme court suggested that a fair value standard approach "mimics" competition in *Duquesne Light Co.* at 308-309.

29. See Bonbright, *Principles,* pp. 215-222.

30. For example the FERC staff report on Regulating Independent Power Producers: A Policy Analysis published October 13, 1987 noted that, "Between 1945 and 1975, fewer than a dozen prudence cases were brought. Since 1975, however, over fifty cases have been undertaken by state PUC's." The staff was using an unpublished report dated 1981 for these statistics, implying close to ten cases per year between 1975 and 1981.

31. In 1987, the electric industry was facing the construction of 33 nuclear power plants, not including coal and other units. Of these, 28 were expected to be completed at a total cost of $92 billion. The remaining units were expected to be cancelled. Of the $92 billion, some analysts expected as much as $40 billion to be at risk for prudence disallowances. See Solomon Brothers, Pending Nuclear Construction Cases, Oct. 31, 1985.

32. *Re New England Power Co.* 31 FERC Para. 61,047 @ 61,084 (1985).

33. Ibid., @ 61,083 (1985).

34. *In re Western Mass. Elec. Co.,* 80 PUR 4th at 501.

35. *In re Consolidated Edison Co. of N.Y., Inc.* Opinion No. 79-1 (N.Y. 1979), 5-6.

36. John Anderson, "Are Prudence Reviews Necessary?" *Public Utility Fortnightly,* CXXVII, 3 (Feb. 1, 1991), 23-36.

37. The Pike County decision, (77 Pa. Cmwlth. 268, 465 A.2d 735) resolved some of these issues as the courts ruled that state commissions could not question the price paid for the power, which was set at the FERC and therefore protected by the filed rate doctrine; states could examine the quantity of supply procured and thus the prudence of the utility's portfolio of supplies.

38. While many local distribution companies were served by multiple pipelines and therefore had had some form of portfolio management function, the fact was that long term contracts had predominated in supply decisions.

39. See, for example, Howard Greenbaum, ed., *Management Auditing as a Regulatory Tool: The New York State Experience* (New York: Praeger, 1987).

40. See, e.g., T. Jamasb and M. Pollitt, "Benchmarking and Regulation: International Electricity Experience," *Utilities Policy* IX (2001), 107-130.

41. Again, we are referring only to the regulation of energy utilities.

42. North Dakota Public Service Commission: *In the Matter of Otter Tail Power Company's Proposal to Implement Performance-Based Regulation,* Case No. PU-401-00-36, (2000).

43. 220 ILCS 5/16-111, Illinois Public Utilities Act.

44. In the US, public power entities can be owned by any level of government. Traditionally, the large wholesale power producers were owned either by the state or the federal government. Local distribution companies, some vertically integrated, are owned at the municipal level.

45. John Maurice Clark, *Social Control of Business* (New York, NY McGraw-Hill Book Co., 1939), p. 250.

46. David Lilienthal, "Regulation of Public Utilities during the Depression," *Harvard Law Review* XLVI, 5 (March 1933), p. 746.

47. For a description of the yardstick proposal, see James C. Bonbright, *Public Utilities and the National Power Policies* (New York: Columbia University Press, 1940).

48. The Netherlands regulator just recently concluded that a closer connection between reasonable profits and actual results may be necessary in future tariff reviews. This seems to indicate a movement away from a pure benchmarking regime. See "Preliminary Findings of Investigation into Profits of Energy Companies," press release, NMa, The Hague, The Netherlands, February 13, 2007.

49. See, e.g., J. Stern, "UK regulatory price reviews and the role of efficiency estimates," *Utilities Policy,* XIII (2005), 273-278.

50. See Jeff Makholm, "Elusive Efficiency and the *X-Factor* in Incentive Regulation," in this section.

51. A typical rate case order for a large utility may run hundreds of pages and be based on thousands of pages of evidence and testimony from all interested parties.

52. The opposite could occur as well, leaving firms with relatively high profit and customers with high prices. However, whichever result occurs, the outcome is harmful to society.

53. 97 PUR 4th 201, Re Pricing and Rate-making Treatment of New Electric Generating Facilities which are not Qualifying Facilities, D.P.U. 86-36-E Massachusetts Department of Public Utilities Oct. 28, 1988.

54. For a comprehensive discussion of the difference between decisional and managerial prudence, see 135 PUR 4th Illinois Commerce Commission, *Re Illinois Power Company,* Docket 91-0024 (September 2, 1992) pp. 238-241.

3

WHY PLANNING A NUCLEAR PLANT IS A GOOD IDEA EVEN IF BUILDING ONE TURNS OUT TO BE A BAD IDEA

Jonathan Falk

Introduction

The nuclear debacle of the 1980s and 1990s led to massive disallowances of nuclear costs when the regulators felt that the money spent on nuclear was not even *ex ante* in the ratepayer's interests. As a result, no new nuclear plant has been begun in the United States since the Three Mile Island incident over 25 years ago. But in a world of increasing concern over greenhouse gases (GHG), planning a nuclear plant—even if not ultimately building one—can be an important hedge against runaway carbon prices. The advent of real options analysis, and particularly of stochastic dynamic programming methods, has provided the tools that can recast the debates over the next generation of nuclear units.

New Interest in Nuclear Power

Speculation on the renaissance of nuclear power in the United States has recently filled both the trade press and popular press. Among the prominent reasons for thinking nuclear is a good idea are these:

- Nuclear power production is a negligible source of greenhouse gases in production.[1] No other technology with this feature is scalable to the needs of a growing economy.
- At the moment, nuclear power is immensely profitable to the owners of nuclear plants. When $13 natural gas sets the marginal price in wholesale markets, nuclear power, with operating costs of no more than a cent or so, reaps large operating profits. Meanwhile,

either (1) the high capital costs of many of those plants are covered by stranded cost agreements or (2) the plants were purchased by companies for much lower capital charges because at the time the forecast wholesale prices were quite low. As a result, heavily nuclear companies are currently reaping outsize rewards.

- New nuclear designs promise large reductions in annual operating and maintenance costs. Inherently safe reactor designs can be run, in principle, with greatly streamlined training, staffing, and process budgets.
- Partial government loan guarantees under the Energy Policy Act of 2005 will subsidize the first six new reactors.

Notwithstanding these palpable incentives to construct a new plant, the history of nuclear plants in the United States casts a giant shadow over the prospects of a revived nuclear industry. Fears concern incremental construction cost, second-guessed (1) by regulators who disallow costs that they find were imprudently incurred, or (2) by markets that will force stockholders to absorb above-market total costs, or, (3) in the worst of both worlds, by both.

Nuclear Power in a Deterministic World

The staged development of nuclear power is an important hedge against runaway carbon prices. It is probably optimal to begin developing nuclear power even if it is quite likely that nuclear power turns out to be uneconomic *ex post*. As much as regulated utilities might want a commitment from their regulators that the costs of nuclear plants will be recoverable, it is impossible to imagine that regulators will be forthcoming. Instead, the typical regulatory dance involves a projection that the given investment will be used and useful and an after-the-fact reckoning which, while it is not supposed to be based on hindsight, inevitably is.

Fortunately, since the era of nuclear plant planning in the 1960s and 1970s, capital planning has been greatly improved by the advent of *real options analysis*. While I do not believe that the use of real options analysis would have changed the decisions that were made over that period,[2] I do believe that real options analysis can substantially recast our debates over the next generation of nuclear units. Carefully calculated expenses should now be recoverable from ratepayers even in the event nuclear power turns out to be the wrong investment.

When a utility uses a real-options greenhouse gas-hedge approach to the recovery of nuclear investment it does not even commit itself to assert that nuclear is *likely* to be an economic choice. Thus, even when things turn out badly, utilities cannot be accused of either lying or incompetence, since their position was that despite the substantial probability that the nuclear investment would be a loser, it was nonetheless (and somewhat paradoxically, though only on first blush) the right thing to do.

This advice might seem strange to those whose familiarity with real-options is embodied in the saying "waiting is better than acting." While that lesson is useful as a pithy summary of real options analysis, it does not tell the whole story. Taken literally, it might be seen as counseling that development of new nuclear plants be postponed until the uncertainties over construction cost are resolved, at least in part. If that were the only uncertainty, this advice would be correct. But there are more critical uncertainties than construction cost, notably the cost of GHG emissions. The real lesson of a full real-options approach for nuclear plants is to wait. The real lesson is that, by increasing the flexibility to respond to uncertainty, expenditures that appear suboptimal in a world of certainty may be worthwhile pursuing today.

If we knew the price at which nuclear power plants could be built and the cost for which power from coal plants, its main US competitor, could be sold, we could figure out, at the margin, whether the next baseload plant should be coal or nuclear.[3] Unfortunately, estimates for the next generation of nuclear plants range from $1,000/kW to perhaps $2,500/kW or more. Estimates of the implicit price of carbon emission range from $0/ton to $100/ton or more. As many analyses have shown, where one stands on the economics of nuclear plants largely comes down to where one stands on the central tendency of these wildly varying estimates. Low capital costs and high carbon prices favor nuclear power, while high capital costs for nuclear and low carbon prices favor coal.[4]

Given these two uncertainties, one might think that the prudent course is to sit on the sidelines and wait and see what happens. That decision would not necessarily be wrong. But nuclear requires a very long lead-time with substantial filings before the NRC and extensive state regulatory proceedings as well. Thus, *if* nuclear turns out to be the correct choice, the fence-sitters will bear years of higher costs before the least-cost alternative can be built.

In fact, investment in nuclear facilities is a staged process. If nuclear investments turn out to be too expensive, the utility can always cancel their plans to go forward. While that investment is lost, it is no different from any other hedge investment—something that you expect to lose under certain states of the world but that decreases losses in other states of the world.

There are two techniques for evaluating the correct response to evolving uncertainty in a series of sequential decisions: financial methods based on continuous-time finance theory and stochastic dynamic programming (SDP) methods based on discrete-time decision theory. Each has its advantages. The finance approach can lean on a very rich and rapidly growing body of work to evaluate financial options, while the SDP approach is fairly easy to tailor precisely to a particular set of facts.

In the case of nuclear plants, I think there are clear reasons to prefer the SDP approach. Unlike the finance methodology, which essentially presumes that information evolves like a random walk over time, the SDP approach is well-structured to consider a series of milestone decision points. Second, the great strength of the finance approach is its use of observed market events to estimate model parameters. The lack of such established markets in the events underlying nuclear construction it quite difficult to seed the finance model.

A "Toy" SDP Model

To see how an SDP model works, consider the following highly simplified scenario. The decision to build a nuclear plant breaks into two stages: (1) NRC design approval and (2) plant construction. In a third stage, the plant is operated and, the Shoreham station notwithstanding,[5] no decisions need to be made after plant completion. Assume that the NRC design approval process costs $10 million and that the cost of the plant is either $1 billion, $1.5 billion, or $2 billion, with equal probabilities. Further assume that the cost of a coal plant (including the present value of necessary emission controls or permits and any higher fuel costs) is either $1.2 billion, $1.3 billion, or $1.7 billion, again with equal probabilities and uncorrelated with the nuclear construction cost. To make the example particularly simple, assume that baseload plants are never on the margin, so that revenues are unaffected by plant choice.

In *ex ante* expected value terms, the decision is quite obvious: Build the coal plant and forego the approval process. An SDP analysis of the problem, however, can take into account the fact that by the end of the approval process, we will have a much better idea of the probabilities, even if those probabilities are still not known with certainty. Thus, we will assume that by the time the approval process is finished, we will have one of the following five states of the world:

	State 1	State 2	State 3	State 4	State 5
Probability	0.200	0.200	0.200	0.200	0.200
Pr(NK)=1	0.200	0.667	0.333	0.400	0.067
Pr(NK)=1.5	0.667	0.000	0.333	0.167	0.500
Pr(NK)=2	0.133	0.333	0.333	0.433	0.433
Pr(CK)=1.2	0.000	0.667	0.333	0.600	0.067
Pr(CK)=1.3	0.000	0.200	0.333	0.300	0.833
Pr(CK)=1.7	1.000	0.133	0.333	0.100	0.100

Each of the five states is characterized by the probability distributions of the cost of nuclear plants (NK) and the cost of coal plants (CK) and its own probability. There are several things to note about this table. First, when we sum across all possible states of the world, the probabilities are exactly as I stated *ex ante*: 1/3 probability of each possible value of NK and CK (that is, each row sums to 5/3 or 1.667). Second, in each state, the probabilities of the NK and CK values each add to 1, so the effect of time is not to change the possible values of nuclear and coal costs, but only to change their probabilities. For example, in State 1 we know that we will have high coal costs with certainty (Pr(CK)=$1.7b is 1.000), and we are twice as likely as before to have the mid-level nuclear prices (Pr(NK)=$1.5b is .667). State 3 corresponds to the case where the intervening period has taught us nothing at all (all probabilities remain at .333).

To implement SDP, we now look at what decision we make in each state of the world, contingent on whether or not we spend the costs to develop nuclear. If we choose not to develop nuclear, the choice is simple. We must build the coal plant no matter what state of the world develops, and the total expected cost of doing so is $1.4 billion.[6]

Now assume we spend the $10 million to get NRC approval. We have the following expected costs in billions of dollars including the $10 million for the NRC approval:

	State 1	State 2	State 3	State 4	State 5
E(NK)	1.477	1.343	1.510	1.527	1.693
E(CK)	1.710	1.297	1.410	1.290	1.343
Difference	0.233	−0.047	−0.100	−0.237	−0.350
Minimum	1.477	1.297	1.410	1.290	1.343

If we find ourselves in States 2 through 5, we find that on an expected value basis nuclear is still more expensive than coal, so we proceed to build the coal plant, in each case also spending the $10 million on nuclear development. But if State 1 develops, nuclear is cheaper by $233 million and we build it instead. The expected value over all of the states of the world is $1.363 billion, $37 million cheaper than $1.4 billion, the EV had we chosen in advance not to develop nuclear and therefore not spent $10 million on nuclear development costs. Thus, the payback on the nuclear hedge, *even though there was an 80 percent chance that the nuclear plant would not be built,* is almost 300 percent. Obviously, this example is highly simplified,[7] but it demonstrates that when relatively small investments can be made that greatly enhance the ability to flexibly commit in the future, such investments may have outsize returns even when they look like poor choices in isolation.

Adding Realism

Converting this example from a toy into a truly useful tool requires discounting cash flows and taking into account the explicit time structure of the model. The two variable, three states-per-variable description of the world needs to be enriched, and the probabilities have to be estimated rather than made up. In addition, the actual decision to construct a nuclear or coal plant probably has dozens of decision points, not two.

An important modeling issue is when to start the investment process and when to proceed to the next milestone. The more decision points, the more critical it is to realistically describe how each uncertainty resolves itself. For example, carbon prices will not be zero one day and $75 the next. When and if the US adopts carbon controls, phase-in periods and extended research will slowly diffuse the true value of carbon reductions into the world. Thus, the choice is not just between investing in nuclear development and not investing. The alternative (familiar as the basic paradigm of real options analysis) is to delay investment to get one more period's information about the likely values.

While all of these details are important, the essential technique of SDP is unchanged. Work backwards from the last decision you will make as a function of the states of the world in which you find yourself then, and use the minimum values thus derived to solve for decisions made one step earlier.

Prudence in the 21st Century

The nuclear debacle of the 1980s and 1990s led to massive disallowances of nuclear costs when the regulators felt (perhaps opportunistically) that the money spent on nuclear was not even *ex ante* in the ratepayer's interests. But this analysis demonstrates that even investments that turn out after the fact to be not "used and useful," are not only prudent investments but are investments it would be imprudent *not* to make. Laying the groundwork for planning the next generation of nuclear plants is almost surely one such prudent investment, especially for regulated utilities: It is a process that should be starting now to help immunize the utility from whatever states of the world develop.

Notes

1. The building of a nuclear plant of course embodies the emission of greenhouse gases.

2. In my opinion, only better (or luckier) foresight would have done the trick.

3. There are of course, lots of other uncertainties, but these two are by far the largest, assuming that the national issue of high-level waste disposal is resolved in some fashion.

4. These analyses ignore the GHG cost of constructing either nuclear or coal plants. The construction cost clearly should take into account the GHG cost embedded in the cost of construction materials. Whether or not it will do so depends on whether (1) the production of steel and cement has to pay GHG costs and (2) the relative amounts of construction materials embedded in the two types of plants.

5. While many plants have been cancelled in various stages of planning and construction, only the Shoreham plant was completed, allowed to go critical and then shut down, incurring decommissioning costs in addition to construction costs without producing any useful output.

6. ($1.2b x .333) + ($1.4b x .333) + ($1.7b x .333) = $1.4 billion

7. Indeed, it's so simple that it can be phrased another way, which may help the reader understand what's going on. In State 1, development of nuclear saves $233 million. There is a 20 percent chance this will happen, so the expected savings is $233 x 0.2, or $46.6 million. In all other cases, the option to build nuclear saves $0. Thus, the development expense has an expected payback of $46.6 million and a cost of $10 million. In the simple model, the $10 million serves as the ante to get into the game. If the potential rewards of the game are high enough, it's a good idea to ante up, even if you win very few hands. In more complicated scenarios, however, the states of the world do not parse quite so easily.

4

PRACTICALITIES OF PRICE CAP REGULATION

Graham Shuttleworth

Introduction

Price cap (PC) regulation—also known as incentive regulation, RPI-X regulation, CPI-X regulation, Performance Based Regulation (PBR), benchmarking or yardstick regulation—is distinguished by the use of a price cap formula for setting the tariffs or revenues of a regulated firm that remains (in whole or in part) independent of that firm's actual costs for a defined period. At the end of that period, the price cap formula is reset to take account of changes in conditions (including, usually, changes in the firm's actual costs). The *level* of the price cap must provide investors with a reasonable prospect of cost recovery, but the *structure* of the price cap must also meet a variety of regulatory objectives. This chapter discusses the practical considerations to be taken into account in designing the price cap formula and how regulators should approach the task of setting the formula for a natural monopoly, given the fundamental principles and constraints underlying any regulatory regime.[1]

In setting price caps, a regulator needs methodologies:

- to forecast a reasonable level of costs,
- to set a revenue formula that tracks costs,
- to determine how allowed revenues should adapt to changes in the pattern of demand, and
- to address special risks and uncertainties.

The following sections describe these tasks in detail, as well as the international best practices in their execution; the incentives for efficiency, quality of service, and long-term investments; and the preconditions for the establishment of a successful regime.

The Necessary Methodologies

Forecasting a Reasonable Level of Costs

Investors in a regulated firm need to be offered a reasonable prospect of cost recovery before they will make the necessary commitment to long-term investment. Where price caps are the preferred regulatory mechanism, it is sometimes suggested that such caps can be set by reference to external, benchmarked costs.[2] However, experience suggests that, even under price cap regulation, it is legitimate—and may be necessary—for regulators to set revenues by reference to (though not always equal to) the regulated firm's own costs.

In the UK, price caps have been applied to regulated utilities for over 20 years. These caps have been reset at different times, and the process of resetting the caps has been constrained by the desire to keep prices in line with actual costs. In 1995, UK energy regulator OFGEM redefined the costs of the electricity distribution businesses at a much lower level, with the effect of lowering price caps. However, by 1999, this method had caused problems because revenues no longer reflected some companies' actual costs. In 2000, OFGEM said, in a consultation paper on the regulation of electricity distribution charges, that:

> To encourage the efficient use of each distribution system, the charges levied by distribution businesses on suppliers should reflect the costs that customers impose on the distribution systems.[3]

On 17 May 2001, a judge in the Supreme Court of the State of Victoria, Australia, ruled that taking firm-specific costs into account at a regulatory review was consistent with both the theory and practice of incentive regulation. Under the law in Victoria, the regulator is prohibited from using Rate of Return (ROR) regulation and must use "price-based regulation adopting a CPI-X approach." The case, between a regulated firm and the regulator, centered on the firm's claim that the prohibition on ROR regulation required the regulator to avoid re-balancing prices in line with the firm's own costs and to set a factor based exclusively on external benchmarks. The judge ruled against the firm.

In 2003, the Dutch energy regulator set out a proposal to set revenues for electricity and gas distribution networks by 2006 on the basis of a benchmark for costs[4] and to update this revenue using a factor derived from the performance of the sector as a whole. However, the method allows the networks to claim extra revenue for "extraordinary and significant investments" and for "regional differences", both of which require explicit attention to actual costs.[5]

One of the arguments Littlechild[6] used in recommending RPI-X-style PC regulation rather than ROR regulation for the UK was that PC regulation has a small cost burden while ROR regulation is costly to operate. Littlechild claimed that the regulator does not need to make "judgements or calculations with respect to capital, allocation of costs, rates of return, future movements of cost and demand, desirable performance, etc." It turned out that this confidence was misplaced. In practice, regulators using PC regulation have to make the same kinds of judgements and calculations, and they incur considerable costs. Armstrong et al. conclude that the scope, complexity and tightness of RPI-X regulation increased over time.[7] In the UK, the costs of regulation are very high,[8] and all across Europe there is concern about the transparency of regulatory judgements.[9]

It is therefore naïve to believe that price caps reduce the burden of regulation by replacing detailed investigations of a firm's costs with the calculation of simple price indices. To offer investors a reasonable prospect of cost recovery, price caps must bear at least some resemblance to the firm's underlying costs. This has been a legal requirement in the US since the early 20th century and is increasingly becoming regulatory practice in other regimes.

Setting a Revenue Formula that Tracks Costs

Cost Pass-Through

The price cap regime usually does not apply to all of the costs of the firm, and in implementing price caps the regulator must decide how much of the firm's revenues will be subject to the cap and how much cost pass-through is desirable. A pure rate-of-return regulatory regime is characterised by full pass-through of costs. However, under price cap regulation, pass-through of costs that are observable and outside of the firms' control may be desirable (and frequently occurs). For example, the price cap applying to end-user tariffs for electricity may allow pass-through of cost items that are not under the control of the distribution company serving the customer, such as electricity contract prices, local property taxes, and charges for transmission (if regulated separately). Armstrong et al. analyse "pure price cap regulation" (a price cap fixed in perpetuity at some predetermined level) and "rate-of-return regulation" (defined as 100 percent cost pass-through) and conclude:

> In almost all cases, it was seen that good price regulation should lie intermediately between these polar extremes, with more cost uncertainty and greater risk aversion on the part of the company implying that a greater proportion of costs should be passed on to consumers.[10]

That is, cost pass-through encourages allocative efficiency by allowing prices to track costs, and it also introduces risk sharing between consumers and investors. Under cost pass-through, the rate of return is unlikely to fall below the cost of capital. This in turn keeps the cost of capital lower, and thus price caps with a degree of cost pass-through can be lower than price caps without such sharing of risks.

In the UK, until 1998, the price control applying to retail electricity prices permitted pass-through of the costs of generation, transmission, and distribution, some 95 percent of all costs. This price control applied to the supply businesses of the Public Electricity Suppliers. Other price caps on the transmission and distribution businesses controlled those charges separately. Between 1990 and 1993 a separate cap linked to the Retail Price Index (RPI) was applied to final consumer prices for electricity, but it was backed up by RPI-indexation of coal-related power contracts. The price controls applying to the electricity distribution businesses in the UK excluded eight categories of service. The categories that generated the most revenue were prepayment meters, extra high voltage charges, and nontrading rechargeables.[11] Other services that were "excluded" from the distribution price cap include special meter reading charges and connection charges. For these services, the distribution companies were allowed to recover the actual costs incurred (including a rate of return on investment). The rationale behind excluding each of these services from the price control is that it is too hard to predict either the costs and revenues or the volume of the service.

Hence, the practice in the UK, a regime famous for its use of price caps, incorporates a number of cost pass-through arrangements.

Updating Price Caps

THE BASIC FORMULAE

To ensure that prices subject to a price cap track costs, the price cap should be updated automatically during the regulatory period to allow for predictable changes in costs. One of the most common mechanisms for updating price caps is known as "RPI-X". Under this formula, the price cap tracks the expected trend in unit costs through an adjustment each year by the rise in input costs less the growth in efficiency. A firm's price cap is adjusted annually for inflation using an independently compiled index of costs (in the UK, the Retail Price Index is favoured—hence the "RPI"). As regulated companies are generally expected to become more efficient over time, price caps are also updated by the expected annual rate of efficiency growth—commonly denoted "X".

The standard formulation of a price cap is as follows:

$$P_t = [P_{(t-1)} * (1 + RPI_t - X)] \pm Z_t$$

Where:

P_t is the price cap for year t and $P_{(t-1)}$ is the price cap for the previous year;

RPI_t is the annual rate of change in the Retail Price Index for year t

X is a factor representing a constant annual rate of change (decline) in the price cap

and Z_t is the adjustment for exogenous changes in conditions (uncontrollable costs, etc.).

Each year, this price cap is compared with the revenue actually recovered by the company, in the form of either a "tariff basket" with fixed weights or an average revenue per unit actually sold ("revenue yield"):[12]

$$\text{Tariff Basket} = \Sigma_i\, T_{it}.Q_{i0}/\Sigma_i\, Q_{i0}$$

where T_{it} is the tariff for service component i and Q_{i0} is a *fixed* quantity set in year 0;

or $$\text{Revenue Yield} = \Sigma_i\, T_{it}.Q_{it}/\Sigma_i\, Q_{it}$$

where Q_{it} is *actual* sales in year t at the tariff for service component i.

The tariff basket, the revenue yield, or a similar measure of average prices must lie below the price cap. These formulae limit the revenue that the company may collect to cover its costs and to earn a reasonable rate of return. The price cap must therefore continue to reflect a reasonable estimate of costs, despite changing circumstances.

RETAIL PRICE INDEX

Including the retail price index (RPI)[13] is one way to ensure that the price cap broadly matches costs, since it allows for general increases in the prices of the firm's inputs (capital goods, materials, salaries and wages). The rate of price changes is usually regarded as too unpredictable to be included as a fixed factor, so price cap formulae use each year's actual figure.

SETTING THE X FACTOR

In contrast to the price index, the X factor is intended to capture the rather more predictable long-run rate of growth in the efficiency of regulated utilities. As these firms become more efficient, their costs per unit decline, and the X factor ensures that the price cap follows the same trend. Because the trend is predictable, the X factor is usually set equal to a single figure for the whole regulatory period between reviews.

In economic literature, the appropriate level of the X factor is the "expected rate of efficiency growth".[14] Best practice is to set the target rate of efficiency growth by reference to average long-term rates of efficiency growth observed in comparable companies. In the US, regulators have accepted calculations of the trend rate of growth in "Total Factor Productivity" as a reasonable basis for setting X. Experts have standardised the method of calculation to the point where the range of possible results is relatively narrow and disputes have only a minor impact. A NERA study of US distribution companies[15] established that their annual rate of increase in total factor productivity had been around 2 percent in recent years. In general, analyses of total factor productivity in utility companies find that the long-term rate of efficiency growth has been 1 or 2 percent per annum. In the absence of other information, this figure would be a reasonable starting point for estimating future efficiency growth. However, the introduction of PC regulation strengthens the incentive to cut costs and may justify adding a "stretch factor" or "consumer dividend" in anticipation of faster growth in efficiency due to these stronger incentives.[16] This stretch factor would amount to no more than another 1 percent, so that a reasonable estimate of expected annual efficiency growth immediately after the introduction of PC regulation would be 2 to 3 percent.

However, the retail price index already includes the effect of efficiency growth in the economy as a whole. For economies in Western Europe, total factor productivity grows about 1 percent per year, which means that input prices rise on average 1 per cent faster than retail prices. To allow for this difference between the RPI (included in the price formula) and the firm's input prices (which determine its costs), the X factor must be reduced by the economy-wide rate of efficiency growth. Hence, one would expect the X factors in an "RPI-X" price cap formula to lie in the range 1 to 2 percent.

In practice, some regulators have set X factors at considerably higher levels and others have set X below zero (i.e., it has allowed prices to rise in real terms, instead of fall). However, these extreme values of X reflect factors other than efficiency growth, such as changes in the definition of costs set out in the accounts. A more transparent approach would have assigned such effects to the Z factor for exogenous changes in conditions. The definition of the X factor is properly limited to considerations of efficiency growth.

Anticipating Forecasting Errors

Regulators need not be concerned about the possibility of underestimating the X factor. Even if a regulated firm beats the regulator's target rate of efficiency growth, the operating costs subject to the price cap are a small part of the firm's total revenues. The effect of beating the target by achieving higher than expected efficiency will be swamped by the effects of the capital intensity of the industry, the long-lived nature of its assets, and the tendency for net asset value to decline even in steady-state conditions, because replacement assets are cheaper than the assets they replace, due to technical progress in asset manufacture. Variations in the rate of return due to unpredictable changes in the growth of efficiency are limited, and they are consistent with the need to provide an incentive for innovation. Regulators can therefore be content with estimating long-run trends in efficiency growth and need not try to anticipate short-term variations.

Benchmarking Methodologies

Some regulators (e.g., regulators in the UK, the Netherlands, and Spain) have tried to adapt benchmarking methods for the purpose of setting X. Benchmarking involves using methods such as Data Envelopment Analysis (DEA) or regression analysis to predict "efficient costs". However, most techniques used to date cannot distinguish between differences in costs due to operating conditions and differences due to inefficiency. Therefore benchmarking is not suitable for setting X, as it leads to arbitrary results. At best, it can be used to check cost forecasts and to identify suitable areas for closer investigation; using it to set revenues independently of actual costs merely provokes protracted disputes and undermines long-term incentives.[17]

ADJUSTMENTS FOR OTHER FACTORS

Including the change in RPI and the X factor explains why PC regulation is sometimes called "RPI-X regulation". However, in practice, price cap formulae often contain a number of other factors intended to ensure that annual revenues adapt to future changes in conditions. If a firm's costs are expected to rise significantly as a result of future commitments on capital expenditure, the price cap may have to be adjusted automatically to avoid financing problems. Furthermore, the overall price cap may be broken down into different segments of the market to allow for the fact that changes in the pattern of demand alter the average costs per unit.

Hence, price cap formulae tend to be somewhat more complex than the term "RPI-X" implies. The complexity derives from the need to allow for and adapt to real-world events, in order to prevent the price cap from deviating too far from average costs, so that it does not have to be abandoned before the end of the regulatory period.

Changes in the Pattern of Demand
Regulators need to decide how revenues will adapt to unpredictable variations in demand. As demand increases, costs will be expected to increase. A price cap provides an automatic increase in revenues, because the revenue allowance is the product of (1) an average price cap and (2) an index of demand. However, the actual pattern of demand (and hence actual costs) may grow in a different way from the index of demand (and hence allowed revenues).

REVENUE YIELD

Average price caps can take many different forms depending on the weights accorded to different elements of a firm's tariffs. The regulator may define the average price cap as a simple average revenue per unit of demand. This means that a single price cap covers all products of a firm. This is known as "revenue yield" and involves predicting revenue per unit.

If the regulated company sells a number of products—such as energy and capacity, or network services at different voltages—the regulator must also specify an index of demand (i.e., a weighted average of various demand measures). Otherwise, the level of "demand" is not uniquely defined.

In the mid-1990s, the UK gas transmission company (Transco) operated under a single average price cap of around 12 pence per therm (p/therm). Within this average, charges to consumers varied widely. Large consumers paid only around 2p/therm, whilst small consumers paid nearly 20p/therm. The mid-1990s saw a rapid expansion in gas deliveries to gas-fired power stations, for which Transco charged around 2p/therm. However, the single average price cap entitled Transco to collect around 12p/therm. To recover the shortfall of 10p/therm, Transco tried to raise charges to small consumers. This policy proved so unpopular that Transco was forced to forego the revenue entitlement.

Hence, "simple" price caps may have perverse and unforeseen effects which require *ex post* correction. These *ex post* corrections undermine the supposed simplicity and incentive properties of such price caps, even if they are justified by the need to recognise a change in circumstances.

MULTIPLE PRICE CAPS

One way to deal with variations in the pattern of demand is to adopt multiple price caps. Multiple price caps impose a separate cap on prices for each individual product or for smaller bundles of the firm's services. In the US, price caps are commonly applied to individual tariffs and charges.

In the UK, the regulator reacted to the problem with Transco's single average price cap by applying separate price caps to large and small consumers. To apply such a breakdown, the regulator must dictate an appropriate allocation of total costs between the various consumers and services.

Note that these price caps need not be the same as the actual tariffs charged by the company. In a price cap of the form where maximum revenue in year t is $\Sigma_i P_{it}.Q_{it}$, any change in the sales volume of service i (Q_{it}) will permit extra revenue of P_{it}, regardless of the tariff for service i. The price cap formula gives the utility the flexibility to redefine its tariffs, but it may have to reset tariffs to meet maximum revenue requirements if the pattern of sales changes during a regulatory period.

TARIFF BASKETS

A further option for regulators is to apply the price cap to a "tariff basket" rather than to actual revenues. The constraint set by a tariff basket is that a weighted average of particular tariffs cannot exceed the cap. Often the weights reflect the revenues from each service in previous years.

In Britain, a tariff basket has been used to regulate British Telecom. For years, the telecommunications provider was subject to an overall tariff cap on the average price of a basket of services, as well as price caps (or "side-constraints") on individual services. Such limits on rebalancing tariffs within a basket are usually implemented where regulators are concerned about undue discrimination or preference being shown to classes of consumer.

In the Netherlands, the Dutch regulator has adopted tariff baskets for electricity and gas distribution networks in the periods since 2000/01 as a way to reconcile legal obligations to use "CPI-X regulation" with legal powers to set tariffs. The form of the control is a tariff basket in which the weights are actual sales volumes ("accounting volumes") in a partic-ular year. The sum over all products gives a measure of what total revenue would be if sales volumes did not change. Any increase (or decrease) in the volume sold at a particular tariff leads to a rise (or fall) in total revenue equal to the associated tariff.

Because tariffs form the basis for this type of control, regulated firms cannot change the structure of their tariffs, and regulators cannot broaden or narrow the scope of regulation, without regulatory approval of both the firm's tariff structure and the firm's tariff basket.

REVENUE CAPS AND HYBRIDS

In the short term, additional demand may be incorporated at little or no extra cost where utility investments are "lumpy" and create spare capacity. Future investments may be fully committed, such that future costs are predictable. The revenue allowance may then be defined as a fixed revenue, rather than a price cap per unit. Under a revenue cap, the firm's total revenues cannot exceed the limit set by the cap.

For example, from 1993 to 2001, National Grid Company (NGC), the electricity transmission company in the UK, operated under a control that defined a fixed annual revenue, indexed to inflation but not to any measure of demand. (Since 2001, the regulator has also allowed NGC to earn additional revenue for every gigawatt by which connected generation capacity exceeds a forecast level.)

Since 1994, distribution (i.e., low voltage network) companies in the UK have received an allowed revenue that is made up of (1) a fixed revenue allowance and (2) a price cap per unit distributed at different voltages. Both the fixed element and the variable price caps are indexed to actual inflation and forecast efficiency growth, with the fixed and variable elements each providing roughly 50 percent of total revenues.

Both the transmission and the distribution formulae emerged out of detailed discussions between regulator and company over the "drivers" that affect future costs, an approach that required the regulator to investigate each company's operations.

CHOICE OF METHOD

In deciding upon the form of a price cap, regulators should choose the methodology that will (1) keep revenues in line with costs (the change in revenue associated with a change in demand roughly equals the associated change in costs) and/or (2) provide incentives to meet demand (the change in revenue associated with a change in demand is greater than the associated change in costs). However, measures of short-term demand may be unrelated to cost, in which case criterion (2) is impractical. Where this is the case, such as for NGC during the 1990s, revenue caps may be preferable, since at least they meet criterion (1). Deciding which methods to use requires detailed investigations into the cost and demand conditions of the regulated firms.

Special Risks and Uncertainties
In addition to taking account of predictable changes in costs, regulators must devise explicit contingent allowances and procedures for unanticipated changes that affect the regulated firm's financial position and that cannot be captured by an index (the Z factor in the formula). Examples include one-off costs associated with restructuring, redundancies, storms, and pensions, or extra capital expenditure that requires explicit acknowledgement.

To avoid unnecessary risk, the regulator and the regulated firm must set out pre-agreed allowances for such unanticipated events, or at least clear procedures for setting such allowances and arbitration rules for resolving any disputes. The presence of such arrangements greatly reduces the firm's revenue uncertainty and the scope for regulatory opportunism.[18] Typical special risk management schemes address uncertainties over capital expenditure and exogenous costs.

For example, the control on the UK's electricity transmission business (NGC) was reformed to deal with variations in capital expenditure. NGC and OFGEM (the UK energy regulator) have consistently failed to agree on an accurate forecast of future capital expenditure on reinforcing the network to accommodate new generators. NGC operated from 1993 to 2001 under a fixed revenue cap (indexed only to RPI and an X factor). Variation in the timing of new connections has in the past led to significant differences in capital expenditure and (less significantly) in NGC's annual costs and profits. Nevertheless, to reduce the problems caused by forecasting errors, the 2001 review of NGC's revenue control instituted an automatic adjustment to NGC's annual revenue cap of £23 million per GW of additional connections by generators, over and above the forecast level. This approach recognises the inherent uncertainty over the volume of new connections, whilst retaining a revenue formula that gives NGC an incentive to minimise costs.

Similarly, an incentive scheme was introduced into NGC's transmission licence in April 1997 for "Transmission Services Uplift" (TSU) to address exogenous costs outside of NGC's control. TSU was defined as the additional costs of dispatch arising because of transmission constraints, plus the costs of ancillary services. NGC had some influence over these costs but could not control them completely. To encourage NGC to operate the system efficiently, it was given the opportunity to earn extra profits by minimising these costs. The incentive was a sliding-scale share in the difference between actual TSU costs and a target agreed in advance with the regulator. Caps and collars were also included to limit the revenues and losses that would arise if uplift were considerably below or above target.

The Incentive for Efficiency under PC Regulation

Some discussions of PC regulation suggest (1) that abandoning the link between revenues and costs allows the regulator to set lower prices than under COS regulation and (2) that lowering prices will by itself encourage greater efficiency.[19] Such reasoning shows a fundamental misunderstanding of the incentives facing a private company. Private companies are motivated by profits. Under PC regulation, the regulated firm can increase its profits by cutting costs to beat the price target set by the regulator. Hence, the ability to raise profits will encourage cost reductions. However, at each review, the price cap must be reset to keep total revenues in line with total costs. These two processes together define the extent to which PC regulation will increase efficiency. Just setting lower prices has no immediate impact on incentives or efficiency, but arbitrary

Figure 1. PC Regulation and Incentives within the Firm

decisions that put cost recovery at risk are certain to lower efficiency in the long run.

Productive Efficiency and the Incentive to Cut Costs

In order to achieve cost reductions, the firm will have to incur some "non-measurable" costs, the most important being managerial resources, which some writers call "managerial effort". The regulator does not have capability to monitor or to control managerial effort,[20] but the regulator can hope to guide it by changing incentives. By offering a higher profit for greater efficiency, the regulator gives the firm's shareholders an incentive to encourage greater effort from the firm's managers—by offering them higher salaries in return for higher profits. The Board of Directors, acting on behalf of the shareholders, can justify awarding the firm's top managers higher salaries if they increase the firm's profits. To the extent that managers have incentives that are aligned with the interests of the shareholders (or are motivated by the threat of takeover), they will respond to price cap incentives by increasing managerial effort. The chain of means and incentives that leads from price cap to efficiency gains is illustrated in Figure 1.

Allocative Efficiency and the Review Procedure

When a regulated firm subject to PC regulation increases its profits by cutting costs faster than expected, the price cap no longer reflects actual costs. Allocative efficiency is maintained by adjusting price caps at the end of each regulatory period—typically varying from three to five years—at which time prices are brought into line with costs. However, resetting the price cap in line with costs affects incentives to reduce costs in the first place.

The longer the lag between the time when a cost saving is made and the time when the price cap is reset to reflect this cost reduction, the greater the proportion of the cost saving that regulated firms are allowed to retain. If each year the regulator immediately passes through cost savings into the next year's prices (i.e., annual Rate of Return regulation), the regulated firm would retain about 7 percent of any cost savings it makes. In contrast, in a regime where prices catch up with cost savings after five years (a typical regulatory period for price caps), the regulated firm would retain, on average, 29 percent of its cost savings.[21]

In some PC regimes, it has been noted that the different proportion of cost savings retained by the firm will bias incentives, so that companies make most savings early on in the regulatory period. This kind of behaviour is unlikely to be efficient. In the US, regulators have no legal basis for allowing revenues in excess of the current level of costs. However, in other regimes—e.g., electricity distribution in Victoria, Australia, or water and sewerage networks in the UK—the regulatory review procedures allow the firm to retain some "unexpected" cost savings made in one regulatory period as higher revenues in the next regulatory period.

Figure 2 illustrates a price cap regime where the regulated utility is allowed to retain part of the "unexpected" extra cost savings after the price cap is reset. In this case, the price cap is reset at a lower level than before, in order to pass some of the extra savings through to customers. However, the firm retains some of the extra savings in the next regulatory

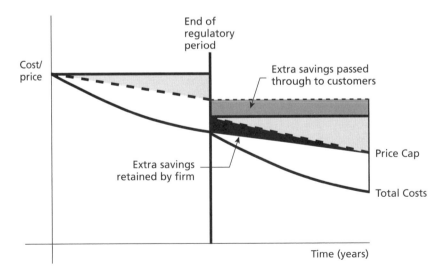

Figure 2.   Price Cap Reviews and Retained Incentives

period. The method of calculating these retained savings would be intended to ensure that the company received the same reward for reducing costs in each year. In this case, savings are retained for no more than five years (the regulatory period) and so are "phased out" by the end of the next regulatory period.

Trade-off between Productive and Allocative Efficiency and the Choice of the Regulatory Period

PC regulation encourages productive efficiency by allowing regulated companies to earn revenues higher than their costs (i.e., to increase profits) when they cut costs below a reasonable target. However, eventually, prices need to be brought back into line with costs to enhance allocative efficiency, to eliminate monopoly profits, and to provide the reasonable prospect of cost recovery needed to encourage long-term investment. Like all regulation, PC regulation involves a tradeoff between these two economic objectives: bringing prices back in line with costs diminishes the incentive to reduce costs.

Therefore, regulators must decide for how long the cap will apply (the length of the regulatory period). Long periods between regulatory reviews provide strong incentives for productive efficiency (cost minimisation) but decrease allocative efficiency. Long regulatory periods also increase the likelihood that unforeseen events will render the current form of the price cap inappropriate.

Typically, price cap regulation is characterised by longer periods between regulatory reviews than Rate of Return regulation. In the UK, regulatory periods of five years are common. However, at various times, the decisions taken at the regulatory review have undermined this separation of price caps into distinct periods. Hence, in practice, the incentives offered by a price cap regime do not depend only on the formula operating within each period, but also on the review process between periods. Some of the processes used at these reviews have also affected incentives.

In 1997, the Monopolies and Mergers Commission (the competition authority in the UK at the time) allowed the regulator to "claw back" part of the capital expenditure "underspend" of utility Northern Ireland Electricity. Underspend is the difference between expenditure predicted at the time of the price review and actual expenditure during the price control period. The claw-back was implemented by offsetting the amount of claw-back against future allowed revenues. In 1999, the regulator of the UK water industry, OFWAT, set a rolling target for the operating expenditure of the water and sewerage companies, i.e., a target that crossed over from one regulatory period and into the next.

Dutch and German legislators have prescribed the length of the period: Regulatory laws in both countries specify the use of price caps for periods of three to five years. In the Netherlands, this formulation of the rule has led to some debate as to whether the regulator is allowed to implement a one-year adjustment at the start of each regulatory period (known in Britain as a "P0-adjustment" because it redefines the year 0 starting point for the price cap).

If revenues in the last year of the previous regulatory period lie above actual costs, regulators will want to reset them at a lower level. However, if one-year adjustments are not allowed, the regulator must achieve the reduction through the X-factor. This form of adjustment tends to confuse discussion of the X-factor, since it no longer represents only the measure of expected efficiency growth but is also a measure of profits to be eliminated. If the regulator ensures that revenues at the end of the next regulatory period are still sufficient to cover forecast costs, the "glide path" from the current year (when revenues are above costs) to the final year (when revenues equal costs) ensures that revenues stay above costs nearly all the time. Regulated firms tend to favour this outcome when they are cutting costs fast enough to outperform the regulator's targets. However, when costs start to rise due to an increase in investment, the position is reversed, and revenues stay below costs nearly all the time. This outcome is less acceptable to regulated firms, is inconsistent with continued investment, and necessitates some reform of the regulatory rules.

Optimal Rates of Sharing Cost Savings with Customers

In the short term, a price cap allows the regulated company to keep 100 percent of any cost savings, a factor that provides a strong incentive for reducing costs. However, many price cap regimes limit the ability of the regulated company to retain such savings over the long term. Some price cap regimes include explicit profit-sharing and, in any case, the regulatory review at the end of each period passes some or all of the savings back to customers. A commonly asked question is how much of any cost saving the regulated firm should be allowed to retain. Unfortunately, there are no straightforward answers.

It is widely accepted in the literature on price caps that there is a tradeoff between (1) the fraction of any cost savings passed to customers and (2) the cost savings that the regulated firm will achieve: the higher

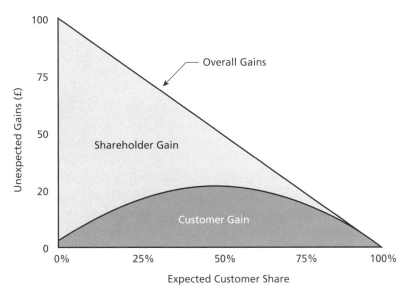

Figure 3. *Relationship between Unanticipated Gains & Consumers Share*

the fraction passed to consumers, the less effort the regulated firm will devote to reducing costs. This tradeoff between cost reduction and profit reduction can be illustrated using a simple example in Figure 3.

Suppose that the cost savings achieved by a regulated firm (relative to some target) are directly proportional to the fraction of these savings that the firm can retain. If the customer receives none of the savings (left-hand side of diagram), the firm cuts costs by 100 percent of what is feasible; if the customer receives all the savings (right-hand side of diagram), the firm doesn't cut costs at all. The downward sloping straight line between these two extremes represents an assumption about how the firm responds to different sharing ratios. The curved line then shows what benefit customers actually receive. On the left-hand side, they receive nothing—a zero percent share of the savings. On the right-hand side, they also receive nothing—100 percent of no savings. In between, the consumers' share peaks at 25 percent—i.e., they receive 50 percent of cost savings equal to 50 percent of the feasible figure. Hence, in this case, the optimal degree of sharing for consumers is 50 percent.

Different assumptions about the shape of the "overall gains" line will give different figures, but most reasonable assumptions would suggest optimal sharing ratios within the middle range (25-75 percent). In practice, most price cap regimes offer incentives that fall within this range, if only because the firm retains 100 percent of savings during a regulatory period and passes through savings at the regulatory review.

Incentives for an Optimal Level of Service Quality

A price cap that rewards a company only for cost reductions, ignoring the quality of service, will almost certainly cause a decline in the quality of service below the level that customers want. Any price cap regime must therefore give the firm an incentive to maintain the appropriate quality of service.

Economic theory is not conclusive on the issue of whether an unregulated monopolist will produce goods that are of a higher, equal, or lower quality than goods supplied competitively. However, under price cap regulation, economic theory predicts that the monopolist will have an incentive to skimp on quality.[22] A monopolist facing a price cap can only increase its profit margins by decreasing its costs, and one way to do that is by lowering quality. If the cost savings are greater than the loss of revenue due to falling demand for the lower quality product, the monopolist will skimp on quality.

Efficient Level of Quality

Marginal Cost of Quality versus Willingness to Pay
All other things being equal, customers prefer higher quality goods and services—but unfortunately all other things are not equal. Higher quality service costs more and raises prices to customers. Faced with a tradeoff between higher costs and higher quality, customers will want quality to increase up to the point at which further increases in quality cost more than they are willing to pay. Generally, as the level of quality increases, it becomes more and more expensive to raise quality by a given amount; at the same time, the value to consumers of additional quality (their "willingness to pay") drops lower and lower. For any given quantity of output, the optimal quality of service is the point where the cost of increasing quality equals the consumers' willingness-to-pay.

To prevent utilities from cutting costs and increasing their profits by letting the quality of service decline, PC regulation may be supported by minimum quality standards and large financial penalties for failing to meet them. Alternatively, the price cap plan can offer financial incentives linked to minor variations in quality of service. Minimum standards may be an appropriate way to encourage a high quality service in relation to safety, because minimum safety standards are usually well defined and consumers' willingness to pay for safety also tends to be very high. Fixing a minimum safety standard for a whole industry will not often lead to unwanted expenditure in individual cases.

In many cases (e.g., the number or duration of interruptions to supply), the benefit to consumers of improving quality is more uniform, so there is no well-defined minimum standard. Instead, it may be more efficient to let utilities adjust quality in response to financial incentives. In practice, a combination of minimum quality standards (to guarantee a minimum quality level) and incentives (to allow choices over the quality of service) is likely to offer the most efficient outcome.

Allowing for Different Valuations and Costs of Quality
What is considered an efficient level of quality depends on the costs of providing quality and on individual preferences. Information about customers' preferences for quality comes from observing the choices they make between cost and quality (either in their market choices or in well-designed surveys where participants must rank alternative price and quality scenarios).[23] However, customers of a utility may have little choice about the service quality they each individually receive. For example, each customer will be subject to interruptions common to other customers supplied by the same transmission line. It is necessary in this situation to think of a "representative customer," who captures the preferences of a cross-section of customers.

The costs of providing quality are likely to differ by individual customer (for example, depending on their location along a transmission line) and for individual distributors overall (for example, depending on their mix of customers, etc.). Figure 4 illustrates how the optimal level of quality (measured on the bottom axis) differs for a given "representative" customer with different costs of providing service quality.

Figure 4 illustrates the relationship between the level of quality provided and (1) the marginal cost of increasing quality (for two distributors) and (2) the marginal willingness-to-pay for additional quality (for the representative customer). For simplicity, we have assumed that rural and urban customers have the same willingness to pay for quality of supply. Willingness-to-pay falls (slopes downwards) at the margin, as the achieved level of quality increases (from left to right). On the other hand, the marginal cost of adding quality increases (slopes upwards) as the achieved level of quality increases (from left to right). In Figure 4, the rural distributor faces more difficult conditions than the urban distributor, so its

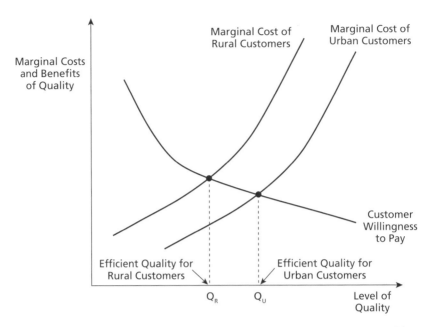

Figure 4.   Efficient Service Quality with Different Costs of Service Provision[24]

marginal costs of adding quality are higher (for any given level of quality). The higher costs derive from the physical characteristics of the network. For example, a rural distributor with more kilometres of line per customer would need to have fewer faults per kilometre of line—and would therefore need to build more robust lines—to achieve that same level of service quality as the urban distributor. In practice, it is more efficient for the rural distributor to operate with a lower level of service quality than the urban distributor, since customers are not willing to pay the extra expense of achieving the same level of quality.

Measures to Achieve Quality of Service under Price Caps

Regulators recognize the lack of incentives for quality of service under a price cap, and they have designed specific measures to achieve their quality targets. In the UK, electricity distribution businesses have always been given general quality targets ("Overall Standards") and have paid compensation to consumers whose own level of service falls below a defined standard ("Guaranteed Standards"). These standards proved to be insufficient. To improve incentives for investment, energy regulator OFGEM began work on an "Information and Incentives Project" after the price control review of the electricity distribution businesses in 1999. Two key objectives of the project were to "strengthen the incentives on the PESs (Public Electricity Supply Companies) to deliver the agreed quality of output and to be able to value better changes in the quality of output."[25] Ofgem has proposed to introduce explicit quality-of-service incentives into the price control regime for each distribution business.[26]

The Dutch regulator is also keen to ensure that price cap regulation (referred to in the Netherlands as CPI-X regulation or yardstick regulation) does not lead to a fall in service quality. The Electricity Law 1998 allows for the inclusion of a "q-factor" in the price cap formula. The chosen format in the law is rather strange (an annual rate of change, rather than an annual adjustment, as one might expect), but the Dutch regulator has adapted it to provide rewards for long-term improvements in the index known as "System Average Interruption Duration Index" (SAIDI), relative to the performance of the distribution system as a whole.

Encouragement of Efficient Long-Term Investment

Any regulator needs to overcome the desire of every monopolist to restrict the quality or quantity of supply in order to minimise its costs. Simple models of a price cap assume that costs and revenues are all contained within one period. However, one characteristic of natural monopoly—one that makes regulation necessary in the first place—is the importance of long-lived investments. In the case of network utilities, a regulatory regime must encourage long-term investment to expand supply. A price cap, which encourages short-term cost minimisation, will not provide the necessary incentive by itself. PC regulation must therefore be augmented by additional procedures that operate over a longer time scale.

Long-Term Regulatory Incentives to Invest

Newbery poses the problem and the answer as follows:[27]

> "What would be needed to persuade investors to sink their money into an asset that cannot be moved and that may not pay for itself for many years? The investors would have to be confident that they had secure title to future returns and that the returns would be sufficiently attractive."

The incentive to invest depends upon the return that investors expect to earn, which depends in turn on the financial incentives to maintain the quality of service and on the procedure for reviewing price caps at regular intervals. Such reviews, even if they happened every five years, would occur around eight times during the life of a typical electricity network asset with a 40-year life. In order to assess whether or not they had "secure title to future returns", investors would need to know at least in principle, how each of these reviews would be conducted and on what basis the price cap would be reset.

The problem of regulatory commitment (as the underpinning for incentives to invest) applies under all forms of regulation, but it is especially important for PC regulation. Given that PC regulation is intended to allow regulated revenues to differ from costs, in order to provide profit incentives, some regulators have incorrectly interpreted PC regulation as a method in which revenues must not be based on costs.[28] Such interpretations create many problems and have ultimately been rejected, though often only after some time.

Implications for Price Cap Review Procedures

In considering the incentive effects of PC regulation, it is therefore important not to focus solely on the incentive properties of a single price cap formula, but on the long-term prospects for revenues offered by the repeated process of setting and revising price caps. In order to offer incentives for efficient long-term investment, individual regulators must be able to offer investors a reasonable prospect that they will be able to recover all the costs of their investment.

- Here, a "reasonable" prospect is one where the regulatory commitment to allow cost recovery uses methods that are (1) *transparent* (explained in a way that lets investors understand what the regulator is offering), (2) *stable* (capable of use at subsequent reviews), and (3) *predictable* (based on objective data and replicable methods, rather than subjective estimates and forecasts).
- "Total cost recovery" means recovery of all the regulated utility's costs, including operating expenses, depreciation (the return *of* capital), and the cost of capital (the return *on* capital).
- In this context, the definition of operating expenses and depreciation requires an *agreed set of accounts,* whilst the allowance for the cost of capital must be *comparable* with that offered by companies

in other sectors that face similar risks and operate with a similar degree of efficiency.

In the United States, these principles are entrenched in administrative and case law.[29] However, in other countries, these principles have only partly (if at all) been embodied in law and are emerging only slowly from the accumulation of rules developed from practical experience with price cap regulation. More than a decade after price cap regulation was introduced into the UK, a UK government Task Force expressed concern that investment was suffering under the current regulatory regime.[30] In theory, incentives for efficient long-term investment would be provided if the regulator made credible commitments to allow firms to recover the cost of investments. In practice it remains a concern, since regulators always retain a right to use their discretion to reject recovery of investments they consider imprudent or inefficient, until the standards for reviewing and rewarding investment are well defined.[31]

Conclusion: Preconditions for Success

Properly applied, price cap regulation can improve productive efficiency by allowing costs to deviate temporarily from prices. PC regulation also achieves allocative efficiency if the price cap formula tracks movements in costs and if periodical reviews reset price caps at levels equal to the new, hopefully lower, level of costs. To ensure that cost reductions are efficient and do not threaten the quality of service, price caps must be associated with certain quality standards and incentives. Finally, firms need to be given long-term investment incentives: They must be offered a "reasonable prospect of cost recovery" by way of stable and predictable methods of regulation.

A review of international experience finds a general consensus that PC has delivered cost savings (productive efficiency). In some regimes, the need to allow costs to deviate from prices during the period when the price cap applies has become confused with a reluctance to recognise the regulated company's own costs when setting the price cap. Certain approaches in which price caps were not based on actual costs have almost certainly damaged long-term incentives for cost recovery. However, this confusion can be (and has been) overcome in many cases. Experience with PC regulation worldwide suggests that there are preconditions that ensure that PC regulation leads to a win-win situation, where both firms and customers benefit.

Scope for Efficiency Gains

The fundamental advantage of PC regulation is the stronger incentive it gives regulated utilities to reduce costs. An industry that operates under a regulatory system that encourages or allows unnecessary expenditure will benefit more from the introduction of price caps than an industry that has already attained high levels of efficiency.

Some authors assume that relatively high electricity prices imply large scope for cost savings. There is certainly a wide variation in average price of electricity around the globe, and countries with high tariffs for domestic and industrial customers seem to offer large scope for cost reduction. However, higher prices and higher total costs cannot be considered as evidence of inefficiency per se. The high costs in certain countries may reflect real differences in operating conditions, rather than differences in efficiency. Only detailed analysis of these conditions would permit a separation of the two effects. Such analysis would entail a very time- consuming and costly process, involving accountants, engineers, and economists, for which there is no shortcut and which few, if any, regulators are prepared to contemplate.[32] In practice, therefore, evidence on potential efficiency gains attainable under PC regulation derives from (1) recognising the shortcomings of the current system of incentives and (2) the belief that PC regulation will accelerate efficiency growth, relative to what was achieved in the past.[33]

Agreed Set of Accounting Principles

Successful regulation requires rules that allow for transparent, stable, and predictable regulation. The lack of agreed accounting principles created many problems for price cap regimes in the UK, since at first it was not clear what costs investors were entitled to recover. Regulators regularly redefined the value of investments or the range of operating expenses attributable to regulated businesses.

Fortunately, most other countries have (or have underpinned regulatory reform with) a set of agreed accounting rules. Some, such as the US Federal Energy Regulatory Commission (FERC) accounting rules, might seem highly detailed, restrictive, and costly to administer. However, without an agreed and established system of accounts, it is not possible to define costs without controversy. Without an agreed definition of costs as the foundation of price caps, the regulator may (indeed, must) adopt ad hoc and changing definitions of costs. The incentives any price cap offers would therefore remain obscure since it would not be clear how savings in one regulatory period would be rewarded or penalised at subsequent reviews. The costs of imposing a stable set of accounts are therefore dwarfed by the costs of regulatory risk caused by the lack of them.

The accounting rules must define the level of costs and allocate those costs among services. For regulatory purposes (regardless of the regime) it is important to have an agreed set of accounting principles to define the level of costs, covering asset valuation, asset lives, and depreciation profiles, as well as the distinction between operating expenditures and capital expenditures. Further, it is also necessary to establish clearly what costs are to be recovered from revenues covered by price caps and what costs are to be recovered elsewhere. Few price caps cover all the services a regulated company offers. Some services may continue to be offered at cost-of-service, because their costs vary in an unpredictable fashion. Other services may have their prices set by a competitive process. Price caps only offer superior incentives if regulated companies know whether costs (and hence cost savings) fall under the price cap or not.

Legal or Institutional Protection of Shareholder Investments

Agreeing on a definition of costs is no use if the resulting information is not used in regulation. In order to ensure long-term investment, regulatory regimes must offer investors a reasonable prospect of cost recovery. This requirement applies to all forms of regulation, but it is especially relevant to discussions of PC regulation. Although regulators have the power to set price caps that allow revenues to differ from actual costs, some regulators have mistakenly interpreted this power as a duty to re-set price caps without regard to actual costs. In fact, PC regulation implies no such duty—and indeed will not function adequately if the process of setting price caps does not reflect actual costs.

Reconciling Price Caps with Obligations to Allow Cost Recovery
In the US, certain constitutional amendments prevent federal and state government agencies from "taking [property] without due process". The Supreme Court has extended these constitutional guarantees over the years to include the process of utility regulation.[34] As a result, regulators in the US must now offer utilities the opportunity to recover their costs and to earn a "reasonable rate of return". Working within this constraint, US regulators have nevertheless managed to set price caps (primarily in the telecommunications industry, but also in the energy sector) and other

forms of performance-based regulation, which allow profits to vary in ways that encourage more efficient performance.

In the UK, the guarantees to investors were enshrined in the duties of regulators. For instance, a primary objective of Ofgem is to promote consumers' interests, but it must fulfil this objective having regard to "the need to secure that licence holders are able to finance the activities which are the subject of obligations imposed" (i.e., regulated activities). Ofwat, the UK water regulator, has a statutory duty to provide a "reasonable rate of return" on the water utilities' capital. Other countries and other PC regimes operate within similar bounds.

A regulatory system that legally defines the rights of utilities to a reasonable prospect of cost recovery helps to ensure that regulatory decisions are consistent with long-term incentives for investment. Adoption of price caps is perfectly consistent with the retention of such rights.

Difficulties Arising from Attempts to Abandon Cost Recovery
While legal statements of principle discourage regulators from adopting ad hoc methods for defining costs, they are not an absolute guarantee. Some regulators have tried to impose flawed methods that endangered cost recovery, but such approaches have proven unsustainable.

For whatever reason, those drafting regulators' duties in UK laws were reluctant to refer directly to cost recovery or reasonable rates of return, with the result that shareholders' rights were uncertain for many years. The history of UK regulation has been a process of gradually removing that uncertainty by developing ever more stable methods. As of 2006, the energy regulator, Ofgem, was still developing detailed standards for judging whether new investments should be recovered from consumers (i.e., prudence review standards). In other cases, regulatory methods not based on cost recovery have faced a more direct challenge in the courts.

- In the US, the attempt by the Federal Communications Commission to set telephone charges on the basis of the TELRIC model of (imaginary) incremental costs was rebuffed by a US Court of Appeals, which argued that Congress, when requiring regulators to base tariffs on costs was "dealing with reality, not fantasizing about what might be."[35] Similar complaints can be made about many methods that ignore actual costs.
- In Victoria, Australia, a judge concluded that the requirement to use price cap regulation was perfectly consistent with the regu-

lator's desire to review actual costs (and indeed that such a review might be necessary).

- In the Netherlands, the regulators' attempt to abandon accounting costs in favour of a benchmark has produced a number of legal challenges, which so far have prompted the regulator to drop plans to set price cap x-factors as high as 7 percent, in favour of an agreed settlement at around 2 percent.

If price caps are to be adopted successfully, it is important not to abandon actual costs as a basis for allowed revenues.

Ability to Commit to Fixed Periods between Reviews

PC regulation means allowing utilities to profit from the cost reductions they achieve over and above the cost target set by the price control, and this ability to earn profits depends on the price cap applying for a fixed period. To provide such incentives, therefore, the regulator must be able to resist pressure to reset the cap within a predetermined period of time. In some cases, the legal framework for regulation does not permit the regulator to renounce the right to intervene when the profits of regulated companies move above or below an acceptable rate of return. Formally, this describes the situation in the US where, for example, the FERC is required to ensure that the prices of regulated services are "fair and reasonable" at all times. However, regulators in the US have used a number of methods to overcome this legal obstacle to setting a price cap:

- First, US regulators have, for example, declared their intention to be "hesitant" to review the price control unless profits are "truly excessive". Where profits are not "truly excessive", the regulator may deem prices to be "fair and reasonable".
- Second, US regulators have devoted time and effort to designing price caps that avoid the need for a review, by including indices, correction mechanisms, and "off-ramps" (i.e., detailed agreed procedures for resolving unforeseen problems without overturning the whole price cap formula). As far as possible, these detailed mechanisms prevent profits from ever becoming "excessive" and avoid the need to invoke a tariff review.
- Third, price caps in the US tend to operate for shorter periods (say three years) than those in the UK (where five years is common), so that problems are less likely to emerge. Because the company is

unable to keep the savings for so long, shortening the period between reviews weakens the incentive for some cost reductions. However, a short-term price cap that is unlikely to be reopened provides better incentives than a long-term price cap that is simply not credible.

These methods are sufficiently useful to be generally applicable and not limited to the US.

Understanding of Cost Drivers and Trends

When costs rise dramatically above revenues, the firm might not be able to finance its activities and the regulator will face pressure to reopen the control in order to ensure that the company is able to provide the necessary services. The regulator will also face strong pressures to intervene if regulated companies are perceived to be making unacceptably high profits. Extreme differences between costs and revenues can arise because costs were measured incorrectly at the beginning of the period or because the X-factor did not accurately anticipate efficiency gains. The preconditions that minimise such risks are agreed accounts, institutional protection of cost recovery, and an open regulatory process.

However, it is more likely that profits vary widely because of the failure of the price control formula to reflect predictable changes in costs. The most notable example of this problem was the price controls of the Californian distribution utilities, which did not allow them to pass through rising wholesale generation prices to final customers.[36] Regulators may have to learn gradually how to incorporate variation in costs in the price control, by including a number of independent indices (like RPI), fixed costs, exogenous factors (like demand), and stable trends (like efficiency growth or "x"). In some cases, it may be impossible to find a suitable formula, in which case uncertainty over future profits may have to be shared explicitly. A profit-sharing formula will weaken short-term incentives, but it may prove necessary in order to prevent "excessive" variation in profit from provoking a tariff review, which undermines the incentives of the price cap.

Thus in order to design a price control that minimises the risk of large variations in profits (i.e., large gaps between revenues, and costs), the regulator must have a good understanding of the different cost components that are associated with a particular service and of the exogenous cost drivers that determine these costs. Under COS regulation, such knowledge tends not to be needed (apart from some knowledge of which costs are fixed and best recovered through capacity payments and which are variable and therefore suited to inclusion in energy charges). The regulator can gain part of this knowledge from understanding the regulatory experience of other countries. But it is also important for the regulator to engage those utilities that will be regulated to help design a cost target that properly considers exogenous factors.

Minimum Quality Standards

Introducing PC regulation will encourage a decline in service quality unless minimum quality standards are enforced or quality incentives are introduced. Quality incentives are not such an important issue under traditional cost-of-service regulation, where the incentive to cut costs is less strong, and indeed COS may lead to overprovision of quality. Under PC regulation, however, quality standards form an integral part of the incentive framework. To ensure that PC regulation does not cause a decline in quality, it is important to measure the quality of service, to set minimum standards or targets, and to provide incentives/penalties for deviating from those standards or targets. Otherwise, the quality of service can decline rapidly.

The types of standards needed are:

- Planning and operating standards covering how the network should be configured:
- Individual customer service standards
- Overall customer service standards

Enforcing service standards requires a clear set of rules defining the standards to be met and the incentives/penalties for deviating from them. Such rules must include (1) clear and objective rules on how companies record information on the quality of service they provide and (2) clearly defined penalties/incentives to give firms incentives to maintain service quality and to compensate consumers.

To provide optimal incentives, the measures, standards, and incentives for improving quality should be based on consumers' willingness to pay. In practice, such information is not often available, so the first set of quality standards within PC regulation usually matches current performance, and incentives are based on the costs of improving service.

Open Regulatory Process

Giving investors a reasonable prospect of cost recovery requires transparent, stable and predictable regulatory methods. One of the cornerstones of the regulatory framework must therefore be stable and predictable procedures and limitations on the scope of regulatory intervention within regulatory periods. However, when resetting a price control, some exercise of regulatory discretion is inevitable. It is important that this regulatory discretion be focused on promoting efficiency while giving firms a reasonable opportunity for cost recovery, and that it not be used in ways that undermine the desired incentives. The following characteristics will help ensure that regulation achieves its intended purpose.

Narrow Mandate
The stability and predictability of outcomes will be enhanced if the regulator has a narrow mandate, e.g., to protect the interests of electricity consumers (by keeping prices low and ensuring certain quality-of-service standards), or to ensure that prices charged by electric utilities are "fair and reasonable" by reference to economic conditions (costs) within the sector. If the regulator must choose from a wide range of regulatory objectives, the scope for regulatory discretion will increase. A narrow mandate therefore allows for a more stable and predictable regulatory process. It also facilitates regulatory accountability, as it makes it easier for an appeals body to evaluate the validity of regulatory decisions. Thus, the regulatory body should look after the interests of consumers as consumers of energy, not as voters or citizens in general, to exclude as many other social concerns as possible.

For this narrow mandate to be effective (and perhaps for it to be legally enforceable), it is helpful if the regulatory body is independent of the government administration and of short-term political pressures in general. Otherwise, the regulatory mandate will be overridden by other objectives relating to interests outside the electricity sector. Thus, a narrow focused mandate may imply the need for *an independent regulatory body*.

Transparent Decision Procedures
Given a narrow and clearly stated mandate, a regulatory authority is held to account more easily if its decision-making process can be laid bare for all to see. To meet this requirement, regulatory processes need to incorporate a process of open consultation with interested parties.

On important matters, it may also be beneficial to allow a cross-examination of other parties that respond to consultations. This practice, which is well established in the US regulatory process, allows flawed reasoning and evidence to be exposed and increases the chances that regulatory decisions will be based on facts and not unsubstantiated opinions.[37] Some regimes (such as the UK) function without such cross-examination, but the lack of assistance from interested parties in appraising arguments places a greater burden on the regulator and increases the chance that decisions will be based on incorrect or irrelevant information.

However the regulator reaches a decision, incentives will be strongest if regulated utilities can see plainly how their revenues relate to their past and future costs. Hence, a further precondition of successful regulation (of all kinds) is the regulator's obligation to explain how decisions have been made, in relation to the available information.

Strict Criteria for Changing the Rules

The need for stability implies that regulators should have to surmount several hurdles before changing rules. The regulator's task at each price cap review should be to provide good reasons for changing the price cap from its current level or for changing the procedure used to set the price cap at the previous review. Each review process should not be a *tabula rasa,* in which the company or the regulator is at liberty to invent new procedures and rules without showing that they are better than what went before. In other words, there are good reasons for placing the burden of proof on those who wish to change the rules.

Accountability

Whatever methods are adopted, the regulatory body has to be accountable to higher independent authorities who can enforce compliance with obligations to use transparent, stable and predictable methods. Typically, regulators are accountable to the courts, but in the UK the Competition Commission (another branch of the executive) provides an alternative route. Given the need to maintain a narrow mandate, it is counter-productive to make regulators accountable to politicians or to political institutions since their decisions will then be affected by extraneous concerns.

Summary

Price cap regulation offers advantages over cost-of-service regulation, provided that it is supported by a number of regulatory institutions.

Some of these institutions are required to successfully operate any regulatory regime, but they tend to be ignored because they are intrinsic to certain methods. For example, detailed attention to cost recovery is intrinsic to cost-of-service regulation, but it mistakenly tends to be given a low priority under some forms of price cap regulation.

I have listed above the preconditions without which price cap regulation will not achieve its aims, although I know that some readers will think that components within it are either obvious or dispensable. Experience of price caps in regulatory regimes around the world has shown repeatedly that regulators face pressure to abandon one or all of these preconditions, but that doing so is always a mistake.

Therefore, when regulators move towards the use of price cap regulation (and especially if they present it as a break with "traditional" regulation of the past), they and the companies they regulate need to ensure that these elements are in place. When putting them in place, they need to learn from the experience of other regulatory systems that have been through this transition. Otherwise, they risk discrediting the whole regulatory system, rather than capturing the benefits that price cap regulation has to offer.

Notes

1. The economic principles of regulation are set out in Graham Shuttleworth and Sarah P. Voll, "Economic Principles of Regulation," in this Section.

2. For an example see DTe (2000), Richtsnoeren (Regulatory Guidelines for the Electricity Sector), February 2000, paragraph 1.29. The Dutch regulator advocates setting prices without regard to costs, arguing that "the solution is to base tariffs not on the firm's own costs, but on the costs of other efficient firms".

3. OFGEM, "The Structure of Electricity Distribution Charges—Initial Consultation Paper" (December 2000).

4. The role of this benchmark is open to dispute, since the allowed revenues emerged from a settlement with the industry as a whole, and this settlement did not describe the precise analysis used to define the revenues of each company. Further, it included a number of compromises over, e.g., the time that each firm had to reach the benchmark.

5. By 2006, no company had succeeded in winning additional revenues for extraordinary and significant investments, but the regulator had already adjusted revenues for the additional costs of particular regional factors (sub-sea cables and local taxes) and was considering whether to make further adjustments for urban/rural differences.

6. S.C. Littlechild, *Regulation of British Telecommunications Profitability* (London: HMSO, 1983).

7. M. Armstrong, S. Cowan, and J. Vickers, *Regulatory Reform: Economic Analysis and British Experience* (Cambridge, MA: The MIT Press, 1994).

8. Ofgem has gone so far as to impose an RPI-X target for its own budget.

9. For the UK, see "Economic Regulators", Report of the Better Regulation Task Force (12 July 2001). The Netherlands and Austria have also seen regulatory appeals against arbitrary choices in CPI-X regulation.

10. Op. cit., p. 45.

11. Nontrading rechargeables generally related to specific requests made by third parties for a company to carry out work on its distribution system (for example, moving lines and cables to accommodate the needs of public authorities or developers). The volume of such work tends to vary unpredictably from year to year.

12. Both of the following formulae show tariff baskets and revenue yields in the conventional format of an average price. In some regulatory systems, e.g., the Dutch electricity and gas networks, the denominator is omitted, so that the formulae define a total revenue, for comparison with the price cap multiplied by the corresponding volume of sales. The use of a revenue formula has the advantage that exogenous costs can be easily added, without conversion into an average price.

13. The Retail Price Index is a particular index of prices commonly used in Britain, where this form of regulation was first defined. Other regimes use a slightly different index, the Consumer Price Index (CPI), and refer to "CPI-X" regulation. (See the Electricity Law 1998 and the Gas Law 2000 in the Netherlands, for instance.) In the US, some regulators use the price index for Gross Domestic Product (GDP-PI or "GDP deflator").

14. For a full discussion of X-factor estimation, see Jeff D. Makholm, "Elusive Efficiency and the *X-Factor* in Incentive Regulation: The Törnqvist v. DEA/Malmquist Dispute," in this Section.

15. J. D. Makholm and M. J. Quinn, "X marks the spot: how to calculate price caps for the distribution function", *Public Utilities Fortnightly* (December 1, 1997), 62.

16. This allowance for the effect of strengthening incentives is separate from any adjustment required to eliminate excess profits, or "inefficiency". Introducing PC regulation does not automatically lead to the elimination of "inefficiency" (i.e., imprudently incurred costs), nor does it provide an alternative justification for preventing their recovery (without some kind of prudence review).

17. For a more detailed discussion of the deficiencies of benchmarking as a regulatory technique, see G. Shuttleworth (2005), "Benchmarking of electricity networks: practical problems with its use for regulation," *Utilities Policy,* volume 13, issue 4, pp. 310-317, December 2005.

18. Regulatory opportunism occurs when regulators take advantage of the powers vested in them to make inefficient decisions. Often such behaviour is driven by

the favourable political appearance of those decisions in the short term, but the consequences are undesirable in the long term.

19. This view is not always expressed as clearly as stated here. Sometimes it appears as the assertion that setting revenues "too high" will allow inefficiency—which implies that lowering revenues would increase efficiency.

20. If the regulator could simply direct management to act efficiently, economic regulation would be unnecessary. Instead, it would be more efficient for the state to run regulated industries—a conclusion which most theoretical and empirical evidence seems to contradict.

21. The proportion captured by the regulated firm declines from the start of the period to the end. If it makes a cost saving in the last year before the price cap is reset, the firm retains the same proportion (7 percent) as under annual ROR regulation.

22. L. Rovizzi and D. Thompson, "The Regulation of Product Quality in the Public Utilities", in: M. Bishop, J. Kay, and C. Mayer, *The Regulatory Challenge* (Oxford: Oxford University Press, 1995).

23. Ordered logit (Choice modelling) is an econometric technique which allows customers' willingness-to-pay to be recovered from information on rankings. See Bill Baker and Paul Metcalfe, "Value of Service in Water Supply" in this volume.

24. We assume that rural customers obtain lower quality of service than urban customers at the same marginal costs, though this is not true in all the cases.

25. Letter to Chief Executives of the PESs from the Director General of Energy Supply, December 1999.

26. See Ofgem, "Information and incentives project incentive schemes—Initial proposals", 4 July 2001.

27. D.M. Newbery, *Privatization, Restructuring and Regulation of Network Utilities* (Cambridge MA: MIT Press, 2000), p. 29.

28. The Dutch energy regulator, DTe, went so far as to write, "The solution (i.e., the best method of setting price caps) is not to base tariffs on the firm's own costs, but on the costs of other efficient firms". See DTe (2000), Guidelines for price cap regulation in the Dutch electricity sector", February 2000, para 1.29 (Dutch version only, NERA translation). This view is proving unsustainable in practice.

29. In the US, the requirement for transparency and objectivity in regulatory decisions is imposed by the Administrative Procedure Act 1946 (Title 5, Chapter 5, sections 511-599). The obligation on regulators to offer regulated utilities the opportunity to recover total costs is encapsulated in the 1944 Supreme Court decision on Hope Gas, *Federal Power Commission v. Hope Natural Gas Co.,* 320 U.S. 591 (1944). The obligation to allow a rate of return comparable with that in other sectors, after adjusting for risks and other factors, is set out in the 1923 Supreme Court decision on *Bluefield Water Company. Bluefield Waterworks & Improvement Co. v. Public Service Commission,* 262 US 679 (1929). Detailed accounting standards have been in place since the 1930s.

30. See "Economic Regulators", Report of the Better Regulation Task Force, 12 July 2001, p/ 19.

31. Karl McDermott, et al., "Rethinking the Implementation of the Prudent Cost Standard" in this volume.

32. As we discussed in section II.A, benchmarking analysis (such as DEA) does not produce a reliable measure of relative efficiency and so cannot form the basis for "stable and predictable" regulatory decisions.

33. See Jeff Makholm, "Elusive Efficiency and the *X-factor* in Incentive Regulation: the Törnqvist v. DEA/Malmquist Dispute," in this Section.

34. In the 1923 *Bluefield Water* case, the Supreme Court established the right of investors in regulated utilities to earn a rate of return *comparable* with that offered by other sectors of the economy. In 1944, the Supreme Court's decision in the *Hope Gas* case imposed an obligation on regulators to offer investors the opportunity to earn this return *after* recovering operating expenditures and depreciation. See above for detailed references.

35. US Court of Appeals, *Iowa Utilities Board v. Federal Communications Commission,* No. 96-3321 (and consolidated cases), 18 July 2000.

36. In the UK, the National Air Traffic Services (NATS) ran into financial difficulties after 2001 as result of the quantity index in its price cap, because air travel was considerably below the forecast level.

37. In an attempt to reduce the cost of regulation, some agencies in the US have adopted shortened procedures which do not involve detailed cross-examination. This omission has raised concerns with the reliability of the information that these bodies use to make their decisions. See Charles F. Phillips, *Regulation of Public Utilities* (Arlington VA: Public Utilities Reports, Inc., 1993), pp. 195-201 for a description of the standard US tariff-setting process, including the right to cross-examination; and the introduction of shortened procedures.

5

ELUSIVE EFFICIENCY AND THE X-FACTOR IN INCENTIVE REGULATION: THE TÖRNQVIST V. DEA/MALMQUIST DISPUTE

Jeff D. Makholm

Introduction

Incentive-based regulation is practiced worldwide, and all applications of it require some form of efficiency or productivity measurement—the *X-factor*. Including this factor in a multi-year regulatory formula allows the formula to survive intact for several years, and this longer regulatory lag between tariff reviews strengthens the incentives on firm performance. The factor, an index number, is intended to permit prices to move between tariff reviews according to an objective and reliable pattern. Differing opinions have arisen, however, on which index number to use.

One index number, the Malmquist Index, has generated considerable interest in some regions (particularly in Australia and Europe) because of its ostensible ability, when used in conjunction with data envelopment analysis (DEA), to distinguish readily between technical change for an industry (which the X-factor is generally held to measure) and efficiency for a particular firm. However, the DEA/Malmquist procedure for separating individual firm efficiency from technical change is inherently unreliable for identifying how inefficient a firm is. Neither the quality of data for regulated firms, nor the essentially idiosyncratic nature of such firms, supports an analysis of the *level* of efficiency of individual utilities. To the extent that regulators attempt to use the DEA/Malmquist procedure to set tariffs to reflect "efficient firm" standards, they inject unsupportable subjectivity and an unreliable methodology into a tariff-making process. The only reliable alternative is to estimate the X-factor directly by measuring long-run rates of change in efficiency indices. The Törnqvist index is best suited to this process, but other similar indices offer similar results.

The X-Factor in the Theory of Price Cap Regulation

Incentive regulation allows automatic or formulaic adjustment to regulated prices between tariff cases. That is, the plan controls the rate of change of the regulated firm's tariffs by adjusting a price cap (or revenue cap) annually according to a predetermined formula. The purpose is to ensure that price changes reflect changing costs the same way as in competitive markets: (1) Changes in industry prices track changes in industry costs and (2) the changes in an individual firm's prices relative to its costs differ from an industry average if its productivity growth differs from the average productivity growth of its industry.[1] This difference between the rate of change in industry prices and in individual firm costs causes a variation in profits. This is the carrot or stick with which the competitive process rewards efficiency gains and punishes firms that are slow to innovate, to reduce costs, or to respond to consumer demands.

The Place of Incentive Regulation in Regulatory Economics

Incentive regulation has been a key part of utility regulation for over 25 years. In that time, many regulated companies in North America and virtually all newly privatized companies around the world embraced under a variety of labels some form of incentive regulation. Generally, incentive regulation plans are characterized by a definite plan period, automatic adjustment for inflation, a productivity adjustment (the X-factor), and sometimes a way to share monetary gains between utilities and customers and/or reward (or penalize) quality of service changes. It is the X-factor that embodies the competition-like constraint to which regulated companies are held under incentive regulation. Imposing that constraint extends the period between tariff cases in an acceptable way and provides the time for cost-savings or sales maximizing incentives to pay off for investors. The X-factor is not an incentive in itself, but it permits regulatory formulae to stay in place longer—and that provides the incentive for more efficient long-term decisions on costs, sales, and investments.

In the early application of price cap regulation in the UK, a general notion existed that the X-factor was a variable simply subject to the regulator's choice. For example, Beesley and Littlechild describe the X-factor as "...a number specified by the government,"[2] as if it were some kind of bureaucratic target. More recent consensus is that the X-factor derives from a regulatory regime designed to limit monopoly utility prices over a defined number of years in a way that mimics the constraints that a competitive firm would face. In discussions on setting the appropriate X-Factor, economists generally agree with the theory set out above and on the two central elements of the relevant Total Factor Productivity (TFP) measures.[3] For example, Loube and Navarro confirm that a price cap plan begins with prices set so that the value of total inputs (including a normal return on capital) equals the value of total output for the company as well as the industry.[4] A number of writers confirm that the purpose of the price cap adjustment formula is to ensure that the constraint of regulated prices mimics the pressures that competition would place on a firm.[5] General agreement also exists among economists that the relevant TFP measure should be based on industry- rather than firm-specific productivity measures.[6]

Theoretical X-Factor Formulation[7]

The standard formulation for implementing price cap regulation is given by equation (5) from Appendix A:

(1) $$dp = dp^N - X + Z$$

where dp denotes a percentage growth rate in price, dp^N is the annual percentage change in a national index of output prices, and Z represents the change in unit costs due to external circumstances (which can be positive or negative).

If the industry achieves a productivity target of X and experiences exogenous cost changes given by Z, the price change that keeps earnings constant is given by equation (1). This price change is given by:

1. the rate of inflation of national output prices dp^N,
2. less a fixed productivity offset, the X-Factor, which represents a target productivity growth *differential* between the annual TFP growth of the industry and the whole economy,[8]
3. plus exogenous unit cost changes, written as the difference between the effects on the industry and economy-wide unit costs of the exogenous event.

To use the industry's productivity performance as a target for an individual company, rewrite equation (1) into the formula:

(2) $$PCI_t = PCI_{t-1} \times [1 + GDP - PI_t - X \pm Z_t],$$

where PCI_t is the value of the price cap index in year t, Z_t is the difference in the effects of exogenous changes on a specific company and on the rest of the economy, and $GDP-PI$ is the national output price index (i.e., "gross domestic product price index").

Simply put, the effect of using the above formula to limit price increases is that earnings remain the same if a company's achieved productivity differential just meets the target X-Factor. Thus a company must perform as well against economy-wide average TFP growth today as the industry as a whole has historically performed in comparison with economy-wide average TFP growth. If a company's productivity growth falls short of the target, its earnings will fall; if it exceeds the target, its earnings will rise. The price adjustment formula that sets this target adjusts output prices by: (1) the change in a national index of output prices less (2) the TFP growth target, measured as the difference between the change in industry TFP and that of the nation as a whole, plus[9] (3) the difference between the effect of exogenous changes on a company's costs and on the costs of the nation as a whole.

Thus, the historical relative TFP growth of the industry and the whole economy is taken as the target for the firm's TFP growth relative to the whole economy. National output price growth and exogenous cost changes are measured annually, but the X-Factor is fixed as the target amount by which TFP growth should exceed historical economy-wide TFP growth. This system of rewards and punishments sets up the same incentives as an unregulated firm would face in a competitive market, where failure to match industry average productivity growth results in lower earnings, and exceeding industry average productivity growth leads to increased earnings.

When turning to the empirical measurement of TFP, it is important to keep two points in mind: (1) the only relevant productivity measure is the *change* in TFP, not the *level* of TFP (discussed in Appendix A); and (2) it is only the *industry average* TFP growth that mimics the constraints faced by firms in a competitive market.

"X-Factor Quantification" and Index Numbers

This X-Factor lies at the heart of the discussion regarding the possible use of the DEA/Malmquist index to regulate utility prices as a component of price cap regulation. The X-Factor is ultimately an index number. Index numbers are found throughout the economy, expressing the value of some entity, like prices or gross national product, at a given period of time and in absolute number form, but related to some base period. Objectively determined incentive regulation uses such index numbers as the X-factor to reflect industry productivity growth.

The first issue concerning the empirical foundation of the X-factor is the use of long historical time trends in its calculations. The conventional assumption among productivity analysts is that the industry productivity and input prices are characterized by a valid and stable trend. This basic view of long-term trends has been adopted by many academic researchers who have studied macroeconomic time series such as GNP, prices, wages, unemployment rates, money stock, interest rates, etc. The issue of whether "structural breaks" disrupt such long-term trends has attracted considerable academic interest,[10] but it would appear that the stable trend hypothesis is a strong one and is most consistent with the search for objectivity in the calculation of a suitable X-factor. Using the longest historical data series consistent with available data allows analysts to identify the magnitude of the trend most reliably.

Since price cap regulation was introduced in the UK in the 1980s, and subsequently in the US in the early 1990s, considerable discussion has attended the choice of the index number to mimic productivity. Most of the literature on index numbers for productivity measurement pre-dates the use of such information in incentive regulation plans. Indeed, all three of the productivity index numbers in general use for price cap regimes were formulated by their named authors decades ago. They are the Fisher Ideal index, used by the Federal Communications Commission (the FCC) for telecommunications incentive regulation in the United States, the Törnqvist[11] index, which forms the basis for many electric utility TFP studies, and the Malmquist index, to which regulators in the Netherlands and Germany have referred on occasion (albeit for a different reasons).

Comparing the Törnqvist with Malmquist Indexes

The popularity of the Törnqvist index follows from its association with "translog" production and cost functions. Simply put, translog functions (which are functions squared in logarithms) were the first to allow economists to study empirically the "U-shaped" cost curves of real-life firms. With such functions, scale and substitution economies could be investigated empirically rather than assumed theoretically. With such flexible, empirically developed models of production technology as a foundation, the theoretical base for index numbers that reflect such production technology is very strong.[12] The translog multilateral productivity index[13] forms the basis for modern TFP studies in the electric power industry, including NERA's.

The Malmquist index in modern regulatory literature is usually mentioned alongside the Törnqvist index in the literature on index number theory. The two indexes are indeed close theoretical cousins. For regulatory purposes, however, various analysts have seized upon a particular feature of the Malmquist index that the Törnqvist does not share: the purported ability to measure the extent of inefficiency of individual utilities against supposedly more efficient peers. However, the use of DEA procedures along with the Malmquist index for the purpose of assessing individual firm efficiencies is not based on index number theory, nor is it consistent with the empirical applications for which it appeared in the literature. In this section I review the use of the Malmquist index by academic efficiency analysts as well as by index number theorists. I show that the use of that index in conjunction with DEA analyses to judge the efficiency of individual utilities is a particular misuse of an index number method, for which no support appears in the theoretical or empirical academic economic literature.

The Malmquist index arose in productivity theory as a more general, less restrictive, way of representing how a production function moves over time. Although it lends itself to the practice, it was not intended as a tool to "differentiate between technical change and changes in productivity."[14] It is not a use for which index number theorists investigated the Malmquist index nor is it supported in that literature.

In general, the Malmquist index measures the change in an industry's total factor productivity over time. It accounts for the fact that technology (i.e., best practice) is continually changing and that a firm's efficiency performance (relative to best practice) is also subject to change. For this reason, calculating this index requires a panel of data for the identification of both technological change and variations in firm efficiency. The Malmquist index describes productivity growth in terms of two components: (1) movements in the best practice frontier (i.e., technological change) and (2) shifts in firm efficiency that narrow or widen the gap between actual and frontier performance.

In comparison, the Törnqvist index does not decompose productivity growth in terms of technological change and efficiency "catch up," but rather in terms of the respective contributions of output and input growth (and their individual components if there is more than one) to the final result. Another important difference between these two estimation methods is that the Törnqvist index relies on cost shares or other value-based weights, which implies the use of price information in addition to quantity series, whereas the Malmquist index only requires quantity indexes to calculate productivity. Other than these differences, and provided that adequate data are available, the Törnqvist and Malmquist indexes should provide similar overall results for industry TFP.

The problem with the use of the Malmquist index is that it enables analysts to make assertions about firm-specific efficiency relating to its two components—one representing the "technology" and the other representing the "firm." The existence of the two components has led analysts to draw conclusions about the efficiency of a particular firm with respect to an industry standard—something that incentive regulation does not call for and that the quality of data to investigate the X-Factor does not support.

Data Envelopment Analysis (DEA) and the X-Factor

DEA combines multiple input and output measures (both monetary and physical) to generate an overall efficiency measure for a company. Mathematical programming methods allow researchers to apply quantitative information of a company and its peer group (i.e., the comparators) to determine relative efficiency performance.

Figure 1 illustrates the basic DEA approach. This figure displays an input-oriented[15] efficiency measurement for a group of 10 companies, which assumes that there is one type of output (e.g., MBTUs delivered) and two kinds of input (e.g., capital and labor). This type of efficiency measure considers the degree to which input quantities can be proportionally reduced without changing the output quantities. The figure plots the combination of inputs (x_1 and x_2) that each company employs to produce a unit of output, which for simplicity is normalized equal to one. Based on the actual behavior of the 10 companies, an envelope curve or efficiency frontier (shown in the Figure) is identified, reflecting the industry best practice. If the production function (which in this case has only two inputs) were to capture all the relevant determinants of cost, then the closer a firm is located to this curve the higher is its level of efficiency. In principle, firms that are located further out can produce the same amount of output with fewer inputs, bringing them closer to the origin and the achievement of higher efficiency. Theoretically, each firm's efficiency level can be measured empirically. For instance, Firm P's score

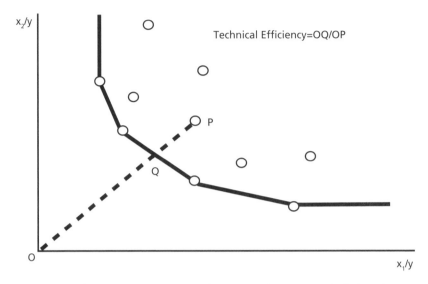

Figure 1.   *Efficiency Measurement with Data Envelopment Analysis (DEA)*

is equal to the ratio OQ/OP. If a firm is located on the frontier, then it obtains the highest possible score, which is equal to one.

Certain analysts (and some regulators) have taken the relative positions on such graphs as Figure 1 as indicating what the X-Factor should be for a particular firm, for instance, by calculating an "efficiency score" for each company equal to the distance from the "efficiency" line. However, these conclusions are inconsistent with the price cap theory that uses a competitive type of constraint for multiyear regulated prices precisely because such conclusions ignore the fact that relative productivity levels are elusive when particular utilities are highly idiosyncratic. Any conclusions about relative efficiency are limited by the caveat that the DEA analysis measures all relative cost drivers. In practice, for utilities in different locations, with different histories, serving different kinds of customers, this is quite obviously not the case. That is, while such an analysis can be useful in gauging the relative efficiency in very similar operations (like McDonald's franchises, which operate from similar shops selling similar, or even identical, products), the same is definitely not true for different utilities selling to different customer bases in different regions of a country (or the world). In such cases, the gap between the company and the frontier could as well be due to any factors not recognized in the analysis and is not necessarily a measure of "inefficiency levels" or "productivity levels."

The DEA/Malmquist Procedure in Efficiency Analyses

Users of the Malmquist index number in regulatory settings frequently refer to the "seminal" 1978 paper by Charnes, Cooper, and Rhodes.[16] This paper is about measuring efficiency "with special reference to possible use in evaluating public programs."[17] In that paper, Charnes, et al. use DEA as a method to chart the comparative efficiency of public programs (decision making units—DMUs). That analysis (the graphical representation is shown above in Figure 1) measures the distance between the presumed efficiency frontier and the position of an individual DMU, implying inefficiency in that unit. They do, however, warn of the method's limitations outside of the public setting, saying

> One limitation may arise because of lack of data availability at individual [decision making unit] levels. This is likely to be less of a problem in public sector, as contrasted with private sector, applications. ... Our measure is intended to evaluate the accomplishments, or resource conservation possibilities, for every DMU with the resources assigned to it.[18]

By acknowledging the need to standardize the "resources assigned to it," as in the case of their school district example, the authors recognize the limitations of their suggested DEA method in situations where input choice or environmental factors cannot be controlled. Despite its limitations for private firms, DEA analysis is a direct analog to the Malmquist index, where the "distance" of a particular firm's observation (in a particular year or for an average of years) is compared to the "envelope." Like DEA analysis generally, the most fundamental problem with using the Malmquist index in this way for different network utilities is that neither all the input choices nor all the environmental factors can be controlled. Individual regulated firms exist in specific local surroundings. The myriad important factors (age, location, vintage of capital stock, idiosyncratic local regulation, etc.) create cost or output differences for particular utilities that their regulatory data does not (and can never hope to) capture. This type of comparison confuses these ubiquitous differences in conditions for significant differences in efficiency.

Federico went right to the heart of the problem of ignoring variations in environment issues:

> In spite of its nice theoretical properties, the Malmquist index is subject to all the shortcomings of conventional measures. It does not take into account environmental [factors], nor possible distortions from the use of benchmark years and the two measures of technical change differ if technical progress on the "frontier" is not neutral. On top of this, the Malmquist index (as the multi-country production function estimates) assumes that all units can attain the same level of production given their factor endowment—i.e., that they belong to the same production function. This assumption may not hold in agriculture, where feasible techniques heavily depend on environment.[19]

What is true of agriculture is true of any business—including network utilities—where local conditions dictate the precise form of investments and operations. The question of environmental factors cannot be disentangled from efficiency in either DEA analysis or its Malmquist equivalent. Sena reviews the various methods and warns about these environmental variables in evaluating the results of either DEA or Malmquist models that purport to identify efficiency for individual not on the frontier:

> However, the main weakness of DEA (namely that it is a deterministic method) is still there and so the computed distance functions may include the effect of factors not related to technical efficiency and technical change. ... The best option left to the researcher is to try to specify the DEA model (underlying the Malmquist index) in the best possible [way]... to minimize the impact of external factors on the computed distance functions.[20]

Sena also identifies another problem with the use of DEA analyses underlying the Malmquist index—that of stochastic shocks in the data:

> DEA does not allow us to model stochastic shocks to production i.e., it is deterministic. Therefore the computed efficiency scores may be biased by factors which are external to the production process. Not surprisingly, some attempts have been made to incorporate stochastic components into the linear programming problem. ...The

data requirements of the chance-constrained efficiency measurement, however, are too many. Indeed it is necessary to have information on the expected values of all variables, along with their variance and covariance matrices and the probability levels at which feasibility constraints are to be satisfied. Therefore, this approach is too informationally demanding to be implemented easily.[21]

The issues associated with bias due to stochastic shocks are genuine and highly problematic for DEA analyses with electric utility data. Appendix C to this paper contains TFP data computed for a 1986 study of electric utilities,[22] using Form 1 data from the Federal Energy Regulatory Commission (the FERC) using the Uniform System of Accounts.[23] The productivity growth figures displayed in the Appendix, generated with a Törnqvist aggregation using the most reliable and consistent data for 39 electric utilities across 11 years, still shows considerable levels of stochastic shocks, particularly in year-to-year comparisons. For example, Kentucky Power for the four years 1973 through 1976 shows TFP yearly growth rates of −22.4 percent, 20.6 percent, −20.2 percent and 28.1 percent. The average TFP growth for Kentucky Power for the 11 years is 3.2 percent, and for those four particular years is 1.6 percent. But a DEA analysis of cost levels in 1974 or 1976 would incorporate very high productivity growth—owing only to stochastic shocks that were reversed in the next year—and those numbers make other companies in those years seem less productive by comparison.

Empirical data from academic TFP studies show that even the highest quality data (from the U.S. Uniform System of Accounts) produces TFP index growth rates for individual companies that are highly sensitive to vagaries and judgments on how company data is reported to governmental agencies. Individual data points for specific companies and years in industry-wide TFP analysis are notoriously unstable, even in the best of circumstances (see the data in Appendix C). The DEA envelope process, or the Malmquist index method, necessarily picks up the instability in individual data points and represents a stochastic error as a shift in technology. Simple noise among a cross-section would be taken as a change in the frontier—an advance of productivity. The more "noise" there is in the data, the more it pushes the envelope, implying inefficiency where none would otherwise be shown to exist. Thus, a simple DEA Malmquist analysis would treat the advances of companies in panel data TFP analyses as a shift in technology and would consider retreats as inefficiency.

In any event, to the extent that particular firms enter and leave the technology envelope on a short-term basis (which is indeed the case with the TFP data I analyzed in Appendix C), that envelope has no reliable significance as an indication of technological possibilities. Given that the envelope encapsulates unreliable individual data points and overstated technical progress, any conclusions based on the technological change and the efficiency "catch up" components of the Malmquist index would be highly unreliable.

Nevertheless, jurisdictions continue to rely on the Malmquist index in their DEA analyses. The Independent Pricing and Regulatory Tribunal (IPART) in New South Wales, Australia, has commissioned a number of regulatory benchmarking studies using the DEA/Malmquist technique.[24] These studies measure DEA production frontiers as a yardstick against which to measure the relative performance of the distributors under IPART's jurisdiction. Recent analyses have also been performed comparing the efficiency of individual Dutch electricity generators.[25] Another analysis was performed for German electricity distributors in the Federal network regulator's (BNA's) 2006 report on incentive regulation.[26] Scandinavian regulators routinely use such studies. These regulatory applications reflect a similar use of the DEA/Malmquist technique, with a similar justification:

> The Malmquist index ... can be decomposed so that the change in total factor productivity may be separated into a shift of the frontier (technical change) and a shift relative to the frontier (change in efficiency).[27]

This reasonable-sounding goal is contrary to the role of productivity in the theory of incentive regulation, as outlined in Section II and Appendix A, and, even if this were a valid pursuit in incentive regulation, it is contrary the advice of Federico and Sena regarding the difficulty of standardizing environmental factors. DEA's adherents seem to like the ease with which it provides "efficiency scores" for particular utilities. But that ease of calculation both contradicts the theory upon which incentive regulation rests and remains inconsistent with the kind of data available for utilities to which DEA is applied.

Summary of the DEA/Malmquist Procedure

Given the characteristics listed above of the Malmquist index and of DEA, any plan to base a price cap on the separation of technological change from company efficiency is going to run into problems than cannot be overcome in an objective manner. The DEA/Malmquist procedure cannot possibly control for all the environmental factors that determine a company's performance. Moreover, random shocks ("noise") in these unexplained factors can lead to further downward bias in the "frontier" and hence to a further underestimate of a company's performance.

The X-Factor remains a highly useful part of incentive regulation. The DEA/Malmquist procedure, however, is a devilishly convenient but ultimately unreliable procedure, inconsistent with the principles of incentive regulation. It is based on assumptions of production technologies and not on theory supported by the economic literature or valid empirical work. It has no support in the economic literature on the theory of index numbers and is contrary to the accepted theory regarding the incentives that price caps are supposed to embody. It is also contrary to the use of the DEA/Malmquist procedure in the analysis of nonregulated businesses where in contrast to network operations the inputs are controlled, and it has manifestly clear and unavoidable empirical problems.

Appendix A

The Derivation of the PBR formula:

Assume the price cap plan begins with appropriate prices so that the value of total inputs (including a normal return on capital) equals the value of total output for the company as well as the industry. For the industry, we can write this relationship as

$$\sum_{i=1}^{N} p_i Q_i = \sum_{j=1}^{M} w_j R_j$$

where the industry has N outputs ($Q_i, i=1,...,N$) and M inputs ($R_j, j=1,...,M$) and where p_i and w_j denote output and input prices, respectively. We want to calculate a productivity target for a company based on industry average productivity growth.

Differentiating this identity with respect to time yields

$$\sum_{i=1}^{N} \dot{p}_i Q_i + \sum_{i=1}^{N} p_i \dot{Q}_i = \sum_{j=1}^{M} \dot{w}_j R_j = \sum_{j=1}^{M} w_j \dot{R}_j$$

where a dot (·) indicates a derivative with respect to time. Dividing both sides of the equation by the value of output ($Rev = \sum_i p_i Q_i$ or $C = \sum_j w_j R_j$), we obtain

$$\sum \dot{p}_i \left(\frac{Q_i}{REV} \right) + \sum \dot{Q}_i \left(\frac{p_i}{REV} \right) = \sum \dot{w}_j \left(\frac{R_j}{C} \right) + \sum \dot{R}_j \left(\frac{w_j}{C} \right)$$

where REV and C denote revenue and cost. If rev_i denotes the revenue share of output i, and c_j denotes the cost share of input j, then

(1)
$$\sum_i rev_i \, dp_i = \sum_j c_j \, dw_j - \left[\sum_i rev_i \, dQ_i - \sum_j c_j \, dR_j \right]$$

where d denotes a percentage growth rate: $dp_i = \dot{p}_i / p_i$. The first term in equation (1) is the revenue-weighted average of the rates of growth of output prices, and the second is the cost-weighted average of the rates of growth of input prices. The term in brackets is the difference between weighted averages of the rates of growth of outputs and inputs. It thus is a measure of the change in TFP. Rewriting the equation for clarity, we see that

$$dp = dw - dTFP.$$

In other words, the theory underlying the annual price cap adjustment formula implies that the rate of growth of a revenue-weighted output price index is equal to the rate of growth of an expenditure-weighted input price index plus the change in total factor productivity (TFP). This equation shows that TFP is the appropriate foundation for a productivity target in the price cap plan: If the price cap plan begins with revenues that just match costs for a company, and if it attains the same productivity growth as the industry (measured in terms of TFP), then that company's revenues will continue to match its costs.[28]

Applying this rule more generally to admit the possibility of exogenous cost events outside of a regulated company's control, we may write

$$dp^* = dw - dTFP$$

where dp^* represents the annual percentage change in industry output prices inclusive of these exogenous costs, and dw represents the annual percentage change in input prices. To raise or lower industry output prices in order to track exogenous changes in cost, we write

(2)
$$dp = dw - dTFP + Z^*$$

where *dp* represents the annual percentage change in industry output prices adjusted for exogenous cost changes, and *Z** represents the unit change in costs due to external circumstances.[29] Thus, to keep the revenues of the industry equal to its costs despite changes in input prices, the price cap formula should (1) increase industry output prices at the same rate as its input prices less the target change in productivity growth, and (2) directly pass through exogenous cost changes.

Equation (2) sets the allowed price change as input price changes less TFP growth adjusted for exogenous cost pass-throughs. If the economy-wide inflation rate were *assumed* to be the measure of the industry's input price growth and the X-Factor were similarly *assumed* to be its TFP growth target, equation (2) would indeed be the basis for the ideal price adjustment formula. However, these two assumptions are incorrect:

1. Broad inflation measures capture national *output* price growth, not the industry's input price growth. So even if the industry were a microcosm of the whole economy, a measure that captures national output price growth would not be an appropriate measure of its input price growth.[30]
2. The *X-Factor* is a target TFP growth rate relative to the economy as a whole (or relative to the TFP growth already embodied in national output price growth). The change in TFP in equation (2) is the absolute TFP growth for the industry. Again, unless economy-wide TFP growth is zero, the *X-Factor* is not equal to *dTFP*.

To get from equation (2) to the price adjustment formula, we must compare the productivity growth of the industry with the productivity growth of the whole economy. It is difficult to measure input price growth objectively. We are unaware of any agency that maintains an index of industry-specific input prices. Further, a productivity adjustment based on company-provided calculations of changes in their own input price index would be controversial and would not necessarily be based on information outside the company's control. However, by comparing productivity growth of the industry with that of the whole economy, we avoid the difficulty of measuring input price growth.

For the economy as a whole, the relationship among input prices, output prices, productivity, and exogenous cost changes can be derived in the same manner as it was derived in equation (2) above

(3) $$dp^N = dw^N - dTFP^N + Z^{*N}$$

where dp^N is the annual percentage change in a national index of output prices, dw^N is the annual percentage change in a national index of input prices, $dTFP^N$ is the annual change in the economy-wide total factor productivity, and Z^{*N} represents the change in national output prices caused by the exogenous factors included in equation (2). Subtracting equation (3) from equation (2) gives

$$dp - dp^N = [dw - dw^N] - [dTFP - dTFP^N] + [Z^* - Z^{*N}],$$

or

(4) $$dp = dp^N - [dTFP - dTFP^N + dw^N - dw] + [Z^* - Z^{*N}]$$

which simplifies to

(5) $$dp = dp^N - X + Z.$$

Appendix B

The Malmquist Index

Figure 2 illustrates the measurement of the Malmquist index, assuming an output-oriented efficiency measure and a constant return to scale technology. To simplify the exposition, I consider one output and only one type of input category. Figure 2 shows the efficiency frontier and a firm's output/input combination for two different time periods. Point 1 refers to initial period (time t), and point 5 pertains to the second period (time t+1). Based on the t-period technology, the firm's initial efficiency is measured by the distance C1/C2, and using the following period technology as reference, it is equivalent to the ratio C1/C3. A similar calculation is made regarding the firm's performance in the following period, so that based on the initial period technology its efficiency is measured as D5/D4, and with the t+1 technology, it is equal to the distance D5/D6. The Malmquist index combines productivity information relative to actual efficiency behavior and best practice frontiers in both periods in order to determine the efficiency change (or productivity growth) between the t and t+1.

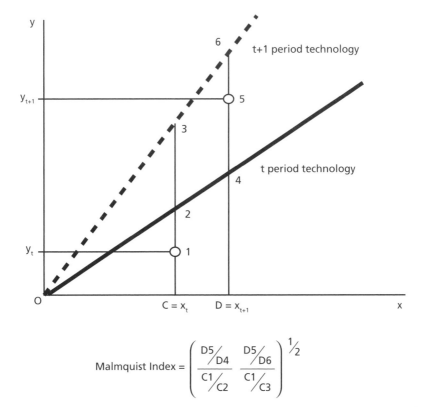

$$\text{Malmquist Index} = \left(\frac{D5 \big/ D4}{C1 \big/ C2} \frac{D5 \big/ D6}{C1 \big/ C3} \right)^{1/2}$$

Figure 2. *Output-Oriented Malmquist Index*

Appendix C

YEARLY GROWTH RATES FOR
TFP INDEX
FOR 39 ELECTRIC UTILITIES

COMPANY	1971	1972	1973	1974	1975	1976	1977	1978	1979	1980	AVG.
POTOMAC ELECTRIC POWER	14.1%	5.5%	-7.2%	-5.4%	-3.6%	3.3%	-8.6%	8.3%	-5.5%	-0.6%	.0%
GULF POWER COMPANY	-0.1%	-8.4%	12.0%	-5.5%	-4.6%	-6.5%	-3.1%	3.5%	3.9%	-11.3%	-2.0%
TAMPA ELECTRIC COMPANY	0.6%	1.1%	3.5%	-7.5%	-5.2%	3.3%	6.2%	0.3%	0.2%	7.6%	1.0%
SAVANNAH ELEC AND PWR CO	-1.7%	-1.5%	1.8%	-12.9%	1.6%	4.8%	0.4%	-9.6%	1.4%	-13.8%	-2.9%
HAWAIIAN ELEC PWR CO	4.0%	2.2%	-0.3%	1.8%	2.9%	0.4%	1.7%	-0.4%	3.0%	-0.1%	1.5%
COMMONWEALTH EDISON	-8.8%	-8.4%	-1.9%	-2.0%	-15.6%	-6.1%	0.9%	-5.7%	-4.4%	-6.2%	-5.8%
INDIANAPOLIS PWR AND LIGHT	-5.5%	-5.1%	3.8%	-1.1%	-6.6%	1.3%	-10.2%	12.8%	1.2%	3.0%	-0.6%
PUB SERV OF INDIANA	1.6%	6.0%	0.4%	-4.7%	2.8%	4.5%	-1.7%	-5.3%	3.3%	-3.3%	0.4%
KANSAS GAS AND ELECTRIC	-6.3%	-5.4%	-2.7%	5.4%	3.6%	-5.8%	10.0%	11.6%	-9.7%	4.6%	0.5%
KENTUCKY POWER COMPANY	6.7%	0.1%	-9.4%	6.0%	-10.2%	13.6%	-6.2%	-5.3%	-6.8%	13.2%	0.2%
KENTUCKY UTILITIES COMPANY	30.5%	-3.4%	4.2%	15.0%	-1.5%	5.3%	2.1%	0.6%	-13.6%	8.3%	4.8%
LOUISIANA PWR AND LIGHT	12.1%	6.3%	0.2%	-4.3%	2.5%	2.1%	-4.9%	-3.2%	-9.9%	-7.4%	-0.6%
DETROIT EDISON COMPANY	-0.7%	-1.8%	1.1%	-0.2%	-3.2%	-4.6%	-0.2%	-1.2%	-2.6%	-6.0%	-1.9%
MISSISSIPPI POWER CO	-6.9%	-7.5%	4.1%	3.1%	-9.6%	1.8%	-14.5%	13.0%	-8.2%	2.1%	-2.3%
MISSISSIPPI PWR AND LIGHT	-3.0%	7.1%	-25.7%	-3.5%	16.4%	15.5%	8.1%	5.0%	-9.7%	1.7%	1.2%
KANSAS CITY PWR AND LIGHT	-0.3%	-2.5%	-3.9%	-11.1%	-5.2%	-3.2%	-6.5%	4.0%	-30.0%	29.4%	-2.9%
UNION ELECTRIC COMPANY	1.8%	.0%	11.5%	-6.5%	10.2%	3.8%	6.4%	-2.2%	-4.3%	-5.0%	1.6%
NEVADA POWER COMPANY	10.8%	-4.1%	-0.7%	8.1%	-2.6%	10.6%	14.5%	-12.6%	0.4%	-1.6%	2.3%
PUB SERV OF NEW HAMPSHIRE	-7.0%	3.2%	-10.1%	-9.4%	2.2%	-2.3%	3.9%	-14.8%	14.6%	-2.1%	-2.2%
PUB SERV OF NEW MEXICO	5.0%	0.1%	-5.4%	2.6%	-0.7%	-16.8%	5.0%	-34.1%	-0.1%	1.1%	-4.3%
OTTER TAIL POWER CO	-8.6%	2.6%	8.6%	-6.3%	14.6%	8.3%	-0.8%	-8.1%	-11.5%	7.8%	0.7%
CLEVELAND ELEC ILLUM CO	8.0%	-1.0%	1.6%	-5.7%	-4.7%	-2.3%	1.4%	-3.5%	-10.2%	-7.1%	-2.4%
COLUMBUS AND SOUTHERN OHIO	1.1%	8.0%	6.2%	-2.8%	-7.8%	4.5%	-1.6%	-6.9%	15.5%	-6.8%	0.9%
OHIO EDISON COMPANY	-6.4%	6.7%	-0.4%	-23.3%	-8.6%	9.0%	-15.4%	10.1%	3.9%	.0%	-2.4%
OKLAHOMA GAS AND ELEC CO	1.0%	4.3%	5.9%	-1.1%	-2.0%	-4.4%	-4.8%	9.4%	-1.6%	0.7%	0.7%
PUB SERV CO OF OKLAHOMA	5.7%	0.2%	-5.6%	6.0%	0.3%	3.3%	-1.5%	-0.2%	-8.4%	4.3%	0.4%
DUQUESNE LIGHT COMPANY	0.9%	2.0%	2.9%	20.9%	-5.2%	5.7%	-1.3%	-17.5%	18.5%	1.2%	2.8%
PENNSYLVANIA PWR AND LIGHT	5.6%	13.7%	10.2%	-4.9%	6.4%	-1.8%	4.7%	-5.5%	-0.4%	-3.4%	2.5%
CENTRAL POWER AND LIGHT	9.2%	-5.1%	0.2%	-4.4%	-4.4%	0.9%	2.5%	4.0%	-3.5%	-3.5%	-0.4%
DALLAS POWER AND LIGHT CO	3.0%	3.4%	0.9%	4.1%	6.3%	4.2%	0.4%	1.2%	2.0%	3.4%	2.9%
EL PASO ELECTRIC CO	0.2%	5.2%	2.5%	0.6%	2.0%	-5.0%	0.3%	-9.5%	6.8%	-10.7%	-0.8%
HOUSTON LIGHTING AND PWR	1.2%	1.5%	-1.5%	-4.1%	-1.6%	1.3%	-2.6%	-3.3%	0.6%	-3.8%	-1.2%
SOUTHWESTERN ELEC PWR CO	0.3%	11.1%	-9.7%	3.3%	-1.3%	-4.0%	0.6%	0.5%	1.2%	-2.2%	.0%
SOUTHWESTERN PUB SERV CO	3.4%	5.2%	-0.9%	1.3%	-3.1%	2.8%	0.1%	-0.9%	-1.4%	5.0%	1.2%
TEXAS ELEC SERV CO	-1.3%	0.6%	-2.1%	5.1%	1.7%	1.6%	-1.3%	5.8%	2.9%	1.0%	1.4%
TEXAS PWR AND LIGHT CO	1.1%	-2.3%	-1.8%	-9.4%	-8.1%	-5.8%	6.0%	-0.8%	-5.8%	1.9%	-2.5%
WEST TEXAS UTILITIES CO	3.0%	5.3%	-2.0%	3.2%	3.9%	1.9%	1.7%	-4.1%	3.0%	2.5%	1.8%
UTAH PWR AND LIGHT CO	-13.4%	21.7%	21.0%	-4.8%	6.9%	-23.8%	31.7%	15.1%	-2.1%	14.6%	6.7%
APPALACHIAN PWR CO	10.5%	26.3%	-3.0%	-11.9%	-9.1%	4.8%	-6.2%	-1.3%	1.7%	1.2%	1.3%
AVERAGE	1.8%	2.4%	0.2%	-1.7%	-1.0%	0.7%	0.4%	-1.3%	-1.7%	0.5%	.0%

Notes

1. The theory of incentive regulation, as derived in Appendix A, deals with the constraints posed by productivity *growth*. The *level* of productivity, as such, is not a focus of the economic concepts that form the basis of incentive regulation.

2. M. Beesley and S. Littlechild, "The Regulation of Privatised Monopolies in the United Kingdom," *The Rand Journal of Economics,* XX, 3 (1989), p. 455; also see M. Armstrong, S. Cowan, and J. Vickers, *Regulatory Reform: Economic Analysis and British Experience* (Cambridge, MA and London: MIT press, 1994), p. 174 for a discussion on the flexibility available to regulators when setting the *X-factor*.

3. That is, (1) changes in industry prices track changes in industry costs and (2) the changes in an individual firm's prices relative to its costs differ from the industry average due to its relative TFP growth.

4. R. Loube, "Price Cap Regulation: Problems and Solutions," *Land Economics,* LXXI, 3 (1995) 288; and P. Navarro, "The Simple Analytics of Performance-Based Ratemaking: A Guide for the PBR Regulator," *Yale Journal on Regulation,*

XIII, 1, (1996) 128. For further discussions on the importance of the correct price level when setting X see J. Bernstein and D. Sappington, "Setting the X Factor in Price-Cap Regulation Plans," *Journal of Regulatory Economics,* XVI, 1, (July 1999) 9, 11; and I. Vogelsang, "Optimal Price Regulation for Natural and Legal Monopolies," *Economia Mexicana, Nueva Epoca,* VIII, 1 (1999) 31.

5. J. Bernstein and D. Sappington, "How to Determine the X in RPI-X regulation: A User's Guide," *Telecommunications Policy,* XXIV, 1, (2000) 64. For additional discussions on the intention to track efficient costs by X tracking the differences in input price and productivity growth rates between the relevant industry and the economy, see Vogelsang (1999) p. 10, Bernstein and Sappington (2000) page 64, J. Vickers and G. Yarrow, Privatization: *An Economic Analysis* (Cambridge, MA and London: MIT Press, 1989) p. 296; and Loube (1995), pp. 289-290.

6. See: Loube (1995), p. 289.

7. This theoretical presentation, derived in Appendix A, is taken from J.D. Makholm and M. J. Quinn, "Price Cap Plans for Electricity Distribution Companies Using TFP Analysis," NERA Working Paper (October 21, 1997) pp. 36-39.

8. This differential is equal to the difference between the electricity industry and economy-wide TFP growth rates only if the rates of input price growth are the same for the industry and the nation, i.e., if $dw = dw^N$.

9. Adjusted for observed differences between input price growth rates for the industry and the nation.

10. In an influential article, Charles Nelson and Charles Plosser postulate that macroeconomic variables are better characterized as "non-stationary" processes that have no tendency to return to a predetermined path, instead of being regarded as variables that fluctuate around a deterministic trend. See Charles R. Nelson and Charles I. Plosser, "Trends and Random Walks in Macroeconomic Time Series: Some Evidence and Implications," *Journal of Monetary Economics* X (1982), 139-162. Pierre Perron, on the other hand, makes one of the most compelling defenses of the "trend-stationary" model, arguing that the empirical evidence validates this model when one accounts for the existence of trend-breaks due to certain "structural shocks" that have lasting effects See Pierre Perron, "The Great Crash, The Oil Price Shock, and the Unit Root Hypothesis," *Econometrica,* LVII, 6 (1989), 1361-1401. Perron finds that the only shocks with persistent effects are the 1929 Great Crash and the 1973 oil price shock.

11. Törnqvist (a statistician in Finnish government service writing in the 1930s) and Theil (an American econometrician) both investigated the validity of index number techniques. The index number used most widely for TFP studies, which is the geometric mean of the Laspeyres and Paasche indexes described in basic economics textbooks, is named after both.

12. In technical terms, the Törnqvist/Theil index number is "exact" for the flexible homogeneous translog aggregator function. The Index is "exact" in the sense that it can be directly related to the properties of the translog. For further reference, see W. E. Diewert, "Exact and Superlative Index Numbers," *Journal of Econometrics,* IV, 2, (1976), 115-146.

13. D.W. Caves and L.R. Christensen, "Global Properties of Flexible Functional Forms," *American Economic Review,* LXX, (1980) 422-432.

14. M. Dykstra, "How Efficient is Dutch Electricity Generation: Current Research," CPB Report (the Netherlands), 1997/4, pp. 45-47 (http://www.cpb.nl/nl/pub/cpbreeksen/cpbreport/1997_4/s3.pdf)

15. DEA also allows the construction of output-oriented efficiency measures, which we describe later on with regard to the issue of total factor productivity. In this case, the relevant question is, by how much can output quantities be proportionally expanded without altering the input quantities used? Output- and input-oriented measures are equivalent only in those cases in which the technology of production exhibits constant returns to scale.

16. A. Charnes, W.W. Cooper and E. Rhodes, "Measuring the Efficiency of Decision Making Units," *European Journal of Operational Research,* II (1978), 429-444.

17. Ibid., p. 429.

18. Ibid., p. 443.

19. G Federico, "Why are we all alive? The Growth of Agricultural Productivity and its Causes, 1800-2000," European University Institute, paper for the Sixth conference of the European Historical Economics Society, Istanbul, 9-10 September 2005, pp. 4-5.

20. V. Sena, "The Frontier Approach to the Measurement of Productivity and Technical Efficiency," *Economic Issues,* VIII, Part 2 (2003), 90. Sena refers to the DEA model "underlying the Malmquist index" in the sense that the latter index is a specific application of the general "DEA model" approach to measuring distance between a particular observation and the frontier. She does not imply that the DEA model and the Malmquist index are anything more than analogues in this respect.

21. Ibid., p. 83.

22. The data in Appendix C appears in J.D Makholm, "Sources of Total Factor Productivity in the Electric Utility Industry," Doctoral Dissertation, University of Wisconsin/Madison, May 1986 (L.R. Christensen, advisor), Appendix 4A, pp. 88-89. Note that the validity of the argument is not affected by the antiquity of the data.

23. The Uniform System of Accounts has been used by the FERC and its predecessors since 1938, as mandated by Congress.

24. See "Efficiency and Benchmarking Study of the NSW Distribution Businesses," IPART Research Paper No. 13, February 1999.

25. See Dykstra.

26. BNA (2006), 2. *Referenzbericht Anreizregulierung: Generelle sektorale Produktivitätsentwicklung im Rahmen der Anreizregulierung (2nd Reference BNA Report on Incentive Regulation: General sectoral productivity movements in the context of incentive regulation),* Bundesnetzagentur, Bonn, 26 January 2006.

27. See Dykstra, p. 1.

28. It is observed often enough that such formulation assumptions might not be appropriate in the case of a recently privatized company, with poorly main-

tained infrastructure, whose costs might be expected to fall faster than the "industry." That would be using the term "industry" too widely, however. It would not be practical to expect productivity growth for a newly privatized company to match that exhibited by a mature, investor-owned industry.

29. Note that Z^* can be positive or negative.

30. Recall that input price growth differs from output price growth by the growth in TFP. Only if national productivity growth were zero could a national output price index be a good measure of national input price growth.

6

MERGERS AND ACQUISITIONS IN THE US ELECTRIC INDUSTRY: STATE REGULATORY POLICIES FOR REVIEWING TODAY'S DEALS[1]

Carl R. Peterson
Karl A. McDermott

Introduction

The debate over the appropriate structure for the electric industry in the United States has been the subject of legislation, policymaking and litigation for years. With the introduction of competition in the wholesale and retail markets for electricity, regulated firms and holding companies of regulated firms are struggling to adjust to new conditions and exploit new opportunities created by changes in government policy toward the industry. These reforms were largely aimed at creating a more efficient industry through providing additional freedom to managers and investors to organize the industry around economic incentives, rather than in response to prescriptive government edicts. This freedom was expected to result in more and varied products and services, more efficient operations and better pricing signals.[2] As should have been expected, utility corporate restructuring efforts have focused on controlling costs to become more competitive while positioning companies to compete in the new market environment through strategic mergers.[3] The extent to which firms are allowed to implant these new organizational structures will have a great bearing on the industry's ability to fulfill the promise of a more efficient industry.

State (and federal) regulators in the US[4] have addressed merger issues for the entire history of the industry.[5] One of the key steps in achieving regulatory approval of a merger[6] is demonstrating that the transaction is in the public interest. With the changing market landscape, both state regulators and utility executives have faced numerous shifts in the rationale for mergers and the source, nature, and measure of expected benefits.[7] The changing context for merger evaluation, including the struggle to create competitive retail and wholesale markets, requires regulators to change the nature of the analytical framework used to assess mergers, as well as the nature of the conditions placed on those mergers. These conditions must continue to protect jurisdictional ratepayers without being so onerous that they thwart a merger deal that is beneficial in the wider context of the evolving industry.

Regulators well understand the concept of cost reduction as one aim of merger activity. However, due to the narrow mandate of the state commissions, the focus on physical and demonstrated cost reductions, and the nature of the administrative process, regulators are less knowledgeable about the role of state regulatory policy as it relates to competitive or strategic mergers. The concepts behind strategic mergers are business related and are less well defined in terms of either traditional merger analysis or what can be demonstrated through sworn testimony. Therefore, while the recent repeal of the Public Utility Holding Company Act of 1935[8] might suggest that merger activity within the industry may increase, the evidence suggests that some state regulators may not yet be ready to approve strategic mergers.

This chapter evaluates recent regulatory review of mergers in the context of the changing structure of the industry. While almost all mergers require approval from multiple regulatory agencies including the Federal Energy Regulatory Commission (FERC) and Federal Trade Commission/US Department of Justice,[9] this chapter focuses on the regulatory approval process at the state level, generally before a state public utility commission (PUC). Section II reviews the types of mergers and their benefits and costs. Section III first addresses the state PUC merger review obligations in the context of regulation and then the merger conditions that have been placed on mergers. Section IV discusses some trends in merger review policy, and Section V provides conclusions.

Merger Types, Rationales, and Costs and Benefits

Mergers and acquisitions, divestures, spin-offs, and joint ventures are part of the changing corporate structure in the electric industry.[10] Each merger type is based on a different rationale, and each offers the potential for different kinds of benefits that vary in size and certainty. Over the past two decades, the types of mergers coming before state regulators have evolved; however, the regulators' policies toward merger reviews and their expectations of potential benefits have not always reflected this evolution.

Merger Typology

Mergers and acquisitions in this industry have taken on five basic forms.

Contiguous companies are mergers between utilities that have abutting service territories. The creation of Centerior in 1986 started the most recent wave of contiguous mergers, followed by Ameren's purchases of Central Illinois Public Service (CIPS), Central Illinois Lighting Company (CILCO), and Illinois Power (IP). Contiguous mergers have traditionally been expected to provide cost savings from staff reductions, joint dispatch of plants, and avoidance of capacity addition, and, when a more efficient firm acquires a less well managed or simply less fortunate firm, imposition of cost controls.[11]

The creation of RTO/ISO systems has reduced the potential for contiguous mergers to cut costs. Mergers between utilities that are members of the same ISO already have their plants dispatched economically, and ISO-sponsored capacity markets remove or reduce the potential for capacity savings when a capacity-short utility merges with a utility with excess capacity. The initial wave of mergers seen in the mid-1980s came about as an attempt to both create the necessary size to reduce average costs and strategically position companies to take advantage of the core competencies of the new firm. However, changing market conditions and policy goals placed limits on these traditional sources of benefits.[12]

Market or geographic extensions are mergers between non-contiguous utilities. Since the late 1990s, FERC has worked to organize regional markets to further promote liquid and sustainable wholesale markets as well as market-based transmission congestion pricing. The merger and acquisition activity that resulted from these actions was generally aimed at integrating the marketing function with the physical delivery and production of power and energy. Examples of market extension mergers are the creation of Xcel, Exelon and AEP/CSW and, in its most extreme form, acquisitions of US firms by foreign utilities such as National Grid, Powergen, and Scottish Power. In these cases, the synergies possible in contiguous mergers are reduced by the lack of overlapping territory. The emphasis instead is on implementing best practices and combining billing systems and corporate functions. In fact, there may be no direct cost savings at all.[13]

Convergence involves merging energy service types, such as gas and electricity, to produce a stronger overall energy supplier. This type dominated mergers in the mid-to-late 1990s. Some electric utilities sought to purchase pipeline firms, ostensibly to support the growth in merchant gas-fired power plant fleets owned by the competitive generation subsidiaries of utilities. Others saw a marketing opportunity to sell electric and gas services across customer groups to boost sales growth. Examples include the Wisconsin Electric purchase of Wisconsin Gas and the merger of the holding companies for San Diego Gas & Electric and Southern California Gas. A convergence merger offers an opportunity to capture some traditional synergistic savings through back office, billing, and marketing economies, while allowing marketing of products across a combined customer base. The mantra became the notion of selling BTUs rather than kWhs or Mcfs. Enron's acquisition of Portland General Electric (PGE) was touted as the first in this wave, although it also represented an opportunity for Enron to show how unbundling should be done to promote retail restructuring and competition.[14] Enron attempted to remake PGE through divesting its generation assets and opening the retail market to competition. It largely failed in this attempt, and while a version of divesture and retail access was approved in Oregon, the state largely rejected the grand plan.[15]

Energy portfolio involves the purchase of a utility by a larger energy firm as part of its energy portfolio. Examples include Enron's purchase of Portland General Electric and Dynegy's purchase of Illinois Power. Other transactions of this type may include integration of retail marketing and regulated business (CalEnergy/MidAmerican), integration of midstream gas assets (Duke/Consumers Energy) or holding company additions (AEP, Southern Company). By diversifying geographically and across energy industries, the merged firms can capitalize on synergies in marketing, co-variation in energy price movements, seasonality in consumption, and other dimensions of the businesses to improve financial growth and stability. This conceptual view may help to explain the large number of electric/pipeline and electric/energy supply mergers that occurred or were proposed in the late 1990s.[16]

Non-utility portfolio is the purchase of a utility by a non-energy firm, in most cases an equity firm, as part of its overall portfolio. These mergers, which first appeared in the 1999-2000 period, used highly leveraged financing techniques to acquire utilities. Examples include Berkshire Hathaway's purchase of MidAmerican Energy, the proposed acquisition of Tucson Electric's holding company, DTE's sale of its transmission assets, and the proposed acquisition of Portland General Electric.

Merger Benefits and Costs

Merger benefits to both shareholders and customers can be categorized along two dimensions: timing and certainty. Timing refers to the pattern of the flow of benefits and certainty refers to the level of confidence in the savings estimates. Some types of mergers have short-term, relatively certain benefits and others have longer-term, less certain benefits. Actual benefits critically depend on the post-merger implementation. For example, the integration of the two companies is always difficult, both technically and culturally.

The nature of the likely benefits differs among the different types of mergers. Mergers of contiguous utilities, market extension, and convergence mergers are likely to have predictable short-term savings associated with specific post-merger activities. Mergers between utilities, especially those in close proximately, are likely to produce at least some short-term, generally one-time, reductions in costs. These come from various sources but may be related to elimination of redundant staff and bureaucracy, expanded scale in purchasing fuel and other inputs, and operational efficiencies such as joint dispatching of power plants.

In contrast, acquisitions for portfolio purposes rely on other factors to create value. These include better strategic management, innovative pricing or product provision, diversification of risks, etc. Such benefits appear over time and may occur more than once.

Mergers create costs as well as benefits. The first major cost category is the acquisition premium. Although regulators are generally very skeptical of allowing direct recovery of merger premiums, many regulatory bodies will use rate freezes or other price regulation methods to provide at least an opportunity to recover the merger premium. The second major cost category is the cost to achieve the merger. This is the cost of implementing the beneficial changes (e.g., integration of supply and information networks, integration of management techniques, etc.).[17] These costs are normally direct costs and are netted from benefits to obtain the net benefits of the merger.

State Merger Review Obligations

Reviewing Transactions Through the Lens of Regulation

Each state's legislation provides the authority[18] for a PUC to review utility mergers and the standards for that review. While each state defines these standards slightly differently, they can generally be summarized as either a *no harm* test or a *net benefit* test.[19] From a non-legal perspective, the *no harm* test essentially gives the management flexibility to organize the entire company, including the regulated utility, as long as any new organization does not harm captive ratepayers or in many cases the operating utility. The *net benefit* test is stricter. It requires that captive customers, and in some cases the regulated utility, benefit in some manner from the transaction. Although regulators are often careful not to define benefits in terms of payments to customers (e.g., rate reductions or some other direct means), in practice, rate reductions tend to be the focus of the regulator's staff and intervening parties in merger proceedings. Because staff and intervenors often advocate for large, upfront rate reductions, regulators are left with the choice of approving the merger without direct rate reductions or approving the merger under the condition of direct rate subsidies to customers. Obviously, the latter approach is far more appealing politically.[20] Although this approach is fundamentally incompatible with the modern US electric industry, rather than fading with the changes in the industry, it is becoming more common, a circumstance that suggests that regulators may be providing disincentives for mergers that are beneficial in the new industry structure.[21]

In some cases a PUC has applied both of these tests (e.g., Oregon) or is allowed to choose between the two standards (e.g., New Jersey).[22] In addition, both legislation and PUC rules often generally require that mergers be in the public interest and support the no harm and net benefit standards with more specific tests that define that public interest. Appendix 1 provides a representative overview of the items that particular PUCs are required to review and the standards to be met in merger approvals.

Typically in reviewing a merger, PUCs have three choices: (1) approve the merger, (2) deny the merger, or (3) approve the merger with conditions aimed at meeting the public interest standard.[23] This conditioning authority represents broad regulatory authority over the proposed transaction. A PUC will review a merger proposal to identify the potential risks, costs, and benefits of the merger. It will then impose merger conditions designed to immunize consumers against the risks or costs and capture some or all of the benefits for them.

Regulators look at their obligations in merger reviews through a lens of regulation that, simplifying somewhat, reflects five traditional regulatory concerns:[24]

- **Revenue Requirement:** *Just and reasonable rates* are set so that utilities are provided the opportunity to recover prudently incurred costs associated with utility service, including a reasonable return on investment.
- **Obligation to Serve:** The obligation to provide service suggests that the utility, as a monopoly provider of service, has an obligation to provide *reliable and safe service* to any customers willing and able to pay a fair and reasonable price.
- **Service Quality:** The utility must assure the regulators that service quality will remain at the pre-merger levels or improve. The general concern of regulators is that the push to achieve post-merger savings could result in cost cutting that would jeopardize service quality.
- **Economic and Social Obligations:** Utilities are granted certificates to provide local service. Their obligations include reasonable treatment of low-income customers, promotion of industrial growth and stability, and even the degree to which a utility is involved with the local community through socially responsible activities. Often the regulator wants reassurance that mergers will not result in managers' attention being directed away from the local needs because of obligations to the larger corporate entity that results from a merger.
- **Benefits to Customers:** Customers are supposed benefit from regulation through the identification of cost-based rates that result from efficient operations. If a merger is supposed to produce cost savings, the customers are entitled to share in those savings.

A typical expression of this lens of regulation can be found in the ACC review of the Unisource reorganization:

> The Commission has a constitutional duty to make and enforce reasonable rules, regulations and orders to protect the convenience, comfort, safety and health of employees and patrons of

public service corporations…. [T]he Commission has [broad] discretion to consider…impairment of financial status, ability to attract capital at fair and reasonable terms…[and] the ability to provide safe, reasonable and adequate service. …The Commission's duty extends to quality of service and safety.[25]

In applying the no harm or net benefit standards, the PUC must be convinced that there exists a set of conditions that could be imposed on the transaction that will fully immunize the customers from any harm or will provide future net benefits. This can be tricky because it requires an assessment of trade-offs across various elements of the merger proposal that are largely unknown and in many cases unknowable. Such an assessment poses particular problems for regulators imbued with the traditional regulatory paradigm that has evolved over nearly 100 years and is based on an industry structure that, largely, no longer exists. For example, does offering a reliability condition dependent on future investment expenditures equal or exceed the value of a current rate reduction or earning sharing mechanism? Two different commissions could come to different conclusions, and it is difficult to predict how any particular regulator will assess these trade-offs. In offering a package of conditions, potential merger partners must examine a regulator's past and current concerns cognizant that in this strategic game, the broad authority conferred by most state statutes hands regulators a very strong bargaining position. Further, they seem more than willing to exploit this bargaining position, especially in light of changes to the industry structure and the recent repeal of the holding company restrictions under PUHCA. It is ironic that the repeal of the PUHCA restrictions may have actually increased the level of scrutiny many mergers will face in the future, thereby providing additional disincentives to mergers that are more consistent with the new structure.

Merger Conditions as a Means to Protect the Public Interest

It is difficult to directly assess the effect of regulator-imposed merger conditions on the probability of a transaction being completed because failure to complete a merger has at least three root causes that may or may not result from regulatory conditions. First is the rejection of hostile takeovers. State commissions may react negatively to hostile takeovers in support of local utility ownership or for other rationales. The proposed merger of Kansas City Power and Light (KCPL) and Kansas Gas and Electric (KGE), for example, resulted rather in the counter merger of

Kansas Power and Light (KPL) with KGE through the formation of Western Resources. Furthermore, the targeted stockholders can also take a negative view of hostile mergers. According to one source, a quarter of the mergers that failed to materialize in the past 20 years were doomed because hostile bids were rejected (e.g., Cal Energy/New York State Electric and Gas). Many others may have failed in the boardrooms before ever coming to public attention.[26]

Second, a merger may fail due to a delay that ultimately exposed the parties to adverse financial conditions. Over half of the reported thirty failures were due to changing financial circumstances.[27] Failures in this class could be Allegheny/Duquesne Energy, and Consolidated Edison/ Northeast Utilities. Any delay may or may not have been caused by a condition placed on the transaction by regulators or simply the length of the regulatory process.

Third, a merger may be terminated due to adverse regulatory conditions or potential adverse regulatory conditions. Examples may be the Exelon/Public Service Electric and Gas proposed transaction or the FPL Group/Constellation merger proposal. The rate reduction the Kansas Corporation Commission (KCC) imposed during the merger bid of Public Service of New Mexico for Western Resources was one of the reasons that the merger failed financially. Other examples include Baltimore Gas & Electric /Potomac Electric Power Company (rate reductions) and Northern States/Wisconsin Electric Power Company (rejected by FERC for market power reasons). More recently, state legislatures have become involved in affecting transactions (Exelon's proposed purchase of Illinois Power in Illinois and the proposed merger of the FPL Group and Constellation in Maryland).

These examples highlight the important role regulatory conditions can play either directly or indirectly in the consummation of transactions. Estimates of merger costs and benefits are inherently uncertain, and the ability of the merger to proceed may be finely balanced. The regulator's authority to impose conditions on the merger is a powerful tool for protecting the public interest. But in setting conditions, PUCs must mind the tipping point where capturing benefits for customers imposes such stringent conditions that they kill a merger that is potentially beneficial to society. It is this larger benefit to society in general that most state PUCs either do not take into account or cannot take into account due to jurisdictional issues or limits on PUC authority through proscriptive legislation.[28]

Policies to Address a Merger Issue

Three merger issues play a central role in virtually every merger, and their treatment is directly related to the regulatory lens and the immunization policies that Commissions are likely to adopt.

The first policy issue is merger premiums and implementation costs. It is fundamental and the regulatory lens is the question of whether cost recovery is responsibility of customers. On one hand, there is the possibility that a merger will turn out to be a mistake. In that case, allowing the costs to be recovered from customers (normally through amortization over a specific period) implies that there is little or no upfront risk to stockholders from proposing mergers. Further, allowing recovery of these costs arguably creates an incentive for acquiring firms to bid uneconomic premiums. On the other hand, allowing cost recovery creates a positive incentive to pursue economical strategic mergers, and generally if the post-merger company turns out to perform poorly, in the long run it is shareholders who are left holding the bag. An obvious example is the case of Enron's ownership of PGE. PGE and its customers were left relatively unscathed by the failure of Enron. It was Enron's owners, and in turn PGE's owners, who paid for the Enron failure. And disallowing merger premiums from rates may thwart mergers that are potentially beneficial not only to both ratepayers and stockholders, but more broadly to society in general.

In attempting to balance these points regulators have employed policies ranging from allowing all premiums and costs-to-achieve to allowing none. One common middle ground has been to allow the successor company to net out the costs-to-achieve and premium from the merger savings calculated over a limited number of years. The use of a net benefit standard allows ratepayers and stockholders to share the benefits in excess of acquisition premiums and cost-to-achieve. Customers are not charged for the cost of any negative net benefit that may occur. Similar ends are achieved with rate freeze proposals that allow stockholders to recoup merger costs for some period of time before the synergy benefits are passed on to customers.

The second fundamental concern is with the certainty and timing of the expected synergy savings. Regulators have to grapple with various degrees of uncertainty when addressing the expected benefits and costs of mergers. In contiguous mergers, dispatch and synergy savings were considered fairly certain. In mergers that involve the adoption of best practice standards, regulators have been more skeptical regarding the timing and size of benefits claimed in merger filings.

Some states have opted for the bird-in-the-hand strategy of immediate rate reductions or credits for customers. Others have employed rate freezes, which implicitly share the benefits between customers and stockholders over the period of the freeze, or cost tracking mechanisms to measure costs through time so that cost-based rate adjustments can be implemented in future rate cases. Still other states[29] have used incentives to deal with cost and benefit uncertainty. Commissions have proposed a sharing mechanism designed to create an ongoing incentive for the utility to pursue cost savings. Potential cost reductions may or may not materialize, but the utility is more likely to work hard to achieve them if it has a chance to share these benefits through earnings sharing mechanisms, rate freezes or other incentive policies. To address these new issues, one approach that might be fruitful is for the merging parties to offer a menu of choices to regulators that in various ways weight future and current benefits. This may provide a regulator the comfort needed to approve the merger while offering a financially neutral approach on a net present value (NPV) basis for the merging parties.

The third major policy issue is quality of service, an area where regulators have traditionally imposed and enforced standards. Virtually all merger approvals involve commitments to maintain or enhance service quality levels. One of two immunization strategies is often employed. The utility may propose a set of service quality standards or targets as a positive part of the merger proposal. Or alternatively, the regulatory attaches to the merger conditions designed to protect the customer from service quality deterioration. These quality conditions represent a set of safety net conditions that protect customers and help ensure that the net effect of the merger is in the public interest with respect to reliability.

In many cases explicit criteria involve the use of CAIDI (Customer Average Interruption Duration Index), which is the SAIDI (sum of all customer interruption durations) divided by SAIFI (total number of customer interruptions). Target levels of service quality or benchmarks and other service quality measures (such as customer service rankings, price, employee safety, etc.) can also be used. Imposing service quality standards may be especially important in cases where the regulator provides for an incentive plan to allow an opportunity to recover merger premiums. Regulators need to be assured that in allowing firms to recoup these premiums, the post-merger firm does not sacrifice service quality and safety. However, regulators also need to be reasonable in their request for service quality metrics. When it is agreed that current levels are sufficient, maintaining current levels of service quality through a system of monitoring and reporting can be an appropriate policy and provide the necessary incentive for the new company to maintain these standards. However, if the regulator deems current levels of service quality insufficient, a better approach is to design an incentive mechanism that will provide the new company the necessary financial inducement to improve service quality and therefore better align the interests of the utility with its customers.

Tools to Address Other Merger Issues

Typically, merger cases before state commissions are not ratemaking proceedings, and therefore the traditional link between costs and prices is often ignored in an attempt to condition the merger in a manner that satisfies the parties and is consistent with local laws and policy. Although costs and prices are not directly linked, the rationale behind rate reductions is the attempt to share with ratepayers the efficiencies identified by the merging parties. In addition to the conditions imposed to implement the commission policies noted above, there are a variety of other tools regulators employ to realize the benefits for customers. Appendix 2 categorizes all these conditions.

RATE LEVELS

Jurisdictions have pursued four common approaches to providing incentives to promote merger savings while at the same time crediting customers for some of those savings:

- Rate credits,[30] often implemented through a specific rider, provide bill reductions for a specific time period (AEP/CSW in Kentucky and Texas).
- Rate reductions are applied to current tariffs (often across the board), either as a one-time reduction or over a period of years (Delmarva/Atlantic Electric in Virginia, Maryland, and New Jersey).
- Cost of service refers either to (1) a pass-through or balancing account mechanism that tracks actual costs over time (AEP/CSW in Louisiana and KPL/KGE in Kansas) or (2) a requirement that a rate case be initiated at a time when merger savings are expected to

decrease the cost structure of the new entity (ConEd/O&R in New York and UE/CIPS in Illinois).

- Implementing alternative forms of regulation such as a price freeze (Boston Edison/CES in Massachusetts) or an earnings-sharing mechanism (UE/CIPS in Missouri and PS CO/SWPSC in Colorado) is often combined with other rate adjustments. The PS CO/SWPSC in Colorado, for example, included a rate reduction as well.

FINANCIAL RING-FENCING

Ring-fencing conditions are designed to wall off the utility from its nonregulated affiliates or holding company and minimize the ability to shift risks associated with unregulated activities to regulated ratepayers.[31] Ring-fencing conditions include:

- **Equity Floors:** This condition requires the utility to hold a minimum level of common equity on an ongoing basis.
- **"Hold Harmless" on Cost of Capital:** This approach requires that the allowed cost of capital[32] for the utility shall not increase as a result of the merger.
- **Dividend Restrictions:** This condition restricts the level or amount of dividends that can be paid to a holding company by the utility.
- **Loan Restrictions:** Loan restrictions limit loans by the utility to affiliated companies or officers of the utility or its holding company.

RING-FENCING: AFFILIATE TRANSACTION RULES

These conditions address the nature and scope of the relationship the utility has with its affiliates. Restrictions may be placed on the type and amount of transactions with affiliated companies, as well as on payment for them. Conditions might include specific cost allocation methods or restrictions on the affiliates' use of utility assets (including labor and information). These conditions may also address issues related to competitive access to information and behavior of the utility in the competitive market.

RING-FENCING: CORPORATE GOVERNANCE

Generally these conditions relate to the make-up and authority of the board of directors of the utility. However, they may also include specific rules on the governing structure of the utility and PUC authority over non-utility investments.

DEGREE OF COMPETITION

In many states that have experienced restructuring, increased competition has jumped to the forefront of merger issues and conditions. Merger applicants have been required to provide market power studies and to undertake power plant divestiture. This issue has been raised even in states where retail competition has yet to occur. For example, the North Carolina Utilities Commission now requires a market power analysis to be conducted by all future merger applicants, even though the state has not embraced retail choice.[33] One of the clearest examples is Pennsylvania, where the restructuring law incorporates new provisions for reviewing the competitive effects of proposed mergers. In the DQE/Allegheny transaction in Pennsylvania, the Pennsylvania PUC relied on its legislation to address competition issues:

> The Electric Competition Act adds an additional approval standard which provides the Commission [PAPUC] with authority to investigate and hold public evidentiary hearings on "the effects of mergers, consolidations, acquisitions or disposition of assets or securities of electricity suppliers...[on] the retail distribution of electricity." 66 Pa. C.S. § 2811(b) Section 2811(e)(1) gives the Commission the authority to approve or disapprove such mergers or acquisitions depending on whether:

>> [T]he proposed merger...[or] acquisition is likely to result in anticompetitive or discriminatory conduct, including the unlawful exercise of market power, which will prevent retail customers...from obtaining the benefits of a properly functioning and workable competitive retail electricity market.

> Finally section 2811(e)(2) provides that:

>> [I]f the commission finds, after hearing, that a proposed merger...[or] acquisition...is likely to result in anticompetitive or discriminatory conduct, including the unlawful exercise of market power...[in] the retail electricity market, the commission shall not approve such proposed merger...[or] acquisition...

except upon such terms and conditions as it finds necessary to preserve the benefits of a properly functioning and workable competitive retail electricity market.[34]

Legislatures and regulators are concerned that retail markets (and FERC and the Congress and concerned that the wholesale market) not be harmed as a result of the proposed transaction. As a result, PUCs may impose conditions that directly affect the competitiveness of these markets including asset divesture, generation-sharing arrangements, special access conditions for competitors, etc.[35]

LOCAL CONCERNS

These conditions address local social/economic issues such keeping headquarters in the service territory, commitments to labor, and commitments to support local community efforts such as charities, education and special arrangements for low-income customers.

OTHER CONDITIONS

Other conditions cover a broad range of concerns, such as resolving issues from past rate cases, requiring adherence to standard practices such as access to books and records and auditing practices, and even the preservation or improvement of the traditional relationships between regulator and the utility. As with cost savings, regulators have a great deal of leverage in extracting special conditions that they would otherwise have no legal authority to require, partly due to the vision that regulators have of utilities in the US. Regulators (and other parties) have traditionally seen utilities as something more than a for-profit company, and this has allowed regulators to impose conditions on utilities that would not be required of competitive firms. Examples include special funding of priority projects, demand side management and demand response programs, funding a variety of studies (management studies, demand response investigations, etc.), and a range of cross-subsidies that may or may not be funded directly by the utility. As business conditions begin to require that utilities operate in a standard commercial fashion, mergers are one place where the traditional approach can be imposed via the conditioning authority of the regulatory body. The question for the industry and its regulators boils down to a question of allowing markets to work or maintaining the special arrangement.

Trends in State Merger Policy

As the industry has evolved, so too have mergers. In past decades, small utilities merged to form larger utilities, and regulators were generally concerned with capturing the benefits of economies of scale. However, as market extension, convergences, and portfolio mergers became more common, the nature of merger costs and benefits changed, and regulators developed new conditions and policies to deal with them.

Prior to 1996, most utility mergers were made in the context of traditional regulation with its focus on physical operations and demonstrated costs, such as lowering dispatch costs and achieving economies of scale. However in the new era, mergers occur for reasons other than cost reductions, though they are still consistent with government policies toward competitive markets and industry efficiency. Unfortunately, at a time when mergers are less likely to have specific upfront cost savings, the trend of merger review appears to be moving toward extracting more benefits for regulated customers:

- **Rate Levels:** Regulators are putting more emphasis on rate reductions even though the mergers are less likely to provide immediate and tangible cost reductions, and they lack good estimates of cost reductions on which to base the rate reduction.
- **Changing Review Standards:** State regulators have refined or toughened the standards under which mergers are reviewed. Examples include:
  - Texas adopted a "more comprehensive public interest standard" because the PUC assumed that competitive pressures would result in costs savings. The PUC also recognized that the transition to competition was important as well and stated that full regulatory oversight was needed during that transition.[36]
  - The Oregon PUC specifically found that the law required a net benefit be provided to customers as a result of the merger, in addition to a no harm standard.[37] Based on the perception that the risks associated with a holding company leverage buyout would not benefit utility customers, the Oregon regulators rejected the acquisition of PGE by Oregon Electric (a holding company funded by the Texas Pacific Group).
  - The Arizona CC found that no conditions could be placed on the proposed buy-out of Unisource (parent of Tucson Electric) by private equity that would meet the public interest standard. The

ACC rejected the acquisition of Unisource by Saguaro (a consortium of Kohlberg, Kravis Roberts & Co. LP, J.P. Morgan Partners, and Wachovia Partners) on the basis that the risks associated with the transaction outweighed the benefits.[38]

— New Jersey adopted a tough bargaining approach toward the proposed PSEG and Exelon deal, prompting the parties to walk away from the transaction. It has been reported that "rate concessions and market power mitigation issues" were at the heart of the disagreement between the parties.[39] As a result, the NJBPU, which had traditionally approached mergers on a case-by-case basis, generally using a "no harm" standard, has modified its administrative rules to include a "positive benefits" standard.

· **Reluctance to Approve Private Equity Deals:** Although several utilities have seen private equity investment, including Dayton Power and Light, Detroit Edison, and MidAmerican Energy, private equity has recently been less successful at convincing regulators of the public interest benefits of their utility purchases. An exception is Berkshire Hathaway.

· **Generic Merger Proceedings:** Several states, including Massachusetts, Oregon, and Louisiana, have found it necessary to review merger policy in a more generic proceeding.[40] These proceedings indicate that merger policy is of the growing importance to state regulators.

Further, it is unlikely that this trend toward more stringent standards and upfront rate subsidies will subside soon. The increasing cost of energy is beginning to be passed on to customers in all jurisdictions. In states that have restructured retail markets, government-imposed rate freezes—many of which have been in place for nearly a decade—are coming to an end. However, rate increases are also occurring in states that have not embraced retail competition, perhaps less abruptly, but nonetheless with similar effects on customer's bills. These conditions impel regulators to look for ways to mitigate rates, and conditioning mergers with upfront rate reductions is an easy regulatory target.

However, these trends are likely to discourage beneficial mergers, or at a minimum, lower the benefits to investors in the short run and to customers over the longer run. In many cases, the regulatory body's use of the traditional lens of regulation to push for upfront rate reductions make deals nearly impossible to consummate in the current climate.

Furthermore, this traditional approach to regulation seems to be pushing firms toward completely separating generation from distribution, thereby implicitly disregarding any benefits of vertical organization.[41] However, the concept of dismantling vertical integration is an "important strategic question" for the vertically integrated merchant power business.[42] If regulatory bodies in the US continue to approach these mergers through the traditional lens of regulation, either there will be an inevitable movement toward divesture of regulated assets or strategic mergers will not occur, and firms will look toward less controversial and potentially less beneficial mergers. Merger partners need to be better prepared to discuss all these issues with regulators and provide innovative packages of conditions that will allow the beneficial mergers to continue and provide the long-term benefits of these new organizations to consumers.[43]

Conclusions

Regulators will continue to view mergers through the lens of regulation. However, their standards must be understood in the context of the new market and the proper role of regulators, and their tools should be fashioned accordingly. The OPUC, while finding that the net benefit standard was required under state law, nonetheless, took the highly unusual step of criticizing the Oregon legislature for misunderstanding the role of regulation and imposing too strict a standard for mergers:

> We would like to make clear that the conclusion reached here is compelled by the statutory language and is not the policy preference of the Commission. In fact, we believe that public policy for mergers and acquisitions should not require a "net benefit" for customers, so long as they are not affected adversely by the change of ownership of the utility. The role of a Public Utility Commission is to protect customers from unjust exactions resulting from the market control that utilities could exercise without state regulation. The form of business enterprise should be of no consequence to the Commission, as long as the utility obeys regulatory mandates and procedures, does not present conflicts with the interests of Oregon customers, does not expose customers to greater risks of higher costs or lower service quality, and is capable of economically and reliably providing the services offered to customers now and in the future. The current statutory standard puts the Commission potentially in the position of second-guessing business decisions of the

companies we regulate, even when these business decisions do no harm to Oregon customers.[44]

We join the Commission's lament. Regulators should be concerned with the service and price standards as applied in their jurisdictions and avoid the all-too-tempting choice of forcing upfront rate reductions on transactions that cannot withstand such pressure. Clearly, the no harm standard allows regulators to place a reasonable set of conditions on a merger without the fear of harm befalling customers or unduly restricting the level and type of merger activity that may improve industry efficiency and operation. Regulators need to understand the larger context within which transactions are now occurring. Without this change in policy, the potential benefits that were expected from restructuring may be delayed or even left unrealized as investors shy away from strategic mergers.

Similarly, regulators need to adapt their tools to the new types of mergers. While there is a perception that the risks associated with some forms of mergers have increased, the question for regulators is whether there is a set of merger conditions that reasonably protects customers and allows them to gain some share of the potential benefits of the merger. However, regulators tend to be, understandably, risk averse, and they have not shown a willingness to trust the tools that are at their disposal to condition deals that may have risk profiles different from traditional utility mergers. For example, in the case of Enron, maybe one of the most notorious corporate failures in recent history, Oregon regulators were largely successful in insulating the regulated utility from its parent company's legal and financial woes. Regulators have the tools to deal with the changing industry environment, but they must be willing to use those tools in different and innovative ways.

In particular, regulators need to adjust their expectations of the size and certainty of the direct benefits from newer forms of mergers, as both are declining. Imposing upfront rate reductions may no longer be a reasonable policy. If it is, the size of those reductions must fit the current environment; it is not appropriate to look back at the past mergers, which were of very different types, to establish reasonable targets. The traditional synergy savings are no longer the primary benefit from mergers in the context of either RTOs or market extension and portfolio mergers.

PUCs also need to adjust their use of some forms of ring fencing. Portfolio mergers are highly sensitive to financial conditions, and regulators' reliance on prescriptive use of financial conditions may result in a failure to consummate a merger. Portfolio companies resist extensive financial control, so that imposing conditions on dividend policy and corporate governance may thwart useful mergers and restrict utilities' access to private capital. This means that standard ring-fencing may be less appropriate in the future as nontraditional players enter the market. However, ring-fencing can be particularly effective in insulating the regulated utility and its customers from the potential harm that could occur as a result of mistakes at the holding company level.

Regulators should not fear mergers and acquisitions. Even in the case of Enron, where its bankruptcy represented one of the worst calamities in the history of the electricity market, the basic ring-fencing provisions that the Oregon commission adopted in Enron's acquisition of PGE succeeded in protecting the PGE customers from any negative fallout from the bankruptcy. The moral of that story is that a simple set of merger conditions can protect customers from harm. There is no need to formulate elaborate sets of conditions that make it harder to predict the effects on company finances and rates. As mergers move into the realm of distant ownership, foreign or domestic, financial/equity firms and the like, elaborate conditions increase the possibility that regulators will miss the opportunity to bring in new management techniques, organizational forms, and financial resources to strengthen weak and strong firms alike. All policymakers recognize that new policies and strategies contain risks, but state regulators can put the appropriate policy protections in place as a counter balance to such risks.

This new attitude may require changes to state law or a new approach by the PUC. Using available tools, regulators can still craft conditions that achieve the dual goals of promoting mergers that improve industry operations and providing benefits to customers. Rather than focusing on benefit-sharing conditions, regulators should emphasize conditions that will adapt to the evolution of the business and the markets. Without these changes in merger policy, the longer-term benefits of industry restructuring are likely to be delayed, potentially indefinitely. And that would cause real harm to customers.

Appendix 1: Selected Standards for the Review of Public Utility Mergers

State	Items to Review
"No Harm Standards"	

Arkansas[a]	Likely immediate impacts on:
	    service quality
	    rates paid by Arkansas ratepayers
	    range of services provided by utility
	Substantially lessen competition in public utility services
	Jeopardize financial condition of utility
	Plans to sell assets that would not be in the public interest

Iowa[b]	Reasonable access to books and records Utility will be able to attract capital Impairment of service quality Ratepayer harms
Louisiana[c]	LA PSC adopted 18 factors including an examination of the net benefits of the merger. However, the Commission has utilized a "no harm" standard to review mergers.
Maine[d]	Rates or services to customers of the former utility will not be adversely affected by the transaction
Kentucky[e]	Acquirer must have the financial, technical, and managerial abilities to provide reasonable service. Is consistent with public interest.
"Benefits or Net Benefits Standards"	
Colorado[f]	"Public interest" is defined by PUC as "consumer and producer welfare maximization." This is defined by the PUC as a matter of historical application.
Oregon[g]	Plan for operating utility as well as experience Funding source Compliance with applicable laws How the acquisition will service the public utility's customers in the public interest

Texas[h]	The reasonable value of the property, facilities, or securities disposed of, merged, transferred or consolidated.
	Whether the transaction will:
	    Adversely affect the heath or safety of customers or employees
	    Result in the transfer of jobs from Texas citizens to workers domiciled outside the state of Texas, or
	    Result in the decline of service
	The public utility will receive consideration equal to the reasonable value of the assets when it sells, leases or transfers assets.
	The transaction is consistent with the public interest.

See Table footnotes on next page.

Appendix 1 Footnotes:

(a) Arkansas Code Ann. 23-3-102 and Docket No. 00-021-U.

(b) Iowa Code § 476.77(3). Net benefit test not required by law. See Order in Docket No. SPU-00-10 at 7, Iowa Utilities Board.

(c) *In re: Commission Approval Required of Sales, Leases, Mergers, Consolidations, Stock Transfers, and All Other Changes of Ownership or Control of Public Utilities Subject to Commission Jurisdiction,* March 18, 1994. In its Order No. U-23327 reviewing the proposed AEP/SEPCO/CSW merger, the Commission noted that its review required that "ratepayers [be] no worse off as a result of the merger…" (at 10.).

(d) Order in Docket No. 99-411, Maine Public Utilities Commission at 4-5.

(e) Order in Case No. 97-300at 5, KY PSC and KRS 278.020(4) and (5).

(f) CO PUC, Decision No. C99-1052, September 22, 1999 (Order defining scope of review).

(g) Oregon Revised Statutes 757.511. OPUC Order No. 01-778 adopted a "net benefit" and "no harm" test. OPUC did not define what evidence would meet the "net benefit" standard.

(h) PURA §1.251(b) referenced in Texas PUC Order in Docket No. 14980. The TXPUC also determined in this docket that the public interest standard should be more "comprehensive" than its previous standard that found a merger consistent with the public interest if it did not "unduly harm the public interest." This includes a finding that a merger must "do more than promise cost savings" and should result in an "improvement" of service (Ibid. at 5).

Appendix 2: Categories of Merger Conditions

Condition Category	Description
Cost Recovery Commitments	These conditions implement the policy prohibiting or limiting the recovery of merger-related costs.
Service Quality	These conditions enforce the PUC's service quality standards by setting specific quality of service standards and might include specific commitments to investment.
Rate Levels	These conditions may apply to current rate levels or may result from a sharing or allocation of merger "savings."
Ring fencing—Financial	These conditions attempt to insulate the utility's financial operations from the finances of an affiliated entity.
Ring-fencing— Affiliate Relationships	The conditions address the nature and scope of the relationship the utility has with its affiliates. This might include specific cost allocation methods or restrictions on the affiliates' use of utility assets (including labor and information).
Ring-fencing—Governance	These conditions may include specific rules on the governing structure of the utility and PUC authority over non-utility investments.
Local Concerns	These conditions address local social/economic issues, such as employment commitments, community support, and maintaining headquarters.
Market Power and/or Other Competitive Issues	This is a broad category that might include specific monitoring of market power in PUC-defined markets or specific issues related to the introduction and promotion of competition in retail markets.
Other	Often these conditions address unresolved issues as well as issues that do not fall into the other categories.

Notes

1. An earlier version of this chapter was published in *Electricity Journal* (1 January 2007).

2. The extent to which this has occurred is a much debated topic with many observers, including some regulators and even some utility executives, professing skepticism. See, e.g., "New England argues restructuring merits; high rates, too much gas, but build cycle starting," *Electric Utility Week* (EUW), October 2, 2006, p. 2.

3. In this chapter, we use the term *merger* to refer to any transaction that modifies the utility or its holding company's organization and requires regulatory approval (this may include mergers, acquisitions, divestures, and joint ventures and reorganizations to the extent that they require regulatory approval). We also use the term transaction interchangeably.

4. Merger policy in the US is a relatively unique approach, in which both regulatory functions (i.e., price regulation and merger oversight) are housed within the same regulatory body. Although there is federal competition policy that is addressed by the Federal Trade Commission and the US Department of Justice, generally each state regulatory body has control over the corporate organization of electric utilities operating in its state.

5. Energy Information Administration, *Public Utility Holding Company Act of 1935: 1935-1992*, DOE/EIA-0563 (Washington, DC: DOE/EIA, 1996), p. 89 reports three distinct merger periods: pre-1930 era (approximately 200 per year), 1936-1975 (less than 15 per year), and 1976-1996 (less than 3 per year). By the authors' count in the post-1996 era, a new merger wave has occurred with the rate jumping to approximately 16 per year.

6. We will not deal directly with the details of one of the primary issues in merger reviews, market power, as that issue is sufficiently complex to need a more complete review. See, e.g., the Market Power section in this volume. *Also see e.g.,* Paul Joskow and Ed Kahn, "A Quantitative Analysis of Pricing Behavior in California's Wholesale Electricity Market during Summer 2000," *NBER Working Paper* 8157 (2001); William H. Hieronymus et al. "Market Power Analysis of the Electricity Generation Sector, *Energy Law Journal,* XXIII, 1 (2002), 1-50; or Richard Gilbert and David Newberry, "Electricity Merger Policy in the Shadow of Regulation," *UCEI Energy Policy and Economics* 019, Berkeley, CA (2006).

7. For example, a survey of utility executives found that significant challenges face merger and acquisition activity in the US including, among other factors, the regulatory landscape and the fallout from the Enron situation. James Hendrickson, "Mergers and Acquisitions as a Vehicle to Create Value in Uncertain Times," *The Electricity Journal,* 16(6), (2003), p. 68.

8. See Energy Policy Act of 2005 (EPAct 2005) and the Public Utility Holding Company Act of 2005.

9. Until recently, this list included the Securities and Exchange Commission. EPAct 2005 transferred the SEC's responsibilities to FERC.

10. Energy Information Administration, *The Changing Structure of the Electric Power Industry 1999: Mergers and Other Corporate Combinations,* DOE/EIA-0562(99), (Washington, DC: DOE/EIA, 1999) provides a summary of the forms of corporate reorganizations that occurred from 1992 to 1998.

11. This opportunity is not uncommon. Given the random nature of geographic certificates, many smaller companies were created than were ultimately warranted by the changing economies of scale of the generation technologies.

12. Whether the new firm actually achieved these goals is a matter for another discussion. For example, James Earl Anderson,, "Making Operational Sense of Mergers and Acquisitions," *The Electricity Journal,* XII, 7 (1999), p. 49 suggests that less than 15 percent of the mergers reviewed achieved pre-merger financial goals.

13. In discussing the situation presented by extreme market extension mergers, one witness in the state of Washington noted in his testimony the following:

    Q: Why are service improvements a more significant issue in this proceeding than in most?

    A: The proposed purchase of PacifiCorp by Scottish Power does not present opportunities for the usual magnitude of cost reductions, since the two companies operate in very different jurisdictions many time zones apart. Scottish Power has not offered a rate reduction or rate cap as part of the merger, and has presented service improvements as a major portion of the benefit to PacifiCorp customers.

    (Testimony of Paul Chernick, before the Washington Utilities and Transportation Commission in Docket No. UE-981627 at 4.)

14. For example see Charles Studness, "Converging Markets: The First Real Electric/Gas Merger," *Public Utility Fortnightly* (Oct. 1, 1996), 12-24.

15. The Oregon Public Utilities Commission approved a version of divesture, although not the version Enron preferred, in Order No. 99-033.

16. The proposed acquisition of The Energy Group PLC by PacifiCorp, Duke/Panhandle, CMS Energy acquisition of Panhandle from Duke, Dominion Resources/Consolidated Natural Gas, and others fit this view. See D. Balto and J. Mongoven, "Deregulation and Merger Enforcement in the Natural Gas Industry," *Antitrust Law Journal,* 69 (2001), 527-568 for a more in-depth look at the issues raised by these mergers.

17. These costs may also include the costs of the transaction (e.g., lawyer's fees, investment banking fees, due diligence costs, etc.).

18. There are a handful of states (e.g., Michigan, Montana, and Florida) that do not provide for merger review by the regulatory body. See "A Regulator's Guide to Electric Mergers and Acquisitions in Florida," (Tallahassee, FL: Florida Public Service Commission, Division of Policy Analysis and Intergovernmental Liaison, 2001), p. 6. At the time of writing, the Michigan Legislature has passed a bill (H.B 6358) that would require utilities to file, 180 days prior to the planned transaction date, any information that is necessary to assess the impact of the proposed transaction. The regulator can then issue "advisory

comments" within 120 days of that filing (i.e., the bill stops short of providing ultimate denial authority to the regulator).

19. Jonathan B. Welch and Marjorie B. Platt, "The Future of Electric Utility Mergers in the USA," *Utilities Policy,* IV, 4 (1994), pp. 255-257 provides an overview of the legal policies toward mergers.

20. It seems apparent that the reason for this focus on rate reductions is the new uncertainty that has entered the industry as a result of industry restructuring. Regulators are looking for a kind of "certainty equivalent" payment, that is, a payment that covers the (real or perceived) incremental risk such that the regulator is indifferent to approving or denying the merger. Of course, the problem is that this payment will differ among regulatory bodies, based on each regulator's risk-averseness, and it may have little or no relationship to actual operating conditions.

21. Kenneth Gordon and Wayne P. Olson, "Removing Disincentives: State Regulatory Treatment of Merger Savings," *The Electricity Journal,* XIX, 8 (2006), 1-7 discusses this disincentive in the context of dividing up "merger savings."

22. See PUC of Oregon (OPUC) Order No. 01-778 and New Jersey Board of Public Utilities (NJBPU) Order in Docket No. EM97020103. However, in the Public Service Electric and Gas Company (PSEG) and Exelon merger, New Jersey determined that a "positive benefits" test should be used and promptly modified its administrative rules to incorporate this new standard. *See* NJBPU Decision in Docket No. EM05020106 and N.J.A.C. 14:1-5.14 (c), effective May 2006.

23. Typical legislative permission for conditioning a merger can be found in the Illinois Public Utilities Act:

    In approving any proposed reorganization...the Commission may impose such terms, conditions or requirements as, in its judgment, are necessary to protect the interests of the public utility and its customers. (220 ILCS 5/7-204(f))

24. These general principles are implemented through specific ratemaking approaches. See, e.g., Karl McDermott et al. "Critical Issues in the Regulation of Electric Utilities in Wisconsin," *Wisconsin Policy Research Institute Report,* XIX, 1 (2006), 1-68; and Karl McDermott et al., "Rethinking the Implementation of the Prudent Cost Standard," in this volume.

25. ACC Decision No. 67454, pp. 28-29.

26. See "Merger and Acquisition Quarterly," C. A. *Turner Utility Reports,* October 2003.

27. Id.

28. While many states require a finding related to "society in general," that is often taken to mean the citizens and businesses of the local jurisdictions. The authors know of no jurisdiction that takes into account the benefits of a transaction to, for example, the regional wholesale market if those benefits could not be localized to that jurisdiction.

29. For example, the Colorado Public Service/Northern States merger creating Xcel Energy. Docket No. 99A-377EG, Decision No. C00-393 February 16, 2000. The mechanism employed was first approved in the merger between Colorado Public

Service and Southwestern Public Service Co. in Docket 95-531EG and Docket no. 95-464E August 23, 1996.

30. These credits are often set to expire at implementation of the next rate case. This mechanism captures benefits that extend beyond the time covered by the analysis in the merger case and provides an incentive for companies to file a rate case if costs have increased significantly.

31. Wayne P. Olson et al. "With Careful Use and Proper Focus, Ring-Fence Regulation Benefits Consumers," Chapter 4 in R. Willet (ed.), *Using New Strategies, Understanding the Issues,* (Houston, TX: Financial Communications Company, 2004) discusses the specifics of ring-fencing applied to the electric utilities.

32. The "cost of capital" is generally taken to mean the rate of return used for ratemaking purposes. It may also specifically refer to debt costs and/or equity costs used in ratemaking.

33. Order in NCUC Docket No. M-100, Sub 129, November 2, 2000.

34. PAPUC Order in Docket Nos. A-110150F.0015 and G-00970574 at 14.

35. See, e.g., ConEd/NU CTDPUC Docket No. 00-01-11, BGE/PEPCO MDPSC Case No. 8725.

36. PUC of Texas, Order in Docket No. 14980, p. 4, 1997.

37. *See* In the Matter of a Legal Standard for Approval of Mergers, OPUC Order No. 01-778, Docket UM-1011 September 4, 2001.

38. OPUC Order No. 01-778, 2001. In both Oregon and Arizona, regulators found that the risks associated with these transactions could not be mitigated to serve the public interest, and therefore they rejected the transactions. This rejection may in part reflect the concerns voiced in the previous footnote regarding the fallout from the Enron situation. See OPUC Order No. 05-114 (March 10, 2005) and ACC Decision No. 67454 (January 6, 2005). One of the authors provided expert analysis to the OPUC of the TPG/PGE merger proposal on behalf of the applicants (i.e., Oregon Electric). *See* Direct Testimony of Karl A. McDermott in OPUC Docket No. UM 1121.

39. *EUW,* September, 25 2006, pp. 7-8.

40. See MA DPU Order in 93-167-A, OPUC Order No. 01-778 Docket UM-1011, and LAPSC General Order 3/18/94.

41. The benefits of vertical integration appear to be substantial in the electric industry. See, e.g., Carl R. Peterson, *"Efficiency in the US Electric Industry: Transaction Costs, Deregulation, and Governance Structures,"* Ph.D. dissertation, (Chicago, IL: Department of Economics, University of Illinois, 2007) or Robert J. Michaels, "Vertical Integration and the Restructuring of the US Electric Industry," *Policy Analysis*, No. 572, (Washington DC: CATO Institute, 2006).

42. See PSEG CEO James Ferland in *EUW,* September 25, 2006, p. 8 after the failure of the proposed Exelon merger, commenting on the difficulty PSEG had with state regulators.

43. One of the problems private equity has had in convincing regulators of the propriety of their proposals is the general concern over the potentially short-term nature of the investments. However, even with proposed conditions to address the potential problems with short-term incentives, such as quality of service standards, equity floors, etc., regulators still seem to be more concerned about the potential profit that private equity might make as a result of the transaction. The implication is that if the holding company makes "excess" profit from its ownership of the utility, it must come at the expense of ratepayers (in one way or another). This zero-sum game approach to regulation is very much embedded in the traditional regulatory paradigm and may be very difficult to overcome.

44. In the Matter of a Legal Standard for Approval of Mergers, OPUC Order No. 01-778, Docket UM-1011 September 4, 2001 at p. 11. The OPUC's lament concerning this standard of review appears prescient in light of its later denial of the TPG/PGE transaction.

7

RETHINKING RATE DESIGN FOR ELECTRICITY DISTRIBUTION SERVICE IN THE US

Hethie Parmesano
Sarah Potts Voll

Introduction

Electric utility restructuring in the US has begun to introduce significant changes in both the operations of regulated firms and the relationship between these firms and their customers. These changes, if wisely orchestrated, can be healthy for an industry that has long been subjected to regulatory regimes that have all too often provided contradictory incentives and policies. Indeed, the introduction of competition has begun to erode the ability of regulators and utilities to maintain rate structures that are not based on economic views of the world. Even the distribution business, long considered the unexciting portion of the sector, is facing competitive threats from technologies such as distributed generation and shifting demand patterns.

The challenge in designing appropriate distribution rates (or distribution components of bundled rates) is three-fold. First, the distribution company must have sufficient total revenue to enable it to maintain and expand the distribution network to provide reliable service. To raise capital for this purpose, the rate structure and revenues must be sufficient to allow the utility to earn a sufficient return on past investment comparable to market rates of return on investments with similar risk.[1] Second, to avoid cross-subsidies, the allocation of the overall revenue requirement to the various categories of customers must recognize the principles of cost causation. Third, to encourage efficient consumption and energy-related investment decisions by consumers, the rate design for each customer class should reflect the structure of the underlying economic costs.

Traditionally in the US, many and certainly the largest utilities provided electric service that bundled generation, transmission and distribution. Pricing was largely based on a backward- looking, fully allocated, embedded cost approach, rather than on the forward-looking economic (marginal) costs of service common in Europe. A typical rate structure, especially for residential and small commercial customers, featured a small fixed monthly customer charge to cover all or a portion of the costs of metering, service drops, and customer accounting and service expenses, and then bundled all other costs into a single volumetric (per kWh) rate. Such two-part tariffs did not—nor did they need to—disaggregate the charges of the generation and wires services because customers had no choice but to take the bundled service. Jurisdictions in the US that have restructured the electricity sector have now unbundled the provision of generation, transmission, distribution and sometimes customer services. Pricing[2] for wholesale generation has become market-based. Pricing for transmission is in flux as FERC and the transmission organizations struggle to establish mechanisms that provide incentives for investment and efficient price signals to system users.

Rate structures for the residual, state-regulated distribution companies, however, have been largely untouched. While in other countries that have restructured the retailer pays the provider of delivery service and is allowed to bundle its costs and structure its prices to consumers any way it wants,[3] in the US, delivery rates are set by state regulators and paid by consumers, whether they are buying generation service from the utility providing distribution service or from a competitive retailer. As existing utility rate caps expire over the coming years, the state commissions will need to address fundamental questions of how to price distribution services in the evolving energy markets. These questions are also important, however, for utilities and regulators in jurisdictions in which service has not been unbundled. Customers with their own generation typically use the utility's delivery system when their own generation units are partly or completely out of service. Because this use is intermittent, standard bundled rates do not adequately compensate the utility for standing by to provide delivery service.

Regulators and utilities that seriously consider the ratemaking issues will find that the traditional two-part tariff is an uneconomic anachronism in a competitive energy sector. Its overemphasis on consumption-based or per-kWh charges neither provides assurance that the distribution company will have an opportunity to recover its prudent investment in its wires system nor imparts accurate information to enable sector participants to make informed consumption and investment decisions. The old structure typically also continues or increases the cross-subsidies that were less apparent when rates covered both the delivery and supply of electricity.

A better way to recover the distribution revenue requirement is to:

- identify the marginal costs of three elements of distribution service for each customer class:
    - distribution costs that vary with the time of consumption (substations and trunkline feeders)
    - distribution costs that vary with the design demand of the customer (primary, transformer, and secondary lines)
    - costs that are specific to the customer (meter and service drop, meter-reading and billing, customer accounting and services);
- develop rate components for each; and
- adjust as necessary to produce the distribution revenue requirement, minimizing the distortion in consumption that results from having charges deviate from marginal cost.

Economic Pricing

The debate over marginal versus embedded costs is hardly new,[4] but it has assumed new importance in the context of retail competition. In many jurisdictions, the delivery company is no longer a part of an integrated utility and earns only the revenues it charges for wires service. If those charges produce less than the right amount of revenue, it is in financial trouble. Correct pricing of the stand-alone delivery service matters.

There are four major arguments for basing utility rates on marginal cost: social welfare benefits, benefits to ratepayers as a whole, limits on cross-subsidies among ratepayers and consistency between the unbundled businesses. The social welfare benefits for basing utility rates on marginal cost stem from the fundamental precept of economic theory that marginal cost pricing results in an efficient allocation of resources. Marginal cost is the cost of the resources needed to produce the next or last small increment of output. It represents the value of those resources in their next-best alternative use. Further, the price willingly paid represents the personal value to the consumer of the next or last small unit consumed. It is an indication of the amount of alternative consumption willingly foregone to consume the unit in question.

When price is equal to marginal cost, consumers and suppliers have access to critical information about how much they should consume and produce—the so-called "price signals." When price equals marginal cost, the cost of the next or last unit exactly matches the value of that unit to the consumer, and, in theory, resource allocation is socially optimal. The resources used to produce the unit cannot be used for another purpose and produce greater consumer satisfaction. If price for marginal units is below marginal cost, consumers will continue to buy additional units even though the satisfaction they receive is below the cost of supplying the additional units. Resources are expended that would have produced greater satisfaction if used to produce something else. If price for marginal units is above marginal cost, consumers artificially constrain their use of the good or service. They forego the benefits they would have enjoyed from consuming more, at a resource cost lower than the value of those benefits.

Utility rates are no exception to the general economic precept. Rates that reflect the marginal cost of service signal to consumers the cost of their consumption decisions. If the price paid for the additional (or saved) unit of gas or electricity service is equal to the marginal cost of supplying it, a consumer deciding what type of appliance to buy or how much to use existing energy-using equipment will make socially efficient choices.

Second, ratepayers as a whole benefit when utility rates are based on marginal cost because economically efficient consumption decisions by individual ratepayers allow the utility to avoid unnecessary, costly expansion of the system. The outcome is lower average rates. For example, certain elements of the electricity delivery system must be sized to meet summer peak-day demands. If the price of electricity delivery service is below marginal cost in the critical summer months, the utility must install additional delivery capacity to meet the peak summer loads that the too-low summer delivery charges have encouraged.[5] The result will be a higher- than-efficient revenue requirement and higher-than-efficient average rates.

Third, marginal cost pricing reduces or eliminates cross-subsidies. Cross-subsidies arise when costs attributable to consumption by one customer or class of customers are recovered from another customer or class of customers. When utility rate design prices marginal use at marginal cost, the revenue received by the utility covers the additional costs of providing the additional service. If price is below marginal cost, some of the additional costs must be borne by someone else—in the short run by utility shareholders and in the longer run by other consumers. If price is above marginal cost, the utility loses more in revenues than it saves in costs when a consumer reduces usage. Again, someone else must make up the difference.

A final reason for basing administered prices on marginal cost is consistency. The cost of electricity service to consumers is made up of two parts—the generation supply portion and the cost of delivery (including transmission, ancillary services, distribution and customer costs). The total cost to the consumer for marginal use will be efficiently priced only if the unbundled electricity supply and electricity delivery are consistently priced.

Generation supply prices are market-based. Competitive suppliers purchase generation on behalf of customers who have chosen non-utility suppliers through a combination of long-term contracts and spot purchases, which may or may not be combined with financial hedges. The prices of all these components reflect the market's expectation of spot prices (marginal cost) over the term of the transaction. Generation supply prices charged by utilities to those customers that do not have a competitive supplier are also related to market prices. In the early stages of retail competition, these prices were administratively set but were generally based on market price estimates. As the transition generation supply arrangements terminate over time, utility generation service will generally be provided through some kind auction process, and the utilities' charges for generation service will also be market-driven prices that reflect the marginal cost of supply in the industry.

The price of delivery is determined through the state (for distribution) and federal (for transmission) regulatory processes rather than in the marketplace. Regulatory policies should ensure that the tariff design of delivery service is as consistent as possible with the existing marginal cost/market pricing of generation service. Consumers make energy decisions based on the total cost of using electricity—both generation service (whether they purchase from the utility or an alternative supplier) and delivery components. Basing the price of the delivery portion on embedded costs or some arbitrary allocation and rate structure when the generation supply portion is a market/marginal cost price is likely to result in inefficient price signals to consumers.

Nature of Distribution Costs and Optimal
Distribution Rate Structure

When developing a marginal cost study for electricity service, three basic principles guide the analyst. First, a marginal cost study represents the going-forward costs associated with small changes in electricity service. The analyst must find answers to the question: How would costs change if the utility needed to supply a small increment (or decrement) of service?

The second principle is that marginal costs are utility-specific. They depend upon the planning and operating policies of the utility under study, the characteristics of its service territory (including geography), its financial situation, and the laws and regulations that govern its actions. The results of the marginal cost study should reflect the constraints applicable to the particular utility.

The third principle is that a marginal cost study should analyze the cost drivers for each component of service—the number of customers on the system, design demands, and energy delivered in peak hours—and use these drivers to compute unit marginal costs. This principle also implies that costs that vary with the timing of the assumed change in service should be time-differentiated.

Applying these three principles to service provided by the distribution company generally leads to the conclusion that most of the cost of providing delivery service is "fixed" and does not vary with usage levels in a foreseeable timeframe. Utilities size most localized distribution facilities in anticipation of the non-diversified demands of customers; economics constrains utilities to use standard size equipment and to provide sufficient local capacity to avoid costly retrofits. The sizing of these types of facilities is based on design loads, and costs do not change with normal variations in customer usage. Only distribution substations and main feeder costs are sensitive to changes in near-term demand—and then only in the peak hours on the local distribution system. These facilities are sized to accommodate the diversified, coincident peak demand of the group of customers they serve. Changes in the diversified peak load ultimately affects investment required in substations and main feeders. The implication for rate design for the typical stand-alone distribution company is that most of the costs should be charged as a fixed monthly charge.[6]

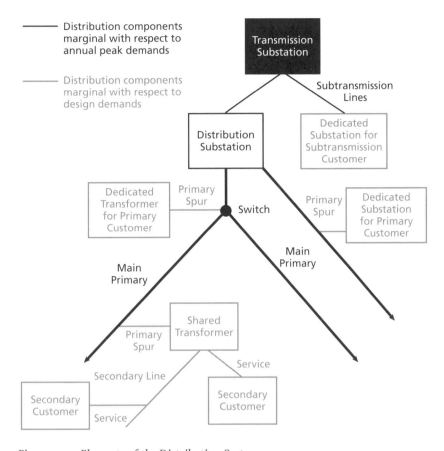

Figure 1. *Elements of the Distribution System*

The diagram above illustrates a typical configuration and indicates which components of the distribution system are design-demand-related local facilities and which are peak-demand-related higher-voltage components.

Thus, the distribution tariff elements for a typical retail customer, and how they are charged in a cost-reflective tariff, break down as follows:

Marginal Customer Costs

These are costs that vary with the number of customers on the system and include annualized investment in and operation and maintenance (O&M) expenses on meters and service drops, customer accounting expenses (such as meter-reading, billing, and accounting), and customer service expenses.[7] These costs vary by customer class but do not vary with changes in usage. They should be recovered in a fixed monthly charge.

Marginal Local Distribution Facilities Costs

These are the annualized costs of the local distribution network (secondary lines, distribution transformers and localized primary lines or "taplines") that vary with the design demand of the customers using the facilities but do not vary with month-to-month changes in demand.[8] The facilities included in this component are sized based on design loads that are not expected to change during the physical life of the equipment and thus do not have to be replaced because of minor changes in loads. These costs should be recovered as a fixed monthly charge per kilowatt of design or contract demand.

Where design or contract demand is not recorded for each customer, reasonable proxies for billing these charges are (1) transformer size for customers with a dedicated transformer, (2) the highest monthly demand recorded in the last 24 months for customers with demand meters, or (3) for customers without demand meters, the standard design demand assumed by distribution planners for that type of customer (residential all-electric, residential mixed electric and gas, very large residential).

Marginal Cost of Distribution Substations and Trunkline Feeders

These components of the system are expanded as regional peak load grows over time. Their costs include both investment and O&M expenses and vary by voltage level of service and by time of use.[9] They are appropriately recovered in time-differentiated energy charges (with enough pricing periods to reflect the varying cost levels on a per-kWh basis) or time-differentiated demand charges assessed per kilowatt of monthly peak load in the various costing periods.

The sum of marginal costs only by happenstance equals the revenue requirement determined by the utility's historical accounting costs. Charges reflecting the discrepancy between the revenue requirement and marginal cost revenues should minimize distortion of the efficient consumption that would result from pricing all elements of distribution tariffs at marginal cost. This generally means adjusting the fixed tariff components (customer and local facilities charges).

Policy Implications

Impact on the Distribution Utility

The primary effect on the utility of aligning its prices with its underlying costs is that it provides the company a more realistic opportunity to recover its prudently incurred costs. The current US practice is to include in per-kWh charges local facilities costs that change only with a major change in a customer's building characteristics or electrical equipment. This practice subjects a large portion of the company's revenues to variations based on the number of kilowatt hours sold. An economic downturn or a cool summer or warm winter will result in under-collection of the fixed costs of the system; the reverse can result in an undeserved windfall profit.

Policy initiatives aimed at reducing electricity usage can also erode distribution company revenues with no matching reduction in its costs for delivery service. Conservation and load management programs and the adoption of residential and commercial building codes and appliance standards are directly intended to reduce the use of energy and especially electricity. These policies and programs typically reduce only the costs of distribution substations and trunkline feeders, not the costs of most of the distribution system.[10] Recovering in fixed charges those costs that do not vary with energy usage eliminates the volatility and long-term erosion of distribution utility revenues unconnected to costs. The more predictable revenue stream will lower the company's risk, which ultimately should translate into a lower cost of capital.

Impact on Consumers

Cost of capital effects aside, a legitimate question is whether most of the benefits to the distribution utility are won at the expense of customers. It is sometimes argued[11] that electricity rates should be primarily volumetric as a matter of fairness so that total bills closely track the amount of electricity used. In particular, consumer advocates often apply this principle to argue further that higher fixed charges place an unfair burden on low-income ratepayers.

However, this notion of fairness to low-income customers, and the lifeline rates that sometimes stem from it, implicitly assumes a direct correlation between income and usage and that low-income customers are by definition low consumers. Studies in several countries have found[12] that this assumption is not necessarily correct. Poor families often include young children and elderly members whose needs for healthy temperatures are inversely related to their incomes, and the affordable housing stock available to them is typically less energy efficient. Apartments for low-income households are more likely to be poorly heated, forcing residents to resort to energy-inefficient electric space heaters. Indeed, the lowest annual electricity users on the system are likely to be the weekend homes of high-income customers, or customers who move to vacation homes for months at a time and during those periods have minimal usage in their primary homes. Nothing in these usage patterns reduces the costs of providing the local delivery network.

Finally, divorcing distribution fixed costs from volumetric charges would make customer bills seasonally more affordable. Charging for distribution services on a per kWh basis forces up bills unnecessarily during winter and summer peaks when energy usage is high.[13]

Pricing for Distributed Generation

Distributed Generation (DG)[14] has the following characteristics:

- It is located within the distribution network, often at the site of a major electricity user, and its energy can usually be consumed without flowing over transmission lines.
- It is usually, but not always, of a smaller scale than most utility-owned or merchant generators.
- It may use a renewable energy source such as solar, wind, mini-hydro or landfill gas, or it may be a combined heat and power (CHP) cogeneration project, which is often based on fossil fuels.
- It is generally not owned by the local utility.

The potential benefits provided by DG can include (1) increasing competition and decreasing market power in load pockets; (2) relieving congestion on the transmission and distribution systems, thereby reducing line losses and generation costs and improving reliability; and, (3) depending on the technology, creating more fuel diversity and less air pollution. Some of these benefits flow from the fact that the generation is distributed; others may result from their renewable fuel source. Policymakers generally consider DG "a good thing" and, when it is economically efficient, economists agree.

An investor determines the economic feasibility of a DG project by comparing its costs, including his upfront capital costs and O&M costs, to the benefits he receives, including revenues from net sales and avoided electricity purchase costs (and for CHP, the avoided cost of steam production using the alternative means). DG facilities generally continue to require electricity (1) for start-up and station use when the generator is not operating and (2) if associated with a customer's load, for stand-by energy during planned and unplanned outages and for supplemental power if the load exceeds the capacity of the generating unit. A DG facility therefore continues to depend on the delivery system for electricity purchases as well as for any sales of excess energy production. The decision to install DG[15] is heavily influenced by the price level and rate structure of the incumbent distribution utility. In theory, if distribution service is correctly priced, the wires company will be economically indifferent to whether the customer uses DG or the electricity grid.

However, incorrect volumetric pricing for delivery service both erodes the distribution company's revenue stream and sends an uneconomically high price signal to customers. Volumetric charges intended to recover both energy and delivery service encourage the customer to install DG because the lower energy purchases from the utility also enables him to avoid paying for delivery even though he continues to incur the fixed costs of the service. Those volumetric charges thus encourage uneconomic bypass[16] by the customer, which erodes the revenues of the distribution company and eventually requires a tariff increase for the utility's other customers. Overpriced volumetric charges also tempt the utility to discourage *economic* bypass where the DG facility would be viable even if it only avoided energy costs because the reductions in revenues are greater than the costs the utility can avoid. Such inefficient behavior by both customers and the utility does not arise when the rate structure properly charges customer-related and local distribution facilities costs as fixed monthly charge per kW of contract capacity and the per kilowatt-hour rate recovers only marginal—and avoidable—costs.

The issue of correct pricing for distribution services has assumed a new immediacy with the passage of the Energy Policy Act of 2005. Section 1251 amends the Public Utility Regulatory Policy Act of 1978 (PURPA) to require that state commissions consider adopting five new standards. Paragraph 11 would require[17] each electric utility to make "net metering service" available to any customer upon request. Net metering is defined as "service to an electric consumer under which electric energy generated by that electric consumer from an eligible on-site generating facility and delivered to the local distribution facilities may be used to offset electric energy provided by the electric utility to the electric consumer during the applicable billing period." That is, a customer's meter will be allowed to run backwards and the customer's sale of energy during the billing period is subtracted from its purchases. If commissions adopting this standard do not restructure distribution tariffs so that per-kWh charges only recover costs that vary with energy use, the utility will not be compensated for providing the distribution infrastructure for either the customer's purchase or sale of electricity.

Examples of this Approach in the US
Structuring distribution charges to reflect the underlying cost structure is rare in the US but not unknown. Examples of tariffs with a significant charge per kW of contract capacity (or a proxy) include:

- **The Sacramento Municipal Power District** applies a facilities charge per 12-months maximum demand or per kW of installed capacity for large general service, time-of-use customers.
- The **Los Angeles Department of Water and Power (LADWP)** has long had a "facilities charge" for nonresidential customers that recovers some distribution costs in a charge per kW, with the billing demand defined as the higher of 50 percent of the capacity of the transformer dedicated to serving the customer or the maximum demand imposed in any of the past 12 months. In designing standby rates for customers with distributed generation, LADWP increased the level of these facilities charges to recover more of the distribution system costs.
- **Southern California Edison**'s delivery service charges include a facilities-related demand charge applied to the maximum 15-minute demand recorded in the billing period. When the customer's meter records little or no energy for extended periods of time or has not recorded a maximum demand in the preceding 11 months, the charge is applied to 50 percent of the customer's connected load. There is an additional distribution demand charge applicable only in the four summer months.
- For large general service customers, **Nevada Power Company** applies a facilities charge per kW to the highest customer billing demand for the highest of the current billing period and the prior 12 monthly billing periods.
- The **New York Public Service Commission** guidelines for delivery standby rates for customers with generation require that the costs

of "local" distribution facilities be recovered by a contract demand charge, rather than a charge based on usage in a given month.[18]

- Most examples apply only to large customers or standby rates, but in 2005 the **North Dakota Public Service Commission** approved a settlement agreement for **Northern States Power** that structures residential natural gas delivery rates as a fixed monthly charge,[19] similar to its design of electricity delivery rates. In his concurring opinion, Commissioner Tony Clark noted:

> It is an accepted ratemaking principle that fixed, non-usage sensitive costs should be recovered through fixed charges and variable, usage sensitive costs should be recovered through variable charges. Unfortunately, regulators and utilities across the country have too often drifted from sound economics in favor of less than straightforward ways of implementing utility rates.

Conclusion

Electric utility restructuring in the US has introduced significant changes in both the operations of regulated firms and the relationship between these firms and their customers. While pricing for wholesale generation and transmission has become more market-based, rate structures for the residual state-regulated distribution companies have been largely untouched. As existing utility rate caps expire and with the renewed interest in distributed generation, the utilities and their state commissions must tackle fundamental questions of how to price distribution services in the evolving energy markets. Serious consideration of the issues of cost and tariff structures and the related financial implications for distribution utilities will lead to the conclusion that the traditional tariffs are an uneconomic anachronism in a competitive energy sector. Their backward-looking accounting costs and their heavy emphasis on per-kWh charges should be replaced by forward-looking, marginally cost-based rates that recognize the principles of cost causation. For the typical stand-alone distribution company, application of these principles will assign most costs to a fixed monthly charge—not a surprising result for wires companies that resemble cable and phone companies more than they resemble their integrated electric utility predecessors.

Notes

1. See Graham Shuttleworth and Sarah P. Voll, "Economic Principles of Regulation" in this Section.

2. For a more comprehensive discussion of pricing for unbundled services, see Kenneth Gordon and Wayne P. Olson, *Retail Cost Recovery and Rate Design in a Restructured Environment,* prepared for the Edison Electric Institute, (December 2004).

3. The structure of distribution tariffs is also important when the buyer is a retailer of generation services. Retailers may choose to recover their distribution expenses from consumers in some way that differs from the structure of the wholesale distribution tariffs they pay, but those who want their retail prices to track their costs will tend to pass through the structure of the distribution (and transmission) tariff. The resulting retail pricing structure cannot be efficient and cost-reflective if the distribution tariff is not efficient and cost-reflective.

4. While marginal cost-based rates have long been the basis of utility rates in England and France, they became an issue in the US in the 1970s. In an environment of general inflation, high energy and construction costs, and competition, rates based on pre-inflationary historical costs led to poor price signals for customers, inefficient uses of resources for society, and repeated revenue deficiencies for the companies. Regulators began to inquire whether it would be more appropriate to use the principles of forward-looking marginal cost for class revenue allocation and rate structure.

5. Of course, additional generation capacity is also required.

6. This is *not* an argument for a mechanism that completely separates sales from revenues by setting a fixed revenue level. Such a revenue cap introduces distortions of its own as it does not recognize that wires costs *are* sensitive to customer and facility growth. Fixing the utility's revenue undermines delivery system reliability as it limits the cash flow availability for infrastructure investments. (An alternative form that allows revenue to increase by a pre-specified amount per customer reduces this problem.) It also reduces rate stability since rates must increase in economic downturns when usage drops and decrease when the economy improves and sales recover—precisely the opposite of price signals that are indicated by the utility's marginal cost. See Eugene T. Meehan, "Affidavit filed on behalf of Central Hudson Gas & Electric Corporation et al.," NYSPSC Proceeding on Motion of the Commission to Investigate Potential Electric Delivery Rate Disincentives against the Promotion of Energy Efficiency, Renewable Technologies and Distributed Generation, Case no. 03-E-0604 (October 24, 2003). The revenue control mechanism applied to British electricity distribution networks uses a 50/50 mix of fixed and volume-related adjustment, thus solving many of these problems.

7. Some of these services, and even the meter itself, may be provided by a competitive supplier. In that case, they must be unbundled so that customers taking generation service from another supplier do not pay the distribution company for services it is not providing.

8. These costs are typically estimated by (1) reviewing sample circuits (either actual circuits or hypothetical ones) serving various configurations of

customers and (2) identifying the replacement cost of the facilities installed there and the design demands of the customers connected to the feeder. These estimates thus reflect the design standards and practices of the utility.

9. These costs are typically estimated by (1) identifying growth-related projects in the distribution budget and (2) dividing the sum of the budgeted expenditures by growth in the sum of substation non-coincident peak demands over the same period. This produces an estimate of the typical investment per kW of peak demand growth. The calculations can be done for the distribution network as a whole, or for sub-regions.

10. Interestingly, while anecdotal evidence describes a reduction of electricity usage per household over time, simply dividing nationwide residential electricity consumption reported on the FERC Form 1 by the number of residential customers shows an increase over the last decade, perhaps suggesting that such programs have not been able to offset the growth in household electronics and larger home size. A state-by-state analysis might produce different results. According to Martha G. VanGeem, "The per capita energy use in California has remained steady due to its active use and enforcement of energy codes for buildings, while energy use in the rest of the U.S. has increased." *Energy Codes and Standards,* at http://www.wbdg.org/design/energycodes (Accessed 1/31/2007)

11. See, for example, Frederick Westin, Cheryl Harrington, David Moskovitz, Wayne Shirley and Richard Cowart, *Charging for Distribution Utility Services: Issues in Rate Design,* Prepared by the Regulatory Assistance Project under a grant from the Energy Foundation for NARUC, Washington DC, 2000.

12. See Matthew Bennett, Dudley Cooke, and Catherine Waddams Price, "Left out in the Cold? The Impact of New Energy Tariffs on the Fuel Poor and Low Income Households," (Center for Management under Regulation, University of Warwick: Coventry, UK, September 2000); and Meg Power, "A Profile of the Energy Usage and Energy Needs of Low-Income Americans," Report for the Association for Energy Affordability, (Economic Opportunity Research Institute, Washington, DC: March 28, 1999). See also Evan Brown, "Energy Performance Evaluation of New Homes in Arkansas," Report prepared for the Arkansas Energy Office, December, 1999, which observed, "Of the 100 homes surveyed, 36 would have qualified for HUD/FHA financing; however half of these homes failed the minimum thermal energy standards. For those more easily affordable homes, energy costs play a proportionally greater role."

13. Many utilities solve this problem by offering budget billing in which customers pay one-twelfth of their estimated annual bill each month, with a true-up at the end of the year.

14. For a fuller discussion of appropriate ratemaking for DG, see Hethie S. Parmesano, "Standby Service to Distributed Generation Projects: the Wrong Tool for Subsidies," *Electricity Journal,* (October 2003), 85-92.

15. As pointed out by Meehan, many of these points about appropriate ratemaking for DG can be applied to the adoption of economic energy efficiency programs. Affidavit, op. cit.

16. "Uneconomic bypass" occurs when a customer leaves (bypasses) a network system (electric, gas, telecom, water) because the price of the alternative is lower than the utility's tariffs but higher than the utility's avoided cost.

17. While this provision requires all state commissions to consider net metering service, many states already offer net metering for customer-owned generation.

18. NYPS Opinion No. 01-4, *Opinion and Order Approving Guidelines for the Design of Standby Service Rates,* Oct. 26, 2001.

19. North Dakota Public Service Commission, *Order Adopting Settlement in Northern States Power Natural Gas Rate Increase Application,* Case No. PU-04-578, June 1, 2005.

II

PUBLIC POLICY

PUBLIC POLICY AND EXTERNALITIES: A FOCUS ON THE ENERGY SECTOR AND CLIMATE CHANGE

Amparo D. Nieto

At the core of the economic regulation of any infrastructure sector is the need to design public policies that remedy market failures. We have discussed the role that public policy plays in key aspects of the energy industry, such as preservation of system reliability and mitigation of market power. This section addresses yet another important reason for public policy—the presence of negative externalities from the production of electricity, particularly air pollution and global warming. A major challenge for today's energy policy makers is to find cost-effective solutions that address environmental concerns, while at the same time ensuring that growing energy demands are met. Increased awareness of the risk of climate change is leading more governments around the world to commit to cutting emissions and encouraging the use of renewable resources. In addition, nuclear power is gaining advocates in the US, Europe and Asia on the grounds that it is a cleaner alternative than coal and gas-fired units and that better technologies are now available to replace the aging nuclear stations.[1]

The governmental push for nuclear power is often not solely based on environmental reasons, but also on a notion that nuclear energy enhances a country's security of energy supply. In the US, the Energy Policy Act of 2005 (EPAct) offers a wide range of public financial aids to build and operate nuclear plants. However, as Dr. Glenn George points out in Chapter 8 "Financing New Nuclear Capacity: Will the 'Nuclear Renaissance' be a Self-Sustaining Reaction?" it is yet to be seen whether EPAct incentives alone will be sufficient to encourage a boom in nuclear construction. According to Dr. George's view, federal subsidies or loan guarantees are not likely to close the gap between what project financiers will seek and what nuclear developers can offer. Corporate boards of directors will need to ensure they have independently assessed all the risks and benefits involved in investing in new nuclear capacity, keeping in mind the large up-front capital investment required, the uncertainty in the wholesale energy markets and the governance requirements of Sarbanes-Oxley.

Developing comprehensive and attractively priced financial packages to investors, as well as creative risk management approaches, will be essential to bridge this gap.

Public policies that encourage increased reliance on renewable resources are also present in the US as well as many other countries. Such policies are intended to make electricity consumers internalize the cost of pollution by specifying the minimum share of demands that must be met with renewable resources, often more costly than traditional resources. This quantity-based approach has materialized in the form of state-wide Renewable Portfolio Standards (RPSs) in the US, and countrywide Renewable Obligations (ROs) in Europe and Asia. Markets for Renewable Energy Certificates (RECs) have consequently arisen and are expanding rapidly. Daniel Radov and Per Klevnas discuss the key elements of the REC markets in Chapter 9 "Renewables Policy: Market-Based Instruments and Portfolio Standards". The authors carefully evaluate alternative public policy choices regarding the design of RPS programs, as well as their inter-actions with other policies that target climate change and air emissions. They also discuss the decisions that need to be privately made to hedge the various risks inherent to these markets.

Market mechanisms can also work effectively in conjunction with policies that impose limits on air emissions from power plants and other stationary sources. A well designed cap-and-trade program can reduce compliance costs significantly as compared to the traditional 'command-and-control' alternatives, because the former allocates emissions reduc-tions among sources in a more cost-effective manner. Firms with the lowest costs to undertake emissions reduction measures will benefit from controlling more emissions and selling their (unused) emission rights to other plants with higher compliance costs. The recent experience with the European Union's Emissions Trading Scheme (EU ETS) for CO_2 and the extensive path-breaking policies for NO_x, SO_2 and mercury emissions in the US offer important lessons on their economic and environmental benefits. Dr. David Harrison, who was actively involved in the design of many of these programs, provides an insightful review in Chapter 10 "Emissions Trading for Air Quality and Climate Change in the United States and Europe". According to Dr. Harrison, the emissions trading approach appears to have been successful in lowering the cost of meeting air emission reduction goals. Emission trading promises to become particularly important as a means to deal with greenhouse gas emissions in the US, under future federal, regional and state policies.

Note

1   In most countries however, long-term storage and nuclear waste disposal
    remain largely unresolved.

8

FINANCING NEW NUCLEAR CAPACITY: WILL THE 'NUCLEAR RENAISSANCE' BE A SELF-SUSTAINING REACTION?[1]

Glenn R. George

Introduction

The Energy Policy Act of 2005 (EPAct) is an important development in the financing of new nuclear capacity in the near- to mid-term in the US. Key features of the Act—including production tax credits, loan guarantees, funding support, and standby support—are intended to provide significant incentives for new nuclear development, construction, and operation.

It remains unclear, however, whether the incentives being offered are sufficient to spur construction of significant new nuclear capacity in light of power market uncertainty, utility investor wariness, and the need to raise significant—and economically priced—capital before a nuclear construction project can be launched. Several observations can be made regarding EPAct from financial and economic points of view:

- Although EPAct contains a number of significant benefits for new nuclear capacity, certain elements—notably details of the loan guarantee program—have yet to be fully defined through the rule-making process.
- Wall Street remains somewhat skeptical of new nuclear financing, in part because uncertainty continues to surround many aspects of the market.
- Securitization and related financial techniques could play an important role.
- Creative approaches to risk management and insurance will also be important.

- Putting elements in place will require frequent and close interaction among energy companies, nuclear consortia, industry groups, bankers, and federal and state regulators and legislators—as well as targeted insight from economic consultants.

Without an aggressive, coordinated effort to resolve these issues and to bring new financial tools and techniques to bear, financing for new nuclear capacity runs the risk of remaining uneconomic in the current environment. The so-called "nuclear renaissance" would then amount to nothing more than construction of perhaps a half-dozen new nuclear power plants, i.e., just enough plants to exhaust the direct subsidies available under EPAct.

The Energy Policy Act of 2005
Ten years of policy effort went into crafting EPAct, viewed by some as the most significant piece of energy legislation in the US since the Public Utility Holding Company Act of 1935. Key financial provisions provided necessary benefits for new commercial nuclear power plants, including production tax credits (PTC), federal loan guarantees, standby support, and funding support. The question is whether these benefits are sufficiently generous to support a nuclear renaissance.

- Electricity from a qualifying advanced nuclear power facility can claim a PTC of $0.018 per kW-hour (not adjusted for inflation) for the first eight years of operation. This applies up to 6,000 MW of capacity put into operation prior to January 1, 2021. Limitations include a $125 million annual cap based on a 1,000-MW benchmark and an allocation process within the 6,000-MW limit.
- The DOE is authorized to provide a loan guarantee of up to 80 percent of the project cost of advanced nuclear power plants, contingent on congressional appropriations for this purpose.
- Standby support is available for delays in the commencement of full operation due to litigation or NRC approval for up to six reactors: $500 million available to each of the first two reactors and $250 million to each of the remaining four, subject in the latter case to a 180-day deductible. Covered costs of delay include principal and interest and the incremental cost of purchased power to replace contracted output.

• Funding support for construction of advanced new nuclear reactors totals $1.18 billion for core nuclear research, development, demonstration, and commercial application activities over the period 2007-2009.

It is important to distinguish at this point between the first new nuclear power plants in the 1,000 MW class—which EPAct directly covers through the PTC (for 6,000 MW of new capacity) and standby support (for the first six reactors)—and those that come thereafter. Indeed, because the subsidies available under EPAct are most generous for first-movers, there has been a rush of sorts among nuclear utilities and other potential developers to announce plans for new nuclear capacity and to pursue site permits from the NRC and a rush among reactor vendors to receive certification for new reactor designs. Without getting sidetracked into a lengthy discussion of specific utilities, vendors, sites, and designs, it is possible to state that approximately 30 reactors of several different designs are currently are currently in some stage of planning by a utility company, consortium, or other developer. Table 1 summarizes the status of these efforts.

The two interrelated questions, then, are whether perhaps six new plants will get built as a result of direct subsidies available under EPAct, and whether significant new nuclear capacity beyond that will be built. For a true nuclear renaissance to take place, substantially all of the plants currently in the planning process, and many others, will need to be built. This is especially true in light of the need for new nuclear capacity to replace existing nuclear plants as they are retired at the end of their lives. Put another way, will investors support construction of six new nuclear power plants in the US, and come back for more?

The DOE Rulemaking Process
The DOE rulemaking process on standby support (EPAct section 638), concluded in the fall of 2006, was key but gaps still remain. The process resolved a number of critical implementation issues, including the nature of the application process and any applicable fees; appropriations and funding accounts; covered and excluded delays; covered costs and applicable requirements; disagreements and dispute resolution; and monitoring and reporting requirements. However, the cost of standby support to developers has not been clarified in the rulemaking process. The loan guarantee program likewise calls for recovery of costs from nuclear

Table 1.   *New Nuclear Plant Status*[2]

Company	Site	Design, No. of Units	Early Site Permit (ESP)	Construction/ Operating License (COL)
Dominion	North Anna	ESBWR (1)	Under review, approval expected 2007	November 2007
TVA (NuStart)	Bellefonte	AP1000 (2)	—	October 2007
Entergy (NuStart)	Grand Gulf	ESBWR (1)	Under review, approval expected 2007	November 2007
Entergy	River Bend	ESBWR (1)	—	May 2008
Southern Company	Vogtle	AP1000 (2)	Under review, approval expected early 2009	March 2008
Progress Energy	Harris; Levy County, Florida	AP1000 (2), Not yet determined (2)	—	Harris - October 2007; Levy County, FL - July 2008
South Carolina Electric & Gas	Summer	AP1000 (2)	—	October 2007
Duke	William States Lee, Cherokee County, South Carolina	AP1000 (2)	—	October 2007
Exelon	Clinton	Not yet determined	Under review, approval expected 2007	Not yet determined
Exelon	Texas, to be determined	Not yet determined	—	2008
Constellation (UniStar)	Calvert Cliffs or Nine Mile Point	EPR (5)	Will go to COL but submit siting information early	4Q - 2007
Florida Power & Light	Not yet determined	Not yet determined	—	Not yet determined
Duke	Davie County, North Carolina	Not yet determined	Under consideration	Not yet determined
Duke	Oconee County, South Carolina	Not yet determined	Under consideration	Not yet determined
NRG Energy / STPNOC	South Texas Project	ABWR (2)	—	Latter part of 2007
Amarillo Power	Vicinity of Amarillo, TX	ABWR (2)	Under development, to be submitted 4Q / 2007	As soon as practicable after 2007
Texas Utilities	Not yet determined	Not yet determined (2-5)	—	2008
Alternate Energy Holdings	Bruneau, ID	Not yet determined	—	2008

developers, but pricing has not yet been determined. Thus, the value of these program elements remains unclear, though the statutory language seems to suggest very generous levels of support.

More importantly, neither the rulemaking process nor EPAct itself addressed two fundamental questions (among others) in financing new nuclear capacity. First, they did not resolve the problem of the timing of capital formation. That is, how does one secure and service several billion dollars in debt and equity for several years before a new nuclear power plant creates any revenue? Although it provides financial benefits spread over time (e.g., production tax credits), EPAct does not provide a mechanism for securing capital *up front* on financially attractive terms. Second, neither the rulemaking nor EPAct dealt with the residual risks. How, for example, does one insure against the possibility that actual First-of-a-Kind (FOAK) costs greatly exceed estimates? Although it mitigates some degree of regulatory timing risk, standby support does not address significant project exposures. Despite its obvious benefits, EPAct does not in itself close the gap between what financiers are likely to seek and what new nuclear developers can be economically offer.

Investor Skepticism

Wall Street remains generally skeptical of new nuclear financing, in part because of uncertainties. *Credit Aspects of North American and European Nuclear Power* opens by observing, "In general, nuclear plant ownership tends to be less supportive of credit quality because it introduces added levels of operating, regulatory, and environmental risks to a business profile."[3] In a similar vein, Thomas E. Capps of Dominion Resources opined, "Moody's would go bananas if we announced we were going to build a nuclear plant."[4] Indeed, many in the financial community considering new nuclear capacity in the North American generation mix[5] see more unresolved than resolved issues.

- How will waste issues and questions surrounding Yucca Mountain be resolved? Is reprocessing seriously back on the table?
- What market structure will surround new nuclear? Is merchant nuclear a possibility? Should nuclear be included in portfolio standards on the basis of supply diversity and security?
- Will the NRC licensing process (10 CFR Part 52) work as designed? What are the pitfalls?

- To what degree will nuclear plant vendors and architect-engineer-constructors guarantee project scope, cost, and schedule, and plant performance? How much "skin" will they put in the game?
- What role will the nuclear consortia (e.g., NuStart, UniStar) play in securing fully integrated financial packages for new nuclear plants? Can anyone be a one-stop shop?
- Will long-term power purchase agreements be available, and can they be monetized?

The burden is on the industry to resolve these issues for investors, not vice versa. Yet nuclear utilities and developers have not yet made a high-profile effort to engage the public and investment community in a dialogue on these critical issues.

Securitization as Part of the Solution

Operating Asset Securitization

Recall that the *timing of capital formation* is the first of the key unresolved issues surrounding new nuclear financing: In general, significant capital is required early in a new power plant construction cycle, yet several years will elapse before revenue is first generated. A key point is that securitization is much more than a mechanism for amortizing stranded costs associated with electric power market restructuring. Rather, it is a generic, widely used, and very powerful financial tool that takes a stream of revenue over time and turns it into a chunk of capital up front. How does it work? In a very simplified, stylized form:

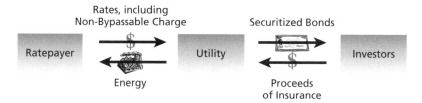

Figure 1.   *Basic Securitization*

Securitized debt—also known as asset-backed securities—is serviced by a dedicated revenue stream from ratepayers. It typically requires legislation that makes the non-bypassable, non-reversible, self-adjusting revenue stream irrevocable by future actions by the relevant public utility commission (PUC).

While most securitization involves the sale of financial assets (e.g., residential mortgages, commercial mortgages, credit card balances, other receivables, stranded cost payments from electric utility ratepayers), *operating asset* securitization is instead the sale of the future revenues from specific operating assets (e.g., bridges, toll roads, public housing, prisons, water projects, electric power transmission lines, local power distribution systems). It requires the certainty of predictable cash flows, a long track record, strong resilience to economic downturns, and high barriers to entry. Investors also have a claim on the operating assets themselves.

Operating Asset Securitization can be illustrated as follows:

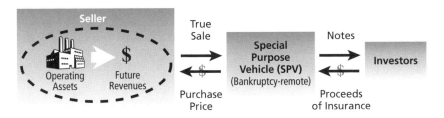

Figure 2.   Operating Asset Securitization

Of critical importance, a higher credit rating means a lower cost of capital, especially compared with alternatives. Of course, pricing depends on the specific transaction structure and its legal underpinnings (e.g., legislation vs. executive order vs. PUC decision) and liquidity support, over-collateralization, and other credit enhancements may also be needed. However, because bondholders have a priority claim over revenues and the underlying assets, the debt generally receives a very high credit rating. A credit rating one or even two notches higher than the applicable corporate rating is generally available—sometimes as high as AAA if supported by the regulatory structure. Securitized debt also has the advantage of generally being off-balance sheet and bankruptcy-remote, and issuing asset-backed securities typically has no impact on the utility's capital structure. Finally, the mechanism offers corporate borrowers the opportunity to increase leverage.

Operating asset securitization allows a very high fraction of future revenues to be extracted as a chunk of capital up front; longer durations allow more capital to be extracted, with any structure over 30 years amounting to a perpetuity. Proceeds could, in principle, be used for any purpose, including dividends to the corporate parent.

Securitization in Energy and Infrastructure Finance
Securitization tools and techniques are being employed in a number of different jurisdictions and in a variety of applications to resolve timing issues in finance, as well as to increase leverage and/or reduce the cost of capital.

- **Transmission Lines**: Securitization was used to finance the Moyle Interconnector in the UK, a £150 million HVDC submarine cable between Northern Ireland and Scotland. Other stand-alone transmission lines (especially those with long-term contracts) could be financed this way.
- **T&D System Ringfencing**: In 2002, Pennsylvania Power & Light made an $800 million "synthetic sale" of its local distribution utility, lowering its cost of capital while at the same time increasing leverage. Similar transactions are common outside the US, for example in the UK water sector.
- **Toll Road Privatization**: Securitization of toll revenue is the methodology underlying transactions involving, *inter alia,* the Chicago Skyway ($1.8 billion for a 99-year lease), the Indiana Toll Road ($3.85 billion for a 75-year lease), and possibly the NJ Turnpike and Garden State Parkway (estimated to be worth as much as $30 billion).
- **Renewable Energy PPAs**: In a multibillion-Euro transaction announced in 2005, the Italian state-owned grid operator (GRTN) securitized above-market off-take contracts on 13.6 GW of energy-efficient power plants that have come on line since 1992 under a government plan to promote development of green energy. Developers were offered 17-year tolling contracts that included an 8-year window during which they are paid an almost 100 percent premium to market-based rates. Many other PPAs globally have been monetized this way.
- **Storm Damage Costs**: In Florida, the Public Service Commission has approved the use of securitization in recovery of hurricane-related costs. FPL ratepayers, for example, will pay a $1.58 average monthly surcharge over 12 years to pay off $906 million in 2005 storm costs and build a $650 million reserve.
- **Environmental CapEx**: The Wisconsin and West Virginia PUCs have allowed the use of securitized debt in financing construction of scrubbers and related facilities on baseload coal plants in the

utility's rate base. Allegheny Energy plans to use this at the Fort Martin station.

Securitization and EPAct

Although there is no "silver bullet," securitization could help close the gap between EPAct's benefits and developers' financial needs. Securitization-type techniques could be used to quantify and monetize the PTC and standby support available under EPAct.

Were it not for the $125 million annual limit (for a 1,000-MW benchmark plant) and the allotment process, the PTC could amount to as much as $142 million per annum for a period of eight years, assuming a 1,000 MW plant, a 90 percent capacity factor, and the need to offset tax liabilities of at least this magnitude every year. In the right transaction structure, it might be possible to sell or securitize this flow and yield nearly $800 million in capital at the time the plant comes on line, or nearly $600 million in capital at the time a construction project is let (i.e., six years before first revenues accrue).[6]

An entire sector of the energy economy—wind—has relied for years on a similar PTC mechanism, with the emergence of tax investors and pure equity investors, each with their own desired rate of return and appetite for risk. Nuclear developers may need to learn from this experience or tap into this network.

Standby support reduces the financial risk associated with plant start-up and concomitant cash flows, although the scope of covered delays and covered costs is as yet unclear. Standby support could be worth as much as perhaps $400 million for start-up of one plant (the first or second one ordered) that is delayed for one year by a covered event (assuming 90% capacity factor and replacement power at $0.10/kWh). This contingent benefit could potentially be used as a credit enhancement in a financing package or as part of a broader project insurance package. Because of its contingent nature, standby support (unlike the PTC benefit) probably could not be directly monetized.

Even if new nuclear capacity is quite expensive—perhaps over $2,000 per kW for the first few plants—the PTC and standby support benefits available under EPAct would appear to be quite substantial relative to the cost of a new nuclear plant. A definitive conclusion in this regard would require significant analysis, reflecting in part the specific technology selected, capital and O&M costs, electricity and uranium fuel price projections, among many other factors. However, it appears likely that construction of the first six plants or so would be economic by dint of EPAct.

Thought Experiment: Securitization of an "Energy Security Charge"

Before turning to the sustainability of the nuclear renaissance beyond the first six plants, it is useful to consider the potential broader applicability of securitization as a mechanism for supporting construction of new nuclear capacity. One can consider, for example, a purely hypothetical "Energy Security Charge" or similar kind of benefit paid to new nuclear generators on the basis of energy (kWh) produced. The structure could be used for regulated or merchant generation assets, though no judgment is offered regarding the advisability of such a structure in either case. The following diagram illustrates one possible structure for securitizing such a charge.

The fact that debt of over $1 billion could be supported by a levy of one cent per kilowatt-hour illustrates the power of the securitization mechanism.

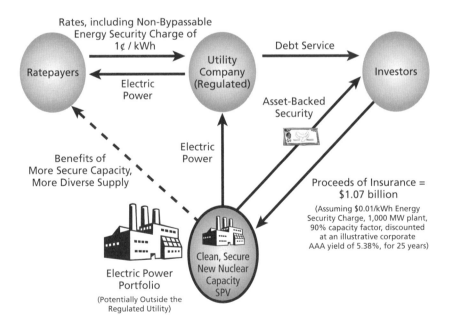

Figure 3. *Thought Experiment: Securitization of a Hypothetical Energy Security Charge*

Risk Management and Insurance

Creative approaches to risk management and insurance will also be key to financing new nuclear plants. *Residual risk* is the second unresolved issue surrounding new nuclear financing and the one that is central to sustaining a nuclear renaissance beyond the first six plants. The risk that the actual FOAK cost will significantly exceed estimated FOAK cost is possibly the biggest exposure not addressed in any way by EPAct.

To pick one example, Westinghouse forecasts that the FOAK AP-1000 will cost perhaps half again as much as the Nth of a kind (NOAK), i.e., beyond unit number four. Similar forecasts exist for other designs.[7] It is possible to calculate the variance of FOAK costs around the best estimate, which represents the risk that actual FOAK costs will differ from estimates. Insurance against FOAK cost overruns can therefore be priced and sold, and the cost allocated among various stakeholders (sponsor, vendor, lenders, insurers, government, etc.) All this would need to be reflected in the web of contractual and other relationships among the parties involved. John H. Gittus, Regent's Professor at UCLA and nuclear syndicate manager at Lloyd's of London, has performed this analysis in the UK and US contexts. It appears that insurance against this residual risk would be available on the market, significantly increasing the likelihood that more than six new nuclear plants can be financed and the nuclear renaissance can be sustained—but much will depend on the required premium, deductible, co-insurance, and other details that pertain at the time.

Even risks that are addressed by EPAct will need to be mitigated once loan guarantees, standby support, and other benefits are no longer available. Creative credit support and enhancement elements will doubtless be required as part of any financial package for a new nuclear plant, until and unless the financial and investor communities become more comfortable and familiar with nuclear financing.

Conclusions

This paper suggests several conclusions regarding financing for new nuclear capacity. First, although EPAct conveys a number of major benefits for new nuclear, key gaps include the timing of capital formation and the residual risk of FOAK cost overruns. Second, the financial and investor communities remain somewhat skeptical of new nuclear financing, in part because of what some view as uncertainty (as distinct from risk) along several key dimensions. Third, securitization and related financial techniques could play an important role in turning revenue streams into lumps of capital. Given the nature of the subsidies available under EPAct, and particularly the PTC and standby support, securitization techniques may be sufficient to get the first six or so new nuclear plants financed and built. And fourth, creative approaches to risk management and insurance will also be quite important, especially if FOAK overrun risk is to be mitigated. If insurance against this risk is available in the market and priced competitively, then plants beyond the first six could be economically financed.

Although the conclusions here appear to be fairly supportive of new nuclear capacity, remaining uncertainties are of such a nature that financing could be unattractively priced—potentially depressing returns for developers, retarding plant deployment, and reducing the number of new plants eventually built. Preparing a comprehensive and attractively priced financial package could take years of effort involving energy companies, nuclear consortia, industry groups, lenders, investment bankers, and federal and state regulators and legislators. Accomplishing all this will require planning, coordination, and frequent and close interaction among stakeholders. Key pieces need to be in place long before any announcement of new nuclear construction can take place without risk of financial backlash from rating agencies, investors, or regulators.

Corporate boards of directors, in particular, will want to ensure they have independently assessed the risks and benefits of investing in new nuclear capacity, given the large capital investment required, the uncertainties involved, and the governance requirements of Sarbanes-Oxley. Remembering the prudence reviews and other regulatory and financial problems that accompanied the last burst of nuclear power plant construction several decades ago, few directors will want to rely wholly on the analysis and conclusions provided by management. There is likely to be significant demand, therefore, for informed, dispassionate, insightful analysis by independent economic consultancies.

Notes

1. An earlier version of this paper, titled *From Streams to Lumps: Transforming Long-Term Incentives into Up-Front Financing for New Nuclear Construction,* was presented at the American Nuclear Society annual meeting, embedded International Congress on Advanced Nuclear Power Plants, held at Reno, Nevada (June 6, 2006).

2. Nuclear Energy Institute, http://www.nei.org/index.asp?catnum=2&catid=344, website viewed January 8, 2007.

3. Standard & Poor's report (January 9, 2006).

4. Quoted in *The Washington Post,* July 24, 2005.

5. It is important not to forget Canada, especially Ontario, is an important part of the North American market.

6. In each case, the calculation assumes the $125 million annual figure, a 1,000 MW plant, 90 percent capacity factor, tax liabilities equal to or greater than the PTC, discounted at an illustrative utility A yield, 5.46 percent and 5.69 percent, respectively.

7. Nuclear industry experience and projections conform closely to the Wright Learning Curve. See T. P. Wright, *Journal of the Aeronautical Science,* 1936. This is a seminal work in the field of learning curve effects, albeit in the field of aeronautics.

9

RENEWABLES POLICY: MARKET-BASED INSTRUMENTS AND PORTFOLIO STANDARDS

Daniel Radov
Per Klevnas

Introduction

Renewable Portfolio Standards (RPSs), which mandate that a minimum amount or percentage of electricity be from renewable energy sources, have been adopted by more than twenty states in the US and by many countries around the world.[1] Policies to encourage the development and exploitation of renewable energy sources are not new. Public policy benefits ascribed to renewable sources include fuel diversity, energy security, better air quality, and reduction in greenhouse gas emissions, as well as local economic benefits such as encouraging a potential export industry or providing local employment. Policies to encourage renewables have included environmental adders, guaranteed or "feed-in" tariffs,[2] public procurement auctions, direct subsidies, loan guarantees, preferential tax treatment, and research and development programs—and many of these policies are still in use.[3]

The development of RPSs and the associated Renewable Energy Certificates (RECs) represents a shift towards encouraging renewable energy sources through market-based approaches. This shift is part of a wider trend away from direct regulation—a trend that applies to electricity producers and retailers as well as to the environmental regulations that affect them. The increasing importance of market-based approaches to environmental policy is reflected not only in the proliferation of RPSs, but also in the continued operation and new development of emissions trading programs and the development of nascent white tag or white certificate programs to encourage investments in energy efficiency.

One of the primary attractions of market-based instruments is that when properly designed, they make it possible to achieve a given target at the lowest cost. Potential suppliers compete for the opportunity to supply market demand and this competition serves to drive down the price to a level just high enough to induce the marginal producer to supply the market. The actions taken are not the result of direct government involvement, but of decentralized decisions by potential suppliers. By contrast, many past approaches to environmental control involved detailed regulation and subsidies, with regulators attempting to pick winners (and also losers) as they provided support or mandated particular actions for individual companies.

Additionally, the increased use of RPS programs indicates a preference for quantity-based instruments in environmental policy. Typically a target is set for the minimum amount of desired renewables generation, and then prices of environmental commodities (credits) are allowed to fluctuate to ensure that this target is met. An attraction of such policies is the flexibility they offer in distributing the cost of achieving targets, as obligations can be distributed through a range of mechanisms. Another appeal arises from the certainty of outcomes—with quantities fixed, the immediate impact of the policy is relatively easy to gauge.

Design of Renewable Portfolio Standard Programs

RPS programs require establishing various ground rules and other program elements. Because they are designed to influence choices for electricity generation, the programs interact with other policies, notably emissions trading programs to limit air emissions and greenhouse gas emissions.[4]

Program Design

Under a typical RPS, suppliers are required to source a given proportion of their electricity from renewable sources. Assuming there is sufficient capacity to meet the requirement, and assuming ideal operation of the market, eligible renewable generating sources will "stack themselves" into a renewables merit order of increasing cost of generation. These sources then compete to supply renewable electricity to meet market demand, which is determined by the policy target. Typically, generators of eligible electricity receive a REC, an official record certifying that a specified amount of renewable electricity has been generated, that can be used not only as a unit of account for compliance purposes, but also traded separately from the energy produced.

Figure 1 illustrates the basic components of a stylized REC program in a competitive electricity market. The electricity market functions as it would without such a program with producers trading in the wholesale market and consumers buying electricity on the same basis regardless of the technology used for its generation. The main difference in the electricity market is therefore the participation of renewables generators that would not otherwise produce electricity.

When RECs are allowed to trade separately from the electricity sold, the RPS quota and rules create a separate market for them. Demand is driven by the quota obligations, and the program regulator needs to monitor compliance, enforce requirements, and register the retirement of certificates or credits to fulfill obligations. Supply to meet the demand for renewables or RECs is met by certain forms of generation that are certified as REC-eligible if they generate and sell electricity. The regulator oversees verification, certification, and issuing of credits, which typically are denominated in terms of an amount of electricity generated from an eligible source. While these stylized elements are common to all RPS

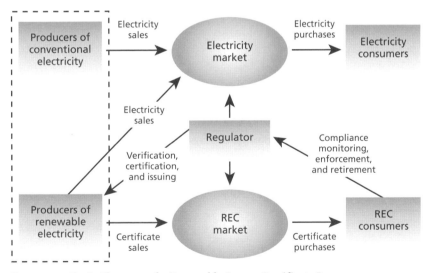

Figure 1.   Basic Elements of a Renewable Energy Certificate Program

Source: Adapted from Isabelle de Lovinfosse and Frédérick Varone, Renewable Electricity Policy in Belgium: Policy Change in the Liberalized Electricity Market, Working Paper No. 4 University Association for Research on Political Action, (Louvain, Belgium: Catholic University of Louvain, 2003).

programs with tradable certificates, RPS programs are relatively complex policy instruments with a large number of design variables.

Creating Necessary Institutions

Introducing an RPS typically requires new institutional arrangements and administrative capacity. In regulated markets, regulatory power over utilities may already extend to introducing and enforcing quotas or other provisions. In many jurisdictions, however, new legislation is likely to be required to create an authority with sufficient power to enforce provisions and ensure the effectiveness of the RPS program and the credibility of the REC market. Participants must comply with the monitoring, verification and reporting protocols for projects, and the trading rules for certificates, while obligated parties must meet their individual targets for eligible electricity.

An important aspect of regulation is the time-horizon of the RPS provisions. Many renewables projects have long lifetimes with high initial capital costs and potentially long payback periods. Investors may fear that, once facilities have been built, there will be a temptation to decrease the original level of support. As with other regulated markets with high up-front costs, ensuring the credibility of the regulatory compact is a key to achieving efficient outcomes. This may involve embedding quota obligations in primary legislation and licenses that are difficult to alter, and setting quotas for long time periods.

Defining Qualifying Technologies

The technologies eligible to generate RECs will depend on the precise objectives of the program. Definitions therefore vary among RPS programs, but almost all include sources with potential for large-scale deployment such as wind power, biomass, tidal/ocean power, and solar energy sources such as photovoltaics. Additionally, eligible energy sources may not be renewable in a strict sense but nonetheless are deemed desirable because of their energy efficiency (e.g., cogeneration or combined heat and power facilities).

Variations in the technologies included often reflect local circumstances. Nevada, for example, awards REC credits for production of solar cells. Renewables certificate policies have been implemented in Europe to comply with the Directive that lays down common EU objectives for the promotion of renewable energy sources, and technology choices can reflect the considerations noted in the Directive:

The Community recognises the need to promote renewable energy sources as a priority measure given that their exploitation contributes to environmental protection and sustainable development. In addition this can also create local employment, have a positive impact on social cohesion, contribute to security of supply and make it possible to meet Kyoto targets more quickly.[5]

Many definitions contain provisions to exclude technologies like large-scale hydro installations that are economically viable without support from the certificate program. Similarly, pre-existing facilities often are not eligible for support through RPS programs, even though this may lead to some inefficiencies. The REC program also co-exists with existing regulation so that arguably if regulatory requirements already stipulate that landfill gas must be used for electricity generation, the inclusion of landfill gas as an eligible technology is unjustified.

Defining and Enforcing Quota Obligations
RPS initiatives vary not only in scope, but also in scale. Early RPS programs typically had relatively undemanding quotas and rapidly resulted in the deployment of technologies that were close to market and easy to integrate with the rest of the electricity transmission and distribution system. The success of early programs led to an international trend to increase requirements, and long-term targets in several jurisdictions now are very high. Table 1 summarizes the target levels of RPS programs in 22 states and the District of Columbia, which range from no explicit target to 33 percent of overall electricity consumed. As the table also shows, some targets are based on installed capacity, whereas others are denominated in terms of electricity generated. Most states with RPS plans have REC trading systems, which may or may not permit compliance using RECs imported from out-of-state. For example, out-of-state sources met more than half of the total RPS requirements during the early years of the Massachusetts program.

There also are differences in the parties subject to obligations. In regulated monopoly markets, obligations are typically on single, vertically integrated utilities. In deregulated competitive markets, most commonly the obligation is imposed on retail electricity suppliers, although there have been examples of obligations in all stages of the supply chain, including generators, the transmissions system operator (Italy), and even

Table 1.   *Renewable Portfolio Standards in the United States*

State	Year Enacted	Date Revised	Preliminary Target	Final Target	Covered Entities	Certificate Trading
Arizona	2001	2006	0.2% by 2001	15% by 2025	Utility	No
California	2002	2005	13% by 2003	33% by 2020	Investor-Owned Utility Municipal Utility	
Colorado	2004		3% by 2007	10% by 2015	Utility Investor-Owned Utility Rural Electric Cooperative	Yes
Connecticut	1999	2003	4% by 2004	10% by 2010	Utility	Yes
Delaware	2005		1% by 2007	10% by 2019	Retail Electricity Supplier	Yes
District of Columbia	2005		4% by 2007	11% by 2022	Utility	Yes
Hawaii	2004		7% by 2003	20% by 2020	Utility	No
Illinois[1]	2005		2% by 2007	8% by 2013	Utility	No
Iowa	1991		none	105 MW	Utility	No
Maine	1999		none	30% by 2000	Utility	Yes
Maryland	2004		3.5% by 2006	7.5% by 2019	Electricity Supplier	Yes
Massachusetts	1997		1% new by 2003	4% new by 2009	Utility	Yes
Minnesota	1997		1,125 MW by 2010	1,250 MW by 2013	Xcel only	No
Montana	2005		5% by 2008	15% by 2015	Utility	Yes
Nevada	1997	2005	6% by 2005	20% by 2015	Investor-Owned Utility	Yes
New Jersey	2001	2004	6.5% by 2008	20% by 2020	Utility	Yes
New Mexico	2002	2004	5% by 2006	10% by 2011	Investor-Owned Utility	Yes
New York	2004		none	25% by 2013	Investor-Owned Utility	Yes
Pennsylvania	2004		1.5% by 2007	18% by 2020	Utility	Yes
Rhode Island	2004		3% by 2007	16% by 2020	Electric Retailers	Yes
Texas	1999	2005	2,280 MW by 2007	5,880 MW by 2015	Retail Suppliers	Yes
Vermont	2005		none	load growth by 2012	Retail Electricity Supplier	Yes
Wisconsin	1999	2006	none	10% by 2015	Utility	Yes

Note: (1) Illinois implements its RPS through voluntary utility commitments.

Source: Barry G. Rabe, Race to the Top: Expanding the Role of U.S. State Renewable Portfolio Standards *(Arlington, VA: Pew Center on Global Climate Change, June 2006).*

end-users (Sweden). Table 2 summarizes some of these features for renewables certificate programs in Europe.

Enforcement of obligations typically relies on penalties for noncompliance, ranging from fines to the threat of revoking licenses. The design of penalties can have important consequences for the functioning of the REC market.

Enabling and Crediting Eligible Generation

Programs also require detailed procedures for the monitoring, reporting, and verifying eligible generation. Crediting also requires registries and tracking systems that allow parties to hold and transfer RECs, as well as retire them to demonstrate compliance. Certificates are usually but not universally denominated in terms of a unit of eligible electricity, e.g., one certificate per MWh renewable electricity output.

Although RPS quotas provide financial support for renewables, as quotas rise it becomes increasingly important to consider other regulatory issues to enable renewables generation to expand to meet quotas. A key issue in this regard is transmission capacity and clarity about who pays for the additional capacity required for renewable generation. Transmission issues are particularly important as many renewable energy sources need to be located close to the relevant natural resources which often are found in remote areas (tidal lagoons, areas with steady and high wind speeds, near suitable biomass resources, etc.). Another issue is the level of public support for or opposition to particular new developments, and expansion of renewables generation may necessitate review of the process for planning permission and licensing in the siting of new facilities.

Designing a REC Market

The flexibility offered by the REC market depends critically on its design. One consideration is whether to allow banking of RECs, so that certificates generated in one compliance period are also valid in subsequent periods. This can provide participants with valuable flexibility to optimize cost over time and encourage early action.

A common concern with RPS programs is that the price of RECs can be volatile, which entails risks for obligated parties who may face very high prices. Conversely, developers of renewable generation projects face the risk of very low prices and therefore less financing than expected. Anticipating this risk, they might only enter the market if a risk premium above the expected average cost of generation is available. To mitigate

Table 2. Features of Renewables Certificate programs in European Member States

Country (Program)	Date of Introduction	Administrator	Target	Obligation (Demand driver)	Average price of REC	Inter-temporal flexibility	Price Mechanism	Plant Eligibility	International Trading	Notes
Belgium (Flanders)	2002	Regulator (VREG)	Rising to 6% in 2010	Suppliers (Quota)	€85 in 2003, 108 since 04/2004	5 years' banking	Price ceiling	Excl. some hydro and all fossil fuels	Regional trading, may be extended to international	Credit metric is CO_2 equivalents
Belgium (Wallonia)	2003	Regulator (CWAPE)	Rising to 8% in 2010	Suppliers (Quota)	€85 in 2003	5 years' banking	Price floor and ceiling	Incl. efficient CHP	Regional trading, may be extended to international	
Italy	2002	Transmissions System Operator (GRTN)	Currently 2%	Generators (Quota)	€99 in 2003 €97 in 2004	3 years' banking	No price restrictions	Excl. fossil fuels; only facilities built after 04/1999; eligibility lasts 8 years	Allowed for import of credits	
Netherlands (Credits)	2000	Transmission System Operator (TenneT)	N/A	Consumers, voluntary (Tax Exemption)	€55 in 2000 but falling thereafter	N/A	Limits effectively set by tax incentive	All renewables, detailed 'calibration' of eligibility	Allowed for import of electricity	Ended in 2005 because of difficulties in establishing market
Netherlands (Groen label)	1998	Industry Association (EnergieNed)	1,700 GWh over five years	Generators, based on past generation (Voluntary Quotas)	€20 in 2000	N/A	No price restrictions	All renewables, including large hydro	Allowed for import of electricity	Ended in 2001 partly because no new voluntary agreement was made
Sweden	2003	Regulator (STEM)	10 TWh annual production (defined as relative quota of 17%) in 2010	Consumers (Quota)	€25 in 2005	Unlimited banking	Price floor and ceiling being gradually phased out	Incl. only non-fossil fuel energy; some hydropower sites ineligible	Compatible with RECS, no international trading	
United Kingdom (Renewables Obligation)	2002	Regulator (Ofgem)	Rising to 10.4% in 2011	Suppliers (Quota)	€55 in 2004-5	Max 25% of obligation from banked credits	Price ceiling close to anticipated market price; "smearback"	Excl. large hydro and some biomass co-firing	No international trading	Scheduled to be in place until 2027. Allows Levy Exemption Credits

Source: David Harrison, Jr., Steve Sorrell, Daniel Radov, Per Klevnas, and Andrew Foss, Interactions of Greenhouse Gas Emissions Allowance Trading with Green and White Certificate Schemes. Report Prepared for the European Commission, Directorate-General Environment (Boston: NERA Economic Consulting, 2005)

these concerns, some programs have included price ceilings as a "safety valve" in the event of very high prices for parties with quota obligations. The price ceiling often takes the form of a buy-out price at which RECs can be bought from the regulator; the same effect would occur with fixed noncompliance fines. Less common are some cases of price floors that guarantee a minimum level of revenue to generators.

One option, used in the UK's RPS program, is a hybrid system that combines a fixed buy-out price with recycling the buy-out revenue to holders of RECs generated from certified generation. This mechanism ensures that the further away the system is from the target renewables level, the higher the value of renewable power—just as with a more traditional program. But it also fixes the maximum costs that that energy suppliers will incur and therefore provides more certainty than a standard RPS. The theoretical economics literature has suggested that there are circumstances where combinations of a quantity (quota) instrument and a fixed fee may be most cost-effective in the aggregate. However, the increasing complexity of such approaches also has drawn criticism.

In addition to these questions of market design, issues also arise related to the integration of RPS programs with cross-border trade in electricity and cross-border trade in RECs. Insofar as the objectives of renewables policy are local (e.g., economic development, energy supply, and local air pollution), they could be undermined if cross-border trading leads to import of RECs without any of the associated benefits.

Relation to Other Public Policy Programs

The policy objectives of RPS programs often overlap with those of other policies. In particular, environmental objectives often can be met in a number of ways, and the presence of multiple policy instruments can lead to complex interactions.[6]

Interactions of RPS Programs with Electricity Markets

Perhaps the most important interaction is the relationship of the REC market to the electricity market. Under competitive conditions, the interactions between these two markets depend on two countervailing effects—one in the wholesale market and the other in the retail. First, retail electricity prices will typically reflect the additional cost of purchasing RECs (which in turn reflect the incremental cost of generation from renewable sources), applying upward pressure on retail prices. Second, for a given capacity of conventional generation, wholesale prices may in fact *fall* in the short term because some conventional wholesale capacity is "crowded out" by the new renewables capacity. This leads to lower demand for conventional capacity and possibly causes a lower-cost generator to set the price on the margin at least some of the time. The net effect on end-user prices depends on the combination of these two factors, which in turn depends on the particular characteristics of the electricity market. Under some circumstances, it is possible that retail prices will fall rather than rise in the short term.

It is important to note, however, that the total cost of generating a given quantity of electricity has risen, reflecting the use of more expensive and subsidized technologies. The potentially lower retail prices result from redistribution from conventional generators to consumers and renewables generators, not an overall lower financial burden. Also, since long-term electricity market prices in competitive markets depend to a large extent on the long-term marginal cost of new entry rather than on short-term conditions, the RPS cannot be expected to depress long-term prices. However, an ambitious RPS quota can significantly delay the entry of new conventional capacity as renewables capacity is built instead.

Interaction with Other Policies through the REC Market
The creation of a market for RECs has important implications for the interaction of RPS programs with other policies. In essence, an RPS supports renewable technologies via the REC price, which must be at least as high as the difference between the price of conventional electricity and the price needed to ensure that the renewable energy quota is met. The higher the quota, the higher the cost of the last MWh of renewable energy that will satisfy it—and therefore the higher the REC price. By the same token, if the price of conventional electricity rises (for example, because fossil fuel prices rise), then for a given RPS target, the price of a REC should fall, since the renewable generator will also benefit from the higher electricity price, and therefore will not need so large a subsidy. This pricing mechanism has important implications for the interaction of RPS programs with other environmental policies. Notably, policies to reduce air pollution—including cap-and-trade programs for pollutants and taxes on emissions—typically have an effect analogous to fuel price increases in that they raise the price of wholesale electricity but do not add to the cost of renewables generators. Thus they cause REC prices to fall. For the purposes of encouraging renewables generation, such policies are non-additional: They do not provide additional support for renewables for a given RPS quota.

These basic relationships can change if the RPS design includes buy-outs or other price-capping mechanisms. Moreover, these relationships are long-term equilibrium relationships and may not hold for any particular shorter-term time period. They become especially important as multiple and far-reaching climate change policies are implemented in a number of countries.

Impact of RPS Programs on Emissions Trading Programs
Many technologies eligible under RPS programs do not lead to the emission of air-borne pollutants such as carbon dioxide (CO_2), sulfur dioxide (SO_2) and nitrogen oxides (NO_x). As most locations introducing RPS programs also have in place policies to reduce emissions of one or more of these pollutants, it is important to recognize the interactions between the two sets of policies.

The effects are particularly striking where a quantity instrument is in place, such as a cap-and-trade program for pollution. This applies to the US Acid Rain program for SO_2, the NO_x Budget program, and the EU Emissions Trading Scheme for CO_2. As designers of cap-and-trade programs intend, these policies help encourage reductions from those sources that have the lowest cost of emissions abatement. There are well-developed markets for emissions allowances and the price is determined by the cost of cutting additional units of emissions to meet the overall cap.

The introduction of an RPS program in this setting relaxes the constraints of the cap-and-trade programs for pollutants because the increase in renewable generation leads to a reduction in emissions from the sources they replace—although, importantly, not to a reduction in overall emissions. This in turn will lead to a fall in the price of emissions allowances—unless the level of the emissions cap is readjusted to reflect the revised emissions expectations. This has been done under Europe's Emissions Trading Scheme. In that case, the emissions allowance price is likely to rise. In either case, the total cost of cutting SO_2, NO_x, or CO_2 pollution is increased because renewables generation is typically not the cheapest emissions abatement option.

Major Future Public and Private Issues
There are a number of issues related to the design and impacts of RPS programs. These include questions about "excess profits," concerns about support for emerging technologies, interactions with other policies, and dealing with concerns about volatility of the support level.

Public Policy Choices

Differentiation of Qualifying Generation

One of the selling points of RPS programs is that once the government or other authority has identified a technology as eligible, there is no further government participation in the promotion or selection of technologies. This feature is attractive because it reduces the risk that a government will try (and fail) to "pick winners." Government backing for projects or technologies that are not the most cost-effective results in inefficiency and waste of taxpayer or private money. RPS programs reduce that risk by allowing market forces to allocate investments in a way that cost-effectively meets policy targets.

But taking a hands-off approach raises other issues. Under most existing RPS programs, technologies are either eligible for renewable credits or not. The least expensive technology, which may even be commercially competitive with conventional generation technologies, receives the same support as more expensive technologies that are only beginning to be commercialized. This can have two important consequences, depending on the characteristics of the market.

EMERGING TECHNOLOGIES

The first consequence is that, if the less expensive technology can satisfy existing targets, the renewables or certificate price will not be high enough to encourage further development of the more expensive technology. Some observers view this as entirely appropriate—why should money be spent on a more expensive way of achieving the same target? Further, they argue that a properly designed RPS system may well be able to support emerging technologies; provided quotas are in place over a sufficiently long time horizon and the program is credible, there will be incentives to look ahead and innovate to meet future targets at lower cost.

Others, particularly proponents of the more expensive emerging technologies, argue that these technologies will become more cost-competitive given sufficient building and operating experience. Meeting future higher renewable targets will require other—currently more expensive—technologies in addition to the existing least-cost option. If these technologies are not supported now, proponents argue, their costs will not decline quickly enough and it will be more expensive to meet future targets. RPS programs, they contend, should not only assist in the deployment of renewables but also have an explicit "technology-forcing" component.

The obvious way to address this concern, if it is to be addressed, is to differentiate technologies in some way. This could be done by having sub-quotas for particular technologies (the New Jersey RPS, for example, includes a "solar carve-out"), or by offering different levels of support to different technologies or technology bands. This approach has been less common for market-based renewable support programs than for non-market-based programs, but it is used in some US States and is being introduced in the UK. Certain "emerging" technologies would receive more certificates than more established technologies. Such provisions typically lead to higher costs, and raise important questions about the merits of technology neutrality and the ability of RPS programs to foster innovation. This essentially reintroduces some aspects of government judgment into the market-based selection process and therefore runs the risk of governments picking winners (and losers) by deciding who should receive a higher number of certificates per MWh produced.

EXCESS PROFITS

A second consequence of the standard RPS design that awards the same price to all technologies occurs where the less expensive technology is no longer sufficient to satisfy the RPS target, so that the price is determined by more expensive technologies. In this case, the less expensive technology can earn profits in excess of what it would need simply to remain in operation. This argument, recently made in the UK to criticize the "Renewables Obligation," could be raised for any sector where differences in costs of production persist, although the fact that government mandate is directly responsible for the "excess profit" may make the case appear different. This concern can be addressed by adopting a differentiation approach.

Another possibility is the imposition of a time limit on eligibility for certificates and for the financial support they offer, depending on the specific technology. Thus an onshore wind development might be eligible to receive certificates for 10 years, after which it would not be eligible. Italy limits the period during which sites are eligible to receive certificates, and in the UK, this approach has been adopted for landfill gas and will be considered in the future for onshore wind.

While this approach might address concerns about potential "excess profits," it would not do much for the first concern about immature technologies.[7] Also, critics of such approaches often point out that the prospect of future profits is a pre-condition for current investment. If investors believe that programs may be modified to correct profits once they arise, there is a risk either that the investment will be deterred or that markets will demand a regulatory risk premium, thus driving up the price of certificates. Indeed, if companies do not trust the durability of program design, the total cost of achieving an RPS quota could increase considerably.

DIFFERENTIATION: SUMMARY

A key consideration in determining whether it is desirable to differentiate eligibility or support or to treat all technologies equally is how the proposal will affect incentives for continued operation and investment. For example, duration limits on eligibility do not appear sensible for technologies where the primary costs are variable (for example, biomass technologies). But all technologies have some operating costs and some capital costs, and it would be difficult to distinguish which technologies should have time-limited support. Moreover, arbitrarily basing the duration of support to technologies on the level of their variable costs would create market distortions—for example, away from high capital cost technologies and in favor of ones with comparatively greater operating costs. Even exclusion of pre-existing facilities may be undesirable if it distorts the way the owners approach upkeep and improvement of existing investments.

Policy Interactions
RPS programs interact in important and sometimes complicated ways with other policies that target climate change and air emissions. These interactions are already important in the European Union, where CO_2 emissions trading has already arrived, and they will become more important in the US if greenhouse gas emissions trading becomes a reality.

Policymakers often do not recognize that once an emissions cap is in place, the emissions benefits of an RPS or other program are likely to be limited. In the short term, emissions reductions attributed to an RPS are not expected to lead to net emissions reductions across a country (or countries) participating in emissions trading, because where the binding cap determines the emissions level, saving emissions in one place simply frees up emissions allowances to be used by another site to cover its emissions. Total emissions remain the same. In the longer term, however, forcing the increased use of renewables may make even tighter caps on emissions feasible.

At bottom, questions about the benefit of separate renewable policies boil down to whether one trusts the market (in this case for CO_2 reductions) to deliver the target at the lowest cost. In Europe, a common argument has been that CO_2 emissions trading is unable to motivate renewables, not only because allowance prices are low but also because of the uncertainty about the future of the cap-and-trade scheme or any successor policy. If the time horizon for renewables projects is significantly longer than pre-existing policies, additional support mechanisms may be necessary. A similar argument is made about research and development into new or immature technologies, contending that such research also constitutes long-term investment that cannot be adequately incentivized by the insufficiently long policy horizons. If RPSs provide greater long-term certainty by setting quotas farther in advance, they may complement the shorter time horizon of other policies. Nonetheless, as other market-based mechanisms internalize more and more of the negative externalities that renewable programs are meant to correct (like climate change, air pollution, etc.) the environmental rationale for maintaining separate renewable support may need to be re-examined.

Price Volatility
Another concern with RPS programs is that the REC market may display large and frequent price fluctuations. Project developers may be deterred from participating because of their uncertainty over the level of support they can expect from an investment. The possibility of higher costs of meeting a given quota has led some to favor "feed-in" tariffs or other support mechanisms for eligible technologies that guarantee the level of support. However, such policies also run the risk of impaired cost-effectiveness, notably if the guaranteed support exceeds that necessary to reach a desired target.

Price controls have been used to mitigate volatility in some RPS programs. Price floor mechanisms, in which the regulator guarantees a minimum price for certificates even if there is no market participant prepared to pay this amount, are relatively rare, reflecting the concern that they may lead to public money being spent unnecessarily. Price ceilings are present in several programs.[8] A price ceiling can protect parties with obligations under a RPS program and the end-users of electricity (to the extent costs of RECs are passed through). However, a ceiling also may deter investment if set too low, and if binding for a significant proportion of time, a ceiling could mean that the amount of renewable generation may fall short of the quota. Mechanisms for controlling volatility thus risk imperiling the achievement of policy objectives.

To a large extent, controlling volatility is a matter of allocating risk between electricity generators, obligated parties, and the regulator or government. The decision to introduce price constraints therefore needs to reflect an assessment of these risks, as well as the extent to which different participants have other means at their disposal to mitigate risk exposure, such as alternative policies for regulators, or long-term contracts, diversification, or other hedging for companies and consumers.

Company Decisions

Understanding and Predicting the Evolution of Prices
REC prices are a key concern of investors in renewable capacity and of suppliers or other regulated entities that need to consider whether to "make or buy" certificates to comply with their obligations. When deciding whether to invest in a particular renewables project or simply rely on the market for RECs, utilities and energy suppliers must consider all of the standard costs associated with investment in generating assets and compare these to the likely revenues from sales of both electricity and RECs.

Forecasting REC prices is complicated by the wide range of technologies eligible to receive RECs—particularly since a number of these have marginal production costs that approach zero once the capacity is built or installed. In a number of states and countries there has been concern that overbuild of such technologies could lead to a collapse of the REC price, increasing the risk to investors. Price forecasting is also complicated by sub-quotas for specific technologies within the larger renewables targets, and similarly by restrictions on the share of a target that may be met by certain technologies.

Hedging Risks Related to Renewable Portfolio Standards
Companies affected by RPSs are likely to be interested in the hedging opportunities provided by the development of environmental commodity markets that are closely related to those in which they already trade and that constitute elements of their core business. Since increases in the price of emissions allowances are likely to be associated with reductions in REC prices, the emissions allowances and renewable energy certificates can be used as hedges against each other as part of a balanced portfolio. Statistical methods can be used to understand these relationships, but a good understanding of the underlying reasons for them is essential to taking advantage of potential opportunities.

Concluding Remarks

The rise of Renewable Portfolio Standards and tradable certificates for renewables reflects a wider trend in environmental policy towards market-based approaches. By imposing quantity targets, RPS programs move support for renewables off public balance sheets and onto the balance sheets of obligated party. A benefit of this approach is that the risk that taxpayer money will be wasted on the "wrong technology" is reduced—but the corollary is that the risks are borne instead by private investors (or other obligated entities). Governments and regulators of course retain the ability to choose winners and losers, and various differences in policy design may have important consequences for who pays and who benefits. Policy design can also mitigate some of the additional risks inherent to market-based approaches.

Decision-makers in both the private and public sectors have only recently begun to consider the complicated interactions between RPS programs and other related programs to achieve environmental targets—including emissions trading and demand-side management or other energy-efficiency support programs. Understanding these interactions—and the opportunities for hedging and risk exposure that they offer—will be key to both policy advocacy and successful private company decisions related to Renewable Portfolio Standards.

Notes

1. In Europe, RPS programs typically go by the title of "tradable green certificate" programs. For the remainder of this chapter, we refer to all such programs with renewable targets and tradable certificates as "RPS programs."

2. "Feed in" tariffs pass through an environmental adder fixed by the government or regulator to guarantee a price level for renewable generation.

3. See International Energy Agency, *Renewable Energy: Markets and Policy Trends in IEA Countries* (Paris: IEA, 2004) for a comprehensive review of policies in OECD countries.

4. See David Harrison, Jr., "Emissions Trading for Air Quality and Climate Change in the United States and Europe," in this Section.

5. Directive 2001/ 77/EC.

6. Fuller exposition can found in Harrison et al., op. cit. and Harrison, op. cit.

7. It might indirectly address some of the issues, however. To the extent that a time-limit proposal reduced the expected earnings from investment in the

lower-cost technology, it could potentially reduce additional investment in it, thereby pushing up the price of certificates—which in turn could improve the prospects for other more expensive technologies.

8. For a discussion of the analogous use of price ceilings within emissions trading, see Henry D. Jacoby and A. Denny Ellerman, The Safety Valve and Climate Policy. MIT Joint Program on the Science and Policy of Climate Change Report No. 83 (Cambridge, MA: MIT, 2002).

10

EMISSIONS TRADING FOR AIR QUALITY AND CLIMATE CHANGE IN THE UNITED STATES AND EUROPE

David Harrison, Jr.
Per Klevnas
Daniel Radov

Introduction and Background

Emissions trading has emerged over the last decade as a major tool for controlling air pollution and climate change in both the United States and Europe. The European Union Emissions Trading Scheme (EU ETS) for carbon dioxide (CO_2) launched in January 2005 has provided important experience and visibility for the approach and highlighted its applicability to climate change policy. Indeed, in the United States and Europe, virtually all of the major current programs and proposals to control CO_2 and other greenhouse gases (GHG)—at least from power plants and other stationary sources—are based upon the emissions trading approach. The United States also has more than a decade of experience with emissions trading programs for other air emissions, and this earlier experience provides important lessons as well.

Compared to the alternative command-and-control approach, the concept of emissions trading is attractive for two major reasons. First, trading lowers the cost of meeting key air quality and climate change objectives. Providing sources with the flexibility to trade the right to emit—rather than requiring all sources to meet given emission standards—means both that the allowance market can be used to determine the least cost means of achieving objectives and that firms have continuing incentives to find cheaper means of reducing emissions. The second reason, and one less generally discussed, is that emissions trading provides environmental gains relative to a command-and-control approach—it provides greater certainty that targets will be met and avoids the environmental effects of giving exemptions to firms that find it difficult to meet the command-and-control standards. Extensive experience with programs over the last decade provides strong evidence that the theoretical economic and environmental gains are achieved in practice.

This chapter explains the concept of emissions trading and how it has been used for air emissions and climate change.[1] We emphasize the importance of learning from the experience with existing programs, both those that have been in existence for decades to deal with air emissions and the recent programs to control GHG emissions. We first provide an overview of the concept, the three major types of programs, and the main elements that are typically specified in developing a particular program. We then summarize the air emissions programs in the United States and the lessons this experience provides. Section III considers applications to climate change, including the existing European cap-and-trade program and various proposals in the United States. Section IV summarizes the key issues that arise with regard to greenhouse gases, including public policy issues involved in designing programs and the issues for private firms subject to a trading program. The final section provides brief concluding remarks.

Concept of Emissions Trading

The concept of emissions trading is simple. A cap-and-trade program sets an aggregate cap on emissions that defines the total number of emissions allowances, each of which provides its holder with the right to emit a unit (typically a ton) of a particular type of emission. The allowances are initially allocated in one of several ways, usually directly to participating sources. Each source covered by the program must hold permits to cover its emissions, with sources free to buy or sell allowances among themselves.

Economic and Environmental Gains
Giving regulated facilities the flexibility to trade emissions allowances reduces the compliance costs of achieving an emissions target, while the overall cap on the level of emissions provides certainty that the emission target will be achieved. Although it is not possible to provide precise measures of cost savings compared to hypothetical control approaches that might have been applied, the available evidence suggests that the increased compliance flexibility of emissions trading yields costs savings of as much as 50 percent.

While some skeptics have suggested that emissions trading is a way of evading environmental requirements, experience to date with well-designed trading programs indicates that emissions trading helps achieve environmental goals in several ways. First, when emission reduction requirements are phased in and firms are able to bank emissions reduction credits, the required emission reductions are achieved more quickly. Second, giving firms with high abatement costs the flexibility to meet their compliance obligations by buying emissions allowances eliminates the rationale underlying requests for special exemptions from emissions regulations based on hardship and high cost. Third, reducing compliance costs has resulted in tighter emissions targets, in keeping with efforts to balance the costs and benefits of emissions reductions. Finally, properly designed emissions trading programs appear to provide other efficiency gains, such as greater incentives for innovation and improved emissions monitoring.

Simple Example to Illustrate the Cost Savings from Emissions Trading
A simple numerical example illustrates how emissions trading can reduce control costs compared to a traditional approach based on setting uniform command-and-control standards. Typically, the cost per ton of reduction rises as the level of reduction required is increased, and this marginal cost could be substantially higher for one plant than another. Assume then that to reduce emissions to meet the standard, Plant I incurs a cost of $1,500 for the *last* ton of emissions reduced, while Plant II spends $3,000 for the *last* ton it reduces. These two facilities might be different plants within the same company, plants owned by different companies in the same sector, or plants in completely different sectors. They might be subject to a common regulatory standard or to completely separate regulations.

The same overall reduction in emissions could be achieved at lower compliance costs by tightening controls at Plant I by one ton and relaxing them at Plant II by one ton. Loosening controls at Plant II by one ton saves $3,000, whereas tightening controls by one ton at Plant I would raise costs by only $1,500, for a net savings in compliance costs of $1,500 to reduce that ton. Under a cap-and-trade program, each source would compare its own emissions control costs with the market allowance price and determine whether it is profitable to control more and sell allowances to others or to control less and buy allowances to cover the additional emissions. The trading mechanism allocates emissions reductions among sources in the most cost-effective manner, relying on individual informa-

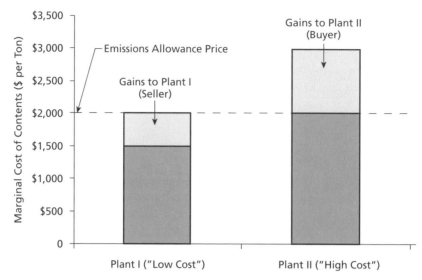

Figure 1. Gains to Plants from the Trade of a Single Emissions Allowance

tion and self-interest—rather than administrative regulation—to determine compliance decisions by each individual source.

Suppose in this simple numerical example that the market price of an emissions credit or allowance were $2,000 per ton, and that the two facilities were initially allocated allowances consistent with the individual emissions levels required under the emissions standard. Figure 1 shows how each of the sources would gain from the market with regard to the last ton controlled.

Plant I (low-cost seller) gains by further reducing its emissions by one more ton than the standard requires and selling the allowance it no longer needs to Plant II; it receives $2,000 for the allowance but pays only $1,500 to achieve the reduction, for a net gain of $500. On the other side of the transaction, Plant II (high-cost buyer) is able to buy the allowance for $2,000 and reduce its compliance costs by $3,000, for a net savings of $1,000. Thus, the total savings in compliance costs of $1,500 for that ton is split between the buyer and the seller; both gain from trading.

Broad Types of Emissions Trading Programs

Three broad types of emissions trading programs have emerged: credit-based programs, averaging programs, and cap-and-trade programs. Although all share the feature of tradability, the three differ in important respects.

Credit-based Programs

Credit-based programs provide tradable credits to facilities that reduce emissions more than required by some pre-existing regulation (or other baseline). They allow those credits to be counted towards compliance by other facilities that would face high costs or other difficulties in meeting the regulatory requirements. Reduction credits are created through an administrative process in which the credits must be pre-certified before they can be traded.

The most significant issue for credit-based programs is establishing the baseline against which credits are calculated.[2] Determining the baseline involves determining what the level of emissions *would have been,* absent the controls for which credits are claimed (e.g., introduction of specific emission control technologies). Early programs developed by the U.S. Environmental Protection Agency (EPA) in the late 1970s and early 1980s led to concerns about "paper credits," i.e., credits for reductions that would have been achieved without the incentive provided by the programs. The response was to limit significantly the credits that were allowed, with the result that these early programs yielded few cost savings.[3] Similar concerns have been raised with regard to the credit-based programs established under the Kyoto Protocol.

Averaging Programs

Averaging programs involve offsetting emissions from higher-emitting sources with lower emissions from other sources, so that the average emission *rate* achieves a predetermined level.[4] Like reduction credit programs, averaging programs provide flexibility to individual sources to meet emissions constraints by allowing differences from source-specific standards to be traded between sources. The primary difference between averaging and reduction credit programs is that reduction credits are created (or certified) through an administrative process whereas in averaging programs, the certification is automatic.

Cap-and-Trade Programs

A cap-and-trade program sets an aggregate cap on emissions that defines the total number of emissions allowances, each of which provides its holder the right to emit a unit of emissions. The permits are initially allocated, typically among existing sources. Each source covered by the program must hold permits to cover its emissions, with sources free to buy and sell permits among themselves. In contrast to reduction credit programs—but similar to averaging programs—cap-and-trade programs do not require pre-certification of allowances: the allowances are certified when they are first distributed. But cap-and-trade programs limit total emissions, a contrast to reduction credit and averaging programs that are not designed to cap total emissions.

Combinations of Types

A trading program might include more than one type of trading mechanism. As discussed below, both the Acid Rain Trading Program and RECLAIM include reduction credit supplements to the basic cap-and-trade program. In addition, a cap-and-trade program might provide for early reduction credits, which allow firms to get credits for voluntarily reducing emissions prior to the introduction of a cap-and-trade program. The credits obtained can be used to meet requirements once the cap-and-trade program goes into force.

Key Elements of an Emissions Trading Program

All three types of emissions trading rely on preconditions to ensure a successful program. First and most importantly, all assume that an emissions control requirement has been put in place that requires emissions to be reduced to levels below what they otherwise would be. Credit and averaging programs will typically require a source-specific standard (e.g., maximum emissions rates); cap-and-trade programs require an aggregate cap on emissions combined with the provision that each source surrender allowances equal to its emissions. Second, the cost savings achieved by all three types of emissions trading depend upon *variability* in the costs of reducing emissions among emissions sources. Differences in emission control costs across emissions sources create the opportunity to reduce costs through trading. Third, in all three types of trading programs the requirements must be both enforceable and enforced. A corollary is that actual emissions or emissions rates must be accurately *measured*—otherwise it would be impossible to enforce the requirements because it would be impossible to determine whether sources were in compliance.

There are various methods of characterizing the many features that must be specified in an emissions trading program, some of which do not apply to all of the three basic emissions trading types. The following subsection lists[5] the major features of emissions trading programs in three major categories: threshold features, design features, and implementation features.

Threshold Features

Threshold features define the cap and set up the basic structure and elements of the program.

- **Cap and budgets.** The cap is the target level of total emissions from covered entities under the emissions trading program. Budgets may be given for groups of emission sources, such as sources in different states or sectors, with the sum of budgets being the total cap.
- **Covered entities** specifies the universe of emissions sources that must participate in the trading program.
- **Geographic or temporal flexibility or restrictions.** Trading among different geographic regions can be restricted if there is evidence that emissions have substantially different effects when emitted in different locations. The trading program can also include options of banking and borrowing. To bank is to reduce emissions more than required in a given year and bank the surplus for future internal use or sale. To borrow is to reduce emissions less than required in a given year and borrow against future reductions, with the borrowed amount supplied by reducing more than required in subsequent years.
- **Opt-in provisions** allow additional sources to opt into the program.
- **Timing** specifies the start date and period of the emissions trading program and includes the possibility of separate phases for the trading program.

Design Features

Design features are the decisions that arise as the program is designed and turned into a specific regulatory program.

- **Allocation of initial allowances** is only relevant in cap-and-trade programs where some method is required to distribute the initial allowances. Common methods include various formulas to distribute initial allowances to participants on the basis of historical information (grandfathering) or of updated information (updating) as well as auctioning the initial allowances. Allocations can also be provided to non-participants (e.g., energy consumers) to compensate for costs they bear.
- **Institutions established to facilitate trading** may include third parties (e.g., brokers) to participate in trading or setting up ongoing auctions to increase liquidity and establish market prices.

- **Banking rules** govern banking and/or borrowing options.
- **Safety valves** are mechanisms to restrict the allowance price from rising above a certain level or to change the provisions of the trading program if the allowance price is above a predetermined level.

Implementation Features
A number of features are developed as the program is carried out.

- **Certification of permits:** This process applies to reduction credit programs, which require emission reductions to be certified before they can be traded.
- **Monitoring and reporting of emissions:** Methods must be designed to monitor and report emissions from each participating source.
- **Compliance and enforcement provisions:** These are developed to determine whether sources are in compliance and enforce the requirements if sources are not.
- **Maintaining and encouraging participation:** These activities aim to keep sources in the program and encourage participation of sources that are given the opportunity to opt in.

Experience with Emissions Trading in the United States

Emissions trading has been used extensively over the past decade to regulate air emissions in the United States. This section provides an overview of the major cap-and-trade programs and the lessons their experience provides.

Overview of Major US Cap-and-Trade Programs for Air Quality

Table 1 summarizes the five major cap-and-trade programs that have been established in the United States. The US EPA has administered all these programs except for the Regional Clean Air Incentives Market (RECLAIM), the Los Angeles air basin program administered by the South Coast Air Quality Management District (SCAQMD).

Acid Rain Trading Program
The largest and best-known cap-and-trade program in the United States is the program for sulfur dioxide (SO_2) created by Title IV of the 1990 Clean Air Act Amendments. It is often referred to as the Acid Rain Trading Program because the major motivation for the program was to prevent acid rain damage. Because of its large scale and high profile, the

Table 1.   *Summary of Major Cap-and-Trade Emissions Trading Programs*

Program	Agency	Type	Emission	Source	Scope	Year
RECLAIM	South Coast Air Quality Management District	Cap-and-Trade	NO_x, SO_2	Stationary	Los Angeles Basin	1994-Present
Acid Rain Trading Program	U.S. EPA	Cap-and-Trade; Reduction Credit	SO_2	Electricity Generation	U.S.	1995-Present
Northeast NO_x Budget Trading	U.S. EPA; 12 states and D.C.	Cap-and-Trade	NO_x	Stationary	Northeast U.S.	1999-Present
Clean Air Interstate Rule (CAIR)	U.S. EPA	Cap-and-Trade	NO_x, SO_2	Stationary	Eastern U.S.	To begin in 2009 (NO_x) and 2010 (SO_2)
Clean Air Mercury Rule (CAMR)	U.S. EPA	Cap-and-Trade	Mercury	Stationary	U.S.	To begin in 2010

Sources: A. Denny Ellerman, Paul Joskow, and David Harrison, Jr. Emissions Trading in the U.S.: Experience, Lessons, and Considerations for Greenhouse Gases (Arlington, VA: Pew Center on Global Climate Change, May, 2003); and U.S. Environmental Protection Agency, Multi-Pollutant Regulatory Analysis: CAIR/CAMR/CAVR. (Washington, DC: EPA, October 2005).

success of the Acid Rain Trading Program contributed more than anything else to the change in attitude towards emissions trading in the 1990s, and it is often cited as an example for other applications.

The Acid Rain Trading Program created a national cap on SO_2 emissions per year from electricity generating plants. During Phase I (1995 through 1999), the 263 electricity generating units emitting the largest volume of SO_2 were subject to an interim cap that required projected average emissions to be no greater than approximately 2.5 lbs. of SO_2 per million Btu of heat input. Phase II, beginning in 2000 and continuing indefinitely, expanded the program to include virtually all fossil-fueled electricity generating facilities and to limit emissions from these facilities to a cap of approximately nine million tons—which implies an average emission rate of less than 1.2 lbs. of SO_2 per million Btu. The final Phase II cap will eventually reduce total SO_2 emissions from electricity generating units to about half of what they had been in the early 1980s.

This cap on national SO_2 emissions was implemented by issuing tradable allowances, each representing the right to emit one ton of SO_2, equal to the total annual allowed emissions, and by requiring that the owners of all fossil-fuel-fired electricity generating units surrender an allowance for every ton of SO_2 emissions. Allowances not used in the year for which they are allocated can be banked for future use or sale. These allowances were allocated to owners of affected units free of charge, generally in proportion to each unit's average annual heat input during the three-year baseline period, 1985-1987. A small percentage (2.8 percent) of the allowances allocated to affected units are withheld for distribution through an annual auction conducted by the EPA to encourage trading and ensure the availability of allowances for new generating units. The revenues from this auction are returned on a *pro rata* basis to the owners of the existing units from whose allocations the allowances are withheld.

RECLAIM

While the Acid Rain Trading Program was being developed, regulators in the Los Angeles air basin were developing RECLAIM as an alternative means of achieving the emission reductions of nitrogen oxides (NO_x) and SO_2 mandated the 1991 Air Quality Management Plan. RECLAIM, approved by SCAQMD after a three-year process, and beginning operation in January 1994, was significant both in some of its provisions and as the first major example of a tradable permit program developed by a non-federal authority. The caps for both NO_x and SO_2 were set higher than expected emissions in the initial years, but the overall caps were reduced steadily so that by 2003, emissions from sources emitting more than four tons of either pollutant would be reduced to about 50 percent below early-1990s emission levels. From 2003 on, the caps have remained constant.

Several features of the design of the RECLAIM program distinguish it from the Acid Rain Trading Program. First, the program covers a heterogeneous group of participants, including power plants, refineries, cement factories, and other industrial sources. Second, the RECLAIM program distinguishes between emissions in two geographic zones. Since emissions in the Los Angeles Basin generally drift inland from the coast, sources located in the inland zone were allowed to use RECLAIM Trading Credits (RTCs) issued for facilities in either the inland or coastal zones, but sources located in the coastal zone could use only RTCs issued for facilities in the coastal zone. Third, the RECLAIM program does not allow banking. It does provide limited temporal flexibility, however, by grouping sources into two 12-month reporting periods, one from January through

December and the other from July through June, and by allowing trading between sources in overlapping periods.

Northeast NO$_x$ Budget Trading Program

The Northeast NO$_x$ Budget Trading program grew out of provisions in the Clean Air Act Amendments of 1990 that facilitated common actions by the District of Columbia and 12 states in the Northeastern United States[6] to control regional tropospheric ozone (smog). The states adopted a cap-and-trade program to reduce NOx emissions from electricity generating facilities having 15 MW of capacity or greater and equivalently sized industrial boilers by about 60 percent from uncontrolled levels in a first phase (starting in 1999) and by up to 75 percent in a second phase (starting in 2003).[7]

A unique feature of the program is that it operates only from May through September, when NO$_x$ effects on ozone concentrations are greatest in this part of the country. Although the environmental objective is to reduce the incidence of ozone non-attainment, the program does not contain provisions that distinguish between the summer days when the ozone standard is exceeded and the days when it is not. Several ideas to address this problem were considered, but none were deemed feasible.[8] Instead, the program relies on the decrease in the overall level of NO$_x$ emissions during the critical summer season.

Clean Air Interstate Rule

The Clean Air Interstate Rule (CAIR) was promulgated by the EPA in 2005 to set new standards on SO$_2$ and NO$_x$ emissions from new and existing fossil fuel-fired electricity generation units in 28 Eastern states and Washington, DC.[9] CAIR establishes two phases of caps for these air emissions, with the second cap lower than the first. Phase I of the NO$_x$ program takes effect in 2009, and Phase I of the SO$_2$ program takes effect in 2010. Phase II for both NO$_x$ and SO$_2$ begins in 2015.

When CAIR is fully implemented, annual SO$_2$ emissions in the covered states are expected to drop by over 70 percent from 2003 levels, and annual NO$_x$ emissions are expected to drop by over 60 percent. Each state covered by the regulation can satisfy its emissions reduction requirement by participating in a cap-and-trade program based on the Acid Rain Trading Program for SO$_2$ and the Northeast Budget Trading Program for NO$_x$. States electing not to join the program are subject to firm caps on their emissions. However, the EPA considers participation in the cap-and-trade program to be the most cost-effective way for states to achieve their mandated emission reductions.[10]

Clean Air Mercury Rule
The Clean Air Mercury Rule (CAMR), promulgated by the EPA on March 15, 2005, sets standards for mercury (Hg) emissions from new and existing coal-fired generating units. Under CAMR, Hg emissions are capped at specific, nationwide levels to be achieved in two phases. The first phase, effective in 2010, establishes a cap of 38 tons per year; the second phase, effective in 2018, caps Hg emissions at 15 tons per year.

EPA expects that the 2010 target for mercury emissions will be achieved largely through the emissions control measures for CAIR. The increased use of flue gas desulphurization to reduce SO_2 emissions and selective catalytic reduction to reduce NO_x emissions also will reduce Hg emissions. Thus, in the early years, Hg emissions reductions will be a "co-benefit" of SO_2 and NO_x emissions reductions. As with CAIR, states may join a national cap-and-trade program to meet their Hg emissions budgets, but if they choose not to participate in the program, their emissions budgets are firm caps.

The cap-and-trade approach for mercury has led to litigation and various state proposals to limit possible interstate trading. While the states are concerned that trading could result in local hot spots, the EPA has concluded that the nature of the atmospheric transport of mercury and its local deposition makes such concentrated effects unlikely.[11]

Implications of Experience with U.S. Air Quality Emissions Trading Programs

The experience of more than a decade with these various U.S. air quality programs provides some guidance on how emissions trading works in practice. The following are conclusions regarding the economic and environmental effects of this experience.[12]

Economic Gains from U.S. Emissions Trading Programs
The economic rationale for emissions trading is straightforward. By giving businesses the flexibility to reallocate (trade) emissions credits or allowances among themselves, trading can reduce the compliance costs of achieving the emissions target. Emissions trading appears to have been successful in its major objective of lowering the cost of meeting emission reduction goals. The high volume of trading observed in nearly all

Table 2.   Abatement Cost and Cost Savings from Title IV Emissions Trading

	Abatement Cost		Cost Savings From Emissions Trading				
	With Trading	Without Trading	Phase I Spatial Trading	Banking	Phase II Spatial Trading	Total Cost Savings	Savings Percent
Average Phase I Year (1995-99)	735	1,093	358			358	33%
Average Phase II Year (2000-07)	1,400	3,682		167	2,115	2,282	62%
Total (13 Years)	**14,875**	**34,925**	**1,792**	**1,339**	**16,919**	**20,050**	**57%**

Source: Adapted from Ellerman et al. (2000).

Note: All costs are in millions of present-value 1995 U.S. dollars. Estimates are based on economic reasoning assuming reasonably efficient markets based on observed allowance prices and abatement (as explained in chapter 10 of the source). Savings percentage is relative to abatement costs without trading. A cost estimate is provided for only the first eight years of Phase II since this is the time period when most of the cost savings from banking were thought likely to be realized.

programs provides circumstantial evidence that participants realize substantial benefits from trading.

Table 2 summarizes the estimates calculated by Ellerman et al. (2000) of cost savings from trading in the Acid Rain Program attributable to different types of trading, i.e., the savings due to spatial trading in Phase I, banking between Phases I and II, and spatial trading in the more stringent and comprehensive Phase II.[13]

On average, spatial trading during Phase I reduced annual compliance costs by about 33 percent from the estimated cost of $1,093 million per year for a non-trading regime in which each affected unit must limit its emissions without any trading. During the first eight years of Phase II, the combination of spatial trading and banking is estimated to have reduced annual compliance costs by over 60 percent, from about $3.7 billion per year. Over the first 13 years of the program, the ability to trade allowances nationwide across affected units and through time is estimated to reduce compliance costs by a total of $20 billion, a cost reduction of about 57 percent from the assumed command-and-control alternative. This estimate is similar to that developed by other researchers,[14] although it is less than the percentage cost savings sometimes claimed for emissions trading programs, including the Title IV SO_2 cap-and-trade program.[15]

RECLAIM and the Northeast NOx Budget Trading program have not been subject to as careful a retrospective review, but both have experienced considerable trading activity, which suggests cost savings. Trading activity in RECLAIM has been substantial, with the overall volume in any given year exceeding the total annual allocation as a result of trading in future vintages. Studies done when the program was introduced estimated cost savings to be about 40 percent.[16] The extensive trading suggests these cost savings have been achieved.

Environmental Gains from U.S. Emissions Trading Programs

Although there were early concerns that emissions trading could compromise environmental quality—indeed, critics had sometimes portrayed emissions trading as a way of evading environmental requirements—in fact, experience to date has demonstrated the opposite. The use of emissions trading actually appears to have *helped achieve* environmental goals. The environmental gains possible with emissions trading are illustrated in Figure 2, which shows that ambient sulfate concentration in the eastern United States has been markedly reduced under the Acid Rain Trading Program.[17]

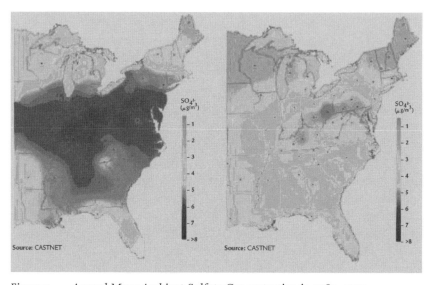

Figure 2.   *Annual Mean Ambient Sulfate Concentration in 1989-1991 (left figure) and 2002-2004 (right figure)*

Source: EPA (2005)

There are five major reasons why the increased flexibility associated with emissions trading can take credit for enhanced environmental performance.

BANKING CREATED INCENTIVES FOR EARLY EMISSION REDUCTIONS

Where emission reduction requirements are phased in and businesses can bank emission reductions—as was the case in most of the prior programs—the required reduction has been achieved faster. The early reductions may defer the achievement of future annual emissions control targets as the banked credits are used. However, as long as a positive discount rate is assigned to the benefits associated with emission reductions, accelerating the timing of the cumulative required emission reductions represents a net environmental gain.

TRADING ELIMINATED NEED FOR SPECIAL TREATMENT OF PLANTS WHERE THE STANDARD CANNOT BE MET

In a command-and-control program, economic hardship or technical barriers can be alleviated only by relaxing the emissions standard. While often justified, these exceptions reduce the regulation's environmental effectiveness because they are one-sided: standards are relaxed to avoid hardships for some facilities, but increased emissions cannot be offset by increasing standards at facilities for which abatement is less expensive or technologically easier. The net result is more emissions than would be produced by regulations that perfectly account for differences in compliance costs.

Allowing businesses for which abatement is costly or even technically infeasible to comply with environmental requirements by buying allowances, effectively paying others to reduce on their behalf, eliminates a feature of command-and-control programs that diminishes their environmental effectiveness. The result is a decentralized mechanism for offsetting emissions that does not detract from achieving the environmental goal.

CAPS PREVENTED EMISSIONS INCREASES DUE TO INCREASED GENERATION

Under an emissions limit approach, the emissions limit is typically expressed as units (tons or pounds) of emissions per unit of fuel burned or unit of electricity produced. Thus, if fuel input or electricity generation increases, the level of allowable emissions increases as well, and total

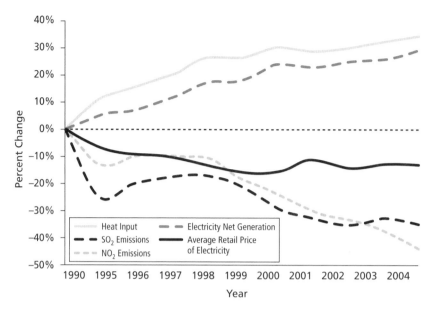

Figure 3. *Trends in Electricity Generation and Emissions from Electric Power Sources*

Source: EPA (2005)

Note: Heat input and emissions data reflect Acid Rain Trading Program units. Generation reflects all fossil fuel-fired electricity-only plants in the United States. Retail price reflects full national values for the electricity-generating sector.

emissions increase. In contrast, under a cap-and-trade program the cap represents a level of emissions, not an emissions rate, so changes in total fuel input or electricity generation do not affect total emissions.

Since the Acid Rain Trading Program began, fuel input and electricity generation have increased by approximately 30 percent, but SO_2 emissions have decreased by nearly 40 percent. These trends are illustrated in Figure 3.

POTENTIAL COST SAVINGS HELPED IN NEGOTIATING
ENVIRONMENTAL TARGETS

The flexibility of trading programs increases the likelihood of gaining consensus on the environmental goal and even adopting a more demanding goal. The allocation mechanism can win over those who might otherwise stand to lose the most from tighter regulations and, all other things being equal, the lower overall costs of achieving the target mean that more reductions are affordable.

The inclusion of emissions trading in the 1990 Clean Air Act Amendments broke what had been a decade-long stalemate on acid rain legislation.[18] The Northeast NOx emissions trading program offered a better means of achieving compliance with the National Ambient Air Quality Standards for ozone, a goal that had long eluded these states (and a number of others) despite ample regulatory authority in the existing Clean Air Act. Similarly, regulators in Southern California adopted emissions trading in both SO_2 and NO_x as a more likely means of achieving the emission reductions that were already required. There also is evidence that the flexibility provided by the Averaging, Banking, and Trading (ABT) programs allowed more stringent emission standards to be set for various categories of mobile sources.

TRADING PROVIDED INCENTIVES TO DEVELOP MORE EFFECTIVE
CONTROL TECHNOLOGIES

Although evidence is limited so far, trading programs should create greater incentives for innovation in emission-reduction technologies than command-and-control regulations. While the latter may force some technological development, there is no incentive to go beyond the standard. Indeed, command and control regulations may be a disincentive because investments in developing more efficient abatement technology might be rewarded only by a tighter standard.

In contrast, the incentive to abate in cap-and-trade programs, where there is no specific standard for any single plant, is continuous across all levels of emissions, and any improvements in abatement technology will result in allowance savings.[19] There is also empirical evidence that the Lead-in-Gasoline Program, a trading program administered by the EPA from 1982 to 1987, led refiners to adopt lead-reducing technologies more efficiently.[20]

Major Greenhouse Gas Emissions Trading Programs and Proposals

The increased national and international interest in emissions trading is largely based on concern about climate change and a consensus that GHGs are well suited to a cap-and-trade program.[21] Once emitted, GHGs reside in the atmosphere for periods measured in decades and centuries. Atmospheric currents ensure that emissions are dispersed quickly in the atmosphere so that atmospheric concentrations of GHGs are relatively uniform over the globe. Uniform mixing means that a ton of a given GHG will have the same effect on atmospheric concentration—and thus on climate change—regardless of whether the ton is emitted in California, New York, or elsewhere on the globe. Thus, trading can—at least in theory—be national and international in scope, and the cost savings commensurately larger as the scope broadens.

The cumulative effect of greenhouse gases and their long duration in the atmosphere also mean that the timing of emissions reductions will not have a significant effect on atmospheric concentrations or climate.[22] Thus, banking offers additional potential for cost savings by using credit-based approaches to bring in sources that would not otherwise be covered by a cap-and-trade program. Although the specific nature of domestic and global measures to address climate change will evolve over time, few environmental problems appear so well suited to emissions trading as GHG emission control.

The major programs and proposals are the Kyoto Protocol and the European Union Emissions Trading Scheme (EU ETS), which is the most significant program to date. Various proposals have also been developed for the United States.

Flexibility Mechanisms under the Kyoto Protocol

In December 1997, representatives from the developed nations of the world met in Kyoto, Japan, and devised a plan for reducing GHG emissions. Signatories to the Kyoto Protocol committed themselves to specific GHG emissions reduction targets with an average emissions reduction of 5.2 percent. The treaty came into force in February 2005 and the first commitment period is 2008-2012.

The Kyoto Protocol includes three flexibility mechanisms that countries can use to achieve part of their emissions reductions:

1. Trading of emission credits between governments;
2. Participation in emissions reduction projects in developing countries (the Clean Development Mechanism, or CDM); and
3. Participation in emissions reduction projects in transition economies (the Joint Implementation or JI).

CDM and JI projects are overseen and approved by the CDM Executive Board and the JI Supervisory Committee, which issue each project's emissions reductions credits (CERs and ERUs). Countries have used both project-based mechanisms to meet the Kyoto requirements because they provide emissions reductions at a much lower cost than domestic emissions abatement measures. Governments and private companies from Europe and Japan have either developed CDM/JI projects on their own or have taken part in carbon funds—public and private institutions investing in CDM/JI projects in order to deliver emissions reduction credits to the fund participants. In aggregate, these funds manage more than $5 billion in capital.

European Union Emissions Trading Scheme

Under the Kyoto Protocol, the EU is committed to reducing its emissions of GHGs by 8 percent below 1990 levels over the period between 2008 and 2012. The European Union Emissions Trading Scheme for Greenhouse Gases (EU ETS) was established in 2003 as a cost-effective mechanism to comply with this commitment.

Overview of the EU ETS

The EU ETS is a cap-and-trade program, and follows the general design outlined above. Its rules identify the installations that are covered by the program, determine how allowances to emit CO_2 are to be distributed to these installations, and stipulate an obligation on each installation to surrender allowances equal to its total emissions in each calendar year. This amounts to establishing a cap on the carbon dioxide emissions from covered installations in the EU.[23] In addition, allowances can be bought and sold, and the resulting market in EU allowances helps lower the overall cost of achieving the cap on emissions.

The first phase of the Scheme runs from 2005-2007, after which the Scheme will operate in five-year phases. The second phase, 2008-2012, thus coincides with the first commitment period under the Kyoto Protocol. The first phase covers large installations in certain industrial sectors (e.g., power generation, refining, iron and steel, cement, glass, lime, bricks, ceramics, pulp and paper) and in particular, all combustion installations with a rated thermal input exceeding 20 MW. Thus, the Directive covers almost the entire power generation sector. In total, the Scheme includes over 11,500 installations, accounting for around 45 percent of CO_2 emissions in the EU, emitting around 2.2 billion tons of CO_2 per year. The Scheme does not currently cover households, transport, or agriculture, other sectors with high emissions. For Phase II, the EU intends to bring aviation into the Scheme, and the European

Commission also has proposed has including maritime shipping at a future date.

Emissions allowances are allocated by each national government, which is required to publish a National Allocation Plan (NAP) for each phase of the Scheme. In the first two phases, allowances are awarded largely free of charge,[24] distributed either on the basis of grandfathering or using industry benchmarks. It remains unclear what allocation methodologies will be adopted for the subsequent phases of the Scheme, though some Member States have announced their intention to auction a larger share of allowances in future years. The Emissions Trading Directive requires that the total quantity of allowances allocated be consistent with the Member State's obligations under the EU Burden-Sharing Agreement (Decision 2002/358/EC) and the Kyoto Protocol. These specify the emissions reductions incumbent on each individual Member State. Member States also have the option of reserving a portion of total allowances for new installations, and many Member States have plans to give allocations to such new entrants in Phase I and beyond.

Experience with the EU ETS Thus Far
It is too early to assess the potential economic and environmental gains from emissions trading of GHGs. The experience thus far illustrates the high price volatility that often occurs at the beginning of major emissions trading programs. In addition, the relatively brief history of the EU ETS has led to a major discussion of the effects the program has on competitiveness, largely as a result of linkages between carbon prices and electricity prices.

ALLOWANCE PRICES AND VOLUMES

Figure 4 shows the price of EU ETS allowances (EUAs) and volume traded each week. The wide fluctuations in price are driven by a variety of factors. The large decline in prices in late April 2006 reflected decreased demand for allowances due to announcements by a number of countries that 2005 actual emissions were considerably lower than expected. The subsequent decline in Phase I prices has been attributed variously to early abatement in the period with higher prices and to lower demand as covered entities had reportedly purchased nearly all of the allowances they need through 2007. Phase II prices have remained at higher levels, reflecting a more stringent cap level for this period, especially after the European Commission demanded less generous allocations from a number of Member States.

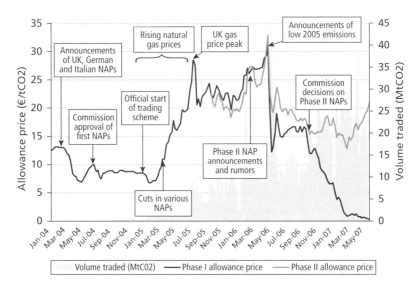

Figure 4.   EU ETS Allowance Market

Source: Data from Point Carbon; commentary provided by the authors.

Table 3 presents the value, volume, and average price of CDM and JI transactions in 2005 and 2006. The total value of transactions of both types roughly doubled year-over-year, supporting the belief held by most observers that these "project-based" compliance mechanisms have successfully established a price signal to encourage GHG reductions in developing countries. As noted, carbon funds, which have been attracted

Table 3.   Value, Volume, and Average Price of CDM and JI Transactions

	2005			2006		
	Value (Millions)	Volume (MtCO$_2$)	Avg. Price ($/tCO$_2$)	Value (Millions)	Volume (MtCO$_2$)	Avg. Price ($/tCO$_2$)
CDM	$2,638	351	$7.52	$5,257	475	$11.07
JI	$68	11	$6.18	$141	16	$8.81
Total	**$2,706**	**362**	**$7.48**	**$5,398**	**491**	**$10.99**

Source: The World Bank and the International Emissions Trading Association, State and Trends of the Carbon Market 2007 (Washington, DC: The World Bank, May 2007).

by the relative price stability of CDM/JI credits, have played a special role in helping these markets to develop.

ELECTRICITY PRICE EFFECTS

One contentious issue is that the EU ETS will lead to increases in electricity prices that benefit electricity companies and undermine the competitiveness of European industry. Early in the discussion of initial allocation, electricity users argued that some of the allowances should be allocated on the basis of electricity use rather than electricity production (commonly called indirect emissions). More recently, power-using sectors, consumer groups and government agencies have advanced various proposals that would limit electricity price increases in various ways.

Since the start of 2005, energy prices, including electricity prices, have increased sharply. While much of this is due to very high worldwide oil and other fuel prices, the impact of the EU ETS on energy price increases, industrial competitiveness, and the profits of electricity generators has become an issue. Higher electricity prices lead to increases in operating margins for some generators ("windfall profits"). Such changes in profits, however, are general features of competitive markets: Operators of nuclear plants may also see their operating margins improve if higher gas prices lead to electricity price increases. To the extent that the EU ETS also leads to higher electricity prices but has a differential impact on the costs of different generation units, it too may benefit some operators while reducing the margins of others.

GHG Trading Programs and Proposals in the United States

Various proposals have also been developed in the United States, including a well-developed program for various northeastern states that is scheduled to enter into force in 2009.

Regional Greenhouse Gas Initiative
The Regional Greenhouse Gas Initiative (RGGI) is a proposal for a mandatory cap-and-trade program covering CO_2 emissions from power plants in ten northeastern states. Beginning in 2009, emissions would be stabilized at current levels through 2014 and reduced by 10 percent by 2018.

At least 25 percent of allowances would be auctioned, and the proceeds would be used to support energy efficiency and renewable energy programs. Companies would be eligible to use project-based emissions offsets up to 3.3 percent of their reported emissions in any compliance period, which represents about 50 percent of the projected average emission reduction obligation. The program also incorporates "safety valve" mechanisms that would relax this limitation to 5 percent if the allowance price exceeds $7/ton and to 20 percent if it exceeds $10/ton; further, if the allowance price exceeds $10/ton for 12 months, the compliance period would be extended by one year.

Congressional Proposals

In addition to regional and state-level initiatives, interest in a federal cap-and-trade program for CO_2 and other greenhouse gases has been growing in recent years. By 2006 11 Congressional proposals had been offered and the current (110th) Congress has seen eight separate proposals in its first several months. Proposals range from covering only electric generation to covering all sectors in the economy, and targets also vary substantially, with one proposal requiring emissions to be cut to 80% below 1990 levels by 2050 and others allowing emissions to grow (albeit at a reduced rate). Many commentators believe that the US Congress will pass a cap-and-trade program for greenhouse gas emissions in the next few years, though the specific provisions of any program are of course uncertain.

Key Issues for GHG Emissions Trading

The emissions trading approach seems destined to be the major policy approach used to deal with climate change. It is likely that the United States will develop a national cap-and-trade program for GHG emissions within the next several years and the European program is likely to evolve as well. Major issues are likely to arise both from a public policy perspective and from the perspective of private firms subject to the programs.

Public Policy Decisions

The public policy issues surrounding the use of an emissions trading program in dealing with climate change fall into three categories: program design elements, effects of a trading program on electricity and energy markets and competitiveness, and linkages among the global programs. The issues are somewhat different in Europe—which already has a program in force—and the United States.

Program Design Elements

While the EU ETS has a well-developed architecture that builds upon experience with prior emissions trading programs, modifications to specific elements of the program will likely be proposed, given the distinctive features of the Kyoto Protocol and the European setting. In the United States, where no program has been definitively determined, there is even greater leeway in designing the program. The following are the major issues likely to arise in program design.[25]

UPSTREAM VS. DOWNSTREAM SYSTEM

A GHG trading program has to determine which emissions should be subject to the program and how the emissions should be accounted for. Prior emissions trading programs have involved regulating direct emitters (e.g., power plants), a system referred to as downstream because these facilities are downstream in the chain of energy production, distribution, and end use. Under an upstream approach, the point of regulation would be the energy producers and suppliers (e.g., coal mining companies, petroleum refiners). An upstream program has the advantage of reducing the number of entities that would be regulated and tends to capture a greater fraction of overall emissions. A downstream program has the advantage of familiarity and of being able to provide direct incentives to reduce emissions from the stack (e.g., carbon sequestration).

CAP LEVEL AND TRAJECTORY

In large part, the cap level and trajectory will determine the stringency of the trading program; therefore the size of the cap and the trajectory for changes are inevitably critical decisions. Under the current EU ETS, the overall cap in each period is the sum of the caps that are set by the 25 Member States, subject to European Commission review and the requirements set by the Directive that established the program. In the US, presumably both would be set by Congress.

INTENSITY TARGET VS. ABSOLUTE CAP

Current cap-and-trade programs involve an absolute cap, a limit on the total level of emissions. Some recent commentators have suggested that the cap should be a *relative* cap that would vary with the level of economic activity. In the US, this approach is referred to as an *intensity* target; the Bush administration called for an 18 percent decline in emissions intensity (per unit output) over 10 years,[26] and the National Commission on Energy Policy has recommended a 2.4 percent annual decline.[27] Unlike an absolute cap, an intensity target does not automatically become more onerous if economic growth is higher than initially had been expected; instead, a conscious choice would have to be made to lower the target.[28] Thus, while an intensity target could achieve the same result as an absolute cap for a given growth trajectory, it also could mitigate (but not erase) fears that an initial lenient cap would evolve into an aggressive one because of unexpected increases in output.

SAFETY VALVE

Some recent emissions trading proposals in the US include a "safety valve", typically a maximum price at which the government would agree to sell additional allowances. Arguments for such a mechanism reflect the view that such a price-based approach is more efficient for addressing the problem of climate change in the face of uncertainty,[29] as well as a concern that a cap-and-trade program would be more politically accept-able if the overall cost were contained. The price can constitute either a penalty or a safety valve, depending on its level relative to the expected market price.

BANKING

Experience provides convincing evidence that allowing banking increases cost savings from emissions trading. Banking can also reduce the volatility of allowance prices because banked allowances provide a buffer against short-term changes in demand conditions. Banking could lead to excessive emissions in the years in which banked allowances are used, and indeed, restrictions on the use of banked allowances are included in the NO_x budget program to avoid high concentrations in emissions. In the case of climate change, however, such concerns are not likely to be rele-vant because of the long-term nature of the issue and the importance of cumulative emissions over decades, rather than the level of emissions in any given year.

ALLOCATION OF ALLOWANCES

The area of greatest interest in policy design for the EU ETS has been the development of the Member State NAPs, and any US program also will have to determine an allocation approach. Specific issues that have proven important in prior programs are:

- What fraction of allowances should be allocated "for free" and what fraction should be auctioned?
- What use should be made of any revenue from auctions? Should the revenues be earmarked for specific purposes (e.g., energy efficiency, technology development)?
- If allowances are allocated first to sectors and then to facilities within each sector, what should be the basis for allocating to sectors?
- What should be the basis for allocating free allowances to individual facilities? Should the factors be based upon historical information (e.g., prior emissions, input, or output) or updated information (e.g., future output)?
- Should a fraction of allowances be set aside for early reduction credits? On what basis should credits be awarded?
- Should allowances be allocated to new facilities? If so, on what basis should the size of the allocation be determined? Should allowances be recovered from facilities that shut down? If so, what should be the criteria for shut-down?
- Should some allowances be allocated to non-participants affected by cost increases (e.g., industries and domestic users whose energy costs would increase)? If so, how should allocations be determined?

Experience suggests that decisions regarding allocation are likely to be contentious but also that it is feasible to develop an allocation plan that can achieve widespread political acceptance.[30] Indeed, the success of Member States in developing the Phase I NAPs is evidence that acceptable allocation plans can be developed, even with the large amounts of money at stake—on the order of 15-60 billion euros in the case of the Phase I NAPs.[31]

Interactions with Markets and Competitiveness Concerns
Public policy is likely to be concerned not just with the design of an emissions trading program for GHGs but also with how the establishment of such a market affects other markets and, more broadly, what effects the program has on the international competitiveness of European or American businesses. Indeed, these issues have already figured prominently in the brief history of the EU ETS.

IMPACTS ON ELECTRICITY AND FUEL MARKETS

The market for CO_2 allowances created by the EU ETS has affected other markets, notably fuel (natural gas, coal) and electricity markets. All else being equal, putting a price on carbon emissions increases the demand for low- and non-emitting fuels (natural gas, renewables) and decreases the demand for higher-emitting fuels (especially coal). Since carbon-emitting fuels are used in producing electricity, a cap-and-trade program for GHGs will inevitably affect electricity prices, although the extent of influence is a complicated conceptual and empirical issue. More complicated relationships may occur. For example, some commentators have suggested that the EU ETS has amplified the market power of natural gas suppliers, and thus increased the impact of higher gas prices on the price of electricity.[32]

INTERACTIONS WITH OTHER ENVIRONMENTAL PROGRAMS

The relationships between the market for CO_2 allowances and electricity/fuel markets mean that the EU ETS will influence related programs and vice versa. Perhaps the most significant of these interactions concern efforts to provide incentives for greater use of renewable energy technologies and for greater energy efficiency. Particularly complex is the set of interactions among the EU ETS and green certificate renewable market programs and white certificate energy efficiency trading programs. [33]

IMPACTS ON COMPETITIVENESS

The experience under the EU ETS has led to extensive discussion of its effects on the competitiveness of European businesses. These concerns are related both to the program's direct effects on the costs of industrial participants and to its indirect effects through electricity price increases. Concerns about the impacts of climate policy on the competitiveness of US business came to the fore during consideration of ratification of the Kyoto Protocol. These concerns have perhaps been the most significant impediment to the development of a program in the US. The US Senate passed a resolution[34] not to enter into any climate treaty that would adversely affect the US economy. Moreover, there is a concern that a modest initial effort would quickly be transformed into a more aggressive program in the future—the proverbial camel's nose under the tent.[35]

A similar concern about the impact on competitiveness has led to proposals in various European countries[36] to change the method of allocating allowances or to limit the translation of carbon allowance prices (and costs) into higher electricity prices. Indeed, some of these proposals would amount to re-regulation of the electricity markets at the same time as Europe is committed to liberalizing electricity markets to increase efficiency and competition.

Concerns about competitiveness and other market impacts could also lead to modifications in the cap-and-trade program. Shifting to auctioned allowances would aggravate rather than mitigate competitiveness concerns and in some cases could also increase price impacts. But other program modifications (safety valves or intensity targets) could reduce the effects of the program on energy markets and on competitiveness of businesses in Europe and the United States.

Linkages between Programs and Other International Considerations
Climate change is an international issue that ultimately will require international coordination. Moreover, there are potential efficiency gains from linking programs, both because of potential cost savings and because linkage tends to reduce leakage, i.e., the shifting of emissions from countries/regions that impose carbon controls to countries/regions that do not.

PROGRAM LINKAGE

As various carbon cap-and-trade programs are developed and proposed, the question naturally arises whether—and how—different GHG emissions trading programs might be linked with one another. The gains from linkage are clear—since gains from trade depend upon differences in costs, linking trading programs with different GHG emissions sources (and thus different GHG abatement costs) promises to increase the overall cost savings from trading. Moreover, linkage can promote efficient emission reductions within and between companies with operations in multiple countries. Options include (1) allowing all market participants (e.g., facilities subject to the cap, brokers, etc.) to trade in all markets, (2) providing specific exchanges/mechanisms for inter-program transactions, and (3) limiting cross-program exchanges to the program administrators (e.g., governments).

Proposals to link different state, regional, national, or international programs must, however, deal with the design features that reduce the compatibility of the programs. One important design issue concerns the presence of a safety valve. If the emissions cap is broken in a program with a safety valve, linking to such a program could break through the cap of the linked programs as well.[37] Other mechanisms designed to contain costs need not have this feature, although some other design elements (such as differences in monitoring and verification procedures) might also lead to difficulties.[38]

INVOLVEMENT OF DEVELOPING COUNTRIES AND LEAKAGE

Virtually all commentators agree that involvement of developing countries in a global climate change regime will be critical, both because these countries will soon account for the bulk of GHG emissions and because these countries are likely to represent the least expensive means of reducing GHG emissions. But developing countries are reluctant to retard their economic growth by imposing stringent carbon restrictions. Various approaches have been proposed to encourage participation by developing countries, notably a growth target that would be equivalent to the intensity targets for a domestic program,[39] but thus far no developing countries have expressed a serious interest in participating in a specific program.

Leakage would be the natural result of incomplete coverage of emissions control and international trade in goods. As the comparative advantage in producing carbon-intensive goods increases outside the countries/regions that impose controls, production of those goods and services will tend to increase in the non-participating countries, thereby increasing carbon emissions. Leakage also can occur because of changes to fuel markets and investment flows resulting from the differential introduction of emissions controls.

Company Impacts and Decisions

The introduction (or indeed, the possibility) of a cap-and-trade program for carbon can have major effects on company decisions and other private considerations. Perhaps the most fundamental change in the shift from the traditional command-and-control approach to a cap-and-trade program is that environmental considerations change from compliance issues to business decisions. A cap-and-trade program means that firms consider the costs of alternatives to reduce their emissions compared to the likely market price of allowances. These considerations—along with the initial allocation of allowances—determine whether firms will be net sellers or net buyers of allowances.

Investment Decisions Under Uncertainty

Since electricity companies and other trading participants make decisions on capital investments that can last for 30 years or more, uncertainty over the future nature of carbon regulation introduces another substantial source of uncertainty in the choice of the lowest cost generation technology. One technology (e.g., pulverized coal) can be the lowest-cost alternative assuming no cap-and-trade program for carbon emissions, while another technology might have lower cost under a cap-and-trade program with high allowance prices. Uncertainties exist not just around the issue of the CO_2 price, but also the level of free allocation and the formula used to determine it—both of which can have significant implications for the value of new and existing assets.

Firms will need to consider more sophisticated analyses of alternatives that take into account uncertainties regarding future carbon controls. Forecasts of allowance prices will allow firms to develop more cost-effective compliance strategies and reduce the effects of uncertainty. Such forecasts can be developed within the firm or purchased from specialists in carbon markets. It will also be important for firms to know the costs of reducing their facility emissions so they can maximize the potential gains from trading under a cap-and-trade program. This information can be used in conjunction with forecasts of likely allowance prices to determine the appropriate strategy for reducing emissions and purchasing or selling allowances.

Participants in the European carbon market have developed futures markets and various derivative instruments to hedge against large price fluctuations. Financial instruments, such as put and call options or the use of forward contracts, are commonly used today to manage price risks in many financial and commodity markets. The potential impacts of higher CO_2 costs could also be hedged through the development of various risk management strategies across related markets (fuels, electricity).

Firms also have opportunities to obtain emissions credits under the JI and CDM programs. Interest in these credit mechanisms has increased, particularly when EUA prices have been high. The use of CDM and JI credits reduce private costs and also influence the market price of EUAs.

Contractual Arrangements
The addition of carbon costs can alter contractual relationships and raise questions about how such additional costs should be incorporated. Most power purchase agreements in European electricity markets have clauses that anticipate the possibility of new taxes, but the carbon costs that arise from a cap-and-trade program are not considered taxes. Thus, the issue of who bears any additional costs and who is entitled to any benefits (e.g.,

of free allowances) is being determined based upon interpretations of contract terms that did not anticipate the development of the EU ETS. Anticipation of a cap-and-trade program in the United States provides an opportunity to provide clarity in these issues when the contracts are determined, even if there is substantial uncertainty whether (and when and how much) such a program might be developed.

Rate Case and Other Considerations for Regulated Entities
The introduction of a carbon cap-and-trade program will require firms in regulated electricity markets to modify their rate case materials. The specifics will depend upon whether allowances are auctioned (and thus included as costs) or provided for free. Companies subject to Integrated Resource Planning requirements in the United States will have to include carbon considerations in their analysis.

Concluding Remarks

Emissions trading has emerged as an important means of introducing cost-reducing flexibility into environmental control programs, reducing the costs and increasing the environmental integrity of regulatory programs. The last two decades have provided a great deal of experience with various forms of emissions trading. Indeed, emissions trading is a feature of virtually every proposal for new initiatives to control air emissions in the United States and, as highlighted by the European program, is the dominant approach in dealing with climate change.

Greenhouse gas emissions trading programs can learn valuable lessons from prior programs relating to cost saving, environmental gains, and the design elements most likely to achieve them. Indeed, emissions trading is especially appropriate for dealing with GHGs. Greenhouse gas emissions mix uniformly and remain in the atmosphere for a long time. Thus, it matters little where or when the emissions are reduced, as long as the required cumulative reduction is made. This characteristic of GHG emissions eliminates the concerns about emission location that have limited the scope of emissions trading in some other programs.

Understanding the lessons from the prior (and ongoing) experience with emissions trading will be important as the use of emissions trading for climate change expands. These lessons apply not only to the policy makers who will design and implement the programs but to private firms that will need to determine their strategy for taking advantage of the flexibility offered by emissions trading. Indeed, taking maximum advantage of this flexibility will enable firms to improve their profits—relative to less flexible regulatory approaches—and at the same time allow will allow the trading programs to achieve cost-saving and environmental objectives.

Notes

1. Sections of this chapter draw on various previous papers and reports, including (1) David Harrison Jr., "Tradable Permits for Air Pollution Control: The United States Experience," in *Domestic Tradable Permit Systems for Environmental Management: Issues and Challenges,* J.P. Barde and T. Jones, eds. (Paris: Organization for Economic Cooperation and Development, 1999; (2) David Harrison, Jr. and Daniel B. Radov. *Evaluation of Alternative Initial Allocation Mechanisms in a European Union Greenhouse Gas Emissions Allowance Trading Scheme.* Report prepared for the European Commission, Directorate-General Environment (Cambridge, MA: NERA, March, 2002); (3) David Harrison Jr., "Tradable Permit Programs for Air Quality and Climate Change," in *International Yearbook of Environmental and Resource Economics,* Volume VI, Tom Tietenberg and Henk Folmer, eds. (London: Edward Elgar, 2002); (4) A. Denny Ellerman, Paul Joskow, and David Harrison, Jr. *Emissions Trading in the U.S.: Experience, Lessons, and Considerations for Greenhouse Gases.* (Arlington, VA: Pew Center on Global Climate Change, May, 2003); (5) and David Harrison Jr., Steve Sorrell, Daniel Radov, and Per Klevnas, *Interactions of Greenhouse Gas Emissions Allowance Trading with Green and White Certificate Schemes.* Report prepared for the European Commission, Directorate-General Environment. (Boston: NERA Economic Consulting, November 14, 2005). The views are those of the authors and not necessarily those of the other co-authors or the sponsoring organizations.

2. See David Harrison Jr., S. Todd Schatzki, Thomas Wilson and Erik Haites, *Critical Issues in International Greenhouse Gas Emissions Trading: Setting Baselines for Credit-Based Trading Programs—Lessons Learned from Relevant Experience* (Palo Alto, CA: Electric Power Research Institute, Inc., 2000).

3. Harrison (2002), op. cit.

4. In the context of GHG emissions, averaging programs sometimes are referred to using other terms, including "intensity-based programs," "rate-based programs" and "relative targets."

5. Derived from Harrison (1999) and Ellerman et al. (2003), op. cit.

6. The twelve are the six New England states (Maine, New Hampshire, Vermont, Massachusetts, Rhode Island, and Connecticut) and the six Mid-Atlantic States (New York, New Jersey, Pennsylvania, Maryland, Delaware, and Virginia).

7. Technically, these phases are the second and third of a three-phase program. The first phase consisted of re-labeling existing technology-based requirements and did not involve emissions trading.

8. Alex Farrell, "The NOx Budget: A Look at the First Year," *Electricity Journal* (March 2000), 83-92.

9. Although CAIR strengthens the cap on emissions from power plants only in Eastern states, the higher allowance prices give power plants across the country an incentive to reduce air emissions beyond levels of reduction without CAIR. Emission reductions at Colstrip are already being achieved because it has a flue gas desulfurization ("SO_2 scrubber") system.

10. 70 *Federal Register* 25228.

11. U.S. Environmental Protection Agency, *Acid Rain Program: 2004 Progress Report* (Washington, DC: EPA, October 2005).

12. This section draws heavily on Ellerman et al. (2003).

13. See A. Denny Ellerman, Richard Schmalensee, Paul L. Joskow, Juan Pablo Montero, and Elizabeth Bailey, *Markets for Clean Air: The U.S. Acid Rain Program* (Cambridge, UK: Cambridge University Press, 2000). Much of the cost savings from spatial trading and from banking are due to intra-utility trading, i.e., trading of allowances among units under common ownership. Ellerman et al. (2000) note (pp. 154-161) that in the first three years of Phase I, from 25 to 30 percent of the allowances needed to cover emissions at affected units with emissions greater than the allowance allocation came from sources external to the utility, or by inter-utility trading.

14. Curtis P. Carlson, Dallas Burtraw, Maureen Cropper, and Karen Palmer. "SO_2 Control by Electric Utilities: What are the Gains from Trade?" *Journal of Political Economy,* CVIII, 6 (2000), 1292-1326 develops estimates of cost savings for Phase I and Phase II years. For 1995 (Phase I), they estimate gains from trade equal to 13 percent of the "No Trading" costs. In 2005 (Phase II), they estimate that overall compliance costs will be reduced by about 37 percent relative to "No Trading" costs. These estimates are similar to those based upon an econometric model in Carlson. See also Robert N. Stavins, "What can we learn from the grand policy experiment? Lessons from SO_2 allowance trading," *Journal of Economic Perspectives,* XII, 3 (Summer 1998), 69-88 for a review of the SO_2 program.

15. Potential cost savings of as much as 95 percent have been estimated for some theoretically possible emissions trading programs (Tom Tietenberg. *Environmental and Natural Resource Economics,* 5th ed. (Reading, MA: Addison Wesley Longman, 2000). Note that a confusion of allowance prices with average incurred costs led official Administration spokesmen to claim cost savings of 90 percent for Title IV (Anne E. Smith, Jeremy Platt and A. Denny Ellerman, *The Costs of Reducing Utility SO_2 Emissions—Not as Low as You Might Think.* MIT/CEEPR Working Paper 98-010 (August 1998).

16. David Harrison, Jr., and Albert Nichols, *An Economic Analysis of the RECLAIM Trading Program for the South Coast Air Basin* (Cambridge, MA: NERA, March 1992).

17. An ancillary benefit is the significant improvement in the quality of environmental data that results from the monitoring requirements of emissions trading programs. Typically, emissions are not monitored under command-and-control regulation since compliance is determined by inspection to ensure that (1) the mandated equipment is installed and working or (2) the mandated practices are being followed. The information obtained from monitoring under trading programs should contribute to better understanding of and solutions to remaining environmental problems.

18. See Ellerman et al. (2000), op. cit.

19. Byron Swift, "How Environmental Laws Work: An Analysis of the Utility Sector's Response to Regulation of Nitrogen Oxides and Sulfur Dioxide under the Clean Air Act," *Tulane Environmental Law Journal,* XIV, 2 (2001), 309-425.

20. Suzi Kerr and Richard Newell, *Policy-Induced Technology Adoption: Evidence from the U.S. Lead Phasedown.* RFF Discussion Paper 01-14 (Washington, DC: Resources for the Future, May 2001).

21. Many economists contend that in theory an emissions tax would be more appropriate for dealing with greenhouse gases, although there is agreement that a tax is not likely to be politically feasible (see, e.g., William Pizer, "The Optimal Choice of Climate Change Policy in the Presence of Uncertainty." *Resource and Energy Economics,* XXI, 3-4 (1999), 255-287; Michael Hoel and Larry Karp, "Taxes and Quotas for a Stock Pollutant with Multiplicative Uncertainty." *Journal of Public Economics,* LXXXII, 1 (2001), 91-114; and Willam D. Nordhaus, *Life after Kyoto: Alternative Approaches to Global Warming Policies,* National Bureau of Economic Research, Working Paper 11889 (Cambridge, MA: NBER, December 2005)).

22. This point about the indifference to the timing of emissions reductions within some control program does not imply that the initiation of some program to control GHG emissions is also a matter of indifference.

23. In addition to allowances allocated by each Member State, allowances may also enter the Scheme through the "Linking Directive" (COM 2003/403). This allows emissions credits generated through the Flexible Mechanisms of the Kyoto Protocol—Joint Implementation (JI) and the Clean Development Mechanism (CDM)—to be valid for compliance within the EU ETS.

24. Auctioning was limited to a maximum of 5 percent for Phase I and 10 percent for Phase II.

25. Program design issues are presented in Pete V. Domenici and Jeff Bingaman, *Design Elements of a Mandatory Market-Based Greenhouse Gas Regulatory System.* White Paper of the Senate Committee on Energy and Natural Resources (February 2006).

26. George W. Bush, Speech at the National Oceanic and Atmospheric Administration (February 14, 2002).

27. National Commission on Energy Policy, *Ending the Energy Stalemate* (Washington, DC: NCEP, December 2004).

28. See William Pizer, *The Case for Intensity Targets,* Resources for the Future, Discussion Paper No. 05-02 (Washington, DC: RFF, January 2005).

29. See, for example, Martin L. Weitzman, "Prices vs. Quantities," *Review of Economic Studies,* XLI, 4 (1974) 477-491 and William Pizer, *Optimal Choice of Policy Instrument and Stringency under Uncertainty: The Case of Climate Change* (Washington, DC: Resources for the Future, March 3, 1997).

30. See Ellerman, Joskow, and Harrison, op. cit.

31. See Barbara Buchner, Carlo Carraro, and A. Denny Ellerman (editors), *Allocation in the European Emissions Trading Scheme: Rights, Rents, and Fairness* (Cambridge, UK: Cambridge University Press, forthcoming).

32. David Newbery, *Climate Change Policy and its Effect on Market Power in the Gas Market,* University of Cambridge Electricity Policy Research Group Working Paper No. 05/10 (Cambridge, UK: EPRG, November 10, 2005).

33. Harrison, Sorrell, Radov, and Klevnas. Op. cit.

34. *Expressing the sense of the Senate regarding the conditions for the United States becoming a signatory to any international agreement on greenhouse gas emissions under the United Nations Framework Convention on Climate Change.* Senate Resolution 98, 105th Congress, First Session (Washington, DC: July 25, 1997).

35. William Pizer, *Climate Policy Design under Uncertainty,* Resources for the Future Discussion Paper No. 05-44 (Washington, DC: RFF, October 2005).

36. See David Harrison, Jr., Daniel Radov, Per Klevnas, and Andrew Foss, *Effects of the European Union Emissions Trading Scheme on Electricity Prices,* Report prepared for the Electric Power Research Institute, Inc. (Boston: NERA Economic Consulting, November 29, 2005).

37. Henry D. Jacoby and A. Denny Ellerman, *The Safety Valve and Climate Policy,* MIT Joint Program on the Science and Policy of Climate Change Report No. 83. (Cambridge, MA: MIT, July 2002).

38. See David Harrison, Jr., Per Klevnas, Daniel Radov and Andrew Foss, *Interactions of Cost-Containment Measures and Linking of Greenhouse Gas Emissions Cap-and-Trade Programs,* Report prepared for the Electric Power Research Institute, Inc. (Boston: NERA Economic Consulting, December 2006).

39. See, for example, Robert N. Stavins, "Forging a More Effective Global Climate Treaty," Environment (December 2004), 23-30.

III

MARKET POWER

INTRODUCTION TO MARKET POWER

Michael B. Rosenzweig

The chapters in this section deal with issues related to market power in the electricity industry. It seems appropriate, even necessary, to discuss at the start the ambiguities associated with the phrase "market power" and to set out our perspective on market power in the electricity industry.

What is market power? Stated perhaps too simply, market power is often conceptualized as *any* ability for a supplier to affect the market price.[1] A supplier with market power is not a price taker. One measure of market power that is often employed is that the market price exceeds the "competitive level" (*i.e.,* the marginal cost of the marginal producer). Our view is that if this definition of market power is applied strictly in practice, it will lead to excess regulatory intervention in markets and thus inefficient outcomes. We believe that market power should only be a matter for regulatory intervention if its exercise is significant and sustained.[2] In the extreme, if no deviation of price from marginal cost is tolerated in the electricity industry because electricity is deemed so important to the public welfare, then the concept of relying on markets to discipline the supply segment of the industry is fatally flawed. In the real world, even competitive markets do not achieve that high standard. Trying to achieve such a standard can only result in overly intrusive and ultimately inefficient intervention in the market.

We should explain why this issue needs to be addressed for the electricity industry. First, a determination that market power exists has profound implications for those alleged to possess it. For example, in US electricity markets, the Federal Energy Regulatory Commission must find that a supplier lacks market power before the supplier is allowed to sell wholesale electricity at market-based rates. Further, any suppliers alleged to possess market power face the threat of price caps and other restrictions on their participation in that market, restrictions that may prevent them from earning a breakeven rate of return. Second, how one defines the pricing behaviour that is indicative of market power plays a key role in how efficiently electricity markets can operate. For example, the typical reaction to difficulties in some markets, particularly the dramatic events in California, is to control the potential exercise of market power by routinely imposing various extra-market mechanisms. These mechanisms include market monitors and automatic mitigation procedures. They all impose costs and constraints on a market that can reduce how efficiently the market functions.

In theory, any deviation from the typical competitive benchmark—price equals marginal cost—is a sign that market power is being exercised. In the real world, however, at any instant in time, price may deviate from marginal cost for a variety of reasons unrelated to a supplier's ability to exercise significant market power over the intermediate or long term.

For example, the simplistic definition of market power does not distinguish between short-run market power and long-run market power. George Hay argues that it is important to distinguish between the two: "The former ... means that there are no good substitutes *at present* ... A firm with [short-run] market power, however, will see its ability to maintain high prices eroded reasonably quickly..."[3] For example, temporary shortages in supply from an unexpected spike in demand or an unexpected outage at a generating facility may allow suppliers to charge prices above the short-run marginal cost of the marginal producer. In these situations, suppliers may be able to affect price in the short term, resulting in market prices above the "competitive level." But economic theory is clear that these types of short-term price increases, in an otherwise competitive market, provide a mechanism to allocate temporarily scarce resources and also provide a signal that new entry may be appropriate over the longer term that will dissipate the deviation from the competitive benchmark. Regulating markets or participant behavior in response to temporary supply and demand imbalances is inefficient if it suppresses the very price signal that leads to an efficient resolution of the underlying resource imbalance.

Moreover, the simplistic definition of market power typically assumes any large player in an industry possesses market power. A large player in a market may have achieved that position in a variety of ways. It may have achieved that position by being the most efficient supplier. It may have achieved that position by being in an industry that is a natural monopoly or is faced with barriers to entry. Or it may have achieved that position by being engaged in various anticompetitive practices such as collusion or predatory pricing. Since a goal of markets is efficiency, it is not economically sensible to restrict entities that acquired their size in the industry by demonstrating greater skill or lower cost. In the other cases, regulatory intervention is justified.

In order to assess when deviations from the competitive benchmark are signs that regulatory intervention is required to mitigate supplier's exercise of market power, we think three questions should be considered.

- Is the deviation from the competitive benchmark significant enough to warrant concern?
- Is the deviation from the competitive benchmark sustainable?
- Is the industry structure such that there may be barriers to entry?

If the answer to any of the three is "no", then the price deviation from the competitive benchmark should not be automatically interpreted as an exercise of market power that warrants regulatory intervention.

How do we propose to define market power that warrants regulatory intervention? From our "leading" questions, it should be no surprise that we believe that market power that needs regulatory intervention is characterized by the ability to affect prices in a significant and sustained manner in the absence of barriers to entry. Affecting prices in a significant and sustained manner can be an outgrowth of the industry's market structure and/or anticompetitive behaviour by market participants, such as collusion and/or predatory pricing. Equally important to our definition is what we believe is *not* market power that warrants regulatory intervention: short-term market power that is the result of changes in market conditions or efficient competition.

To make this definition more concrete, the terms "significant" and "sustainable" must relate to measurable criteria. As a simple example, suppose a certain geographic region has a large number of players, each of which submits bids to supply wholesale electricity. Suppose that the hourly market clearing price during the year is $25 per MWh during hours when the market was competitive. Suppose further that during certain hours of the year some players may be able to exercise market power, which, if exercised, would result in a market clearing price above $25 per MWh. Whether regulatory intervention is warranted in those hours in which some players may be able to exercise market power depends on:

- **How frequently market power can be exercised:** A handful of hours a year can have a very different implication for the merits of regulatory intervention than 50 percent of the hours in a year.
- **How predictable are the times in which market power can be exercised:** Knowing that the hours in which market power can be

exercised are always hot summer days can have a very different implication for the merits of regulatory intervention than if the hours are scattered randomly throughout the year.

- **How significant is the price increase that results from the exercise of market power:** Knowing that the price increase is only 5 percent greater than the competitive price can have a very different implication for the merits of regulatory intervention than if the price increase is 100 percent greater than the competitive price.
- **How high are the barriers to entry in the market:** Knowing that entry is easy and would be likely in response to a price increase has a very different implication for the merits of regulatory intervention than if entry is difficult.

Our proposal is that events that are infrequent (*e.g.,* occur less than 5 percent of the time), unpredictable, and do not increase market clearing prices above their competitive level by more than 5 percent are not in need of regulatory intervention.[4] Importantly, if markets have no significant barriers to entry, then sustained market power is unlikely to be an issue. If market clearing prices are sustained above the market clearing price at which entry would be profitable but does not occur, then suspicions about the exercise of market power are justifiably aroused. If entry occurs, of course, market power will be efficiently mitigated. If these thresholds are exceeded, then further investigation would be warranted to determine to what extent regulatory intervention is necessary to mitigate the price increases. So, for example, in the context of wholesale power markets, we would propose using the entry price for a baseload coal unit as the benchmark entry price. This would avoid issues about how many hours in a year the benchmark unit would operate and also the difficulty of arriving at the "competitive price" and the associated debates over methods and models.

Our approach to defining the conditions that justify mitigating market power by imposing regulatory restrictions can be applied to a variety of situations facing the electric power industry.

First, it clearly is valid for natural monopolies in the electricity sector. It is widely, although perhaps not universally, accepted that there are elements of the electricity sector that are natural monopolies. By definition, a natural monopoly is able to exercise significant and sustained market power, and thus the efficient response to a natural monopoly is to impose regulation. As discussed in another section of this monograph, such regulation should be done in an innovative way in order to provide as much of the discipline and incentives of a competitive market as possible.

Second, our approach applies to transient load pockets. A transient load pocket is a sub-market that forms when the larger market temporarily separates; it is of interest only when suppliers are able to affect the market clearing price in that load pocket. Transient load pockets should not rise to a level warranting regulatory intervention unless the condition is significant and sustained. In addition, any regulatory approach undertaken should ensure that price signals for solving the problem efficiently (e.g., encouraging new entry) are not smothered.

Third, our approach can be applied to droughts in hydro dominant systems. The standard reaction to droughts is to cap prices. To the extent droughts lead to significant and sustained price increases, price caps may prevent the appropriate price signals from being sent that would otherwise encourage new entry of non-hydro generating capacity. While there may be a justification for price caps in order to control uneconomic transfers of wealth or for equity considerations in this situation, using price caps to mitigate temporary market power is not justified.

Finally, our concept can be applied to incomplete electricity market designs. The potential for market power to be exercised is disciplined, in part, when the demand-side of the market is able to adjust its purchasing decisions in reaction to higher prices. Higher prices encourage the demand side of the market to purchase less. We believe that higher prices are often blamed on the exercise of market power, when in fact those prices can be explained by the inability of the demand side to respond to higher prices and discipline suppliers by purchasing less. We will not repeat that discussion here but simply note that the administrative intrusions into power markets in the form of capacity requirements, capacity markets, market monitors, and automatic mitigation mechanisms are attempting to fix the wrong problem in an inefficient and expensive way. The problem is not the exercise of market power; it is flawed design. In these situations, the efficient solution is to fix the market design.

Notes

1. Purchaser market power, in the extreme monopsony, is an important issue but not the focus of this section of the monograph.

2. Others have raised this issue in different regulatory contexts. See, for example, George Hay, "Market Power in Antitrust," *Antitrust Law Journal,* Vol. 60, Issue 3, pp. 807-827.

3. Ibid., p. 818. Emphasis added.

4. A similar type of bright line is employed by the US Department of Justice and the Federal Trade Commission in merger analysis. The Horizontal Merger Guidelines, first published over 20 years ago by the US Department of Justice and the Federal Trade Commission, provide a bright line mechanism for businesses and antitrust practitioners to assess whether a proposed merger is likely to result in market power (see http://www.ftc.gov/bc/docs/ horizmer.htm). While not a tolerance level for a post-transaction price increase, the Guidelines approach seeks to determine whether a proposed merger is likely to result in a small but significant increase in price that is sustained over a non-transitory period of time. In practice, a small but significant increase in price is typically defined as a 5 percent price increase over pre-transaction level prices and a non-transitory period of time is typically defined as two years.

11

MARKET POWER ISSUES IN THE AUSTRALIAN ELECTRICITY MARKET

Ann Whitfield

In common with electricity industry restructurings around the world, Australia's competition reforms and its formation of the National Electricity Market (NEM) resulted in the disaggregation of the formerly vertically integrated State electricity businesses and horizontal disaggregation in the competitive generation and retail sectors. Since restructuring, considerable merger and acquisition activity has begun to reverse the disaggregation restructuring, and the trend towards further consolidation is likely to continue. As a result, market power issues are becoming increasingly important in the Australian electricity market. To date, however, the Australian experience in analysing market power in the electricity sector indicates a need for a more rigorous approach to the requisite analyses, including the development of quantitative modelling approaches that will be widely accepted.

Background

The competition reforms undertaken in Australia and the formation of the NEM resulted in disaggregating (frequently referred to as unbundling) the formerly vertically integrated State electricity businesses into separate distribution, transmission, generation, and retailing elements. In the competitive generation and retail sectors, horizontal disaggregation (ensuring sufficiently widespread ownership) was intended to address market power concerns—although the extent of horizontal disaggregation differed across states. In most states, most of electricity sector assets have been corporatised but remain in the hands of the public sector. In contrast, Victoria privatised its electricity sector assets,[1] and initially entrenched the disaggregation of the sector in legal cross-ownership restrictions to prevent subsequent vertical or horizontal re-aggregation.[2]

Since restructuring, however, there has been considerable merger and acquisition activity, influenced in part by the relaxation of the Victorian cross-ownership restrictions. Cross-ownership has been permitted since 2001 in Victoria if the Australian Competition and Consumer Commission (ACCC) formally or informally approve the merger.[3] The ACCC, Australia's anti-trust body, assesses all mergers under §50 of the Trade Practices Act 1974, which prohibits mergers when they are likely to result in a substantial lessening of competition in a market. As interpreted by the ACCC for the electricity sector, this standard remains a work in progress with several challenging questions still unresolved.

Two recent mergers in the NEM have raised competition issues, the first in relation to vertical aggregation of generation and retail businesses and the second in relation to horizontal aggregation within the generation sector. In 2003, the Australian Gas Light Company (AGL), which owns a retail electricity business in Victoria and has substantial retail interests elsewhere in the NEM, proposed to acquire a stake in Loy Yang A, a Victorian base load generator. The ACCC opposed the acquisition on competition grounds. AGL took the case to the Federal Court and Justice Robert French found[4] that the merger would not be expected to result in a substantial lessening of competition and could proceed.

In 2005, China Light and Power (CLP) proposed to acquire the generation interests of Singapore Power, an Australian non-regulated energy asset. If successful, CLP would add peak load generation to its existing base load portfolio. The ACCC investigated and announced on 30 March 2005 that the horizontal merger did not give rise to competition concerns, and it would not intervene.

In its decision on the CLP merger, the ACCC concluded that it was "acutely aware of increasing consolidation in the energy sector. The ACCC remains firmly committed to close scrutiny of all acquisitions that involve significant vertical integration in energy supply chains or horizontal aggregation at any level."[5]

The ACCC's commitment to close scrutiny of vertical and horizontal aggregation highlights the need for a robust and generally accepted framework for the analysis of the competition impact of such mergers. The analysis of merger activity in the two substantive cases considered to date still leaves open important questions of how market power should be assessed in the electricity sector, and in particular:

1. What weight should be placed on standard concentration ratios in the analysis of generation mergers?
2. In competition policy analysis in the electricity sector, how should the market be defined and to what extent is it reasonable to identify temporal sub-markets?
3. What role can quantitative analysis be expected to play?

Use of Standard Concentration Ratios

The ACCC's general merger guidelines contain safe harbour provisions that set out concentration thresholds below which the ACCC is unlikely to take any further interest in a merger[6] because considers it unlikely that the merger would substantially lessen competition. However, the merger is not covered by the safe harbour provisions if, post-merger, the combined market share of the four (or fewer) largest firms is 75 percent or more (the so-called CR4 threshold) and the merged firm will supply at least 15 percent of the relevant market. The ACCC will want to further consider such a merger proposal to satisfy itself that it will not result in a substantial lessening of competition. The ACCC will also examine a merger if the merged firm will supply 40 per cent or more of the market.

However, analyses of the two electricity sector merger cases in Australia to date and related debates on generator market power in the NEM have concluded that standard concentration ratio analysis may be of limited value in the market power analyses in generation markets. The ACCC itself has stated that it "is very mindful that the same conclusions that might be drawn from concentration measures in other industries cannot be drawn from concentration measures in electricity generation."[7] Strategic combinations of generation assets can confer the ability to profitably affect price, even at relatively low concentration ratios because of several key factors: (1) electricity is non-storable, (2) demand is highly inelastic, (3) demand response capacity is lacking, and (4) a large change in price can be achieved through withholding generation capacity at certain times (especially in the presence of transmission constraints).

And indeed, the approach taken in analysing generation mergers internationally confirms the limited applicability of standard concentration ratio analysis. In Europe, in the case of Vattenfall's acquisition of Elsam and Energi E2 assets[8] the European Commission stated that:

In this particular case, and in the context of analysing the effect of the concentration on the market for electricity, the Commission has also applied other types of analysis than calculation of market shares, which in its view in this case arguably provide for a better way of assessing the likely effect of the transaction on consumers.

Similarly, in the US, there have been calls for the FERC to consider using its own simulation models in addition to its standard market definition and concentration ratio analysis.[9]

The implication is that the standard CR4 threshold in the ACCC's safe harbour provisions is of limited use for screening generation mergers. At the very least, the ACCC should carefully consider the definition of the 'generation market' used for any concentration ratio, including such temporal limitations as identifying peak and off-peak markets.[10]

More generally, the peculiar characteristics of the electricity market suggest a likely need to directly analyse the expected changes in the ability and incentive of generators to affect prices in the NEM by withholding capacity, even where concentration ratios remain low. And this step suggests the need for a clear analytical framework for assessing generation mergers, encompassing the impact of interconnector constraints and hedging contracts on generators' incentives.

Market Definition

The question of market definition in Australia's analysis of generator market power also remains to be definitively resolved. The NEM is a wholesale market for electricity covering six interconnected regions. The regions are state-based, and a spot price is determined for each region on a half-hourly basis via the wholesale electricity exchange operated by the National Electricity Market Management Company (NEMMCO). When the interconnectors are not constrained, the spot price differs between regions only by regional loss factors. When the interconnectors between regions become constrained, regional spot prices differ. It is common for generators and retailers to enter into hedging agreements (i.e., derivatives contracts) against the spot price, in order to manage the risk of uncertain future spot price movements.

In the case of AGL's acquisition of Loy Yang A, the ACCC found that the wholesale electricity market was regional and that, due to the presence of interconnector constraints, the relevant market in the AGL case was confined to Victoria. It also determined that the hedging market was separate from the electricity wholesale market operated by NEMMCO.

In contrast, Justice French concluded that there was a NEM-wide market for generation,[11] and that hedging activity should be considered as being in the same market as the operation of the wholesale electricity exchange:

> The geographic market is not to be determined by a view frozen in time or by observations based on short-run timescales. The NEM is an evolving market that is intended and designed to operate as a single market for electricity throughout the regions it covers. Transient price separations between those regions may define temporally limited submarkets, which can be referred to for the purposes of competition analysis.... In my opinion...having regard to the structure of the market and the extent to which its major participants operate across regional boundaries, I am satisfied that there is one NEM-wide geographic market for the supply of electricity, and associated with that entry into electricity derivates contracts.[12]

Later, in its analysis of CLP's proposed acquisition of Singapore Power's generation assets, the ACCC again diverged from Justice French's view that the relevant market was the entire NEM. The ACCC defined the appropriate market for the proposed CLP merger as the market for the supply of wholesale electricity in Victoria and also in the combination of South Australia and Victoria.[13] While noting that this definition differed from Justice French's broader definition, the ACCC opined that its definition better addressed the competition issues arising in the case, which were related to the horizontal acquisition of generating capacity, rather than the vertical aggregation issues in the AGL case. The ACCC's conclusion on market definition was driven by its view that interconnectors can be constrained, and that this can have a significant effect on industry behaviour:

> The ACCC also took into consideration the existence of times when even if the interconnectors are not constrained, the fact that they are able to become constrained can have a significant effect on industry behaviour. Use of data solely relating to the frequency and severity of interconnector constraints for the purposes of geographic market definition may not give adequate recognition to the ability of players in one region to exercise market power up to

the point where inter-regional flows of electricity through the interconnectors threaten to become a competitive constraint.[14]

In short, the ACCC concluded that the *ability* of generators to cause interconnector constraints might enable them to exercise market power in obtaining more favourable outcomes in the hedging market; the generators might not need to actually act in a way that would result in an interconnector constraint.

However, in his AGL decision, Justice French had considered whether (1) the opportunities to 'spike' the pool price with a view to increasing forward contract prices and (2) the fact that a generator responds to those opportunities from time to time constituted evidence of market power. He found, contrary to the ACCC:

> There is here a distinction to be drawn between what was referred to as 'transient market power' and 'persistent but intermittent' market power. It may also be that that distinction is able to be reflected in the concept of temporal sub-markets and what is elsewhere described as the inter-temporal variation of market power.
>
> ....
>
> I do not accept that such inter-temporal market power reflects more than an intermittent phenomenon nor does it reflect a longrun phenomenon having regard to the possibilities of new entry.[15]

It is instructive to consider how other jurisdictions approach the definition of market power in the electricity sector. US regulatory precedent would support a market definition narrower than the entire NEM, as the FERC merger guidelines define separate markets for peak and off-peak periods. Specifically, the FERC endorsed the Federal Trade Commission's view that:

> [B]ecause transmission constraints may bind during peak demand periods... applicants should justify the use of a broad geographic market with evidence that the market definition remains viable during peak times. If not... the market definitions should be narrowed for peak periods.[16]

In an analysis of market power for a generation portfolio in the PJM market,[17] the FERC accepted both the proposition that there were many geographic and load-based markets within PJM and the possibility that the generators could act strategically to cause some transmission constraints within PJM to bind.[18]

In Vattenfall's acquisition of the Elsam and Energi E2 assets,[19] the European Commission considered Vattenfall's argument that the market for generation of electricity should be defined as at least pan-Nordic in scope, but found three major reasons against the broader market definition. First, the Commission noted that, as a result of congestion of interconnections in the Nordic region, "there are a certain number of hours during which the behaviour of dominant firms within a certain Nord Pool area is insufficiently constrained by the competitive dynamics of the neighbouring areas."[20] Second, the variation in the number of congested hours results in variations in the level of price between each pair of countries in the region and over time (both intra-day and longer term). Therefore, while the average annual price difference in a region may be low, price differences may be higher between certain countries and at certain times. Third, the Commission's market investigation indicated that "congestion can be foreseen (and might be influenced) by market participants, and that congested periods between two areas are not a transitory but rather a recurrent phenomenon."[21]

Based on these observations the Commission found that a potential conclusion would be to define several separate markets, one for each configuration of congestion pattern between the two countries in question. Alternatively, the market definition could define a market for each price area with producers in other regions treated as sources of immediate supply side substitution.

From the above discussion, it is apparent that Justice French's thinking in the AGL case differs from the subsequent market analysis by the ACCC in electricity merger cases and from market analysis in the European and US electricity sectors. It is a further example showing that the analysis in Australia to date remains incomplete. As a result, both potential merging parties and regulatory agencies are uncertain about the courts' future treatment of key market definition questions.

Use of Quantitative Analysis

Because it is recognized that strategic combinations of generation assets can confer the ability to profitably affect price, even at very low concentration ratios, some way to assess the scope and incentives for such behaviour will inevitably be a part of assessing market power in the generation market. Therefore, some form of quantitative modelling of the market and the pre- and post-merger outcomes is probably inevitable.

Justice French, however, was dismissive of the relevance of much of economic modelling of the market presented during the AGL v ACCC case:

> The Court has been exposed to sophisticated econometric evidence seeking to mathematically model bidding and pricing behaviour in relevant markets. It has been necessary, paying due respect to the amount of thought and expertise which underlies those contending positions, to keep firmly in mind that the Court's decision must be based upon the best view it can form of the commercial realities of risks, incentives and behaviour and so on of the operation of the competitive process with and without the proposed acquisition.

And further:

> But in a market, which is globally regulated through a central auction based pricing and dispatch mechanism subject to differing regional regulatory regimes defined by State law and affected by a variety of external variables affecting both supply and demand, the past and future of pricing strategies by market participants are not to be judged by econometric models alone, however sophisticated. The Court is concerned to make judgements about competition in a living commercial setting whose actors operate upon conjectures and predictions that may prove to be wholly or partly incorrect and that may be, from an economists perspective, irrational.[22]

Notwithstanding the views expressed by Justice French, quantitative assessment is well established in analysing market power in the electricity sector in the other markets where NERA works, particularly in the US and Europe.

In the US, mergers must be approved by at least three separate authorities. The US Department of Justice (DOJ) has general responsibility for the approval of all mergers in all industries, and the Federal Energy Regulatory Commission (FERC) has specific responsibility for mergers involving wholesale electric markets. The regulatory authorities in the states directly affected by the merger also have a say. The DOJ merger guidelines are explicitly mirrored in the FERC 1996 Merger Policy

Statement (MPS), which gives additional detail on the sorts of analyses that FERC expects. Applicants typically use transportation models and sensitivity or scenario analysis to explore market definition outcomes under different assumptions about key parameters. The MPS does not require that any particular model or modelling approach be used. Its Appendix A sets out general methodology, and its Appendix B specifies data sources available at the time the MPS was issued to be used in future competitive analysis.

In Europe, quantitative analysis has been used in a number of instances, both in descriptions of a static market and with regard to merger analyses. Supply Function Equilibrium (SFE) modelling has been used to predict the outcome of proposed mergers in three prominent cases dealing with competition policy: *Sydkraft/Graninge* before the European Commission,[23] *Nuon/Reliant* before the Netherlands competition authority (NMa)[24] and Elsam/NESA before the Danish Competition Authority (DCA).[25] Quantitative modelling has also been used to analyse whether generators have the potential to exercise market power. The Scandinavian competition authorities published a report[26] in 2003 that concluded that, on the basis of an SFE model of the Nordic electricity spot market, there is potential for Nordic generators to exercise market power.

The analysis of market power also needs to be considered in a hypothetical, or 'what if', context. Given the existence of the hedging market, the exercise of market power by generators needs to be considered in terms of the *potential* to affect outcomes in the electricity market, as well as the *actual* outcomes in that market. The ability of the generator to affect outcomes in the electricity market gives it the power to command higher prices in the hedging market even though the observed outcomes in the electricity market will be the same. The inescapable conclusion is that this type of analysis calls for the use of quantitative modelling techniques.

However, recognizing the validity of Justice's French's comment about the complexity of the modelling presented in AGL, it is important that quantitative modelling does not become a 'black box'. The assumptions incorporated into the models and the outcomes that result all need to be explicable in terms of the commercial drivers or incentives and the behaviour of parties in relation to those incentives. With that caveat, it is likely that the further exploration of quantitative modelling approaches to market power would encourage the development of a more comprehensive and rigorous assessment of market power issues within the electricity market in Australia.

Conclusion

Market power issues in the electricity market in Australia are becoming increasingly important as acquisitions and new investment see a reconsolidation in generation and retail activities. This trend can be expected to continue.

A rigorous approach to the analysis of market power issues must to established, given the peculiar characteristics of the electricity market that make more traditional approaches to competition policy analysis less applicable to it. The US and Europe offer invaluable experience that could be drawn upon in developing such an approach.

Notes

1. Electricity sector assets have also been privatized in South Australia, via long-term concession agreements.

2. Section 68 of the Electricity Industry Act 2000 (Victoria) prohibits a distribution, generation, or transmission licensee from holding a controlling or substantial interest in another distribution, generation, or transmission licensee ('prohibited interests').

3. Section 68(8) of the Electricity Industry Act 2000 empowers the Essential Services Commission in Victoria to determine that it is satisfied that the ACCC has considered an acquisition and that the ACCC has notified the person that it does not intend to take action in relation to the acquisition under section 50 of the Trade Practices Act 1974. In such cases the proposed acquisition is not considered to be a 'prohibited interest'. See also Electricity Industry (Prohibited Interests) Regulations 2003.

4. *Australian Gas Light Company v Australian Competition and Consumer Commission,* 19 December 2003.

5. ACCC, *China Light & Power's Proposed Acquisition of the Australian non-regulated energy assets of Singapore Power, Public Competition Assessment,* 14 April 2005, p. 9.

6. ACCC Merger *Guidelines,* June 1999, p. 44. However the ACCC reserves the right to still investigate the merger if, for example, it disagrees with the market definition (and therefore the calculation of concentration ratios) submitted by the parties.

7. ACCC, CLP, p. 8.

8. Case NO COMP/M.3867—Vattenfall/Elsam and Energi E2 assets Notification of 18 October 2005 pursuant to Article 4 of Council Regulation NO 139/2004, Paragraph 34. In this case the Commission utilised a merger simulation model to assess the effect of the merger on electricity prices.

9. See for example, D. Moss, Electricity Mergers, Economic Analysis and Consistency: Why FERC needs to change its Approach, American Antitrust Institute Working Paper 04-02, January 2005, pp. 28-29.

10. This is considered further in section 3.

11. Note, at the time of the French Decision, Tasmania had not become a member of the NEM.

12. AGL v ACCC, p. 387.

13. ACCC, CLP, p. 4. The CLP acquisition also included the gas and electricity retailing assets of Singapore Power, and the ACCC public competition assessment therefore also considered the appropriate definition of the retailing market. This is not discussed in this Chapter.

14. Ibid.

15. AGL v ACCC, pp. 456, 493.

16. FERC Final Order, 18 CFR Part 33 (FERC Order No. 642), pp. 33-34.

17. The PJM market covers all or parts of Delaware, Illinois, Indiana, Kentucky, Maryland, Michigan, New Jersey, North Carolina, Ohio, Pennsylvania, Tennessee, Virginia, West Virginia, and the District of Columbia.

18. FERC, Order *Approving PJM Supporting Companies' Request For Market-Based Pricing Authority,* March 1999, pp. 16-17.

19. Case NO COMP/M.3867—Vattenfall/Elsam and Energi E2 Assets Notification of 18 October 2005 pursuant to Article 4 of Council Regulation NO 139/2004.

20. Case NO COMP/M.3867, Paragraph 25.

21. Case NO COMP/M.3867, Paragraph 27.

22. AGL v ACCC, pp. 9, 498.

23. Case No COMP/M.3268, 29 September 2003, available at http://europa.eu.int/comm/competition/mergers/cases/decisions/m3268_en.pdf.

24. Both a Cournot simulation model and an SFE model were used. The NMa's decision after its phase II investigation is available at http://www.nmanet.nl/nl/Images/11_25355.pdf. The parties appealed the remedies imposed by the NMa, and the Court of Rotterdam annulled the NMa's merger decision in May 2005.

25. The DCA's decision is available at http://www.ks.dk/publikationer/konkurrence/2004/elsam-nesa.

26. Report of the Nordic Competition Authorities (June 2003), *A powerful competition policy: Towards a more coherent competition policy in the Nordic markets for electric power.* Available at http://www.kkv.se/bestall/pdf/rap_power-comp2003_summary.pdf. For a rough description of the model see Eltra (2003) available at http://www.eltra.dk/media(15185,1033)/Beskrivelse_af_Eltra%27s_Markedsmo del_MARS-GB-okt03.pdf.

12

THE ASSESSMENT OF MARKET POWER IN EUROPE'S WHOLESALE POWER MARKETS[1]

Fernando Barrera

Introduction

The assessment of market power in the wholesale electricity market in Europe is prone to inconsistency and error. Reasons for the inconsistency include (1) the number of countries and institutions, (2) their different degrees of independence from political powers, (3) the public-service character of the industry, (4) the role of the state in European countries, and (5) the changing paradigm in European electricity markets. The mistakes arise from not fully understanding the particularities of the electricity market or the importance of market rules when applying the traditional tools of competition policy analysis to this industry.

In the European Union (EU), antitrust cases may have a country or a common-market dimension, depending on the relative national market share of the undertakings' business. Although the institutional boundaries of an antitrust case are well established in the EU by the Council Regulation (EC) Nº 139/2004 on the Control of Concentration between Undertakings and although the assessment of market power follows some general principles, practice might not follow the regulations. As the degree of independence varies across Member Country Competition Authorities (MCCAs), treatment across jurisdictions and between countries and the European Commission may also differ.

In the case of agreements and abuse of dominant position, the member state is, in practice, applying European Commission (EC) legislation,[2] so there is less scope for inconsistent treatment. But in country decisions on mergers, although the decisions are generally based on European legislation, the authorizing legislation is national. The merging parties may therefore argue for the case to be analysed by the EC or by the

MCCA, depending on the independence or previous record of the MCCA.[3] Hence, the rules for deciding which authority has jurisdiction over the case become very important.

As cross-country operations are more common and the decisions of the Court of First Instance[4] become precedent, the opportunities for inconsistent decisions will be reduced. However meanwhile, there is still a great deal of overzealous analysis of market power in Europe, a too-restrictive approach to market definition, and an analysis that ignores how industry rules affect the traditional competition policy analysis.

This essay reviews decisions taken by some member countries and the EC defining the relevant market and assessing market power in the wholesale generation market. It explains possible inconsistencies as well as the problems of using anti-trust techniques without due consideration of the specific nature of the power industry.

Competition Policy in the Power Market

Electricity as a product is normally considered radically different from other products. In particular, its non-storability and the very low elasticity of demand raise the possibility that demand may not intersect supply at some times, forcing the system operator as the default supplier to set the price.[5] As a result, over the years regulators have introduced a number of rules of behavior and price formation. These rules determine the level of competition in the market, making the assessment of the market rules a very important component of competition policy analysis. Normally, the tools of competition policy analysis are applied across sectors without much consideration of the specific characteristics of the sector. In dealing with electricity and other regulated sectors, the analyst must understand the rules in place and how these rules alter the behavior of market agents before conducting traditional analysis. Depending on the rules that are chosen, a given industry structure can have different impacts on industry conduct. Therefore, the usual structure-conduct-performance paradigm requires an additional step: a structure-rules-conduct-performance approach.

For example, the analysis of production offers and prices as a measure of market power will only be useful in markets where prices are set at the intersection of demand and the last accepted production offer. In pay-as-bid markets, production offers reflect the generator's expectation of market price and not its production costs, so the analysis of the gap between production offers and prices is simply an analysis of forecasting accuracy.[6]

Similarly, it has been known since Green and Newbery's 1992 analysis of the British market that the contract position of the generating companies can alter the incentives to manipulate prices in the spot market.[7] Once the company's production is under contract, it has less incentive to profit in the spot market. The contract prices, set in advance, will be the main determinant of the company's revenues, and increases in the contract cover thus dilute the incentives to increase prices in the spot market.[8] Vertical integration between retail sales and wholesale generation has an effect similar to contract cover. An integrated generator with x percent sales being the retail sales of its affiliated retail arm behaves in the same way as a generator with x percent contract cover, so that the higher the retail market share, the lower the incentives to exploit market power in the spot market.

Other market rules that affect the analysis of market power are explicit capacity remuneration systems (that encourage higher reserve margins than in "pure energy" markets), the way imbalances are calculated (whether they discriminate against small producers), the liquidity of the contract market (energy sales by new entrants will be easier in liquid markets), and market transparency.

Failure to acknowledge the existence of these market rules will under or over estimate the degree of market power in the electricity market. Competition authorities need to collect evidence and specific knowledge from the industry before applying the tools of competition policy analysis to an assessment of market power in this industry.

Definition of the Relevant Market

The EC's approach to defining the relevant market is based on a simple sequence that first defines the relevant *product* market and subsequently, the relevant *geographic* market.[9] This framework is generally applied by the MCCAs, though compared to other jurisdictions the number of cases concerning the industry is limited, as markets have only recently been liberalized.[10]

Energy Markets

Wholesale electricity markets encompass the electricity produced at power stations (including imports) for the purpose of sales to retailers, to consumers, or to an organized market. In some cases,[11] the EC has separated this market into (1) the electricity that is sold under competitive conditions (the Conventional Market), and (2) generation that has been subsidized by deliberate government incentives, mainly generation from renewable energy sources.[12]

The EC generally concludes that the wholesale electricity market is, in fact, no larger than the national market. This position is based on the observation that imports in most European countries do not currently exert a strong competitive constraint on national producers, given the limited interconnections between EU countries. The EC considers that the observed differences in the level of prices between neighboring countries constitute evidence of market separation. It stresses that, despite the efforts to harmonize liberalization across the states, wholesale market regulations across the EU are still very heterogeneous, a fact that further contributes to market separation.

However, for certain countries, it is not at all clear that the relevant market is national. In the EDF/AEM/EDISON case,[13] the EC noted the frequent level of congestion on the Italian transmission network. Also, an investigation on the degree of liberalization of the electricity sector in Italy[14] concluded that the wholesale market should be separated into four different regional submarkets: North, Macrosouth (mainland of Italy except for the north and Calabria), Macrosicily (Sicily and Calabria), and Sardinia. This conclusion is supported by a statistical test that quantified the residual demand of each zone[15] and showed that in these regions a hypothetical monopolist would be able to exercise market power for hourly periods, at most. Residual demand curve analysis was developed by Bushnell et al.[16] It identifies a supplier as pivotal when, in a given hour, the available capacity of the remaining generators (including imports) is less than the demand in that hour. The measure of pivotality is the number of hours in a given period that the supplier can be deemed to be necessary for demand.

We do note that the residual demand test itself has problems. It assumes that the fuel used to generate is available at all times and this is not the case for technologies that can only generate when the fuel is available (wind, solar, run-of-river). It would be more accurate to use actual generation rather than capacity. Of greater concern, the index gives the same value to a single megawatt as to all the megawatts of the supplier, and it is clear that, depending on the number of megawatts available, the incentives to exercise market power are very different (varying from none to many). Finally, it is clear that monopolizing a market for a single hour cannot be regarded as a profitable activity (in the sense of sustained exercise of market power) so the authority would need to analyze the number of hours when the test reveals market power.

In contrast to the Italian market, the Nordic competition authorities—Norway, Sweden, Denmark, and Finland—concluded that for most time periods the relevant market includes all four countries.[17] Using 2001 data, the investigation analyzed the relationship between (1) the constraints in the interconnection capacity among their national transmission networks in certain time periods, and (2) the price differentials in the electricity spot markets across the Nordic countries. The study found that, during the time periods in which the capacity constraints of the interconnection were binding, the prices of electricity in the wholesale market differed across the countries in the area. And in those time periods in which there were no congestion problems in the interconnection facilities, the prices of the national spot markets tended to converge. In particular, in the majority of the sample time periods—52 percent—there were no congestion problems in the interconnection facilities, and therefore the spot markets of the Nordic countries cleared at similar prices. The Nordic MCCA concluded that, if the time dimension is considered, the correct geographical definition of the wholesale market for most of the time should not be less than the area encompassing Norway, Denmark, Sweden, and Finland.

Ancillary Services

The ancillary services product market consists of the reserve capacity and other services that the Transmission System Operator requires to meet its obligations for maintaining the quality and reliability of the electricity supply. In general, the EC has decided that the ancillary services are national in scope.[18] Nevertheless, the EC introduces some caveats for certain EU countries on whether the market for these services should be geographically disaggregated, (e.g., the Italian ancillary services market might be considered regional due to the capacity limitations of the transmission network). Like its wholesale energy market, the Italian ancillary service market must be separated into geographical zones (coinciding with the areas that the Italian Transmission System Operator uses for the procurement of such services). Similarly, the Spanish Administrative Competition Court (Tribunal de Defensa de Competencia), in its decision on the proposed merger of ENDESA and IBERDROLA,[19] decided that the ancillary market services in Spain should be divided into different zones, also coinciding with the areas that are used by the Spanish Transmission System Operator to procure the services.

However, many of the transmission constraints in Europe are transient due to entry, ease of removing the constraint, the active role of transmission companies, and the incentives they have to remove the constraint, etc. This transient nature should caution against overly restrictive market definitions like those made in Spain and Italy.

The Assessment of Market Power

In contrast to other industries (e.g., telecoms), the EC has not produced general guidelines for the evaluation of market power in the electricity sector. Nonetheless, the EC's decisions represent an important point of reference for the MCCAs, and an analysis of relevant decisions and reports produced by the EC and the MCCAs provides a general overview of the practice of market power assessment in the electricity sector in Europe. Most market power assessments have been focused on the wholesale electricity market, and these decisions consider that concentration is affected by barriers to entry and by the unilateral and coordinated effects of vertical integration. In addition, some states have attempted the of ex-ante regulation of market power.

Assessing Market Concentration in the Wholesale Electricity Market

The assessment of concentration in the wholesale market relies initially on the calculations of market shares in terms of both production and capacity. These indicators are often combined with data on the technology mix of generation units. Both the composition and the structure of generation assets are used as an insight to evaluate the capability of suspect undertakings to strategically influence the market price, especially in the spot market. For example, the Italian electricity regulator and anti-trust authority reported the market share of ENEL in terms of installed generating capacity based on conventional mid-merit plants (*i.e.,* thermoelectric plants and hydropower in Italy).[20]

The concentration index recommended in the general guidelines of the EC on the assessment of horizontal mergers[21] is the Herfindahl-Hirshman Index (HHI), which indicates differences in market shares and hence concentration. The guidelines refer to the following circumstances:

However, the guidelines claim that the thresholds are only an initial indicator of the absence of competition concerns. Thus, relative concern still exists where the post-merger HHI is greater than 2,000 and the change in the HHI is less than 150, but also where, for example:

Table 1.   *HHI EC Thresholds (merger guidelines)*

Stance	HHI post merger	Change in HHI
No concern	<1,000	Any
No concern	1,000-2,000	< 250
Relative concern	> 2,000	< 150

Source: Guidelines on the assessment of horizontal mergers under the Council Regulation on the control of concentrations between undertakings (2004/C 31/03)

- a merger involves a potential entrant with a small market share;
- merging parties are important innovators and this is not reflected in their market shares;
- there is significant cross-shareholding among the market participants;
- indications of past or ongoing coordination or facilitating practices are present; or
- one of the merging parties has a pre-merger market share of 50 percent or more.

In some cases, MCAAs have criticized this approach, arguing that the indicator has to be adjusted by some additional factors in order to provide a more accurate estimate of concentration. For example, in its comments on the merger guidelines,[22] the Norwegian antitrust authority argued that using HHIs in the electricity sector without adjusting for any measure of capacity might lead to erroneous estimates of market concentration. The anti-trust authority suggested a hypothetical example:

- If two companies, which produce at full capacity, merge and after the transaction do not intend to reduce the combined output level, the unadjusted HHI might overestimate the change in concentration even if the merged entity is producing at the competitive market level.
- Similarly, if the two companies have excess capacity, and after they merge reduce their output, the unadjusted HHI might underestimate the level of concentration.

A joint report[23] by the Nordic Authorities—Norway, Denmark, Sweden and Finland—on applying competition policy to the electricity sector also mentioned the need for adjusting the HHI to include cross-ownership effects. In discussing an example used in the report, the authorities notes:

> External investors with diversified ownership in more than one company in the relevant market would be less inclined to compete aggressively and more inclined to take the profitability of the whole market into consideration.

There are clear problems associated with the EC's use of HHI based on installed capacity. Not all installed capacity translates into a potential to exploit market power. Examples are hydro plants that are limited by their water inflows, wind generation limited by the wind, and gas turbines that, given their high variable costs, operate a limited number of hours. In all these examples, installed capacity is clearly an overestimation of the plant's potential to exploit market power. Thus, however limited the EC's use of the HHI, it is at least preferable to use actual generation as a proxy for market power rather than installed capacity.

Similarly, not all hours of the day are relevant to calculate concentration ratios. Different technologies compete at different parts of the demand curve. The US Federal Energy Regulatory Commission, for example, has developed an alternative structural analysis that differs by demand levels to reflect the fact that storage is not possible and supply has to be adjusted instantaneously.[24]

However, even if generation figures are used, a number of problems remain. What is important in the assessment of market power is the generation that can be profitably withdrawn from the market and, in reality, not all generation can be withdrawn.[25] Nuclear plants are too inflexible to be withdrawn, and due to their low variable costs they tend to operate regardless of market price conditions. The production decisions of run-of-river plants are chiefly determined by water inflows. Combined cycle gas turbines in Europe tend to buy their gas through long-term gas contracts with take or pay clauses of around 70 to 80 percent. Even though these plants are very flexible in their capacity to adjust output, the cost of withdrawing the plant and reducing production is the possibility of failing to comply with their take- or-pay obligations. Although peaking plants in some countries buy their gas or fuel oil in interruptible contracts, the fact that they operate few hours reduces the effects of their withdrawal.

For all these reasons, HHI-based analysis is prone to errors and, most likely, would overestimate market power. As an alternative approach to quantifying market concentration—and subsequently market power— some MCCAs recommend the use of simulation models to analyze the wholesale markets and support their decisions in competition policy cases. For example:

- The Nordic competition authorities recommend the use of simulation models like the ELTRA model. This model allows for hourly simulations of the effects on prices, production, demand, and exchanges in the Nordic wholesale market under different competition scenarios.

- The Spanish MCCA (the TDC) argued in the ENDESA/IBERDROLA case[26] that using HHIs was not adequate for evaluating market concentration in the context of the merger. Therefore, it assessed the impact of system operations using a model based on one developed by Borenstein and Bushell[27] previously used to simulate the Californian wholesale market, and one created by Marín and García-Díaz[28] that simulates the outcomes of the Spanish wholesale market on the basis of a model of oligopolistic competition.

- The Dutch Competition Authority (the NMa) hired consultants to develop simulation models to assess the effect of the merger of RELIANT and NUON on the Dutch wholesale market. The merged entity would become one of the largest undertakings in the market, accounting for 20 to 30 percent of domestically generated electricity. The models tried to reproduce the strategic behavior of the merged company in the competitive bidding of the Dutch wholesale market. Combining the price and quantity predictions of the model with a qualitative analysis, NMa concluded that the merger would be conducive to an increase of the price level in the electricity wholesale market. Therefore, the NMa subjected the merger to structural conditions. The merging parties appealed the decision to the Court of Rotterdam. The Court annulled the NMa decision, finding that there was no strong evidence to support a finding that the merged firms would adopt the strategic behavior that the NMa models assumed. The Court also rejected NMa's international evidence that the envisaged behavior had taken place in other countries.

In spite of the advantages of market simulation models, analysts need to be aware of the perils in using them to assess market power. Some of the most important limitations are (1) the problem of multiple equilibria, (2) the instability of some of the equilibria, (3) the impact of having to assume continuity in the supply functions and (4) the probability that the analysts may have left out some important aspect of the market being analyzed. In practice, when well specified and when their limitations are acknowledged, the models are a good starting point for analyzing the qualitative existence of market power, but their usefulness for analyzing remedies or regulatory interventions is more limited.[29]

Moreover, in many instances the assessment has not properly considered the contract position of the parties, which can drastically reduce incentives to increase the market price.

Ex-ante Regulation of Market Power

Competition authorities have also introduced ex-ante rules to assess market power, failing to understand that each merger should be based on its merits and that attempting to establish *a priori* rules for merger analysis is a flawed exercise. The two clear examples are the Spanish Competition Tribunal "1+1=1 doctrine" and the attempt of the British energy regulator OFGEM to introduce a Market Abuse License Condition (MALC) in the license of generators. The 1+1=1 doctrine, in which the merging parties should propose remedies that leave the market structure unchanged, has been applied in a number of failed mergers in Spain since the market was liberalised.

The UK Competition Act 1998 follows European practice in prohibiting cartels and abuse of a dominant position, and the Financial Services and Markets Act 2000 provides a general basis for scrutiny of traders' behavior in all financial markets, including markets for electricity contracts. OFGEM believed these powers to be inadequate due to the "special characteristics" of electricity, and during much of 1999 and 2000 pressed for increased powers over the market behavior of generators.[30] OFGEM wanted to be able to penalise abuse of substantial market power, as defined by OFGEM.

When AES and British Energy objected to the inclusion of the MALC in their licenses OFGEM referred them to the Competition Commission (CC). Following an extensive inquiry, the CC rejected OFGEM's attempt to impose the MALC on AES and British Energy because of the lack of evidence and a concern that OFGEM's proposed powers would create uncertainty and deter normal competitive behavior.

The MALC was nothing less than an attempt to re-invent competition policy on a new and untried basis. OFGEM attempted to establish guidelines on the forms of behavior that might be considered an abuse. Since in practice the behavior could be both pro- and anti-competitive, OFGEM also tried to describe a procedure for identifying abuses: (1) check whether the generator possesses substantial market power; (2) check whether the generator has exercised substantial market power; (3) check whether the generator's behaviour has harmed consumers. In practice, however, each step in this process reduced to one narrow question: To what extent has the generator raised prices above the competitive level? As such, OFGEM departed from the broad framework of market analysis adopted by competition authorities, and in particular, the concept of dominance.

Advocates of basing regulatory decisions on objectivity rather than discretion welcomed OFGEM's failure to introduce the MALC. The problem with OFGEM's approach is that it amounts to ex ante regulation, as the regulator must be able to determine the competitive price at all times. As Shuttleworth and Williams observed

> After all, if government officials knew exactly what competitive outcomes should look like, period by period, it would be unnecessary to institute competition itself; the officials could merely mandate a competitive outcome. It is precisely the lack of such omniscience that led the government to open generation to competition in the first place.[31]

Given that competition policy analysis is constructed on the premise of *ex-post* regulation because anti-competitive conduct can take many forms and any breach has to be proved, this type of *ex-ante* and, by definition, generalised approach to competition policy is a bad idea and an arbitrary way to constrain business decisions.

Conclusion

The inconsistencies in assessing market power in the European electricity sector, especially in merger cases, stems from the nation-based authorizing legislation and its implementation by authorities with varying degrees of political independence. Presumably, the inconsistencies will gradually disappear as individual cases are appealed and the decisions of the Court of First Instance become precedent. However, lack of consistency is not the only problem in assessing market power. Other problems include (1) using antitrust techniques that ignore the peculiarities of the sector, (2) narrowly defining the market based on transient conditions, (3) employing an index that measures the capacity of production rather than actual production, and (4) overlooking the impact of established market rules and contractual relationships. If consistently applied, these actions ensure consistent errors. However, initiatives like OFGEM's attempt reinvent competition policy on a sector-specific basis are not the solution either. Rather, as they develop geographically uniform anti-trust policies, tools, and techniques, the EU competition authorities must adapt their analyses of the electricity industry in ways that acknowledge the special characteristics of the sector.

Notes

1. I would like to thank Daniel Paredes for research assistance in the preparation of this paper. I have benefited from discussions on the subject with Oscar Arnedillo and colleagues in NERA's Madrid office and from comments by the editor. I have also benefited from colleagues in NERA's European offices who produced most of the worthwhile commentary in competition policy cases in the electricity sector in Europe. Needless to say, all errors are my own.

2. Articles 81 and 82.

3. See for example the Gas Natural takeover bid for Endesa where Endesa preferred the EC to the Spanish competition authorities because the final decision in Spain rests with the government.

4. Most EC decisions are appealed to the Court.

5. See Stephen Stoft, *Power System Economics: Designing Markets for Electricity* (Piscataway NJ.: IEEE Press, Wiley Interscience, 2002).

6. Marginal system price markets are also easier to monitor by authorities due to their transparency and the fact that offers are based on costs rather than expectations.

7. Richard J. Green and David M. Newbery, "Competition in the British Electricity Spot Market," Journal of Political Economy, C, 5, (October, 1992), 929-53 were analyzing contracts for differences in the early British spot market through which suppliers received the same price regardless of the spot market price. Such contracts effectively turned the spot market into fixed price contracts.

8. This is not to say that a 100 percent contract cover will make the generator indifferent with respect to the spot market price. The reasons is that the generator, by increasing the spot price, could alter market expectations and result in

an increase in forward and contract prices. However, because prices in the forward market do not only depend on prices in the spot market, it is unlikely that all the increase in the spot price will be translated to the forward market. It is clear that exercising market power in the forward market is more difficult than in the spot market, so the authorities would need to consider the link between spot and forward prices before assessing market power. See, for example, Stoft, S. (2002) *Power System Economics*, p. 350.

9. See the EC Notice on the definition of the relevant market for the purposes of Community competition law—O J C 372. In the Notice, the EC clarifies that the application of the concepts of product and geographic market must rely on the well-known SSNIP test—Small but Significant and Non-transitory Increase in Price.

10. See Case COMP/M.3729—EDF/AEM/EDISON, and COMP/M.3440—EDP/ENI/GDP, available in http://europa.eu.int/comm/competition/index_es.html.

11. See Case COMP/M.2434—Grupo Villar/EnBW/Hidroeléctrica del Cantábrico, COMP/M.2620—Enel/Viesgo, COMP/M.2684—EnBW/EDP/Cajastur/ Hidrocantábrico, and COMP/M.2819 Canal de Isabel II/Hidrocantábrico/JV, available in http://europa.eu.int/comm/competition/index_es.html.

12. See Radov and Klevnas for a description of the EU regulations promoting the use of renewable energy sources, in this volume. For the purposes of market definition, the subsidized nature of the product has made the EC consider the energy sold under these conditions distinct from that sold in the competitive market.

13. See Case COMP/M.3729—EDF/AEM/EDISON

14. Jointly carried out by the Italian sector regulator and the national competition authority: Autorità per l´energie elettrica e il gas and Autorità garante della concorrenza e il mercato. "Indagine conoscitiva sullo stato della liberalizzazione del settore dell´energia elettrica." February 2005.

15. The residual demand is calculated by subtracting the regional capacity of importation—from other regions—to the regional demand level.

16. James Bushnell, Christopher R. Knittel and Frank Wolak, "Estimating the Opportunities for Market Power in a Deregulated Wisconsin Electricity Market".

17. Konkurrencestyrelsen, Konkurresverket, Konkurrasetilsynet, Samkeppnisstofnun, Kilpailuvirastro. "A Powerful Competition Policy: Towards a more coherent competition policy in the Nordic market for electricity power," 2003, available at http://www.kkv.se.

18. In the decision for the case EDF/AEM/EDISON - COMP/M.3729—EDF/AEM/EDISON, it is stated "[...] In previous decision, the Commission has always considered that ancillary services markets are national in scope".

19. See the case C60/00—ENDESA/IBERDROLA, available in http://www.tdcompetencia.es.

20. *Op cit.*

21. Guidelines on the *assessment* of horizontal mergers under the Council regulation on the control of concentrations between undertakings, available in http://europa.eu.int/.

22. http://www.konkurransetilsynet.no/archive/internett/avgjorelser_uttalelser/arkiv_2003/H2002-1169_horizontal_mergers.pdf.

23. Konkurrencestyrelsen, *Konkurresverket,* Konkurrasetilsynet, Samkeppnisstofnun, Kilpailuvirastro, Norway and Finland. "A Powerful Competition Policy: Towards a More Coherent Competition Policy in the Nordic Market for Electricity Power" (2003) available at http://www.kkv.se.

24. FERC (1996), Merger *Policy* Guidelines, Appendix A.

25. The Spanish competition tribunal took this view in the assessing the merger between Unión FENOSA and Hidrocantábrico "the analysis should take into account to what extent different technologies can be withdrawn from the market" *Informe del TDC en el Expediente de Concentración Económica C 54/00 Unión Eléctrica Fenosa-Hidroeléctrica del Cantábrico,* 2000, p. 25. In the end, the analysis was not carried out but the authorities should remain open to that possibility.

26. See Case C60/00 ENDESA/IBERDROLA, available at available in http://www.tdcompetencia.es.

27. S. Borenstein and J. Bushnell, "An empirical analysis of the potential for market power in California's electricity industry," (1997) available in www.ucei.berkeley.edu/ucei.

28. P. Marín and A. García-Díaz, "Strategic bidding in electricity pools with short-lived bids: an application to the Spanish market," Discussion paper nº 2567 (2000) available at www.cepr.org.

29. For example, the Spanish government commissioned a study to analyze possible regulatory measures to reduce the presumed market power of Spanish generators in the so-called White Book of the wholesale market. The model presented did not mention the existence of multiple equilibria in the solution of the model nor did it justify the choice of a single equilibrium outcome (made using stability analysis) over the others.

30. This is based on Graham S. Shuttleworth and Iestyn Williams, "UK Competition Commission rejects tighter regulation of generators," *NERA Energy Regulation Brief* (January 2001).

31. Ibid.

13

TOO MANY COOKS AND NO RECIPE MAKES A BAD BROTH

Jonathan Falk

Introduction

The assessment and mitigation of market power in electricity in the US has two primary problems. *First,* jurisdiction for market power is divided among many partially distinct and partially overlapping regulatory bodies, each with its own regulations and methodologies. Some of these regulations are unique to electricity; others are unique to state regulation; others are the generic market power methodologies applicable to any industry. In the presence of well-defined rules, this multiplicity of jurisdictions might be inefficient and redundant, but it would at least be understandable.

However—and this is the *second* problem—each of these entities has wide scope to make up the rules as they go along. This creates a regulatory scheme that is not only inefficient but haphazard and thus introduces added costs and (at least partly) undiversifiable uncertainty into the electricity industry. These elements, in turn raise the required returns on capital. While it is probably impossible to measure this effect precisely, it is possible that electricity costs more than it would in a world with a deregulated electricity wholesale market with essentially no electricity-specific market power regulation at all.

This paper will attempt to survey the panoply of market power methods and try to create a framework in which the regulation of market power in electricity can be understood. Section II notes various definitions of market power in electricity, a brief introduction intended to accompany Michael Rosenzweig's piece within. Section III sketches out the paths by which market power intervention is assessed and mitigated. Section IV details the varying parties and the scope of assessment roles. Section V discusses the public policy issue.

In essence, I believe there is little if any purpose served by the over-lapping regulatory structure in US electricity and very little need for special regulatory schemes to accommodate the special requirements of electricity. Abandoning regulatory layers is politically unrealistic, however. What might be feasible is a more precise delineation of specific scope for specific agents, as well as an increase in transparency by at least one of those agents, FERC.

Market Power Defined

Every aspect of market power in electricity in the US is controversial. Not surprisingly, this controversy begins with the very definition of market power. Among the definitions:

- Market power is the ability to the affect the price profitably.[1]
- Market power to a seller is the ability profitably to maintain prices above competitive levels for a significant period of time.[2]
- Market power is the ability to significantly influence market prices and cause them to vary from competitive levels for an extended time.[3]
- As in all industries, an electricity producing firm exercises market power when it reduces its output or raises the minimum price at which it is willing to sell output (its offer price) *in order to change the market price.*[4]

These are all similar definitions, but the nuances matter. All of them deal with the firm with market power changing the market price. Some definitions characterize that price as the market price; others as the competitive price; still others use the term "workable competition." The central point is that in **perfect** competition (an idealized construct) all firms act as price takers. But how is the concept of market power in electricity to be defined when a system is short, or nearly short, of capacity to meet the demands of customers? Much confusion arises in this situation, largely because the analogy with perfect competition breaks down; the paradigm of perfect competition assumes perfect mobility of resources and therefore assumes that shortages and shortage costs do not exist.

Paths of Intervention

There are four different pathways through which regulators can intervene to thwart the potential exercise of market power: mergers and acquisitions, transitions to competitive markets, market pricing authority, and market operations.

Mergers and Acquisitions

When two firms merge, regulatory authorities attempt to ensure that the resulting firm will not be able to exert excessive market power. Generally, the regulators compare indices of likely competition for the industry with and without the merger, paying careful attention to several types of potential market power.

Horizontal Market Power
Horizontal market power is the ability to sustain price increases from excessive control of a particular link in the electricity supply chain, which runs from fuel to wholesale generation to retail markets.

Vertical Market Power
Vertical market power is the ability to somehow use concentrated ownership of different parts of the supply chain to harm competition, usually by denying competitors who lack similar integration across the supply chain access to either production inputs or markets for output. Five links are particularly scrutinized.

WHOLESALE-RETAIL

Wholesalers need access in some fashion to retail customers. An entity that controls both wholesale and retail markets may have the incentive to shut other wholesalers out of its retail markets.

WHOLESALE-TRANSMISSION

Wholesalers must have the ability to sell to markets. Combined ownership of wholesaling with transmission opens the possibility that an entity owning both wholesale power and transmission will deny access to its transportation system to competing wholesalers or somehow give its own wholesale operation preferential access to the transmission system.

TRANSMISSION-RETAIL

For retail customers to avail themselves of the cheapest supply, they need to ensure that competitors can reach them. Again, control of the transmission system by a retailer may allow it to foreclose retail competition.

FUEL-WHOLESALE

The bulk of electricity production is powered by only a few fuels: coal, gas, uranium, and favorable water geographies. Control of access to these fuels by an entity that also competes in power generation may hamper the competitive process by restricting economic access to fuel.

ELECTRIC-GAS

Electricity and gas are competitive power sources for some industrial processes as well as for residential heating and cooking use. Control of both sources may hamper the ability of final customers to choose the most efficient option in favor of the one with greatest financial reward to the seller.

Competitive Market Transition

Where there is a transition from a vertically integrated cost-of-service regulated market to one that has at least some aspects of a competitive market, regulators attempt to ensure that the opening market structure is not likely to be unduly burdened with market power concerns.

Market Pricing Authority

Once the competitive market in the US is up and running, the market participants must still petition for the right to sell at market rates. This showing requires a prospective analysis that indicates that market power is not likely to be a significant problem.

Operations

Finally, regulators can explicitly scrutinize the observed results of electric markets, and they can intervene either through rules or through investigations to modify those outcomes to better comport with the regulator's notion of a market not subject to the exercise of market power. Traditionally, the exercise of market power has been completely legal as long as the entity makes no attempt to leverage its market power into other related markets. The clearest statement of this position is in the US Supreme Court case of Verizon Communications v. Law Offices of Curtis V. Trinko, LLP:

> The mere possession of monopoly power, and the concomitant charging of monopoly prices, is not only not unlawful; it is an important element of the free-market system. The opportunity to charge monopoly prices—at least for a short period—is what attracts "business acumen" in the first place; it induces risk taking that produces innovation and economic growth.

Indeed, the typical regulatory oversight of markets deals with fraud, not market power. The long history of price regulation of electricity, however, has induced a focus on the operations of electricity markets and a strengthening of the duties and responsibilities of market monitors. These bodies are directly empowered by regulators to take actions in cases of the purported operational exercise of market power. Operational pricing mitigation will be discussed below.

Regulatory Bodies

The four pathways to potential market power enforcement can be taken by no fewer than five entities, whose jurisdiction partially overlaps.

US Department of Justice

The US Department of Justice (DOJ) has two roles in market power assessment and mitigation. As enforcer of the Sherman and Clayton Acts, it has primary responsibility to stop combinations in restraint of trade and attempted monopolization. It assesses the likely competitive impact of mergers and gives an *imprimatur* to mergers or denies it. Where the DOJ disapproves of a merger, the merging parties are free to challenge that decision in court, but this is an onerous and often unsuccessful venture, so in practice the DOJ exercises its powers to negotiate with merging parties to find acceptable mitigation to preserve competition.

The DOJ's market power inquiries are guided by merger guidelines, which are actually the clearest statement of what is permitted in a merger. A product market is defined, and a Herfindahl-Hirschman Index (HHI) is constructed. The HHI is the sum of the square of market shares of each entity in this market. The change in HHI resulting from the merger is then compared to certain thresholds—low HHI changes are given a safe harbor, high HHI changes are deemed probably uncompetitive, and an area in between warrants further study. There are also a variety of other criteria, *e.g.,* a rule that allows a merger if, but for the merger, one of the companies would go out of business.

Major disputes in many mergers revolve around product definition, but DOJ antitrust analysis does not stop with these tests; it will also examine cost savings from a merger. If a merging party can demonstrate that prices will fall after a merger due to cost savings, the DOJ could allow a merger to proceed.

The DOJ has another responsibility in operations. Explicit collusion or price fixing between putative competitors is also within their purview. They can file criminal charges against those alleged to have fixed prices.

The DOJ responsibility covers all mergers, not just mergers in electricity. DOJ's Antitrust Division has developed a number of tools to help assess mergers. By and large, however, these methods are not industry-specific. To the extent that electricity mergers present unique problems in antitrust analysis, the DOJ is least well positioned to analyze them.

Federal Energy Regulatory Commission

FERC's authority to investigate market abuse comes from the Federal Power Act and the Energy Policy Act of 2005. Section 206 of the Federal Power Act requires that prices be "just and reasonable"; Section 203 requires FERC approval of the transfer of ownership of assets over which FERC has jurisdiction. The Energy Policy Act gives FERC the power to investigate "market manipulation." FERC's jurisdiction in these areas covers only the wholesale generation and transmission of power. Retail regulation is left to the states.

Merger Authority Under Section 203
In evaluating mergers, and particularly the associated HHI changes, FERC uses the Delivered Price Test (DPT), a variant of the market power tests developed by the DOJ. In the DPT, analysts define a number of relevant geographic and time-differentiated markets, *e.g.,* the PJM Eastern market in shoulder hours. They then calculate simultaneous import capacity into this market and allocate it to various entities. After making an assumption about the likely clearing price for electricity in this market before the merger, they define a set of units that can deliver power economically to this region simultaneously at a price 5 percent above this clearing price. They then use the ownership of this set of units to define HHI levels

before and after the merger. Changes in this HHI level are then compared with the DOJ thresholds.

While it might seem that this method is a transparent way to evaluate mergers, in practice the method turns out to hinge on a host of assumptions that both dictate the results and are difficult to assess objectively. In an important paper, Diana Moss[5] finds that analysis of the same markets, sometimes even by the same economists, yields wildly different estimates of the underlying HHI values and, by extension, the changes in HHI associated with mergers.

Market-Based Rate Authority

As malleable as are the FERC standards under their merger authority, the Section 206 authority to generate "just and reasonable" prices is explicitly up for grabs. FERC is manifestly dissatisfied with its prior methodology for assessing market power when deciding whether to allow market prices to set rates. A variety of approaches seem to be slowly coalescing into a Supply Market Assessment (SMA) calculation that combines HHI measurements with so-called "pivotal supplier tests," in which the absolute necessity of a particular generator's output in order to fulfill demand makes a market putatively uncompetitive.

It is difficult to know where this process will end, beyond the safe prediction that wherever it ends up, intervenors will feel justified in protesting any result they don't like. Prominently espousing this view is Frank Wolak, who in the oddly named article, "Sorry Mr. Falk: It's Too Late to Implement Your Recommendations Now,"[6] argues that no matter what procedures FERC puts in place, their obligation is to ensure "just and reasonable" prices after the fact. Thus, it is not necessarily a winning argument to contend that prices determined in markets considered *ex ante* to be structured in a reasonable way ought to be *ipso facto* "just and reasonable."[7] Owing to the long history of regulation, political meddling in the process of electricity prices is endemic to any attempt to introduce competition into electricity. Politicians deem low prices to be a sign of competitive forces at work while high prices prove inadequate competition leading to unjust enrichment. As long as this potential for a no-win situation persists for electric utilities, the long-run cost of utility investment will rise so that the risk-adjusted return is set at a level at which the utility industry can attract capital.

FERC recognizes this problem. In the cases related to the California debacle, FERC has consistently refused to go back and attempt to reset market derived rates, even when they have suspected (but have not yet attempted to prove) that the prices were derived as a result of horizontal market power, a proposition that remains controversial even today. Nonetheless, it is unsettling when, with no evidence of market manipulation, the political representatives of ratepayers demand that particular malefactors be compelled to disgorge "unjust" profits.

Market Manipulation

The Energy Policy Act has put new regulations in place to stop market manipulation. The Act is not explicitly directed at market power but rather at suspect trading practices, such as wash sales and the misstatement of trading revenues and indicative market prices. However, the basic rubric for market manipulation could easily be expanded to include market power, particularly should a jurisdiction mandate a cost standard in bidding. In that case, the exercise of market power would mean a misstatement of cost, which could then be deemed to be market manipulation.

State Regulators

State regulators are responsible for retail tariff setting. Except for large industrial users—which some states have freed from the tariff-setting process in order to encourage them to find the best deal available—the majority of loads are still subject either to *de jure* lack of competition or a *de facto* single supplier. The state interest in protecting these customers with few retail options gives its regulators the authority to judge mergers.

State regulatory assessment of mergers is pretty much *sui generis* by state. Broadly speaking, however, there are two primary objectives. The first is to capture as many efficiency savings from the merger as possible to pass along to ratepayers. The argument for this is that the ratepayers paid for the assets and thus are entitled to the savings. The second objective is political and revolves around out-of-state ownership of utility resources and local employment consequences of the merger. The State of Oregon, for example, turned down an attempt by an investment firm to purchase the Portland General Electric Company out of the Enron bankruptcy on the grounds that (1) out-of-state owners would get tax savings that would not be passed along to Portland residents, (2) out-of-state owners would have insufficient incentive to make Oregon-based investments, and (3) the focus of the management would not be local. The regulators preferred PGE to be owned by a bankrupt Enron.

By and large, these state issues have little to do with market power. Since the state maintains the ability to set retail rates, the state can control any problems of market power at retail.

Occasionally, however, real market power questions arise in a state in which retail rates are essentially set not by a tariff process but by annual auctions. In the thwarted Exelon-PSEG merger, the State of New Jersey was concerned about the increased concentration of generation ownership. We may expect to see more state interventions in mergers in those states without an explicit tariff process.

Independent System Operators

While FERC arguably has some authority over the exercise of market power in the operation of electric systems, for the most part it has contracted out this responsibility to Independent System Operators (ISOs). ISOs, which in the US are aggregations of utility control areas, form a market nexus for FERC grants of authority to sell at market prices. Thus, before authorization is given, the ISO must demonstrate through FERC filings that the ISO's market rules will not be unduly influenced by market power. In particular, all ISOs are required to have a market monitor who both observes the performance of the market, making periodic reports on the state of the market, and enforces market rules for the mitigation of market power where and when it is deemed to exist. Thus, it is the ISO market monitoring function that is primarily responsible for controlling the operational exercise of market power.

The rules that these market monitors enforce are not uniform. Each ISO has its own definition of when normal market rules ought to be suspended and when generators will be constrained in how they can bid. This lack of uniformity is the symptom of a groping for a "best" way to organize these markets; it is not an adaptation of some ideal set of market rules to local market conditions. FERC proposed a standardized market design that would have imposed a uniform framework on the operation of competitive electric markets, including rules for the mitigation of market power. However, this initiative dissolved for several reasons, prominently the fear by state regulators that the standardized market design would threaten their ability to run retail markets as they wanted.

Thus, all changes to market rules at an ISO, including those related to market power mitigation, must be reviewed at FERC for consistency with the "just and reasonable" standard. Since this standard itself is quite opaque and since FERC does not want to discourage any potential adoption of the ISO model, it is not surprising that there is a wide zone of acceptable market power mitigation schemes.

The US and State Judicial Systems

Finally, private parties who allege anticompetitive behavior can invoke the Sherman and Clayton antitrust acts at the Federal level, as well as various state antitrust laws. Favoring these suits is the fact that, if successful, the plaintiffs receive treble their assessed damages. Plaintiffs can be either competitors or customers, but the customers must be direct customers, not those whose purchases are embedded in some other product.

The Public Policy Issue

Market power is potentially a problem in electricity, but it is also a potential problem in every other commodity sold in a market. Yet no other market has the range of assessments and interventions that electricity does. This would make sense if either of the following two propositions were true:

- Electricity is more susceptible to market power than other industries.
- Market power in electricity does more economic damage than other forms of market power.

In fact, it is fairly easy to show that neither of these propositions is true. At least over the last 30 years, the electric industry has seen rapid technological change so that generally new competitors are more efficient than the older generators with substantial market shares. Most areas of the country are characterized by fairly robust transmission systems in which differences in price between regions can be quickly arbitraged away. Electricity is traded in both spot markets and long-run markets, each of which disciplines the other.

In terms of efficiency, the fact that electricity has fairly low observed elasticities[8] means that the efficiency losses from the exercise of market power are fairly small. While electricity itself is a vital commodity in modern economies, it is a quite small input to most industrial production and a small part of the typical household budget. Finally, we have only just begun to explore the robust possibilities for demand-side controls by consumers. If people have the ability to respond to prices when they are unwilling to pay more than six cents per kilowatt-hour for power, then there is no way to use market power to profitably extract prices above six cents.

Why, then, are we so worried about market power in electricity that we set up controls to monitor and mitigate that exceed those in any other industry? And why, in that assessment, do we use inconsistent and vague standards that make it impossible for producers to know when they are behaving illegally? The answer (given the lack of demand response) is an overhang of regulation: since the *raison d'être* of regulation was to control prices, it is a difficult habit to give up (particularly when, undisciplined by demand, the result is politically unacceptable high prices). The decision to carry out a mix of partly regulated, partly deregulated structures within the electric system gives regulators more than just an excuse to keep their fingers on the scale—it gives them an obligation to do so.

In contrast, consider airline deregulation in the United States. After extensive study, it was decided to end the scheme of pervasively regulated airfares in the United States. Alfred Kahn of the Civil Aeronautics Board came to the conclusion that there were no half-measures that would work in airline price deregulation: The only way to get out of the pricing business was to get out of the pricing business. That doesn't mean that airline passengers and competing airlines are now unprotected; they are simply protected by the same antitrust laws that protect all other consumers and competitors in all other industries. There is no special filing for just and fair airline prices because there is no one to complain to.

A second reason for the pervasive regulation of electricity pricing schemes is that we have so many very expensive, very complicated engineering models of what an electricity system and market ought to be. This encourages a regrettable mindset in which divergences between price observations in the real world and price predictions of a model are taken to be proof of flaws in the world, not in the model. Thus in California, the standard assessment of excess pricing comes from comparing a model to actual prices, not from any attempt to determine whether the actual outcome itself was really the result of the exercise of market power. Virtually no evidence has been presented that it was. The actions of Enron, for example, are often cited as proof of nefarious activity. But Enron owned almost no electricity generation in California and made very little money in aggregate in trading electricity. They did take a very large position in natural gas and associated electricity output, making large sums of money as gas prices rose and losing essentially all of it when gas prices later collapsed. None of their vilified trading schemes had anything other a beneficial effect on electricity prices as far as I, or anybody else, have been able to determine.[9]

That said, a plea for FERC to get out of the market power aspect of the electricity business would surely fall on deaf ears, particularly given the perception that DOJ is not well positioned to analyze the unique problems presented by electricity mergers. But there is no reason they have to. Substituting transparent rules for its current complicated and inconsistent rules would go a long way to eliminating the major negative effect of the excess of cooks. The problem develops when new entrants cannot know what behavior is legal and what behavior is illegal, when they cannot depend on the stability of a pricing regime in order to have some way of estimating the probability that they will earn a return on new investment, and when a cost-reducing merger is unconsummated for fear of the regulatory costs of gaining approval in at least three separate jurisdictions: DOJ, FERC and the State Commission. All of these negatives result from the current approaches and raise the cost of capital, or, equivalently, raise the hurdle rate required to get companies to invest in electric power rather than in something else.

By introducing a set of simple, transparent rules, the FERC can keep its hand in market power determination without interfering excessively with proper economic incentives. If the recipe is rigid enough, the number of cooks is less of a problem.

Notes

1. Steven Stoft, *Power System Economics: Designing Markets for Electricity* (Piscataway, NJ: IEEE Press, Wiley Interscience, 2002), Chapter 11.

2. US DOJ Merger Guidelines, Section 0.1
   http://www.usdoj.gov/atr/public/guidelines/horiz_book/01.html

3. California ISO Department of Market Analysis (formerly Surveillance) FAQ, http://www.caiso.com/surveillance/faq/

4. Severin Borenstein, James Bushnell, and Frank Wolak, Diagnosing Market Power in California's Deregulated Wholesale Electric Market, http://www.ucei.berkeley.edu/ucei/PDF/pwp064.pdf, August 2000 (italics in original).

5. "Electricity Mergers, Economic Analysis and Consistency: Why FERC Needs to Change Its Approach," AAI Working Paper 04-02, available at http://www.antitrustinstitute.org/recent2/348.pdf

6. *The Electricity Journal,* August/September 2003, pp. 50-55.

7. However, it undoubtedly represents a plausible interpretation of the FERC obligation under the Federal Power Act. The Ninth Circuit Court of Appeals has recently addressed this issue regarding FERC action after the California crisis, in which the decision argues that FERC in fact may have such an obligation. As if this writing, the Ninth Circuit has not yet definitively ruled that contracts signed at the end of the California crisis are presumptively valid, but has instead directed FERC to see whether or not the level of such contracts were the result of market power.

8. This reflects the fact that the great majority of customers do not see prices in real time or near real time and cannot react effectively to changes in prices.

9. See Falk, "Substituting Outrage for Thought," *The Electricity Journal* (31 August 2002), 13-22.

IV

SECURITY OF SUPPLY

SECURITY OF SUPPLY:
HOW TO ENSURE CAPACITY ADEQUACY

Sean Gammons

The issue of security of supply has recently shot up the agenda in the public debate about the electricity industry, as it has in the wider energy debate. In the case of the electricity industry, the catalysts have been the major supply interruptions in California in 2000 and 2001, the blackouts that hit the north-east US and Italy in 2003, and the blackout that hit Germany, France, Belgium and other parts of the continental European system in late 2006. Also driving the debate forward is the need for decisions about replacing ageing nuclear and coal-fired power stations across the world.

Security of supply has many dimensions, including security of fuel supplies, the availability of adequate generation capacity, the maintenance of a reliable delivery system in the form of transmission and distribution lines, and even the extent of foreign ownership of the industry's assets. The papers in this section focus on one aspect of security of supply: how to ensure that adequate generation capacity is available to meet peak demand, or "capacity adequacy" for short.

Why is this issue of particular importance in the electricity industry, and why does it remain so contentious? Part of the reason may lie in the specific technological conditions of the industry. Electricity cannot be stored economically, and hence an electricity system needs enough installed capacity to cover the small number of hours of peak demand during a year. Demand in most other hours of the year is much lower than in these peak periods, so an industry with an adequate level of installed capacity operates with a large capacity surplus most of the time.[1] In regulated systems, utilities accept an obligation to ensure continuity of supply on condition that the regulatory agency allows them to recover their costs. Once a utility has built enough capacity to meet the established reliability target,[2] the regulator may be tempted to disallow some of the investment costs incurred by the utility,[3] and this risk may deter the utility from investing in the first instance. However, this well-known example of the "hold-up" problem stems from the regulatory agency's problem in committing to a policy, rather than from the specific techno-logical conditions of the industry.

In a market system, a pattern of operation that requires the provision of excess capacity most of the time puts the industry on an economic "knife-edge" in the following sense. In the periods of excess capacity (i.e., most of the time), too much capacity is chasing limited demand, and hence, marginal cost pricing tends to be the order of the day, squeezing the margins earned by baseload capacity.[4] In the few hours of peak demand, when capacity is scarce, prices need to rise to high levels to allow the peaking capacity that is only needed in those few hours to recover its full costs, including capital investment costs. The high prices in these few periods may also be needed to remunerate the investment costs of base-load capacity, which sees its margins squeezed in most other hours of the year. Hence, ensuring capacity adequacy in a market system is not just about ensuring there is enough capacity around to meet peak demand; it is also about ensuring investors have incentives to build and maintain adequate baseload capacity, and thus ensure the long-term sustainability of the industry.

The other reason that the issue of security of supply and capacity adequacy remains contentious may lie in the institutional history of the industry. The concept of an electricity market is itself still relatively new. Electricity markets, where they exist, have grown out of long-lived government-owned or government-controlled monopoly institutions. In the past, consumers knew who to blame if the lights went out: the local utility and the politicians who controlled it. Anticipating this response, politicians and utility managers reacted by designing the electricity system to supply, possibly oversupply, adequate generation capacity. Today, politicians across the US, Europe and many other parts of the world have delegated the provision of electricity supply to the market, partly in an effort to ensure that generation capacity is not oversupplied. However, as discussed by the papers in this section, consumers have been slow to adjust to this new paradigm. They still tend to blame politicians when things go wrong, thus making politicians prone to intervene in the market, often with controversial short-term solutions like mandated capacity procurement and/or price caps.

In many restructured electricity markets around the world, the creation of incentives to ensure capacity adequacy has been at the heart of decision making. For example, the original Electricity Pool of England and Wales had a "capacity payment" built into the pool price, a number of US markets have explicit capacity obligation mechanisms built in, and Spain has an explicit capacity payment mechanism. There are also some markets that operate without explicit capacity payment or obligation schemes, but where the creation of incentives to ensure capacity adequacy has been no less central. For example, the national electricity market of Australia has no such scheme, but Australia consciously designed its market rules to reflect marginal costs and allows prices to rise to very high levels during periods of capacity scarcity in order to provide incentives for adequate investment. Similarly, the Electric Reliability Council of Texas is noteworthy in the US because it continues to operate without an explicit capacity mechanism by setting the cap on its energy-only market at a very high level.

However, in a range of other markets, particularly in Europe, the creation of incentives to ensure capacity adequacy has been virtually absent from the debate about restructuring electricity markets. This difference in emphasis stems from the different model of restructuring that dominates in Europe. For the most part, wholesale markets in Europe have emerged not by regulatory design but as an adjunct to the creation of retail competition, which is mandated by the EU electricity directives. Many of the European power exchanges and over-the-counter markets, such as Powernext, the EEX, and the APX, have emerged in response to the particular demands of producers and traders: to provide vertically integrated incumbents with some extra flexibility to optimise their production and to give small new entrants a means of managing their imbalances in markets where imbalance prices are often set at punitive levels.[5] These power exchanges and markets were not designed at the outset to provide a reliable source of bulk wholesale power for supply to end-users.

The unwritten assumption in most European markets seems to be that the big incumbents will continue to ensure security of supply, provided they are allowed to recoup their incremental investment costs through their retail tariffs, and—and this is the part that never gets written down—that they are allowed to maintain their existing market positions. Indeed, it may be no coincidence that in much of the recent debate, many European governments have seemed to conflate the creation of so-called "national champions" with achieving security of supply. In addition, European governments have given themselves the fallback option of running public tenders for new capacity in the event that the traditional arrangements fail. (In the past few years, for example, the Irish and Greek governments have resorted to such procedures.)

To that extent, the need for wholesale market prices to provide incentives for capacity adequacy has remained off the agenda in Europe. However, as retail markets open in Europe and become more competitive, both through regulatory initiatives aimed at removing regulated tariffs and unbundling networks and through the slow growth of new entrants, producers will need to be able to rely on the wholesale market to recoup their investments, just as oil majors rely on the crude market to recoup their upstream investments. Hence, the question of how to provide incentive for capacity adequacy through the design of wholesale markets must soon rise to the top of the agenda in Europe, as it has done already in some other markets.

The conventional wisdom about electricity markets—which is challenged by one of the papers in this section—is that demand is highly unresponsive to price, or "price inelastic" in the lexicon of economists, and hence that electricity prices need to rise to very high levels in periods of peak demand in order to ration scarce capacity—see Chapter 14 by Kathleen King and Hethie Parmesano, "Conditions for Efficient Investment in Capacity" in this section for a fuller description of this theory.

It is sometimes argued that the high level of price volatility exhibited by energy-only markets makes them prone to market failure, a susceptibility which needs to be corrected through some form of regulatory mechanism. For example, some observers claim that the unpredictability of price spikes acts as a deterrent to investment. They contend that an energy-only market cannot *guarantee* capacity adequacy because it depends on the response of investors to price signals and those responses cannot be predicted with certainty. That dependence alone, they argue, constitutes a market failure. However, the flaw in this reasoning is that such arguments apply equally to other capital-intensive industries without creating the grounds for regulatory intervention in the market.

If there is a problem with energy-only markets, it is not market failure but the risk of regulatory failure due to a form of the "time consistency" problem, first popularised by the Nobel Prize-winning economists Edward Prescott and Finn Kydland in their research on monetary policy.[6] Its occurrence in nascent electricity markets is the central theme in this section. Applied to energy-only markets, the "time consistency" problem translates as follows: Politicians and regulators cannot be trusted to allow energy-only markets to work as intended. As capacity becomes scarce, the risk is that politicians and/or regulators step in to prevent the price spikes that are needed to incentivise investment, either by imposing price caps or arranging ad hoc capacity procurement tenders (cf. the examples of Ireland and Greece and many US markets).

In other industries or sectors where the time consistency problem arises, mechanisms have been adopted that attempt to tie the hands of the politicians or the regulator.[7] Hence, it should come as no surprise to learn that one of the intellectually defensible approaches to dealing with the time consistency problem in the electricity industry is to tie the hands of the regulator through some form of explicit capacity payment mechanism (CPM), which forces the regulator to commit to a procedure for approving the industry's investment requirements and the arrangements for cost recovery. All such mechanisms have at their heart some form of capacity targeting, although the target is sometimes used in a formula that fixes a capacity payment rather than as an explicit capacity obligation. Hamish Fraser discusses the criteria that should govern the choice of a CPM in Chapter 15 "Capacity Payment Mechanisms: How to Pick the One That's Right for You". Recent CPM approaches in the U.S. include setting up multi-year forward capacity auctions and building in locational incentives to promote efficient co-ordination of generation and transmission investment. Amparo Nieto and Hamish Fraser review these innovative CPM designs in Chapter 16, "Locational Electricity Capacity Markets: Alternatives to Restore the Missing signals".

The other intellectually defensible approach to dealing with the time consistency problem is to design a wholesale market with the systems needed to ensure that demand response is capable of rationing capacity before prices can spike to the levels that attract regulatory interventions. Decreasing costs of computing power, together with innovations in metering technology, have made it cheaper to collect and transmit the real-time pricing information that is needed in order to expose customers to the real costs of their consumption decisions. In addition, a number of recent empirical studies have suggested that relatively limited demand response programmes targeted at the largest customers can induce much more elasticity in the market demand curve than conventional wisdom assumes. Michael King, Kathleen King and Michael Rosenzweig review this evidence and its consequences for electricity market design in Chapter 17, "Customer Sovereignty: Why Customer Choice Trumps Administrative Capacity Mechanisms."

First, however, Kathleen King and Hethie Parmesano review the conditions that are necessary to ensure efficient investment in capacity, taking into account the risks that investors face. Their paper is instructive in another way too: Through a series of examples, it illustrates the great variety of approaches to ensuring capacity adequacy that have been tried in different parts of the world. This paper and others in this section highlight the amount of experimentation that is still going on in this field of electricity market design.

The best choice of approach to capacity adequacy will depend on the specific market conditions in each market, and hence the papers in this section do not proffer a "one-size-fits-all" solution. However, they do provide a clear view of the general principles that market designs, regulatory regimes, and political processes must adhere to if markets in electricity can have any hope of succeeding. We hope that together they will provide a valuable guide to decision making.

Notes

1. The industry actually needs to carry a surplus of capacity even during the few hours of peak demand, to ensure capacity is available to cover unforeseen outages.

2. The standard to which regulated utilities must comply may be defined in terms of a loss of load probability (LOLP) or loss of load expectation (LOLE), which may be set at, say, eight hours a year (or less than 0.1 percent of the hours in the year), or more simply, a percentage of reserves over annual peak.

3. This temptation may arise because the social costs of this form of opportunistic action may not materialise until many years later, possibly long after the incumbent regulator or regulatory commission have moved on.

4. "Baseload capacity" is capacity that runs during most of the hours of the year.

5. Imbalances are the difference between a supplier's actual metered volumes and its nominations, which get settled with the transmission system operator (TSO) at defined imbalance prices. In most European markets, there is a tendency among the TSOs and the regulators to see imbalances as a form of free-riding behaviour, and hence to impose punitive imbalance prices (i.e., very high prices for deficits) as a deterrent against relying on "the system" as a source of supply close to real time.

6. "The essence of the time consistency problem is as follows: a policy which economic policymakers regard as the best option in advance, when it can influence households' and firms' expectations about policy, will often not be implemented later on, when these expectations have already been formed and shaped private behavior. Economic policymakers will therefore revise their decision, so that the policy they ultimately conduct will be worse than if they had had less

discretion in policy choice. This result does not hinge on policymakers being guided by objectives different than those of citizens at large; rather, the difference appears in the constraints on the economic policy problem at different points in time." *The Prize in Economics 2004 — Information for the Public,* http://nobelprize.org/nobel_prizes/economics/laureates/2004/public.html, visited on 22nd January 2007.

7. The best known mechanism is probably "inflation targeting" by independent central banks, where governments have delegated the job of setting interest rates to independent central banks who are given a legal duty to ensure inflation is maintained at a certain target level, backed up with various sanction mechanisms. In this setup, the government's hands are tied because they hand over decision making on interest rates to a central bank that is required to follow a mechanical set of rules. A new government may always seek to introduce new laws to take back control over interest rates, but it would incur significant costs to do so (e.g., delaying other government legislation). Hence, such a mechanism creates a credible long-term commitment, which may become stronger over time as the benefits of such a system become established. The European Central Bank and Bank of England currently operate under such a framework.

14

CONDITIONS FOR EFFICIENT INVESTMENT IN CAPACITY[1]

Kathleen King
Hethie Parmesano

Introduction

In a competitive electricity market, efficient new investment in generation will take place if investors expect revenues sufficient to cover their
costs over the long term, including profit appropriate to the risk of their
investment. For a variety of reasons, however, many electricity markets
are not competitive. Elements of regulation, market power, and other
impediments to competition remain and price spikes have led to regulatory interventions that tend to discourage investment by reducing the
returns to generators and/or increasing regulatory uncertainty.
Furthermore, the risks that attend wholesale power markets have led to
short-term volatility exceeding that of other commodities, and in the US,
to severe boom-and-bust cycles.

The concern is that energy-only markets, particularly in their current
state—with ad hoc regulatory interventions and risks that are difficult to
hedge—will not provide incentives for sufficient investment in generating capacity. As a result, more markets are turning toward capacity
mechanisms. However, there are a few examples of markets that do not
rely on capacity mechanisms, and early indications are that investment or
disinvestment is occurring when warranted by the supply-demand situation as reflected in energy prices. These markets raise the question of
whether it is necessary to provide additional regulatory or administrative
mechanisms to ensure efficient investment in imperfectly competitive
power markets. The answer depends on the assumptions about what the
future holds and about whether such regulatory or administrative mechanisms produce a better, or just a different, outcome than market forces.

Competitive Markets and the Power Market

The conditions for efficient investment in a perfectly competitive market are clear in theory. There is a decades-old literature that concludes that efficient investment will occur in a competitive energy-only market without regulatory interventions such as required reserve margins and price caps if the expected value of generation prices over time is equal to the marginal running cost of the marginal generating unit plus a shortage cost component.[2] In competitive markets with a fully operating demand component, this shortage component raises the total price sufficiently for consumers to reduce the level demanded to match the available supply. If the sum of the shortage components of market prices over the year is expected to be at least as high as the annualized cost of new peaking capacity (and this situation is expected to persist over a sufficiently long period), new investment will be cost effective and will take place. That is, investment will occur when expected market prices provide sufficient revenues to cover the costs of new generation, and the cost of the new capacity will be equal to the value consumers place on that capacity.

Further, if the sum of the shortage components is expected to stay below the annualized cost of new peaking capacity, not only will new capacity not be added but existing capacity that does not expect to cover its avoidable costs will be retired or mothballed. Thus, when either excess or less-than-optimal capacity is expected, investors will eventually respond to expected spot prices of energy and adjust capacity back to the optimal level.

The real-world intuition for this result in typical unregulated markets is that investors make decisions based on forward-looking estimates of market outcomes, which govern the return they expect to receive. It is reasonable to suppose that investment in such markets is relatively efficient since investors have many opportunities to invest and bear the risks and rewards of their investment decisions.

The competitive, unregulated market of the theory, however, does not characterize much of the power industry. Historically, the power industry has generally been either government-owned or government-regulated. Although the process of restructuring has begun, elements of regulation, market power, and other impediments to competition remain, with some markets closer to effective competition than others. The demand side of the market has not been completed in many regions.[3] Decisions to open retail markets in the US have been reversed or suspended,[4] leaving many regions subject to a combination of market and regulatory forces.

Many of the regulatory responses are a reaction to particular perceived problems, such as price spikes or prices that are too low to support new investment. Those responses are often developed in politically-charged decision-making processes, rather than as part of a carefully considered regulatory regime. In the response to price spikes, there has been little recognition that efficient prices in energy-only markets must provide for a shortage component, which at any point in time reflects the marginal value of additional capacity. Often, the price spikes themselves have been exacerbated by lack of demand-side response, by regulatory policies that discourage investment, or by the real or perceived exercise of market power during times of high prices. In many markets, these spikes have led to interventions such as price caps on generators, market power mitigation measures, and re-cutting politically unpopular market outcomes. These particular interventions reduce the margins received by generators, increase uncertainty about future regulatory actions, and discourage investment.[5]

Thus the efficient decision-making process in unregulated competitive markets is undercut in restructured power markets. Not only do investors have more limited opportunities to invest—both because of the lumpiness of investment and because of their relative inexperience in nascent competitive markets for power generation—but regulatory intervention and changes in market structure have driven a wedge between the assumptions that guided investors' decisions and the resultant risks and rewards.

Risks in the Power Industry

The risks that investors face in power generation markets differ from those in industries that feature liquid markets for sale of the relevant product. While market institutions are developing to manage some risks to some degree, other risks, particularly those caused by regulatory uncertainty, are more difficult to manage.

Market Risks

The nonstorability of power, combined with limited or no demand response, creates volatility in power market prices that exceeds the volatility in typical financial markets.[6] The long-term liquid markets that would allow investors to hedge the risks on long-lived generating assets have been slow to develop in some markets.

Power market participants in a number of regions are developing solutions to the lack of long-term liquid markets. In some cases, large industrial customers have contracted with generators to obtain certain energy supplies at fixed prices.[7] Australia has an active contract market for generation.[8] The combination of retailing and generation functions in the same company also provides a natural hedge. Retail prices are more stable than wholesale prices, and retail customers do not switch suppliers as quickly as wholesale customers. In Britain, the industry has aggressively reintegrated since the expiration of the Government's Golden Shares in the 12 Regional Electricity Companies so that by late 2005, all six of the major companies owned both generation and retail supply businesses, and all but one of the six also owned multiple distribution networks.[9] In the US, some retailers, such as Centrica in the Energy Reliability Council of Texas (ERCOT), have begun to acquire generation to balance their customer obligations. Many other US energy holding companies that compete in restructured markets have continued to own both subsidiaries that control generation and subsidiaries that serve retail customers in competitive markets.

Non-Market Risks

Continued regulatory interventions in many jurisdictions have introduced uncertainty about future regulatory and administrative policies. Regulatory intervention often appears to be arbitrary and unpredictable and thus impossible to price or hedge against. Contracts or hedges that are fairly priced under one regulatory regime may no longer be fairly priced in the wake of regulatory actions such as imposition of price caps, changes to the rules governing capacity requirements, or introduction of locational energy pricing. In addition, regulatory intervention that reduces price spikes reduces price volatility and hence decreases the value of capacity while discouraging a true market for capacity. Regulatory intervention may thus undermine the development of market mechanisms to ameliorate uncertainty. After all, why should a retailer purchase a hedge in the form of a long-term capacity contract if the regulators have historically acted to provide one?

Furthermore, while regulatory intervention that increases market price volatility tends to increase the market value of capacity, monetizing the value of that capacity requires risk markets (forwards and options) and risk merchants.[10] To the extent that risk markets do not exist to price or hedge these risks, the financing may not be available to build an efficient level of capacity. Investors who may be willing to take on market and physical sources of risk may be unwilling to take on and unable to hedge regulatory risk. In order to allow market mechanisms to emerge and function effectively, regulators must have the patience and fortitude to refrain from changing the generation market rules for potentially lengthy periods of time.

Such regulatory patience and fortitude has been in short supply in some parts of the world, but not in all. Significant price spikes and even rolling blackouts have not led to government intervention in a number of countries. For example, early in the process of deregulation in the US, prices in the Midwest reportedly spiked above $4,000/MWh in the summers of 1998 and 1999 due to weather and in 1998 due to transmission and credit events.

Prices rose to A$9,000 per MWh in South Australia (SA) in late November 2004, when temperatures were at 37 degrees Celsius, network outages reduced supplies from NSW and VIC, and Pelican Point stopped generating. There were additional price spikes in early December 2004 due to high temperatures in Sydney. Prices reached almost A$10,000 per MWh in NSW and A$900 per MWh in Victoria, despite the fact that the weather was mild in Victoria. In late March 2005, there were widespread blackouts in SA due to equipment faults.

Prices in ERCOT spiked to $990/MWh in February 2003 as unseasonably cold weather in the Midwest interrupted gas delivery, causing outages at a number of gas-fired generators. Rolling blackouts occurred in April 2006 in ERCOT because of high demand due to unseasonably hot weather combined, with maintenance and unplanned generation outages.

Although there was an investigation of the summer 1998 Midwestern US events, these price spikes and rolling blackouts did not result in the kinds of interventions seen elsewhere (price caps, retrenchment from competitive markets, capacity requirements). It should be noted, however, that they occurred for only a number of hours or days. The high prices and volatility in the Western US markets in 2000 and 2001 that triggered retrenchment from retail competition lasted for months. And the impetus for administered capacity mechanisms in the Northeastern US appears at least in part to spring from the revenue concerns of generation owners.

Are Regulatory Mechanisms Necessary to Encourage Investment in Generating Capacity?

To counter the potential for underinvestment created by regulatory interventions and unhedgeable or poorly hedgeable risks, many wholesale markets are turning toward capacity mechanisms. Capacity requirements and capacity payment mechanisms are designed to ensure that sufficient investment occurs to meet regulator-determined reserve standards.[11] Ironically, in a situation of excess capacity, creating an administered mechanism to provide more revenue to generators will tend to slow the exit of inefficient plants[12] from the market and thus depress market prices for a longer period.

The recent theoretical literature on capacity requirements and capacity payments takes into account both uncertainty and other distortions.[13] This literature finds that underinvestment may result from a binding price cap, monopolistic investment behavior, lumpiness of new investments, and investor risk-aversion, combined with lack of long-term liquid markets for hedging risks. Depending on the existence of other distortions, capacity mechanisms can either distort investment decisions or move back toward the efficient investment path, although at the cost of other distortions relative to the competitive equilibrium. Further, depending on assumptions regarding investor foresight, investment cycles may occur in energy-only markets. Capacity payments may mitigate these cycles at the cost of other distortions, such as a distortion in the percentage of capacity that is peaking versus baseload. Generally, the findings of this literature depend on the specific underlying assumptions. In determining whether this literature makes the case for capacity mechanisms, readers must not only decide which assumptions are the most realistic portrayal of a particular set of market circumstances and investor behavior, but must also weigh the social costs of the distortions potentially alleviated with the social cost of the distortions potentially created by the capacity mechanism.

Looking beyond the theoretical literature to market experience, there are a few examples of markets in which regulators have not intervened extensively. Indications are that without capacity mechanisms in these markets, investment or disinvestment is occurring when warranted by the supply-demand situation and energy prices.

The Australian National Electricity Market (NEM)[14] is an example of an energy-only model with minimal interventions. Spot prices are currently subject to a cap of A$10,000 per MWh, which has remained in place since 2002 despite the initial intention to raise it to A$20,000 per MWh.[15] In addition, like virtually all system operators, NEMMCO has the power to intervene in the market when system reliability is threatened.[16] Even though the NEM does not incorporate a capacity mechanism, investment in new generation occur as the supply and demand outlook has tightened. Since the beginning of the NEM in 1998, generators have invested in over 5,000 MW of new capacity.[17] Over 16,000 MWs of new generation investment are proposed for the period to 2013, of which 3814 MWs are either under construction or in the advanced planning stages.[18] The pattern and level of prices over the year are generally considered to be at the "long-run new entrant level." While the market has to date been largely successful in encouraging new investment, the question of whether there should be some form of capacity mechanism is periodically re-considered by the Australian Energy Market Commission.[19] A review of capacity mechanisms in particular, concluded in 2002, found that no change to Australia's energy-only market design was warranted.[20]

Until 2001, the Electricity Pool of England & Wales linked generation capacity payments to the Loss of Load Probability. Since 2001, the British Electricity Trading and Transmission Arrangements (BETTA[21]) eliminated any explicit capacity payment mechanism, and the only remuneration for capacity derives from the price of energy bought and sold in the market. The market price at times of market shortage is underpinned by the penalty prices charged for energy supplied to traders who run a deficit.[22] The experience is mixed. In the first year without explicit capacity payments (2002), capacity and reserve margins increased. In the following year, spark spreads[23] also fell, as did capacity and reserve margins. Reserve margins in 2004 remained slightly below 25 percent, lower than the reserve margins in all but one year since the restructuring of the market began in 1991. So far, there have been no moves to take the initiative for investment in generating capacity out of the hands of private investors, although concerns about rising gas prices, increasing carbon emissions, and slow development of renewable energy sources have led to discussions at government level of a "nuclear option." If reserve margins continue to be adequate without government intervention, Britain will provide an example of sufficient investment without administered capacity mechanisms.

A comparison of recent changes in capacity in the New England ISO (NE-ISO, in the New England region of the US) and ERCOT is also instructive. Both markets were considerably overbuilt in the early 2000s. The similarity ends there, however. ERCOT is an energy-only market while the NE-ISO has a capacity requirement and active bilateral capacity markets with monthly and deficiency auctions conducted by the ISO. In March 2006, after years of discussion, ISO-NE generators and most of the load representatives agreed to establish a forward capacity market.[24] Physical differences exist as well between the two markets. The NE-ISO has access to hydro in Canada and there is the possibility of sales to New

York from selected locations in the NE-ISO. By contrast, ERCOT is effectively an island.

The reserve margin in the NE-ISO, which was a 28 percent in 2003,[25]
had fallen to about 20 percent by summer 2005.[26] The reserve margin in
ERCOT in 2003 was 38 percent,[27] and had fallen to under 17 percent by
summer 2005. In fact, on April 17, 2006, rolling blackouts were required
because of high demand due to unseasonably hot weather, combined with
maintenance and unplanned generation outages.[28] In both markets, load
growth had outpaced forecasts, but the dramatic decline in the reserve
margin in ERCOT is primarily due to the mothballing of 5 to 8 GW of
uneconomic older generators.[29] There was no similar wave of older units
leaving the NEPOOL market, a fact that can be attributed at least in part
to the uncertainty over the future value of installed capacity. Generators
were unlikely to exit the NEPOOL market until the oft-debated structure
of its capacity payment mechanism was finalized, in hopes that such a
payment might provide significant revenue. In ERCOT, where the potential for capacity payments was not held out, generators have reacted
quickly to adverse market conditions. Whether they will react as quickly
to invest when market conditions improve remains an open question.

In conclusion, in a wholesale market with significant distortions and
unhedgeable risks, it is not immediately apparent whether introducing
additional distortions results in a more or less efficient outcome. In this
environment, is it necessary to provide additional regulatory or administrative mechanisms to ensure efficient investment? The answer depends
on assumptions about what the future holds.

Important considerations include:

- What other regulatory interventions are likely in the future, and
  what are the risks associated with these? Regulatory stability is
  important for the development of effectively competitive markets.
  Certain regulatory and political choices, such as regular imposition
  of generation market price caps, may so stifle market responses
  that additional regulatory intervention is required.
- Is a stable combination of regulation and market forces possible or
  will the regulatory framework continually be changed when regulators or governments do not like the outcomes?
- Will the demand side of the market be completed? Will demand
  response reduce the temptation for regulatory intervention by
  reducing the frequency and amplitude of price spikes?

- Is the power generation industry inevitably subject to boom-bust cycles? The recent bust in some jurisdictions, which was the result of investor inexperience and over-exuberance, may not be repeated to the same extent as the market matures, and it appears that these markets are recovering. Even if the industry is inherently cyclical, do the cycles distort investment decisions, and are the transaction costs and potential distortions created by the cycles sufficient to warrant regulatory intervention, with its own distortions?
- Will long-term liquid markets develop to improve the efficiency with which the risks associated with investment in long-lived generation assets can be managed?
- In the absence of interventions, will financing be available for new generation when the supply-demand balance and market prices justify it? If so, will the risk premium required be politically acceptable? Will it be a higher cost than the costs introduced by regulatory intervention?
- Do the capacity mechanisms under consideration distort investment decisions or move back toward the efficient investment path? Do they create other distortions? What are the costs and benefits of the distortions that are created or mitigated? Will the capacity mechanism chosen be stable or subject to periodic regulatory changes?

In addressing the question of whether regulatory or administrative intervention is needed to ensure sufficient investment, it is necessary to weigh the costs and benefits of encouraging investment in generating capacity and mitigating investment cycles against the distortions in consumption, production, and investment decisions that the regulatory or administrative policies under consideration cause or reduce. The fact that markets without interventions or administered capacity mechanisms are working in some parts of the world suggests that, unless seriously flawed, the markets should be given a chance to work. There is no reason in principle why market forces cannot deliver sufficient generation capacity. Indeed, the capacity mechanisms implemented to date seem to be required primarily to offset other regulatory interventions that have had the effect of discouraging efficient investment in capacity.

Notes

1. Acknowledgements: The authors are indebted to our colleagues in Australia and in Europe for their extensive contributions and for sharing their knowledge of and insights into their own markets. In particular, we would like to thank Greg Houston, Director and Jennifer Fish, Consultant in NERA's Sydney, Australia office; Oscar Arnedillo, Director, Madrid; Graham Shuttleworth, Director, and Sean Gammons, Associate Director, London; and Francesco Lo Passo, Director, and Marcella Fantini, Consultant, Rome. Any errors or omissions are of course the responsibility of the authors.

2. For example, Michael A. Crew and Paul R. Kleindorfer, *Public Utility Economics,* (New York: St. Martin's Press, 1979), pp. 108-115.

3. See Michael J. King, Kathleen King, and Michael B. Rosenzweig, "Customer Sovereignty: Why Customer Choice Trumps Administrative Capacity Mechanisms" in this volume.

4. Examples in the US include California, Arizona, Nevada, Montana, New Mexico, Oklahoma, and Arkansas. Many more states that were considering opening their retail markets have shelved those plans.

5. In July 2003, NERA conducted a small survey for the Northeastern ISOs of merchant generators, financiers, and investors regarding the role and structure of capacity markets in ensuring sufficient generation will be present to meet future energy demands. The stability of market and regulatory structure and the sanctity of contracts (particularly those with regulatory or governmental entities) were cited as a major factor influencing whether new generation will be built, after the existence of long-term contracts for the generation off-take, and the supply and demand balance. In fact 70 percent of respondents cited these stability and contract sanctity issues even when they were not specifically raised in questions. Specific concerns cited ranged from changes in the definition of ICAP or UCAP to specific instances of an ISO changing the posted prices after entering into contracts and then re-cutting the contract, to the State of California's re-cutting contracts it entered into during a time of market turmoil. Of the 56 long-term contracts negotiated between the California Department of Water Resources and various energy companies between February and August 2001, 34 have been renegotiated. (http://www.platts.com/Electric%20Power/Resources/News%20Features/ california%2orefund/index_2.xml). Whether or not these regulatory/ governmental actions were warranted, respondents viewed themselves as being in a "heads they win, tails I lose" situation.

6. The market price of a kWh of electricity can range from negative (in hours when generators need to keep a unit operating in order to have it available the next day when prices will be high) to $4000 or more.

7. For example, TVO, an organization of large industrial customers in Finland, has combined with some municipal utilities to build a nuclear plant to avoid price volatility due to changing hydro conditions. A similar deal has been discussed in France, where a new nuclear plant would be backed by a 20- to 30-year contract between large industrial customers and EdF.

8. In Australia, generators and retailers or large industrial customers protect themselves from spot market movements by entering into financial or derivative contracts for differences, whereby one party makes a commitment to pay the counter-party an amount that is calculated by reference to the spot price. The general effect of these contracts, which are believed to account for the vast proportion of generator output in the NEM, is to swap market-determined financial obligations for an agreed, fixed, contract price.

9. At the time of writing, the six major companies are: BGT, Powergen, Scottish and Southern Energy, npower, EDF Energy, and Scottish Power. The six account for 99 percent of the retail supply market [*Domestic Retail Market Report—September 2005,* 6 February 2006, page 8] and 68 percent of generating capacity [*Platts Powervision,* First Quarter 2006]. All but BGT also own multiple distribution network companies [*Domestic Retail Market Report—September 2005,* 6 February 2006].

10. Options increase in value as volatility increases. A holder of an option, however, can only monetize the value of the option (or get cash for it now) if there are markets on which the option can be traded.

11. See Hamish Fraser, "Capacity Payment Mechanisms: How to Pick the One that is Right for You" in this volume.

12. Plant with forward-looking maintenance and running costs that exceed the expected value of the energy and capacity it provides.

13. See Audun Botterud and Magnus Korpas, "Modelling of Power Generation Investment Incentives Under Uncertainty in Liberalised Electricity Markets," Department of Electrical Engineering, Norwegian University of Science and Technology, 2004; Audun Botterud, "Long-Term Planning in Restructured Power Systems: Dynamic Modelling of Investments in New Power Generation under Uncertainty," Department of Electrical Engineering, Norwegian University of Science and Technology, Ph.D. Thesis, 2003; S.S Oren, "Ensuring Generation Adequacy in Competitive Electricity Markets," University of California Energy Institute, Energy Policy and Economics No. 7, Berkeley, CA; D. Bunn and E. R. Larsen, "Sensitivity of Reserve Margin to Factors Influencing Investment Behaviour in the Electricity Market of England and Wales," *Energy Policy* 20 (1992) 420-429; A. Ford, "Cycles in Competitive Electricity Markets: A Simulation Study of the Western United States," *Energy Policy* 27 (1999) 637-658; P. Visudhiphan, P. Skantze, and M.D. Ilic, "Dynamic Investment in Electricity Markets and Its Impact on System Reliability," *Proceedings of the Market Design 2001 Conference,* Stockholm, Sweden, 2001; L.J. De Vries, "Securing the Public Interest in Electricity Generation Markets: The Myths of the Invisible Hand and the Copper Plate," PhD Thesis, Technical University Delft, Delft, Netherlands; A. Botterud, "Optimal Investments in Power Generation under Centralised and Decentralised Decision Making," *IEEE Transactions on Power Systems* (2005); and S. Skrede and H.O. Iglebaek, "Capacity Expansion in Deregulated Power Markets," MSc Thesis, Norwegian University of Science and Technology, Trondheim, Norway.

14. The NEM is the single interconnected power system that includes Queensland, New South Wales, the Australian Capital Territory, Victoria, South Australia, and Tasmania. It does not include either the Northern Territory or Western Australia. A capacity mechanism is in place in the Western Australian

Wholesale Electricity Market. However, this is an isolated market with one dominant generator, and supplies cannot be drawn from neighboring systems in times of crisis. For further information see http://www.imowa.com.au/reserve_capacity_overview.htm

15. At the completion of its first review in 2000, NECA recommended that VoLL be increased from $5,000 per MWh to A$10,000 per MWh in September 2001, with a further increase to A$20,000 per MWh in April 2002. See ACCC, "VoLL, capacity mechanisms and removal of zero price floor," Final Determination (20 December 2000). It is worth noting that, while the generating assets in Victoria and New South Wales have been privatized or placed in long-term vesting contracts, most of the other generating assets in Australia have been corporatised but remain in public ownership.

16. In order to ensure reliability of supply, the market and system operator NEMMCO has set a reliability standard of 0.002 percent of unserved energy— meaning that over the long term, supply must be no less than 99.998 per cent of demand. When reserves fall, or appear likely to fall, below the minimum reserve levels required to meet the reliability standard, NEMMCO has the power to intervene in the market by (a) acting as a "reserve trader," and/or (b) requiring generators to provide additional supply at the time of dispatch to meet minimum reserve levels. As a reserve trader, NEMMCO purchases ahead of time the additional reserve generation it forecasts will be needed at the time the market is dispatched to meet minimum reserve levels. NEMMCO has used its reserve trader powers only twice since the start of the NEM. In both cases it entered short-term contracts for reserve capacity to meet summer peak demand but did not find it necessary to dispatch any of these contracts.

17. ESSA, Electricity Australia 2000. Excludes capacity from the Northern Territory and Western Australia.

18. ESSA, Electricity Gas Australia 2006, Appendix 2a.

19. See AEMC Reliability Panel, Comprehensive Reliability Review Issues Paper, May 2006 at http://www.aemc.gov.au/electricity.php?r=20051215.142656.

20. See NECA, Capacity Mechanisms: The Options, August 2002 at http://www.neca.com.au/SubCategoryco81.html?SubCategoryID=232.

21. Until 2005, BETTA was known as the New Electricity Trading Arrangements, or NETA, and only covered England and Wales, like the old Electricity Pool. In April 2005, the rules were extended to cover all of Great Britain, i.e., England, Scotland, and Wales, and the system acquired its new name.

22. That is, traders who generate or buy less than they sell or supply to consumers.

23. The spark spread is the difference between the market price of electricity and the price of natural gas or other fuel used to produce it, expressed in similar units.

24. The settlement was approved by the FERC on June 16, 2006. The NE forward-capacity auction will procure capacity three years ahead to allow time for new entry. See Amparo D. Nieto and Hamish Fraser, "Locational Electricity Capacity Markets: Alternatives to Restore the Missing Signals" in this volume for a discussion of this approach.

25. ISO New England 2003 CELT Report.

26. ISO New England 2005 CELT Report.

27. 2003 Report on the Capacity, Demand, and Reserves in the ERCOT Region.

28. 2005 Report on the Capacity, Demand, and Reserves in the ERCOT Region.

29. 2003 and 2005 Reports on the Capacity, Demand, and Reserves in the ERCOT Region.

15

CAPACITY PAYMENT MECHANISMS: HOW TO PICK THE ONE THAT'S RIGHT FOR YOU

Hamish Fraser

Introduction and Background

Ultimately, the primary public policy objective of all electricity markets is simple: to ensure security of supply at the lowest sustainable cost. Around the world, regulators, government agencies, and others are concerned that a market for electrical energy alone might not provide the needed economic signals for the maintenance of installed energy capacity, the construction of new capacity as needed, and the participation of demand resources. A key challenge for a generator who wishes to enter the market is to convince prospective lenders that the investment risk can be evaluated and that the risk is reasonably low. But future energy market revenues are inherently uncertain, and thus expectations of revenue might not be sufficient to ensure that new investment is timely. In turn, under-investment or late investment by resource providers can have serious repercussions for prices paid by customers and for supply adequacy. In addition, prices in energy markets are potentially volatile, a fundamental concern of many policy makers.

A Capacity Payment Mechanism (CPM) is intended to calm the volatility while ensuring supply adequacy through meaningful economic signals to generators and demand-side resources. These economic signals should lead to socially efficient decisions on new investments, on maintenance of existing capacity, and on demand response. However, there is no "best" capacity solution. The best CPM for any particular jurisdiction, (country or market), is a function of the specific conditions in that jurisdiction. Broadly speaking, while the same issues may apply across all jurisdictions, the relative importance of the issues differs from one place to another, and as a consequence the best choice of CPM may differ.

Capacity Payments Mechanisms as a Response to Market Failure

Many electric markets are grappling the issue of how to ensure supply adequacy and protect against undue price volatility. While addressing in part a common problem, the underlying causes can be quite different, for example, retail prices that are set by governments far below the cost of new entry, or the need to create extra forms of payment to generators to compensate for politically imposed caps in energy markets. At their core, the main arguments favoring CPMs have the sometimes unspoken premise that supply adequacy is a shared good. This view is sometimes nothing more than a statement about a historical situation, but it is further justified by the fact that in a retail competition environment, to the extent that aggregate supply is inadequate, random curtailments will be imposed on customers, even those who have contracted with a distributor or retailer that has adequate resources. Since everyone shares the same transmission system, there is no easy way the system operator can discriminate physically between customers of a distributor or retailer able to serve load and those of a distributor or retailer unable to meet its commitments. Further implied in this statement is that in the short-term demand is independent of price and that supply and demand are balanced in the operating time frame through physical (noneconomic) rationing.

It is useful to compare the noneconomic rationing of supply that can exist in electricity markets with the way that most other types of market ration scarce supply, and in particular to pose the question: *How might system reliability and market price volatility become unacceptable to stakeholders in the electricity industry, and not in other industries?* The answer rests with the fact that in most other markets, demand is a function of price, and price rations supply. Other markets can be represented by diagrams of supply and demand curves, with the market-clearing prices and quantities. When demand increases, prices rise, and as a result, some of the customers who would choose to consume at the initial price now choose not to consume. Similarly when demand falls, prices fall, and at the lower prices some of the customers who would choose *not* to consume at the initial price now decide they *will* consume. The implication of the demand response is that the market is "reliable", i.e., customers self-determine the level of reliability they want. If any customer requires greater continuation of uninterrupted supply than the market average, then that customer will pay more on average than other customers. Another implication is that this price-sensitive demand reduces market price volatility. When prices would otherwise be very high, the demand response *reduces* the quantity consumed and *reduces* the price accordingly. Likewise, when prices would otherwise be very low, the demand response *increases* the quantity consumed and *increases* the price accordingly.

Contrast this situation with electricity markets, where system conditions can change quickly in the short term, yet there is virtually no mechanism by which customers can react to short-term changes in price. For the most part, final electricity consumers face fixed averaged prices and simply have no incentive to respond to changes in the wholesale price. Most do not face actual hourly wholesale prices, and very few even have hourly meters.[1] Further exacerbating the lack of demand response, the supply side of the industry can only respond to high prices by building new generating plant in the long term (two to three years lead time). As a result, energy-only markets can produce very volatile short-term prices. Most of the time, price might be based on the Short-Run Marginal Cost (SRMC) of generation. But when the prices spike, they can spike to very high levels because there is little on either the supply or the demand side to constrain them.

While policymakers accept that an important objective of the market is that price should signal the need to finance new capacity, most argue that the signal should not result in extreme price spikes when that capacity is needed. Nor should it result in unacceptable economic impacts, such as large transfers of wealth within a short period of time for little or no efficiency benefit. They are therefore inclined to impose price caps in energy-only markets to limit spikes to socially acceptable levels.

But the imposition of price caps is not the answer—at least, it is not the answer in the long term, and it is not the full answer in the short term. While price caps may stem unreasonable wealth transfers, they can deny generators the ability to recover their total costs—i.e., their fixed costs over and above SRMC—and therefore they reduce the incentives for generators to invest the amounts necessary to assure required levels of reliability.

A further problem with relying on price spikes to provide the necessary investment signals is the uncertainty due to the unpredictability of load and forced outages. Each price spike hour contributes to the recovery of fixed costs for all generators in an energy-only market so that a reasonably accurate estimate of outage hours and prices is a prerequisite for investors to estimate whether the fixed costs of a new investment will be recovered. But in practice, the number of outage hours is especially diffi-cult for a generator contemplating entering the market to estimate, particularly when it is very likely that there are only a few hours in which prices spike. Further, the hours will be highly auto-correlated. When an extreme condition exists in a particular hour, the next hour is likely to exhibit that condition as well. There could be no outages for many years, and then in one year there might be many in a row.[2] This uncertainty and this pattern of uncertainty increase the investment risk for a generator, and this risk translates into a considerable uncertainty surrounding the level of capacity that the market will induce participants to build.

An important objective of electricity market reform is to provide incentives that ensure an acceptable level of reliability.[3] It can be impos-sible, or nearly impossible to achieve this objective in an energy-only market, given (1) the extent to which demand is not responsive to price and customers cannot self-determine the level of reliability they want, and (2) a situation where new entrants are uncertain whether they can recover their fixed costs. Where the consequences of shortages are shared in a way that has nothing to do with a customer or a distributor or retailer having arranged an adequate supply, then there is a good argu-ment for using a CPM.

If price spikes and the lack of *short-term* demand response were not sufficient reasons by themselves to use CPMs, lack of demand-side partic-ipation in energy markets in the *long-term* is another market failure that leads to CPMs. The development of retail markets in many jurisdictions, including most of the US, has been stunted. There are few commercial counterparties with whom merchant generation investors can sign long-term power purchase agreements. The forward markets that do exist for multiyear contracts tend to be quite illiquid.[4] But generators entering a market cannot finance projects based on spot market sales alone. Suppliers of both equity and debt require some degree of revenue certainty over a multiyear period before they will finance a new power plant with an economic life of 20 to 30 years. Until a long-term demand side of the market develops, some other means of financing capacity must be found.

Finally, while some electricity markets have so far managed to operate quite successfully without a CPM, these markets appear to be mostly exceptions to the norm. For example, the BETTA market in Britain does not have a CPM, but it began life with a considerable capacity surplus that may in part have been encouraged by pre-BETTA CPM provisions. Britain also has developed an enviable level of demand response since full retail competition was completely implemented in 1999. And in any event, potential CPMs continue to be investigated in Britain.

New Zealand does not have a CPM. However, as a hydro-dominant system it has investigated equivalent mechanisms to deal with "dry years" and was recently forced to adopt an ad hoc scheme to build a small peaking plant in response to a dry year adequacy problem.

Australia is perhaps the best example of a market with no CPM. Prices are allowed to spike to levels that are high by international standards. However, much of Australia's generating capacity is state-owned, so investment incentives may be different. Some parts of Australia also have a reasonable amount of demand response. To the extent that either customers or the retailer has time-of-use meters and settlement is done on the basis of hourly consumption by a retailer's customers (rather than by use of general load profiles), the *retailer* has the incentive to make arrangements with customers willing to have their load curtailed (rationed) during high-priced hours. Customers pay fixed prices specified in their contracts, but retailers offer discounts for interruptibility and curtail service to participating consumers when the wholesale market price is high.

CPMs and Market Structure

There is no universally accepted capacity solution. Virtually every capacity mechanism in the world, including each CPM in the US, remains under review. The criteria that can be used as yardsticks to measure the effectiveness of a proposed CPM are largely the same one jurisdiction to the next, as are the building blocks that are needed to make up a capacity mechanism. The trick is that every market is different, and it is necessary to build a solution that meets the specific needs unique to each market. The relative importance of each criterion will depend on the state of industry restructuring and the type of market, as well as specific regional issues.

There is little need for a CPM in vertically integrated systems or in single buyer markets where Independent Power Producers compete to sell contracts to a monopoly retail supplier. The vertically integrated system was the US model for over 100 years, and it is still the model in many US states and other countries; and the single buyer market is a typical first step of restructuring. Since prices and investment decisions are almost fully regulated in these types of systems, the most important criterion is capacity adequacy. This is achieved through a regulator-imposed requirement on the utilities, with corresponding tariffs approved to allow costs to be recovered. The contracts in single buyer markets are typically Power

Purchase Agreements for the life of the plant and typically include sales of capacity as well as energy. The CPM function is often little more than a requirement that the monopoly retail supplier demonstrate to its regulator that a minimum level of installed capacity has been procured at minimum overall cost. Because market energy prices are not relied upon to attract entry at this stage, the main consideration in these markets is capacity adequacy and the definition of who is responsible for ensuring capacity adequacy.

CPMs are also unnecessary when the market is fully competitive—i.e., when there is not just the legal right for retail consumers to choose, but rather when there is also deep and liquid competition on the demand side without large numbers of retail customers remaining on regulated default tariffs. As demand-side participation builds up, demand response should be able to ensure reliability, and the main concern of policymakers will be stable prices rather than adequate capacity.

The most relevant market structure for the use of CPMs is one that includes wholesale competition but not yet the demand responsiveness of full retail competition. In this structure, generation is fully competitive and is not regulated through cost-of-service, and the incumbent generator(s) are no longer obligated to ensure adequate capacity. The purchasers are distribution companies and perhaps a few large customers. This is a common situation. It applies to much of North America and Europe. A role of the regulators is to provide incentives that result in capacity sufficient to meet an acceptable level of reliability. This should be achieved through an efficient mix of the right type of new capacity constructed at the right time, and increased availability of existing capacity. Other objectives of the regulators are to ensure that price signals are reasonable and do not result in extreme price and bill spikes and unacceptable economic impacts when more capacity is needed.

In essence, regulators design CPMs in a competitive wholesale market by requiring the buy side of the industry to pay an insurance premium for protection against the outages and price spikes that would occur when capacity is scarce. With a CPM, generators should face reduced volatility in short-term market energy prices. At times, prices could be driven down to variable cost levels, and at other times, they may be tightly capped to prevent undue market manipulation and to limit price spikes to socially acceptable levels. Instead of recovering capital during periods of scarcity and very high prices, the CPM seeks to mitigate those periods and provide for capital recovery through the insurance premium. That premium will provide an incentive for the construction of capacity that will, in time, avoid periods of scarcity.

Regulators may consider tradeoffs between various objectives. For example, if a market starts life with sufficient capacity, then price stability and concerns over gaming, fairness and simplicity could weigh heavily in the choice of CPM. In a liquid market with relatively sophisticated mechanisms for forward contracting and risk control, and perhaps some limited form of real-time pricing to load, concerns about ensuring a particular level of reserve might be somewhat replaced by concerns about the efficiency of the price signals to long-term investors.

The particular choice of the CPM will also depend on the type of market. Some CPMs may be easier to implement in a centralized pool-based market than in a decentralized physical bilateral contract-based market. For example, a CPM that is based on making payments for capacity availability might be harder to implement in a bilateral market where availability might not be continuously monitored and under the control of a central entity.

Specific regional issues may also affect the choice of a CPM. Where two jurisdictions are adjacent and have significant levels of trade, it might be unwise to have CPM arrangements that are substantially different. This was once the case among PJM and the markets to the west and south, and it led to price incentives to market participants that were inconsistent with the intended capacity market rules.

There is little question that it is useful to consider some form of CPM in any jurisdiction that has introduced wholesale competition and where the demand side is less than fully developed. There are a number of examples where the pricing mechanisms that have been adopted have been unsuccessful in driving long-term investment decisions in new generation. Ireland and Greece have recently experienced capacity shortages resulting in the need for administrative procurement processes. In some jurisdictions, there was a rush to build new capacity as soon as the market opened. In other jurisdictions, the market opened with an excess of reserves already in place, but there is now concern that future capacity requirements might not be forthcoming: Load growth, plant retirements, and a lack of appetite for new investment by companies (many of whom are now bankrupt as a result of initially rushing into some markets and driving prices down) potentially combine to convert current excess capacity into deficits within a few years. Large markets, such as some regional US markets, Britain, and even Russia, fall into this category.

Criteria for Designing and Evaluating CPM Alternatives

This section describes the criteria that can be used to evaluate CPM alternatives. Not all the criteria will necessarily be simultaneously achievable; however, an analysis of the extent to which each one is achievable, with a weighting based the relative importance placed on each one, will help determine the best overall CPM choice for a particular jurisdiction.

Capacity Adequacy/Reliability of the System

The chosen CPM must provide for adequate installed generating capacity to meet a defined reliability standard. It must encourage the construction of capacity that the market might otherwise not elicit because of the uncertainty of capital recovery. Additionally, the CPM should encourage short-term availability when required and should encourage efficient maintenance scheduling of installed capacity.

Efficient Price Signals for Long-Term Investments

The CPM should avoid distorting investment decisions. It should not "double pay" generators through its capacity and energy payments. It should achieve capacity adequacy consistent with efficient energy market signals and without interfering with market forces other than those related to the provision of capacity. Overall prices should efficiently signal when, where, and what types of new generators are required—and efficiently signal when, where, and what market exit is appropriate.

Price Stability

Compared to an energy-only market, the CPM should reduce market price uncertainty and reduce risk premiums to investors. In jurisdictions with advanced retail access, wholesale market energy prices are critical because expectations of these prices flow directly into the retail price offers made by competing retailers and into the prices of direct purchases, swaps, and contract hedges available to large users. These energy prices must be set by competitive forces but must be at levels that do not require extraordinary demand response to ration supply and do not involve excessive wealth transfers from buyers to sellers at peak time periods. Prices that must spike to levels well above SRMC in order to maintain the required capacity adequacy/reliability of the system might *not* meet these requirements. These price spikes may occur during prolonged periods of shortage, alternating with prolonged periods of surplus, so that the resulting price fluctuations flow through into unacceptable variation in the retail prices. The CPM must therefore take some of the volatility out of the energy market by shifting the revenue required to attract investment away from energy price spikes, and should replace these revenues to generators (and equivalently, these costs to customers) with another mechanism.

Susceptibility to Gaming

The chosen policy proposal should not be susceptible to gaming, where individual market participants, acting in their own best interests, can cause outcomes inconsistent with the objectives of policymakers. The chosen policy proposal should rather be incentive-compatible, so that market participants, by acting in their own best interests, should have incentives to cause the desired outcomes. The chosen policy proposal should not rely unduly on noncompliance penalties to force these outcomes.

Fairness

The CPM should not unfairly discriminate between participants. For example, if a CPM meets the first criterion of providing adequate capacity and reducing the likelihood of involuntary load curtailment, then it is likely that the CPM will have decreased the number of times that the installed reserve margin falls to critical levels. However, a CPM will inevitably result in cost increases associated with greater reliability for distributors, retailers, and electricity users in times when capacity *is not* scarce and lower prices when capacity is scarce. A fair scheme would maintain reasonable proportionality between the payments made to achieve adequate capacity and the benefits received from attaining it. Buyers in the electricity market should pay in proportion to the benefit they receive, and all generators who contribute to greater reliability in exchange for reduced price spikes should be rewarded proportionately.

Simplicity

The CPM should be transparent, predictable and simple to administer. This is not just an aim in itself; it is also a prerequisite for the scheme to offer better incentives for long-term investment.

Building Blocks of a CPM

Various choices need to be made to build up complete CPM alternatives, which can then be evaluated against the design criteria. This section describes the main choices and then provides a checklist of the key attributes.

Nature of Scheme

The two major alternatives with respect to the overall nature of a CPM are:

1. Schemes that fix a capacity payment (or payment formula) and make the payment available to generators willing to offer capacity at that price, and
2. Schemes that set a quantity of capacity required to ensure adequacy and either impose an obligation on market participants to provide such a quantity or have a central buyer procure such a quantity.

The two schemes may share many common elements, but they are fundamentally different. In the first, the payment is fixed and the quantity of capacity available to the market depends on the willingness of generators to offer capacity at that fixed price. In the second, the quantity of capacity is fixed, and the payment is determined by the cost of the marginal supplier. A hybrid of these two schemes is also possible.

The key attribute of a fixed capacity payment is that a central authority specifies either a payment level or a formula as a supplement to energy payments. That payment is then made to generators who provide the capacity product. With the fixed payment scheme, generators, who are deciding whether to keep existing plants open or develop new plants, are able to factor capacity payments into their economic decision-making process, in addition to their projections of energy market revenue opportunities. Provided that the capacity payment is set sufficiently high to cover the fixed cost of maintaining or developing generation plants above what a generator would expect to be able to recover from the energy and ancillary services markets, the CPM would be expected to make it profitable for new plants to enter the market when additional capacity is required. The payment can be set in advance and reset periodically, or it can function via a formula that automatically updates. For example, in the old England & Wales pool, the CPM was implemented half-hourly based on day-ahead projections of half-hourly loss of load probability (LOLP) and a value of lost load (VOLL) established by the regulator.[5] A fixed payment scheme can also be designed so that the capacity payment to each eligible unit of generation capacity is set for a period of time and announced in advance. A methodology is needed to determine the initial payment level and the timing and method for resetting the payment level. Spain, Chile, Argentina, and Ireland all have schemes that set a fixed capacity payment in advance and for a set period.

In the alternative fixed quantity method, a central authority establishes a quantity of capacity that is needed, most often by a loss of load expectation (LOLE) analysis. An acceptable LOLE might be something like eight hours per year, meaning that on average the required level of capacity will meet total demand in all but eight hours per year.[6] Having identified the required amount of capacity, the central authority can assign a capacity obligation to each distributor/retailer and assess a penalty if it fails to contract for sufficient capacity. Or, the central authority can procure such capacity through a competitive process such as an auction or an Invitation to Tender (ITT).

Hybrid mechanisms combine elements of the two approaches so that the capacity price is formed by the intersection of an administratively determined capacity demand curve and the curve of prices offered by suppliers. The New York ISO, for example, produces downward-sloping demand curves and requires each load serving entity (LSE) to possess or purchase enough capacity to cover the capacity quantity at the point where the curves cross, in proportion to its share of the forecast peak demand. At the target quantity, the capacity price is the estimated annual cost of a new peaking unit less that unit's energy market margins. The downward-sloping demand curve represents the decreasing marginal value of additional capacity. If the supplies are plentiful, the LSEs might be obliged to purchase more capacity than the target level, but at a lower price. Conversely, when supplies are limited, LSEs might purchase less than the target level but at a higher price.

Product Definition

The next step in designing a CPM, whether fixed payment, fixed quantity, or hybrid, is to define the product. While the product is generally called "capacity", there is no universal definition of what that term means. It is necessary to define in detail the generator's obligations in providing capacity, how compliance with those obligations will be monitored, and the buyer's obligations, including the details of the payment scheme. Essentially, the definition of the capacity product is a description of the terms and conditions as embodied in a capacity contract. Note however that the capacity contract need not be an explicit bilateral contract, but may be established as part of the market rules. The principal features of the product design are the term, the lead time, performance provisions, and the contractual relationship.

Term

A significant factor is the term (tenor, or length) of the contract, that is, the period for which the mutual commitments apply. The term is the duration for which a payment is fixed, either as embedded in market rules or in explicit contracts with generators. Longer terms can be an important factor in mitigating the risk that investors face with capacity investments.

When capacity payments are embedded in the market rules, the term is usually indefinite because the payment scheme will apply until regulators, legislators, or ministers change the rules. However, even when the term is indefinite, the payment may be fixed for a certain amount of time—six months, a year, or a number of years. Alternatively, the market rules may call for a central authority to enter into an explicit capacity contract with each generator, setting forth mutual obligations. In that case, a key element of the contract would be the term, which could also vary from a period of months to a period of years.

Lead Time

The lead time is the period of time between the date upon which mutual commitments are formally agreed and the date by which a generator must have capacity available and the performance provisions first apply. The length of the lead time may vary from nothing to a period of years. Longer lead times can allow new entrants to compete for capacity payments; however, the total quantity of capacity required to achieve a particular minimum LOLE standard is less certain when the lead time is longer.

Performance Provisions

Performance provisions are the obligations of the generator and define what a generator must deliver to receive payments and avoid penalties. Since a main objective of capacity is often to meet a supply adequacy standard measured in LOLE, the performance requirements are typically geared to factors that enable LOLE to be reduced by the development and maintenance of generation capacity. Key aspects of these provisions include:

- **Demonstrated Maximum Net Capability (DMNC):** A generator's capacity payment will generally be based on its DMNC. The DMNC might be established by periodic tests that require a generator to demonstrate that it can produce power at a given level for a given duration at specified ambient conditions. The old England & Wales pool avoided periodic tests by setting the generators' availability equal to their declared level. The DMNC was subject to a cap equal to the registered capacity for which they paid transmission tariffs until the plant suffered a forced outage, after which the cap was set equal to the maximum level of output achieved since the outage.
- **Primary energy source availability:** The ability of a generator to reduce LOLE will depend not only on its DMNC, but also on the availability of its primary energy source (fuel). Generators with virtually unlimited primary energy sources contribute to reducing LOLE based on DMNC and mechanical availability. However, generators with limits on fuel availability (such as hydro plants and wind turbines) can reduce LOLE only when fuel is also expected to be available. The equivalent capacity that an energy-limited source contributes to reducing LOLE can be computed by modeling the energy source limit.
- **Mechanical Availability:** Mechanical availability, represented by a forced outage rate and maintenance requirements, affects the degree to which generating capacity can be relied on to reduce LOLE. All else being equal, capacity with higher forced-outage expectations or greater maintenance requirements contributes less per unit of DMNC to reducing LOLE and is usually eligible for a lesser payment than capacity that is more available. CPMs usually require (1) that performance be tracked and verified with respect to scheduled maintenance and forced outage and (2) that this performance in some way affect the payment or trigger a penalty.
- **Deliverability:** In order to reduce LOLE, the output of the plant must be deliverable under peak conditions. Since some plants may be unable to operate at full output at peak times due to network constraints, capacity requirements or payments could be defined on a locational basis. Alternatively, the plant could be required to meet a defined deliverability standard, and—particularly if the inter-

connection requirements do not require new generators to provide transmission upgrades—it is advisable to check how much of a plant's potential output is deliverable to all load under peak conditions.

In sum, a CPM should ensure that generators have incentives to build and maintain capacity consistent with their contribution to reducing LOLE. It is not necessary to impose standards with respect to actual availability under adverse system conditions. As long as maintenance is coordinated, forced outages are random and primary fuel availability has been realistically represented, it is expected that some plants will be unavailable during times of greatest need, and the risk that a plant is unavailable when needed does not have to be assigned to the plant owner.

There remains a question of providing appropriate short-term incentives to encourage generators to be available when they are most needed. Such incentives should derive primarily from the energy market, where prices rise at times of system stress. Therefore, the need to build short-term incentives into CPMs emerges only if energy market (and operating reserve market) prices are unable to perform this function—for example, if they are capped too tightly.

Contractual Relationship
As discussed previously, the obligation of the generator will be part of some type of contract, either an explicit bilateral contract or a more general contract in which the CPM is incorporated into the market rules. An explicit bilateral contract would probably be with a central buyer/authority and would be standard across all generators. Explicit contracts are desirable where the term is fixed and sellers could view the contract as providing certainty, or where there are penalties for nonperformance that require generators to offer financial security—penalties that might be easier to enforce as part of an explicit contract. For example, some CPMs envisage that generators are selected several years in advance of need and that they can commit to building plants on the basis of receiving capacity payments. Such schemes usually involve a financial security that would be forfeited if the plant is not built on time.

Payment Level

Both the level and the structure of the payment need to be determined, and these differ between the schemes that fix the payment and the schemes that set the quantity.

Fixed Payment CPM

For schemes that fix the payment, decisions must be made about (1) the principle to be used to set the payment, (2) the choice of the entity responsible for setting the payment, and (3) the applicable regulatory or legal review procedures. If the CPM specifies a formula, any subjectivity in the setting of input parameters must be minimized and clearly set out, and the process for modifying the formula must also be decided.

Economic theory suggests that the capacity payment should represent the difference between two market prices:

1. energy-only market prices that can rise to include the value of unserved load and that would prevail in a competitive market where there were no limits on energy prices; and
2. the energy market prices that result from the market rules as they are implemented and as they may constrain prices to be effectively capped by the marginal cost of production.

In a market with just the right amount of capacity to meet the efficient LOLE target, this level of the capacity payment should equal the annual carrying cost of a new peaking unit (currently represented by a combustion turbine) less the expected net revenue that such a unit could earn in the energy and ancillary service markets.[7] Capacity prices set at this level should be just sufficient to encourage efficient entry and exit of the right amount of capacity.[8]

Thus, the capital required to develop a new peaking unit would be compensated in two ways. First, a portion would be expected to come from the margins available from operating in energy and ancillary service markets. Second, the amount not provided by those margins would be captured through the capacity payment. A combination of this capacity payment and energy market opportunities would induce and support efficient development of more capital-intensive plants, both intermediate and baseload. Those plants would have lower energy costs and would earn greater margins from energy sales than a peaking plant. These greater margins would induce and finance investment in the higher capital costs of intermediate and base load plants.

This economic theory, however, only applies when supply and demand are in balance. When available installed capacity *exceeds* the amount required to meet the efficient LOLE target, the value of the lost load that would have been reflected in the unconstrained energy prices drops exponentially below the annualized cost of peaking plants. When the available installed capacity is less than the target amount, the value of the lost load that would have been reflected in energy prices rises exponentially above the annual cost of peaking capacity. Hence, raising the capacity payment when capacity is short and reducing it when capacity is long, would (on a short-term basis) equilibrate the capacity payment with the value of lost load that would result from competitive unconstrained energy prices. It would also introduce an element of price volatility.[9] However, it is still possible to adjust the capacity payment on a longer-term basis, say for a year, to reflect the supply/demand balance. Reducing the capacity payment where there is surplus capacity will signal to the market that no additional capacity is required. Increasing the capacity payment when there is too little capacity will signal that more capacity is needed.

Fixed Quantity CPM

In a fixed quantity CPM, there is no administrative setting of the payment level. Instead the quantity of capacity that will be remunerated is fixed and set equal to the LOLE target. The price is then determined by a competitive method, an ITT or auction; Offers are accepted up to the target level and a clearing price is determined that is paid to all generators. The tender process can be done for any lead time and for any contract term.

A fixed quantity scheme with a tender is substantively different from a fixed payment scheme. With a fixed payment, the price is set in order to induce the target amount of capacity and the result is an amount of capacity which may be higher, lower, or equal to the target. In the fixed quantity scheme, the amount of capacity achieved matches the target, but the price is the unknown and it may be higher, lower, or equal to the price assumed when the target level of capacity was chosen, depending on how competitive the market is, how well the tender has been structured, and whether the lead time is sufficient to allow potential new entrants to compete. In theory, given a competitive market and well-designed tender or auction, the price that results from the tender or auction should be the same as the efficient capacity payment.

Hybrid Mechanism CPM

The major task in a hybrid CPM is setting the capacity demand curve. The mechanism combines elements of setting the price in a fixed price method and setting the quantity in a fixed quantity method, in order to determine a target point through which the administratively determined capacity demand curve passes. The key additional decisions are the slope of the curve and the maximum price (if any) that is applied.

Links to the Other Markets

The methodology for payments for the capacity product must recognize the links between the capacity market and the energy and ancillary services markets. The rationale for the capacity market is that prices in the energy market will not rise to reflect the true value of lost load, or will not do so with sufficient certainty, and hence will not induce sufficient entry. If the constraints (caps) on the energy price were so tight that energy prices rarely rose above marginal production costs, something close to the full annual carrying cost of a peaking unit would need to be reflected in the capacity prices. The capacity payment would be lower if it were expected that energy prices could rise substantially above marginal production costs. Thus, a critical link to the energy market is that the level of capacity payment must reflect constraints and conditions in the energy market generally and more specifically, factors that suppress energy prices (e.g., bidding limits, price caps, mitigation schemes).

The level of the capacity payment should also reflect other factors that influence energy prices, such as supply conditions, short-run demand inelasticity, etc. These factors can be observed over time, but it is difficult to determine the value of these factors when initially setting a capacity payment level prior to market experiences in the energy market.

Proper consideration of expected energy prices in the capacity payment level is critical. If energy profits are *understated* in setting the capacity payment level (by the central authority in the fixed price method, or by the generators in the fixed quantity method), customers will pay twice for a portion of the capacity payment: once for the portion that is in energy price and a second time in a higher-than-needed capacity payment. But if energy price expectations are *overstated,* new peaking generators will not recover investment cost, and the resulting levels of entry would be inefficiently low and supply adequacy would be unacceptable.

A possible solution is to force energy prices toward marginal cost so there is no double payment. However, this solution comes at a cost since energy prices that reflect scarcity serve important short-term efficiency purposes. They signal consumers to use electricity efficiently and generators to maximize output (e.g., postpone maintenance and operate above rated capacity for short periods). A price-capping mechanism that constrains price to marginal costs sacrifices these signals (and may require that the signals be reproduced in the CPM). This situation highlights a threshold CPM issue: whether it is the CPM or the energy market that is to be the primary tool for maximizing efficient management of short-term availability. Once facilities are constructed, generators still face short-term decisions as to the extent of availability. They could elect to save costs by not being available to run during off-peak periods. One view of a CPM is that the mechanism is a "stick" with which the central planner can specify minimum levels of availability and penalize generators that fail to deliver that availability. An alternative view is that the energy/ancillary services market prices are sufficient "carrots" to encourage generators to be available when market prices signal the need. The CPM encourages sufficient entry, but once installed, availability to generate would only be insisted upon in defined instances of system stress. For example, in PJM, a unit with a low forced outage rate that contributes more to meeting the system LOLE target is credited for capacity purposes with more MW than an equivalent unit with a higher forced outage rate. Eligibility to sell capacity prospectively is thus affected by the historic forced outage rate. Hence there is an incentive for good availability. There is, however, no link in the short term between capacity payments and actual availability, and there is no capacity incentive to be available in any specific hour other than during system emergencies. The short-term incentives to be available come almost entirely from the energy and ancillary services markets. Prices in these markets, even when capped, are well above maximum short-term production costs and provide short-term availability incentives.[10]

Payment Structures

Capacity vs. Availability Payments
As was just described, the design of CPM payment structure assumes either that energy (and ancillary service) markets are the primary tools to encourage short-term availability or that the CPM payment structure itself will be the primary tool. Payment structure options include:

- **Unforced Capacity Payment:** Under this methodology, each unit is paid a fixed annual capacity payment in equal monthly installments based on its unforced capacity (capacity times one minus the forced outage rate). The unit earns the payment by establishing DMNC through tests and establishing a forced outage rate history.

An open issue is how to measure forced outage for units that operate infrequently.

· **Availability Payment:** Under this approach, a unit earns the payment by being available for each (say) half-hour. Available units are paid the capacity payment on an annual basis divided by the number of half-hours in the year, divided by one minus a target on availability factor, say 10 percent. Hence a unit available 90 percent of the target would receive the full capacity payment. Higher or lower availability results in higher or lower revenue. Units are still required to demonstrate DMNC, but their payment is based on declared half-hourly availability up to this DMNC. This methodology is appealing if the energy market caps are too tight to sufficiently encourage short-term availability. It is inefficient, however, to the extent that it might require plants that could be shut down in off-peak periods to remain available just to receive the payment.

· **Shaped Availability Payment:** A variant of the second method bases payments on declared availability by half-hour. The aggregate payment level available to a generator that was available for 90 percent of all half-hourly periods would be equal to the full annual capacity payment level. However, payments would be shaped to reflect seasonal and diurnal loss of load probabilities. This methodology would still require that generators be available in each half-hour to earn a capacity payment, but the shaping of such payments mitigates the potential inefficiency of requiring generators to be available. A peaking generator with material standby costs can decide to be unavailable in low-load periods at a lower economic cost than under the second option.

Contract for Difference Payment Structures

It is very difficult to estimate the net operating margin that a peaking unit would expect. Understating the margin would result in customers overpaying; overstating it would result in an insufficient incentive for entry. Both are significant problems.

A payment structure that potentially mitigates this problem is a one-way Contract for Difference (CFD). Under a one-way CFD, a strike price is predefined, and the capacity payment to a generator is offset by the imputed margins the generator can earn in the energy market over and above the strike price. The CFD offsets, calculated for every half-hour, are summed and subtracted from the capacity payment the central authority gives the generator at the end of each month. The strike price (and other CFD parameters, if any) would be common across all CFDs, so that from the perspective of the central authority, all capacity is considered equal and is priced accordingly. For example, the strike price might be based on the variable cost of a high variable cost unit, and the monthly capacity payment would be offset by the sum over all half-hours of the excess of market prices over this CFD strike price.

The use of such a CFD payment structure can be beneficial because it lowers the overall risk associated with the CPM. The net capacity payment hedges both customers and generators against market volatility. Instead of estimates of expected profits, a more realistic reflection of profits applies. If energy prices are in excess of peaking operation costs for a significant number of periods, the net capacity price paid would decline while energy prices and profits would rise (avoiding double payment). If on the other hand, prices provided few profit opportunities for peaking generators, net capacity prices would stay at the full level, but energy profits would be low. Under this structure, neither customer nor generator bears the full risk of an inaccurate projection of energy market margins for peaking units, and the CFD structure will stabilize the price volatility.

The CFD payment structure does, however, present design issues of its own:

- There is a tradeoff between reducing volatility on the one hand, and long- and short-term economic signals on the other. The lower the strike price, the greater the price stability as increases in energy prices above the strike prices will be offset by reductions to the capacity payments. However, the strike price must be high enough so that the energy margin (the difference between the strike price and a unit's variable operating cost) net of the CFD offset payment is positive for virtually all generators that generate. Otherwise, some generators will not be profitable, and the pattern of revenues is unlikely to promote efficient entry if peakers are in fact needed.
- With all generators having the same CFD, the strike price effectively caps the short-term energy market prices. No unit would have an incentive to bid above the strike price in the spot market since the difference between its energy payment and the strike price is subtracted from its capacity payment.[11] Therefore, setting the strike price too low (for instance, at a level related to the variable cost of a peaking unit) would dampen the effectiveness of

short-term price signals in the energy market. The strike price should be set high enough to enable the energy market to reflect tight market conditions: to signal to customers not to consume, and to producers to generate when their output is most needed. Alternatively, it might be desirable to reduce the impact of the CFD offset formula, perhaps by multiplying by a fixed factor set between zero and one.

- CFDs are really only viable in centralized pool-based markets. In decentralized physical bilateral contract markets, which do not necessarily have a transparent spot price, there may be no reliable reference price from which to set the CFD offset payment.
- Finally, a decision must be made whether to index the strike price to any fuel price index. Under a CFD, a generator's energy margin is the difference between the strike price and its variable operating costs (which are largely fuel). Indexing the strike price to a fuel price index might be beneficial if it makes the margin more predictable, but this might be impossible to do if a wide range of plant types share the same CFD.[12]

Penalties

Penalties are closely related to payment structures. Payment structures that tie very closely to actual performance are usually not accompanied by penalty provisions. Payment structures that rely on self-declaration and assumed performance in the absence of contrary evidence usually have penalty provisions. For example, energy markets generally have no penalties. Units that fail to generate do not get paid. However, operating reserve markets often have penalties because operating reserve is very often not called to show that it can produce. A generator declares and is paid for reserves, usually without any short-term test of whether it can perform. A penalty applies when the reserve is called upon and does not perform, as it calls into doubt whether past declarations of operating reserves were misrepresentations. Nonperformance penalty provisions are required for any CPM to ensure that market participants actually deliver the capacity they promise.

Special Considerations for Fixed Quantity CPMs

The payment level in a fixed quantity scheme is set by competition rather than by an administrative process. The solicitation for the required capacity specifies the product design (i.e., payment mechanisms, penalties, any CFD provisions, and performance security). Bidders compete to provide the product, thus setting the price for capacity. In theory, the competitive process price is more efficient than an administrative price. In practice, all the same issues apply. Uncertainty over potential energy market margins or the continued structure of the CPM will be reflected in the offer prices. Informed offers may well come about only after a few years of experience, and early uninformed offers may well be unacceptably high.

A primary concern in designing a competitive process to set prices involves market power. Increasing the lead times to the point where new entry is possible should limit price and control market power somewhat because the market to develop new plants is generally competitive. However, where ownership of existing generation is highly concentrated, realistically efficient entry may not be able to limit the influence of a dominant portfolio player on a capacity procurement for a fixed, highly inelastic quantity. A CPM that sets the capacity price by an ITT or auction must be closely monitored to see if there is a need for market power mitigation.

Recovery of Capacity Payments

All costs of the electricity industry are ultimately recovered from customers, and so a remaining issue is how the costs of the CPM will be recovered from customers. This includes both the allocation of capacity cost responsibility among customers and the settlement mechanisms used to collect the capacity charges and pass them on to generators (and the management of credit risk). Three common alternatives are: (1) a customer-specific allocation rule that apportions capacity costs to distributors/retailers based on their customers' load profiles, (2) allocation and settlement of capacity costs in the same way as transmission Use-of-System charges, and (3) inclusion of capacity costs in a pool price uplift.

Issues that should be addressed in choosing a recovery mechanism include:

- Is the capacity price known before the consumption decision is made?
- Does recovery reflect cost-causation?
- Does the mechanism require time-of-use metering?
- Is the mechanism administratively complex, and in particular what happens when the consumers switch their retailer?

Alternative 1—Customer-Specific Allocation Rule: This rule might allocate capacity costs to customers based on of their contribution to the capacity need. If the capacity need is defined by capacity sufficient to meet a reliability standard at the times of peak hours of the year, then a reasonable method might be to allocate costs according to customer load in those peak hours. Such a method would then require a means of measuring load in those individual peak hours, at least by class of customer, and perhaps individually for large individual customers. Capacity costs can be allocated to distributors/retailers on the basis of load at the peak times, and the distributor/ retailer would then be responsible for passing through its cost allocation to its customers.

The obligation can be set *ex post* or *ex ante*. A disadvantage of *ex-post* is that actual peak load can be uncertain at the level of individual distributors/retailers. The allocated obligation and cost to individual customers would also be uncertain. If the peak hours are identified in advance (*ex ante*), the determination of those hours should also be somewhat unpredictable (or alternatively, spread over a numbers of days), so that participants would not be able to game the system by identifying the individual hours concerned and dropping load for short periods of time.

Another option is to estimate the probability of each hour being the monthly (or annual) peak, use that probability to trigger the retailer's cost responsibility, and use time-differentiated retail tariffs that reflect these probabilities. The advantages of this alternative are that it accurately aligns causation with responsibility for payment, and it has international precedent. A disadvantage is that there has to be a way of fairly allocating costs when customers switch their retailer. If the peak for the year occurred in January and Retailer A incurred the capacity charge for a particular customer, the customer should not be allowed to switch to Retailer B in February unless either (1) it had already paid its full share of the total capacity cost or (2) an obligation equal to the amount of the unpaid capacity obligation for the year was transferred from Retailer A to Retailer B. In the US Northeast, the latter method is used—the payment obligation at the customer level is set ex ante, and a monthly obligation "follows" customers when they switch retailer.

Alternative 2—Use-of-System Methodology: Recovering capacity costs in the same way as transmission Use-of-System charges has the benefit of simplicity because pricing and settlement mechanisms already exist, and extra time-of-use metering might not be needed. And because Use-of-System charges are generally charged on a per MW basis, this approach approximately aligns causation with responsibility for payment, albeit more weakly than Alternative 1. This method would also need a means of allocating payment obligation to customers that switch suppliers, although the same method as for Use-of-System charges might be used.

Alternative 3—Include Capacity Costs in the Pool Uplift: This method involves estimating the total MWh of load in a year and then dividing total annual capacity costs by that total MWh level to get a capacity uplift charge to apply to all energy consumption in the year. The difference between actual capacity payments made to generators and the amounts recovered from customers—caused by differences between estimated and actual annual MWh load—could be "trued up" between years. In any event, these differences are likely to be small—in the order of 1 percent or 2 percent.

The advantage of this method is its simplicity. The level of capacity cost allocated to a customer would be unambiguous, regardless of its peak load or choice of retailer. The main disadvantage is that cost-causation is not aligned with responsibility. Customers with a high load factor (i.e., low contribution to the capacity requirement) or that provide diversity (i.e., do not peak at the time of the overall system peak) would pay the same per MWh capacity charge as customers with high contribution to the capacity requirement. A variant of this approach is to improve the alignment of cost-causation by applying per-kWh capacity adders to the pool price only in pre-defined "peak" hours within peak seasons.

Checklist

Once a final high-level CPM design is decided, many detailed design issues will then need to be resolved. At a minimum, the following check-list should be completed:

Quantity:
  • Who decides how much to buy, when, and how?
Product:
  • What is the basic product definition? If physical, what capacity
    qualifies; if financial, what is the structure?
  • What are the linkages between the contract and the energy market?
  • Who controls dispatch of the facility?
  • What is the length of the contract?

Performance:
- Who are the sellers, how do they qualify and what is needed to ensure they perform?
- Who are the buyers and what provisions ensure that the buyers perform in accordance with the needs of the system?

Purchasing/Pricing:
- How do buyers purchase the product and when?
- What financial arrangements support the purchase?
- Do they purchase for their own account or on behalf of other market participants?
- How are prices determined?

Who Pays?
- How is the scheme funded? Who are the payers? If the buyer is an intermediary how are funds transferred between the payers, the buyers and the sellers?

Conclusion

Once reasonable CPM alternatives have been developed for a particular jurisdiction and the relative importance of each criterion has been established for that jurisdiction, the next steps are to evaluate the alternatives and select the best one. This evaluation process should involve an analysis of expected outcomes of each alternative, with a matrix of scores for each criterion against each alternative. Then, by analyzing the relative weights of the criteria factored by the scores given, it should be possible to narrow down the choices and even identify the best solution.

In practice, the relative importance of the criteria should heavily influence the evaluation process, and the state of industry structure should strongly influence the decision. Initially as the industry is restructured, capacity adequacy concerns dominate, leading to a tendency to adopt fixed quantity methods. As markets mature, price stability can be more important and there is a tendency more towards hybrid CPM models (or perhaps a fixed payment CPM). In fully developed markets, there may be no need for a CPM at all so long as there is sufficient demand response.

The selection of the right CPM for a particular jurisdiction should be the result of a structured process where (1) the criteria listed above are prioritized, (2) sensible alternative CPM solutions are developed using the building blocks described above, (3) and the evaluation process carefully scrutinizes those alternatives against the specific objectives of the jurisdiction concerned.

Notes

1. The lack of demand response is not isolated to a few electricity markets. Electricity markets virtually *everywhere* lack demand response. When supplies are exhausted and load must be shed from the system, it is not an ordered list of willingness-to-pay that specifies who will be cut off; rather the process is basically arbitrary. (Some jurisdictions do have some rules, such as shutting off industrial customers first, not shutting off critical health services, etc., but basically the customer tends to have little say in the matter.) As a result, shedding load is highly economically inefficient.

2. The price uncertainty does not only exist in the spot market; it finds its way into the longer-term contracts markets as well. Since future contract prices are based upon the expectation of future spot prices, there is a corresponding uncertainty as to future contract prices.

3. That is, an acceptably low level of Loss of Load Probability (LOLP).

4. Some countries have jumped to full retail competition with no fixed regulated default service tariff, and the result has sometimes been vertical integration of generation and retail businesses. The generators do not have life-of-plant contracts, but they do have assurance in the form of a "natural hedge" provided by their retail load.

5. This formula produced a level of additional revenue that proved volatile and difficult to predict. Furthermore, the payment was subject to manipulation by withholding small amounts of capacity. Absent gaming concerns, however, such a formula adds to the energy price an amount equal to the expected value of load that may not be served in each half-hour period, and is considered to provide an efficient short-term price signal. The rules adopted for England and Wales applied a degree of smoothing to limit half-hourly volatility, but prices were nevertheless regarded as quite volatile. Generators would need to forecast the highly uncertain level of revenue from such a scheme for use in investment decision making.

6. Failing to meet demand does not mean that the system faces a catastrophic failure or system blackout. It means that the system cannot meet the demands of all customers, so some must be cut off. In practice, some years would record more than eight hours of outage, but many years would record less.

7. Although such a unit would be near the last dispatched, it is likely that in practice the energy price will on occasionally rise above the unit's operating cost and provide an operating profit opportunity in the energy market.

8. For an explanation of the rationale behind this conclusion, refer to Sally Hunt, *Making Competition Work in Electricity* (NY: Wiley Finance, 2002), Appendix E.

9. The ultimate extension of this method is be to base half-hourly prices on LOLP and VOLL—as was done in the old England & Wales pool.

10. Links also exist between the CPM, the energy market, and the gas market and between the CPM and the transmission arrangements in the market rules.

11. This has the ancillary value of mitigating market power.

12. In addition, rules might be necessary to specify certain hours in which the CFD offset does not apply—for example, during outages. (Alternatively the CFDs could be firm.) Similarly, since unit commitment is potentially a System Operator decision, designers might chose not to apply the CFD offset based on ex post prices if a unit had bid a lower price but not been selected.

16

LOCATIONAL ELECTRICITY CAPACITY MARKETS: ALTERNATIVES TO RESTORE THE MISSING SIGNALS

Amparo D. Nieto
Hamish Fraser

Introduction

The reliability problems in an interconnected electricity system ought to be solved or avoided through an efficient combination of investments in transmission, generation, and demand-side alternatives. However, if market participants are to make efficient investments and usage decisions, the market needs to send the proper price signals. Prices need to reflect the true economic value of incremental energy and capacity in any *time period* and *location*. Unfortunately in most electricity markets, this is not the case. Even in restructured markets, regulatory arrangements to ensure adequate generation capacity are generally still needed.

The theoretical and practical arguments for establishing electricity Capacity Payment Mechanisms (CPMs) have been widely accepted in many regions of the US, Europe, and elsewhere. Most markets are incomplete because they are missing important players? the end-users. Demand response has been slow in coming since only a small volume of demand is exposed to market prices or is able to signal how much they are willing to pay for a given level of reliability. Most customers do not ration their demand when market prices are high simply because they do not see these prices. Instead, their rates reflect generation costs averaged over long daily or seasonal periods. This averaging of prices is due not only to equipment constraints (lack of interval metering or real-time communication) but also to the perception that customers will not be willing to accept even limited levels of exposure to actual short-term market price volatility.[1]

The lack of a meaningful demand side leads to reliability concerns and market price volatility. When economic signals of scarcity conditions are not delivered to end users, the demand curve is inelastic, and with nothing to constrain prices, energy market prices can spike to very high levels. Energy regulators typically react by imposing price (or bid) caps in the energy market[2] so that in hours when the system is most stressed, there is no scarcity price signal to elicit efficient generation entry or demand-response initiatives. In addition, low volatility risk in the energy market severely reduces the incentive for retailers to sign long-term bilateral contracts with generators.[3]

In absence of new entry, the system reserve margin will continue to decrease while the associated shortage costs increase. Until demand response is facilitated and market prices reflect the underlying marginal costs of energy and capacity, a "second best" solution (i.e., a CPM) is needed to mitigate this social deadweight loss. The next question for economists is: What is the second best?

There is no universal agreement on the ideal CPM design for electricity markets, and different schemes work better in different conditions. However, a common feature of most CPMs worldwide is that they fail to acknowledge the *locational* value of capacity, producing a uniform capacity price for an entire region or country. A CPM without a locational dimension tends to exacerbate network congestion problems and worsen the capacity in specific locales, even while it resolves the problems in the aggregate.

The theoretical arguments for Locational Marginal Prices (LMPs) for energy are well established and widely implemented. Location-specific energy pricing is justified as a market-based means of promoting short-term allocative and productive efficiency, as well as long-term efficiency in the location of generation, transmission, and demand. LMPs signal to generators where their power will be most valuable, to merchant trans-mission investors where new lines will be needed, and to industrial firms where power consumption is less costly. A locational Capacity Payment Mechanism, therefore, should not be particularly controversial at least not conceptually.

In theory, the economic value of capacity as part of a reliability solu-tion is defined by the marginal ability of that capacity to reduce Loss of Load Expectation (LOLE). LOLE analysis looks at the volatility of demand and reliability of generator capacity to determine how many hours a year, on average, demand is likely to exceed capacity. If the output of a hypo-thetical plant in the region is deliverable on an equivalent basis when and where it is needed, regardless of where the plant is located, then the value of capacity will be constant across a region. In practice however, some plants may be unable to operate at full output at peak times due to network constraints. With a single capacity price for the entire region, there is no generation entry in load-pockets or import-constrained areas, and the transmission constraints worsen over time as load grows. These areas become increasingly vulnerable to high peak demand periods due to extreme weather conditions or unplanned outages of generation capacity. The US illustrates these problems well. In the first years of restructuring, power plant construction boomed, yet the adequacy of generation capacity was not uniform within each region. Most plants were built in low-cost areas rather than in load pockets where they are most needed.

In the rest of this paper, we explore the range of traditional and innovative alternatives that have been implemented in the US and abroad to solve locational capacity problems. First, we examine methods outside of a CPM construct. Next, we look at types of centralized CPM schemes with built-in locational incentives. We evaluate their relative merits from the point of view of the signals provided to market participants and their potential impact on the efficiency of the market.[4]

Locational Capacity Solutions Outside a CPM Construct

Electricity sectors around the world implemented methods to provide locational incentives long before the locational CPM constructs were introduced. Methods include reliability must-run contracts, special bidding arrangements, local ancillary services markets, merchant transmission, locational access charges, and non-wires solutions.

Reliability Must Run (RMR) Contracts

In instances where capped energy market revenues fail to compensate the operating and avoidable fixed costs of necessary local resources—typically old, high-cost peaking units with low capacity factors—cost-based payment mechanisms can be applied on a case-by-case basis to keep these units available.[5] In US markets such as New England, PJM and California, typical compensatory local reliability mechanisms have taken the form of "Reliability Must Run" (RMR) contracts between the ISO and selected units located in load pockets. The main attraction of the RMR mechanism is that RMR contracts are only signed with those generating units that need them and where those units are also needed for system reliability purposes.

There are a number of problems with RMR contracts. In particular it may be difficult to identify those units that (a) need a particular level of price guarantee in order to remain in operation and (b) must be kept in operation in order to maintain acceptable levels of reliability. A central entity should make a very detailed and potentially extraordinarily complex unit-by-unit analysis of the entire system, including the avoidable fixed and variable cost levels of individual units, the reliability consequences of having/not having each unit, the strategic response by market participants to alternative compensation or closing for each unit, the market power implications of each options, etc. In practice, the selection of RMR units is usually a more pragmatic and ad hoc, and this can lead to disputes.

Further, the mixture of reliance on cost-based regulation for some generators and reliance on market-based forces for others can interfere with the dynamic efficiency of the generation markets. By providing the RMR generators with out-of-market contract payments, as opposed to letting locational market prices signal the higher value of capacity in a constrained area, market forces are unable to properly fulfill their function of signaling the true scarcity value of energy to either load or generation. Generally, neither the load in the constrained area nor potential entrants are aware of the extra cost associated with RMR contracts, since these costs are typically spread to all consumers in the region in the form of uplift charges.[6] Over time, the uneconomically low market prices within load pockets may overstimulate demand, requiring ever higher out-of-market generation. Ideally, RMR contracts should only be used as a temporary mechanism to ensure they do not indefinitely delay the retirement of an inefficient unit.[7]

Special Bidding ("PUSH")

In 2003 PPL and Devon Power applied to FERC for RMR status on some specific units in New England. ISO-New England required these units to remain available for reliability purposes even though they were not viable at prevailing market prices. As part of the prevailing complex rules relating to market power mitigation in Designated Congestion Areas, price caps had been imposed based on the annual cost of a new combustion turbine unit divided by the number of hours it was expected to operate during the year. Recognizing the need for cost recovery, FERC changed the rule and introduced a new mechanism called "Peaking Unit

Safe Harbor" (PUSH) as a temporary measure in New England, pending an alternative and more permanent solution.

PUSH was designed to allow a generator that had operated at a capacity factor of 10 percent or less in 2002 a safe harbor bid price based on the sum of its variable cost and fixed costs. The fixed cost component for 2003 was calculated by dividing the unit's annual fixed costs by the number of MWh it generated in 2002. The generator could therefore recover its costs in 2003 if it ran for the same number of hours (and had the same costs) as in 2002. These prices were also allowed to set the LMP.

In theory, the PUSH approach is more efficient than RMR contracts in that it allows the market price in the congested area to increase up to the level that compensates the marginal unit. However, it has encountered problems of its own. As fuel prices increased after 2002, expensive peaking units tended to run less and less. As they did not achieve their 2002 capacity factor levels they did not fully recover their costs. FERC had assumed that, because under LMP all generating units in a region would receive a price equal to the highest accepted PUSH bid, then it would be possible for a unit to receive a price greater than its own PUSH bid and that the risk of under-recovery was therefore balanced by the risk of over-recovery. But this does not appear to have happened. Because these units often run at minimum levels when they do run, they are not deemed to be price-setting units under ISO-New England pricing rules, even if their PUSH bids are higher than the unit actually dispatched on the margin.

Local Ancillary Services Markets and "Scarcity" Pricing

An important aspect of reliability is ancillary services, particularly operating reserves (i.e., generators that are either spinning or able to come on line within a specified time to prevent real-time imbalances between supply and demand). In markets with LMP, operating reserves should be jointly optimized and priced with the energy markets, and ancillary service markets should recognize local operating reserve requirements.[8] A co-optimized system of energy and operating reserves that recognizes local constraints can potentially provide more efficient market-clearing prices during reserve shortage hours and thus encourage the investments and operational decisions that make it more likely that a unit will be ready when it is needed. Such prices might, for example, encourage more investments in quick-start units or units with faster ramping rates in import-constrained areas. Unfortunately, because price caps are likely to limit energy prices in these same periods, they also blunt the incentives and the effectiveness of locational signals.

Local operating reserve markets affect another mechanism used in some electricity markets, the "scarcity pricing mechanism." The NY-ISO uses an administrative scarcity price adder when the system as a whole is experiencing shortages of operating reserves (typically $1,000/MWh). When scarcity pricing is triggered, the resulting high prices provide market revenue to owners of generation capacity that is operated during a limited number of hours of very high demand, reducing the need for RMR contracts. However, in order to be effective, it is essential that this mechanism be triggered by the physical realities modeled by the ISO, both in the day-ahead and in real time. In other words, the dispatch algorithms used in the day-ahead and real-time markets need to recognize the locational reserve requirements that the ISO must adhere to when operating the system. The scarcity pricing mechanism would then raise prices in areas that do not fully meet local reliability requirements, even when system capacity is sufficient to meet load and operating reserves in the region as a whole. However, as long as the scarcity price cap is still significantly lower than the value of lost load (VOLL),[9] this approach can only complement, and not replace, a locational capacity payment mechanism.

Merchant Transmission and FTRs

Transmission is an entirely different approach to ensuring capacity adequacy in constrained areas, but it can perform a reliability function equivalent to that performed by generation. When the underlying economic value of capacity differs between two regions, additional generation capacity may be warranted in the region with the higher capacity value. It is possible, however, that the most efficient solution would be new *transmission* between the regions so that a capacity-deficient region can benefit from the capacity surplus in an adjoining region. A better system of Financial Transmission Rights (FTRs) could help bring about transmission solutions more regularly.

Most LMP energy markets issue FTRs that entitle their holders to a refund of congestion costs (the difference in LMPs at the source and sink of the transmission path). In PJM and New York, merchant transmission investors expanding the capacity of the transmission system can also be granted FTRs to provide incentives for decentralized transmission expansion. In practice, however, there has been a great deal of skepticism about the ability of FTRs to fulfill this role, or even to contribute to the process of capacity expansion. There are several reasons for this skepticism:

- Congestion rents drop dramatically when transmission is added.
- It is difficult to give property rights to merchant investors in a network when the construction of one piece of equipment in one part of the network alters transfer capabilities in many other parts.
- Central planners err on the side of caution; thus centrally planned transmission investments are made before the FTRs get a chance to do their job.
- Most importantly, price caps in the energy market limit FTR values to below their economic value and below the true value of transmission at the time.

One effect of the price cap in the energy market is that it fails to signal the true value of additional transmission investment. For example, in a region where all import capability is used to full capacity and the region runs out of generating capacity, prices will be capped at the regulatory imposed level (e.g., $1,000/MWh in the Northeast markets). Assuming the price of power in the exporting region is $100/MWh, because that region still has available low-cost generating capacity, then transmission is valued at $900/MWh in that hour. This may be well below the true value of transmission at the time, given the true value of lost load. While outage events are rare, it is precisely this value of mitigating high-value and rare events with transmission that should be signaled to potential transmission investors.

Electricity FTRs in the US have traditionally been short-term (one-year duration), although FERC recently approved long-term FTRs.[10] However, the key challenge remains how to better signal the true economic value of transmission to meet locational generating capacity requirements.

Locational Access Charges

Another alternative to help ensure adequate capacity in constrained areas is to send capacity price signals via the regulated transmission charges. Starting with the premise that both generators and customers pay for access to the grid (recovery of embedded transmission costs), specific locational access charges can be devised to encourage generators to locate in areas that will help to solve congestion problems. Annual access charges for generators in Ireland, for example, are currently based on the so-called MW-mile method. Based on a load-flow analysis, the model rewards generators producing reverse load flows and imposes charges on those that increase dominant flows. The level of cost allocated to a generator depends on the distance and direction of resultant changes in power flows due to the existence of that generator. With these locational access charges, the regulator aims to correct for the lack of locational energy and capacity prices in the generation market. A major disadvantage of this approach is that locational access charges are reassessed every year, and the potential for significant annual changes creates additional risk for generators. There are also short-term efficiency drawbacks in that the locational access charges reflect embedded rather than marginal transmission costs and market energy prices are not locational. As a result, the price in any given hour can be inconsistent with the marginal costs of efficient generator dispatch.[11]

A more appropriate time to give generators a locational capacity signal via transmission pricing is before the investment costs are sunk. "Deep" connection charges are effectively locationally in that they recover from new generators the cost of any transmission upgrades necessary to accommodate their plants. In contrast, "shallow" connection charges recover only the costs of the dedicated transmission facilities and do not signal the cost of ensuring deliverability. PJM's deliverability requirements for new generators represent a form of deep connection charges. New capacity resources must be deliverable to the whole system, including portions of the system that may have a capacity deficiency. If the output of a new generating unit is not deliverable from its chosen location, it must pay for the necessary transmission enhancements. This approach presumes that all generating capacity should be deliverable everywhere in the system on an equal basis. However, if under the most efficient allocation of resources the value of incremental capacity is different in different locations, imposing deep connection charges would be inefficient. Total system costs could be lowered and the same reliability standards met without imposing this deliverability constraint.

The "Non-Wires Solutions" Procurement

Other non-CPM methodologies for helping to ensure capacity adequacy in constrained areas fall into the category of "Non-Wires Solutions" (NWS), or "Transmission Alternatives." NWS may include payments to new generation located within a constrained area, distributed generation, payments for committed demand reductions, or any network arrangement that allows grid investment to be deferred or avoided. In the US, state regulators often mention NWS as potentially useful mechanisms that should be part of regional transmission planning process. NWS initiatives have been particularly popular in BPA and the Northeast, which have a history of reliance on energy efficiency, demand reduction, and distributed resources.

The NWS approach serves as a centrally operated mechanism in which generation and transmission solutions compete against each other, ideally with the lowest-cost combination projects emerging from the process. The ISO or regulator determines (a) the net market benefits of investments in transmission assets as compared to NWS and (b) the most appropriate choice in each location, taking grid reliability standards into consideration.

NWS has generally proved difficult to implement. New administrative arrangements should be clear and economically sensible and should be implemented in a way that does not distort markets that primarily rely on decentralized decision making. However, like RMRs, the process by which non-wires generation solutions get ISO-sponsored payments may not be compatible with a competitive marketplace.[12] In addition, the selection process is often arbitrary, mostly due to the practical difficulties of comparing transmission with generation and load alternatives. Transmission investment is lumpy and tends to provide more capacity than generation solutions. Therefore the choice of timeframe assumed for the deferral of the transmission project is a key factor. Short deferral periods work against non-wires alternatives, particularly generation-based options.

Locational Capacity Solutions Integrated with a CPM

A locational dimension can be introduced into CPM schemes (centralized capacity requirements and/or payments) to recognize that the economic value of incremental capacity in an import-constrained area or zone might be greater than the regional capacity value. The choice of a particular CPM design requires a case-by-case examination of the particular characteristics of the system and the stage of restructuring. In any case, the overarching objectives of any CPM are:

- Reliance on market-based principles, to the extent possible, as opposed to regulator-imposed solutions;
- Consistency with least-cost and reliable dispatch, providing efficient availability incentives for generators; and
- Provision of price signals that approximate the *true* economic value of capacity by time period and by location to guide required investments for reliability.

The best CPM will be the one that is most likely to achieve capacity adequacy without sacrificing other goals of the overall capacity solution. Thus, assessing the relative merits of alternative CPM proposals requires a careful analysis of their impact on a number of key areas and should answer to the following questions:

- What efficiency distortions are introduced in the market (energy prices and quantities, level of reliability and cost) by the elements of the capacity payment construct?
- How effectively can the locational capacity payment work to solve load-pocket constraints?
- Can transmission and generation solutions compete under the approach?
- Do locational compensatory schemes alleviate or increase market power concerns?
- How does the CPM affect other energy policy goals, such as reduced volatility in capacity prices?

In principle, CPMs in electricity markets take three major forms: a fixed regulated payment made to all available capacity (price-based CPMs), a regulatory-mandated capacity quantity imposed on all load-serving entities of the system (quantity-based CPMs), or a hybrid CPM scheme, where the capacity price is set by a formula that links price to actual capacity levels.

One major drawback of price-based CPMs is that when the price is fixed, the quantity of capacity delivered by the market can be highly uncertain, and such uncertainty undermines the reliability objective, one of the main policy reasons for creating a CPM.

US capacity markets have traditionally adopted the quantity-based approach. The ISO creates demand for capacity by imposing a minimum capacity requirement for the region or pool. Each Load Serving Entity (LSE) is then required to provide a share of the regional reserve requirements, generally based on its previous year's contribution to system peak. The main disadvantage of quantity-based approaches is the extreme volatility of price outcomes, with capacity prices fluctuating from $0 in surplus periods (because there is no demand for incremental capacity) to the deficiency charge or administrative penalty in periods of shortfall.[13] This high volatility creates risk for both consumers and investors and ultimately increases the cost of capacity or the cost of meeting a reserve margin target.

A hybrid CPM approach was used in the previous England and Wales Pool, and was pioneered in the US by the New York ISO. The advantage of a hybrid approach is that it can be structured to limit the price volatility of quantity-based CPMs and reduce the quantity uncertainty of the fixed-price CPM. The parameters are set to achieve a target level of installed capacity, and LSEs purchase more or less capacity relative to the target, depending on the capacity price. Hybrid CPMs may be used to implicitly set a capacity price cap to limit market power. A disadvantage of hybrid designs is that they are likely to be particularly sensitive to regulatory intervention, and subsequently they tend to increase the perceived regulatory risk.

Locational Capacity Demand Curves

Some locational hybrid CPM schemes in the US rely on ISO-administered capacity demand curves. All generators located within a capacity zone that participate in the ISO auction are entitled to the resulting zonal capacity price. The auction uses a downward-sloping demand curve, whose price parameters are set by the ISO, not the actual buyers' bids. The "markets" are cleared for all zones at the same time and all LSEs are charged the local clearing price for the capacity purchased on their behalf. The auction results in higher prices in the transmission- constrained zones, providing more revenues to generation owners in those areas. Consumers in the constrained areas bear the extra cost. New York currently operates a capacity demand curve, with monthly auctions that clear the market in three distinct zones: two load pockets (New York City and Long Island) and the rest of New York state.[14] PJM's proposal (Reliability Pricing Model - RPM) also includes a regulated demand capacity curve and establishes different prices by capacity zone (Locational Delivery Areas).[15]

In 2004, the New England ISO proposed an administrative capacity demand curve, called "Locational Installed Capacity Payment" (LICAP), aiming to reduce the ISO's increasing reliance on out-of-market relia-bility contracts. The LICAP would involve separate capacity auctions for three import-constrained zones (Northeast Massachusetts, Southwest Connecticut, and remainder of Connecticut), one export-constrained zone (Maine), and the remainder of the New England pool ("Rest of Pool"). FERC initially approved the LICAP proposal, but it was later aban-doned due to strenuous opposition by state regulators and customers who argued that it was a costly administrative approach that would not provide assurance of new capacity in load pockets.

The goal of an administrative capacity demand curve is to minimize the probability that installed capacity will fall below a specific minimum level, its "Objective Capability." The New England ISO's demand curve was designed to provide generators with higher price signals when actual capacity was near that minimum (112 percent of expected peak load). When actual capacity levels fell below the Objective Capability, the curve assumed that consumers would be willing to pay up to two times the cost of new entry (*Efficient Benchmark Capacity Cost,* EBCC).[16] The clearing price would be determined by the point of the demand curve corresponding with the total installed generation capacity in the zone (regardless of whether some of those units were temporarily de-listed), adjusting for exports and imports to and from other zones.

We see a number of problems with such a capacity demand curve. The first problem has to do with the short-term nature of the capacity obligation. Since the capacity offered and purchased is based on monthly markets, there are no price signals for long term investment, and investors may perceive revenue streams as too uncertain. The second problem is that, economically speaking, the efficient level of capacity should reflect consumers' VOLL. Under the LICAP demand curve, there would be a positive capacity price for capacity beyond the target capacity level (up to about 128 percent of the peak load). As a result, payments could be made for capacity at a greater cost than the value of the incremental reserve to the consumer. Such potential overpayment in the NE-ISO proposal was, in part, a consequence of the ISO's uncertainty about the level of capacity that the demand curve would encourage.

The third problem is that an administrative demand curve is a heavily regulated approach. Excessive regulatory uncertainty can increase the cost of capital of generators and reduce investment below the level desired by the regulator. The main argument in favor of a demand curve approach is that it reduces price volatility and thus allows developers to better predict their ICAP revenues and finance new capacity. However, the regulatory nature of the curve might work in the opposite direction and increase risk associated with plant investment. For example, a regulator might redefine the slope of the curve at some point to reduce the payments to generators and the clamoring of consumers.

The New York ISO ICAP demand curve, in operation since 2002, appears to have met its immediate objectives of reducing price volatility and improving the transparency of the ICAP markets. However, it remains to be seen whether an ICAP demand curve with monthly capacity obligations will meet its longer-term objective of encouraging sufficient capacity region-wide at a reasonable cost.

Locational Forward Capacity Auctions

Typically, quantity-based CPMs have been designed with one-year time horizons. A novel approach within the group of quantity-based CPM schemes is ISO-operated capacity auctions that use multiyear commitment periods. The problem of price volatility fades away with a multiyear forward capacity auction, and such auctions can be designed to accommodate locational constraints. Under these schemes, the ISO is still responsible for performing forecasts of the amount of capacity (ICAP) required in the region (or locations within the region), but it does so for three or four years in the future. If the auction is designed so that it occurs with sufficient time in advance of the actual performance date or commitment period (say, three to four years) both existing and potential new entrants will be able to compete for the same product and the price will reflect long-term (improved) surplus conditions.[17] This has three important positive effects:

- Expanding the pool of competitors to include entrants reduces market power concerns. The increased competitiveness can lead to lower capacity costs and to generators' offers that reflect their expectations of revenue in energy and ancillary service markets.
- The three-year lead promotes stability of capacity prices, which will tend to oscillate between the fixed O&M costs of existing plants (in periods of surplus capacity) and the long-run marginal cost of capacity. If new capacity is required, the auction capacity price will rise to the level required to attract entry. The capacity-clearing price therefore will vary around the competitively derived (incremental) cost of new entry.
- It encourages innovation. Existing generators compete with current and future resources, which may encourage them to upgrade or invest in new technologies by the time compliance is required.

A multiyear forward capacity auction may be combined with administrative demand capacity curves. For example, PJM's Reliability Pricing Model (RPM) proposal would involve auctions for capacity products to be delivered four years later, using an administered capacity demand curve. However, forward capacity auctions that rely on ISO demand capacity curves still retain the regulatory risk associated with a heavily regulated approach. A particular form of capacity auction that employs a *market* rather than an administrative process for capacity procurement, while also accommodating congestion problems, is the "Descending Clock Auction (DCA)."

How Forward "Descending Clock Auction" Schemes Work
Under a DCA scheme, each year the ISO runs a descending-clock auction to find enough resources to meet the region's ICAP in the commitment year (e.g., resources needed in the summer of 2012 will be auctioned in the spring of 2009). The auction begins with the ISO naming a price, and suppliers indicate the quantity of capacity they are willing to offer at that price. If there is more capacity supply than needed, the auctioneer lowers the going price for the following round the "clock ticks down." When the total amount of MWs submitted is just as large as the capacity needed to meet the required ICAP, the auction closes. The winners will be the bidders in the last round of the auction and will receive the auction-winning price for each kW of capacity committed.

The clock auction can accommodate multiple zones or multiple products by running several simultaneous clocks that tick down at different speeds, depending on the excess supply for each of them. For example, if there is excess supply in zone A but not in zone B, the going price for zone A will be lowered in the subsequent round, but the price for zone B will stay the same. Bidders are still not allowed to bid more in a round than they bid in a previous round but this restriction is only valid for the whole auction and not for each zone. Subject to not creating aggregate excess demand, bidders are allowed to switch their bids from zone A to zone B and then switch back in a later round. In this way, the market will determine the relative prices between A and B and the entrant can make an informed decision as to where to build the plant. The auction will close when there is no excess supply in either zone.

We see numerous advantages to this market design.

- A capacity DCA potentially requires less regulatory intervention than a LICAP-demand curve mechanism, therefore lowering regulatory risk. It can also accommodate retail load switching for LSEs.
- The dynamic character of zonal designations enables state regulators and load to identify and take actions to eliminate transmission constraints. Therefore the auction may provide a useful locational

economic signal to all market participants to solve constraints and locate where needed.

- A descending clock auction format (in contrast to simultaneous sealed-bid uniform price auctions) can provide a more efficient outcome, as it can better address the decision-making problem that bidders face when they enter the auction. The auction process ensures that the ISO purchases capacity from the lowest opportunity-cost resources (the bidders in the last round). The more efficient, least-cost resource can simply wait for the less efficient resource provider to withdraw from the auction.

- Finally, a DCA approach presents advantages over adequacy methods that rely on bilateral contracting because the bidding process reveals crucial information. In an open-auction format, bidders learn valuable information about other bidders' estimates as the auction proceeds and bidders drop out. A bidder may use such information to modify its expectations of energy and ancillary service market revenues as well as its expectations of system excess supply at a given price level.

Illustrating a Locational DCA: The New England FCM

A locational Forward Capacity Market (FCM) was adopted in New England in 2006 and can be used to discuss the implications of this promising capacity DCA approach.[18] The first auction is expected to be held early in 2008 for a commitment period beginning June 1, 2010.

The FCM contains a locational component that allows prices to differ between import- and export-constrained zones within New England. Before each auction, the ISO evaluates the need for a locational component. If transmission limits (including transmission upgrades that are predicted to be on-line by the commitment period) are expected to bind, the ISO designates capacity zones, and separate but simultaneous auctions are held for each zone to meet the "Local Sourcing Requirement". Potentially, the auction will stop the clock at a higher price in an import-constrained zone or at a lower price in an export-constrained zone. Each year the ISO will determine a zone's capacity requirements in proportion to its contribution to the NE Control Area's coincident peak in the previous year. The starting price of the auction is two times the agreed value of Cost of New Entry (CONE) of $7.50/kW-month ($15/kW-month).

The NE FCM also includes a locational element in that it recognizes the potential capacity element in the hourly LMP energy prices. Payments for capacity will be reduced by an amount known as the "Peak Energy Rent" (PER), computed as the revenues from 12-month rolling average LMPs less the variable costs of a hypothetical benchmark combustion turbine unit.[19] Because the PER will be linked to energy LMPs, given transmission constraints, PER will vary by location.

Other elements of the FCM include:

- **Commitment Period:** Existing generators accepted in the auction will only commit capacity resources for one year at a time, while new capacity will be able to lock in a compensation at the market-clearing capacity price for up to five years. The goal is to provide a predictable return on the investment for the initial years of operation.
- **Availability Conditions:** Generators would be paid for any capacity purchased from them, but not if the capacity is unavailable when needed. On any critical day, a resource can have its compensation reduced up to 10 percent of annual FCM payment if it is not available during shortage events, and, in any month, a resource can lose up to two and one-half months of its annual FCM payment. The forfeited capacity payments would be distributed among the generators that actually performed during the shortage events.
- **Reconfiguration auctions:** The ISO will conduct annual reconfiguration auctions one and two years prior to the commitment period to allow suppliers who had previously been selected in an FCM to exchange that obligation with other suppliers. Seasonal and monthly reconfiguration auctions will also be held during the commitment period. The ISO can use these reconfiguration auctions to buy additional capacity resources or sell back resources it may no longer need. Reconfiguration auctions mitigate risk to resource providers as their supply commitments come due, especially the risk of large deficiency charges.

Challenges of Locational CPMs: Looking Ahead

Notwithstanding the advantages of DCA-based auctions, there are challenges ahead as to how these schemes will effectively work. Four areas in particular will need further review to increase the probability that CPM schemes can succeed in restoring the missing locational signals.

Will Locational Incentives Work?

Locational forward capacity schemes such as the one approved for New England take into account transmission upgrade proposals expected to be operative by the start of the commitment period. These transmission proposals will be an important factor in final auction capacity prices by zone, but it is unclear how incentives for merchant transmission will work. Both the ISO-NE and the PJM proposals use Capacity Transfer Rights (CTRs) to hedge congestion costs (differences between zonal capacity prices) for each interface. The details of the CTR allocation process have not yet been established, but incentives to invest in transmission upgrades through CTRs may be limited. The same problems that limit the effectiveness of FTRs associated with capped energy LMPs may also apply to merchant transmission. Centralized transmission planning decisions compensated at regulated, postage stamp rates will still have a major impact on how effectively the locational capacity payments can solve locational problems.

It is essential that these transmission projects not be mere speculations. If approved transmission projects suffer delay, the locational price signals will not reflect the actual needs in an import-constrained zone in the year for which resources were committed. A system of penalties for failing to complete the promised project would need to be devised (perhaps, by allocating the extra capacity costs arising from reconfiguration auctions to those parties who failed to build).

At the same time, if new entrants accepted in the zonal capacity auction are aware that a Transmission Owner is planning to build transmission lines sometime after the three- year lead-time period, they will also be aware that the completion of the transmission project will depress the zone's capacity price. If generators are to internalize expectations of future zonal capacity prices, the system operator must make sure that these plans are transparent at the initial state of TO's planning process.

Another source of competition in local markets would be the participation of demand-response in the multiyear capacity auctions. However, it remains to be seen how demand-response participation would work in the capacity auctions, especially as customers are generally unwilling to commit to demand reductions several years in advance.

Definition of Capacity Zones

Locational CPMs can help market participants form expectations of congestion costs by zone. This information may be useful to LSEs in signing long-term bilateral contracts to hedge capacity costs corresponding to the area where they are located. However, setting the criteria and defining the zones is not a straightforward matter, and the choices affect both reliability and the transfer of risk among parties. A potential problem with forward auctions and locational schemes is that the actual value to the system of resources committed through long-term contracts would be affected by any changes in capacity zones from year to year, leaving parties exposed at the point of the commitment period to the risk that the locational capacity price will change. Unless a very transparent and objective process is devised, the risk is even higher if the definition of capacity zones is subject to regulatory proceedings, as is the case in New England, where the stakeholder process provides for consultation with state utility regulatory agencies. Any uncertainty arising from lack of objective processes may deter the LSEs from local bilateral contracting.

Finally, constraints could warrant different energy prices by node within a zone. When that occurs, broader zonal prices can create incentives for investment and operational decisions that are inconsistent with the reliability needs. Whether the zonal capacity auction eliminates the need for additional out-of-market compensation schemes for local generators important for reliability will depend on (a) how successfully the ISO draws the capacity zonal boundaries and (b) how accurately the boundaries reflect the actual constraints that limit the deliverability of power on the grid. Other locational considerations include the need to coordinate with any locational forward operating reserve (spinning reserve) markets and with interconnection policy. For example, with a policy of "deep" interconnection charges, the generator internalizes the cost of reinforcement in its capacity bid.

Local Market Power

It is difficult, and often contentious, to distinguish between prices that reflect true scarcity conditions and prices that result from the exercise of market power (capacity withholding). In the NE FCM design, incumbent generators will have little opportunity to affect price. An FCM auction will control market power by subjecting existing generators to competition from the potential new power plants and merchant transmission, whose bids will set the auction clearing price. In addition, the market monitor will review offers by existing capacity suppliers for signs of the exercise of market power and will make the prices public so that developers can estimate how much new capacity will be needed and propose new projects to compete with existing capacity resources.

Local market power mitigation should in principle follow the same methodology employed for system-wide market power, but the situation is particularly tricky in small markets. The key to the locational capacity scheme is to define zones broadly enough so that competition can work and generating units can be scaled efficiently. In practice, if a potential new, efficient unit is oversized for the load pocket, there is a trade-off between having a more costly, smaller-scale new unit to fit the peak load growth (leading to higher local capacity prices) and carrying out transmission upgrades so that larger units can export to outside areas.

Further, controlling market power by putting incumbent generators at the mercy of the price-setting actions of new generators only works if the new entrants are willing to act as price makers. However, a new generator with a guaranteed contract from some other entity might have very little incentive to act as a price maker in the FCM and be content rather to be a price taker. If too many new units are price takers, there may be few bidders in the FCM and the market could collapse. The potential for this problem is exacerbated if there is no need for many new units in the first place. In small geographic markets like New England, which only grows about 600 MW a year, it is likely that new units will be added infrequently so the system's ability to contain market power through the bids of new entrants is limited.

Link to Energy Markets

In equilibrium, the clearing price in the capacity auction should be expected to equal the capital costs of an efficient new entrant peaker, less the rents that such peaker would expect to earn in the energy market (the PER). In the presence of an explicit PER adjustment mechanism, generators will internalize the expected PER reduction when submitting bids in the capacity auction. In order to avoid jeopardizing the intended goals of the locational CPM, the PER, as a minimum, should meet the condition that real-world units must be capable of remaining as efficient as the benchmark generator over time. If there is a new, more efficient technology built, revenues to existing less efficient units will be lower, reflecting the fact that they are now less valuable.

Depending on the specific design, PER approaches could potentially hinder the efficiency of the energy markets. When a PER adjustment is established so that it effectively acts as a Contract for Difference (CFD) (that is, so that any difference between the spot price and the strike price is effectively deducted from energy market revenues to avoid double payment), there is a risk that generators will not have incentives to offer energy prices above the strike price. Taken to the extreme, one could expect the spot energy price at or below the strike price at practically all hours. This outcome would create poor short-term generation availability incentives and demand response in the energy market. Availability incentives would largely rely on administrative (penalty-avoidance) decisions, at the expense of market-based signals of scarcity. The New England FCM's 12-month rolling averaging approach may mitigate this effect somewhat, but it nevertheless deserves some careful analysis.

Conclusions

The first-best solution in existing electricity markets requires enabling the demand side to work, along with regulatory willingness to let market prices rise when the marginal cost of supply increases. Unfortunately, this is not the case in many jurisdictions. The current price caps in the energy markets send distorted price signals and limit incentives for long-term bilateral contracting. Until the conditions for such a first-best solution are in place, regulators and independent system operators must continue to look for regulatory capacity mechanisms that approximate the economic value of incremental capacity (time and location-differentiated). The goal is to promote efficient coordination of generation and transmission investment while at the same time reducing concerns over price volatility and market power.

In this paper we have explored the range of traditional and innovative locational capacity mechanisms implemented in the US and abroad. We have found that non-CPM solutions, such as cost-based payments directed to specific generators, tend to present efficiency problems or are otherwise limited in their success in providing the required incentives. In contrast, well-designed CPMs with built-in locational incentives hold promise for signaling the economic value of capacity to potential investors.

Locational CPMs are not a perfect substitute for LMP energy-only markets. First, they do not provide real-time hourly marginal capacity cost signals as an energy-only market would. Second, the CPM reliability target is still generally chosen by the ISO or a central authority, instead of reflecting the level of reliability that consumers are willing to pay for. Nevertheless, with the proper design, local capacity price differentials between zones can be expected to improve incentives to build required generation and/or transmission infrastructure. If they are effective, the underlying loss of load probability during high peak hours should not be systematically higher than in a first-best solution scenario.

The choice of the right locational capacity program involves an analysis of the specific characteristics of the sector, as well as important decisions internal to the scheme. Capacity demand curves often translate into purely administrative capacity prices. Locational CPM mechanisms that rely on market-based principles such as forward capacity auctions with a three- or four-year lead time effectively allow the market (the new entrant) to set the capacity price. Further, descending clock capacity auctions present additional merits over other CPM options, as the bidding process reveals crucial information of the opportunity cost of new resources.

Despite the apparent advantages of these innovative locational CPM schemes, their effectiveness as a long-term capacity solution remains to be seen. We have highlighted the four key areas that will need further work in order to increase the likelihood that locational CPMs can succeed in restoring the missing signals. The stability of these programs will also be a crucial factor in ensuring that market participants gain confidence in the scheme and generators can rely on CPM as a source of adequate returns on investment. To the extent that locational CPMs provide stable capacity prices and ensure system reliability over time, they are a step in the right direction. If the New England FCM proves successful, other jurisdictions should consider introducing a locational dimension to CPMs, always with the caveat that no CPM approach can be regarded as "the one-size-fits-all" solution. Finally, locational CPM schemes, combined with innovative retail pricing options that reflect the higher opportunity costs at scarcity times by area, can further expand demand-side participation when and where is needed. The goal, as we argued here, is to have sufficient price-responsive loads so that eventually, efficient market-driven reliability levels will obviate the need for regulatory capacity requirements.

Notes

1. Recently, however, there has been increasing focus worldwide on deploying interval metering and implementing dynamic rate programs on a large scale. For further discussion on this subject see *Responding to EPAct 2005: Looking at Smart Meters for Electricity, Time-Based Rate Structures, and Net Metering.* EEI, by Ken Gordon, Wayne Olson, and Amparo D. Nieto, May 2006.

2. In the US, for example, generation bids are capped at $1,000 per MWh in New York, New England, PJM, and Texas, or $400/MWh in California.

3. Even in the context of uncapped markets, the uncertainty in the frequency with which prices spike means that generators may decide against building new capacity unless they can rely on long-term contracts to cover their fixed costs. (Spot market revenues alone may not form a sound basis on which to plan for generation investment, unless the expected economic profit is substantial).

4. Performance-Based-Regulation (or PBR) approaches are not part of the scope of this paper. In cases where non-profit ISOs and RTOs plan and operate the transmission system, the focus is necessarily shifted toward providing incentives to market participants.

5. They can also be applied in load pockets that are not workably competitive.

6. This is the case, for example, in New England. In PJM, the extra cost associated with RMR payments is charged to the specific local load zones.

7. PJM ISO recognized this need and developed rules that would allow a unit to defer retirement *for a limited period*. The ISO builds the transmission to operate with the retirement, and RMR payments only apply until the transmission is complete.

8. ISO-NE, for example, is planning to implement real-time markets with co-optimized locational energy and reserves.

9. Studies to survey the VOLL show that the value varies by type of customer. However, at the margin, the VOLL that would set the market price in an hour of insufficient capacity would be the highest accepted demand bid in the market. A VOLL as high as $10,000 per MWh is sometimes used in planning studies to set installed reserve requirements.

10. Order 681 requires RTOs to make available long-term TFRs that assure rights for a minimum of 10 years. FERC left open the question of whether the 10-year minimum could be satisfied with shorter terms that include assured renewals for at least 10 consecutive years.

11. The pool-based market proposed for the island of Ireland will require making "constraint payments" to those generating units that were scheduled in an Ex Post Unconstrained Schedule (EPUS) but did not actually run because of transmission constraints.

12. For example, when the California ISO (CAISO) attempted an NWS project in 2001, a number of stakeholders saw this process as a return to a central planning regime and claimed that such decisions should be left to the market.

13. Under most RAR rules, if an LSE does not satisfy its resource requirement, it is assessed a deficiency penalty, which sets a de facto capacity price cap.

14. An LSE in New York City must procure 85 percent of its ICAP from in-city generators. On Long Island, 93 percent of the Island's peak load must be supplied by local capacity. A generator located in another jurisdiction but committed to the load pocket via an AC or a DC line also qualifies towards the locational requirement.

15. In addition, PJM-ISO would use deliverability requirements to ensure that a generating unit is actually providing a value to the system when it is needed. The PJM proposal would have two zones initially and more zones (up to 23) later.

16. The NYISO's demand capacity curve is also capped at 2 x EBCC, but it reaches that maximum price at a lower level of reserve margin.

17. As is the case in most of the CPMs in the US, LSEs can still self-supply through their own resources or bilateral contracts, which will be taken into account by the ISO to offset the LSE's projected capacity-obligation. Reductions in demand through energy efficiency and dispatchable demand response programs would also qualify as capacity.

18. The forward capacity market was proposed by NE generators, ISO-NE and four out of six NE states. It was approved by FERC on June 15, 2006. NERA reviewed similar DCA proposals and provided advice to ISO-NE, ISO-NY and PJM in 2003 and 2004.

19. The current NY-ISO ICAP market includes a PER adjustment, but it is based on a *forecast* of PER energy and ancillary services rents over a year, assuming long-run equilibrium (i.e., assuming that installed capacity reserves equal the reserve requirement).

17

CUSTOMER SOVEREIGNTY: WHY CUSTOMER CHOICE TRUMPS ADMINISTRATIVE CAPACITY MECHANISMS

Michael J. King
Kathleen King
Michael B. Rosenzweig

Introduction

The Issue

In a market economy, price is the communication mechanism between producers and consumers. Prices signal millions and billions of individual consumption and production decisions and are formed through the interaction of producers and consumers. Competition among producers and decisions by consumers result in "efficient" prices in that the economy produces what consumers want, with neither too many resources being dedicated to products or services that consumers do not value nor too few to those that they do value. Price rations existing capacity and signals the need either to invest in additional capacity or to retire plant rendered obsolete from technological competition or from lack of market demand.

Regulators and politicians have been reluctant to rely on market forces in power markets and to accept the prices that result. Rather, they have implemented price caps and created market monitors to police power markets; they have resorted to the bludgeon to obtain results that they deem acceptable. The most recent incarnation of the interventionist tendency is the development of administrative capacity mechanisms and/or the imposition of reserve margin obligations on load-serving entities (LSEs).

The felt need for such market intervention grew from the price excursions experienced in a number of the formal power markets, coupled with the deep sense that electricity is too important to the welfare of customers to be subject to tradeoffs based only on price. The California debacle set the stage for much that followed. We can and have debated the reasons for that disaster, from the innocent to the nefarious. But the one thing that must be clear to everyone is that the post-debacle administrative invasion of power markets is the consequence of the unwillingness of politicians (at the behest of their constituents who are also electricity consumers) to accept the reality or even the prospect of high prices.

The reason most often proffered by economists for the inconvenient tendency of prices to spike just when customers most ardently want to consume electricity is the apparent lack of demand response to tight supply. During periods of system stress induced by supply imbalance, wholesale power prices rise—sometimes to stratospheric levels—yet consumers show little restraint in their consumption. The lack of consumer response to high prices should not surprise anyone, since consumers do not see the price. Few if any customers in any particular market are on real-time tariffs. Some[1] have labeled the lack of demand response a "market failure" and argue that administrative requirements and mechanisms are necessary to ensure the availability of sufficient capacity to serve the demand that may be present, whether or not that demand is price responsive.[2] The lack of a robust price-responsive demand, however, is a failure of design and will—not a flaw inherent in power markets.

Principal Theses of this Chapter

There are two principal theses of this chapter. First, markets should be designed to expose customers to prices that reflect the value of power so that demand response is the primary and predominant mechanism employed to ration capacity, to ensure that needed capacity is built, and to control market power. Experience has shown that markets that lack a robust demand side are ripe for failure.[3] When extreme demand puts the system under stress, there is no way to signal consumers to reduce consumption, and consumers thus have no reason to restrain their use. As a result, prices can and in fact have soared to stratospheric levels as the cost of meeting additional demand reflects the cost of interrupting other customers or using the most expensive generating units. Furthermore, without the discipline of an active demand side, suppliers can become price setters instead of price takers, exacerbating the tendency of prices to soar.

The entirely predictable consequence of soaring prices is a public outcry against both "unscrupulous profiteers" and the economists who recommended competitive markets. Unfortunately, rather than addressing the flaw directly, policymakers have tried to "patch" the problem through administrative mechanisms. Regulators have intervened to protect the public and, in the US, allegations of market manipulation and the exercise of market power have led governors and law enforcement authorities to intervene as well. The discomfort with high prices led to the array of mechanisms to assure that such excursions would not repeat: price caps, market monitors, etc. In turn, these interventions created economic conditions that chilled the enthusiasm for investment in incremental system resources. This led to new mechanisms to patch this new hole in the "market" process: capacity markets and capacity obligations.[4]

Our second thesis is that these nonmarket-based approaches are effectively a partial retreat towards administered markets and that this retreat from market principles is unnecessary and leads inevitably to less efficient capacity investment decisions.[5] A major benefit of moving from the traditional regulated utility paradigm should be the market-based determinations of capacity needs that are clearly superior to even the best guesses of regulators. The most efficient way to redesign a market flawed by a lack of a demand response is to provide a means for that response—not to abandon market economics for central planning (even in the guise of "faux-market" mechanisms) and lose the key benefits of introducing markets. The usual apology given by those economists designing Band-Aids for incomplete markets is that achieving demand response is too expensive. But this conclusion is based on old technical information and on the further false assumption that adequate demand response requires the participation of every customer—two presumptions that this paper refutes.

This chapter contends that there are theoretical and practical reasons to consider addressing the capacity adequacy issue through the demand side (by addressing the design failure directly). Specifically, we argue that theory suggests and experience proves that capacity can be efficiently used and rationed if consumers are given price signals to which they will then respond. There are two ways that consumers' response to prices affects the power system in a beneficial manner. First, prices ration scarce capacity, ensuring that those consumers who most highly value consumption obtain the commodity, while those who are less ardent in their desire to consume forego some portion of what they otherwise would choose to use. Second, exposed to the fluctuations in prices, consumers will contract for an economic amount of reserve capacity. And, since such capacity would reflect the economic value customers place on the availability of reserves, additional capacity will only be built if the prices cover a sufficient portion of the investment cost. Customer-determined levels of reserves eliminate the need for capacity mechanisms and the ad hoc pricing mechanisms created to make these ancillary markets appear to be providing efficient levels of investment.

Empirical studies show that consumers do, in fact, respond to prices that reflect scarcity. Further, consumer response can be enhanced by the development of technology that enables consumers to control their load and respond to price changes. Implementation of broad-scale demand response programs is becoming more cost-effective as technology has improved and the costs of metering and data management have dropped. Finally, even if implementing demand-response for all consumers is not cost-effective, the amount of demand response necessary to address capacity reserve issues is often quite small and may currently be provided through programs targeted at the largest and most price-responsive customers.

Given the guidance provided by theory, the results of experience, and the changes in the cost and capabilities of metering technology, we contend that decision makers addressing the capacity adequacy issue should first look at the cost-effectiveness of demand response before embarking on a second-best solution of supply-oriented administrative measures. Were the topic of this paper broader, we might also argue that the other administrative interventions that burden currently incomplete markets would also be redundant with a robust demand side giving customers the tools to protect themselves from the capricious vagaries of a power market.

Organization of this Chapter

In Section II, we discuss the theory of consumer demand and why a properly designed demand response can be relied upon to ration available generation capacity and lead to optimal expansion decisions that eliminate the need for capacity obligations, capacity markets, and administratively determined "market prices" for capacity. Section III discusses the empirical studies and concludes that consumers do, in fact, respond to prices that reflect the scarcity of generation capacity. In Section IV, we show that the technology that enables demand response has improved in both performance and cost. This includes both metering systems to provide better price signals to consumers and technology that enhances their response to price. Section V shows that even if it is not possible to implement demand response programs for all customers, capacity adequacy can be addressed through targeted programs involving the largest customers. In the final section, we draw together our conclusions.

Theory Shows that Customers Should Be Exposed to Real-Time Prices

Our central argument is that demand response is an indispensable element of an efficient power market—whether or not that market includes customer choice of supplier. There is significant theoretical support for this argument since the markets that are of interest are those where wholesale prices are determined on a real-time basis. Prices in these markets generally reflect the marginal cost of the highest-cost producer whose output is purchased. And customers who see these marginal cost-based prices make efficient consumption decisions, and in the process they provide signals for efficient investment to suppliers. Moreover, the existence of demand responsiveness is a sufficiently powerful mechanism that it can eliminate the price spikes and the specter of market power that compel policymakers to intervene in power markets in ways that ultimately defeat the benefits of having a market.[6]

Not Exposing Customers to the Cost of Their Consumption Decisions Results in a Market Failure

The status quo in power markets around the world tends to shelter consumers from the real-time cost consequences of their consumption decisions. Since consumers do not see a price that reflects the current cost of meeting their demand, they cannot weigh the value of service they receive against the cost of supplying that service. At times of system stress, consumers see a price that is much less than the cost of providing the service, and even if they were to adjust their consumption downward, their bill would not directly reflect the value of the cost savings. As a result, most consumers "appear" insensitive to prices that signal scarcity, and they are less likely to invest in technology that might shift their load to periods when the cost of production and wholesale prices are likely to be lower. Yet this result arises predominantly because consumers do not see a price signal nor would they directly benefit if they responded to it!

Since consumers do not receive a price reflecting the marginal cost of supplying them under conditions of scarcity, it is not surprising that consumers fail to signal their preferences for reliability. This market failure is not new; it existed prior to the restructuring of the power industry. Some restructuring initiatives have included a competitive retail market where consumers either (1) were exposed to real-time prices or (2) could subscribe to a rate plan that shielded them from price risk and included a premium that paid the retailer to assume the risk. But this solution was never fully implemented in most US markets. The solution, rather, has been to intervene administratively in the markets. First there were price caps, and then came market monitors. The most recent focus has been on attempting to determine what amount of additional capacity "should" be present, and then trying to assure that such capacity is built by developing mechanisms to compensate the owners of reserves. This places the administrator or regulator in the position of guessing consumers' preferences.

Charging Customers a Price that Reflects Time-Differentiated Marginal Cost Results in Allocative Efficiency

A fundamental tenet of economics is that markets can efficiently allocate resources to produce the goods and services that consumers demand. The central factor ensuring this efficiency is that goods and services end up priced at their marginal cost—that is, the cost of producing an additional increment of the good or service. If consumers see prices that reflect the marginal cost of producing each good or service they might be interested in consuming, they can then value the consumption of each—and the resulting mix of goods and services produced and the allocation of resources required to produce them will be economically efficient.

Why is pricing all goods and services in the economy at their marginal cost likely to result in efficient allocations of resources? The reason has to do with the ability of the market system to aggregate the choices of individual consumers. If prices for all goods and services reflect their marginal cost, then consumers can make their consumption decisions on the basis of the value received from the good or service relative to the cost that the economy incurs to provide it. The result is the combination of goods and services that yields the greatest value to all the participants in the economy. This is achieved by allowing consumers to "vote" through their consumption decisions on the mix of services that yield their greatest satisfaction (value received) given the price they pay (and their income). If the price paid reflects the cost society incurs to produce the next unit of each good and service, the result can be shown to be the "best" result. What is vital to this market theory is the existence of a demand side. Simply, a market without a functioning demand side is not a complete market and cannot be expected to operate effectively or efficiently.[7]

Charging Consumers Market-Based Prices Results in Efficient Capacity Decisions

In addition to the short-term allocative efficiency, effective markets also display dynamic efficiency, the efficient use of resources over time. If generators receive their revenue based on prices revealed by an effective market (including the scarcity component), they will invest efficiently in generating capacity. The volatility inherent in unconstrained power markets does not inhibit—but rather promotes—efficient investment in capacity. In fact, allowing a market to respond to power price volatility is essential to efficient pricing of capacity for two reasons:

- Volatility of power prices leads to development of risk markets where the risks of price volatility can be quantified, priced, and allocated to those most able to manage them.
- The development of risk markets supports investment in capacity by providing a market value for capacity based on consumer preferences for the risk mitigation that capacity may provide.

Electricity is a unique good in that there are few methods to store it and none (yet) that are cost effective on a large scale. Instead, electricity must be produced and demand and supply must be balanced in real time. The result is that prices tend to be quite volatile. However, consumers and producers often do not wish to be exposed to price volatility and prefer predictability. A consequence is the development of risk markets, notably forward markets and the development of derivatives. These risk markets not only provide the mechanisms for consumers and producers to manage and efficiently allocate risks, they also provide a mechanism for producers and consumers to form expectations on the future price of power and its likely volatility.

One might ask whether contracting in the forward markets for delivery of power at a future date at a pre-determined price reduces the incentives for consumers to respond to real time market prices. Does the development of risk markets reduce the effectiveness of demand response in assuring the adequacy of capacity? The answer is no. The development of risk markets actually facilitates investment in capacity by providing an explicit mechanism to monetize the worth of capacity. The owner of a call option in a derivative contract has the right, but not the obligation, to take delivery of the commodity (here, electricity). Similarly, the owner of the power plant, of the physical capacity, has the right, but not the obligation, to turn the power plant on and take delivery of the output of the plant. Just like the derivative contract, the value of the output is the price of the physical commodity at the time of delivery.

If consumers see price risk that is too high or volatile to manage without contracting, they have the opportunity to go to the risk markets either directly or through an intermediary and contract forward or purchase options to manage their risk. And the intermediaries can contract with producers to hedge the risk physically. Further, because the value of forward contracts and derivatives is tied to the expectations of future spot prices, the prices formed in risk markets provide useful information for investment. Producers can look to the markets to determine if it is reasonable to invest and can contract to cover some, if not all, of the risk of investment.

If peak demand were nearing available capacity, the expected volatility of spot prices would be expected to rise, raising the value of derivatives and forward contracts as well as the value of power plants. This would serve as a signal to invest. In fact, consumers would be more likely to contract in the risk markets as volatility increases. This demand for risk mitigation is likely to provide greater financial assurance that investment will pay off. Conversely, if there is an abundance of capacity, volatility will be reduced, and consumers are less likely to contract in risk markets. The result is to depress forward prices and the value of derivative contracts, serving as a signal to producers that they should withdraw or retire uneconomic capacity.

An Effective Demand Side of the Market Has the Potential to Neutralize Market Power and Price Spikes

The furor over price spikes and allegations of the exercise of market power has sparked significant academic interest in the role of demand response in power markets. Vernon Smith, one of the fathers of experimental economics, coauthored a study to test the ability of demand-side bidding to control the supply side of a market in the context of an experimental construct. The results of the study support our thesis that demand response could eliminate the primary justifications for the extra-market interventions in power markets that themselves distort the market outcomes. The paper concludes that:

> [W]e also find that the introduction of demand-side bidding in a two-sided auction market completely neutralizes the exercise of market power and eliminates price spikes. The obvious policy conclusion is that empowering the wholesale buyers provides a completely decentralized approach to the control of supply-side market power and the control of price volatility.[8]

Of course, empowering wholesale buyers requires that retail customers be free to respond to prices as well.

Similarly, an analysis of the Norwegian power market, a market generally deemed to be effective and efficient, found that the existence of an "active demand-side" was an integral part of the market's design that "mitigates market power".[9]

Administrative Capacity Mechanisms Result in Inefficient Outcomes

Because time-differentiated marginal cost pricing reflects both the cost and the reliability of electricity supply, theory suggests that the proper amount of capacity will be built if producers and consumers see prices that reflect the real-time cost of power. Compare and contrast that design to the current situation in which customers neither pay nor see prices that reflect the cost of their consumption decisions. The result under current conditions is that customers often consume power at times when the value they receive from their consumption decision is far less than the cost society bears to produce the power. Yet the administrative solution to this problem—require some entity to supply more capacity than the energy prices would justify and spread the cost over all consumers—simply places the veneer of reliability over the ugly problem of inefficiency. Instead of asking customers to curb consumption that is of less value to them than the cost incurred, the administrative solution simply requires plant that costs more than the value to consumers of ensuring that the lights stay on, adding additional cost in the process.

The alternate solution is to charge customers time-differentiated prices that reflect the cost of supplying service. Customers who do not value the service at the level of cost reflected in their prices will curtail their consumption. And should supply be insufficient to meet demand, the price can rise above production cost to include a scarcity component to allocate available capacity to those who most value consumption at that moment.

Some argue that consumers do not respond to prices or that they lack cost-effective technology to track and respond to prices. We address these issues in the next two sections.

Empirical Studies Show that Customers Respond to Price

For more than three decades, energy economists have been conducting studies to determine whether consumers respond to time-varying prices and, if so, to quantify the magnitude of their response. Initial debate in the industry about whether customers adjust their consumption to prices at all was settled by early research, which showed that customers do respond to changes in energy prices.[10] Prompted in part by the Public Utilities Regulatory Policies Act of 1978, researchers turned their attention to the question of whether consumers would respond to price differentiated by the time of use. Experiments were initiated, and researchers again found that there was a small but significant response to price. In general, these studies found that time-varying prices affect energy consumption decisions in both the short and long run.

Work in the early 1980s[11] advocating spot pricing of electricity, coupled with advances in metering technology, encouraged the exploration of pricing structures that dynamically reflect the marginal cost of power to consumers. These pricing options are often called real-time pricing (RTP). Initial interest in RTP programs was focused on very large customers, where the RTP program could often be used to respond to competitive pressures.[12] Subsequently, utilities sought to develop dynamic pricing structures that could be delivered cost effectively to smaller customers, including residential customers. These pilot programs, conducted in the late 1980s and 1990s, all showed that consumers do respond to dynamic prices.

The number of utilities offering RTP programs in the US has grown from a handful in the early 1990s to roughly 70 by 2004, with 2,700 customers and 11 GW of non-coincident peak demand (equal to 1 percent of installed capacity in the US).[13] Further, critical peak pricing programs have been introduced to extend dynamic time-varying pricing to more and smaller customers. Dynamic pricing has interested utilities and competitive retail suppliers whether or not the jurisdiction was pursuing greater retail competition. The three largest RTP programs in existence today in the US are in the still-regulated Southeastern Electricity Reliability Council—at Georgia Power, TVA, and Duke Power. In fact, Georgia Power's RTP program is the nation's largest, having grown to encompass one-third of the utility's peak demand, with 1600 customers and 5 GW of participant peak demand on the program. But real-time pricing programs also exist in deregulated markets. For example, some Northeastern providers-of-last-resort (POLR) use RTP as the POLR rate with customers who have real-time meters and can observe the RTP. Recent interest in demand response has also led to analyses measuring the effects of various forms of customer curtailment options on operations in ISOs. The programs are growing because they work—that is, when consumers are given a price signal, they respond to it.

The many time-varying pricing programs initiated since the 1970s vary in the customer classes eligible for participation, the number of customers allowed (or required) to participate, and other particulars. However, they can generally be grouped into one of four distinct categories: Time-of-use pricing (TOU), economic curtailment pricing (ECP), critical peak pricing (CPP), and real-time pricing (RTP).

TOU programs originated to differentiate between relatively predictable differences in the cost of service at different times of the day, week, and year. They priced pre-defined and fixed blocks of time—usually on-peak and off-peak but sometimes further segmented to establish super-peak and mid-peak periods—to reflect the costs during that period. Generally TOU programs were voluntary, although in some locales, utility commissions and utilities required mandatory participation for large customers. Because the technology requirements are modest for TOU programs, this pricing scheme has been in existence longest, and there is a wealth of experience with it.

ECP programs are intended to mitigate extreme wholesale power price events. Under such programs, LSEs will typically notify subscribing customers the day before an expected high-price event, offering a payment to reduce their load below a pre-determined level. Customers can then choose whether or not to accept the offer. The most common ECP programs are offered by system operators and are called at times when system reliability is in danger, which are generally also times of high prices. Their predecessor programs were the interruptible programs that utilities have operated for decades.

CPP programs are similar to ECP programs in that they seek to mitigate occasions of tight power supply and correspondingly high wholesale power prices. Rather than an offer of payment for load reduction, customers are notified in advance of critical peak periods during which their rates will rise to a predetermined level, allowing customers to adjust their consumption accordingly. Typically, these rate programs have defined annual limits on the number of critical peaks an LSE may declare.

RTP programs are intended expose customers to the actual hourly cost of procuring power, allowing them to adjust their demand accordingly. Typically, these prices are based on the expected utility system marginal cost, day-ahead prices as reported by trade publications or (within the territory of an ISO/RTO) actual market prices. Often RTP programs will include mechanisms for customers to mitigate their exposure to dramatic price swings. For example, they may establish a customer baseline under an existing rate structure and charge customers real-time market prices only for demand that exceeds the baseline, while compensating them at market prices for reducing demand below the baseline.

However they are implemented, the experience with all four of these pricing mechanisms has been consistent: Consumers do respond to prices, and while the response of an individual consumer may be small, the aggregate impact of customer response can have a dramatic impact on demand.

Technology Has Changed, Expanding Both the Potential Customer Base for Demand Response Programs and the Response to Price Signals

In recent years, technologies that facilitate demand response have fallen in cost and improved in technical capabilities. As a result, the expansion of demand response programs to a wider range of customers is more promising now than it has been historically. Roughly speaking, enabling technologies fall into two categories:

- **Interval meters with two-way communications capability:** These allow customers to access information about their usage and time-varying prices while enabling utilities to reflect that usage and pricing in customer bills.
- **Technologies that enhance the customer's ability to respond to pricing signals:** These include energy information tools that help customers plan demand response, as well as load controllers and automated demand response systems, smart appliances, and on-site generation.

Metering and Advanced Communication Technologies Have Become Less Costly and More Capable

Until recently, the high cost of advanced metering infrastructure (AMI) was a significant barrier to adopting dynamic time-varying pricing programs for all but the largest customers. However, the costs of AMI technology (both the meter and the information systems necessary to manage the data) are now falling. For example, during PPL's AMI Project, which began rollout in the spring of 2002, capital costs for the project were estimated to be $123/meter.[14] Two years after the PPL project, based on data collected from several eastern US utility procurements, the cost had fallen to $107/meter.[15] A 2005 study of the PPL project found that the hardware costs had fallen further to $98/meter.[16]

But while this trend highlights the continually falling prices of the "smart" meters (meters capable of two-way communication), new functionalities tend to increase the cost per meter, ultimately resulting in a near-static price of $100/meter.[17] The enhanced capabilities of these metering systems often bring needed capabilities to the metering infrastructure. Some of these metering systems enable distribution automation functions, such as capacitor bank switching, load balancing, regulator and tap changer monitoring, transformer load management, and automated outage management.

The costs of the metering systems and the costs of providing these additional capabilities are joint costs, and a proper cost-benefit analysis must consider these joint products of the communications infrastructure. As a result of the falling or static prices and greater capabilities of metering technology, the net benefits of dynamic pricing are positive and sizeable even for residential and medium C&I customers (between 25 and 500 kW) and even for a utility that has not yet installed the AMR technology needed to support dynamic pricing.[18]

Indeed, a number of utilities, including Hydro One, Hydro Quebec, ENEL, Niagara Mohawk, and the California utilities PG&E, SCE, and SDG&E, have recently found the installation of advanced meter reading technology to be cost effective. The Italian utility ENEL, which is installing 30 million interval meters with AMR, expects its €2 billion investment to pay for itself in about four years. The California utilities have all filed business case analyses showing that the benefits exceed the costs for the wider deployment of advanced metering infrastructure and dynamic pricing programs. The California Public Utilities Commission has determined that PG&E's application to recover the costs associated with an advanced metering system was reasonable, in the public interest, and likely to be cost effective. In particular, the Commission found that:

> A voluntary critical peak pricing tariff for residential and small commercial or industrial customers with under 200 kW demand will provide PG&E with up to 15 critical peak events per summer season for customers to reduce their load in exchange for an incentive pricing option. Certain customers, primarily those with significant air conditioning load, can reduce their total bill by up to 10% in exchange for a 25% reduction in their load just during the critical peak periods. Other customers can benefit too....

> There was sufficient credible evidence demonstrating that PG&E's proposed AMI is likely to be cost effective over its useful life.[19]

Technology Enables Users to Increase Their Response to Price

Historically, demand response programs have tended to focus on large customers, albeit on a broad range of types of facilities.[20] Technological innovation and the diffusion of automated controls, storage systems, etc., are designed to enhance the ability of customers both to understand their energy usage and to more easily control it. As a result, these technologies possess a significant potential to alter consumption patterns and to enable more customers to participate in and respond to dynamic pricing programs.

California's Statewide Pricing Pilot (SPP) program[21] offers some insight into how consumers can use enabling technologies to respond to pricing information. The most dramatic impact on load reduction in the SPP program came from households with smart thermostat technology. One group in the variable critical peak pricing portion of the study consisted entirely of households with central air conditioning and smart thermostat units, while a second group consisted of households with considerably lower saturation rates for central air conditioning and significantly lower penetration of smart thermostat technology. The total peak-period load reduction for the smart thermostat group was 27.23 percent[22] compared with a 15.76 percent reduction for the group of consumers with substantially lower smart thermostat penetration. According to the study's authors, "roughly 60 percent of the total impact is due to the enabling technology and roughly 40 percent is due to price-induced behavioral response over and above the technology-driven impact."[23] Further, the 27.23 percent reduction is more than twice the reduction achieved by a third group in the study. Participants in the fixed critical peak pricing group were not offered enabling technologies and only managed to reduce their peak-period energy use an average of 13.1 percent.

The Gulf Power CPP program has capitalized on the finding that automated controls greatly enhance demand response in CPP programs. Programmable automated controllers for heating and air conditioning units, water heaters, and pool pumps were an integral part of Gulf Power's CPP program.

In other demand reduction technologies, "smart window" systems, which affect building lighting and temperature needs, can reduce peak demand for commercial buildings by 20-30 percent.[24] In 1999, energy consumption for air conditioning and lighting in commercial buildings accounted for 25 percent of California's statewide peak demand.[25] A three-hour test of five commercial and institutional facilities with demand response technologies performed in 2005 showed that energy consumption had dropped an average of 10 to 11 percent. The facilities included a variety of structures that have not typically been the focus of dynamic pricing programs: a supermarket, office buildings, a cafeteria, and a library. End uses that helped reduce consumption were primarily fans and set points on the HVAC, although one facility used overhead lighting and door heaters.[26]

The results of surveys of demand response program participants in New York and California provide some additional interesting insights on how customers in these programs incorporate technology into energy management activities. They reported that web-based data systems help customers to access and respond to price signals and meet load reduction targets, but the means of responding have tended to be low-tech (or manual), rather than automated.[27] However, while, a study of the 2002 results in NYISO suggests that automated responses were more effective than manual ones in reducing demand, the difference was not statistically significant.[28] Further, although 45 percent of the large Niagara Mohawk customers on real-time pricing installed technologies to facilitate demand response, most of them did not understand or take advantage of the full potential of their technology.[29] In general, customers need more help to understand demand-response pricing programs.[30] This finding suggests that if these barriers can be overcome, existing programs and technologies can yield significant additional demand response.

But importantly, obtaining an effective level of demand response does not require universal adoption or sophisticated implementation of these technologies. To the extent that a sufficient response can be achieved from a targeted customer class, the impact of any barriers to adoption and implementation by small customers may be neutralized.

How Much Demand Response Is Needed to Assure Adequate Capacity?

We hope that by now we have convinced the reader that theory suggests that *customers should* be on time-differentiated dynamic rates or prices that reflect the marginal cost of service, that *customers do respond* to such rates, and that *technology is available* to implement such pricing structures and enhance the customer's demand response. Yet despite all of this evidence, regulators, system operators, utilities, and generators have all advocated supply-side strategies to assure adequate generation capacity. Some have failed to see the connection between the lack of a demand side and price excursions. Others have argued that it is impractical or cost inefficient to implement demand management schemes sufficient to provide for generation adequacy.

It may or may not be the case that it is cost inefficient to require all customers to be placed on time-varying pricing. Alternatively, it may or may not be the case that, no matter the merit of the economic argument, it is politically impossible to place all customers on mandatory time-varying pricing even in the presence of risk markets that allow them to manage their risks. But the question that we now address is, how much demand response is enough? Can capacity adequacy be addressed by designing demand response programs that are implemented for only a segment of customers?

We are not aware of any example of a fully functioning competitive electricity market in the US. Generally, the demand side of the market has not been completed, and regulatory and administrative interventions often distort economic signals on the supply side as well. The good news is that the amount of demand response that can currently be made available is sufficient to enable a functioning market to emerge. This results from the nature of price spikes. In clearing-price markets, price spikes occur at times of scarcity when the price is highly sensitive to system conditions.[31] At such times, a small change in the balance of supply and demand can produce very large changes in market price. A small increase in demand causes price spikes as load increments are served by the least efficient, most costly generating units or by interrupting or curtailing usage by other customers. When the system operator must interrupt load to relieve system stress, the market price of power reflects its scarcity value. Thus, small decreases in demand due to demand response eliminate the need to use involuntary interruptions, and at such times, small reductions in demand can create large reductions in price.

The effects of price responsive demand on market prices have been studied through simulation. One such simulation of the electricity market in the MAIN region of the Midwest United States found that if 10 percent of the region's demand had been exposed to real-time prices and had a price elasticity of demand of -.2, the high prices observed in June 1998 and July 1999 would have been reduced by 50 percent or more.[32]

Simulated Reductions in Price That Due to Real-Time Pricing

Price Without RTP ($/MWh)	Price With RTP ($/MWh)	Percent Change
$10,000	$2,656	-73%
$7,500	$2,171	-71%
$5,000	$1,632	-67%
$1,000	$515	-49%

Source: Caves et al., op. cit.

Other studies go even further, finding that demand response could eliminate the ability of suppliers to exert market power[33] and that the few examples that have been observed show that when the system is under stress, a reduction in demand of 2 to 5 percent could reduce prices by half or more. A demand response of this magnitude could focus on relatively few of the largest customers in the system, although the precise number is a parameter that will need to reflect the specific nature of a particular market.[34] The reductions in price are substantial, substantial enough that one could have confidence that they would ameliorate the concerns that lead to uneconomic administrative interventions in power markets, with their deleterious effect on capacity adequacy.

A variety of targeted programs have proven successful in providing demand response. Many of the largest customers, accounting for substantial amounts of load, already have advanced metering and communications capabilities, so new metering infrastructure is not required to implement demand response programs for them. Moreover, programs targeting a small number of customers who account for a large portion of peak demand can significantly reduce load at times of system stress.[35] For example, when the price rose to $450/MWh in its RTP program, Public Service of Oklahoma experienced an 18 percent reduction in peak demand; and at a price of $250/MWh, Duke's RTP customers experienced between 25 and 33 percent reduction in peak demand. Georgia Power has attained between 300 and 350 MW of load reduction when prices are at $100/MWh. These are significant load reductions, on the order of the output from a large power plant.

Similarly at the ISO level, during the August 2006 heat wave, PJM reported that on August 2, when PJM set a new record of 144,796 MWs of consumption, demand response reduced wholesale energy prices during the highest usage hours by more than $300/MWh for a reduction of $230 million in payments for energy on that day. Demand response throughout the week resulted produced price reductions that PJM estimated to be equivalent to over $650 million in payments for electricity.[36]

To Ensure Capacity Adequacy, We Need Demand Response, Not a Surreptitious Partial Return to Regulation

Demand response mitigates price excursions and the ability of suppliers to exercise market power (should they have it). By completing the market—that is, providing price signals to customers and allowing them to make consumption decisions in response to them—regulatory and administrative interventions can be relaxed or removed. Price caps, automatic mitigation procedures, and similar measures focus on protecting consumers in the short run from politically unpopular price excursions and the perceived or actual exercise of supply-side market power. But they also erode incentives for supply-side investment in the market that would mitigate market power and price excursions in the long run. As the demand-side response programs are implemented and expanded, the amount of regulatory and administrative intervention oversight can be reduced.[37] As regulatory and administrative interventions are phased out and investors develop confidence that demand response will limit the political incentives to intervene, market signals regarding efficient investment in generating capacity will begin to work.

We all know that *functional* markets work. It is almost universally accepted that power markets have "failed" because they lack half of a market—an effective demand side. The failure of market designers to complete the market has condemned power markets to always "fail". This approach is bad market economics, and administrative intervention is simply a replay of central planning—a proven failure from which restructuring was to rescue us. It ignores the advances in technology that make widespread implementation of demand response feasible. And it ignores the crucial fact that widespread adoption is not even a necessary prerequisite to completing the demand side because small reductions in demand are sufficient to discipline price. In sum, relying on demand response instead of administrative intervention is practical if the political barrier can be overcome.

There is considerable baggage associated with administratively determined capacity markets. Some "wise old sage" must determine how much capacity is required and must impose on someone obligations to support that capacity. The costs of the capacity must be socialized and spread to a defined group of customers through a non-bypassable charge. The capacity obligation must be a sufficiently long-term commitment in order to convince an investor to sink capital into a new power plant. And even with all of this baggage, there are no examples we know of where capacity mechanisms in organized markets have actually led to investment in generation.

Further, this baggage comes without the benefits that were present under regulation. With regulation, there was the surety that if the investment were prudently incurred, the investor would be allowed a reasonable opportunity to earn not only the return of their capital but also a return upon it. Yet the path of administrative capacity mechanisms has devolved to one where the investor bears the risk of administrative changes to the mechanism without the protection of regulation. And one additional caution: It is not at all clear that this partial return to regulation will result in a structure that is capable of producing the benefits of a market or whether we will end up with a single-buyer arrangement with long-term contracts for supply.

It is our view that we should either decide to rely on markets or accept that we will always face issues of capacity adequacy. Either we believe that markets work or we don't. Let's decide. If the former, the focus should be on educating the political decision makers so that they can make proper choices. If the latter, let's admit our failure and go back to overt regulation of capacity issues—the proper economic approach where markets do not work (at least for such a key input factors as power). Sitting on the fence, especially a picket fence, as we are doing now, is always painfully suboptimal.

The authors strongly believe that there is no reason to return to regulation. In fact, the evidence shows that capacity adequacy is best addressed by letting the customers choose. What has been lacking to date is the will to let customers do what is best—make these decisions on their own.

Appendix

In this section, we will first discuss the experience with static (TOU) pricing and then turn our attention to the dynamic pricing programs of ECP, CPP, and RTP.

The Early Experience with TOU Rates Showed that Customers Respond to Price Signals and Encouraged the Pursuit of Dynamic Pricing Programs

In the 1970s, utilities and the Federal Energy Administration (a precursor of the Department of Energy) undertook rate experiments to determine if customers would respond to a time-differentiated rate. Studies of these experiments showed that customer load response was statistically significant and that amount of customer response (in the form of shifting load from the on-peak period to the off-peak period) varied depending on customer appliance holdings and business type.[38] They generally showed that instituting TOU pricing results in a significant gain in welfare as measured by estimating the changes in producer and consumer surpluses. For example, in their 1984 analysis of 4000 C&I customers on TOU rates at 10 US utilities, Park and Acton found welfare gains of over $1000 per year per customer on average, with metering costs of $65 per year per customer.[39]

The result of the research with TOU rates was twofold. First, although a number of utilities implemented TOU rates for their customers they found it difficult in practice to make the rates mandatory, due to concerns expressed by customers, regulators, and advocates. Utilities generally adopted TOU pricing as a mandatory program only for the largest customers and then offered voluntary TOU programs that customers could opt into. Second, the discovery that customers would respond to time-differentiated prices encouraged the industry to explore pricing options that would better reflect the dynamic costs the utility incurred.

Customers Respond to Dynamic Time-Varying Pricing as Well

Dynamic pricing structures send customers a price signal that reflects the costs that are being currently experienced. These prices represent the marginal cost of power, including the marginal costs of production and distribution, and, if additional capacity is likely to be needed, the long-run marginal cost of additional infrastructure as well. Customers can then react to these price signals by choosing to adjust their electricity consumption based on the value they receive from consumption. In this sense, dynamic prices are notably different from static TOU rates and traditional demand-side management programs, e.g., interruptible load tariffs, which allow utilities to curtail customer demand unilaterally.

Whatever the form of the price signal sent to customers, at its root it must be market-based and time-sensitive if demand is to efficiently communicate with supply. Real-time pricing programs communicate to customers price signals that are dynamically determined to reflect the current marginal cost of serving load. Critical peak pricing and curtailment pricing programs can achieve this goal of market efficiency only if the frequency and price levels at which "critical" events are called by utilities are periodically adjusted; otherwise, consumers will not value their consumption based on the costs that the electrical system is incurring.

Currently, there are numerous efforts across the United States to apply one or more of three dynamic pricing approaches—economic curtailment programs (ECP), critical peak pricing (CPP) and real-time pricing (RTP)—in some form. A survey of some notable programs for which information is available illustrates that the dynamic pricing programs have gained momentum and that customers do respond to dynamic price signals. It also becomes apparent that the three approaches can converge when put into practice.[40]

Economic Curtailment Programs (ECP)
Most of the ECPs are offered by system operators who may chose to call for load reductions for either economic reasons (e.g., it is cheaper to curtail load than to serve it) or when the system is under stress. The New York ISO, PJM, and the New England ISO offer ECPs.

The NYISO maintains programs through which large loads (or aggregated smaller loads) may offer their curtailable loads into the wholesale power and capacity market. Under the Emergency Demand Response Program, loads are paid the greater of $500/MWh or the power market price for curtailment. The Installed Capacity-Special Case Resource Program allows customers willing to curtail to participate in the unforced capacity market. Both programs give participants at least two hours notice. By August 2004, there were 2,059 participants in the programs, providing a total of 1,562 MW of curtailable load.[41]

PJM runs both an Economic Load Response Program and an Emergency Load Response Program. The Economic Load Response Program provides the choice of a day-ahead option or a real-time option. Under the day-ahead option, participants may receive the day-ahead locational marginal price (LMP) for load reductions scheduled a day in advance. Under the real-time option, participants may receive the real-time LMP for load reductions during times of high prices.[42] By December 2004, there were 2,119 MW participating in the economic load response program and 1,783 customers in the emergency load response program.[43] In the first week of August 2006, demand response reduced wholesale energy prices by more than $300/MWh during the highest usage hours for a reduction of $230 million in payments for energy for the day and over $650 million in payments for electricity for the week.[44]

ISO-NE currently offers several demand response programs for large customers, two of which are ECP programs. In the Real-Time Demand Response Program, customers must comply with curtailment events given either 30 minutes' notice or two hours' notice. These customers receive payment for their curtailment efforts ranging from $0.35/kWh to $0.50/kWh, as well as market-based ICAP payments. Real-Time Profiled Response Program participants are required to interrupt their load within two hours of receiving instruction from ISO-NE and are compensated according to the locational marginal price in their Load Zone.[45]

All participants in the ISO-NE demand response programs, except the Real-Time Profiled Response group, must use interval metering to record the customer's usage in designated intervals and an Internet-based system for program communications.[46] NEPOOL provides financial support for customers to install the appropriate technology. A test of the Real-Time Demand Response Program for customers on 30-minute notice reported interruption of 349.42 MW out of 763.41 enrolled MW, or a 45.8 percent load reduction. Facilities with on-site generation capabilities accounted for 61 percent of the overall curtailment. In 2004, ISO-NE compensated curtailments on "56 distinct days for a total of 2,132 event hours and resulting in 9,216 MWh of load curtailments."[47] Approximately 40 percent of the assets enrolled in the price response program curtailed.

CPP Programs
CPP originated in the 1980s. Some of the earliest trials were conducted by Électricité de France and are offered under their Tempo tariff option. Generally a CPP program offers a standard pricing scheme with a twist: Under certain conditions, the price will deviate from its designated price

to a higher level and the customer receives a signal that a higher price is prevailing. In its Tempo option, for example, EDF provides customers an illuminated device that indicates blue, white, or red depending on whether the price (conditions) are normal, moderate, or very high. Obviously, a CPP program has numerous moving parts, including (1) the number of pricing levels, (2) the existence of constraints on the number of times that prices can be moved to those levels, and (3) the method for notifying the customers. Results of CPP programs in the US are from trials conducted in California, from a Gulf Power program, and from early tests by GPU and AEP.

California's Statewide Pricing Pilot (SPP) program was a trial conducted in 2003 and 2004, in which a sampling of residential, commercial, and industrial customers were put on one of several TOU tariff structures. All classes of consumers reduced both their peak and total energy consumption in response to price signals, with those subject to CPP rates achieving between 13 percent and 27 percent load reductions depending on the penetration of enabling technologies. Customers that were given technology to automatically control portions of their demand in response to price signals reduced their peak and total loads more than those who were not. It is notable that a survey of participants conducted in 2003 reported that about 80 percent of residential customers and 70 percent of commercial customers preferred their CPP or TOU rate to their original inverted tier rate. The survey also reported that customers understood time-differentiated rates more easily than they understood traditional block rates.[48]

Gulf Power has offered CPP pricing to its residential customers since 2000.[49] Notable for its deployment of advanced metering and home automation technology, the program has achieved load reductions of 40 percent to 60 percent during critical peak periods. As of the end of 2004, the program had 6,000 participants, with enrollment expected to reach 10 to 12 percent of residential customers (40,000 to 50,000 customers).

GPU and AEP also conducted pilot CPP programs in the early 1990s. AEP found critical period reductions of almost 60 percent of customers' peak load during the winter and GPU had similar results.[50]

RTP Programs
In the 1990s, the first utilities implementing industrial and large commercial real-time pricing programs in the US included Pacific Gas & Electric Southern California Edison, Niagara Mohawk Power, Georgia Power,

Oklahoma Gas and Electric, Public Service Company of Colorado, Pennsylvania Power and Light, Florida Power and Light, Duke Power, the Tennessee Valley Authority, and Consolidated Edison.[51] The Electric Power Research Institute and several of the utilities undertook a number of studies to document the impacts of these programs as well as the impacts of pool price contracts in England and Wales.[52] Studies of these programs[53] generally come to consistent conclusions:

- Demand response differs widely across industries, between customers within industries, and over time.
- Customers who are most responsive are those with on-site generation, with discrete production process that they can shift, formerly interruptible customers, or customers in specific—generally energy-intensive—industries. This finding indicates the importance of technological factors in demand response.
- Between one-quarter and one-half of all customers on the various programs are price responsive, and customer responsiveness may vary from month to month as they choose the amount of electricity to reduce given the value of electricity to them at any given time.
- Demand response in aggregate is consistently statistically significant.
- Aggregate elasticities estimated in the various studies, while significant, are relatively small, of an order of magnitude of 0.10, although individual customer elasticities vary from insignificant to over 1.00.[54]
- Given the size of the price excursions in high-priced hours in many of the RTP programs of 1000 percent or more, a small price elasticity translates into a substantial amount of load reduction.
- Customers volunteer for RTP programs to save money overall.

These findings have implications for the level of success—both in terms of participation and of demand response—that one might expect from dynamic time-varying pricing programs in current competitive markets. Many restructured markets in the US have had transitional features that suggest that participation in or load response from RTP programs during the transition to competition were a lower bound on future results. First, many states froze, capped, or set rates so that customers would see bill savings from restructuring. As a result, customers would realize lower savings from RTP during the transition than prior to restructuring and would have less incentive to participate in a dynamic pricing program. Second, the variation in prices in many wholesale markets was relatively small early in this century because of excess capacity. As a result, any demand response would have been smaller than we would expect as the supply tightens. Nevertheless, a variety of programs have been successfully instituted in restructured markets.

RTP programs offered by system operators and utilities are producing demand reductions that can be relied upon to both mitigate market prices and relieve capacity shortages during periods of system stress. The programs that are listed below are not exhaustive, but rather represent the types of programs and results achieved.

SYSTEM OPERATOR PROGRAMS

The NYISO offers its Day-Ahead Demand Response Program, in which loads greater than 1 MW (individually or through aggregation) may bid into the day-ahead power market and receive market prices for their curtailment. In 2004, 26 customers participated.[55]

ISO-NE currently offers two demand response programs that should be considered RTP programs. Day-Ahead Demand Response Program participants must offer at least 1 MW of curtailment into the Day-Ahead Energy Market and receive the Day-Ahead Zonal Price if the curtailment bid clears.[56] Participants in the Real-Time Price Response Program reduce energy consumption (from 100 kW to 5 MW) on a voluntary basis during times specified by the ISO-NE and are compensated at the applicable Real-Time Zonal Price.

A relatively new market administrator, the Midwest Independent System Operator (MISO) began full operation of its energy markets on April 1, 2005. Its market-based approach to dynamically priced demand response is similar to that of the three northeast ISOs. In MISO's day-ahead and real-time balancing markets, "demand response resources" are allowed to submit bids to curtail demand. These resources must be dispatchable (able to reduce demand) in accordance with instructions from the ISO, and they are treated like a generating resource. To ensure performance, they must have telemetry adequate to allow the ISO to measure demand reductions.[57]

UTILITY SPONSORED PROGRAMS

Georgia Power has offered some form of real-time pricing tariff options to commercial and industrial customers since 1992 and has the largest program in the US with more than 1,600 customers accounting for as much as 5,000 MW of demand. Over 80 percent of eligible customers enroll in one of several day-ahead or hour-ahead rate programs based on Georgia Power's avoided cost of power procurement. Studies cite reductions in load of 30 percent during periods of moderately high prices (e.g., $0.30/kWh), and 60 percent in the few hours in which prices exceeded $1.00/kWh.[58] Other utilities also have RTP programs based on avoided costs, and although none have achieved the market penetration of Georgia Power's program, many have shown substantial load reductions at high price levels:[59]

Table 1. *Load Reductions Experienced by Utilities with Real-Time Pricing Programs*

Utility Real-Time Program	Load Reduction (MW)	Price Level ($/kWh)
Public Service Co. of Oklahoma (AEP)	18% of Peak Demand	$0.45
Cinergy	40	$0.20
Duke Power	25% - 33% of Peak Demand	$0.25
Commonwealth Edison (Exelon)	16% - 30% of Peak Demand	$0.10
Florida Power and Light	< 5	$0.40
Kansas City Power and Light	3.5 16.2	$0.80 $0.94
Georgia Power	300–350	$0.10
Tennessee Valley Authority (TVA)	200–300	$0.04

Niagara Mohawk Power Corporation has used a real-time tariff as default for its customers over 2 MW since 1998, employing a customer baseline (CBL) mechanism that bills (or pays) market power rates for consumption above (or below) CBL levels. A 2004 in-depth study of the program[60] found patterns of load response that are generally similar to findings in earlier studies of response to traditional RTP programs offered by vertically integrated utilities. Elasticities of substitution were 0.11 for industrial customers, 0.30 for government/educational customers, and insignificant for commercial customers. A later study[61] of 119 customers found slightly higher elasticities of substitution of 0.16 for industrial customers, 0.10 for government/educational customers, and 0.06 for commercial customers. The study also found that 45 percent of customers could respond to prices, 45 percent have invested in

DR-enabling technology, and 10 to 20 percent have entered into financial hedging arrangements.

Neither study found a correlation between price responsiveness and the installation of energy management systems, peak load management devices, or energy information systems; however, on-site generation was associated with higher price responsiveness. The earlier study suggested that customers do not understand the full potential of the technology they have installed. The later study asked about the uses to which customers put their DR-enabling technology and found that most used them for facility/process control and automation and/or to reduce overall electricity costs. Sixteen percent reported using EMCS/PLM to respond to high hourly prices and 23 percent used EIS.

While PJM runs demand-side response programs at the system operator level, a substantial amount of load also participates in dynamically priced or curtailable contracts offered by both competitive and distribution LSEs. According to the 2004 Price Sensitive Load Survey, 3,658 MW of load is dynamically priced or on LMP pricing (of which 302 MW is residential load), 550 MW is interruptible or curtailable, and 1,117 MW responds to price through some other mechanism.[62]

In 2003-2005, Commonwealth Edison offered an RTP tariff to residential customers through Energy-Smart Pricing Plan, a pilot program managed by the Chicago Community Energy Cooperative. Customers faced hourly energy prices that consisted of the ComEd Zone day-ahead LMP (capped at 50 cents/kWh) with adders for capacity, losses, and miscellaneous costs, plus an access charge to cover distribution costs. Customers could view the next day's prices after 6 p.m., and were notified by email or automated phone calls if the prices were expected to exceed 10 cents/kWh the next day. For the summer of 2003, participants saved an estimated average of 11 cents on their electricity bills, reduced usage by almost 20 percent when prices exceeded 10 cents/KWh, and gave the program a 98-percent satisfaction. For the hot 2005 summer, savings were 3 to 4 percent of electricity usage with an average price elasticity of 4.7 percent, a reduction of 15 percent at the summer peak. Price elasticities of 4.2, 8.0, and 4.7 percent were found for the summers of 2003, 2004, and 2005, respectively. Following the pilot program, ComEd has continued to operate a real time pricing program through its web-based www.thewattspot.com program. The Cooperative currently manages a similar program for the Ameren Illinois Utilities (Power Smart Pricing) as well as providing energy management and price response information.[63]

Notes

1. See, for example, Peter Cramton and Steven Stoft, "A Capacity Market that Makes Sense," *Electricity Journal,* XVIII, 7 (August/September 2005), 43-54.

2. Our Australian colleagues argue that this line of reasoning does not apply to Australia since customers and politicians are prepared to accept market based prices even in the light of price excursions to very high levels. In this view, the need for demand response as a prerequisite for a well functioning power market is misplaced since there is no imperative for extra-market intervention.

3. In contrast to the California experiment, some markets—such as those in the UK and Norway—have mechanisms that allow for at least some consumers to react to changes in prices at least on a day-ahead basis.

4. In some market designs in the US, such mechanisms were a legacy of the regulated industry structure.

5. It is not just capacity expansion that is delayed. Efficient withdrawal of inefficient capacity could be (and we might argue has been) delayed by administered capacity mechanisms.

6. See Stephen J. Rassenti, Vernon L. Smith, and Bart J. Wilson, "Controlling Market Power and Price Spikes in Electricity Networks: Demand-side Bidding," Interdisciplinary Center for Economic Science, George Mason University, 4400 University Drive, MSN 1B2, Fairfax, VA 22030; Tor Arnt Johnsen of Statistics Norway, Shashi Kant Verma of McKinsey and Company, Inc.; and Catherine Wolfram of Harvard University, "Zonal Pricing and Demand-Side Bidding in the Norwegian Electricity Market," presented at the POWER Fifth Annual Research Conference on Electricity Industry Restructuring, March 17, 2000, Berkeley, California.

7. R. G. Lipsey and K. Lancaster, "The General Theory of Second Best," *Review of Economic Studies,* XXIV (1956/1957) 11-32 showed that when the marginal cost pricing rule was not followed in all sectors of the economy, marginal cost pricing in a specific sector does not necessarily result in allocative efficiency. This is because the distortions in those sectors not following the rule may influence the results in the other sectors. However, as Richard Schmalensee, *The Control of Natural Monopolies* (Lexington Books: 1979) p. 30 points out, the amount of data and analysis needed to show that some other "second-best" pricing rule results in allocative efficiency generally is not present. Nor have analysts conducted the extensive analysis to show that application of marginal cost pricing in the electricity sector would, in fact, be inefficient. Finally, marginal cost is the fundamental pricing scheme in restructured power markets. So to argue against marginal cost pricing is to reject the restructuring process, which of course is also one way to resolve the capacity adequacy issue in the context of competitive power markets.

8. Rassenti, Smith, and Wilson, op. cit., fn. 6.

9. Johnsen, Verma and Wolfram, op. cit., fn. 6.

10. See, for example, L.D. Taylor, "The Demand for Electricity: A Survey," *Bell Journal of Economics,* 6 (1975) and "Decreasing Block Pricing and the Residential

Demand for Electricity," *Institutional Studies of the Demand for Energy,* ed. by W.D. Nordhaus (New York: North-Holland Publishing Company, 1977); and An extensive review of the pre-1977 literature, covering 30 studies, can be found in Douglas R. Bohi, Analyzing Demand Behavior. *A Study of Energy Elasticities* (Baltimore: Resources for the Future, 1981). Subsequent studies included D. McFadden, C. Puig, and D. Kirshner, "Determinants of the Long-Run Demand for Electricity," *Proceedings* of the Business and Economics Statistics Section, Part 1, American Statistical Association (1977), 109-119; Roberta Barnes, Robert Gillingham, and Robert Hagemann, "The Short-run Residential Demand for Electricity," *Review of Economics and Statistics,* LXIII (1981), 541-552; A. Goett and D. McFadden, "Residential End-Use Energy Planning System (REEPS), EPRI, EA-2512, Research Project 1221-2 (July 1982); Jeffrey A. Dubin and D. L. McFadden, "An Econometric Analysis of Residential Electric Appliance Holdings and Consumption," *Econometrica,* LII, 2 (1984), 345-362; and Jeffrey A. Dubin, "Evidence of Block Switching in Demand Subject to Declining Block Rates—A New Approach, *Social Science Working Paper* 583, California Institute of Technology (1985).

11. See Fred C. Schweppe, Michael C. Camaranis, Richard D Tabor, and Roger E. Bohn, *Spot Pricing of Electricity* (Kluwer Academic Publishers: Boston, 1988).

12. For example, one of the utilities to drive development of RTP has been Georgia Power, possibly reflecting the fact that, in Georgia, since the 1970s, large new customers have had a one-time choice of supplier.

13. Galen Barbose, Charles Goldman, and Bernie Neenan, "A Survey of Utility Experience with Real Time Pricing," Ernest Orlando Lawrence Berkeley National Laboratory, LBNL-54238, December 2004. In the Appendix, we briefly review various experiences with time-varying pricing.

14. Ward Camp, Distribution Control Systems, Inc, Case Studies— Pennsylvania Power & Light, Idaho Power Company, Florida Power & Light; www.energy.ca.gov/demandresponse/documents/2004-09-30_workshop/ 2004-09-30_AMI.PDF.

15. Chris King, eMeter, "Advanced Metering Infrastructure (AMI)— *Overview of System Features and Capabilities,*" September 30, 2004; http://www.energy.ca.gov/demandresponse/documents/2004-09-30_ workshop/2004-09-30_AMI.PDF.

16. "Interview with Ward Camp, Vice President, Distribution Control Systems, Inc." September 27, 2005.

17. "Interview with Chris King, Chief Strategy Officer—eMeter Corporation." September 30, 2005.

18. See Ahmad Faruqui and Stephen S. George, "The Value of Dynamic Pricing in Mass Markets," *The Electricity Journal,* July 2002, 45-55 on the cost effective-ness of TOU, CPP, and Extreme Day Pricing (EDP).

19. California Public Utilities Commission, *Decision 06-07-027 July 20, 2006,* pp. 64, 67.

20. Charles A. Goldman, Michael Kintner-Meyer and Grayson Heffner, "Do 'Enabling Technologies' Affect Customer Performance in Price-Responsive

Load Programs?," *Proceedings* of the 2002 ACEEE's Summer Study on Energy Efficiency in Buildings, LBNL-50328 (August 2002), pp. 10-11. For example, of the 56 survey results summarized by the study (covering demand response programs in California and New York), the average summer peak demand per facility was 1.4 MW; 8 different facility types were included in the survey: agricultural, government, health, industrial, lodging, office, recreational, and retail. Also see the description of participants in a survey of approximately 30 demand response programs in Charles A. Goldman, Grayson Heffner and Galen Barbose, "Customer Load Participation in Wholesale Markets: Summer 2001 Results, Lessons Learned and 'Best Practices'," LBNL-50966 (February 2002), pp. 11-12.

21. July 2003–December 2004 for 2500 customers in variable and fixed critical peak pricing programs.

22. "Impact Evaluation of the California Statewide Pricing Pilot," Charles River Associates (March 16, 2005), p. 108.

23. Ibid.

24. Ibid., p. 2.

25. "Active Load Management with Advanced Window Wall Systems: Research and Industry Perspectives," Proceedings from the ACEEE 2002 Summer Study on Energy Efficiency in Buildings: Teaming for Efficiency (August 2002), publication date: June 2002, p. 3.

26. Naoya Motegi, Mary Ann Piette, David S. Watson, Osman Sezgen, Laurie ten Hope, "Measurement and Evaluation Techniques for Automated Demand Response Demonstration," Ernest Orlando Lawrence Berkeley National Laboratory, LBNL-555086, August 2004, *Proceedings* of the 2004 ACEEE Summer Study on Energy Efficiency in Buildings, A subsequent re-test of these five facilities resulted in a three-hour savings of 5 to 30 percent per building. In addition, 15 more buildings were included in the study. The energy reductions for the additional buildings ranged from 0 percent to 40 percent. In all, energy reductions totaling almost 4 MW (out of approximately 22 MW of expected peak demand) were reported for the 20 facilities. "Findings from the 2004 Fully Automated Demand Response Tests in Large Facilities," September 7, 2005, pp. v-vii & 34-37. In a separate case study (referenced below) of the effect of installing an energy information system Enterprise Energy Management Suite, at University of California at Santa Barbara, reductions of 16 percent in peak demand, 14 percent in summer usage, and 10 percent in gas usage were reported, resulting in a calculated payback period of 1.2 years. Naoya Motegi, Mary Ann Piette, Satkartar Kinney, Jim Dewey, "Case Studies of Energy Information Systems and Related Technology: Operational Practices, Costs, and Benefits," International Conference for Enhanced Building Operations, October 2003.

27. Goldman, Kintner-Meyer and Heffner, op. cit., pp. 9-10.

28. Neenan Associates, et al., "How and Why Customers Respond to Electricity Price Variability: A Study of NYISO and NYSERDA 2002 PRL Program Performance," LBNL-52209 and PNNL#14220 (January 2003), pp. 4-25 – 4-26.

29. Galen Barbose, Charles Goodman, and Bernie Neenan, "A Survey of Utility Experience with Real-Time Pricing," LBNL-54238 (December 2004), p. 33.

30. Ibid.

31. In the short run, a desirable level of reliability is obtained because the "lights go out" when consumers make an explicit choice to turn off the lights. This outcome results from the consumer deciding that the cost of consuming electricity exceeds the consumer's willingness to pay for it. In the long run, the pattern of price spikes (reflecting consumers' willing to pay for electricity) will determine the level of investment in supply-side resources in the market. Hence, through short-run consumer responses to prices, you obtain the long-run level of reliability that consumers are willing to pay for.

32. D. Caves, K. Eakin, and A. Faruqui, 2000. "Mitigating Price Spikes in Wholesale Markets Through Market-Based Pricing in Retail Markets," *The Electricity Journal.* 13(3), 13-23.

33. Rassenti, Smith, and Wilson, op. cit.

34. Michael B. Rosenzweig, Hamish Fraser, Jonathan Falk, and Sarah P. Voll, "Market Power and Demand Responsiveness: Letting Customers Protect Themselves," *Electricity Journal,* XVI, 4 (May 2003), 11-23. A discussion of these issues is also contained in: Rosenzweig, Fraser, Falk, and Voll; "Demand Response Measures: Using Market Forces to Fix Electricity Market Failures," NERA Energy Regulation Brief, Rosenzweig, et al., 2003; and "Comments of Michael Rosenzweig, Hamish Fraser, Jonathon Falk, and Sarah Voll on SMD," FERC Docket No. RM01-12-000.

35. Table 2 in the Appendix shows utilities with targeted real-time pricing programs that have attained significant peak reductions.

36. "Early August Demand Response Produces $650 Million Savings in PJM," *The Energy Central Network* (August 17, 2006).

37. Rosenzweig, Fraser, Falk, and Voll, op. cit.

38. Representative articles from this vast literature include: Douglas W. Caves, Laurits R. Christensen, and Joseph A. Herriges, "Consistency of Residential Customer Response in Time-of-Use Electricity Pricing Experiments," *Journal of Econometrics,* (26) 1984, 179-203; Douglas W. Caves, Joseph A. Herriges, and Kathleen A. Kuester, "Load Shifting Under Voluntary Residential Time-of-Use Rates," *The Energy Journal,* 10(4) 1989, 83-89; Joseph G. Hirschberg and Dennis J. Aigner, "An Analysis of Commercial and Industrial Customer Response to Time-of-Use Rates," *The Energy Journal (Special Electricity Issue)* 4 (1983) 103-126; and Rolla Edward Park and Jan Paul Acton, "Large Business Customer Response to Time-of-Day Electricity Rates," *Journal of Econometrics,* 26 (1984) 229-252.

39. According to Park and Acton, the $65 per year cost is calculated based on a cost of $600 per meter, 15-year service life, and an 8 percent real discount rate.

40. For example, many of the ECP programs offered by ISOs compensate customers at the market price of power for load curtailments and reductions. This is

substantially similar to a true RTP program in that marginal customer consumption is valued at the market price of power.

41. "NYISO 2004 Demand Response Programs," Attachment 1 to the NYISO Seventh Bi-Annual Compliance Report on Demand Response Programs and the Addition of New Generation in Docket No. ER01-3001-00, December 1, 2004.

42. PJM website, http://www.pjm.com/services/demand-response/demand-response.html, queried on October 24, 2005.

43. "PJM Demand Side Response Program," http://www.pjm.com/committees/working-groups/dsrwg/downloads/20041221-item-5-price-responsive-load-survey-ytd-dsr-stats.pdf, queried on October 24, 2005.

44. "Early August Demand Response Produces $650 Million Savings in PJM," *The Energy Central Network,* (August 17, 2006).

45. "ISO New England Load Response Program, Manual, Revision: 6," prepared by ISO New England, Effective Date: February 1, 2005, pp. 1-5.

46. "An Evaluation of the Performance of the Demand Response Programs Implemented by ISO-NE in 2004," prepared for ISO New England, by RLW Analytics, December 29, 2004, pp. 1-4.

47. Ibid., 2-10.

48. "Statewide Pricing Pilot (SPP): Overview and Design Features," October 5, 2004, reporting on "SPP End-of-Summer Survey Report," Momentum Market Intelligence, WG3 Report, January 21, 2004, pp. 23-24; and "Residential Customer Understanding of Electricity Usage and Billing," Momentum Market Intelligence, WG3 Report, January 29, 2004, p. 16. A later report (Rocky Mountain Institute, "Automated Demand Response System Pilot: Final Report," March 31, 2006) restated and updated the load reduction results. It reported that during summer months high consumption customers with the Advance Demand Reduction System (ADRS) reduced load on event days by 43% in 2005 and by 51% in 2004, while they reduced load on non-event days by 29% in 2005 and 32% in 2004 relative to control customers. High consumption customers without ADSR reduced load during summer 2004 by 17% on event days and by 12% on non-event days.

49. The discussion below is drawn from the following references: Severin Borenstein, Michael Jaske, and Arthur Rosenfeld, "Dynamic Pricing, Advanced Metering and Demand Response in Electricity Markets," Center for the Study of Energy Markets Working Paper 105, Berkeley, California, October 2002; Brian White, "GoodCents Select: Program Overview," apparently dated January 6, 2005; Lisa Schwartz, "Demand Response Programs for Oregon Utilities," Appendix A, prepared for the Oregon Public Utility Commission, May 2003; and Dan Merilatt, GoodCents Solutions, Inc., "Critical Peak Pricing—Gulf Power's Experience," September 2002.

50. See, for example, Ahmad Faruqui and Stephen S. George, "The Value of Dynamic Pricing in Mass Markets," *The Electricity Journal,* July 2002, 45-55.

51. King (1993), "The Impact of Real-Time Pricing: Evidence from the British Experience," Presented at the Southern Economic Association Conference, November 16, 1993, reports that, as of March 1993, at least 13 US utilities had customers on some form of RTP and at least three utilities had an RTP program but did not yet have customers on the service. At the same time, hundreds of customers in England and Wales were taking service under Pool Price Contracts with half-hourly-varying prices. By the end of 2004, over 70 utilities had RTP programs (See Barbose, Goldman, and Neenan, "A Survey of Utility Experience with Real Time Pricing," Ernest Orlando Lawrence Berkeley National Laboratory Working Paper LBNL-54238, December 2004, http://eetd.lbl.gov/ea/EMS/EMS_pubs.html).

52. The quantitative impacts of these programs are documented in the EPRI *StatsBank* Database.

53. Robert H. Patrick and Frank A. Wolak, "Estimating the Customer-Level Demand for Electricity under Real-Time Market Prices," NBER Working Paper 8213, April 2001, http://papers.nber.org/papers/w8213.pdf.; Joseph A. Herriges, S. Mostafa Baladi, Douglas W. Caves, and Bernard F. Neenan, "The Response of Industrial Customers to Electric Rates Based upon Dynamic Marginal Costs," Review of Economics and Statistics, 1993; Kathleen King, "The Impact of Real-Time Pricing: Evidence from the British Experience," Presented at the Southern Economic Association Conference, November 16, 1993; Kathleen King and Peter Shatrawka, "Customer Response to Real-Time Pricing in Great Britain," *Proceedings* of the 1994 ACEEE Summer Study on Energy Efficiency in Buildings, vol. 4, 195-203; Ahmad Faruqui, Joe Hughes, and Melanie Mauldin, "Real-Time Pricing in California: R&D Issues and Needs," prepared for the California Energy Commission, January 8, 2002; Galen Barbose, Charles Goldman, and Bernie Neenan, "A Survey of Utility Experience with Real Time Pricing," Ernest Orlando Lawrence Berkeley National Laboratory Working Paper LBNL-54238, December 2004, http://eetd.lbl.gov/ea/EMS/EMS_pubs.html; Peter M. Schwarz, Thomas N. Taylor, Matthew Birmingham, and Shana L. Dardan, "Industrial Response to Electricity Real-Time Prices: Short Run and Long Run," *Economic Inquiry*, XL(4) October 2002, 597-610; Jay Zarnikau, "Customer Responsiveness to Real-Time Pricing of Electricity," The Energy Journal, XI (4) 1990, 99-116; C. Goldman, N. Hopper, O. Sezgen, M. Moezzi, R. Bharvirkar, B Neenan, Roisvert, P. Cappers, and D. Pratt, "Customer Response to Day-ahead Wholesale Market Electricity Prices: Case Study of RTP Program Experience in New York, Prepared for the California Energy Commission, July 2005.

54. Note that the size of the price excursions themselves may limit the measured elasticity. Even if customers shut down entirely (i.e., reduce load by 100 percent) when prices soar by 1000 percent, their measure price elasticity (= % change in load / % change in price = 100%/1000%) will only be 0.10.

55. "NYISO 2004 Demand Response Programs," Op. cit.

56. "ISO New England Load Response Program, Manual, Revision: 6," prepared by ISO New England, Effective Date: February 1, 2005, p. 1-1.

57. Business Practices Manual for Energy Markets Instruments, Version 5, April 5, 2005, pp. 4-16 – 4-17.

58. See Steven Braithwait and Ahmad Faruqui, "Demand Response: The Ignored Solution to California's Energy Crisis," *Public Utilities Fortnightly*, March 15,

2001, and Steven Braithwait and Michael O'Sheasy, "Customer Response to Market Prices—How Much Can You Expect When You Need it Most?," EPRI International Energy Pricing Conference, July 2000.

59. Barbose, et al. (2004). op. cit.

60. C. Goldman, N. Hopper, O. Sezgen, M. Moezzi, R. Bharvirkar, B Neenan, R. Boisvert, P. Cappers, and D. Pratt, "Customer Response to Day-ahead Wholesale Market Electricity Prices: Case Study of RTP Program Experience in New York," Prepared for the California Energy Commission, July 2005, previously published Ernest Orlando Lawrence Berkeley National Laboratory Working Paper LBNL-54761, June 2004; also reported in Charles Goldman, Nicole Hopper, Osman Sezgen, Mithra Moezzi, Ranjit Bharvirkar, Bernie Neenan, Donna Pratt, Peter Cappers, and Richard Boisvert, "Does Real-Time Pricing Deliver Demand Response? A Case Study of Niagara Mohawk's Large Customers RTP Tariff," Ernest Orlando Lawrence Berkeley National Laboratory Working Paper LBNL-54974, August 2004.

61. C. Goldman, N. Hopper, R. Bharvirkar, B Neenan, R. Boisvert, P. Cappers, D. Pratt, and K. Butkins, "Customer Strategies for Responding to Day-Ahead Market Hourly Electricity Pricing," Prepared for the California Energy Commission, Ernest Orlando Lawrence Berkeley National Laboratory Working Paper LBNL-57128, August 2005.

62. J. Polidoro, "Price Responsive Load Survey Report," May 16, 2005, http://www.pjm.com/committees/working-groups/dsrwg/downloads/20050516-item-3-price-responsive-load-survey-report.pdf, queried on October 24, 2005.

63. The energy cooperative website at http://www.energycooperative.org; Summit Blue Consulting, LLC, "Evaluation of the 2004 Energy-Smart Pricing Plan Final Report," March 2005, http://www.energycooperative.org/pdf/ESPP-2004-Evaluation-Final-Report.pdf and "Evaluation of the 2005 Energy-Smart Pricing Plan Final Report," August 2006, http://www.energycooperative.org/pdf/ESPP-Evaluation-Final-Report-2005.pdf, queried May 18, 2007; and Anthony Star, Assistant Manager, Community Energy Cooperative, "The Energy-Smart Pricing Plan" Presentation to the Mid-Atlantic Distributed Resources Initiative Demand Side Management Working Group, June 8, 2005, http://www.pjm.com/committees/working-groups/dsrwg/down-loads/20050608-madri-plan.pdf; queried October 24, 2005.

V

PROCUREMENT

REGULATED PROCUREMENT PROCESS IN A WORLD OF COMPETITIVE MARKETS: DEVELOPING THE RIGHT PROCUREMENT STRATEGY

Kurt Strunk

The theme of this book is markets and regulation in juxtaposition. The procurement of competitive generation services by regulated distribution companies underscores this juxtaposition. In markets throughout the Americas, Europe, Africa, Asia, and Australia, utilities are taking important decisions regarding the procurement of generation services. In many of those jurisdictions, regulated distribution companies purchase generation services in a competitive wholesale market where generators and/or power marketers sell at market-determined rates. While the utility's procurement costs are based on market-determined prices, the generation component of the distribution company's tariff is regulated. To recover the cost of procurement a utility needs regulatory approval of the prudence of its procurement decisions—both the products procured and the procurement method. In this context, a distribution utility needs to develop its procurement strategy to carefully manage, on the one hand, the regulatory risks, and, on the other hand, its operating risks as a buyer in the competitive generation market.

Procurement strategies are vital because the stakes involved in procurement choices are high. Generation services typically comprise over half of the total delivered cost of power and in most jurisdictions their cost is passed through to customers without a markup. A cost disallowance for procured generation services can easily eliminate an entire year of distribution earnings. The experience of distribution companies in the Western United States in 2000 and 2001 illustrates just how serious the consequences of failed procurement decisions can be. A crisis in the Western power markets drove formerly healthy utilities across the West into financial distress and Pacific Gas & Electric into bankruptcy, events that ultimately cost customers dearly. In contrast, many of the procurement models NERA examined in the chapters that compose this section show that, when designed and implemented properly, a procurement model can work well for all stakeholders—customers, utilities, wholesale suppliers, retail suppliers, and other interested parties.

The consequences of procurement decisions not only impact the rates paid by customers but influence the structure of the industry as well. The effects of procurement decisions on the wholesale market and the retail market can be subtle but are always important. In the wholesale market, the strategies of regulated utilities to procure generation services can affect the nature of competition. For example, to the extent the distribution utility elects to procure a product that is not commonly traded in the wholesale market, the market may develop around the distribution company's need. Suppliers providing that service to the distribution company may wish to lay off certain risks to other suppliers, further affecting the types of transactions that take place in the wholesale market. Distribution utilities may execute supply contracts with new power plants, thus directly impacting the wholesale market (although as discussed in the section on security of supply, restructured markets are more likely to solve the new capacity question either by leaving it to the market or by organized efforts of the Transmission System Operator/Independent System Operator).

Strategies of the regulated utilities to procure generation services will also affect the competitiveness of the retail market to the extent that consumers are able to procure generation services directly from non-utility retailers. The utility's procurement policies and their regulatory treatment will determine the level of the utility's retail generation rate, which establishes for non-utility retailers the price to beat and the benchmark against which their retail contracting strategies are developed.

However for some readers, even the notion of a distribution company having a procurement strategy may sound strange. This is because distribution companies in some jurisdictions do not procure generation service. For example, in England and Wales and in Texas, distribution companies have no supply obligation and are not in the business of providing generation service. In other jurisdictions, the distribution company may buy energy but not be responsible for the purchasing decisions. This is the case in Brazil, where the distribution companies do have an obligation to serve but where they buy energy through government- imposed procurement auctions. The Brazilian government designs and runs the auctions, specifying the products and the terms of the solicitations, leaving the distribution companies with little say in the procurement decisions. Similarly, in Italy, the distribution companies have an obligation to serve and to supply generation service but are not responsible for procuring this generation on behalf of those customers. The Italian procurement function is instead assigned to a single-buyer, who procures on behalf of all distribution companies. Another example is Spain, where the distribution utilities procure the generation needs of their default service customers but have no flexibility in their purchasing strategy, because the quantities, type of contract, and the timing of the purchases are specified by the Spanish regulator. In jurisdictions such as these, one might reasonably conclude that a procurement strategy for distribution utilities is not necessary or relevant. Nevertheless, NERA has found in its consulting work that it is vitally important to develop a robust procurement strategy, even where another entity is making procurement decisions on the distributor's behalf. It is important that the distributor understand the implications of those decisions and influence those decisions to assure its own well being. For these reasons, we believe procurement is among the most important issues facing the power sector today.

The chapters in this section analyze the key decisions necessary to develop a robust procurement strategy, and to gain insight into (1) the elements that have made certain procurement models succeed or flounder and (2) what models work for which operating environments. The chapters examine both the experience of procurement models both in the United States and in other countries. In the United States, the issue of procurement has been litigated extensively in regulatory proceedings, and substantial effort has been made to optimize procurement.

Chapter 18 "Default Service Procurement: The US Experience with Full Requirements" examines the drivers of the trend in the United States to move toward full requirements procurements and away from utility portfolio management in those instances where wholesale markets are increasingly competitive and sophisticated. It explains why it does not make sense, in the context of well-developed wholesale markets, for the utility to have its own trading floor and trading staff to procure a portfolio of products that could be supplied by the competitive market. Nevertheless, it recognizes that the full requirements solution may not be the best procurement mechanism for all utilities and that certain circumstances merit other approaches.

Chapter 19 "Procurement from Affiliates: Regulatory Constraints in the United States" explains the Federal Energy Regulatory Commission's (FERC's) standards for approval of a contract between a distribution utility and an affiliated wholesale generator. The FERC's affiliate contract policy calls for transparent procurement mechanisms that allow affiliates and non-affiliates to compete on a level playing field. The chapter summarizes and evaluates the FERC guidelines for competitive procurement, which have shaped the procurement strategies of utilities in the United States.

Chapter 20 "New Jersey versus Maryland: Is there a "Best" Competitive Bid Process?" compares the New Jersey model to the Maryland model, highlighting the differences in (1) bidding process: auction versus RFP, (2) pricing to customers: bid prices versus translation mechanism, (3) risks to suppliers: credit requirements and other risk differences, and (4) supplier versus distribution company responsibilities. In drawing these contrasts, the paper clarifies the key issues that must be decided in designing a full-requirements procurement.

Chapter 21 "Open Auctions as the New Trend for Power Procurement: An Analysis of the New Jersey BGS and the Brazil "Old Energy" Auction Designs" discusses this new trend and compares the power procurement auctions in Brazil to those in New Jersey, highlighting how choices regarding the design of the auction can be critical to the procurement outcome.

Any procurement strategy contains defined building blocks. As illustrated in the figure below, a procurement model should include, first, an

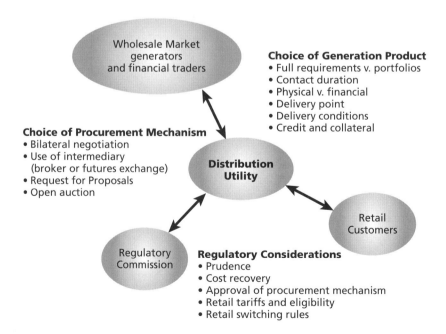

appropriate choice of which products to procure, second, an appropriate choice of the procurement mechanism through which those products are procured, and third, a regulatory mechanism to assure recovery of all reasonable costs incurred to effect the procurement.

These elements are discussed below in the context of the papers that follow.

Product Design: Product design refers to the details of the services being procured. There are a myriad of options for the type of product procured and the structure of the deals, all of which affect the final cost to customers. Key product design decisions include: Should the utility assemble its own portfolio or should it procure full requirements service and rely on suppliers to build portfolios? If it elects to assemble its own portfolio, what products should that portfolio include? Should the utility use short-term or long-term contracts? If it elects to procure full requirements, what are the key commercial terms in the contracts? Terms may include customer segments covered, contract duration, assurances that the supplier will provide reliable supply, credit protection for the utility and customers, allocation of risks among the supplier, the utility, and the customers.

Several papers in this section address product design. "Default Service Procurement: The US Experience with Full Requirements" compares full requirements procurements to the assembly and management of a supply portfolio and examines what is driving the industry toward full requirements procurements where wholesale markets are increasingly competitive and sophisticated. "Maryland versus New Jersey" illustrates how subtle differences in product design can affect the suppliers' view of the procurement and the procurement outcome. "Procurement from Affiliates" shows how the US regulators require that the choice of product design be made in a way that does not give an advantage to any specific bidder, particularly affiliated bidders.

Procurement Process: The utility procurement process also requires important decisions that are not independent of the choices made for product design. For example, if the utility elects to assemble its own supply portfolio, it must assess what procurement mechanisms to employ to assemble the portfolio: To what extent will the utility pursue direct negotiations with suppliers, seek to use brokers to facilitate transactions, tap existing exchange traded or over-the-counter markets for standard products, or issue its own solicitations for non-standard products? Similarly, if the utility chooses to pursue full requirements, it needs to decide the frequency of procurements and the solicitation format. The choice of solicitation format can have material impacts on the overall procurement cost. Depending on the circumstances, certain solicitation formats are more effective in creating a competitive bidding environment, which drives down procurement costs.

If there is no pre-existing market for the product(s) being procured, the utility must create a market mechanism for procurement. In this context, utilities often rely upon market mechanisms like an auction or a request for proposals (RFP). Of course, if there is already an established market for the product, there is no need to create a market mechanism and the utility may simply enter that market as a buyer. Should the utility directly participate in the market, managing its own portfolio, it will need risk management policies and procedures, as well as the technology to assure that management is receiving correct and timely information. In contrast, with a full requirements product, the utility transfers the risks and rewards (and the portfolio analysis and risk management functions) to the supplier. The choice of product is therefore intertwined with the choice of how the utility will procure and what in-house resources will be required.

"New Jersey versus Maryland" examines the differences between the procurement processes chosen by the utilities in these two states and compares the use of an RFP procurement process to the use of an auction. "Open Auctions as the New Trend for Power Procurement" provides two case studies of the use of open auctions to implement successful procurements and shows how subtle differences in the designs of those auctions can affect the procurement outcome. The case studies examine open auctions that were adopted and implemented under very different regulatory and market conditions.

Regulatory Approvals: As important as careful planning of the product design and procurement process is the attention that both the utility and the regulator must pay to the regulatory treatment of the costs of generation services procured by the utility. Assurance of recovery of prudently incurred costs is fundamental to the financial integrity of the utility; without it, the utility cannot provide customers reliable service at reasonable costs.

Under certain types of procurements, the utility may be subject to traditional *post facto* prudence reviews. In this case, contemporaneous documentation of analysis and decision making will be critical. An alternative to *post facto* prudence reviews is approval of the procurement strategy and process on an *ex ante* basis. This option has been employed by distribution utilities operating in Maryland, the District of Columbia, and New Jersey for their full requirements purchases. Pre-approval was also used in Ireland, when the default generation provider (the retail supply arm of the Electricity Supply Board) sought assurance from the regulator that any above-market costs associated with long-term contracts that it executed pursuant to an initiative of the regulator would not be disallowed. A more thorough analysis of prudence issues is provided in the section on regulation in this volume.

"Procurement from Affiliates" evaluates the FERC guidelines for competitive procurement and explains the standards in the US that utilities need to meet to obtain the FERC approval of a contract between a load-serving utility and a wholesale generation affiliate. US federal regulatory policy, spelled out in case precedent, sets forth strict rules under which distribution utilities may purchase from affiliated generators or power marketers. Hence, where affiliate purchases are a possibility, the assurance of cost recovery also involves compliance with the affiliate standards. The rules are quite specific and recommend an open and transparent solicitation to assure that all suppliers have an opportunity to compete to serve the load of the distribution utility and that there is no undue favoritism toward the affiliate.

"Maryland versus New Jersey" examines regulatory approval considerations in these two those states. Similarly, "Default Service Procurement: The US Experience with Full Requirements" explains how regulatory approval is one driver in the trend toward full requirements procurement.

Finally, as the papers illustrate, procurement strategies will differ depending the utility's specific characteristics and particular goals, existing market conditions, and especially its regulatory and operating environment. Not all jurisdictions require the distribution utility to offer generation supply; not all jurisdictions have separated generation from distribution; not all utilities have access to a workably competitive wholesale market; and not all utilities are subject to retail access. The nature of the utility's obligation, the degree of vertical integration, the terms of existing long-term power purchase agreements, the structure of the wholesale and retail markets in which the utilities operate—all are factors that will affect a given utility's determination of the appropriate procurement strategy. The risks for integrated utilities that merely purchase to supplement an owned-generation portfolio will differ from the risks to a wires-only utility that procures its entire generation needs in the wholesale markets. The development of a procurement strategy must take that into account.

"**Default Service Procurement:** The US Experience with Full Requirements" explains why certain US utilities have found the full requirements product to be part of a successful procurement strategy. However, this product strategy is not the only one and may not be the right one. Building a portfolio of contracts is a model that has worked in other jurisdictions. Regulators in Argentina have allowed the distribution utilities to build their own portfolios and determine the appropriate duration and quantity of the forward contracts they enter into, as well as the share of their needs that are met through spot market purchases. In New York, the distribution utilities construct portfolios on behalf of their default service customers. These are procurement models that have worked in specific circumstances and specific regulatory climates.

We hope you enjoy the papers in this section, which highlight why individual procurement approaches have been successful and unsuccessful for utilities in certain circumstances, and why utilities in other circumstances have elected to proceed otherwise.

18

DEFAULT SERVICE PROCUREMENT: THE US EXPERIENCE WITH FULL REQUIREMENTS

Kurt Strunk

Introduction

In the US jurisdictions that have pursued restructuring, there is a striking trend in the procurement policies of incumbent distribution utilities obligated to continue to serve customers who do not or cannot choose a non-utility generation provider. The norm for these utilities is to procure generation requirements for their default service customers on a full-requirements, forward term basis. That is, they have elected to structure their solicitations for default service to ensure that all of their load is served by competitive entities and there is no residual tranche for which they retain responsibility. Utilities in New Jersey, Maryland, the District of Columbia, Virginia, Delaware, Massachusetts, Maine, Pennsylvania, Rhode Island, and Illinois currently procure or are planning to procure full requirements power to meet their obligations to serve default service customers.

The primary reason that utilities in these jurisdictions have chosen, and their regulators have approved, full requirements procurement, is that the utilities want to focus their resources on delivery services. Generation companies and/or power marketers can take on the responsibilities and manage the risks of assembling a portfolio of owned generation or contracts. From the regulator's perspective, the clean separation of generation and distribution mitigates concerns about conflicts of interest and the possibility of undue advantages in serving retail customers.

The full requirements approach is not, however, a one-size-fits-all solution: It will not work for every operating environment. Wholesale markets may not be sufficiently well developed to support full-requirements procurement. Utilities may have large portfolios of rate-based generation that are well suited to meeting the needs of their customers, rendering full-requirements procurement unnecessary. Similarly, in jurisdictions without retail access, the rationale for choosing a full-requirements product on the basis of its impact on the development and operation of a retail market simply does not apply.

Section II of this chapter examines common elements of the full-requirements procurement processes that have been adopted by restructured markets in the US. Section III describes more fully the rationale for selecting a full-requirements procurement process. The fourth section evaluates certain alleged drawbacks that are often cited those who advocate active portfolio management by the utility and compares the two approaches. The fifth section summarizes my conclusions.

Common Elements to Full-Requirements Procurements in Restructured US Markets

Three common situational considerations have underpinned the decision of utilities to pursue full-requirements procurement in restructured US markets:

- The utilities own little or no generation;
- The utilities are part of strongly functioning Regional Transmission Organizations (RTOs), such as PJM, or the New England ISO, which perform centralized economic dispatch functions and administer spot electricity markets.
- The retail market has been liberalized in the utility's service territory, and all (or nearly all) customers have the freedom to choose a non-utility supplier of generation services.

In addition, a high-level comparison of the procurements reveals numerous common elements in the way they are structured, although there are substantial differences in the details of how they have been implemented.

- **The cost of utility procurement is the foundation for retail rates:** A large number of US utilities that have elected to procure full requirements have been through a transition period where they were subject to rate freezes or rate caps. As these transition periods end and rate freezes or rate caps expire, their retail rates for generation services are determined by the direct results of the procurement method selected and reflect, with limited exceptions, a pass-through of the costs of the generation services procured.

- **The full-requirements load is divided into tranches:** The utilities have sliced up the load responsibility into "tranches." Each tranche represents a fixed percentage of the total default service load requirements of the utility so that suppliers provide a "vertical" slice of the load curve. Generally speaking, the US procurements have set the percentages so that each tranche corresponds to about 25 MW to 100 MW of peak load, assuming normal conditions and no migration of customers off of the utility default service rate. This provides an opportunity for multiple suppliers to serve the load, and so diversifies the risk of supplier default and encourages competition among suppliers in the wholesale market.

- **The procurements are for short-term or medium-term supply:** No full-requirements procurement in a restructured US market has been structured to include contracts longer than five years, and contract term is generally for three years or less. Contracts tend to be shorter for large customers.

- **The form of the payment to suppliers of generation services is a single $/kWh price:** For service to small customers, the utilities have often structured the payments to suppliers in terms of a single charge for energy taken.[1] This per kWh generation rate is an all-in rate, including compensation for the costs of supplying capacity, ancillary services, and in some cases transmission.

- **Rolling procurement is used for securing the supply requirements of small customers:** The full-requirements procurement processes for small customers in the restructured US markets have largely been designed to use rolling (or "laddered") procurements. In a rolling procurement, only a fraction of the load is procured at one time, and the final retail rates paid by customers reflect the average prices obtained through multiple procurement processes. Rolling procurements therefore require vertical tranches, as a rolling procurement is obviously not possible when 100 percent of the load is procured at a single point in time.

The Full-Requirements Products Squarely Meet the Goals of the Utility and its Regulator

In NERA's experience working with utilities and regulators, the choice of product must further the goals of the procurement process. Hence, product design should be considered within the context of designing a procurement process that meets a broad set of goals or guiding principles. We have identified eight goals that are common across jurisdictions and discuss how the full-requirements product advances each of these goals, particularly in the US.

Reliable Supply

The overarching goal common to all stakeholders is the procurement of reliable supply. Reliability requires generating plant sufficient to serve the load and an adequate transmission grid to deliver the generation to the load. Historically, it was the utility that was responsible for assuring that sufficient generation and transmission were built. However, following restructuring, the US utilities electing to pursue full-requirements procurements have been members of FERC-approved RTOs. These RTOs not only perform centralized economic dispatch functions and administer spot electricity markets, but also ensure capacity adequacy and resource deliverability through a centralized planning process.[2]

Transferring the generation and transmission planning function to the RTO gives the utility greater flexibility in structuring its full-requirements procurement contracts and allows them to be structured as financial risk management contracts. The physical delivery obligation embedded in the contracts merely transfers to the RTO, and the supplier becomes responsible to the RTO for any failure to deliver. This contractual structure meets the goal of assuring reliable supply, without tying the contract to a specific generation facility or a specific set of generation facilities. Financial players with strong balance sheets can compete with generation owners to supply the full-requirements load of the utility, thus increasing the number of competitors and the downward pressure on supply costs without in any way compromising reliability.

Utilities that are not in RTOs and that remain responsible for generation and transmission planning may well prefer to tie their procurement contracts to physical generation plant. Financial contracts that delegate physical delivery obligations to the RTO do not make sense absent an RTO market. As noted previously, full requirements may not be the right choice for utilities in such situations.

Development and Operation of Retail Energy Markets

A primary goal of regulators in jurisdictions that have implemented retail access is to assure the proper functioning of the retail markets, including efficient entry and exit by suppliers. Efficient entry, for example, reflects a supplier's ability to supply at a lower cost or its ability to provide customers with greater value. Entry based on opportunities created by over-priced default service is not efficient. By pricing default service at the market rate resulting from the competitively procured full-requirements contract, regulators can minimize nonproductive customer switching to inefficient entrants.

Procure Low-Cost Supply for Customers, Consistent with Market

When divided into tranches and viewed in the context of a well-developed wholesale market, the full-requirements can by provided by multiple suppliers. The product can be supplied by generators with a portfolio of physical assets, or by financial players with a portfolio of contracts and financial hedges. Designing a product that is appealing to this broad set of potential suppliers assures that when the product is procured, there will be strong competition among suppliers, competition that drives down costs for customers.

Although one goal is to reduce costs for customers, it is important that those costs still reflect the market. Market prices encourage efficient consumption and conservation decisions and meet other goals *vis-à-vis* the impact on the retail market. The utility cannot and should not be expected to procure at costs that are below those that are available in the marketplace.

Encourage Fair Opportunity for any Wholesale Supplier to Serve Load

The product procured by the distribution utility (and the process by which the utility procures the product) must be designed to encourage maximum participation by competitive suppliers. Therefore, the full-requirements procurements implemented in restructured US markets have featured standardized supply contracts. Standardized contracts preclude negotiation over terms and conditions; the suppliers that are chosen to serve load are those suppliers who are willing to serve it at the lowest cost, according to a common set of terms and conditions. Standardized contracts send an important signal to potential suppliers that they will be able to compete effectively because they know that competition will be based on price alone, rather than on specific nuances in commercial terms that could favor one supplier over another.

Protect Small Customers from Market Price Volatility

The full-requirements procurement processes in the US generally use rolling (laddered) procurements to secure generation supplies for small customers. Since only a fraction of the load is procured at one time, the final retail rates paid by customers reflect the rolling average prices obtained through multiple procurement processes.

Put Supply Risk Management Function in the Hands of Competitive Entities

Providing default generation service at a fixed price requires that the supplier actively manage price risk. Competitive entities that undertake to serve the load of default service customers must assemble supply components in the competitive wholesale market and must assess and price the risks of customer switching, of load fluctuations due to weather, etc. Assigning the portfolio and price risk management function to competitive suppliers subjects the function to the discipline of the market and removes any inefficiencies of regulating a service that is vigorously competitive.

Ensure Financial Integrity of the Distribution Utility

Generation costs and revenues can exceed 50 percent of total distribution utility cost and revenue and are thus an order of magnitude greater than distribution utility earnings. As the distribution utility typically earns no profit from supplying generation service, it should not bear the risk of nonrecovery of generation costs.

The full-requirements product helps protect the financial integrity of the distribution utility by reducing the regulatory risk of its purchased power program (i.e., the risk that procurement costs would be deemed imprudent and disallowed). While under US regulatory practice the utility can never evade the prudence standard, the full-requirements product reduces regulatory risk by assigning the portfolio management decisions to the supplier. The utility, therefore, is never in the position of being second-guessed for its portfolio management choices. It must of course demonstrate the prudence of its decisions to proceed with full-requirements procurements and or the implementation of its procurement procedures, but the approach appropriately allocates the supply cost and associated cost recovery risks and does not jeopardize the financial integrity of the purchasing utility.

Clean Break of Generation and Distribution Functions

An important factor in the decision of US utilities to procure full requirements is the desire to have a clean break between generation and distribution. The distribution companies do not want to be in the generation business, and they seek generation companies and/or power marketers to take on the responsibilities and manage the risks of assembling a portfolio of owned generation or contracts. It is worth noting that they have elected to structure their solicitations to assure that all of the load is served by competitive entities. They do not want to bid out a portion of the load and retain the responsibility of assembling the portfolio requirements for a residual tranche that was not taken by the competitive market. In their view, the portfolio management function, when housed within the regulated utility, carries an asymmetric risk/reward tradeoff— "heads you win, tails we lose"—and therefore they seek no residual obligation for the utility.

Problems with the Portfolio Management Approach

Critics of the full-requirements approach generally argue that the distribution utility should purchase a portfolio of financial and physical hedging products, with the total cost and prudence of the purchases determined after the fact. This alternative utility portfolio management approach is the primary alternative model put forth for post-transition utility default service generation product.[3] While in the full-requirements model, the portfolio management function is in the responsibility of competitive suppliers selling at market-based rates, in the utility portfolio management model, this function remains with the regulated utility, subject to regulation. However, the utility portfolio management alternative has several major shortcomings.

Preparedness: Staffing and Infrastructure

In well-developed wholesale markets, the trading that is necessary to support the supply of utility default service customers requires sophisticated staff and trading infrastructure to manage market, credit, and operational risks. For the most part, regulated distribution utilities have neither the staff nor the infrastructure to manage these trading risks. Competitive entities that manage energy supply portfolios invest substantially in systems and information sources (reports in the trade press suggest investments of millions of dollars) to support their trading operations. A regulated utility may not wish to make such investments in trading infrastructure, particularly if their corporate strategy is to exit the generation business.

Where utilities have divested generation assets or transferred them to an affiliate, the staff that had the skills to interact with the wholesale market often went with the asset to be employed by the new owners. Even if those employees had remained at the utility, absent substantial retraining it is unlikely that they would be qualified to manage the trading risks of meeting the generation needs of default service customers in a well-developed wholesale market. The portfolio manager's tool box (i.e., the products commonly traded in a wholesale market) are dramatically different in today's wholesale markets from the products that were available in the days of integrated utility portfolio management, with economy energy trading at split-the-savings rates. Moreover, the risks of procuring supply for customers in a retail access world —where the degree of migration off of or onto the utility's generation rate is unknown and uncertain—are vastly different from the risks of rounding out a portfolio of rate-based generation. Hence, with or without generation assets, a regulated distribution utility generally will not have the staff or the infrastructure needed to assume the trading and risk management responsibilities associated with managing a supply portfolio for default service customers.

In contrast, there are dozens of competitive wholesale power suppliers that are capable of supplying a full-requirements product. This segment of the marketplace—that aggregates financial and physical electricity products and provides risk management services—contains many established firms equipped with the systems and personnel to properly manage price and volume risks. The New Jersey Board of Public Utilities noted that there were 25 bidders participating in the competitive auction to supply full requirements to the customers of the New Jersey distribution utilities. FERC has authorized market-based rate authority to over 500 entities. There is no reason to believe the distribution utility is in a position to manage this risk as well as a group of established trading and marketing firms.

Competitive Pressure versus the Threat of Prudence Disallowance

From an economist's perspective, the portfolio management function should be regulated only if it is a natural monopoly or there is another special situation where a market is not producing an efficient outcome. Economists know that regulation is less effective than competition in achieving an efficient allocation of resources and prices that correctly reflect economic realities. There is no evidence that the service of assembling a supply portfolio and managing its risks is a natural monopoly, nor is there evidence that the market is not producing an efficient outcome.

Furthermore, portfolio management is a particularly ill-suited candidate for regulatory oversight. Regulation that relies on a retroactive review of portfolio management provides incentives for utilities to make decisions that are within the range of reasonable options and that a reasonable person would select from information that was reasonably knowable at the time. These incentives naturally lead to well-considered decisions that avoid risks and that stay with tried and true approaches. Such decisions need not be optimal or even result in a favorable outcome for customers relative to other decisions that could have been made at the time. Competitive suppliers of the portfolio and price risk management service can and will consider all options to manage the portfolio and can use any and all hedging instruments. However, survival in a competitive market requires a winning strategy. Competitive pressures encourage rapid response to changing situations, encourage novel approaches to hedging, and reward the taking of well-calculated risks. Customers can be expected to benefit from lower prices if the full gamut of strategies is brought to bear on managing the supply portfolio, and if the competitive discipline of the market is allowed to select those entities that excel at this management function.

Impact on the Retail Market

Under the utility portfolio management model, with its *ex post* prudence review of the utilities' portfolio management decisions, the rates are not knowable with certainly in advance. In contrast, procurement of a full-requirements product on a forward term basis enables regulators and customers to know in advance and with certainty the costs of the default service. This allows customers to make informed switching decisions and encourages retailers to compete against the utility's "price to beat," which is known *ex ante*.

Conclusion

The striking trend towards full-requirements procurement is rooted in a rationale that applies sound economics and sound regulatory policy. Use of full-requirements procurement in restructured US markets has demonstrated that it is the optimal choice for utilities with access to a competitive wholesale market. It clearly has advantages over its most often proposed alternative, the utility portfolio management model. Nevertheless, it is not appropriate for all utilities. If wholesale markets are insufficiently developed or utilities own significant generation to serve their load, full-requirements procurement may not be possible or desirable. Ultimately, the appropriate procurement approach is utility-specific.

Notes

1. While it is common to use a single per kWh rate to compensate suppliers for serving small customer load, Maryland has structured their full-requirements procurement differently. In Maryland, suppliers actually bid on the retail rate components, and winning suppliers are paid the components that they bid. The retail rates provide for separate demand and energy charges.

2. The PJM website (www.pjm.com) explains: "PJM ensures the reliability of the largest centrally dispatched control area in North America by coordinating the movement of electricity in all or parts of Delaware, Illinois, Indiana, Kentucky, Maryland, Michigan, New Jersey, North Carolina, Ohio, Pennsylvania, Tennessee, Virginia, West Virginia and the District of Columbia. PJM, acting neutrally and independently, operates the largest competitive wholesale electricity market in the world. PJM manages a sophisticated regional planning process for generation and transmission expansion to assure future electric reliability." Similarly, the ISO New England website (www.iso-ne.com) describes its role, "ISO New England helps protect the health of New England's economy and the well-being of its people by ensuring the constant availability of electricity, today and for future generations. ISO New England meets this obligation in three ways: by ensuring the day-to-day reliable operation of New England's bulk power generation and transmission system, by overseeing and ensuring the fair administration of the region's wholesale electricity markets, and by managing comprehensive, regional planning processes."

3. Another alternative that has been proposed—and was implemented in Texas—is the assignment of default service customers to a non-utility provider of last resort. In the Texas case, this requires that the non-utility providers of last resort perform the billing, customer inquiry, and metering functions, which many suppliers that are suited to serve the default service load are not interested in performing. Further, many regulators are wary of customer assignment without customer consent. For these and other reasons, it has not been pursued in other jurisdictions.

19

PROCUREMENT FROM AFFILIATES: REGULATORY CONSTRAINTS IN THE UNITED STATES

Kushal Patel

Introduction

In February and July of 2004, the US Federal Energy Regulatory Commission (FERC)[1] issued precedent-shaping decisions on a number of affiliate transactions. FERC expanded the jurisdictional scope of its review by ordering that all future transactions involving any sales between regulated US public utilities and their affiliates shall be subject to the standard set by FERC's 1991 *Edgar*[2] decision. The standard memorialized in the *Edgar* decision is designed to assure that a public utility does not enter into a higher-cost transaction with an affiliate when less costly options are available from nonaffiliated entities. An affiliate seller could demonstrate that the ratepayers would not be subject to higher costs as a result of the transaction through the use of benchmarks, data on non-affiliate pricing, or evidence of head-to-head competition.

By 2004, FERC's goal had evolved from protecting a utility's captive ratepayers from affiliate abuse to "the development of vibrant, fully competitive generation markets" that do not foreclose existing merchant generators, new entrants, or nonaffiliated suppliers.[3] With the explosive growth during the last 20 years of non-affiliate independent suppliers, public utilities now have greater non-affiliate options than ever before to meet their energy, capacity, and ancillary services requirements. Faced with this myriad of non-affiliate suppliers, FERC is prodding utilities with supply resource needs to rely on market-based mechanisms for procurement and is discouraging them from directly awarding contracts to affiliates.[4] It has pledged to undertake a thorough review of all affiliate transactions to ensure that independent suppliers are not denied equal competitive opportunities.[5]

Utilities that wish to enter into contracts with affiliates, either power purchase agreements (PPAs) or the purchase of assets, thus face new and challenging constraints that can potentially threaten full cost recovery. The *Edgar* standard provides a safe harbor for these transactions that allows utilities to avoid or at least minimize the risk from FERC of *ex post* challenges, disallowances, and outright rejections of the procurement results. But to be eligible, utilities must rethink their traditional procurement processes and consider open competitive solicitations that level the playing field to squarely satisfy the requirements of the order. FERC has offered one sure way to achieve fast-track review and approval of an affiliate transaction. Its 2004 *Ameren* and *Allegheny*[6] decisions have provided guidelines on *Edgar* compliance for US public utilities: The transaction in question must be the result of an open, well defined, and transparent competitive solicitation process conducted by an independent third party.[7]

This chapter reviews the development of FERC's policy regarding affiliate transactions and present several case studies illustrating how existing competitive solicitations have met the *Edgar* standard by following the competitive solicitation guidelines memorialized in the *Allegheny* decision. While they focus exclusively on US regulatory policy, the solicitation design frameworks that have evolved and the guidelines that reflect best practices in the US can be used in non-US jurisdictions. The US approach to affiliate transactions avoids undue risk, complication, or ambiguity regarding the overall fairness and results of the process, and proactively mitigates any concerns regarding favoritism or possible abusive affiliate self-dealing.

Development of the Policy

Edgar

In 1991, FERC sought to assure that Boston Edison had chosen the lowest-cost supplier from the options available in the market, taking into account both price and nonprice terms, and that it had not given unjust preference to its affiliate, Edgar Electric Energy.[8] It set a standard that the seller must show that customers of the affiliated regulated entity will not experience higher costs as a result of an affiliate transaction. Under *Edgar*, there are three principal ways that the seller may demonstrate that the transaction is free from such abuse. The first is "evidence of direct head-to-head competition between [the seller] and competing unaffiliated suppliers either in a formal solicitation or in an informal negotiation process."[9] This head-to-head competition should assure that the transaction is above suspicion and is disciplined by the competitive market and therefore does not distort the market. When the applicant relies on a head-to-head competitive process, the *Edgar* standard requires it to demonstrate that (a) the competitive process was not designed and implemented in a way that provided the affiliate an undue competitive advantage; (b) the evaluation did not unduly favor the offer from the affiliate, with a particular emphasis on the evaluation of nonprice factors; and (c) the affiliate was selected based on some reasonable combination of price and nonprice factors.

The second type of evidence permissible under *Edgar* is reference to the prices that nonaffiliated buyers were willing to pay for similar services from the generator. (This type of evidence has seldom been relied on.)

A third type is benchmark evidence of the prices, terms, and conditions of comparable transactions made by nonaffiliated sellers. *Edgar* sets the following criteria for the comparison group of transactions:

1. The transactions must occur in the relevant market.
2. The transactions must be contemporaneous with the instant transaction.
3. The transactions must involve services similar and comparable to those involved in the instant transaction.
4. The applicant must demonstrate that the instant transaction is as favorable to the buyer as the comparison group transactions, considering both their price and nonprice terms.
5. The applicant must clearly and fully explain all assumptions used to evaluate both.
6. The comparison group transactions must not incorporate the effect of the exercise of market power by a party to the instant transaction.

Expansion of the Edgar Standard

The *Edgar* standard first applied only to market-based tariffs, but in February 2004 FERC expanded *Edgar's* scope of transactional review in its *Mountainview*[10] decision. Southern California Edison was proposing to purchase power from Mountainview, which it was in the process of acquiring, at cost-based rates. FERC accepted the agreement with some modifications, and, more significantly, held that henceforth it would apply the *Edgar* standard to all affiliate power transactions of duration of one year or greater, whether filed as cost-based tariffs or market-based tariffs. In extending *Edgar* to cost-based transactions, FERC recognized that due to various supply conditions, including competitive supply entry and transmission open access, market-based tariffs in several parts of the country could be lower than cost-based tariffs. FERC intended to assure that captive ratepayers pay no more than market value in these situations. It also expressed its concern for the wholesale market itself: "Affiliate preference could discourage non-affiliates from adding supply in the local area, harming wholesale competition and, ultimately, wholesale customers."[11] FERC restricted resale of Mountainview output to spot market sales bid at the marginal cost of each unit, noting that otherwise Edison, which would be assured of full cost recovery from Mountainview, could bid below cost, lowering the clearing price below a competitive outcome and dampening competitive price signals.

In *Mountainview*, FERC noted that under its current policy all that was required was that the cost-based formula was just and reasonable, and therefore the expansion of the *Edgar* standards would only apply prospectively. On May 28, 2004 in Docket No. PL04-6-000 FERC held an open technical conference and requested comments to discuss solicitation processes for power procurement in general and the *Edgar* standard in particular. FERC invited interested parties to comment on a number of solicitation issues, including the questions of whether the *Edgar* standard was sufficient to assure no preferential or abusive affiliate dealings, whether a competitive solicitation process should be designed collaboratively, and whether an independent third party should monitor and/or administer a competitive solicitation. On July 28 and 29, FERC issued two orders further expanding the scope of the *Edgar* decision and establishing new guidelines to standardize the analysis of future transactions between public utilities and their affiliates.

First, the *Ameren* decision applied the *Edgar* standard to Section 203 transfers of FERC-jurisdictional assets from a generator to an affiliated regulated utility. In previous cases,[12] FERC had been concerned that the regulated utility might serve as a safety net for merchant generators who, if market conditions turned unfavorable and they could not recover their costs from market rates, could sell their assets back to the utility at book costs to be recovered by the utility's cost-based rates.[13] Hence, whether it is the buyer in a PPA or the buyer of a generating plant, in all cases the utility must now provide evidence sufficient to meet the *Edgar* affiliate transaction standard.

FERC's actions regarding utility acquisition from affiliates arguably overlap the role of the state public utility commissions, whose purview includes prudence reviews of utility expenditures.[14] FERC, however, asserts that its role is a different and necessary addition to state review. While state commissions have the opportunity in prudence reviews to assure *ex post* that no above-market costs from affiliate transactions are passed on to ratepayers, FERC review is *ex ante:* it occurs before the transaction is consummated and can prevent any harm to market competition. In *Ameren*, FERC determined:

> While effective state regulatory review can prevent excessive rates to the retail customers of the acquiring utility, it is not a remedy for the anticompetitive effects of affiliate preference, which harm all customers. The possibility of eventual regulatory review does not prevent the exercise of affiliate preference before the transaction occurs. We are also not convinced that such eventual regulatory review of rates is an effective remedy for anticompetitive effects that arise at the time affiliate preference occurs. Ultimately, all customers are harmed because competition is undermined.[15]

FERC cited decreased efficiency, increased market power, and increased entry barriers as three areas of potential harm to competition that could ensue if affiliate transactions are not screened and determined to be free from competitive distortion in the first place.[16] FERC further spelled out new constraints on utilities' supply planning, if that includes the possibility of an affiliate transaction. In order to meet FERC's competition objectives, utilities were encouraged to include open, transparent, competitive solicitations in their supply planning processes to assure that customers are getting the least-cost supply resources available in the market. To avoid all suspicion of affiliate preference, FERC recommended that the solicitations be conducted by an independent third party, although the decision fell just short of making such solicitations mandatory.[17]

In *Allegheny*,[18] FERC was asked to approve an affiliate contract awarded as a result of a competitive Request for Proposals (RFP) process in Maryland for full-requirements service.[19] In its decision, FERC made clear that it would apply the same standards it had used in *Ameren* for sales of assets between affiliates to evaluate proposed sales of energy from a marketer to an affiliated load-serving utility. It clearly articulated and memorialized its strong preference for head-to-head competition to assure that the transaction was above suspicion, was the least-cost option for the utility, and did not distort the market or otherwise repress competition.[20] While all three types of evidence permissible under *Edgar* could still be used by applicants seeking to demonstrate the reasonableness of an affiliate transaction, FERC's preference was clear, and it reiterated the four guidelines governing future solicitations involving head-to-head competition that it had expressed the day before in *Ameren*:

A. **Transparency:** the competitive solicitation process should be open and fair.
B. **Definition:** the product or products sought through the competitive solicitation should be precisely defined.
C. **Evaluation:** evaluation criteria should be standardized and applied equally to all bids and bidders.
D. **Oversight:** an independent third party should design the solicitation, administer bidding, and evaluate bids prior to the company's selection.

Head-to-head competition is viewed as the most compelling evidence of *Edgar* compliance and lack of affiliate favoritism because it leaves no doubt that the utility considered all available options and chose the least-cost one. When independently monitored and evaluated, well-defined head-to-head competition between affiliates and non-affiliates directly and unambiguously determines the market price for a given service or product and allows all observers such as regulators and non-affiliates to understand and appraise the results.

Possible Solicitation Scenarios

FERC's 2004 *Allegheny* guidelines are intended leave a utility considerable room to design its own solicitation, but whether utilities will be able to implement them easily or effectively depends on their operating environment. The guidelines call for well-defined products, a goal that is easier to achieve in some markets than in others. Certain power products lend themselves to standardization. If a utility's need can be met through a standard product with standard terms and conditions that apply to any winning bidder, there will be no dispute about differences in nonprice terms between the offers of affiliated and nonaffiliated suppliers. A standard product can be put to bid in an open and transparent solicitation in which price is unambiguously the determining factor in the selection of winning bidders. Hence, with standard products, the FERC criterion of evaluation transparency is easily met, although utilities must still take care to ensure that the choice of commercial terms for the standard contract does not provide unjustified preference to the affiliate.

However, the solicitation will not always involve a standard product. A utility operating in certain circumstances may wish to solicit bids on a PPA that is asset-backed, either tied to the construction of a new facility or backed by an existing plant, or alternatively, may wish to acquire assets directly. When the solicitation design and evaluation must take into consideration differing qualities and values of several assets, the goals of product uniformity, evaluation objectivity and transparency are more difficult to achieve. In this case, a utility may face substantial challenges with respect to product design and bid evaluation. These need not be insuperable. Decades of industry experience with Independent Power Producer (IPP) contract solicitations in the US and abroad provide solutions to many of these challenges. In the case of nonstandard products, however, extreme care must be taken at the solicitation design stage.

Example of a Compliant Solicitation: Auctions

The 2006 Illinois auction for full-requirements default service or provider of last resort service (POLR) contracts[21] provides an excellent example of an open and transparent process, free from affiliate bias. As FERC observed when it authorized an affiliate to make market-based sales to its regulated distribution company affiliate in advance of the solicitation: "We find that the [Illinois Auction Proposal] satisfies the Commission's concerns regarding affiliate abuse because the IAP, as proposed, is consistent with the guidelines for competitive bid processes set forth in *Edgar* and *Allegheny* and will result in just and reasonable rates."[22] The approach to product design and solicitation design taken by the public utilities in Illinois demonstrates how a solicitation can meet FERC's competition objectives and readily comply with the *Edgar* standard by incorporating the *Allegheny* guidelines.

Background

In 1997, the Illinois General Assembly passed the Electric Service Customer Choice and Rate Relief Law of 1997, which gave customers the opportunity to purchase power from the supplier of their choice and initiated restructuring of the state's electric power industry. During the transition period, set to end on December 31, 2006, rates to customers were frozen and the Illinois utilities supplied their customers on the basis of long-term power supply contracts. Commonwealth Edison Company (ComEd), and the three Ameren Illinois Utilities no longer own generation in Illinois though they continue to serve as the providers of last resort for electric service for customers who do not choose an alternative electric supplier.

In preparation for the end of the transition period, the Illinois Commerce Commission (ICC)[23] held a series of meetings and workshops to examine the future of the electric market in Illinois, public policy issues surrounding restructuring of the electric industry, and critical questions concerning procurement of supply to serve customers in the post-2006 environment. The Post-2006 Final Report recommended that, for large utilities with no generation such as ComEd and Ameren, the Commission should endorse a vertical tranche auction.[24]

In February 2005, ComEd and the Ameren Utilities filed proposals with the ICC for procurement of supply for its customers in the post 2006-period.[25] They proposed to use a competitive procurement process in the form of an auction that would determine the wholesale prices for different customer rate classes. Based on the auction results, retail rates would be set through a fully transparent pre-established/approved rate-making process. One essential goal was to provide full-requirements service, i.e., energy, capacity, ancillary services, and certain other transmission services, to customers at a cost consistent with market conditions. Another goal was to further the development of markets by providing an opportunity for new entrants to compete by aggregating supplies at wholesale and providing a full-requirements, price-risk-managed service to retail customers. ComEd and Ameren would gain access to greater diversity of supply, and their customers would no longer face the financial risks associated with utility construction programs, stranded cost, and volatile market prices. The competitive procurement process permitted the utilities to accurately set market values and put all suppliers on an equal footing. It also harnessed powerful incentives for the utilities to stabilize and minimize their power supply costs. On January 24, 2006, the ICC approved the use of an auction to be held in September 2006.

Design of the 2006 Illinois Auction

The 2006 Illinois Auction was a simultaneous, multiple round, descending clock auction, where all products within the Illinois Auction were put on offer at the same time over the course of multiple rounds of bidding.[26] The products are divided into two Sections: the Fixed Price Section (generally smaller customers who pay a fixed retail rate) and the Hourly Price Section (generally larger customers who pay a real-time rate based on hourly energy prices). Bidders register for either section or both. A bidder registered for both sections may bid on all products; a bidder registered for only one section may bid only on the products in that section. Bidding is conducted simultaneously for both sections, but each section is evaluated separately, and bidding may end in one section before the other. Each section contains two groups, one for the products of the Ameren Illinois Utilities and one for the products of ComEd. A product is a specific category of load for a specific supply period.

The fixed price products have multiple supply periods designed with the goal that future supply periods will be for three years. On a forward basis, one-third of ComEd's and Ameren's smaller customer fixed-price load will be bid out during each auction in order to reduce the sensitivity of retail rates to the price from any single auction. This practice minimizes ratepayer shocks and volatility (as well as possible regulatory and political backlash). For larger customers, Hourly Price Section contracts are for one year, during which the prices for capacity and ancillary services are fixed but the energy prices fluctuate in accordance with the wholesale spot markets for energy administered by the applicable Regional Transmission Organization.[27]

Each auction is managed by an independent Auction Manager, who is subject to ICC approval. In addition, the ICC Staff and their consultants oversee the auction and advise the ICC before it approves the auction results. In each round of the auction, the Auction Manager announces a price for each product. Bidders declare the number of tranches that they are willing to supply for each of these products at the announced prices. If the number of tranches bid is greater than the number of tranches needed for a product, the price for that product is reduced (ticks down) for the next round. In the next round, bidders are given information on the general progress of the Illinois Auction and an opportunity to bid again. Bidders can revise their bids for a product when its price falls by reducing the tranches of load they are willing to serve or by switching their offer from one product to another.[28] The auction ends when bidding has ended for each section, all product prices have stopped ticking down, and no bidder can change its bid. Tranches are tentatively awarded to the winners, pending execution of the applicable utility Supplier Forward Contracts.[29] All the winners for a product receive the same clearing price, which is the lowest price at which bidders are collectively willing to supply all the tranches in that product.

Regulatory Oversight of the Auction Process

The Illinois auction involved considerable regulatory oversight during both the auction proposal and its implementation stages. The ICC Staff and its consultants helped develop many of the auction parameters and other processes and directly monitored the conduct and results of the auction. An evaluation of the 2006 Illinois Auction against FERC's four guiding *Allegheny* principles demonstrates how the auction reflects the best practice in solicitation design in the US and compliance with the *Edgar* standard.

TRANSPARENCY

FERC calls for a competitive solicitation process that is open and fair. It defines transparency as the free flow of information: "No party, particularly the affiliate, should have an informational advantage in any part of the solicitation process."[30] Transparency is also an important factor in evaluating and selecting the winning bidders.

The Illinois Auction maintains transparency—free flow of information—through the use of a publicly accessible website managed by the independent Auction Manager. The website contains (1) an overview of the Illinois Auction, (2) auction guidelines, (3) such detailed data as hourly load data and customer switching statistics for each Illinois utility, (4) the filed tariffs, (5) the Supplier Forward Contracts to be executed by winning bidders, and (6) all other information necessary for bidders to participate effectively. It can be viewed by any interested party and thus guarantees fair and equal access to the largest universe of potential bidders.

All communication, such as e-mail, the website interface, and telephone calls between interested parties and the utilities, is conducted through the Auction Manager. Questions and answers are posted on the website under the rubric "frequently asked questions." The absence of direct communication between bidders and the utilities and the anonymous basis of bidder questions assures the integrity and impartiality of the process. Telephone communication with the Auction Manager was permitted, and potential bidders were encouraged to attend four information sessions prior to the auction. Two of these sessions were open to any interested party, two were for potential bidders only, and all were monitored by the ICC Staff. At the sessions, the Auction Manager made presentations and distributed information packets, which were subsequently made available on the website. The sessions included an opportunity for in-depth questions and answers. These communication practices fulfill FERC's goal that the solicitation be well promoted and that the rules be clearly presented to all bidders in a transparent manner.

In addition, in order to "enhance the fairness and transparency of the entire process,"[31] the Illinois Auction allowed for public comment on the auction design through the ICC regulatory process. Interested parties could participate, on equal terms, as intervenors in the proceeding before the ICC and voice any issues, concerns, or comments on the auction design and process. The ICC then was the final authority on whether or not to approve the auction and whether changes to the design or process were required. Intervenor suggestions and comments incorporated in the final design of the auction included the length of the product supply periods and the final customer makeup of each of the products.

Finally, to ensure fair and equal treatment of all winning bidders and eliminate the potential for favoritism, the auction prohibits post-bid negotiation.

DEFINITION

FERC states "[t]he product or products sought through the RFP should be defined in a manner that is clear and nondiscriminatory. The RFP should state all relevant aspects of the product or products sought."[32] The Illinois Auction provides for a clear and explicit product definition, which consists of full-requirements power for a "slice" or "tranche" of each utility's provider of last resort load.

The exact product is made known to all bidders in the form of the executable Supplier Forward Contracts, which are posted on the Illinois Auction website and spell out in exacting contractual detail the product terms and conditions, with no room for ambiguity. The use of a standard agreement for all suppliers allows any potential bidder to play on a level playing field with any other bidder, affiliate or not, and assures no bias in the auction process. A standard supplier agreement also vastly simplifies the selection of winning bidders, as selection is made on price terms alone. These contracts were also open to review and comments during the initial ICC proceeding, as well as several months before the September 2006 Auction.

EVALUATION

FERC found that "[t]o fulfill the evaluation principle, RFPs should clearly specify the price and nonprice criteria under which the bids are evaluated."[33] The Illinois Auction is designed to select those bidders who are willing to supply POLR service at the lowest cost to customers. It reveals a clear, unambiguous price for each product, so the evaluation is transparent. Evaluation of nonprice criteria such as financial integrity, relevant regulatory or regional transmission organization approvals, etc., is not an issue because the standardized contract means that all bidders, affiliate or not, will be supplying the product under the same nonprice terms. These nonprice terms involved substantial input from various parties and intense regulatory scrutiny to ensure that they do not favor the affiliate over other potential bidders.

In addition, the Illinois Auction provides for a pre-auction bidder qualification process to assure that all potential bidders meet certain stipulated minimum requirements. The pre-qualification process is important to the fairness of the process and evaluation because it assures that all price bids considered in the auction are from suppliers who are qualified and meet the necessary minimum requirements to be counterparties to the Supplier Forward Contracts. After pre-qualification, the Auction Manager filters all information. Certain confidential information about the auction is available only to those bidders that have passed the pre-qualification, the Auction Manager, and the ICC Staff and its advisors. ComEd and Ameren themselves are restricted from viewing certain information that could conceivably be used to render preferential treatment to an affiliate.

OVERSIGHT

FERC's fourth principle calls for "an independent third party...able to make a determination that the RFP process is transparent and fair and that the RFP's issuer's decision is not influenced by any affiliate relationships."[34] In the Illinois Auction, FERC's requirement for independent oversight and evaluation is fulfilled by the Auction Manager,[35] who ensures that no abuse of an affiliate relationship occurs, that all potential bidders receive fair and equal treatment, and that the guidelines and rules of the auctions are followed in an unbiased manner. The Auction Manager has oversight authority, has no financial interest in the bidders (especially in affiliates of ComEd and Ameren), and is not paid on the basis of the outcome of the auction. By controlling the flow of information from potential bidders and any other interested parties to the utilities, the auction manager can deny ComEd and Ameren prior access to any information that might give an unfair advantage to their affiliates, unambiguously preserving the integrity and fairness of the auction process.

Asset-Specific Transactions

While the Illinois Auction provides an excellent example of a solicitation that complies with *Edgar,* this type of solicitation will not fit all utilities. There are specific circumstances—the existence of well-developed spot and forward markets and an appropriate regulatory regime—that make non-asset-backed, full-requirements auctions possible in Illinois. Utilities elsewhere will need to design procurement processes that take into account local market conditions and the prevailing regulatory frame-work. They too can design solicitations that meet the *Edgar* standards and *Allegheny* principles, but the nature of the transaction may be different.

An asset-specific solicitation (i.e., for a physical product) can mimic many of the design features of the Illinois Auction, either specifically for *Edgar* compliance or more generally to minimize any charges of favoritism or any risk of *ex post* regulatory scrutiny and disallowances. For example, the use of a public website is an effective means of providing information to interested parties on a nondiscriminatory basis. The use of an independent third party for bid evaluation remains a means of complying with the FERC requirements and assures that the bid evaluation is unbiased and fair.[36]

The key areas that will differ for asset-specific transactions are product design and evaluation. The product design will require considerable forethought to ensure that the type of capacity sought includes all resources that might provide a competitive source of power for the utility. Similarly, choices with respect to how the contract allocates risks (availability, fuel price, transmission, residual value, force majeure, etc.) must be defensible and unbiased.

The design of an objective evaluation process is critical. FERC anticipates that it is feasible to have an evaluation that compares different types of supply resources in a single solicitation and that the evaluation can be transparent and well documented. The best approach to evaluating very different bids in a single solicitation is to quantify (monetize) all factors that are reasonably subject to quantification (which the most significant factors generally are). For example, one can quantify in a common measure of cost any difference in availabilities or dispatch restrictions, or for that matter, different dispatch costs. A system planning model can be used to compare the bids in terms of their present value or levelized cost per kWh. For factors that are not quantifiable, the utility may elect to set minimum threshold requirements, much like the bidder qualification process in the Illinois Auctions.

While more complicated than solicitations for standard products, asset-specific solicitations can be designed to meet FERC's competition requirements and the *Edgar* standard. However, careful analysis and forethought in solicitation design are imperative to ensure both a successful outcome for the utility and a fair competitive process.

Application of the Allegheny Principles

The *Edgar* standard requires regulated public utilities to chose the least-cost option if the transaction involves an affiliate. FERC has demonstrated in several cases its seriousness in applying the *Allegheny* guidelines of transparency, definition, evaluation, and oversight in determining whether an affiliate transaction has met the standard in a fair and unambiguous manner. Two examples are the case of Conectiv Energy Supply, Inc. ("CESI") in Virginia and the auctions for Basic Generation Service in New Jersey.

Virginia
The CESI case demonstrated FERC's seriousness in applying the *Allegheny* guidelines in their entirety. In late 2004, CESI sought FERC approval[37] of wholesale power sales to its regulated distribution company affiliate, Delmarva Power and Light (Delmarva).[38] It was awarded a contract as a result of an RFP process, initiated and administered by Delmarva for full-requirements service to Delmarva's default Standard Offer Service (SOS) load in Virginia.[39] Nine suppliers qualified to bid in Delmarva's RFP, and seven well-known energy suppliers submitted bids. CESI was chosen as the winning bidder and sole supplier for Delmarva's SOS load obligation and subsequently filed with FERC seeking authorization to make market-based sales Delmarva pursuant to the PPA awarded in the RFP solicitation. CESI asserted that the solicitation followed the guidelines delineated in FERC's *Allegheny* decision, especially that it was a direct head-to-head competition on a price-only basis. The RFP solicitation had been designed to mirror as closely as possible the RFP solicitations used by the Allegheny

utilities in Maryland to meet their SOS obligations, since those solicitations had previously satisfied FERC's concerns of possible affiliate abuse.

In its December 30, 2004 Order, FERC accepted the PPA between CESI and its affiliate Delmarva for filing subject to refund; however, it did *not* approve it and instead set it for a public hearing. Even though the RFP had met the criteria of transparency, definition, and evaluation, Delmarva had failed to meet the oversight criterion to FERC's satisfaction. Delmarva had not used an independent third party to design the solicitation, administer the bidding, and evaluate the bids, and as a result FERC found that the Commission was "unable to determine that no affiliate received undue preference during any stage of the RFP."[40] FERC noted, for example, that prospective bidders had been required to submit a credit application and associated financial information.

> Without independent third-party oversight, such criteria could be used to limit potential competitors from submitting bids. On this basis, the Commission's preliminary analysis indicates that the PPA ... may be unjust, unreasonable, unduly discriminatory or preferential or otherwise unlawful [and that such] issues of material fact...cannot be resolved based on the record before us and are more appropriately addressed in the hearing ordered below.[41]

Commissioner Kelliher dissented, stating that the Delmarva RFP solicitation was in essence the same process reviewed and approved in the *Allegheny* decision, that no protests were filed by any of the nonaffiliated bidders in the Delmarva RFP, and that the RFP met three of the four *Allegheny* criteria in their entirety. He emphasized his "view that the four criteria set forth in *Allegheny* constitute guidelines the Commission will consider on a case-by-case basis in evaluating an RFP in an affiliate situation rather than a 'bright-line' test that must be satisfied to avoid a hearing."[42] Nevertheless, Kelliher held that a public hearing was unnecessary because the Delmarva RFP was similar to Maryland's *Allegheny* RFP, which had been previously reviewed and approved by FERC.

The case was settled, with the FERC trial staff, CESI, and Virginia Attorney General agreeing that the 2004 process had been free from affiliate abuse and undue preference. However, Delmarva agreed to file a plan for future bidding in Virginia that would contemplate "in any future RFP for wholesale supply, Delmarva will use an independent third party monitor as part of the RFP process pursuant to the guidelines outlined in

Allegheny.[43] As a result, the 2006 Delmarva Virginia RFP solicitation was identical to the 2004 RFP process except that an independent third party was used to monitor the process. Accordingly, in 2006 FERC ruled that the RFP was consistent with the *Allegheny* criteria, including the oversight criterion, and that it satisfied any concerns regarding affiliate abuse.[44] Generally speaking, it is safe to say that, absent any transactional or market idiosyncrasies, FERC will expect utilities seeking approval of an affiliate transaction in a timely, swift, and relatively risk-free manner to adhere to the *Allegheny* guidelines in their totality.

New Jersey

Since 2002, utilities in New Jersey have conducted auctions for default Basic Generation Service (BGS) that are substantially similar to the 2006 Illinois Auction. FERC reviewed the New Jersey BGS solicitation in connection with filings[45] submitted by the winning affiliated suppliers seeking approval of market-based sales to their affiliates pursuant to the BGS Supplier Master Agreement. As expected, FERC applied the *Edgar* standard regarding least-cost affiliate transactions, using the *Allegheny* guidelines in its review for possible undue affiliate preference and abuse. In its approval of market-based sales by PSEG Energy Resources & Trade LLC to its regulated public utility affiliate, Public Service Electric and Gas Co.[46] FERC explicitly stated that the New Jersey BGS Auction had satisfied "the Commission's concerns regarding affiliate abuse"[47] as it had met each of FERC's *Allegheny* criteria for unbiased solicitations:[48]

TRANSPARENCY

FERC noted the BGS auction achieved transparency in the design stage through its collaborative process involving informed parties with diverse interests, its on-the-record, public New Jersey Board proceeding and its use of an auction website that allowed for easy access to critical information. The independent auction administrator who answered questions from interested parties and posted them on the auction website also added to the transparency. The Commission was thus able to find that "the design, administration, and bid evaluation phases of the BGS auction were transparent."[49]

DEFINITION

The auction materials clearly defined both the products and the pro forma contracts, including bidder qualification criteria and the bid evaluation method prior to the solicitation. "Bidders had knowledge of the process through which they could bid and through which their bids would be evaluated before they were called upon to submit them. Thus, the Commission believes that the BGS auction was clearly defined."[50]

EVALUATION

The bids were selecting based only on price were evaluated by the independent consultant and the results were reviewed and certified by the New Jersey BPU. "Thus, the Commission believes that the bids were evaluated in the BGS auction based on standardized criteria and that those criteria were applied equally to all bids regardless of affiliation."[51]

OVERSIGHT

An independent consultant[52] developed the auction design prior to the first auction in 2002 and was responsible for its administration. The BPU exercised general oversight authority and retained a separate independent consultant as an advisor who reported directly to the Board. FERC found that the presence of the independent third party as well as the involvement of the Board and its independent advisor "provided sufficient independent third-party oversight of the design, administration, and bid evaluation stages of the BGS auction."[53]

Conclusion

FERC's core belief, stated in *Ameren,* is that the "public interest requires policies that do not harm the development of vibrant, fully competitive generation markets."[54] A corollary is that utilities with resource needs should rely on market-based mechanisms for procurement and that direct contracts with preferred affiliates undermines the ability of independent generators to enter the generation market and ultimately undermines the market itself. FERC has therefore pledged to thoroughly review all affiliate transactions to ensure that independent suppliers are not denied equal competitive opportunities.

FERC decisions have made clear[55] that US public utilities should strive to adhere to the safe harbor guidelines represented by the *Allegheny* guidelines for *Edgar* compliance as much as feasible when seeking or even contemplating an affiliate transaction. Otherwise they risk *ex post* disputes with non-affiliates, other regulatory agencies, and consumer advocacy groups as well as delays at FERC in affiliate transaction approval and outright FERC transaction denial. If a public utility can follow the

Allegheny guidelines, then it should effectively avoid unnecessary and often extremely costly regulatory processes and litigation by proving unambiguously to all parties concerned that it has indeed chosen the least-cost option on behalf of its ratepayers without undue preference to an affiliate, or any other entity for that matter.

While these affiliate standards and guidelines are specific to the US, they can be used to design or implement regulatory policy or solicitations in non-US jurisdictions. They are particularly suited to situations where there is potential for perceived favoritism, such as a sale or transfer of services or assets from one affiliated entity to another when other non-affiliate options exist for those same services or assets. The standards and guidelines FERC has adopted provide a clear, accepted, and tested standard by which to judge the efficacy, results, and overall fairness of a solicitation or asset transfer. By using standards and guidelines similar to *Edgar* and *Allegheny,* a regulated entity can successfully spin off or transfer assets to an affiliate with a sound expectation of being able to enter into agreements for full-cost recovery at a later date without undue risk or complications. The regulated entity can prove unambiguously to the applicable regulatory bodies and other interested parties that these agreements represent the non-preferential and unbiased least-cost option for the utility and its customers and that the transaction has done nothing to harm the development of vibrant, fully competitive markets.

Notes

1. FERC is an independent agency under the US Department of Energy (DOE) charged with (among other things) regulatory oversight of public utility affiliate and wholesale transactions.

2. Boston Edison Company Re: Edgar Electric Energy Company, 55 FERC ¶ 61,382 (1991). *(Edgar)*

3. Ameren Energy Supply Company et al., 108 FERC ¶ 61,081 (2004). Opinion at 59. *(Ameren)*

4. Ibid.

5. Ibid. at 59-63.

6. Allegheny Energy Supply Company, LLC, 108 FERC ¶ 61,082 (2004) *(Allegheny)*

7. *Ameren* at 68-84 and *Allegheny* at 22-35.

8. *Edgar* at 62,168-62,170.

9. Ibid. at 62,168.

10. Southern California Edison Company 106 FERC ¶ 61,184 (2004). *(Mountainview)*

11. Ibid. at 59.

12. See for example FERC's Cinergy decision, Cinergy Services Inc., 102 FERC ¶ 61,128 (2003) at P 24. *(Cinergy).*

13. Ibid. at 23.

14. See Karl A. McDermott, Carl R. Peterson and Ross C. Hemphill," Rethinking the Implementation of the Prudent Cost Standard." in this volume for more information on prudence reviews.

15. *Ameren* at 48.

16. Ibid. at 68.

17. Ibid. and *Cinergy* at P 24.

18. *Allegheny Energy Supply Company, LLC,* 108 FERC ¶ 61,082 (2004) *(Allegheny)*

19. See the Chantale LaCasse & Thomas Wininger, "Maryland versus New Jersey: Is there a 'Best' Competitive Bid Process," in this volume for more information on the Maryland RFP.

20. *Allegheny* at 18. See also *Cinergy* at 23-24.

21. See Kurt Strunk, "Default Service Procurement: The US Experience with Full Requirements" and LaCasse & Wingerer on full requirements service and default service auctions, respectively.

22. Commonwealth Edison Company et al., 113 FERC ¶ 61,278 (2005).

23. The ICC is the state agency with regulatory authority over the Illinois public utilities, such as the authority and oversight of utility rates and cost recovery applications, etc.

24. A tranche is a fixed percentage of load, and it can be thought of as a vertical slice of ComEd's and Ameren's load curve or a "slice of system" product.

25. See details in the ICC dockets 05-150 (ComEd) and 05-160, 05-161, and 05-162 (Ameren Utilities).

26. For more information on simultaneous descending clock auctions, see LaCasse & Wininger and Georgina Martinez, "Open Auctions as the New Trend for Power Procurement," in this volume.

27. For more information on this type of auction in other jurisdictions, see the chapters by LaCasse & Wininger and Martinez.

28. The small customer load procured in the Fixed Price Section is separate from the larger customer load procured in the Hourly Price Section. There is no switching between the Fixed Price Section and Hourly Price Section products.

29. Contracts for Fixed Price Section products were executed on September 20, 2006.

30. *Allegheny* at 23.

31. Ibid. at 24.

32. Ibid. at 27.

33. Ibid. at 29.

34. Ibid. at 34.

35. NERA first provided litigation support in the initial procurement docket with the ICC and subsequently was approved by the ICC as the auction manager.

36. An example of a recent asset-backed solicitation that incorporates many of the features of the Illinois Auction, such as the use of a public website and the use of an independent auction manager, is the January 2007 General Electric (GE) auction for 300 MW of transmission rights from a variable frequency transformer in New Jersey to New York City. For more information on this solicitation, see www.lindenvftauction.com.

37. Conectiv Energy Supply, Inc., 109 FERC ¶ 61,385 (2004) *(CESI)*.

38. CESI and Delmarva are both wholly owned subsidiaries of Pepco Holdings, Inc. CESI is a power marketer that owns no generation, transmission., or distribution facilities, but has authority to sell power and energy at market-based rates. Delmarva is a regulated distribution utility that owns no generation.

39. Under the Virginia Electric Utility Restructuring Act, Delmarva is required to provide default service or standard- offer service until 2010 to any customer that does not choose an alternate supplier. (*See* § 56-576 et. seq. of the Code of Virginia)

40. *CESI* at 18.

41. Ibid.

42. Ibid., Dissenting Opinion of Joseph T. Kelliher, at 1-3.

43. Conectiv Energy Supply Inc., 112 FERC ¶ 63,007 at 6.

44. Conectiv Energy Supply Inc., 115 FERC ¶ 61,222.

45. These filings involved applicants requesting a waiver, to the extent necessary, of the applicable provisions in their codes of conduct and market-based rate tariffs to permit affiliate transactions pursuant to contracts entered into as a result of the New Jersey statewide bidding process. Public Service Electric & Gas Company and PSEG Energy Resources & Trade LLC, 111 FERC ¶ 61,152. *(NJ BGS)*

46. See LaCasse & Wininger and Martinez in this volume for more details on the New Jersey BGS Auctions.

47. *NJ BGS* at 7.

48. Ibid. at 10-13.

49. Ibid. at 10-11.

50. Ibid. at 10-11.

51. Ibid. at 11.

52. NERA has been the independent consultant for the New Jersey auctions since 2002.

53. In an order dated June 1, 2006, FERC has also approved affiliate transactions made pursuant to the most recent New Jersey BGS Auctions, which took place in February 2006. Public Service Electric and Gas Company, PSEG Energy Resources & Trade LLC, and Exelon Generation Company, LLC, 115 FERC ¶ 61,282.

54. Ameren at 80.

55. To date, FERC has approved at least US$15 billion (approximately) worth of affiliate transactions in solicitations using the *Allegheny* guidelines.

20

MARYLAND VERSUS NEW JERSEY: IS THERE A "BEST" COMPETITIVE BID PROCESS?[1]

Chantale LaCasse
Thomas Wininger

Introduction

Against the backdrop of a highly organized and well-functioning wholesale market, power sector restructuring at the state level in the United States has often given each function of the traditionally integrated utility its autonomy. Generating assets are sold or transferred to competitive entities that will buy and sell in wholesale markets. Marketing and trading operations stand alone to manage transactions at the wholesale and sometimes at the retail level. The wires part of the utility, responsible for distribution services to retail customers, becomes an electric distribution company—an EDC. Only the EDC remains squarely within the ambit of the state regulator.

Saying that an EDC is a wires-only company means that the only assets it owns are wires. However, that does not necessarily imply that its only function is to distribute electricity over its wires. In many restructured states in the United States, an EDC also retains the obligation to provide electricity service to any retail customer not served by a retail electric supplier. The EDC does not fully perform the function of a retail electric supplier; it cannot market or tailor its offerings to customers' needs. It simply must stand by to supply any retail customer that has failed to choose a retail electric supplier, or that has ceased to be served by a retail electric supplier, for example as a result of a bankruptcy. This is in contrast to countries like England and Wales where the power sector has been thoroughly and successfully restructured and the distribution companies retain no obligation to supply electricity services to customers taking distribution service.

In most US states whose power sectors were being restructured, the expectation was that retail electric suppliers would flock to retail customers and that few (if any) customers would remain the burden of the EDC. This expectation has not been met. True, many larger commercial and industrial customers have arranged supply for themselves with retail electric suppliers that offer savings or cost certainty through a longer term contract, or a service that is tailored to the customer's usage pattern. However, residential and small commercial customers by and large remain default customers, continuing to take electricity service from the EDC. Perhaps for many, the cost of evaluating alternatives outweighs any economic benefit from taking service from a retail electric supplier, and perhaps competitive retail electric suppliers can market more cheaply to larger customers. The result is that the EDC must provide a safety net electricity service for a majority of customers.

In many restructured states, the EDC serves its default customers by procuring full- requirements supply from wholesale market participants, usually through a structured competitive solicitation process. But within the common paradigm of procuring full- requirements supply for default customers are different strategies and approaches to procuring this supply. The strategies adopted by the Maryland EDCs on the one hand, and those adopted by the New Jersey EDCs on the other, provide an instructive contrast. A review of these two strategies highlights the factors that could guide the decision on the aspects of the procurement process. However, we find that this review does not allow us to make a pronouncement on a definitive "best" procurement method—rather, we conclude that varying methods for procurement exist to suit the varying goals, circumstances, and predispositions in different jurisdictions.

The Choice of Full-Requirements Supply

Typically, an EDC in a restructured electricity sector no longer has generating assets to support and hedge the requirement to provide electricity service to default customers. The EDC acts as agent for its customers in a transaction for power whose value is tied directly to the number of customers and the load left on default service and this value can be many times the size of the EDC's distribution revenues. Its regulator then decides whether the EDC can pass on to its default customers all of its costs of purchasing electricity services, examining the soundness of the EDC's decisions and evaluating the resulting rates to default customers.

To fulfill its obligation to default customers, the EDC could directly acquire a portfolio of products from the wholesale market and manage this portfolio in view of the risks of changing power costs and of customers leaving and returning to default service. However, the EDC typically no longer has the trading personnel necessary to support this portfolio management function. Further, all portfolio management decisions could be subject to review by the regulator after the fact. Alternatively, the EDC can contract with wholesale market participants so that the ultimate suppliers are responsible for the portfolio management function. Suppliers have the personnel and a variety of options to hedge price risks and any other risks associated with supplying default customers that may or may not be available to the regulated EDC. Suppliers may even have assets tailored to perform this function. Set up to trade and to hedge power competitively, wholesale market participants are better placed to manage the risk of providing default supply than are regulated entities, and they can do so more efficiently.

One way to structure the contract with wholesale market participants is to make each supplier responsible for supplying a share of all needs of default customers at each instant. Together, all suppliers meet 100 percent of the needs of default customers. This is a full requirements supply.[2] It stands in contrast both to contracts for fixed quantities of energy, and to separate contracts for each service required by default customers (energy, capacity, ancillary services). The EDC can harness the competition in a well-organized and well-functioning wholesale market Specifically, the EDC has an incentive to reduce its power supply costs by devising a competitive bidding process that promotes competition among the entities that will become the ultimate suppliers so as to obtain wholesale prices that the regulator is willing to allow the EDC to fully recover in rates.

So far, this situation describes that of many EDCs. In all restructured US states (except Texas), EDCs retain responsibility for serving default customers. In many of these, such as New Jersey, Maryland, Delaware, and Illinois, the EDC procures full-requirements supply through a structured competitive solicitation process. But different EDCs implement this common procurement process through different strategies and approaches. The strategies adopted by the Maryland EDCs on the one hand, and the strategies adopted by the New Jersey EDCs on the other, provide an instructive contrast of the diversity of strategies in this regard. The Maryland EDCs use a Request for Proposal (RFP) as their competitive solicitation process, which is similar to the process commonly used to procure new capacity. The New Jersey EDCs use an auction approach that shares much with the method used to sell licenses of radio spectrum and little with other procurements in the energy sector. The Maryland EDCs retain the ultimate responsibility to supply default customers and remain the retailer in the view of the independent system operator. The New Jersey EDCs contractually pass all responsibilities on to wholesale market participants, and it is the wholesale market participants that are the retail electric suppliers in the eyes of the system operator. Maryland EDCs share risks with their wholesale suppliers by shielding them in part from the risk of customers leaving default service with the EDC for a retail electricity supplier. The New Jersey EDCs share the risks differently and transfer to the wholesale market participants all risks associated with the possibility of customers leaving default service. Maryland EDCs procure supply for different rate classes separately over several bid dates. The New Jersey EDCs conduct a single statewide solicitation for much more aggregated groups of customers.

These contrasts illustrate that contract features can be specified in various ways to carve a different share of risks among the counter-parties (namely, the EDC and the wholesale market participant that supplies default customers). There is also a multitude of ways to design a bidding process to harness the competition among wholesale market participants. The way in which bids are solicited and evaluated, the amount and type of regulatory oversight, and the timing of the bid are all features that can distinguish one bidding process from another.

When Illinois was studying how it would procure supply for its default customers, interveners often contrasted the "Maryland model" with the "New Jersey model." The differences in the procurement strategies used by the EDCs in these two states (and the differences in strategies across various states in general) have gained more notoriety and prominence than the basic similarity of competitively procuring full requirements supply. The Maryland and the New Jersey EDCs have come to different conclusions as to the "right" sharing of risks between the EDCs and the ultimate suppliers through the design of the full-requirements contract; and the "right" environment to spur competition through the design of the bidding process. But are these differences indeed more important than the basic similarity in the approach? Will differences in the design of the same basic full-requirements procurement process yield a different result? These are the questions that we address below.

We begin by providing, in the context of the restructuring and deregulation of each state, additional details that further contrast the approaches to procurement in New Jersey and Maryland. We examine along the way some of the key decisions in the design of these procurement approaches. We review the pros and cons of two contrasting bid processes, of two ways to set retail rates, and of various distributions of risk among the EDCs and the wholesale market participants. This review is instructive in highlighting the factors that could guide the decision on each of these aspects of the procurement process. We do not use this review to make a pronouncement on a definitive "best" procurement method—rather, we conclude that varying methods for procurement exist to suit the varying goals and predilections of the regulatory bodies in different jurisdictions.

New Jersey and Maryland Procurement Approaches in Context

New Jersey Auction

Power sector restructuring in New Jersey was undertaken in the late 1990s by the legislature, the regulatory agency—the New Jersey Board of Public Utilities (the Board)—and the four investor-owned utilities—Atlantic City Electric, Jersey Central Power & Light, Public Service Electric and Gas, and Rockland Electric Company. The utilities either elected to sell their generation assets or to transfer them to affiliates, and each became an EDC. Each EDC retained the default obligation to provide electricity service to any customer that did not specifically choose a retail electric supplier. The enabling legislation gave the name Basic Generation Service (or BGS) to the electricity service provided by the EDC.

Following the advent of retail choice in 1998, the New Jersey legislation called for a four-year transition period during which retail rates charged by the EDC were frozen. During the fourth year of this transition period (August 1, 2002 through July 31, 2003), the Board called upon the EDCs to make a proposal on how to procure BGS competitively—i.e., how to procure electricity service for their default customers from wholesale market participants at competitive prices. The EDCs jointly proposed a standard contract and an auction in which wholesale market participants would compete to provide BGS. A single auction process would procure supply to serve the load of all four EDCs in the state simultaneously. A standard statewide contract would transfer to the wholesale market participants who won at the auction all risks inherent to procuring electricity service for default customers. After the transition period, the EDCs sought for the Board to continue to auction the right to serve default customers in the same manner, except that the resulting auction prices would be directly used in setting the unbundled electricity rate. Each year since the end of the transition period, the Board has approved the continuation of the auction process and has accepted its results.

The product in the New Jersey auction is full-requirements supply. A wholesale market participant that wins at the auction is responsible for serving a given percentage of an EDC's BGS load, whatever the load may be. Thus, a wholesale market participant who wins 10 percent of an EDC's BGS load is responsible for providing all of the services necessary to serve 10 percent of that EDC's load. It bears the risks associated with the load level, which can be affected by weather, by customers choosing a retail electric supplier, etc. In the first auction, wholesale market participants specified their bids in tranches, where a tranche for an EDC was a specific fraction of the EDC's total default service load in every hour of the year for all customers at a fixed price. In subsequent years, there have been two auctions: one for tranches of the load of small customers, and the other for tranches of the load of large customers.

The contract to supply BGS load—either for residential and smaller commercial customers, or for larger commercial and industrial customers —is between an auction winner and an EDC acting as an agent for its default customers. The contract is finalized in advance of the auction, and all winners sign the exact same contract with the EDCs. The contract is pre-approved by the state regulator in a proceeding during which the regulator accepts feedback from potential suppliers and acts as mediator between the EDCs and the wholesale market participants. After the proceeding, the contract is non-negotiable. Through the contract, the auction winners will function as load serving entities. They assume the responsibility of serving the retail customers, establishing all accounts and all guarantees with the independent system operator to be able to do so. The EDC remains responsible for distribution service.

The "large" commercial and industrial customers are covered by an auction in which energy is priced to the hourly market. The contracts are for one year, and the wholesale market participants bid to supply capacity, transmission, and ancillary services at a fixed price in $/MW-day. Wholesale market participants supplying residential and smaller commercial customers bid an all-in wholesale price in $/MWh. Every year one-third of the load is at auction for a three-year term, and the remaining two-thirds are supplied by three-year contracts from previous auctions. This term-averaging approach insulates smaller customers from short-term fluctuations in the wholesale market. The remainder of this chapter focuses on this auction for retail supply to smaller customers—which are the majority of default customers.

Bidders submit their bids through a "simultaneous descending clock" auction. This auction is simpler than it sounds. In each round, the auction manager announces a price for the load of each EDC. A bidder bids by submitting the number of tranches of each EDC's load that it would be willing to serve at the announced prices. If overall the supply bid for an EDC is more than what is needed, the price for that EDC decreases (ticks down) in the next round. Bidders submit bids at the new prices in the next round. As the prices decrease from round to round, the amount of load that the bidders are willing to serve declines. Bidders can switch their bids from one EDC to another. The auction ends when suppliers are willing to supply just the right amount of load for each EDC. The auction ends for all EDCs at the same time.

The determination of winners at the auction is straightforward: Bids are evaluated on a price-only basis. The winners for an EDC are those bidders that bid tranches when the auction prices tick down to the lowest prices at which wholesale market participants are still willing to supply all the tranches of that EDC's load. Prices will vary across the EDCs. Bidders may switch their bids from one EDC to another from one round to the next, an arbitrage that works to align prices with the market's perception of differences in the costs to serve the various EDCs.

The price set at the auction is a wholesale price that is then converted into the retail rates paid by customers of the EDCs. Retail rates vary for different classes of customers depending on the cost to serve the class. For example, customers in a class that is more expensive to serve than the average of the system may pay 1.2 times the auction price per megawatt-hour, while customers in another class may pay 0.8 times the auction price. The auction price, shaped to account for seasonal cost difference, determines the payment to the supplier. The supplier receives a summer price (the auction price times a factor greater than one) during four summer months, and a winter price (the auction price times a factor less than one) during the remaining winter months. If the EDC paid all auction winners exactly the auction price, and if all customers paid to the EDC exactly the auction price, the revenues and payments would naturally be aligned. However, since this is not the case, the amount that the EDC pays its suppliers may not match the revenues collected from its customers. Any difference is reconciled through a charge or credit to default customers, depending on whether the amount due to the suppliers exceeds or falls short of the amount collected based on the retail rates.

The Board is involved in all key policy decisions regarding the procurement process. It has final say on the two key documents that govern the process, the contract that is signed by the EDCs and the auction winners, and the auction rules that regulate the conduct of the bidding process. The Board also has final say on the results of the auction, including the discretion to reject them entirely. The Board, along with its staff and consultants, judges whether the auction process was conducted in accordance with the process put in place. The EDCs retain an auction manager[3] who is responsible for carrying out the auction process as approved by the Board. The auction manager administers the qualification of bidders and the bidding process, and disseminates information about the auction to potential wholesale market participants and to all stakeholders.

Maryland Request for Proposals

The Maryland context that gave rise to a full-requirements procurement process corresponds in many ways to the context in New Jersey. Like New Jersey, Maryland has four investor-owned utilities: Allegheny Power, Baltimore Gas & Electric, Delmarva Power and Light Company, and Potomac Electric Power. The power sector in Maryland was restructured through legislation in 1999 and through multi-party settlements that were approved by the Maryland Public Service Commission in 2000. The legislation provided for a phase-in of retail customer choice beginning in July 2000 and ending in July 2002, during which the utilities sold or transferred their generation assets. Each EDC retained the obligation to serve default customers at the frozen rates that were agreed to in the restructuring settlements. During the phase-in period, the EDCs served their default customer load through supply plans that included contracts with affiliated generators or power marketers.

Upon expiration of these supply contracts, each EDC was required by the state legislation to procure supply for default service load competitively. Each put forth a plan to procure power through a series of requests for proposals (RFPs). The RFPs would be held on multiple dates. This structure provides flexibility: if any portion of loads fails to be competitively procured on a given date, it can be procured again at a later date. Customers are divided into a residential class as well as three types of non-residential customers classified on basis of size. Each RFP would procure supply for at least one of these types of customers for one or more terms.

As in New Jersey, wholesale market participants in these RFPs bid to supply full-requirements service: They bid to supply a percentage of an EDC's load for a particular customer type, whatever the load may be. However, there are differences between New Jersey and Maryland in the services that are required of wholesale market participants. In Maryland, the EDCs retain responsibility for network transmission services and for the interface with the independent system operator as the load serving entity. Further, for nonresidential customers, the EDCs provide some protection to wholesale market participants against the risk of customers migrating to a retail electric supplier from default service or of customers migrating back to default service from a retail electric supplier. For any load exceeding a given threshold, wholesale market participants are paid a variable price pegged to the market (rather than the fixed price they bid). This mechanism protects winning suppliers against customers returning to default service when market prices are rising while the price of default service is fixed. This threshold is established when the contract is signed and updated when a sufficient amount of load leaves default service to take service from a retail electric supplier.

While in New Jersey the auction determines wholesale prices and the auction prices are later used to derive the specific retail rates, in the Maryland RFP the bids themselves are in the form of a list of retail rates. The bidders directly specify the prices to be paid by customers, including their own seasonal (and in some cases, time-of-use) differentiations.

Bidding takes place through a sealed-bid submission process. Bidders are provided with a standardized bidding spreadsheet on which they enter the details of their bids. Each bidder sends its bidding spreadsheet to the EDC. The EDC converts the list of bid prices into a single present value of the projected cost stream according to a pre-determined formula that was communicated to bidders before they bid. The EDC calculates an average price and ranks the bids on the basis of this single number. The winning bidders are those whose bids yield the lowest average price. The state regulator reviews the bids and, on the advice of its consultant and staff, can decide either to accept or to reject the bids. A winner is paid the retail rates that it itself bid. Consumers in a given rate class pay the average of the bids for that rate class.

Contrasting Key Elements of the Procurement Approaches

Setting up a successful procurement process, one that will harness the competition among wholesale market participants, that will be fair to all participants, that will be transparent to stakeholders, and that will deliver results that meet or beat expectations, is both a conceptual and a managerial challenge. There is a multitude of features of the procurement process that may impact its results. For example, the intensity with which the economic opportunity is promoted to prospective wholesale market participants may influence participation, which in turn will affect the amount of competition and therefore the ultimate prices. There are many different ways to reach out to potential wholesale market participants, including releases in the trade press, ads in print media, information sessions for press or for wholesale market participants, email announcements, and direct contact. The effectiveness of each of these methods depends on many factors, such as whether the procurement process is new or well known to wholesale market participants.

The diligence with which information is disseminated can also affect whether the process is fair to all prospective suppliers. For prospective wholesale market participants, their perception of the fairness of the process can in turn determine their willingness to participate in this or in future procurement processes of the same kind. The transparency of the process to all stakeholders and the ability of the state regulator to monitor the auction process can affect both the confidence of prospective wholesale market participants (and their participation) and the confidence of the state regulator that the results obtained meet expectations and should be accepted.

It is not surprise that EDCs in different states take different avenues to promote the opportunity to prospective wholesale market participants or to set up a process to ensure that information is disseminated fairly and efficiently. Many procedures can be established to achieve these objectives. Decisions on issues of this kind are likely to depend on the context, on the particular regulatory situation faced by the EDCs, and on the particular history of the procurement process. Comparing the procurement approaches in New Jersey and Maryland is interesting because the EDCs in the two states are in very similar situations, yet they have made very different decisions on the most crucial, the most core elements of the procurement process.

When deciding on a procurement approach, the New Jersey and the Maryland EDCs were on quite similar trajectories in restructuring the power markets. The territories of the New Jersey and the Maryland EDCs are part of the same system operator—the PJM Interconnection—with the same wholesale market participants. The legislation enabling retail choice and providing for a transition period toward the new structure incorporated fundamentally the same approach in both states. The plans for procurement in the interim period were also similar. The timing of the restructuring and the timing of the first open procurement process were almost identical. Some of the utilities in both states are in fact affiliates of each other.

And yet, the EDCs adopted starkly different approaches on how bids would be submitted. The New Jersey EDCs opted for procuring all needed supply for a given year through a single statewide auction while the Maryland EDCs opted for several RFPs due at several different dates. The bid product is fundamentally different. The New Jersey Auction determines a single wholesale price for each EDC while the Maryland RFP yields retail rates for different customer types. The sharing of risks between the wholesale market participants and the EDC inherent in the standard contract is also different. The New Jersey EDCs contractually pass on all risks to their suppliers while the Maryland EDCs explicitly take on some of the volumetric and transmission price risks. The bid product, the bidding process, and the contract are by any measure the fundamental elements of any procurement process, and the EDCs in these two states have taken contrasting approaches to each of these elements.

While it is easy to imagine that many different approaches to, say, promotion of the procurement process could yield results that are equally good, one would expect that different decisions on key components of the procurement process would have different expected results. Is one approach better than the other? In the next section we examine these key components and assess the factors that could lead a decision maker to elect one approach rather than another.

Bidding Process

The contrast between the Maryland procurement approach and the New Jersey procurement approach is most evident in the choice of the bidding process.

The Maryland EDCs use a series of RFPs, typically with each EDC holding several RFPs to procure its needed supply. Bidders qualify with each EDC separately to participate in its RFPs. In a given RFP, the EDC procures supply for a given percentage of the load of a customer type or for several customer types (residential, or nonresidential in a given size bracket). Bidders in an RFP submit their bids to the EDC by filling out an electronic spreadsheet where the bidder fills out the number of blocks on which they are bidding and their price bids. Bidders know that their bids will be evaluated on the basis of a single quantitative measure (an expected cost stream or equivalently an average price) for each quantity block. All bidders submit their electronic forms at once on a given day.

Auction theorists call this type of bidding process a sealed bid auction. One can think of the auction as equivalent to each bidder writing down a number on a piece of paper, sealing the paper in an envelope, and the EDC opening the envelopes to pick the lowest number. There is a single round of bidding for a particular customer type on a particular date. No bidder has solid information about any of its competitors or even about how much supply it is bidding against. If supply is being procured for various customer types, the bidder has no information on which customer types other bidders are intending to supply and no information regarding other bidders' bids.

In a sealed bid auction, a bidder that formulates a bid to maximize expected returns will likely seek to form expectations about the number of bidders competing against it and about their likely bids. The bidder takes into consideration that a slightly higher price bid increases profit— but at the same time, a higher price reduces the chances that the bidder will win and realize that profit. With little to no information about the competition, doing well in such an auction—in the sense of not regretting one's bid after the fact—takes a fair amount of sophistication or luck. Winning is the sought outcome—but if winning is paired with having price bids that are well below the rest of field, the bidder has left money on the table and will regret winning so handily. Losing may be the right outcome for a bidder who is at a cost disadvantage—but if losing is paired with the realization that the bidder would have been able to match the highest accepted bid, the bidder will regret that greed has gotten in the way of a good profit opportunity. In both of these cases, if the bidder had been able to change its bid in response to the bids of the rest of the market, it would have done so.

In contrast, a bidder participating in a simultaneous descending clock auction does have the ability to change its bid in response to bids by the rest of the market. In New Jersey where this auction format is used, bidders submit bids on multiple products over the course of multiple rounds. The loads for all the EDCs (each of which is a product) are put on offer through a single process. In a round, each EDC announces a price for its load, and the bidders bid at these prices. A bidder bids by stating the number of blocks or tranches that it is willing to supply at the announced prices. Once all the bids are in, the number of blocks is tabulated and compared to the number of blocks needed. If more blocks are bid than are needed for an EDC, the price for that EDC will be reduced in the next round—it "ticks down," like a descending clock. Before bidders have to bid again in the next round, bidders are told the new prices (from which they can immediately determine which EDCs have excess supply and which do not). Bidders are also provided a range of excess supply for the entire auction. In the next round, bidders can bid again. A bidder is not given bid-specific information about any other bidder; however, the bidder is given dynamic feedback about what "the rest of the market" is doing. The bidder can use the information to maintain its bids, to switch bids from one EDC to another, or to decrease the number of blocks it bids altogether.[4] The mechanism is illustrated in Table 1 below.

In round 1, the price for the load of each EDC is 10¢/kWh. A hypothetical bidder might bid 10 blocks of PSE&G, 2 blocks of JCP&L, 0 blocks of ACE, and 1 block of RECO. This bid would be submitted online through specialized auction software. When the bidding window ends and bids for all bidders are tabulated for round 1, all EDCs have more supply bid than needed, except for ACE. The prices for all EDCs except ACE will be

Table 1.   *Simultaneous Descending Clock Auction Example*

	EDC[5]	Price (¢/kWh)	Blocks bid	Blocks needed	Excess supply
Round 1	PSE&G	10.000	75	30	45
	JCP&L	10.000	27	15	12
	ACE	10.000	5	5	0
	RECO	10.000	2	1	1
	EDC	**Price (¢/kWh)**	**Blocks bid**	**Blocks needed**	**Excess supply**
Round 2	PSE&G	9.500	55	30	25
	JCP&L	9.762	25	15	10
	ACE	10.000	20	5	15
	RECO	9.985	7	1	6

reduced in round 2. The amount by which the price decreases is a function of the amount of excess supply. Note that bidding does not close for ACE: Bidders have an opportunity to switch their bids from other EDCs to ACE in response to ACE's price being higher than the price of other EDCs in round 2. Before the bidding window for round 2 opens, bidders are told the prices for the next round, as well as the fact that excess supply for the entire auction is in the range of 56 to 60 blocks. In round 2, some bidders switch their bids toward ACE and RECO, and away from PSE&G and JCP&L. There is excess supply on all EDCs and all prices will tick down for round 3. Prices continue to tick down and bidders continue to bid until there is just enough supply for each EDC.

Auction theorists call this kind of auction structure an "open auction" to contrast it with a sealed bid or closed auction. Open auctions are multi-round bidding processes during which bidders get market information and learn something about the competitive environment, and then have the opportunity to incorporate this information into their bids in the next round. On a theoretical level, the rationale for open auctions is that they reduce uncertainty for bidders. Reducing bidders' uncertainty allows them to be more aggressive in their bidding and tends to result in lower prices. Also, because bidders can switch across EDCs, they can arbitrage away any price differences among EDCs not tied to differences in cost, thus ensuring that all EDCs are valued in accordance with the market.

However, the open auction can only work well with sufficient competition at the outset. It is the competition among bidders willing to serve load at the prices of the opening rounds that ticks the prices down to their competitive levels. If there are few competitors, an open auction without additional competitive safeguards[6] could disappoint. If bidders realize that competition is weak and adjust their bidding strategy in response to this information, the auction could close at prices that would compare unfavorably to a sealed bid process. At the extreme, if there were a single bidder, at least with a sealed bid process that bidder might believe it faced competition and put in bids to beat the expected competition. With an open auction, prices would never tick down from their opening levels and the auction would end immediately.

Auction theorists and practitioners have devoted a substantial amount of research to analyzing various bidding processes to determine which yields the best prices. Not surprisingly, the answer is: it depends.[7] Both descending clock auctions and RFPs can work well, and one option may yield better results than the other in a given context. The characteristics of the competition as well as the number and characteristics of the products are all considerations that can tip the balance in one direction or the other.[8] In comparing the procurement processes of the New Jersey and the Maryland EDCs, the most important factor to explain the different bidding processes may be the policy decision for New Jersey to have a single statewide process and for Maryland to have many different processes for the different EDCs. A single statewide process is a single chance for all wholesale market participants to come and compete, generating the type of competition that can best harness the advantages of an open auction. In contrast, various smaller procurements held at different times can yield varying degrees of competition against which a sealed bid process reduces the potential downside risks. Also, perhaps New Jersey policymakers were more willing to trust a novel bidding process and the strength of the competitive market, while those in Maryland preferred a bidding process more familiar from asset divestiture and other past procurements in the energy sector. Neither opinion implies a judgment on what the "best" process is—rather, they are different risk assessments of the bidding process, and with each assessment comes a tailored procurement approach.

Bid Price

The bidding processes in New Jersey and in Maryland are different not only because the way bids are submitted and processed is different, but also because the form of the bid(s) is different. In New Jersey, bidders bid amounts of load they are willing to serve at all-in ¢/kWh *wholesale* prices. In Maryland, bidders submit a list of *retail rates* for energy blocks they are bidding on. Ultimately, in both states, the results of the competitive process determine the rates that customers will pay. In New Jersey, the single wholesale price resulting from the auction is put through a prism that yields a retail rate that is different for each customer class and that varies by season and sometimes by time of day. This prism is a series of ratios of the cost of the class to the cost of the entire system: Multiplying the auction price (standing in for the cost of the system) by this ratio then yields a retail rate scaled to the auction results. In Maryland, no translation is needed as bidders bid at retail directly. The average of all winning bid retail rates for a given customer class, season, and sometimes time of day directly determines the retail rate paid by that customers class for that season (and time of day).

At first glance the prism may seem like a clumsy mechanism. Even if based on ratemaking principles and carefully executed with appropriate data, why use this translation mechanism when bidders could bid market retail rates directly? It would seem appealing to have the market determine retail rates rather than have to construct them after the fact from a wholesale price. However, this view implicitly assumes that bidders have all the proper incentives to bid a price for each rate component that reflects the relative costs of various customer classes or seasons. But this is not necessarily the case, and the bidder's strategy may be something else entirely. The bid rates are never individually considered in the evaluation of the bid; instead, they are converted into a single number, the present value of the predicted cost stream from the rates specified by the bidder. The calculation of the present value requires assumptions about usage, and the bidder's strategy may rest on its perception of the validity of those usage assumptions. If a bidder believes that these assumptions are wrong, the bidder can bid high on classes for which it believes usage has been underestimated and low on classes for which it believes usage has been overestimated, to maintain or lower the present value for the purposes of its ranking. If its usage forecast is more accurate than the formula, this strategy can be used to improve its chances of winning, while also increasing its likely revenue, should it win. Such a strategy would mean that bid prices would have little to do with the relative costs to serve the various classes or seasons.

Another consideration is the information that bidders have regarding retail rates as they are bidding. The levels of the retail rates matter to bidders because these rates will determine the customer's economic incentive to leave default service to find a retail electric supplier. Thus the rates will factor directly in the bidders' assessment of the amount of load they will have to serve. In the New Jersey bidding process, bidders receive in advance the translation mechanism from wholesale auction price to retail rates. At each round a bidder could calculate the retail rates for that round's wholesale prices and readjust its projections of load as a result. Bidders probably do not do that, but they can dynamically adapt any assumptions about customer migration as the auction unfolds. In the Maryland bidding process, a bidder bids retail rates and, based on its own bids, can make predictions about the amount of load to be served. However, a bidder lacks any information about the other potential winning bids that will be included in the average to determine the actual retail rates. Bidders must form expectations about the prices of competing bids or proceed with incomplete expectations; either way, the process increases uncertainty for bidders.

Both methods strive to obtain market retail rates, but both methods have shortcomings. Whether one is better than another for yielding retail rates that are consistent with the market and with market fundamentals is in the end an empirical question. But comparing past solicitations does not necessarily inform a judgment in this regard given the many design differences.

Sharing of Risks

The Maryland EDCs shoulder a certain amount of risk that the New Jersey EDCs contractually pass on to the wholesale market participants that win at the auction. Although we will not review all contract differences here, we have already mentioned that the Maryland EDCs take responsibility for network transmission and remain the load serving entities in the eyes of the independent system operator. The load serving entity is responsible for establishing a certain relationship with the system operator that requires, among other things, meeting certain creditworthiness requirements. Finally, the Maryland EDCs shelter wholesale market participants from some of the risks associated with nonresidential customers migrating on and off default service.

In New Jersey, wholesale market participants bear all the risks, including migration risk, in keeping with the principle of allowing the competitive market to shoulder as much risk as it can efficiently handle. All else being equal, the Maryland EDCs' approach, which reduces some of the risks that wholesale market participants face, should make those market participants willing to bid lower, yielding better prices. However, the Maryland EDCs do not shoulder this portion of the risk for free: They are compensated for this risk from their customers. In principle, the Maryland approach would yield better prices than the New Jersey approach only if the Maryland EDCs were better at managing the risks than wholesale market participants, or if the information regarding customer migration were so poor that sheltering the wholesale market participants from that risk had great value. This could be the case, for example, in a jurisdiction's very first procurement process, when very little data would be available on customer behavior and their propensity to choose a retail electric supplier.

Are Maryland's electric customers better off paying their EDCs to bear migration risk? While this is an empirical question, it is likely that in some regulatory contexts, the decision would also be heavily influenced by politics and corporate culture. EDCs passing on responsibilities to wholesale market participants could be perceived as abandoning their historical role as providers for their customers and shirking their duties under the spirit (if not the letter) of the pre-competition regulatory framework. Again, this discussion does not imply a judgment on what the "best" sharing of risk is—rather, it illustrates that the procurement approach can be tailored to the various considerations that may be important to state regulators and to all stakeholders.

Conclusion

In some states of the United States, the regulated EDCs must enter into large transactions to procure supply for their default customers. These EDCs have an incentive to set up a competitive procurement process for full-requirements supply to minimize the risks of a transaction that can be very large indeed compared to its distribution revenues. EDCs in this situation have developed interestingly different strategies for setting up a competitive bidding process and defining the product upon which wholesale market participants bid. The different strategies adopted by the Maryland EDCs and the New Jersey EDCs provide an instructive contrast. We have used this contrast not to make a pronouncement on a definitive "best" procurement method—such a method is too dependent on the context for such a pronouncement to be made—but instead to highlight certain key decisions that can be made in the procurement process and to discuss the factors that go into the design of these elements. We have reviewed the pros and cons of two contrasting bid processes, of two ways to set retail rates, and of various distributions of risk among the EDCs and the wholesale market participants.

Because of the differences in the procurement method—the differences in terms, in the customer classes being bid, in the elements being included in the bid—simply comparing the final prices does not yield an apples-to-apples comparison. In the end, the regulatory bodies in different jurisdictions have chosen varying methods for procurement to suit their specific circumstances, goals, and predilections. Yet the differences between the procurement processes themselves are not so striking as the similarities. In both of the cases studied here, the EDCs use the competitive market to transfer risks to those best suited to manage them and to get the best prices for customers. Differences among the distributions of risk and the solicitation methods employed pale in comparison to the underlying concept of using a competitive procurement process. At the heart of this process lies the principle that head-to-head price competition among suppliers will determine prices for customers. The definition of full requirements will vary, different regulatory bodies will come to differing conclusions as to what the optimal distribution is, and the bidding process may be different, but the tools used to procure supply for customers at competitive prices all come from the same set of economic principles.

Notes

1. An earlier version of this paper appearing the *Electricity Journal,* XX, 3 (April 2007).

2. See Kurt Strunk, "Default Service Procurement: the US Experience with Full Requirements," in this volume.

3. NERA has served as the auction manager in New Jersey since its inception.

4. For a complete explanation of this process, see New Jersey's Auction Rules, located at http://bgs-auction.com/bgs.bidinfo.ar.asp.

5. ACE stands for Atlantic City Electric, JCP&L for Jersey Central Power & Light, PSE&G for Public Service Electric and Gas, and RECO for Rockland Electric Company.

6. The New Jersey process in fact does incorporate a number of additional competitive safeguards.

7. See, for instance, Paul Milgrom and Robert J. Weber, "A Theory of Auctions and Competitive Bidding," *Econometrica,* L, 5 (1982), pp. 1089-1122; John McMillan, "Selling Spectrum Rights," *Journal of Economic Perspectives* (Summer, 1994), pp. 145-162; R.G. Riley and W.F. Samuelson, "Optimal Auctions," *American Economic Review* (June 1981), pp. 381-392.

8. In any case, it is not possible for an outside observer to compare the results of the Maryland and New Jersey approaches. The winning bids in Maryland are not publicly released; only the averaged rates that customers in each class will pay are made public.

21

OPEN AUCTIONS AS THE NEW TREND FOR POWER PROCUREMENT: AN ANALYSIS OF THE NEW JERSEY BGS AND THE BRAZIL "OLD ENERGY" AUCTION DESIGNS

Georgina Martinez

Introduction

Adoption of open auctions is a new trend for power procurement. In this paper we analyze the energy procurement auctions of New Jersey for the provision of basic generation service (BGS) for non-shopping customers and the Brazil energy auctions for the purchase of energy needs of the regulated market. These two auctions are representative examples of how open auctions have been implemented under very distinct market models and regulatory circumstances, and they illustrate the most recent variants in auction design for power procurement. The New Jersey BGS auction was the first descending clock auction format implemented for energy procurement; the Brazil Old Energy auctions, which combine the open auction and the sealed-bid auction formats, were the first hybrid approach auctions implemented for energy procurement. We analyze New Jersey BGS and Brazil auctions with particular emphasis in auction design and its effect on the outcome of the auctions.

As an introduction to open auctions, we first briefly discuss auctions and their defining features and provide an overview of the origins of open auctions in the electricity industry. We then analyze the New Jersey and Brazil auctions, their regulatory background, design and outcome. We discuss Brazil's adoption of the hybrid approach as an effort to overcome some peculiarities in the Brazilian generation sector and conclude that a simpler design, such as the one adopted for the New Jersey BGS auctions, may produce better results.

Open Auctions as Competitive Procurement Processes

Evolution from RFPs into Auctions

Prior to open auctions, energy was procured through administrative processes and traditional Requests for Proposals (RFPs). Typically, winners were evaluated and selected based on a review and scoring of the bidders' price and nonprice factors, which consisted of descriptions of their business plans, quality of proposals, and financial proposals. The subjectivity of the price and nonprice criteria and the desire for more objective and transparent processes for the selection of winners gave rise to a variant of the traditional RFP, the price-only or sealed-bid RFP. In sealed-bid RFPs, the proponents or bidders are first asked to comply with a set of qualification standards and only those proponents that pass the qualification stage compete on a price only basis. Once past the qualification stage, winners are selected based on measurable and objective qualification criteria, usually price factor(s). The price-only evaluation stage of a sealed-bid RFP consists of a one-round auction in which bidders submit their price bids and the winners are those bidders offering the lowest price.[1] A sealed-bid RFP is also called a sealed-bid auction. One-round auctions are termed "closed" auctions. In a closed auction, bidders bid only once on a single round and cannot see the bids of others (hence, the name, sealed-bid).

The winning bidders in sealed-bid RFPs can be paid under a variety of pricing rules. Under a second-price pricing rule, the winner receives the bid of the second-lowest bidder. Under a pay-as-bid scheme, bidders submit bids for various quantities at various prices and winners are paid their actual bids.[2] In a Uniform Price Auction, bidders submit their bids, the auctioneer aggregates the bids and determines the clearing price at which demand equals supply, and bidders bidding below the market clearing price become winners and are paid the market clearing price for all units won.

A variant of the sealed-bid RFP is the open auction consisting of multiple rounds. Open auctions can be ascending price[3] or descending price[4] depending on whether the auction is used to sell or to purchase an item. An open auction where more than one product is offered at once is called simultaneous ascending or descending auction. In a descending price auction, prices start high and descend over several rounds. Bidders indicate the amount of each product they wish to supply at each round as the price goes down successively until everyone stops bidding. The winning bidders are determined based on the bids of the closing round of the auction, which is the first round with no new bids submitted for any of the items. Open auctions operate under a uniform pricing rule where all winning bidders are paid the closing price of the auction for each product.

Both sealed-bid RFPs and open auctions work well, and both can be designed to achieve the ultimate goals of a competitive procurement process, which are fairness, transparency, and efficiency. In a well-designed RFP or open auction, bidders are provided with equal access to information about the business opportunity and clear rules to follow. Both sealed-bid RFPs and open auctions used for the procurement of energy have a qualification stage with clearly specified criteria to qualify bidders to participate in the next phase. The auction design will clearly spell out the price rules under which the bids are evaluated—so that bidders know they will compete under an objective evaluation and selection process—and how the final price paid to bidders will be determined. All bidders and stakeholders to the process can observe how winners are selected and ensure that no participant has an advantage over another.

However, open auctions are not only transparent; they also tend to achieve more efficient results than sealed-bid RFPs, especially when used for the purchase of multiple related items of uncertain value, such as the procurement of the load for more than one distribution company or for more than one contract delivery period or for more than one customer segment. An efficient market outcome is characterized by similar—and low—prices for similar products. Greater uncertainty about the value of the item at auction tends to result in higher price differentials for similar products. In sealed-bid auctions, bidders are only given one opportunity to bid and once bids are submitted, they cannot be revised. Bidders may have to guess what other bidders are bidding, and those with poorer information will tend to do worse than those who are better informed. In contrast, open auctions allow bidders to obtain information throughout the multiple rounds of the auction, revisit their bids, and compete on more equal grounds.

The type of information provided to bidders between rounds will vary from one auction design to another. However, usually bidders are given information on the going price for each product and some measure of excess supply or demand in the auction, so they can intelligently revise their bids for the next round. Additionally, in most open auctions where several substitute items are auctioned at once, bidders are allowed to switch from one product to another as prices decrease, and prices decrease faster on those products receiving a higher number of bids. Bidders can then revise their offers and switch bids among products as relative prices among products change. As a result, similar products will tend to sell for similar prices. Open auctions also tend to achieve the lowest prices possible, because the auction closes only when bidders have bid the price down to the point that they are not willing to supply the item or service at a lower price.

Sealed-bid RFPs are a good option when only one item is needed, when the load for auction is small, or in mature markets where there is little uncertainty regarding the price of the product. Simultaneous descending price auctions are most likely to provide added economic benefits when several related items are at auction, and the process benefits from the ability to revise bids based on new information as the auction proceeds.

A major criticism of open auctions is that the auction design can give place to collusion or signaling among bidders. According to Paul Klemperer,[5] open auctions are particularly vulnerable to collusive, predatory, and entry-deterring behavior. In an open auction there is a strong presumption that bidders with the lowest cost structures will win, so weaker firms with higher cost structures have little incentive to enter the auction. In a sealed-bid auction, the outcome is less certain. Advantaged bidders may want to make a higher profit and therefore may not bid their lowest price, thus increasing the chances for a weaker bidder with a higher cost structure to win.[6] Klemperer also argues that a sealed bid auction with uniform pricing is more prone to collusive behavior than a sealed bid auction with discriminatory pricing.

Background to the Open Auction and its Adoption in the Electricity Sector

Open auctions have their origins in the US Federal Communications Commission (FCC) 1994 decision to replace traditional administrative procedures with auctions for the sale of licenses to acquire spectrum rights across the US.[7] These auctions used a simultaneous ascending clock auction format where bidders bid to purchase one or more blocks available for each market. Throughout the last decade, following the successful precedent of the FCC auctions, some 21 countries around the world adopted open auctions to sell spectrum rights in the telecommunications sector.

Today, complex open auctions are being adopted successfully for the procurement or sale of energy in liberalized electricity markets. Alberta, Canada, implemented the first open auction in the energy sector, a Simultaneous Ascending Auction (SAA), for the sale of Power Purchase Arrangements (PPAs) in 2000. In 2002, New Jersey adopted a variant of the

SAA for its Basic Generation Service (BGS) Auction to procure basic generation to serve default service costumers in the state.[8] This auction was the first to use the format of a Simultaneous Descending Clock Auction (SDCA). The SDCA introduced a clock feature where the Auction Manager suggests one price for each product on every round, and bidders bid for the right to supply the product(s) at prices suggested by the auctioneer. If at a given price, bidders are willing to supply more than the quantity demanded, that price will "tick" down in the following round. Bidders can revise their offerings for a product when its price falls by reducing the quantity they are willing to supply. Or, if several products are involved, bidders can switch their offer from one product to another. The bidding continues until bidding on all products has stopped and the offered supply equals the demand for all products. Bidders are paid the closing prices.

In Texas, the power generating companies use variations of the SDCA to sell capacity entitlements. Since 2001, as an alternative to divestiture, the Public Utility Commission of Texas has required open auctions for the sale of capacity by generators affiliated with incumbent utilities. In 2004, the Ohio Commission required FirstEnergy to carry out an SDCA as a market test to the rate stabilization plan filed by the Company.

Outside the United States, Électricité de France has used ascending auctions for the sale of Virtual Power Plants (VPPs) and Power Purchase Arrangements (PPAs) to independent generators since September 2001. The Nuon auction in the Netherlands (2004) and the RWE auction in Germany (2006) each used an open auction for divesting generating plants. Nuon introduced a variation on the typical open auction by following the ascending auction format by a sealed-bid round. Other applications of open auctions in the international scene are the Eletrabel generation VPP auction, the Italian Aquirente Unico Financial Contract for Differences Auctions, the Ruhrgas gas release program in Germany, and the UK emissions trading scheme auction.

The Open Energy Auctions of New Jersey and Brazil

The New Jersey BGS Auctions

Regulatory Background to the New Jersey BGS Auctions
While a main goal of US deregulation has been to provide consumers with direct access to more competitive markets for generation services, the deregulating states have also recognized the need to ensure the procurement of economical and reliable power supply for their non-shopping retail

ratepayers. Most have turned to competitive procurement processes, mainly RFPs and auctions. The first open auction to purchase the energy needs for non-shopping retail customers was the 2001 Basic Generation Service auction (NJ BGS Auction), proposed by the four New Jersey electric distribution companies (EDCs).

New Jersey's retail competition, initiated in August 1999, included a four-year transition period with a pre-established decreasing price for BGS offered by the EDCs.[9] The New Jersey Board of Public Utilities (BPU) directed each of the EDCs to file by August 1, 2001, specific proposals to implement an RFP process to procure BGS for Year 4 of the Transition Period (August 1, 2002 – July 31, 2003). In response, the EDCs jointly proposed a competitive solicitation process using an open auction featuring a descending clock format instead of an RFP. Other parties initially opposed the proposed format, noting that it had never been tested and was therefore potentially risky. However, the EDCs and their advisor[10] argued that the purpose of the competitive procurement was to procure supply for BGS customers at the lowest cost consistent with market conditions and to further the transition in New Jersey by opening the provision of BGS energy supply to energy trading and marketing companies. Pointing to the results from the open auctions used by the FCC, Alberta, and other governmental agencies throughout the world, they demonstrated that the open auction process was viable and efficient and that it could achieve the desired results. The BPU agreed, concluding that most of the concerns raised by opposing parties were concerns that could be raised for any RFP process and were not unique to the proposed descending clock auction format.

The SDCA Auction Design
The auction design for the first New Jersey BGS auction was based on the Simultaneous Multiple Round (SMR) auction developed for the FCC and subsequently used in Alberta, but with three modifications. Since the NJ BGS auction was for procurement rather than sale, it was structured as a descending rather than an ascending price auction. Second, at the close of each round, bidders are provided with information on the next round prices and a measure of excess supply remaining in the auction. (All other information, such as other bidders' bids, bidder identities and exact measure of excess supply is kept confidential.) Third, the Auction Manager can reduce the volume being procured.

The load to be procured through the auction is offered as one or several products for each of the four EDCs, and the products are split into tranches. In a round, the Auction Manager announces a price for each of the product or products available for each of the four EDCs. Bidders respond by bidding the number of tranches that they are willing to serve. If the number of tranches bid is greater than the number of tranches needed for an EDC product, the price for that product is reduced or "ticks down" for the next round. Prices decrease by a given percentage of the previous price, based on the level of excess supply specific to each product. Prices do not tick down for products for which there is no excess supply. When a price falls, bidders can either reduce the number of tranches they are offering to supply or switch among products. Although bidders may not increase the total number of tranches bid, they may increase the number bid on one or more EDCs while reducing the number bid on other EDCs. Switching between EDCs maintains the appropriate price difference equilibrium among the products available for each EDC. These switches are allowed as long as they do not result in an EDC with fewer bids than needed.

The switching rule is one of the main features of the BGS auctions, one that mimics a fluid, unregulated market seeking equilibrium. It allows bidders to switch from one product to another depending on how they value each product and to adjust their bids as the relative prices among products change throughout the auction. The prices of products that receive more bids decrease at a faster pace. As the prices for those products can decrease more than prices for the less popular products of each round, some bidders may then switch bids to higher-priced products. When these products start receiving more bids, the price for these products will start to decrease at a higher rate until other products become more attractive to bidders and bidders again switch to other products. The bidding continues as long as there is excess supply for at least one product and prices continue to tick down from one round to the next. This process continues until the total number of tranches bid equals the number of tranches needed, and bidding from all bidders stops. The winners are the bidders holding the final bids when the auction closes, and they are paid the closing prices per MWh.

The Auction Manager's power to reduce the volume of the auction is intended to ensure a competitive bidding environment. For the auction to proceed, supply must exceed demand, so that bidders can compete to supply by reducing the number of tranches they are willing to supply as prices tick down. Therefore, prior to the start of the auction, the Auction Manager asks bidders to indicate how many tranches they are willing to

supply at maximum and minimum starting prices. Based on this information, the Auction Manager sets the starting prices of the auction to
ensure sufficient supply for a competitive process. The Auction Manager
can decide to reduce the auction volume based on the total number of
tranches bid in the first round, the full volume, and a measure of the
concentration and distribution of bids in the first round.[11] The purpose is
both to ensure a competitive process and specifically to prevent bidders
from overstating their interest with their first round bids and then
dramatically curtailing supply during the auction. The Auction Manager
will reduce volume in the first round of the auction should a bidder
reduce the number of tranches, so that the supply is lower than or close
to the quantity demanded. The Auction Manager may also reduce the
volume during the first 10 rounds of the auction if a bidder suddenly
withdraws a fair amount of tranches, thereby suddenly reducing competition and keeping prices high.

NJ BGS Auctions Results

Since the first auction in 2002, each February the New Jersey EDCs have
conducted BGS auctions, and through the successful SDCA model, they
have procured several billion dollars of electric supply.

In February 2002, the New Jersey utilities conducted an SDCA for the
purchase of 17,000 megawatts for 12-month contracts. The auction began
on February 4, 2002 and finished on February 13, 2002 after 73 rounds of
bidding. In this first BGS Auction more than 20 energy trading and
marketing companies competed to provide full-requirements service to
BGS customers. Table 1 below shows the number of tranches procured by

Table 1.   Auction Results of NJ BGS Auction of 2002

EDC	BGS Peak Load Share (MW)	Number of Tranches Available[12]	Number of Winners	Number of Tranches Won
PSE&G	9,608	51	10	1 to 15
JCP&L	5,146	96	9	1 to 15
ACE	2,370	19	4	1 to 5
RECO	440	2	2	1 to 3
TOTAL	**17,564**	**170**		

each EDC, the number of winners for each EDC, and a range of tranches won by each of the winning bidders.

The second BGS auction took place in 2003 and followed the same format as the first, but the load was split between the BGS-FP Auction, a fixed price service auction for residential and smaller commercial customers, and the BGS-CIEP Auction, an hourly service auction for larger commercial and industrial customers.[13] The FP auction was comprised of a 10-month product and a 34-month product for each EDC, chosen to allow alignment of future procurements to the PJM year, which begins June 1st.[14] The 2004 BGS auctions included one-year and three-year products as a transition towards procuring one-third of the load each year on a three-year basis. Twenty-six bidders participated in the two auctions. The 2005 BGS auctions included one-year products and attracted 25 different bidders. One tranche was not secured through the auction, and the BPU set the price for this tranche at the highest closing price of the other three EDCs. Tables 2 and 3 summarize the results of the NJ BGS auctions.[15]

Table 4 shows the number of winning bidders for each of the NJ BGS auctions and the number of rounds for each of these auctions. The number of rounds in each auction varied depending on the level of competition in the auction and the rate at which the prices decreased.

Table 2.   *Summary of Results of NJ BGS FP Auctions*

		Final BGS-FP Auctions Final Price (¢/kWh)					
EDC	**2002**	**2003 10-month product**	**2003 34-month product**	**2004 one-year product**	**2004 three-year product**	**2005**	**2006**
Total FP Peak Load Share (MW)	17,564	10,320	5,062	5,180	5,338	5,132	5,558
PSE&G	5.11	5.39	5.56	5.48	5.52	6.54	10.25
JCP&L	4.87	5.04	5.59	5.33	5.48	6.57	10.04
ACE	5.12	5.26	5.53	5.47	5.51	6.65	10.40
RECO	5.82	5.56	5.60	5.57	5.60	7.18	11.11

Table 3.   *Summary of Results of NJ BGS CIEP Auctions*

Final Prices BGS-CIEP Auctions Final Price ($/MW-day)				
EDC	**2003**	**2004**	**2005**	**2006***
Total CIEP Peak Load Share (MW)	2,672	2,712	2,883	2,960
PSE&G	60.00	52.01	22.62	0.50
JCP&L	65.25	54.98	25.38	0.48
ACE	56.10	49.90	39.76	0.39
RECO	59.80	57.69	20.47	0.50

*2006 auction prices were final DSSAC Price ($/MWh)

Table 4.   *Summary of Rounds and Winning Bidders for NJ BGS FP Auctions*

	Number of Winners				
	2002	**2003**	**2004**	**2005**	**2006**
FP	15	15	12	7	10
CIEP		8	6	6	3
	Number of Rounds				
	2002	**2003**	**2004**	**2005**	**2006**
FP	73	14	71	13	17
CIEP		15	52	71	15

The Outcome

The NJ BGS Auctions have been deemed extremely successful. The BPU evaluated the results and approved them within 48 hours of the close of each auction. It found that the auctions had achieved market-efficient prices and were extremely transparent.[16] The auctions each attracted multiple winning bidders, with each EDC being served by a different set of very diverse suppliers, lowering the risk of default by any single supplier. All EDC products have sold for similar prices so that at the end of the auction, bidders felt the process was fair and transparent: No winning bidder ended up taking less than other winning bidders for the same product.

The results of the NJ BGS auctions would have been hard to achieve through alternative procurement processes. Each year, the design and performance of these auctions have been carefully analyzed and refined to improve the next year's NJ BGS auction to better reflect market conditions and achieve more efficient results. For example, residential and small commercial load and large commercial load were separated (after 2002), the terms of the product have varied, and the price decrements have been revised to better control the pace of the auctions and to allow bidders enough time to make decisions in each round. Some changes have been made in pre-qualifying and in auction administration to maximize the level of participation.

Brazil "Old Energy" Auctions

Regulatory Background to the Brazil "Old Energy" Auctions
Brazil began to restructure its electricity sector at the beginning of the 1990s after realizing that the government's resources would be insufficient to satisfy the needs of the growing economy. The new electricity model envisaged the introduction of competition and the reliance on private investors, who would assume control of generation, distribution, and retail services and of the development of new infrastructure. The sector was unbundled, an independent system operator with functions of market operator was established, and an independent regulatory agency (ANEEL) was created. Under this model, the electricity distribution companies purchased their electricity from both the then-privatized and the state-owned generation companies and used bilateral transactions to cover any medium-term shortfalls. In the wholesale electricity market, imbalances of electricity were settled at the prevailing (monthly) spot price. Energy prices for regulated customers were capped at a reference value set by ANEEL, and the distribution companies absorbed any differences.

In 2001, the country experienced a national electricity shortage. From May 2001-March 2002 blackouts were avoided through a rigorous rationing regime. The shortage and subsequent rationing exposed the vulnerability of the distribution companies and consumers to price increases inherent in the model. Therefore, in July 2003, the government announced a new model for the electricity market, designed to (1) protect regulated customers and the distribution segment from price variations, (2) tailor the power supply to actual demand, and (3) achieve the lowest market prices possible through a transparent procurement process. The new model distinguishes between regulated markets for captive consumers and unregulated (free) markets for large users. Generators are allowed to sell to either market but can enter the regulated market only via competitive regulated auctions. It also distinguishes between "old energy" auctions, for un-contracted energy from plants built before March 2000, whose inherited vesting contracts were expiring, and "new energy" auctions, in which generating companies bid on concessions to build new power plants and provide "assured energy" to the regulated market.[17] The auctions are conducted by the Chamber of Compensation for Electric Energy (CCEE), in accordance with rules set by the Ministry of Mines and Energy (MME).

In the regulated market, the "old energy" auctions were designed for the distribution companies to procure eight-year contracts with start dates of 2005, 2006, 2007, 2008, and 2009, with a requirement that they purchase 100 percent of their load for the five-year planning horizon. These are forward contracts backed by firm capacity. The distribution companies pool their purchase of power to supply their captive consumers and sign bilateral contracts with each generator selling in the auction for a pro-rata quantity of the power proportional to its share of the pooled demand. This diversifies the risks for the distribution segment, since each distribution company is contracted with all participating generators.

The Hybrid Auction Design for "Old Energy"

One of the characteristics of the Brazilian wholesale electricity market is that it is mixture of federal/state-owned and private companies, with different levels of costs, profitability and incentives. Privatization of generating sector had stalled with only 20 percent of the capacity purchased by private investors. The other 80 percent remained in either federal or state hands. The predominance of publicly owned units results in several anomalies for the wholesale market and for any auction process, including the opportunities for collusive, predatory, and entry-deterring behavior noted by Klemperer. In particular, the large publicly held generators had better information on both the total demand and the cost structure of their competitors. Perhaps as a result, Brazil adopted a hybrid framework for the auctions consisting of two phases that combined two different types of auction formats: a descending clock auction followed by a sealed-bid auction.

The goal of the auctions was to fully contract the amounts declared by the distribution companies. The total demand was divided into products corresponding to the eight-year contracts starting on different years. Each product was split into lots (tranches) of 1.0 MW, which represented the smallest bid that could be offered for a product.

In Phase I of the auction—the descending clock auction phase—CCEE begins by announcing the prices for each of the products, and bidders respond by offering the number of lots they are willing to supply for each of them at the going price of each product. Lots offered are not specific to any one distribution company. Products are considered "open" when more lots are offered than demanded and "closed" when fewer lots are offered than demanded. Bids associated with open products are considered "free" and can be bid again for the same product or for different products in subsequent rounds. Bids associated with closed products cannot be re-bid elsewhere in the round immediately following. However, from one round to the next, products can go from being open to closed as bidders reduce the number of lots bid on a product, and from closed to open if those lots are then bid on a closed product. Bidders switch their bids among products as prices decrease, and prices decrease until they go below a reserve price, which is the highest price CCEE is willing pay for a lot of energy.[18] Each bidder's total bids in a round cannot exceed his total bids in the previous round, and once a bidder withdraws lots from the auction, those lots cannot be bid back in.

The only information known to the bidders is the current price and whether a particular product is open or closed. Bidders do not know the reserve price, total demand, the price decrement formulas for price reduction between rounds, or the measure of over-demand. The measure of over-demand, also known as the reference supply, equals the total forecast demand scaled up by a factor greater than one to guarantee excess supply at the beginning of Phase II of the auction. This artificial demand is then taken out of the auction during Phase II to provide bidders with an incentive to bid prices in Phase II lower than their lowest price bid at the end of Phase I. Phase I ends when the total bids for all the products available are equal to or below the total quantity, including the amount of over-demand, and the current price of every product is below the reserve price. If this second condition is not met, the CCEE reduces the demand for that particular product so as to reach at least the reserve price, beginning with the products with later start dates of supply.

Phase II of the auction consists of one round where bidders can only bid the quantity offered at the close of Phase I at prices lower than the last price offered at the end of Phase I. At the start of Phase II, bidders know whether a product has excess supply or excess demand, whether a product is open or closed. Phase II is designed under a pay-as-bid scheme. Therefore the CCEE calculates the clearing price, and all bidders bidding below that price are winning bidders and are paid their actual bid prices. Additionally, bidders that have bids for open products may make "alternate" bids for closed products, which are applied if they do not become winners in their first choice(s) of open product(s).

Results of the Brazil "Old Energy" Auctions

The first "old energy" auction to procure contracts starting in 2005, 2006, and 2007 took place in December 2004. Called Mega Leilão (Mega Auction), it involved 17,000 MW and contracts for start years 2005, 2006, and 2007. The second auction, to procure eight-year contracts for the years starting in 2008 and 2009, took place on April 2005. Only the 2008 product was procured as CCEE excluded the 2009 product from Phase II due to insufficient supply. Two additional auctions took place in October 2005, resulting in 102 MWs sold by five winners for a three-year contract starting in 2006 and 1,166 MWs sold by 10 winners for an eight-year contract product starting in 2009. Even so, the volumes offered did not satisfy demand, as buyers of the eight-year contracts still met less than 40 percent of their requirements for the 2009-2016 period.[19]

Table 5 summarizes all the "old energy auctions," their estimated volume, the volume sold, and the number of winners.

Table 5.   *"Old Energy" Auctions in Brazil*

Auctions for Old Energy	Date	Products	Estimated Volume	Volume Sold	Buyers	Sellers	Winners
1st Auction	December 7, 2004	Three products of 8-year contracts starting in 2006, 2007 and 2008	17,715*	17,008	35	18	12
2nd Auction	April 2, 2005	Two 8-year contracts starting in 2008 and 2009	2,650e	1,325	34	16	10
3rd Auction	October 11, 2005	One 3-year contract starting 2006	1943	102	5	13	5
4th Auction	October 11, 2005	One 8-year contract starting 2009		1,166	17	15	10

* Source: Dutra and Menezes, "Lessons from the Electricity Auctions in Brazil," The Electricity Journal, XVIII, 10 (December 2005), p. 18 and Summary results 1st, 2nd, 3rd and 4th Leilao at the Câmara de Comercialização de Energia Elétrica- CCEE website at http://www.ccee.org.br/leiloes_mae/leiloes_existente/

FIRST "OLD ENERGY" AUCTION, DECEMBER 2004

Table 6 summarizes the monetary results of Phases I and II of the first auction. At the end of Phase I, two of the products were closed or fully supplied and one of the products was open. As required by the auction rules, final prices offered during Phase II were lower (between 7.98 percent and 2.97 percent) than the closing Phase I prices. The pay-as-bid scheme of Phase II of the auction resulted in final price differentials of 20 percent between the lowest and highest bid for the 2005 product, 15 percent between the lowest and highest bid for the 2006 product, and 17 percent between the lowest and highest bid for the 2007 product as shown in Table 6.

In this first auction, 35 distribution companies bought energy and 18 generation companies offered to sell. However, in terms of concentration, the federally owned generation companies, Furnas and Chesf, together won 56 percent of the lots in the auction, and the state- owned generator Cesp won 11.75 percent of the lots. Privately owned generators only won 6.61 percent of the load. Furnas bid the highest prices in Phase II, very

Table 6.   Results of Phase I and Phase II of 1st "Old Energy" Auction of December 2004

	Products		
	2005-08	2006-08	2007-08
Sold Lots (17,008 MW)	9,054	6,782	1,172
Phase I			
Average Closing Price R 21 (R$/MWh)	$62.10	$71.00	$77.70
Status	Closed	Closed	Open
Phase II			
Average Closing Price (R$/MWh)	$57.51	$67.33	$75.46
Min Price Offered	$51.73	$60.35	$66.05
Max Price Offered	$62.10	$69.98	$77.70
Price differential between Min and Max price offered	20.05%	15.96%	17.64%
Price differential between phase I and phase II of auction	7.98%	5.45%	2.97%

close to the closing price of Phase I; Chesf offered the lowest prices for all products. Table 7 presents the detailed results by seller, which highlight the highest price paid by sellers in bold.

Table 7.   Detailed Results by Seller for the First "Old Energy" Auction, December 2004

		Products			Total	
		2005-08	2006-08	2007-08		
Seller	Type of Seller	Closing Price (R$/MWh)	Closing Price (R$/MWh)	Closing Price (R$/MWh)	Sold Lots	Percentage of Total
FURNAS	Federal	$60.94	**$69.58**	**$77.70**	5,753	33.83%
CHESF	Federal	$52.79	$60.35	$66.05	3,692	21.71%
CESP	State	**$62.10**	$68.37	**$77.70**	1,998	11.75%
ELETRONORTE	Federal	$56.00	$63.90	$77.00	1,550	9.11%
COPEL GERAÇÃO	State	$57.50	$67.62	$75.44	1,429	8.40%
CEMIG	State		**$69.58**		927	5.45%
CEEE	State	$57.47	$67.87		412	2.42%
EMAE	State	$60.84	$69.21	$75.75	123	0.72%
CDSA	State				0	0.00%
CEC	State				0	0.00%
CERAN	State				0	0.00%
CGTEE	State				0	0.00%
			Subtotal Federal and State		**15,884**	**93.39%**
LIGHT	Private	$51.73	$61.12		510	3.00%
DUKE	Private	**$59.98**	**$69.98**	**$75.98**	490	2.88%
ESCELSA	Private	$57.00	$64.00		114	0.67%
TRACTEBEL	Private			$70.89	10	0.06%
TEC	Private				0	0.00%
BREITENER	Private				0	0.00%
			Subtotal Private		**1,124**	**6.61%**

Source: Summary results by seller for 1st Leilao at the Câmara de Comercialização de Energia Elétrica- CCEE website at http://www.ccee.org.br/leiloes_mae/leiloes_existente/

SECOND "OLD ENERGY" AUCTION, APRIL 2005

The second auction for old energy produced less favorable results. The 2009 product was excluded from the auction as a result of the automatic demand reduction feature triggered when total supply bid is lower (here, less than 50 percent) than the initial demand.[20] Thirty-four distribution companies and 16 generators participated. The auction resulted in 1,325 MW sold for the 2008 product and 10 winning bidders.[21] According to news releases, a number of companies left the auction early as most of the small private generators found the reserve prices too low and therefore did not win any lots.[22] Price differentials for winners in the auction narrowed compared to the first auction, with a 6.37 percent difference between the maximum and minimum final prices.

Largest winners were again the federal- and state-owned generators, Chesf and CESP, which bid at the closing price of Phase I. The lowest bidders were Enersul and Tec, private generators. Table 9 presents the detailed results, by seller.

Table 8.   Results of Phases I and II of the Second "Old Energy" Auction, April 2005

	Products	
	2008-08	2009-08
Sold Lots (1,325)	1,325	0 sold
First Phase		
Average Closing Price R 46 (R$/MWh)	$99.00	$63.30
Status	Closed	Excluded
Average Closing Price R 59 (R$/MWh)	**$83.50**	
Status	Closed	Excluded
Second Phase		
Average Closing Price (R$/MWh)	**$83.13**	
Min Price Offered	$78.50	
Max Price Offered	$83.50	
Price differential between Min and Max price offered	6.37%	

Table 9.   *Detailed Results by Seller for Second "Old Energy" Auction, April 2005*

Seller	2008-08 (MWh)		2009-08 (MWh)		Total
	Lots Sold	Closing Price (R$/MWh)	Lots Sold	Closing Price (R$/MWh)	Lots Sold
CHESF	450	83.5	–	–	450
CESP	170	83.5	–	–	170
TEC (private)	150	81.55	–	–	150
CDSA	133	83.48	–	–	133
CEMIG GERACAO	105	83.5	–	–	105
CGTEE	104	83.5	–	–	104
ELETRONORTE	90	83.47	–	–	90
COPEL GERACAO	80	82.32	–	–	80
CELPA	23	83.5	–	–	23
ENERSUL	20	78.5	–	–	20
CEC	–	–	–	–	0
CERAN	–	–	–	–	0
FURNAS	–	–	–	–	0
TERMOPE	–	–	–	–	0
DUKE ENERGY (private)	–	–	–	–	0
TRACTEBEL (private)	–	–	–	–	0
Total	**1,325**	**83.13**	**0**		**1,325**

Source: summary results by seller for 2nd Leilao at the Câmara de Comercialização de Energia Elétrica-CCEE website at http://www.ccee.org.br/leiloes_mae/leiloes_existente/

THIRD AND FOURTH "OLD ENERGY" AUCTIONS

The third and fourth auctions took place in October of 2005 to sell energy available for delivery dates of January 2006 and January 2009. This energy had been offered at the two previous auctions, but the market had failed to reach equilibrium, leaving both supply available and the load of some distribution companies uncovered. Seventeen distribution companies and 12 generating companies participated. The three-year contracts with 2006 start dates resulted in the sale of 102 MW by five

Table 10.   *Results of Phases I and II of the Third and Fourth "Old Energy"*
                   Auctions, December 2004

	Products 3rd auction	Products 4th auction
	2006-03	2009-08
Sold Lots	102	1,166
First Phase		
Average Closing Price (R$/MWh)	$64.30	$96.00
	Round 19	Round 1
Second Phase		
Average Closing Price (R$/MWh)	**$62.95**	**$94.91**
Min Price Offered	$62.76	$91.80
Max Price Offered	$63.89	$96.00
Price differential between Min and Max price offered	1.80%	4.58%
Price differential between first and second phases of auction	**2.14%**	**1.15%**

Source: Summary results by seller for 3rd and 4th Leilao at the Câmara de Comercialização de Energia Elétrica- CCEE website at http://www.ccee.org.br/leiloes_mae/leiloes_existente/

generators to five distribution companies. The largest seller in this auction was Duke, a private generator, which sold 66 MW at an average price of R$62.76/MWh. This price was below the R$67.33/MWh average for 2006 contracts transacted at the December 2004 auction, but the contracts were for only three-year rather than eight-year terms. In the fourth auction, 1,166 MW of eight-year contracts starting in 2009 were sold by 10 sellers to 17 distributors. The average price was R$94.91/MWh, much higher than the reserve price set for the April auction. Even so, the eight-year contracts satisfied only 40 percent of the requirements for the 2009-2016 period.[23] The top seller of 2009 contracts was Tractebel.

The Outcome
The old energy auctions in Brazil had mixed results. While more than 20,000 MWs were contracted through the auctions and the auctions resulted in a diverse set of winners comprised of federal- and state-owned and privately owned generation companies, the amount contracted was below demand, at least for the 2009-2016 period.[24] The first auction

was the most successful, where 17,008 MWs were offered for the total estimated demand of 17,715 MWs for the three products available. The prices submitted in Phase II by Furnas and CESP, two of the largest winners, were very close to the closing price of Phase I. Most likely, they could have submitted lower bids closer to Chesf's. Probably Furnas and Cesp were aware that competition was limited and that they could still win a fair number of the lots without having to bid more competitive prices. On the other hand, the higher prices bid did allow the smaller private generators with probably higher cost structures to sell a percentage of their energy. Out of the 12 winners, private generating companies (Duke, Escelsa, Light and Tractebel) won 6.61 percent of the available lots. In a traditional open auction, prices would probably have decreased until only the least-cost providers would have won, and private generation companies may have been outbid.

Price differentials between the maximum and minimum final price offered by winning bidders in Phase II were less pronounced in the second auction, possibly because bidders were able to observe the final prices and price differentials of the first auction. Bidders going into Phase II knew that competition was limited and, not surprisingly, offered prices barely below the closing price of Phase I: indeed 7 of the 10 winning bidders offered prices as high as the prices of the closing round of Phase I. While higher prices were expected for this auction, it is difficult to know how much of the higher price was due to the later starting delivery dates of the products and how much was due to the inability of the auction design to prevent collusion.

Analysis of SDCA and the Hybrid Auction Designs

Comparison of the SDCA and Hybrid Designs

There are a number of similarities between the open auction design used in the New Jersey BGS Auctions and the design of the Brazil Old Energy Auctions: The starting prices are revealed, prices tick down if there is excess supply, and everyone knows the going prices at each round of the auction. There are also several technical differences worth noting. Table 11 summarizes the key differences.

More broadly, the bidders in the first phase of the Brazil auctions have significantly less information than the bidders in the NJ BGS auctions. In the Brazil auction model, the reference supply consists of the total demand, multiplied by a factor higher than one, but neither the total

Table 11. *Main Differences Between NJ BGS Auctions and Brazil*
"Old Energy" Auctions

NJ BGS Auctions	Old Energy Auctions in Brazil
One-phase auction consisting of a simultaneous descending clock auction.	Two-phase auction, hybrid model with a descending clock auction as first phase and a sealed-bid auction as second phase.
Bidders know total volume at the start of the auction.	Bidders do not know total volume.
Volume reduction if quantity supplied on first round or subsequent rounds falls below a parameter called the initial eligibility ratio.	Volume reduction if reserve price (known only to the auction administrator) is not met.
Prices bid are specific to each of the products available for each EDC.	Prices bid are not specific to a distribution company, but specific to each product term available in the auction.
Each distribution company receives the price bid for each of the products specific to each EDC.	All distribution companies sign contracts with all winning generators and receive the same prices for their pro-rata portion of each product in the auction.
Uniform price auction, where all winning bidders of a product get paid the same amount	Phase II is a pay-as-bid auction, where all winning bidders get paid the amount they bid.
There are load caps to prevent a bidder winning all supply.	There are no load caps.
No reserve prices	Reserve prices are set for each product are but known only to the auction administrator.
Switching is allowed only from open products to closed products.	Switching is allowed from open to closed products and vice versa.
A measure of excess supply is provided to bidders.	No information on amount of excess supply is provided to bidders.
Bidders do not know price decrement formulas; however, bidders do know that prices decrease at a higher rate depending on level of excess demand.	Bidders do not know price decrement formulas.
Auction ends on phase I with uniform pricing.	Auction ends on phase II, the sealed-bid phase, with discriminatory or pay-as-bid pricing.

quantity demanded nor the reference supply (nor their reserve prices) is revealed to bidders. In the NJ BGS, bidders know the total demand, and they see the going prices for each round and a measure of excess supply at the end of each round. A second difference between the two auctions is that, although both auctions have a volume reduction feature, the triggers are different. In the NJ BGS the administrator may reduce the total volume of the auction if the total supply offered during the first round or subsequent rounds of the auction falls below the eligibility ratio pre-set parameters. In the Brazilian auction, volume is reduced if the bids do not reach the reserve price.

A third difference is in the reserve price. There is no reserve price in the NJ BGS. In Brazil, the reserve price plays a significant role although its purpose is not clear. Usually a reserve price serves as an independent valuation of the lots for bidders. However, in that case, the reserve price would need to be announced. Keeping the reserve price secret increases the chances that bidders will make a mistake (by not meeting the reserve when they would have been willing to do so) and that the auction will fail. This may have occurred in the second "old energy" auction, where almost half of the estimated demand went unfilled.

A fourth difference, which may have resulted in not trivial outcome in Brazil, is the contingency plan if the auction volume is cut back. In New Jersey, if the auction volume is cut back, the distribution companies purchase necessary services to serve BGS load through the PJM-administered markets. Bidders know that their only opportunity to guarantee the sale of their supply is through the auctions. In contrast, Brazilian generators knew there would be a further opportunity to re-bid their supply in subsequent auctions. Anticipation that lots could be sold at a later time may have affected the participation of bidders in the first auction, increasing the chances that the auction would be less competitive or even fail. Thus, market participants knew that after the 2004 auction there would be another auction in 2005, and some generators decided to withdraw from the first auction in hopes of getting better prices in 2005.

The final difference between the two auctions is, of course, that the NJ BGS auctions only have one phase, consisting of a simultaneous descending clock auction (SDCA) format, and the Brazil "old energy" auctions use a hybrid approach consisting of two phases: a descending clock auction phase followed by a one-round sealed-bid auction. This second phase was apparently intended to respond to the criticism of observers like Klemperer who argue that open auctions alone are vulnerable to collusive, predatory, and entry-deterring behavior. A sealed bid auction offers the possibility that advantaged bidders may want to make a higher profit and therefore may not bid their lowest price, thereby opening a window of opportunity for a bidder with a higher cost structure to compete.

Was the Hybrid Design Superior to a SDCA for Brazil?

The goal of the Brazil auctions for old energy was to fully contract the amounts declared by the distribution companies and achieve the lowest market prices possible, using a transparent process. Therefore, the auctions were designed to allow large and small, public and private generators to compete. Given the strong presumption that in an open auction the strong bidders with the lowest cost structures will win, weaker firms with higher cost structures have little incentive to enter the auction. The addition of a sealed-bid phase was intended to attract smaller bidders (privately owned generators) by increasing their chances of winning lots, as it allowed large bidders (federal- and state-owned generators) with lower cost structures to bid a higher price. In the first phase of the auction, large publicly owned generators were allowed to set the selling price for second phase, and in all probability, real competition did not occur until this second, sealed-bid, phase.

Further, since the only information bidders obtained during the first phase regarded bidders' own bids and the going prices for the products, the first phase mainly determined the maximum amount of lots they were allowed to offer in the second phase. This result could have been obtained more simply without having the first phase of the auction. The CCEE could have just revealed the reserve price and asked bidders to name the maximum amount of lots they were willing to supply at that price. The CCEE could then have set the starting prices and number of tranches a bidder could bid in the second phase. The auction also offset one of the main advantages of open auctions: providing bidders with enough information to avoid large price differentials among similar bidders. Bidders were left to guess how low to bid in the second phase, with the result that the price differentials among winning bids were as large as 20 percent between the highest and lowest winning bid in the first auction.

This hybrid approach produced mixed results. The pay-as-bid pricing scheme in the sealed-bid phase may have deterred large bidders from colluding; however, the lack of information provided to bidders during Phase I and the incorporation of a sealed-bid final round defeated one of the main goals of an open auction, achieving transparency and efficient results. Nor did the auction design necessarily result in the lowest possible prices. Better price discovery would have enabled bidders to make better-informed bids, fostered more aggressive bidding and hence lower prices, and reduced the winner's curse.[25] Indeed, so little information was provided to bidders during the first phase of the auction that the results in the second phase would probably have not been much different had the first phase not occurred. The real competition took place in the second phase, the sealed-bid round of the auction. Until then, bidders may have not needed to make meaningful bids. Most likely, the bids of the large public generators, who by the end of the first phase had the highest number of lots allocated to the products, determined the closing prices of the second phase. Further, the competition in the sealed-bid phase was among large generators who could anticipate their opponents' strategies and in general had better information and therefore an advantage over the smaller and less informed players.

Conclusion

The specific hybrid approach adopted in Brazil does not appear to have added value to the open auction design. Rather, combining these two types of auction formats may have negated many of the advantages of the open auction and exacerbated the negative aspects of the sealed bid auction. In general terms, a design like the one implemented for the "old energy" auctions in Brazil tries to combine the advantages of open auctions—favoring transparency and competition—with the advantages of a sealed bid auction—deterring collusion and predatory behavior from bidders. It is not clear that this auction design prevented collusion. Nor does it appear that this particular hybrid approach was the best choice to ensure that small generators could compete against the large federal- and state-owned generators in Brazil's energy market.

There are other alternative design features that could have been added to a traditional open auction and could have achieved more efficient outcomes. For instance, there are numerous examples of auctions that deal with a broad mix of bidder types in terms of size, skill and information availability. Such auctions can be designed to provide an equitable opportunity for the smaller bidders by "setting aside" some of the volume to be auctioned for smaller participants facing different cost structures. This is the method used by the United States Treasury in selling T-bills and notes by auction. Smaller bidders can opt for the set-aside and simply indicate an amount that they wish to purchase. The price is determined as a function of the auction outcome. Also, the FCC has used set-asides to encourage the participation and success of small players, called designated entities or small bidders, in more than 20 spectrum auctions. In some of the spectrum auctions, the FCC has set aside a few blocks in which only designated entities or small businesses can bid. These designated entities can bid on set-aside licenses and/or are granted a bidding discount when bidding on open licenses, allowing them to compete on equal footing against large bidders. The FCC believes that without special treatment, these small businesses would find it difficult to compete with the large market incumbents.

In Brazil approximately six or seven large bidders represent 85 to 90 percent of the available resources with sizes and cost structures that are very different from those of small bidders or private generators. The auction could have remedied the price distortion and reduced the substantial disadvantage of the private generators by permitting smaller suppliers (e.g., those whose assets represent less than 3 to 4 percent of the volume of demand) to designate what volumes they wished to provide for each product. These volumes would not have been part of the auction. The price for these volumes could have been the reserve price (or alternatively, the current price when the first phase ended, the highest price in the second phase, or the weighted-average price of the second phase).

As shown by the New Jersey and Brazil auctions, there will be much additional variation and innovation in the design of open auctions to test different auction features and explore what works best. However, a lesson to be learned from the New Jersey BGS auction experience and the "old energy" auctions in Brazil is that such variations must ensure that they do not negate the basic principles behind the use of open auctions—transparency, efficiency, and fairness. Auction design does matter, and a simple descending clock auction design in Brazil, with some added features to offset the disparity between large state-owned generators and small private generators, could have achieved better results while at the same time preserving the ultimate goals of open auctions.

Notes

1. Lowest price bidders become the winners when the auction is for the procurement of a service or item. Highest price bidders become the winners when the auction is for the sale of an item.

2. Auctions that use the pay-as-bid pricing rules are also known as discriminatory auctions.

3. Ascending price auctions are also known as English auctions and are the best known formats of auctions, commonly used for the sale of art work.

4. As procurement electricity auctions involve the purchase (not sale) of electricity, this paper focuses on descending price auctions used for the purchase of an item or service.

5. Paul Klemperer, "Collusion and Predation in Auction Markets," University of Oxford - Department of Economics; Centre for Economic Policy Research (CEPR) (February 2001).

6. Ibid., p. 7.

7. Simultaneous Multiple Round (SMR) auctions adhere to the format previously explained of simultaneous ascending price auctions where multiple items are sold at once. In the case of the spectrum auctions, multiple licenses for several regions across the US were auctioned simultaneously through the use of complex open auctions.

8. Default service customers are those that do not elect to be provided service by a third party.

9. Public Service Gas & Electric Company (PSE&G), Atlantic City Electric Company (ACE), Jersey Central Power & Light Company (JCP&L), and Rockland Electric Company (RECO).

10. NERA Economics Consulting, which has served as the Auction Manager to all the New Jersey BGS auctions that have taken place to date. The BPU was in charge of reviewing and giving final approval to the BGS auction process and of monitoring the conduct of the auction. The Auction Manager's role is to run the process itself and to keep the BPU fully informed during the whole process.

11. The Auction Manager uses a confidential set of guidelines to decide whether to cut back the auction volume and to determine the magnitude of any necessary cutback. If the auction volume is cut back, it will be cut back to the number of tranches bid in Round 1, divided by a parameter called the target eligibility ratio, which represents a desired ratio of tranches bid to the auction volume. The precise value of this parameter depends on various factors, such as the number of bidders and characteristics of individual bids. The Auction Manager may further cut back the Auction volume on the basis of the bids as the auction progresses, if such additional volume cutback is necessary to ensure a competitive bidding environment.

12. A tranche for one EDC represents a given fixed percentage of that EDC's BGS Load. A tranche in the BGS-FP Auction is expected to be close to 100 MW of peak demand. No bidder was allowed to purchase more than 60 tranches across products.

13. BGS-CIEP auction determines a Capacity Charge measured in $/MW-day. It is not a term-price service, but a service that is priced to the hourly market. The capacity obligation is the unforced capacity requirement for the aggregate group of BGS-CIEP customers determined in accordance with the EDC and PJM

practices on a daily basis. A tranche in the BGS-CIEP Auction is expected to be close to 25 MW.

14. PJM Interconnection is a regional transmission organization (RTO) in the US electric system. PJM ensures the reliability of the largest centrally dispatched control area in North America by coordinating the movement of electricity in Delaware, Illinois, Indiana, Kentucky, Maryland, Michigan, New Jersey, North Carolina, Ohio, Pennsylvania, Tennessee, Virginia, West Virginia, and the District of Columbia.

15. In 2003-2005 BGS-CIEP Auctions determined the capacity price. The 2006 BGS-CIEP Auction determined the Default Supply Service Availability Charge (DSSAC), non-bypassable capacity charge paid to CIEP suppliers representing a premium for assuming migration risks. It is a delivery charge applicable to all Transmission General Service, CIEP, and customers with Peak Load Shares equal to or greater than 1250kWh.

16. Jeanne M. Fox, "New Jersey's BGS Auction: A Model for the Nation," *Public Utilities Fortnightly,* CXLIII, 9 (September 2005), 16-19. Commissioner Fox has served on the NJ BPU since 2002.

17. See, A. Oliveira, E Woodhouse, L Losekann, and F Araujo, "The IPP Experience in the Brazilian Electricity Market," Program on Energy and Sustainable Development, Working Paper #53 (October 2005), pp. 23-27.

18. If the reserve price for a product is not met, the MME is not obligated to procure that product.

19. "Brazil's 3rd & 4th energy auctions sell 1,268 MW; few private firms participate," *Platts Global Power Report* (20 October 2005).

20. Dutra and Menezes, "Lessons from the Electricity Auctions in Brazil," *The Electricity Journal,* XVIII, 10 (December 2005), p. 18.

21. "Brazil's 3rd & 4th energy auctions sell 1,268 MW; few private firms participate," The McGraw-Hill Companies. *Global Power Report.* Publication Date: 20-OCT-05.

22. Energy auction prices lower than expected. Power in Latin America, Publication Date: 20041217 Issue No.: 150 Volume No.: Page No.: 8 The McGraw-Hill Companies.

23. *Brazil's 3rd & 4th energy auctions sell 1,268 MW; few private firms participate.* Op. cit.

24. *Brazil's 3rd & 4th energy auctions sell 1,268 MW; few private firms participate* Publication Date: 20-OCT-05 Op. cit.

25. In this case, the winner's curse is when a bidder ends up winning, but its price bid is much lower than other bidders' bids.

VI

WATER AND TRANSPORT

22

ESTIMATING CUSTOMERS' WILLINGNESS TO PAY FOR SERVICE QUALITY: THE EXAMPLE OF WATER SERVICE RELIABILITY IN LONDON, UK

Bill Baker
Paul Metcalfe[1]

Estimates of customers' willingness to pay for service quality increments can, and we argue should, play an important role in the decisions of regulators and regulated companies. This chapter looks at the formation and use of such value estimates. While it focuses on a recent application of the Stated Preference (SP) approach to valuing water service reliability in London, UK,[2] such value estimates are important not only in the water sector, but in any industry where consumers have little opportunity to exercise their preferences for service quality.

Introduction

Many utility services are operated within regulatory regimes designed to ensure that utility companies invest and operate "efficiently" and that the prices charged reflect the costs of providing service. Delivery of the service via a shared network makes the quality of service much the same for different customers. Where there is no retail competition, customers cannot act on their preferences for different degrees of service quality by switching between suppliers offering different packages of quality and price. How then can regulators and utility companies know they are providing an appropriate level of quality? How do they balance the incremental costs and benefits of proposed quality improvements? How do they appraise investments that improve service quality?

Water in England and Wales is supplied by 20 or so investor-owned companies. The quality of the water delivery on each water supply network is necessarily fairly homogeneous. While opportunities for retail competition have increasingly been introduced to the sector, to date, a negligible number of customers have switched supplier. Economic regulation is in the hands of the Water Services Regulation Authority (known as Ofwat) which, along with the land-use and environmental authorities, must consider the merits of proposed water investments including those that will improve water service reliability. The water companies and their engineering advisors are adept at forming estimates of the financial costs of capital investments which will improve service reliability. Increasingly, the non-financial costs are being estimated and brought into the appraisal and there is now a desire to estimate and take account of the benefit of improved service reliability as well.

Estimates of the benefit of increased reliability can be useful in several ways within a regulatory regime for a water utility. For example:

- In considering increased expenditure on asset renewal, it would be useful to know the worth to the customers of lowering the outage risk and hence of lowering the asset failure risk.
- In considering a proposal to build increased water abstraction or storage capacity, it would be useful to know the value to the customers of enhanced reliability of supply given the chances of drought events.
- In calibrating incentive rewards to be granted to a regulated company for service quality outperformance, it would be useful to know the benefit the customers gain from that extra service quality.
- In proposed local implementations of national improvement policies, it would be useful to know the locations where the resulting benefits to the customers would be low relative to the costs. This would suggest that a different approach would be better.

There are several good examples in England and Wales of water service benefit estimation using the SP approach. One was an element of the Leading Edge Asset Decisions Assessment (LEADA) initiative, undertaken by Yorkshire Water in support of the 2004 Periodic Review of their regulated water and wastewater price cap. In order to derive estimates of benefits to use in the cost-benefit assessment of its investment proposals, Yorkshire Water estimated customers' willingness to pay for service improvements of various kinds. The willingness to pay results allowed the company to better prioritise and time the investments in its business plan, and to better justify its case to Ofwat for a revised price cap.

The study surveyed 1000 households and 500 businesses to form monetary estimates of the benefits of service quality increments.[3] One of the quality attributes investigated was reliability of water supply. The study showed that, on average, Yorkshire households were willing to pay £3.20 per year and Yorkshire businesses were willing to pay £16.90 per year to reduce the risk of experiencing a disruption event of "2-3 *months of no running water on the premises"* from one occurrence in 500 years to one occurrence in 750 years.

Two further interesting studies involving SP were undertaken in 2004 and 2006 for ActewAGL,[4] the water and wastewater services operator in Canberra, Australia. These aimed at assessing whether the current levels of reliability and other quality attributes were appropriate, given customers' valuations of quality of service. As expected, the first study showed that customers placed a high value on experiencing minimal service interruptions. However, it also showed that customers placed high values on a number of other less obvious attributes, such as notice of an interruption and the method of handling customer calls. The second study examined customers' willingness to pay to reduce drought period water-use restrictions in any year, across the range from continuous restrictions through to virtually no chance of restrictions. The study found that households were on average willing to pay an additional 32 percent of their annual water bill to increase the water service reliability level across the range.

Another water service reliability valuation was the study on willingness to pay that NERA conducted in London, UK, in connection with the proposed desalination plant at Beckton in the estuary of the Thames River. The next section describes the SP approach in general, and the following sections use the Beckton study to show what is entailed in applying the approach.

The Stated Preference Approach

When markets are competitive, customers' valuations for different qualities of service are revealed through the difference in the prices they pay for different quality. Where customers cannot express their valuation of service quality through market behaviour, the prices paid will not provide this valuation information, so other methods must be used to estimate the value customers place on quality of service. The SP approach relies on surveying customers as a basis for estimating service value.

The two main SP techniques used to estimate the value of service are *choice experiments* (also referred to as *choice modelling*) and *contingent valuation*. Both approaches collect survey data on respondents' attitudes, socio-economic characteristics, and uses of the service, as well as their willingness to pay (or to accept compensation) for changes in service quality (more generally, changes in the attributes of the good or service in question). However, the two techniques differ in their approach to obtaining the respondents' estimates of willingness to pay.

Contingent valuation (CV) methods ask people directly how much they are willing to pay (or to accept as compensation) for a change in a particular quality attribute or impact. CV questions can be phrased in a number of different ways, such as

- open-ended questions ("How much would you be willing to pay?"),
- discrete yes/no choice questions ("Are you willing to pay £x?"),
- yes/no questions presented in a series, and
- presentation of payment cards where respondents are asked to choose a monetary amount from a proffered list.

By contrast, in choice experiments (CE) respondents are asked to say which of two or more fully described service alternatives they prefer. CE methods work by examining the trade-offs that people make between different bundles of service attributes. Setting one of the attributes to be a payment means the respondents make trade-offs between money and each service attribute. From the set of answers, analysts can derive respondents' willingness to pay.

In CE applications, a utility function representing respondents' preferences (trade-offs) is first fitted to the whole set of respondents' choices. Provided consumers' preferences meet some mild regularity conditions, in the second step the trade-off with money (*i.e.,* the willingness to pay) can then be found for each attribute. Appendix A sets this out. When well applied, CE methods can generate good estimates of willingness to pay for service quality attributes, including the reliability of water supply.

Stated Preferences in Practice: Valuing Extra Reliability from Extra Capacity

England and Wales is not a part of the world typically associated with droughts and water shortages. However in 2006, millions of people in the South-East of England experienced water use restrictions ranging from garden watering bans to prohibitions on car washing and window cleaning. For a number of years now, Thames Water, the water supply company for London and the Thames Valley, has been concerned about the adequacy of its sources of supply in times of drought. The current regulated water tariffs do not produce a demand response in times of drought: Most households pay for water via an invariant property tax, and it is illegal for the water company to meter them against their wishes. Also, the tariffs for businesses and households that are metered do not increase in times of drought. To improve water supply reliability during dry periods, Thames Water sought permission from Ofwat and the land-use authorities to construct a desalination plant—the Beckton plant—for use in times of drought.

As part of demonstrating the need for this plant to the land-use authorities, Thames Water commissioned NERA's water group to estimate the economic value of avoiding the water use restrictions that may occur, absent the availability of the Beckton desalination plant or equivalent capacity improvements.[5]

The SP valuation work began with extensive qualitative research, including discussions with focus groups of household customers and in-depth interviews with business customers, to inform the development of the survey approach and the instruments to be used (questionnaires, choice cards, etc.). Table 1 describes four levels of water-use restrictions that the statutory framework specifies be used in succession in case of drought in London.

The qualitative research suggested that restrictions at Levels 1 and 2 were of little concern to customers. Customers were more concerned about restrictions at Level 3, and much more concerned about restrictions

Table 1.   *Water Service Restriction Levels in London, UK*

Level	Nature of Restrictions
1	Advertisements asking people to save water and slight reductions of water pressure in some places
2	A ban on the use of sprinklers to water gardens
3	A ban on so called "non-essential" uses, including car washing and the use of hosepipes for watering gardens
4	Rota cuts, or full cut-off, of water supply to premises of households and businesses

at Level 4. The SP investigations therefore focused on the risk of restrictions at Levels 3 and 4.

Following two pilot surveys, fieldwork for the main survey collected responses from 302 London households and 152 London businesses. The samples were designed to be representative enough so that the responses could be used as the basis for aggregate valuation estimates for all London customers.

The SP survey employed choice experiments in which each respondent made 12 selections, each between two alternatives. Each alternative included a statement about each of five attributes: the likelihood and duration of water supply restrictions at Level 3 and at Level 4, and the annual water bill. The statement placed each quality attribute at one of a small number of pre-set quality levels. The range of levels covered both those currently applying for water service in London and those that would apply if the Beckton plant was built.

In addition to making the 12 choice modelling pair-wise selections, as a check each respondent was asked a sequence of contingent valuation questions. For a set quality improvement in terms of a lower risk of restrictions, respondents were asked if they would pay increasing amounts to have this, until they said no.

We fitted utility functions to the whole set of respondents' pair-wise choices and found fitted functions that were convincing in economic terms. Each function had a form and coefficients that satisfied the statistical criteria of goodness of fit and that were statistically parsimonious. From the household and the business utility functions, we then derived the customers' willingness to pay to reduce the risk of supply restrictions.

The SP responses and fitted functions passed a range of validity tests including:

- **Content validity:** Examination of the survey responses showed that respondents had a good grasp of what they were being asked to consider and gave sensible answers to the choices they were presented with.
- **Convergent validity:** The responses were consistent with other findings within the study and in other studies.
- **Expectations validity:** The responses and valuations varied as one would expect with wider explanatory variables, such as customer income and size of the customer's water service bill.

Estimates from Household Choice Experiments

Our preferred model for representing *households'* utility allowed separate parameters to be estimated for different income groups and for respondents who did not provide income data. Table 2 presents NERA's preferred model.

The pseudo-R^2 and the log-likelihood values for the model indicated an acceptable fit for this type of model.[6] The coefficients on the expected number of days of Level 3 and Level 4 restrictions were negative, highly significant, and differed in size, indicating that respondents were much

Table 2.   *Choice Modelling Estimates for Residential Customers*

Variable	Definition	Results
p3d3	Expected number of days of Level 3 restrictions per year; equals the probability multiplied by the duration of Level 3 restrictions.	−0.0165 (5.30)**
p4d4	Expected number of days of Level 4 restrictions per year; equals the probability multiplied by the duration of Level 4 restrictions.	−0.477 (8.38)**
£bill_inc1	Equal to annual water and sewerage bill, measured in pounds, for those respondents with income less than £20k. Equal to zero otherwise.	−0.0164 (11.21)**
£bill_inc2	Equal to annual water and sewerage bill, measured in pounds, for those respondents with income between £20k and £40k. Equal to zero otherwise.	−0.0073 (7.29)**
£bill_inc3	Equal to annual water and sewerage bill, measured in pounds, for those respondents with income greater than £40k. Equal to zero otherwise.	−0.0065 (7.78)**
£bill_miss	Equal to annual water and sewerage bill, measured in pounds, for those respondents with missing data on income. Equal to zero otherwise.	−0.0061 (6.15)**
Observations	Number of Observations (302 x 12)	3624
Respondents	Number of Respondents	302
Log-Likelihood	Measure of Goodness of Fit	−2328.99
Pseudo R^2	Measure of Goodness of Fit	0.07

Source: NERA analysis.

Notes: Absolute value of z statistics in parentheses. "*" stands for significant at 5% and "**" for significant at 1%. Dependent variable is "spchoice", the probability that a respondent n will choose alternative i, when offered alternatives i and j. The model is estimated in logit form.

more concerned about Level 4 restrictions than about Level 3 restrictions. The income group coefficients were significant and negative, showing that all income groups preferred lower bills to higher bills.

From these results for the utility function, we calculated how much residential customers are willing to pay for water supply reliability. Our measure of supply reliability is the statistical expected day, calculated as the probability of a drought water-use restriction event multiplied by its average duration. For example, if at the starting point there is a 0.1 chance of a restriction event in any year, and the likely duration of an event would be 100 days, then we calculate that there are 10 expected days of restrictions each year. A risk reduction of one expected day could be achieved by lowering the likely duration of an event to 90 days or by lowering the chance of a restriction to 0.09 each year.

Measured this way, we understand from Thames Water that the current reliability level for water service in the London area is around 1 expected day of Level 4 restrictions per year. NERA estimated that London households, on average, are willing to pay £1.85 per year for each reduction of one expected day of Level 3 restrictions, plus £53 per year for each reduction of one expected day of Level 4 restrictions.

Estimates from Business Choice Experiments

Our preferred model for estimating the utility expressed in the London *businesses'* choices is shown in Table 3. It weights for the effect of business size, grouping business customers into three classes:

- The smallest businesses with fewer than 10 employees,
- Mid-size businesses with between 11 and 200 employees, and
- The largest business customers with more than 200 employees.

The largest customers exhibited very high willingness to pay to avoid restrictions, especially the severe Level 4 restrictions. To produce conservative valuation estimates, we used a utility function that capped the extra annual amount large businesses would be prepared to pay to avoid restrictions at 100 percent of their annual bill for Level 4 restrictions, and at 6 percent of their annual bill for Level 3 restrictions.

The business SP utility model had an acceptable fit. The coefficients on the expected number of days of Level 3 and Level 4 restrictions per year were negative, highly significant, and differed in size, confirming that

Table 3.   *Choice Modelling Estimates for Business Customers*

Variable	Definition	Results
p3d3	Expected number of days of Level 3 restrictions per year; equals the probability multiplied by the duration of Level 3 restrictions.	−0.0207 (4.88)**
p4d4	Expected number of days of Level 4 restrictions per year; equals the probability multiplied by the duration of Level 4 restrictions.	−0.3715 (4.73)**
%bill_emp1	If no. of employees is less than 10, equal to annual water and sewerage bill as a percentage of current bill. Otherwise equal to zero	−1.3301 (5.32)**
%bill_emp23	If no. of employees is between 11 and 200, equal to annual water and sewerage bill as a percentage of current bill. Otherwise equal to zero	−0.5697 (2.34)*
Observations	Number of Observations (149 x 12)	1788
Respondents	Number of Respondents	149
Log-Likelihood	Measure of Goodness of Fit	−1199.69
Pseudo R^2	Measure of Goodness of Fit	0.03

Source: NERA analysis.

Notes: Absolute value of z statistics in parentheses. "*" stands for significant at 5% and "**" for significant at 1%. The dependent variable is "spchoice", the probability that a respondent n will choose alternative i, when offered alternatives i and j. The model is estimated in logit form.

businesses were more concerned about Level 4 than about Level 3 restrictions. The coefficients on the dummy variables for small and medium business size are significant and negative, confirming that willingness to pay to avoid supply restrictions, as a proportion of the annual water bill, increases with business size.

From the utility function, we estimated that on average, London businesses are willing to pay £48 per year for each reduction of one expected day in Level 3 restrictions, plus £845 per year for each reduction in one expected day in Level 4 restrictions. The unit of risk again is the statistical expected day, formed here just as for households.

CE-based Total Benefit of Improved Service due to the Beckton Plant

By applying these household and business valuation estimates to the reduction in supply restrictions that the Beckton water treatment plant would bring about in future years,[7] extrapolating the sample results to the full affected London population of households and businesses and summing over these, NERA estimated that London water customers value the increased reliability at £226 million in the first year of plant availability and about £3,521 million in present value terms over the life of the plant. This is many times the capital and expected running cost of the plant.

Estimates Based on Contingent Valuation Responses

We also fitted utility functions to the CV responses and derived willingness to pay estimates for households and businesses with this methodology. These models conformed well to economic norms and fitted well in statistical terms, having highly significant coefficients with the expected signs. The CV results suggest that on average, London households are willing to pay £31 per year for each reduction of one expected day of Level 4 restrictions, and London businesses on average are willing to pay £145 per year for each reduction of one expected day in Level 4 restrictions.

For both households and businesses, the CV estimates of willingness to pay for one expected day reduction in Level 4 restrictions lie below the corresponding CE estimates. This difference is larger for businesses. But the CV total benefit figure, aggregated to reflect the value to all affected London consumers of the increased reliability provided by the Beckton plant over future years, is still several times the cost of the Beckton plant.

There are plausible reasons for the difference between the CE and CV estimates. The CV estimates of the willingness of households and businesses to pay are likely to be biased downwards because respondent customers express an element of protest that they—as opposed to some other unspecified party—would be expected to pay for the reliability improvement, at a time when water company performance is under scrutiny in the general media. The CE method is less prone to such protest influences.

The table below presents a summary of the study's reliability value estimates.

Table 4.   *Household and Business Willingness to Pay for Water Service Reliability*

Value per Expected Day of Restrictions	Level 3 £ per customer per year	Level 4 £ per customer per year
Households		
Choice Modelling	£2	£53
Contingent Valuation	N/A	£31
Businesses		
Choice Modelling	£48	£845
Contingent Valuation	N/A	£145

Source: NERA estimates.

Stated Preference Methods in Future

The value of water service reliability in London was derived by rigorous application of SP techniques in a context where it is not possible to rely on market values. It is one of a growing number of such studies in the UK and elsewhere. It illustrates that it is possible to successfully address difficult aspects of benefit estimation, such as dealing with risks and aggregating different peoples' valuations, to produce benefits estimates that will aid decision making.

Over time, accumulating sets of estimates for different service quality attributes, times and locations will allow cross-checking and increasingly build confidence in the stated preference methods and their results. We expect to see much more use of SP-based benefit estimates in the water sector and other regulated utility sectors in future. The techniques should also be particularly useful, for example, in defining appropriate capacity reserves in electricity markets where reserve levels are prescribed by regulation.

Appendix A: Utility Function Specification

When a simple linear utility function is used, the utility that customer n obtains from, or ascribes to, service option i is represented as:

$$U_{ni} = \sum_k \beta_k x_{nik} + \gamma bill_{ni} + \varepsilon_{ni}$$

where x_{nik} is the level of the kth attribute of alternative i presented to customer n; β_k is the parameter reflecting the relative importance of attribute k on average for the population; $bill_{ni}$ is the level of customer n's annual water bill under alternative i; γ is the parameter reflecting the marginal utility of income on average for the population; and ε_{ni} is a random error term. With this utility formalisation and given some modest assumptions about the error term, the probability that a respondent n will choose alternative i, when offered alternatives i and j, is given by the logit formula:

$$Prob\ (choice_n = i\ |\ x_{ni1}, x_{ni2}, .., x_{niK}, bill_{ni}) = \frac{e^{\sum_k \beta_k x_{nik} + \gamma bill_{ni}}}{e^{\sum_k \beta_k x_{nik} + \gamma bill_{ni}} + e^{\sum_k \beta_k x_{njk} + \gamma bill_{nj}}}$$

Given a dataset of observed choices between pairs of alternatives (i, j, and so on), the β and γ coefficients in this model may be estimated by maximum likelihood methods. More complex constructions allow nonlinear utility functions to be fitted and systematic variations in respondents' preferences to be modelled.

Respondents' marginal willingness to pay for improved service attribute levels is derived from the estimated model coefficients. In the simple linear model where one of the attributes of the alternative is its price (e.g., the impact of the alternative's changes in water service attributes on the customer's bill), the researcher divides the estimated coefficient on any other attribute (e.g., the expected duration of water use restrictions) by the estimated coefficient on the price (or the bill) to obtain the respondent's marginal willingness to pay for changed levels of this service attribute.[8]

Notes

1. Currently, Dr. Bill Baker heads NERA's water practice, and Paul Metcalfe is a special consultant in the practice.

2. The London reliability study was funded by Thames Water Utilities Limited. The authors gratefully acknowledge the assistance of Ken Train, Sarah Butler, and Accent Market Research Limited with that study.

3. Accent and CREAM, "Yorkshire Water Services: Final Report" (2002).

4. See D. Hensher, N. Shore, and K. Train, "Households' Willingness to Pay for Water Attributes," *Environmental and Resource Economics,* XXXII, (2005), pp. 509-531, and D. Hensher, N. Shore, and K. Train, "Water Supply Security and Willingness to Pay to Avoid Drought Restrictions," *The Economic Record,* LXXXII, 256 (2005), pp. 56-66.

5. Note that NERA does not estimate those economic costs which would be borne by especially sensitive or special needs customers (e.g., those with home dialysis water supply requirements), because these would be avoided or largely mitigated by Thames Water's drought management approach. Nor does NERA estimate changes in economic costs which may arise through wider environmental effects paralleling water supply disruptions (e.g., fish kills from low river flows caused by extra abstractions from rivers during droughts).

6. The pseudo-R^2 statistic is calculated as the difference between the log-likelihood of the model and the log-likelihood of a model containing only a constant term, divided by the log-likelihood of the model containing only a constant term.

7. Using figures for the extent of restrictions supplied by Thames Water.

8. For further details on choice modelling, and on its use for estimating the value of water supply security, see respectively, D. McFadden, "Conditional Logit Analysis of Qualitative Choice Behaviour," in *Frontiers in Econometrics,* edited by P. Zarembka (New York: Elsevier, 1974), pp. 105-142; Hensher, et al. (2005); and Hensher, et al. (2006).

23

TRANSPORT ECONOMICS

Emily Bulman
John Dodgson
Stuart Holder

Introduction

This chapter shifts the emphasis away from the energy sector to consider application of economic techniques to another sector of the economy, albeit one that is a major user of energy, namely the transport sector. In particular, we consider how economists have advocated use of economic techniques to optimise use of transport capacity. Transport capacity is expensive to install and is generally fixed in the short run, so it is important that best use be made of capacity. Demand for use of capacity varies in time, peaking at certain times of the day, week, and/or year with low demand in periods in between. At peak, demand for travel or freight transport may exceed capacity, and so some rationing device is needed. In practice this rationing device is most commonly congestion: Users of the capacity impede each other's progress, so that their own costs rise. In some cases such as the "bottleneck" case in highways, physical capacity in terms of the number of road vehicles that can pass a fixed point in a given period may actually fall.

Decision makers, both in public bodies such as highway authorities and in private transport companies such as railroads or bus companies, will continually need to consider whether they are operating the right level of capacity, or whether they should expand capacity through investment in new highway lanes or new railroad tracks or new buses. In making these decisions, they will use investment criteria that compare expected future benefits with expected future costs. Public bodies are likely to consider social costs and benefits, using some form of cost-benefit analysis or multi-criteria analysis, while private firms are likely to concentrate on the impact on expected future profitability. But whatever the investment criteria, the expected value of benefits will depend on the expected future use of the improved facility, and this in turn will depend on the prices that will be charged to use the capacity, that is, the road tolls, rail freight charges, bus fares, etc. In turn, the prices and other mechanisms to allocate capacity will determine how well the facility is used and how well it provides benefits both to operators of the infrastructure and to its users.

The theme of this chapter is the different ways to achieve optimal use of existing transport infrastructure. We consider use of three different types of transport infrastructure, highways, airports, and railroad tracks, and consider the alternative mechanisms recommended by economists. In doing so, we need to identify the physical coordination problems and take account of the nature of the decision makers involved in the market place.

In the highway sector, there are large numbers of individual decision makers—individual car, truck, van, and bus drivers—who make their own decisions within a framework of traffic rules, speed limits, and some limited physical coordination from automatic traffic signals. The rules of the road have grown up over many years, and this mechanism works well as long as traffic levels are not so high that individual vehicles impede each other's progress. But once they do and congestion sets in, then this mechanism works less well since individual decision makers have no incentive to take into account the costs that their actions impose on other road users.

In the airports sector, decisions cannot be left to individual vehicle operators. There have to be mechanisms to ensure physical separation of aircraft, both on the ground and in the air. Airlines are obliged to operate within air traffic control systems and regulations, and individual airports operate systems to allocate the take-off and landing slots and the terminal and remote stands to the different airlines using their facilities. Where demand for airspace and facilities exceed capacity, mechanisms need to allocate capacity among competing potential users. In general, allocation and use of capacity must be agreed in advance, though with sufficient operational flexibility to deal with day-to-day variations in schedules as flights vary from scheduled times.

Finally, the problems of physical coordination appear to be greatest in the rail sector. From the very earliest days of the railway, it was realised that infrastructure and operations needed to be coordinated within vertically integrated organisations that combined operation of the track and signalling with operation of trains. This coordination could achieve safe operation of different trains on each company's network while also enabling the company to plan the operation of different types of trains to ensure that more profitable operations received priority over less profitable ones. This model of rail operation is the one that persists to the present in North America, but it has increasingly been superseded in Europe and Australia by a model based on vertical separation, with different train operators on the same network, and with priorities and payment for the use of the network at least partly established through a price mechanism.

The purpose of the rest of this chapter is to explain how economic mechanisms can contribute to determining best use of transport capacity in the different circumstances faced in these three different parts of the transport sector.

Charging for Highway Use in Congested Conditions

Principles of Highway Congestion Charging

Highway congestion is a serious problem around the world, both in major towns and cities and on the highway network. Congestion is a classic example of what economists call externalities. By their actions, economic agents impose costs on others, which they ignore because they are not required to pay compensation. As a result, their level of activity will be higher than that which is economically efficient.

This happens in road transport because the capacity of any highway is limited. When traffic levels are low, additional vehicles will be able to join the traffic flow without getting in the way of existing vehicles, so that the average speed of the traffic will not be affected as the traffic flow rises (measured, for example, in vehicles per lane per hour). But eventually, when traffic flow exceeds what is termed the maximum free-flow traffic level, the addition of an extra vehicle to the flow will impose delays on the other vehicles, so that average traffic speed will fall. The average travel time per trip increases (and time has a value) while operating costs such as fuel use may also rise under "stop-start" driving conditions.

All this means that the observed traffic flow will exceed the economic optimum where the additional *value* of an extra trip as measured by the demand curve equals the marginal social *cost* of each extra trip. The marginal social cost of an extra trip includes the marginal private cost borne by the road user, plus the external cost that the marginal road user imposes on all other road users. Ignoring environmental costs such as noise or air pollution, this external cost is equal to the increase in the cost per trip of each existing road user multiplied by the number of vehicles in the flow suffering this extra congestion cost.

For many years, economists have advocated the use of congestion charges to bring marginal social costs and marginal private costs into balance, not to eliminate congestion but to achieve *economically efficient* levels of congestion. For this to work, we need to measure the extra costs of congestion, in particular by providing a value for travel time, but also (with the help of highway engineers) the way in which increases in traffic flow on a particular type of road or through a particular type of junction reduce overall traffic speeds and increase vehicle operating costs.

The theory of highway congestion charging was set out in a 1961 paper by Alan Walters in the journal *Econometrica*.[1] The British Government took up the idea soon after setting up the Smeed Committee chaired by Reuben Smeed, a distinguished highway engineer. In 1963 this Committee found that road pricing was "technically feasible and economically desirable," and advocated a system of congestion charging in London. After 40 years and much intervening debate, in February 2003 the Mayor of London introduced a daily congestion charge in central London. In the meantime, a more sophisticated form of electronic metering had been introduced in Singapore, and cities in Scandinavia had introduced less sophisticated cordon charging systems.

In order to understand both the technical arguments for road congestion charging and the slow rate of introduction, it is useful to set out the economic logic of the approach and a clear explanation of who gains and who loses from the introduction of a congestion charging mechanism.

Figure 1 illustrates the basic economic theory. The horizontal axis of the two diagrams shows traffic flow per hour per lane on a road. The top part shows an engineering relationship known as a speed-flow curve for the highway. This is initially flat for lower levels of traffic flow (F) as speed (v_0) is not affected as additional vehicles join the flow. But then at higher flows speeds decline and the curve slopes downwards, eventually becoming very steep as the maximum capacity of the road is reached.

Once the maximum free-flow speed is reached, average speeds fall and travel time increases so that the "generalised cost" per trip, including both time and operating costs rises. Thus, beyond flow F_0, the average cost per trip or the marginal private cost per trip (MPC) rises. Each road user will travel as long as their own (private) benefit from making the trip exceeds their own private cost, so that the traffic flow equilibrium will be at flow

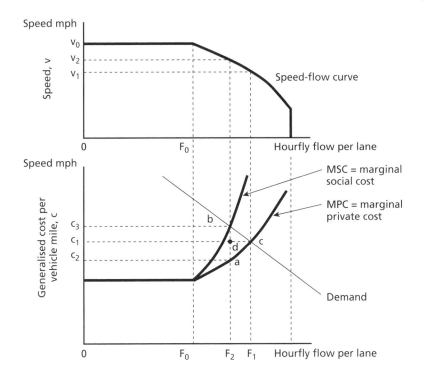

Figure 1.   *Road Congestion Charging Model*

F_1, where the demand curve crosses the MPC curve. However, this is not the economically efficient flow, because the marginal trip at flow F_1 imposes a greater cost on all road users than the benefit to the marginal road user. The optimal flow is at flow level F_2, where the marginal social cost curve, including both private and congestion costs, cuts the demand curve. This can be achieved by imposing a charge equal to ab on each vehicle using the road.

There are real benefits of such a solution. The resource cost (made up of time and other resources like fuel) of each trip falls from c_1 to c_2. This creates a real resource saving benefit equal to area $c_1c_2$da.

On the other hand, traffic flow falls from F_1 to F_2, and those users who are dissuaded from using the road because of the toll suffer a loss of "consumer surplus" equal to area dbc. In addition, road users as a group are worse off because the total cost they pay per trip, including the charge, rises from c_1 to c_3, so they suffer a loss of consumer surplus equal to area c_1c_3bc. The agency implementing the charge incurs the real costs of administering the charge (not shown on the diagram), but gains the toll revenue (which is equal to area c_2c_3ba), which might be spent on transport (for example, improving transit to give car users an alternative) or in other sectors of the economy or to reduce other parts of the tax burden on individuals.

Congestion Charging in London

Transport for London (TfL), the agency reporting to the Mayor and responsible for transport services in London, introduced a congestion charge in February 2003. The charge is levied in a 22 square km (8.5 square miles) central zone encompassing the City of London (the financial district) and the West End (which includes the Oxford Street shopping area and theatreland). Vehicles entering or travelling in the zone on week-days between 7:00 a.m. and 6:30 p.m. are subject to the daily charge that was originally set at £5 a day ($9) and was then increased to £8 a day ($15) in July 2005. The charge can be paid without penalty up to 10 p.m. on the day of travel at a garage or store, or by telephone, SMS text messaging, on-line, or interactive voice response (IVR). However, many types of vehicles and users are exempt, including taxis, buses, vehicles with a disabled sticker, motorcycles and scooters, and emergency vehicles. In addition residents of the central zone are able to purchase a weekly ticket at effectively a 90 percent discount.

Enforcement is by cameras and licence plate recognition. On purchasing a ticket a user provides the vehicle registration number. The registration numbers of vehicles travelling in the charging zone during the charging period are recorded, and penalty payment notices are sent to owners of vehicles not recorded as having paid the charge or being exempt. The standard penalty is £100, or £50 if the charge is paid within 14 days (and £150 if not paid within 28 days).

Before the charge was introduced, there was concern that car users would not have an acceptable alternative means of transport (which would in turn reduce the elasticity of demand for car travel and hence the effectiveness of the scheme in reducing traffic). So steps were taken to improve public transport. London has an extensive underground/subway system, but lines into central London were already heavily used in peak hours. Therefore, the main emphasis was on improving bus services,[2] which would also benefit once congestion charging was in place because reductions in traffic flow levels would improve traffic speeds. In addition, improving bus services would encourage some shorter-distance subway passengers to transfer onto buses and so free up some underground capacity for use by longer-distance travellers transferring from cars as a result of the congestion charge. In addition to investment in alternative modes, there was extensive preparatory work in signing the congestion zone so that road users would be aware of where they could pay, and in remodelling junctions on the inner ring road on which charges would not be paid.[3]

Congestion charging is widely considered a success.[4] It has reduced traffic flows in central London, resulting in increased average speeds. The evidence suggests that this reduction in traffic was real, and congestion was not simply moved around to other parts of London. TfL's detailed monitoring programme has shown that:

- Traffic flows have fallen. In both 2003 and 2004, traffic entering the charging area was 18 percent below what it had been in 2002, the last year before the charge was introduced. But car traffic between 2002 and 2003 fell by a third, while numbers of taxis increased by 17 percent and buses by 23 percent. Traffic on the inner ring road was higher in 2003 than it had been in 2002, but fell slightly between 2003 and 2004.
- Congestion within the charging zone, measured by the difference between travel time at night when roads are uncongested and travel time in the charging period fell by 30 percent compared with 2002. The main impact seems to have been achieved through reduced queuing time at junctions. Congestion in the periods before and after the charging period have been reduced, and has also fallen (though more in 2003 than in 2004) on the inner ring road[5] and on main radial routes into central London.
- Travel by bus has increased in London. People entering the central zone by bus increased 37 percent between 2002 and 2003. Up to a half of this increase was due to the introduction of the congestion charge, but reliability of bus services into the central zone has also increased partly as a result of freer traffic flow conditions.
- Road accidents and emissions of key traffic pollutants such as NO_x and particulate matter have been reduced.
- Residents and others in the charging zone are generally positive about the changes in their local area as a result of the scheme, particularly the reduction in congestion but also improvements in air quality, noise, traffic levels, and public transport provision.

- Despite concerns expressed by some central London retailers about loss of business as a result of the charge, the net impact of the scheme on the London economy appears to have been broadly neutral.
- After payment of operating costs, the scheme generated net revenues of £97 million in 2004/05 (total revenue was £190 million, costs £93 million), most of which was spent on improving bus services.[6]

Furthermore, the Mayor, who had staked his personal reputation on the charge, was re-elected in June 2004. Finally, from 2007, the existing zone is being extended westwards to Kensington and Chelsea, doubling the size of the zone, and further testifying to the perceived success of the scheme.

NERA's Work on Congestion Charging

NERA has contributed to the development of congestion charging in Great Britain at two levels. First, we designed a national system of congestion charging on the road network in England for the Government's think-tank, the Commission for Integrated Transport (CfIT), to show how congestion charging might reduce traffic flows, increase speeds, and generate benefits on what has been acknowledged to be one of the most congested road networks in Europe. Second, we helped Transport for London assess how extension of congestion charging across London would generate additional benefits above those in the existing central area scheme.

In both these applications, NERA has developed models based directly on the framework set out in Figure 1 to show both the optimal congestion charges and the effect of particular charge levels on particular types of roads and at particular times of the day or week. These charges are based on charges per vehicle-mile, rather the existing London Congestion Charge, which is based on the cost of travelling in a particular area. Consequently, the congestion charges in the NERA models are more closely related to actual congestion imposed by vehicle use.

Table 1 shows some results of our work at the national level.

The NERA technical study for CfIT in 2002 was important in changing the public and political debate in the UK surrounding paying for road use. While there has been a clear national consensus regarding the problem of congested roads in the UK for a number of years, the policy solutions to this issue have historically focussed on the supply-side and the building of new road capacity. NERA's study helped CfIT refocus the national debate on the need for a more balanced approach that acknowl-

Table 1.   Impact of a National System of Road Congestion Charges in England

	London			Other Conurbations			All England
	Central	Inner	Outer	Inner	Outer	Motorways	
Charge per car mile (pence)	54.6	35.5	21.1	11.0	4.3	3.5	4.2
Reduction in traffic (%)	-18.5	-15.9	-11.5	-12.3	-5.6	-2.6	-4.2
Increase in speeds (%)	13.7	11.6	13.4	8.0	2.0	3.2	2.9
Toll revenue (£m)	243	574	1021	357	525	1140	5666
Travel time benefits (£m)	103	288	524	112	116	332	1875
Increased reliability (£m)	26	72	131	28	29	83	469
Losses to those no longer travelling (£m)	22	36	69	25	25	52	313
Net benefit before collection costs (£m)	107	324	586	115	120	363	2031

Source: G. Copley and J. S. Dodgson, "Evaluation of a National Congestion Charging System," Proceedings of the Institution of Civil Engineers, Transport 157, Issue TR2 (May 2004),117-123.

edges that building more roads is not a sustainable solution and that measures need to be taken to ensure that car users think seriously about their levels of use. Following publication of the study, momentum in the debate has grown and has been bolstered by the widely held view that the Central London congestion charge has been a success. In the summer of 2004, the UK Department for Transport took an important step forward in the national debate by publishing its *Road Pricing Feasibility Study*, which examined how a scheme may work and the challenges it would face. Importantly, the study suggested that a national scheme could be feasible in 10 years' time.

Since the publication of the feasibility study, the Department has made it clear that it considers road charging to be an important component of its proposed approaches to tackle congestion on roads in the UK. To support this position and to further the political argument, the Government has actively engaged with local government by encouraging them to adopt sub-national schemes in their jurisdictions. Through the *Transport Innovation Fund,* central government has provided local authorities with funding to pursue the kind of successful policies that appear to have worked in central London.

In addition to our work for CfIT on a national charging system, NERA developed a model for Transport for London of the indicative impacts of congestion charging on traffic levels across London. This model, known as SOCCAR, provides TfL a user-friendly means for understanding the impact of particular charging levels on different road types and in different time periods in the central area charging zone, inner London, and outer London. The model has helped TfL study potential future charging scenarios alongside their assessments of possible new technologies for congestion charging. For example, TfL has produced the following illustration: The introduction of charges of about £1 per mile in central London, about 50 pence per mile in inner London, and about 25 pence per mile in outer London could reduce congestion across Greater London by up to 40 percent.

Using Market Mechanisms to Allocate Airport Slots

The Problem of Congestion at Airports

Large urban areas generate substantial demand for air travel. But the noise and pollution that it creates means that nearby residents typically oppose plans to increase airport capacity so that airports close to urban areas are often congested. Some congestion is inevitable. Even airports that have excess capacity for much of the time can experience severe congestion. Like other forms of transport, demand for air travel is highly peaked so airports may operate close to capacity for just a few hours a day and have low demand at other times. In such circumstances, a major expansion of infrastructure or facilities may not be financially or economically justified.

Where capacity is scarce, unrestricted access to airports would result in aircraft queuing and the potential for long delays. In practice, serious delays are usually avoided because access to airports is rationed by allocating airport capacity (slots) to specified flights, typically according to administrative criteria. In particular, airlines are ordinarily entitled to retain the slots that they have used in the previous season.

Thus, airlines impose costs on other airlines through their use of the facilities—either in the form of delays or by preventing other airlines from accessing the airport. As airport charges do not reflect such externalities, allocation of capacity can be suboptimal. In this section we consider how airport capacity can be allocated efficiently in theory, and how this can best be achieved in practice.

Efficient Allocation of Airport Capacity

Figure 2 illustrates how airport capacity may be allocated. The figure shows three curves:

- The demand for use of the airport.
- The marginal private cost borne by each airline using the airport, consisting of airport charges (reflecting the cost of airport infrastructure and services), the airline's own internal costs (staff time, etc.), and the costs an airline bears as a result of delays occurring at the airport.

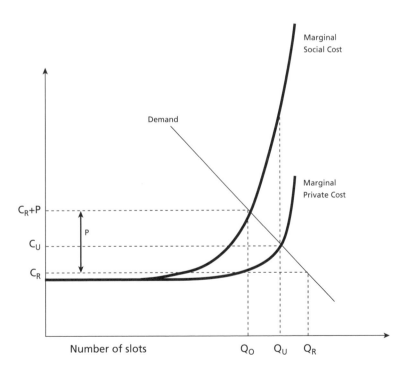

Figure 2.   *Demand for Airport Capacity for a Peak Hour*

- The marginal social cost of an additional aircraft using the airport. This differs from the private cost because it also includes the external costs that each aircraft imposes on other aircraft in the form of delays, as well as the costs it imposes on wider society, for example, in the form of noise pollution.

In the absence of capacity charging or rationing, the problem is analogous to highway congestion. Unconstrained demand Q_u would occur where the demand curve crosses the marginal private cost curve. The optimal use of the airport occurs where the demand curve crosses the marginal social cost curve, at Q_O. This demand would be achieved by charging airlines price P for use of the airport capacity, a price partially offset for the airlines that continue to use the airport by cost savings due to reduced delays ($C_u - C_R$).

In practice, however, scarce capacity is administratively rationed at most airports. If the airport were to ration peak capacity to Q_O slots (the optimal number) without imposing a slot charge, it would reduce delays and hence private costs would fall to C_R. But at C_R, demand would increase to Q_R. Hence {$Q_R - Q_O$} flights would be denied the opportunity to use the airport during the peak. If the slots were allocated to those airlines that valued them most, the allocation would be efficient and equivalent to levying a charge P, but nothing in current allocation practice guarantees such an efficient result. Administratively allocating a slot to an airline not willing to pay P inevitably denies the slot to an airline that is. Such an allocation is inefficient because the slot could be traded, leaving both airlines better off as a result of the sale, a classic case of an improvement in efficiency and social welfare. The principal insight here is that:

Slots would be allocated efficiently if and only if they were used by airlines willing to pay price P for them.

Although airport capacity allocation has many parallels with highway traffic congestion, the interdependencies are more complex. Most airport traffic is scheduled, planned, and marketed months in advance, so that airlines require certainty that they will be able to run their services. A hub airline will wish to time a wave of arrival flights a short time before a wave of departure flights to permit convenient passenger transfers. A non-hub airline may wish to use a single aircraft to undertake two or more return flights in a day, and so would require four slots spaced at convenient intervals. An airline's demand for a particular slot is often contingent on its ability to obtain one or more other slots. For example, for an airline to use an arrival slot, it also needs a departure slot some time later for its onward or return journey. If the airport at the other end of its route is also coordinated, the timing of slots at each airport is interdependent.

Although a highly informed airport coordinator might conceivably be able to allocate slots efficiently without payments, the complexities of slot demand and practical information constraints mean that efficient allocation is best achieved through a form of market mechanism. NERA carried out a major study for the European Commission examining how market mechanisms might improve the allocation of airport slots. This study provided the main research resource for the Commission's 2004 consultation on slot allocation.[7]

Current Practice for Allocating Airport Capacity

At over 200 airports worldwide, airport slots are allocated by airport coordinators following a code of practice set by the International Air Transport Association (IATA). The system is not followed in the US, where antitrust laws prohibit airports from practising slot allocation except for four specified high-density airports. Under both the IATA and the US systems, airlines have "grandfather rights" to slots: If an airline had been allocated a particular slot in the previous season, it would also be allocated the slot in the subsequent season, if it so requested.

Slots that are not allocated according to grandfather rights are known as "pool" slots and are allocated by the coordinator. Coordinators are often required to favour airlines with a limited presence at the airport (a new entrant): The EU offers 50 percent of pool slots to new entrants and, prior to 2000, the US allocated 25 percent. In addition, national governments often reserve certain slots for subsidised flights to more remote regions. Given the complexities, slot scheduling for each season takes many iterations of requests and offers between airlines and coordinators over a number of months, as each coordinator tries to balance the needs of different airlines.

In general, airports worldwide do not charge for airport slots. In the European Union, the purchase of slots is explicitly prohibited, though there is some legal uncertainty as to whether payments can accompany the (legal) practice of exchanging slots. For example, payments accompanying exchanges of slots at London Heathrow have been made quite openly. In the United States, it is legal to buy and sell slots that have already been allocated, though the Federal Government may suspend slots at any time, so the normal rights of property ownership do not apply. Authorities have been at pains to emphasise that airlines cannot be considered to own their slots.

Many airports and commentators consider these existing administrative systems for slot allocation (in the absence of monetary trading) highly inefficient. Since an airline that does not use an allocated slot is not liable for airport charges, it has little incentive to release slots for which it has limited use. As a result, large numbers of sought-after slots are not used, and the difficulty of obtaining slots frustrates efforts to develop new services. This view was supported by NERA's analysis of airport data for the European Commission:

- At the most congested airports, schedules changed little from one season to the next (62 percent of slots were used in the same way as the previous season, whereas only 7 percent were used for entirely new services), whereas at other airports there was greater variation (48 percent of slots were used in the same way as the previous season, whereas 22 percent were used by entirely new services).[8]
- Although small aircraft tend to generate less revenue than larger ones and hence represent an inefficient use of scarce runway capacity, they were quite widely used during peak times at congested airports (8 percent of peak slots were used by aircraft with fewer than 50 seats, 16 percent had fewer than 100 seats).[9]
- Tellingly, 6 to 9 percent of the slots allocated to airlines (in the sample of airports for which there were data) were then not used.[10]

Some US airports have been subject to a different form of inefficiency, caused by unconstrained airport access. The Aviation Act AIR-21 of April 2000 gradually phased out slot restrictions at high-density airports (Chicago O'Hare, John F. Kennedy, and LaGuardia). By November 2000, with 300 new flights operating at LaGuardia, delays had increased by over 230 percent. Such queuing for capacity is inherently inefficient because airlines are not paying for the delays they are imposing on other airlines. New slot restrictions, however, quickly abated the problem.

Using Market Mechanisms to Allocate Slots

Market mechanisms can be used, in theory, to achieve an efficient allocation of airport slots. They may take the form of a primary mechanism replacing the administrative allocation with a payment scheme,[11] and/or they may take the form of a secondary mechanism, where airlines trade slots with each other or with third parties once the primary allocation has been made.

Primary Allocations

POSTED PRICES

Under a system of posted prices, the coordinator or airport would levy a charge for each slot. The charges would be fixed according to a transparent system of tariffs published some months prior to the start of the season. This would reduce the extent of excess demand and ensure that sought-after slots were not allocated to low-value services. Airlines would bear the charge for slots allocated to them, irrespective of whether the slots were actually used, thus also alleviating the problem of airlines failing to use the scarce slots that have been allocated to them.[12]

The system would require airport operators to forecast demand some months in advance, and in the first few seasons there would be little information about the way airlines would be likely to respond to higher prices. To reduce the risk of setting prices too high and slots remaining unsold, prices may be deliberately set on the low side. Hence prices might still fail to clear the market and there would still be excess demand for some slots.

This mechanism would be relatively straightforward to implement and would also provide incentives for airlines to use slots efficiently. But there is a risk that such charges could lead to disputes, challenges, and possible retaliation by states that have not implemented a similar system.

AUCTIONS

Under this mechanism, airlines would bid for the slots they required, and the coordinator would allocate slots to the highest bidders. The auction could be restricted to pool slots or to a proportion of total slots, with the remainder allocated using grandfather rights. Auctions are widely used in other sectors and have been considered by the Federal Aviation Administration as a possible means of slot allocation.[13]

In theory, large-scale auctions could achieve the most efficient allocation of slots possible and would have a relatively early impact. In practice, however, unlike telecommunications and other licences, auctions would be highly complex for both the organisers and the airlines. Airline bidding strategies would be unavoidably complicated. Airport slots at different times may not be good substitutes for each other, and there are significant demand interdependencies. At a minimum, airlines would require a departure slot a certain length of time after the arrival slot, to allow for efficient turnaround. It may wish to schedule a frequent service, with several evenly spaced flights a day. Moreover, if the destination airport is also congested, the airline would need to coordinate its bidding strategy for the two airports concerned. Thus, barriers to participation and the strong possibility of administrative error could undermine the scope for efficient allocation of slots.

Unless such auctions were restricted to pool slots, they might have a disruptive impact on airline schedules, and co-ordination problems might occur because of the need to hold several auctions (for slots at different airports) at the same time. They might also provoke challenges and retaliation by states that did not hold such auctions, and they would be strongly opposed by many airlines because they could involve the suppression of grandfather rights.

Secondary Trading

Secondary trading occurs following the initial allocation of slots by airport coordinators. Exchanging slots with other airlines allows carriers to adapt their schedules and make better use of their overall slot portfolio. It also safeguards them against the risk of ending up with slots they cannot use. It thus complements administrative allocations and auctions that are applied only to a proportion of slots. Trading typically consists of a financial transaction between airlines or their agents and may form part of a larger package of cooperation, often within the context of an airline alliance, which removes the constraint that the slots be of equivalent worth. It has been practiced for some years at high density airports in the US and to a limited extent in the UK.

The risk in bilateral negotiations is that potential deals might not take place, either because buyers and sellers could not identify each other or because airlines were reluctant to sell slots to their competitors. The first of these problems might be reduced by independent agents acting as facilitators and monitoring each airline's willingness to buy or sell slots. Concern that airlines would be reluctant to sell to competitors, however, is reinforced by the US experience of secondary trading. The high-density airports where the systems operated were characterised by high slot holdings of incumbent airlines and little new entry. This outcome could have resulted either from the slot allocation regime or might simply reflect efficient slot allocation. As most potential slot sellers will be airlines wishing to reduce their presence at the concerned airport, they would not be competing directly with airlines who wished to increase theirs, and therefore should not be inhibited about releasing slots.

Secondary trading is likely to have low implementation costs and is unlikely to interfere with existing slot allocation and scheduling proce-dures. But because airlines are confronted only with an opportunity cost rather than a cash outflow, the response in some cases might be delayed or might not occur at all. Secondary trading might be less successful than primary trading mechanisms in promoting a more efficient use of slots.

Impacts of Market Mechanisms

NERA considered the potential benefits of moving towards an efficient system for allocating slots. Given data constraints, NERA measured effi-ciency gains by estimating the increase in passengers using the airport that may result from the introduction of market mechanisms.

The estimate was derived by considering five European airports in detail and by segmenting demand for slots into eight categories (for example, hub carrier short haul, hub carrier long haul, low-cost carrier, charter). Demand was forecast for each of these categories, and NERA derived an elasticity of demand with respect to the charge for a slot for each of the eight categories by taking into account, *inter alia,* airport charges as proportion of total flight costs. The slot price was then increased until demand equalled supply, and the change in the mix of flight categories was used to determine average passenger loadings and hence the number of passengers using the airport. We also used cross-elasticities to determine the extent to which flights might be rescheduled to use lower-cost slots at off-peak times.

Overall, we estimated that the number of passengers using major airports in Europe would increase by 7.3 percent as a result of using an ideal market mechanism to allocate the slots. At highly congested airports, the increase would be 6.3 percent—slots are already intensively used throughout the day at such airports, so the main change would come from the mix of aircraft using the slots. At airports that were congested at peak times only, the number of passengers would increase by 8.5 percent—resulting from a change in the mix of aircraft using slots, from more use at off-peak times, and also from fewer slots being allocated but then remaining unused.

We then estimated how these changes might differ for each of the market mechanisms. As shown in Table 2, secondary trading may be less effective than an ideal market mechanism because airlines may not be inclined to sell slots even though they would profit from doing so. Posted prices may not be fully efficient because they would be prone to forecasting errors. Auctions may also fall short because of the difficulty of bidding for the full set of slots required to fit particular schedules. In the low case for auctions, the efficiency gains may be marginal because of the significant risk of airlines making major bidding errors or being unwilling to participate.

We concluded that these mechanisms increase the concentration of airlines using the airport as a hub. This reflects both the hub airline's tendency to value the slots more than other airlines—at least in part reflecting an efficient allocation—and the fact that it would be able to use the mechanisms more effectively. For example, potential trading partners may approach the hub airline first. Overall, we concluded that each of the market mechanisms would deliver material benefits, though auctions may be difficult to adopt in practice, and mechanisms that transferred wealth from airlines to other parties would be subject to legal dispute.

Table 2.   Summary of Main Properties of Market Mechanisms for Airport Slots

	Secondary trading	Higher Posted prices & secondary trading	Auction of 10% of slots & secondary trading
Approximate estimate of impact on passenger numbers			
Low case	2.2%	4.1%	0.4%
Central case	**4.0%**	**5.0%**	**4.1%**
High case	4.8%	5.8%	4.6%
Implementation costs	very low	moderate	very high
Other factors			
Potential for instability in airline schedules	very low	low	high
Likelihood of increased concentration at hub airports	moderately high	moderately high	very high
Consistency with existing scheduling procedures	good	moderately good	poor
Risk of international disputes, challenges & retaliation	low	high	very high

The Allocation and Pricing of Rail Infrastructure

Introduction: Rail Infrastructure Allocation

The problems of how to allocate capacity on the rail network among competing users, and how to charge for the use of the network, have assumed greater importance in recent times. For many years, such problems rarely if ever arose because most rail services were provided by vertically-integrated organisations that were responsible for providing both the rail network and the trains that ran on it. Where trains did run on other companies' networks (for example, in the US and Canada), the commercial arrangements were often negotiated between the parties with relatively little regulatory control over tariffs or the terms and conditions of access.

More recently, vertical separation between infrastructure provision and train operation has become more common. This has occurred in two main situations. Some countries (including Australia, Sweden, and the UK) have voluntarily implemented vertical separation, usually as part of a more general restructuring of the rail industry, which often also involved some private sector participation. Vertical separation can facilitate competition in downstream markets, either competition within the market where different train operators compete directly with each other, or more usually, competition for the market, where different organisations bid for time-limited franchise contracts or similar rights to operate certain train services. Other countries have introduced vertical separation, in some cases somewhat reluctantly, in order to comply with European Union directives that aim to make it easier for rail services (especially freight services) to operate across national boundaries and to liberalise rail freight markets.

Vertical separation raises important questions about (1) the allocation and pricing of access to the rail network and (2) the pricing and capacity allocation principles that might be applied where an infrastructure manager is supplying network access to a number of independent train operators. The manager must develop a common charging and capacity allocation framework that can be applied to all train services using the network.

This is somewhat different from the situation that occurs where a vertically integrated rail organisation allows other train operators to use its network. If such access is mandated, difficult issues arise in relation to the pricing of such access (since the vertically integrated supplier may be providing network access to train operators that compete with it in downstream markets). Indeed, the "efficient component pricing rule," which has been proposed and to some extent used to determine interconnection charges between telecom operators, was originally developed in the context of rail infrastructure access.

But such situations have not generally arisen in rail industries. Where the infrastructure manager is vertically integrated (i.e., it also operates trains), the requirements to provide network access to potential competitors are often weak and sometimes voluntary (as in the US and Canada). In such cases, there is often considerable flexibility about charging principles (for example, the application of stand-alone cost ceilings, which in practice permit a wide range of charges to be applied below the ceiling). And where the infrastructure manager is subject to stronger requirements to provide network access to its potential competitors, it is often required also to deal with its "own" train operator on an arms-length basis and subject to the same terms and conditions as it applies to independent train operators. So all train operators pay access charges.

The Problem of Allocating Rail Network Capacity

Especially where the infrastructure manager is either independent or required to treat all train operators equally,[14] and when several train operators are seeking access to the network and not all their requirements can be met, it may be necessary to establish rules or procedures about how to allocate capacity. However, deciding between competing demands for network capacity can be a difficult exercise, not least because of the complexities arising where operators want to use the same network facilities to run different types of service.

One problem is that rail network capacity itself is difficult to define and measure. The number of trains that can use a particular part of the network depends on technical constraints such as the minimum separation (or "headway") that must be maintained between trains, which in turn depends on factors such as the signalling equipment installed on the route. Then, within these constraints the number of trains that can be accommodated will depend on the precise nature of the traffic seeking to use the route and the order in which the trains are scheduled.

Figures 3 to 6 illustrate the problems with simple "train graphs." The vertical axis refers to physical locations along the route, the horizontal axis refers to time, and each line shows the planned path of an individual train. These graphs show one of the simplest examples possible, a single uni-directional route with uniform line speed and a single intermediate station stop.

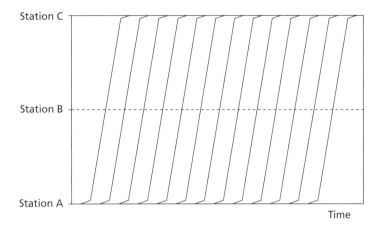

Figure 3.　　*Train Graph with Fast Services*

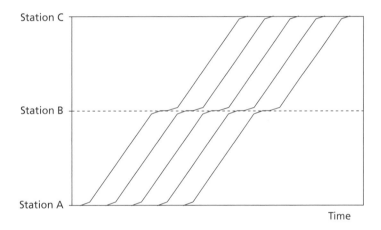

Figure 4.　　*Train Graph with Slow Services*

The maximum use of capacity is generally achieved when all train services are identical. They travel at the same speed, use the same type of
rolling stock (so they share the same braking and acceleration characteristics), stop at the same stations for the same amount of time, and take
exactly the same route. Figures 3 and 4 show simple cases where identical
services use the route. These are either fast non-stop services (Figure 3) or

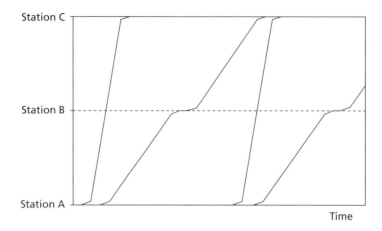

Figure 5.   *Train Graph with Alternating Fast and Slow Services*

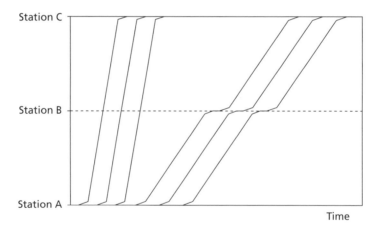

Figure 6.   *Train Graph with Flighted Fast and Slow Services*

slower stopping services (Figure 4). In both cases, however, the uniformity of the traffic allows a relatively large number of trains to use the route.

Figures 5 and 6 then illustrate both fast and slow trains using the route. In Figure 5 these services are alternated, whereas in Figure 6 the services are "flighted" so that several fast trains run in quick succession, followed by several slow trains. The situation shown in Figure 5 often arises in practice, because users of both the fast and slow services generally prefer a service spaced at regular intervals (rather than, for example, three trains in quick succession followed by a long gap with no services). But alternating services carries a penalty in terms of the lower number of trains that can be accommodated.

In practice, the situation facing real-life train schedulers is very much more complex than these simple examples. Among other complications:

- Routes diverge, converge, overlap, and cross each other. On any particular route, services may enter the route at particular junctions and/or leave at others. The timetables on different routes around the network need to be coordinated to allow for such interactions.
- At many locations, trains using junctions need to cut across the path of trains travelling in the opposite direction. Space needs to be left in the timetable to accommodate such conflicting movements.
- There are many different types of trains, not just the fast/slow versions shown above. They may have quite different running speeds, stopping patterns, and acceleration/deceleration capabilities (especially, for example, heavy freight trains).
- As well as the headway necessary to maintain a safe separation between trains, additional allowances must be inserted to allow for "resilience," so that the timetable is not unduly disrupted by individual trains running late and the day-to-day perturbations that are normal on a complex and congested rail network.
- On more complex routes, operators will typically look to maintain connection opportunities for passengers to change trains part-way through a journey.
- Some train operators (especially freight) may require access rights to run particular services but may not be able to specify exactly when the train will run.

Thus train timetabling is a complex task, often undertaken manually by timetabling experts and very often involving only incremental changes from an established timetable that has been tried and tested over a number of years. It relies on specialist knowledge and non-market based processes to decide, for example, which trains should be "first on the graph" on the basis that the services (often long distance or with complex routes) would be difficult to fit into a timetable that was already partially complete.

Could Prices or Auctions Be Used to Allocate Rail Network Capacity?

In theory, a variety of market mechanisms can be considered potential candidates for allocating capacity where there is excess demand for train paths. In broad terms, these approaches involve either (1) pricing, that is, some form of pre-determined tariff so that train operators can calculate how much it would cost them to run a particular service or (2) auctions, a process whereby train operators can indicate the value that they attach to particular train paths, thereby revealing the allocation that generates the highest value.

In practice, except in extremely simple cases, it is highly unlikely that either approach could be used to efficiently allocate scarce rail network capacity. Whereas the allocation of scarce airport take-off and landing slots discussed in Section III involves just the node at each end of a journey, the problem of allocating scarce rail network capacity can apply at every location along a route, with the many complexities noted above.

To use a pricing mechanism to allocate scarce capacity between competing users would require a pricing system that could generate a price for any train path that an operator might require. The infrastructure manager would need sufficient information about train operators' likely demands for these paths at different times of day even to create a market-clearing schedule of prices for a "standard" train path. This in itself would be extremely difficult. But also, there is no such thing as a standard train path. In addition to differences in speed, stopping patterns, etc., even minor retimings of identical train paths could either create or remove conflicts with other services. We see only one exception to the unsuitability of using pricing to allocate capacity: Levying rail infrastructure charges on the basis of planned services (for which the infrastructure manager has allocated capacity) rather than on the services that actually run, would discourage train operators from reserving scarce capacity that they may in fact not use.

The use of auction mechanisms also raises major potential problems, but in theory at least it could provide a mechanism through which train operators could express their requirements and their willingness to pay for these, and the auctioneer could compute the set of feasible allocations that generates the maximum value. Borndörfer et al. show the hypothetical application of a simultaneous ascending combinatorial auction to a small part of the German rail network.[15] Bidders can specify flexible time requirements (for example, frequencies rather than specific departure times), require connections between services, and specify rolling stock diagrams. At each round of the auction, the highest value feasible allocation is calculated.

However, we believe that applying this approach to real-world situations would be extremely difficult and probably impossible. Train operators would be concerned with many more variables than those considered by bidders in Borndörfer's paper. The process of drawing up bids, addressing interactions between different services and deciding how much to bid for each would be complex and possibly intractable. Moreover, this would need to be repeated at each round of the auction. It is also likely to be computationally infeasible. We note, for example, that the authors carried out quite simple tests involving bids for 946 pre-defined candidate train paths but with varying degrees of freedom around the precise departure time. When the time window for each slot was increased to five minutes, it took three days to compute the results of a single round. Though interesting from a theoretical point of view, and despite recent advances in auction design, we believe the prospects for using auctions to allocate scarce rail network capacity are very remote.

Instead, therefore, where capacity allocation problems have arisen in practice, they have sometimes been addressed through analysis focused on the particular location and the specific services seeking access, rather than through more generic approaches that could be applied to all conflicts. This has included

- Government decisions, backed up by varying degrees of economic analysis, about the services that should be allowed to run (and sometimes funded by the government);
- Specific regulatory decisions that examine the merits of the different services that operators wish to run but cannot all be accommodated; and
- Detailed studies in the UK resulting in "Route Utilisation Strategies" that seek to establish the best use of the available infrastructure along particular routes. These studies are unusual in that they can recommend changes (or even removal) of existing services and assess the relative merits of possible new services.

In other cases, however, potential capacity allocation problems have been resolved through the application of administrative rules rather than analysis. These include operational decisions about which trains should be "first on the graph" and political decisions about particular types of services that should have priority over others. However, an implicit system of grandfather rights is also common, such that potential new entrants will simply be told that there is no room on the network for their service rather than having any opportunity to argue the case that their proposed service should displace others that are currently using the network (for example, because it would generate higher net benefits).

Pricing of Rail Infrastructure

Even if the pricing mechanism cannot be used to allocate scarce capacity on the rail network, rail infrastructure charges can still play a valuable role in encouraging the efficient use of less congested parts of the network. But the prices need to be set correctly. If infrastructure charges are too high, potentially viable traffic (i.e., traffic that could afford to pay the additional costs that it creates) could be priced off the network. Equally, infrastructure charges that are too low could result in inefficient use of the network—either by services that generate no additional value, or because there are too many services in total and therefore the level of congestion is inefficiently high.

The efficient infrastructure charge for a train operator seeking to run an additional service is the short-run marginal cost (SRMC) of that service.[16] SRMC covers costs such as:

- the marginal wear and tear (hence increased maintenance costs or advancement of renewals) imposed on the track and other assets by the additional train;
- for an electric train, the traction current consumed;
- any additional operations costs, reflecting for example increased work for signallers and train planning staff; and
- any costs imposed on other users of the network.

The latter can be important in cases (which are common) where capacity is theoretically available but the network is actually already congested. The costs include both the costs that the "new" service might impose on existing services if it runs late and therefore disrupts them, and also the increase in expected delays that will result simply because the network is even more congested and therefore has less resilience to recover from any disruption that does occur (even if it is not caused by the new operator). The UK is unusual (though not unique) in that it has introduced a component of its track access charge that attempts to capture such costs, but in practice it has proved difficult to estimate these costs at the level of detail originally envisaged.

A more general difficulty with SRMC pricing is that it generally leads to a very low level of cost recovery. In Europe, SRMC is typically estimated at around 10 to 20 percent of average cost. The conflict between the objectives of efficient pricing and of cost recovery is one of the main challenges that infrastructure managers and governments have had to address when introducing track access charges. A few governments, mostly in Scandinavia, have been willing to fund the difference between marginal and average costs, though even in some of these cases this is being reviewed. Elsewhere, even if some government subsidies are available, the infrastructure manager needs to set access charges higher than marginal cost for at least some train operators in order to meet its cost recovery target.

Where prices (in any industry) have to be raised above marginal cost, the two standard approaches used to minimise the adverse impact on economic efficiency are two-part tariffs and variable mark-ups over marginal cost. In a two-part tariff, each user pays a fixed charge (usually the same for each user or class of user) plus a variable charge based on their consumption. The variable charge remains at marginal cost and therefore promotes efficient consumption decisions. But this approach can only be applied where the fixed charge will not lead to a significant number of potential consumers reducing their demand to zero. When applied to intermediate goods such as rail infrastructure, it can also distort competition between firms in downstream markets (e.g., large and small train operators). Where it is possible to use two-part tariffs without pricing some train operators off the network or distorting competition, this approach may avoid the efficiency loss from pricing above marginal cost. But such circumstances are rare—the main examples are France, where SNCF faces little or no meaningful competition, and in the UK, where the fixed charge is paid by franchised passenger operators who know what the fixed charge will be in advance and therefore simply factor it into their franchise bids.

Variable mark-ups over marginal cost are based on Ramsey Pricing principles, which state that the mark-up for each consumer should be inversely proportional to that consumer's elasticity of demand. The main way the principles have been implemented in practice is through mark-ups that vary among different market segments or broad types of customers. In some countries, access charges do vary by factors that may be related to the underlying demand elasticities—these include the type of service (e.g., freight, local passenger, long-distance passenger, high-speed passenger) and route. But it is not clear that these charges are based on differential mark-ups over marginal cost rather than simply an adjustment to the average charge per train required to meet the cost recovery target, or that the mark-ups fully reflect the price elasticities of different types of traffic.

Pricing and Investment

Our theme in this chapter has been the importance of considering the contribution of pricing and other techniques of economic allocation to improving efficiency within the transport sector by improving use of existing capacity. Nevertheless, decision makers cannot therefore neglect investment decisions. While different allocation mechanisms will alter investment priorities over the coming years, they will not avoid the underlying need to consider how far capacity should be altered to cope with changing transport demands.

Notes

1. See A. A. Walters, "The Theory and Measurement of Private and Social Cost of Highway Congestion," *Econometrica*, XXIX (1961), 679-699.

2. Improving bus services across the whole of London was a specific objective of the Mayor's transport strategy. NERA had advised TfL London Buses in development of its bus strategy for London.

3. One concern was that the central area congestion charge would simply divert the traffic and hence the congestion to other parts of London.

4. Results are taken from TfL's Third Annual Report, published in April 2005: TfL *Central London Congestion Charging: Impacts Monitoring: Third Annual Report,* April 2005.

5. The benefits of traffic management measures appear to have outweighed the impact of some increase in traffic flow.

6. By law, the net revenues must be spent on furthering the Mayor's Transport Strategy.

7. NERA, *Study to Assess the Effects of Different Slot Allocation Schemes,* (January 2004), http://europa.eu.int/comm/transport/air/rules/doc/2004_01_24_nera_slot_study.pdf, published as European Commission *Commission Staff Working Document—Commercial slot allocation mechanisms in the context of a further revision of Council Regulation (EEC) 95/93 on common rules for the allocation of slots*

at Community airports. 17/9/2004. http://europa.eu.int/comm/transport/air/
consultation/doc/2004_12_01/2004_consultation_paper_en.pdf

8. From NERA (2004). Table 4.1.

9. Ibid., Section 4.4.2.

10. Technically, these slots were returned to the coordinator after the slot return
    deadline. Ibid., Section 4.3.

11. While the payment would be made to the coordinator, the coordinator would
    probably not retain the revenue, but use it, for example, to fund improvements
    to airport infrastructure.

12. Dusseldorf airport has explored the concept of levying a slot reservation fee.

13. Federal Aviation Administration (2001), *Notice of Alternative Policy Options for
    Managing Capacity at LaGuardia Airport and Proposed Extension of the Lottery
    Allocation.* Published in the Federal Register of 12 June 2001.

14. In the European Union, EC Directive 2001/14 requires that, where the infra-
    structure manager is not independent of all train operators, responsibility for
    ensuring that infrastructure capacity is allocated on a fair and non-discrimina-
    tory basis shall be assigned to an independent body.

15. R. Borndörfer, M. Grötschel, S. Lukac, K. Mitusch, T. Schlechte, S. Schultz, and
    A. Tanner, "An Auctioning Approach to Railway Slot Allocation," *Competition
    and Regulation in Network Industries, Special Issue on Recent Trends in the
    Privatization and the Regulation of Network Industries,* I:2 (2006), 163-196.

16. For a discussion of how SRMC might be applied in practice, see NERA (1998),
    An Examination of Rail Infrastructure Charges. This is a report for the European
    Commission that provided the basis for many of the charging principles
    included in EC Directive 2001/14.

CONTRIBUTORS

Bill Baker

Dr. Bill Baker is a Director of NERA and leads NERA's world-wide water and wastewater practice. He has been involved with the issues of network industries for more than twenty years and has extensive experience in water and wastewater, utility, and resource and environmental sectors in all parts of the world. His roles on projects have ranged from providing expert testimony to directing large multi-disciplinary research studies. He has directed projects for water companies or investors in the private sector, as well as for state-owned operators, governments, regulators and international agencies. Dr. Baker has provided advice and testimony on structural reform, the introduction of competition, the development of regulatory frameworks, privatization by sale and by concession, price control mechanisms, cost, efficiency and tariff studies, demand and will-ingness-to-pay estimation, investment appraisal, merger approvals, financing, valuation, financial and risk modeling, and the cost of capital.

Fernando Berrera

Dr. Fernando Barrera is a specialist with more than 10 years experience in the economics of the energy industry. His background combines teaching and research work in microeconomics and energy markets at the University of Oxford and Universidad de Los Andes in Colombia with consulting experience at NERA and Europe Economics. To this blend of academia and consulting work he adds his practical energy regulation background acquired when he served as an independent regulator at Colombia's energy regulation commission (CREG). His work in energy includes wholesale market design, analysis of reliability payments, regulation of transmission and distribution, and retail market analysis and design. His first hand experience in the analysis of wholesale markets spans the UK, Spain, Italy, Portugal, Argentina and Colombia. In wholesale markets he has conducted a number of competition policy projects on the competitive behaviour of power generators in merger analysis and abuse investigations.

Emily Bulman

Emily Bulman is a senior consultant specialising in applying economics to the transport sector. She advises on economic regulation, principally in the rail and air transport sectors, and on matters of public policy. Based in London, she has worked extensively on the London congestion charge, and road pricing more generally. In the rail sector, she has advised on the regulation of rail fares, alternative contractual arrangements and incentive structures, financing, capacity allocation, demand forecasting and policy appraisal. She was one of the main authors in NERA's study on using market mechanisms to allocate airport slots, and has also advised on various aspects of airport regulation. She has managed important studies for the European Commission, the UK Department for Transport, Transport for London and the Land Transport Authority of Singapore. She has degrees in mathematics from the University of Cambridge, and in transport economics from the University of Leeds.

John Dodgson

John Dodgson is a Director in NERA's London office and Head of the European Transport Team. He joined NERA in 1997. Before that he was an academic at the University of Liverpool, where he lectured in microeconomics, public finance and transport economics. He also published in a range of economics journals, including the Economic Journal, European Economic Review, Explorations in Economic History, and the Journal of Transport Economics and Policy. At NERA John has directed a number of major projects for the European Commission, in both the postal and transport sectors. He has also led projects in the aviation, public transport, rail and road sectors, for a range of public and private sector clients in both the UK and in other countries. Particular transport specialties are appraisal and evaluation, railway economics, and highway congestion pricing. In the postal sector John has worked for postal operators and regulators, including postal regulators in The Netherlands, Singapore and the UK.

Jonathan Falk

Jonathan Falk, a Vice President in NERA's Energy Practice, has advised a wide variety of industry participants on the statistical modeling of investment, industry structure, and short- and long-run pricing. He has substantial experience in dispatch modeling for complex electric systems, especially the development of software for large linear programming-based marginal cost models. He helped create novel insurance products to transfer price risk in electric markets. Mr. Falk has also statistically estimated the value of reliability in restructured electric markets, studied market power questions in emerging electricity markets and estimated the social benefits of real-time pricing options. His work has addressed valuation, optimization, and the financial risks associated with restructured electric markets. He has advised on the structure of market rules, including benchmarking contracts between affiliated entities, and has created models to value flexibility in utility planning. Finally, Mr. Falk has lectured and written as well on game-theoretic strategies in electric market bidding for both energy and capacity.

Hamish Fraser

Hamish Fraser specialises in electricity industry restructuring, electricity market investment analysis, and the development of electricity market trading rules. He is based in New York and has provided advice to government agencies, system operators, regulators, power companies, and other electricity industry organizations in more than 25 countries including the U.S. He has participated in the design of detailed market rules in a number of jurisdictions including in the US New York and PJM, Greece, Mexico, Spain, and New Zealand. Mr. Fraser has also led many electricity market valuation assignments, and has provided market and regulatory strategy advice to numerous utilities in the electricity industry, including over 30 in the US, over the course of 17 years. Mr. Fraser received a B. Sc. with first class honors in Operations Research (Master of Commerce equivalent) from the University of Canterbury in New Zealand in 1990.

Sean Gammons

Mr. Gammons is an Associate Director in NERA's European Energy Practice. He specializes in electricity and gas market regulation, restructuring, competition policy, litigation, and valuation work for corporate and government clients. Mr. Gammons has particular expertise in using computer-based economic models to assist clients in anticipating market evolution and analyzing complex strategic decisions. In the past several years, Mr. Gammons has led a large number of due diligence and valuation exercises in support of potential acquisitions or green-field investments, including for power generation companies, wind energy projects, gas storage facilities and gas interconnectors. His other past assignments have spanned merger cases, contract disputes, pricing and regulatory strategy, and cost-benefit studies of new policy proposals or rule changes.

He holds an MSc in economics from University College London, a BA from Oxford University, and a Diplôme d'Ingénieur from the ENSPM in Paris.

Glenn R. George

Glenn R. George has over two decades of experience in the global energy sector as a policy-maker, manager, entrepreneur, investment banker, and consultant. He is a Vice President in NERA's Energy M&A Support and Financing practice. As an energy consultant, he specializes in corporate finance, regulatory affairs, M&A strategy, and infrastructure finance, with an emphasis on market restructuring, energy efficiency, asset securitization, nuclear power, and cross-border transaction support. Prior to joining NERA, he was co-head of the Global Energy Group at Nomura Securities. He previously held senior consulting positions at PA Consulting Group and PricewaterhouseCoopers, and was a co-founder and senior officer of energyLeader, an innovative start-up company.

Prior to entering consulting, Dr. George served in leadership, policy-making, and program management positions in the U.S. Government, including nuclear facility oversight, congressional liaison, and naval ship design, procurement, and regulation. He holds an engineering degree and an M.B.A. (both with Distinction) from Cornell and the Ph.D. from Harvard.

David Harrison

Dr. David Harrison, Senior Vice President and head of NERA's global environment practice, has participated for more than 25 years in the development of emissions trading programs. He was a member of advisory committees for RECLAIM and for the Acid Rain Trading Program in the US. In Europe, Dr. Harrison co-authored a major study for the European Commission on the initial allocation of allowances under the EU ETS. Dr. Harrison and NERA colleagues assisted the UK government in the development of their National Allocation Plan for the EU ETS. He has assisted numerous companies in the U.S., Europe and Japan in assessing the impacts of carbon trading programs and lectures frequently on emissions trading programs in the U.S. and at numerous international events.

Before joining NERA, Dr. Harrison was an Associate Professor at the John F. Kennedy School of Government and on the senior staff of the President's Council of Economic Advisors. He holds a Ph.D. in Economics from Harvard University.

Ross C. Hemphill

Ross C. Hemphill specializes in pricing design, cost of service analyses, and regulatory strategies for electricity and natural gas utilities. With over 25 years' experience in these areas, he has testified on behalf of utilities, state jurisdictions, and customers in regulatory proceedings and legal disputes. Prior to joining NERA, Dr. Hemphill was a Vice President at Laurits R. Christensen Associates. He has also held the positions of Director of Pricing and Resource Strategies at Niagara Mohawk Power Corporation and Manager of Economics & Law at Argonne National Laboratory. Dr. Hemphill has published articles on pricing design in *Public Utilities Fortnightly* and *Resources and Energy,* as well as reports for the Edison Electric Institute, the National Regulatory Research Institute and the American Public Power Association. Dr. Hemphill obtained his PhD in resource economics from the Ohio State University in 1988, and his MS and BA in economics from Indiana State University and Lewis University, respectively.

Stuart Holder

Stuart Holder is an Associate Director in NERA's London office. He specialises in the economic analysis of transport markets. His work covers regulation, access charging, privatisation, cost and revenue modelling, pricing, and competition issues. Stuart made major contributions to high profile NERA reports for the European Commission on airport slot allocation and rail infrastructure charging, and has led a wide range of NERA projects in the rail, airport, air traffic control and other transport industries. He assisted the UK Government during its 2004 review of the rail industry and following its decision to place Railtrack in administration, and has advised on airport regulation in countries including Ireland, Italy, Portugal, South Africa and the UK. Stuart has also worked on projects involving regulatory reform in developing countries, including major studies for the Asian Development Bank and the World Bank in Malaysia and Côte d'Ivoire, and is co-author of an influential journal article on regulatory governance.

Kathleen King

Dr. King has over two decades of experience as an energy economist both as a consultant and in industry. Her work has included litigation support, commercial consulting, and transaction support.

In litigation and arbitration cases she has addressed damages and lost profit calculation in disputes over power plants and contracts, as well as environmental compliance, and energy trading practices. Her work on energy trading practices includes valuation of trading companies, assessment of trade data, contract evaluation, and assessment of strategies and practices of trading organizations. Her experience in wholesale power markets includes market assessment, price forecasting, asset valuation, and economic due diligence. Her experience in retail electricity markets has focused on product design and evaluation for regulated, transitioning, and competitive markets. She was instrumental in the design, implementation or analysis of most of the early two-part real-time pricing programs in the U.S. and analysis of Pool Price Contracts in the U.K.

Michael J. King

Mike King, Senior Vice President, has extensive experience in electric wholesale markets, electric utility restructuring, strategy, and regulation. Mr. King's practice focuses on four areas: wholesale power markets, competition in power, environmental regulation of generation, and incentive regulation. Mr. King has served as an advisor in the acqusition of over 20 GW of generation throughout the world, and assisted in raising over $40 billion in debt frinancing. He has served as an expert witness in contract breach and environmental litigation cases appearing in Federal court as well as before arbitration panels. He has advised companies and regulatory bodies on the structure and implementation of incentive regulation schemes, including both Performance Based Regulation and energy efficiency incentives. Prior to joining NERA, Mr. King served in senior management roles at PA Consulting Group, PHB Hagler Bailly, and Synergic Resources Corporation. He holds a M.A. in Economics from the University of Wyoming.

Per Klevnas

Mr. Klevnas is a Consultant in NERA's Energy and Environment Group specialising in the analysis of economic issues associated with environmental regulation. His recent work has concentrated on the development of market-based approaches to greenhouse gas regulation, including through numerous assignments for the European Commission and the UK government in connection with allowance allocation, market impacts, and policy interaction under the European emissions trading scheme. Mr. Klevnas also has assisted private clients in Europe and the U.S. evaluate how environmental regulation will affect them and the wider economy, including in the automotive, electric power, forest and paper, and other sectors. His work in this areas includes modelling the market and firm impacts of alternative programme designs and the cost savings available from market-based mechanisms. Mr. Klevnas also has assisted with the modelling, evaluation and design of market-based environmental regulation in transport, renewables, and energy efficiency policy.

Chantale LaCasse

Dr. Chantale LaCasse is a Senior Vice President with NERA Economic Consulting. Her practice concentrates on serving NERA's energy industry clients, with a focus on helping clients design, implement, and manage auctions. Dr. LaCasse has testified as an expert witness before state regulatory agencies on matters related to auctions and the design of procurement processes. She has provided conceptual advice to utilities and regulators on the design of energy auctions and she has developed detailed rules for their implementation. She has been involved and managed auctions in several jurisdictions in the United States, including New Jersey, Illinois, Ohio and Pennsylvania, as well as in other countries such as Canada and Ireland. Before joining NERA in 2001, Dr. LaCasse was a successful academic in Canada; she trained Ph.D. students in game theory and she conducted research in auctions and other issues in economic policy.

Jeff D. Makholm

Dr. Makholm specializes in the economics of regulated infrastructure industries in the energy (electricity, gas, and petroleum products), transportation (pipelines, railroads, and airports), water, and telecommunications sectors. He has directed projects regarding such infrastructure businesses in the US and more than 20 other countries

Dr. Makholm has provided expert testimony and reports on over 200 occasions for electricity companies, gas distributors, gas and oil pipeline companies, or regulatory bodies involved in administrative, civil, and international arbitration cases concerning competition and market power, tariff design, financing, and cost of capital. He participated in key hearings before the Federal Energy Regulatory Commission, which lead to US gas and electricity industry restructuring. He has also testified on market and regulatory issues before the Supreme Court in Victoria, Australia and before the High Court and Parliament in New Zealand.

In addition, Dr. Makholm participated in key gas industry reforms in the Europe, Central and South America, Australia/New Zealand and China.

Georgina Martinez

Ms. Martinez is a Senior Consultant at NERA, where she has served as an economic consultant for the energy and telecommunications industries in the US and abroad. Ms. Martinez has provided consultancy services with regards to design and implementation of auctions and bidding strategy.

She has been a key member of the NERA team implementing descending clock auctions and sealed-bid RFPs to procure energy for retail customers in the states of Illinois, New Jersey, Ohio and Pennsylvania. She also served as advisor for buyers participating in energy auctions in Brazil and Canada. In the telecommunications sector, Ms. Martinez has provided bidding strategy advisory services to buyers participating in spectrum auctions in Australia, Austria, Canada, Colombia, Mexico, Switzerland, the UK and the US. On the sellers' side, Ms Martinez was member of the team that designed the Italian and the Singapore 3G auction and has served as advisor to Industry Canada's Spectrum Management Division.

Karl McDermott

Dr. McDermott specializes in public utility regulation. His projects have included advising the members of the Southern Companies, Commonwealth Edison, Wisconsin Electric Power Co., and MidAmerican Energy, LG&E, and SoCal Gas on issues regarding rates design, prudence reviews, regulatory and merger policy as well as restructuring. He has also assisted a number of East European countries including Macedonia, Poland, Romania with efforts to develop appropriate regulatory structures and in the privatize and restructure the electric supply industry. Prior to joining NERA, he served as Commissioner on the Illinois Commerce Commission during the negotiation of the Illinois restructuring law. Dr. McDermott initiated the Commission's investigation into the alternative restructuring options and has made a number of presentations on restructuring issues. Dr. McDermott has lectured extensively in Eastern Europe and South America on regulatory methods, regulatory reform and restructuring. He has published articles in The Electricity Journal. Dr. McDermott obtained his PhD in economics, University of Illinois.

Paul Metcalfe

Paul Metcalfe is a Special Consultant in NERA's Energy, Environment, Transport, and Water Global Practice in London. He advises public and private sector clients on economic aspects of policy-making, regulation, and business planning. His expertise covers non-market valuation tech-niques, economic appraisal, environmental economics, supply-demand planning, cost and tariff analysis, and econometric modeling.

In a recent projects: he advised a UK government department on the design and conduct of a major stated preference study to value a national program of improvements to rivers, lakes and coastal waters; and, on the use of economic instruments for achieving policy goals; he recently advised a number of UK water utilities on economic aspects of supply-demand planning for water and wastewater services, economic aspects of metering in the water industry, and best practice approaches to forecasting domestic and non-domestic water demand; and, he conducted econometric demand and cost modeling studies for clients in the rail, water, pharmaceuticals, local government and air traffic control sectors.

Amparo D. Nieto

Amparo Nieto is a Senior Consultant at NERA, specialized in the economic regulation of electricity and gas industries. Since 1995, she has advised energy regulators, governments and utilities around the world on energy policy reforms, involving competitive wholesale trading arrangements, transmission pricing and retail tariff restructuring. Her consulting experience includes projects in the U.S., Canada, Spain, Ireland, Argentina, Brazil, Mexico, Barbados, India, Greece, and Kenya. In recent years, Ms. Nieto has been involved in the review of generation capacity markets in the US, and the development of market power mitigation strategies in Ireland. She teaches seminars on marginal cost modeling and dynamic pricing, and has conducted many studies for the design of electricity and gas time-of use tariffs, real-time and critical peak pricing rates, and market-based demand response programs. Ms. Nieto has presented numerous papers on energy regulatory issues at the NERA *Marginal Cost Working Group* and other industry forums.

Hethie Parmesano

Dr. Hethie Parmesano is an expert on electricity, gas, and water industry costing, pricing, sector structure, and regulation. In recent years she has been involved with projects dealing with regulation, restructuring, and privatization of state-owned utilities in a variety of different settings, including the U.K., Spain, India, Ireland, Japan, Kenya, Greece, El Salvador, Argentina, Barbados, Brazil, Cambodia, and Mexico. Dr. Parmesano also has extensive experience with costing, pricing, and restructuring issues in the U.S. and Canadian utility industries. Her work both in the U.S. and abroad has involved issues such as efficient utility service pricing, regulating distribution companies, implementation of retail access, transmission pricing, rate structure for Provider-of-Last-Resort service, backup rates for distributed generation, real-time pricing and other innovative pricing options. She teaches seminars on costing and pricing topics, directs a NERA-sponsored industry group called the Marginal Cost Working Group, and has testified widely on utility matters.

Kushal Patel

Kush Patel currently works as a Consultant in NERA's energy practice. Mr. Patel has been involved with a number of energy related projects primarily focusing on electricity procurements in deregulated markets serving as a member of the auction management teams of the New Jersey BGS and Illinois Auctions. Mr. Patel has also been involved in energy contract review/analyses, benchmarking studies, and prudence reviews in addition to contributing to the creation and analysis of hedging strategies, economic damage modeling, and generation asset modeling. He holds a Bachelor of Arts degree in Economics, a Bachelor of Engineering degree in Materials Sciences, and a Master of Engineering Management degree from Dartmouth College.

Carl R. Peterson

Dr. Peterson's practice focuses on retail electric markets, incentive-based regulation, pricing public utility services and regulatory strategy. Prior to joining NERA, Dr. Peterson spent six years at the Illinois Commerce Commission (ICC) providing expert testimony on rate design and merger applications and was a senior technical advisor to two Commissioners. Internationally, Dr. Peterson has worked on electric sector reform in Eastern Europe, China and Kazakhstan.

Dr. Peterson has authored an array of reports and papers addressing issues in the electric and natural gas industries. His work has been published in *The Electricity Journal, Natural Gas and Electricity* as well as numerous edited volumes.

Dr. Peterson received BS and MS degrees in economics from Illinois State University and completed his PhD in economics at the University of Illinois at Chicago. Dr. Peterson is an invited lecturer at the Institute for Public Utilities at Michigan State University and has also taught under-graduate economics courses.

Daniel Radov

Mr. Radov's work concentrates on environmental economics, with a particular focus on emissions trading, climate change, and economic issues associated with air quality regulations. His clients come from a range of industries, including electric power generation and retail supply, automobile and engine manufacturing, forest and paper products, agro-chemicals, petroleum products, and the public sector. He has helped electricity companies in the US, Europe, and Asia understand the effects of emissions trading, renewables policy, and energy efficiency requirements, and has used complex economic models to assess the environmental implications of emissions regulations for auto manufacturers. He has also helped the European Commission and the UK Government design and implement the European Union's Emissions Trading Scheme, and develop and evaluate other climate change policies such as renewable support and energy efficiency.

Mr. Radov holds a BA from Williams College, an MPhil from the University of Cambridge and a MSc in Economics from University College London.

Michael B. Rosenzweig

Dr. Michael B. Rosenzweig is a Senior Vice President and the Chair of NERA's Global Energy, Environment, Transport, Water and Auction Practice. He is an expert on finance, regulation, and energy, specializing in restructuring, regulation, privatization of state-owned utilities, and regulation of electric utilities. Other areas of interest include due diligence for asset acquisitions, transmission pricing and access, strategic planning for utilities, market rules, ancillary services, and tariffs.

Dr. Rosenzweig has directed projects addressing strategic issues related to bulk power market, demand response, competition, transmission access, and pricing. He has directed projects restructuring electricity markets in India, where he served as project director of four major power sector reform projects, Latin America, Eastern Europe and the US. He has testified before international arbitration tribunals (both the International Centre for Investment Disputes and International Chambers of Commerce), US District Court, the Federal Energy Regulatory Commission (FERC), Congress, and local regulatory bodies.

Graham Shuttleworth

Graham Shuttleworth is based in NERA's London office. He studied economics at the Universities of Cambridge and Oxford, England, and has worked at NERA for nearly 20 years. In that time, he has provided expert reports for regulatory hearings, contract arbitrations, and disputes over property taxes ("rates"), and has appeared as an expert witness before a number of panels, arbitrators, and tribunals. He has amassed a wide range of experience in the economics of network regulation, energy market rules, and contract design in the electricity and gas sectors. Recently, he has worked on the regulation of network tariffs and on the analysis of competition in energy markets. In 1996, Mr. Shuttleworth co-authored (with Sally Hunt) a book on "Competition and Choice in Electricity Markets". Mr. Shuttleworth has worked on these topics throughout most of Europe, as well as in Australia, Asia, and Latin America.

Kurt Strunk

Mr. Strunk has extensive experience working on strategic, regulatory, and corporate financial issues in the energy industry. In the US, he has advised utilities on sector restructuring, contract and asset valuation, hedging and risk management, and regulatory strategy. Mr. Strunk has also advised governments, regulators, and energy companies on issues relating to industry structure, regulation, and sector reform in Latin America and Europe. He was a member of the NERA team working on sector restructuring in Spain and also coauthored the white paper outlining structural reform of the Mexican power sector, developed for the Mexican Congress. In Ireland, Mr. Strunk advised on the development of wholesale power contracts and on the design of new capacity solicitations. Mr. Strunk serves as a consulting and testifying expert in regulatory proceedings, commercial litigation, and arbitration proceedings. He has testified before public utilities boards in the US and Canada and has prepared expert reports and testimony in a Federal court proceeding.

Sarah Potts Voll

Sarah Voll is an expert on utility regulation and restructuring issues. She specializes in the design and operation of independent regulatory commissions in emerging markets and has advised newly privatized utilities on their interaction with their regulators. She has also provided litigation support for international investment disputes in infrastructure industries. Dr. Voll served as the Chief Economist and Executive Director of the New Hampshire PUC where she was active on the National Association of Regulatory Utility Commissioners' staff committees on economics and finance, water, and executive directors.

Her publications include *Plough in Field Arable* and, with co-author John Voll, *The Sudan: Unity and Diversity in a Multicultural State*. She was a co-author and Chairman of the Marginal Cost Group for NARUC's *Cost Allocation Manual for Electric Utilities* and has published articles on utility regulation and reform, agricultural development, water, independent power production and rate design.

Ann Whitfield

Ann Whitfield is an Associate Director with thirteen years experience working as an economist for both private consultancies and government. She joined NERA's London office in 1996 and relocated to NERA in Sydney from September 1998. Her particular areas of expertise are utility regulation and energy market design. She has worked for a range of Australian clients, including both regulators and utility businesses. Ms. Whitfield has advised on the competition policy implications of several merger and acquisition projects in the Australian utilities sector. She was recently part of the team advising the Australian Energy Market Commission on the national rules for electricity transmission. Ms. Whitfield holds a first class degree in philosophy, politics and economics from Oxford University and a masters in economics from the London School of Economics.

Thomas Wininger

Thomas Wininger is a Consultant at NERA, based in New York City. He has extensive experience with auction design and administration in the energy sector, energy contract analysis, prudence reviews, statistical analysis of generation asset revenues, and benchmarking studies. He has been a part of the auction management team for the New Jersey BGS auctions, the recent Illinois auction for ComEd and Ameren, the Pennsylvania Power RFP, and the FirstEnergy Competitive Bidding Process in Ohio, among others. Mr. Wininger's work on competitive procurement process design has included assisting with testimony in regulatory proceedings regarding power procurement, designing auction rules that govern solicitation of load, and managing conduct during the bidding processes themselves. Prior to his work with NERA, Mr. Wininger studied economics and English at Dartmouth College in Hanover, NH, where his work focused on financial analysis and game theory.

INDEX